Women in World Christianity

Women in World Christianity: Building and Sustaining a Global Movement

Gina A. Zurlo

WILEY Blackwell

Registered Offices
John Wiley & Sons, Inc., 111 River Street, Hoboken, NJ 07030, USA
John Wiley & Sons Ltd, The Atrium, Southern Gate, Chichester, West Sussex, PO19 8SQ, UK

For details of our global editorial offices, customer services, and more information about Wiley products visit us at www.wiley.com.

Wiley also publishes its books in a variety of electronic formats and by print-on-demand. Some content that appears in standard print versions of this book may not be available in other formats.

Library of Congress Cataloging-in-Publication Data
Names: Zurlo, Gina A., author.
Title: Women in world Christianity : building and sustaining a global movement / Gina A Zurlo, Gordon-Conwell Theological Seminary.
Description: Hoboken, NJ, USA : John Wiley & Sons, Ltd., 2023. | Includes bibliographical references and index.
Identifiers: LCCN 2023000268 (print) | LCCN 2023000269 (ebook) | ISBN 9781119823773 (paperback) | ISBN 9781119874775 (epdf) | ISBN 9781119874782 (epub)
Subjects: LCSH: Women in Christianity--Textbooks. | Women in church work--Textbooks.
Classification: LCC BV639.W7 Z87 2023 (print) | LCC BV639.W7 (ebook) | DDC 270.082--dc23/eng/20230517
LC record available at https://lccn.loc.gov/2023000268
LC ebook record available at https://lccn.loc.gov/2023000269

Cover image: *Silence (The Worshipper)*, Nalini Jayasuria. Courtesy of The Overseas Ministries Study Center at Princeton Theological Seminary ©2001
Cover design by Wiley

Set in 9.5/12.5pt STIXTwoText by Integra Software Services Pvt. Ltd, Pondicherry, India

This book is for the women of my family who came before me,
  Carmella Guerra DiMarco (1938–1994)
  Renée DiMarco Zurlo
  Ivette Carrion DiMarco

those journeying with me,
  Angela Carmella Silver
  Jacquelyn Mari DiMarco
  Joanna Morgan DiMarco

and those that will journey after me,
  Elisa Renée Bellofatto
  Ashley Ann Bodecker

Contents

Acknowledgments   *x*
List of Tables   *xii*
List of Figures   *xv*

Introduction: Why Women in World Christianity?   *1*
Gender and Quantitative Research on World Christianity   *2*
Women in the World Today   *4*
Is World Christianity a Women's Movement?   *6*
Contents of This Book   *7*

Part I   Women in World Christianity by Continent   11

1 Women in World Christianity   *13*
World Christianity, 1900–2050   *14*
World Christianity by Major Tradition, Family, and Denomination   *19*
Dynamics of Religious Change   *24*
Women in Christian History   *26*
Women in Social Scientific Research   *28*
Women in Theology   *31*
Conclusion   *32*

2 Women in African Christianity   *35*
Christianity in Africa, 1900–2050   *37*
Women in African Christianity: Past and Present   *42*
African Women in Theology   *49*
Conclusion   *50*

3 Women in Asian Christianity   *54*
Christianity in Asia, 1900–2050   *56*
Women in Asian Christianity: Past and Present   *62*
Asian Women in Theology   *70*
Conclusion   *71*

4 Women in European Christianity *76*
Christianity in Europe, 1900–2050 *78*
Women in European Christianity: Past and Present *84*
European Women in Theology *91*
Conclusion *92*

5 Women in Latin American and Caribbean Christianity *97*
Christianity in Latin America and the Caribbean, 1900–2050 *98*
Women in Latin American and Caribbean Christianity: Past and Present *105*
Latin American and Caribbean Women in Theology *112*
Conclusion *113*

6 Women in North American Christianity *117*
Christianity in North America, 1900–2050 *118*
Women in North American Christianity: Past and Present *124*
North American Women in Theology *132*
Conclusion *134*

7 Women in Oceanic Christianity *138*
Christianity in Oceania, 1900–2050 *139*
Women in Oceanic Christianity: Past and Present *145*
Oceanic Women in Theology *150*
Conclusion *152*

Part II   Women in World Christianity by Tradition and Movement   157

8 Women in Catholicism *159*
Catholics, 1900–2050 *160*
Women in Catholic History *164*
Vignettes: Catholic Women Worldwide *166*
Conclusion *176*

9 Women in Orthodox Christianity *181*
Orthodox, 1900–2050 *182*
Women in Orthodox History *187*
Vignettes: Orthodox Women Worldwide *191*
Conclusion *194*

10 Women in Protestant Christianity *197*
Protestants, 1900–2050 *198*
Women in Protestant History *202*
Vignettes: Protestant Women Worldwide *205*
Conclusion *211*

11 Women in Independent Christianity *215*
Independents, 1900–2050 *216*
Women in Independent Christian History *220*
Vignettes: Independent Women Worldwide *223*
Conclusion *228*

12 Women in Pentecostal/Charismatic Christianity *231*
Pentecostals/Charismatics, 1900–2050 *232*
Women in Pentecostal/Charismatic History *237*
Vignettes: Pentecostal/Charismatic Women Worldwide *239*
Conclusion *245*

13 Women in Evangelicalism *248*
Evangelicals, 1900–2050 *249*
Women in Evangelical History *254*
Vignettes: Evangelical Women Worldwide *256*
Conclusion *259*

Part III   Women in World Christianity by Select Topics **263**

14 Christianity and Gender-based Violence *265*
Gender-based Violence and Discrimination Worldwide *266*
Christianity and Gender-based Violence *268*
Christian Responses to Gender-based Violence *272*
Conclusion *279*

15 Christian Women and Ecology *284*
Global Ecological Challenges *285*
Gendered Impacts of Ecological Challenges *286*
Christian Responses to Ecological Challenges *287*
Conclusion *295*

16 Christian Women and Theological Education *300*
Historical Vignette: Women and Theological Education in the United States *301*
Women and Theological Education Worldwide Today *302*
Conclusion *311*

17 Christian Women and Peacebuilding *316*
What is Peacebuilding? *317*
Christianity and Peace *319*
Vignettes: Christian Women in Peacebuilding *320*
Conclusion *326*

Conclusion *330*
Further Research *332*

Appendices *334*
Glossary *345*
Index *352*

Acknowledgments

In 2019, I gave a lecture to a group of Doctor of Ministry students on how to be intelligent consumers of quantitative data on religion. Around the table sat ten pastors of local Protestant churches, their male DMin mentors, and me, the lone woman in the room. I invited each pastor to provide a description of his congregation. Each detailed his church's history, ethnic makeup, denominational affiliation, size, and special ministries.

Not a single one said anything about gender.

Upon pointing out the omission of this very basic demographic fact, they all replied:

"Oh yeah, my church is mostly women."

I'd like to acknowledge the women in churches worldwide, many mere afterthoughts, who pray, teach, cook, clean, minister, empower, submit, learn, and carry out acts of service under the radar, overlooked, without complaint nor fanfare, without being told, and without credit. I acknowledge all the female academics who have painfully watched panels of men completely overlook the gendered dynamics of a subject, who have participated in initiatives as the token woman, and have been misnamed or mistitled. I acknowledge the prodigious women who are called the assistant of a man even though they're equal to or outrank him. I acknowledge all the women who have been sexually harassed while working incredibly hard to achieve their dreams. I've been in every one of these scenarios, and countless similar others. This book is for us.

In 2018, the initial idea for the Women in World Christianity Project came to me in Bogotá, Colombia, while attending yet another global Christian conference with very few women present. Amanda Jackson was there when I first asked the question, "If World Christianity is supposedly a women's movement, where are the women?" She became the project's first enthusiastic supporter. The Louisville Institute (2019–2021) and the Religious Research Association (2019–2020) provided generous financial support for the project.

This book would not have been possible without the Center for the Study of Global Christianity (CSGC). Research assistants Nadia Andrilenas and Jane Kyong Chun worked on the literature review, survey development, and survey administration. Shela Chan tracked down endless citations and verifications, drafted reflection questions, and served as a conversation partner about women in the church, theology, and the academy. Michael Hahn and Noah Karger provided essential copyediting and proofreading. CSGC codirector Todd Johnson promoted this project from its onset, always a fierce defender of women's rights in his own life and work. The CSGC's data analyst, Peter Crossing, produced most of the tables and graphs that appear in this book. Christopher Guidry helped prepare the photos. Thanks to my colleagues and friends who offered constructive feedback on portions of the manuscript: Annalisa Butticci (Europe), Soojin Chung

(Asia), Jeremy Hegi (North America), Graham Joseph Hill (Oceania), and Michèle Miller Sigg (Africa). Numerous staff members at Wiley-Blackwell assisted with this manuscript, including Catriona King, Marissa Koors, Hannah Lee, Clelia Petracca, Mandy Collison, and Laura Adsett.

Dana Robert, my mentor at Boston University School of Theology, asked the question at the core of this book, "What would the study of Christianity in Africa, Asia, and Latin America look like if scholars put women into the center of their research?" Fingerprints of her pioneering research and expert advising are throughout this book, and I am honored to be a part of her legacy in the study of Christianity, mission, and gender. My friend, Michèle Miller Sigg, was the first to ask in 2013, "Why are there no women in your *World Christian Database*?" Thanks to her loving and relentless insistence, now there are. My sister, Angela Silver, and my closest friends, Julie Pacheco, Jessica Indelicato, Stephanie Tomasulo, Katherine Boylan, and Michelle Mahoney, have been journeying with me for years, providing emotional support, spaces to vent, childcare, and anything necessary to ensure my success.

I'd like to thank my parents, Mark and Renée Zurlo, who made tremendous sacrifices to ensure my sister and I had everything we needed to make good choices and find our place in the world. Finally, thank you to my husband, Christopher Bodecker, who is always surrounded by women, human and feline: our daughters, Elisa and Ashley, and our cats, Luna and Lyla. Love you all.

List of Tables

1.1 World religions, 1900–2050. *15*

1.2 Christianity and percent Christian female by global North/South, 2020. *16*

1.3 Countries with the most Christians, 1900 and 2020. *17*

1.4 Countries with the most Christians with percent Christian female, 2020. *17*

1.5 Countries with the highest and lowest percent Christian female, 2020. *18*

1.6 Major Christian traditions, 1900–2050. *20*

1.7 Major Christian traditions with percent Christian female, 2020. *21*

1.8 Christian families with percent Christian female, 2000 and 2015. *21*

1.9 Largest denominations with percent Christian female, 2015. *23*

1.10 Largest non-Catholic denominations with percent Christian female, 2015. *23*

2.1 Religions in Africa over 1%, 1900–2050. *37*

2.2 Christianity in Africa by region, 2020. *37*

2.3 Countries in Africa with the most Christians, 2020. *38*

2.4 Countries in Africa with the highest percent Christian female, 2020. *38*

2.5 Christian families in Africa, 2000 and 2015. *39*

2.6 Largest denominations in Africa, 2015. *40*

3.1 Religions over 1% in Asia, 1900–2050. *55*

3.2 Christianity in Asia by region, 2020. *56*

3.3 Countries in Asia with the most Christians, 2020. *57*

3.4 Countries in Asia with the highest percent Christian female, 2020. *57*

3.5 Christian families in Asia, 2000 and 2015. *59*

3.6 Largest denominations in Asia, 2015. *60*

4.1 Religions in Europe over 1%, 1900–2050. *77*

4.2 Christianity in Europe by region, 2020. *78*

4.3 Countries in Europe with the most Christians, 2020. *79*

4.4 Countries in Europe with the highest percent Christian female, 2020. *79*

4.5 Christian families in Europe, 2000 and 2015. *80*

4.6 Largest denominations in Europe, 2015. *82*

5.1 Religions in Latin America and the Caribbean over 1%, 1900–2050. *98*

5.2 Christianity in Latin America and the Caribbean by region, 2020. *99*

5.3 Countries in Latin America and the Caribbean with the most Christians, 2020. *99*

5.4 Countries in Latin America and the Caribbean with the highest percent Christian female, 2020. *100*

5.5 Christian families in Latin America and the Caribbean, 2000 and 2015. *101*

5.6 Largest denominations in Latin America and the Caribbean, 2015. *102*

5.7   Largest protestant and independent denominations in Latin America and
the Caribbean, 2020.   *102*

6.1   Religions in North America over 1%, 1900–2050.   *118*

6.2   Countries in North America with the most Christians, 2020.   *119*

6.3   Christian families in North America, 2000 and 2015.   *120*

6.4   Largest denominations in North America, 2015.   *121*

7.1   Religions in Oceania over 1%, 1900–2050.   *140*

7.2   Christianity in Oceania by region, 2020.   *140*

7.3   Countries in Oceania with the most Christians, 2020.   *140*

7.4   Countries in Oceania with the highest percent Christian female, 2020.   *141*

7.5   Christian families in Oceania, 2000 and 2015.   *142*

7.6   Largest denominations in Oceania, 2015.   *143*

7.7   Catholics and Anglicans in Australia and New Zealand, 1901 and
2013/2016.   *146*

8.1   Catholics by continent, 1900–2050.   *161*

8.2   Catholics by continent with percent female, 2020.   *162*

8.3   Countries with the most Catholics, 2020.   *162*

8.4   Countries with the highest percent of Catholics, 2020.   *163*

8.5   Countries with the fastest growth of Catholics, 2020.   *163*

8.6   Largest Catholic denominations, 2015.   *164*

8.7   Catholic workers, 2020.   *168*

9.1   Orthodox by continent, 1900–2050.   *183*

9.2   Orthodox by continent with percent female, 2020.   *184*

9.3   Countries with the most Orthodox, 2020.   *185*

9.4   Countries with the highest percent of Orthodox, 2020.   *185*

9.5   Countries with the fastest growth of Orthodox, 2020.   *186*

9.6   Largest Orthodox denominations, 2015.   *186*

10.1   Protestants by continent, 1900–2050.   *198*

10.2   Protestants by continent with percent female, 2020.   *199*

10.3   Countries with the most Protestants, 2020.   *199*

10.4   Countries with the highest percent of Protestants, 2020.   *200*

10.5   Countries with the fastest growth of Protestants, 2020.   *200*

10.6   Largest Protestant denominations, 2020.   *201*

11.1   Independents by continent, 1900–2050.   *217*

11.2   Independents by continent with percent female, 2020.   *218*

11.3   Countries with the most Independents, 2020.   *218*

11.4   Countries with the highest percent of Independents, 2020.   *219*

11.5   Countries with the fastest growth of Independents, 2020.   *219*

11.6   Largest Independent denominations, 2015.   *220*

12.1   Pentecostals/Charismatics by continent, 1900–2050.   *233*

12.2   Pentecostals/Charismatics by continent with percent female, 2020.   *234*

12.3   Countries with the most Pentecostals/Charismatics, 2020.   *235*

12.4   Countries with the highest percent of Pentecostals/Charismatics, 2020.   *235*

12.5   Countries with the fastest growth of Pentecostals/Charismatics, 2020.   *236*

12.6   Largest Pentecostal/Charismatic denominations, 2020.   *236*

13.1   Evangelicals by continent, 1900–2050.   *250*

13.2 Evangelicals by continent with percent female, 2020.   *251*

13.3 Countries with the most Evangelicals, 2020.   *251*

13.4 Countries with the highest percent of Evangelicals, 2020.   *252*

13.5 Countries with the fastest growth of Evangelicals, 2020.   *252*

13.6 Largest Evangelical denominations, 2015.   *253*

14.1 Gender-based violence in countries with the most Christians.   *269*

14.2 Countries with the highest Gender Inequality Index scores.   *270*

14.3 World Watch List 2022: 50 most difficult countries to be a Christian.   *271*

16.1 Global Survey on Theological Education, enrollment (2011–2013).   *303*

16.2 Headcount enrollment by gender in the Association of Theological Schools, 2021–2022.   *309*

16.3 Full-time faculty by gender in the Association of Theological Schools, 2021–2022.   *310*

List of Figures

1.1 Christianity in the global North and South, 1900 and 2020.   *14*

1.2 Christianity by major Christian tradition, 1900 and 2020.   *19*

1.3 How do you think the chances of women and men compare when it comes to getting a ___ position in a congregation? (global).   *30*

1.4 Thinking of the ___ position in your congregation, is this person male or female? (global).   *30*

2.1 Christianity in Africa by major Christian tradition, 1900 and 2020.   *39*

2.2 How do you think the chances of women and men compare when it comes to getting a ___ position in a congregation? (Africa).   *41*

2.3 Thinking of the ___ position in your congregation, is this person male or female? (Africa).   *42*

3.1 Christianity in Asia by major Christian tradition, 1900 and 2020.   *58*

3.2 How do you think the chances of women and men compare when it comes to getting a ___ position in a congregation? (Asia).   *61*

3.3 Thinking of the ___ in your congregation, is this person male or female? (Asia).   *62*

4.1 Christianity in Europe by major Christian tradition, 1900 and 2020.   *80*

4.2 How do you think the chances of women and men compare when it comes to getting a ___ position in a congregation? (Europe).   *83*

4.3 Thinking of the ___ in your congregation, is this person male or female? (Europe).   *83*

5.1 Christianity in Latin America and the Caribbean by major Christian tradition, 1900 and 2020.   *102*

5.2 How do you think the chances of women and men compare when it comes to getting a ___ position? (Latin America and the Caribbean).   *104*

5.3 Thinking of the ___ in your congregation, is this person male or female? (Latin America and the Caribbean).   *104*

6.1 Christianity in North America by major Christian tradition, 1900 and 2020.   *119*

6.2 How do you think the chances of women and men compare when it comes to getting a ___ position? (North America).   *123*

6.3 Thinking of the ___ in your congregation, is this person male or female? (North America).   *123*

7.1 Christianity in Oceania by major Christian tradition, 1900 and 2020.   *142*

7.2 How do you think the chances of women and men compare when it comes to getting a ___ position? (Oceania).   *144*

7.3 Thinking of the ___ position in your congregation, is this person male or female? (Oceania).   *145*

8.1 Catholics by continent, 1900 and 2020.   *160*

9.1 Orthodox by continent, 1900 and 2020.   *184*

10.1 Protestants by continent, 1900 and 2020.   *199*

11.1 Independents by continent, 1900 and 2020.   *216*

12.1 Pentecostals/Charismatics by continent, 1900 and 2020.   *234*

13.1 Evangelicals by continent, 1900 and 2020.   *249*

Introduction: Why Women in World Christianity?

"Women have comprised the majority of Christians globally, at least for the last three centuries for which we have statistics. 'World Christianity' could be considered 'as a Woman's Movement' (Robert 2006), so it behooves scholars and practitioners to observe women's dynamics closely to ascertain significant patterns in the development of worldwide Christianity."

Angelyn Dries (Dries 2016, p. 315)

Mary's Magnificat is the longest speech by a woman in the New Testament. It is recorded in Luke 1:46–55 (NIV) at her visit with her cousin, Elizabeth; both the women pregnant with prophets, and for Mary, the anticipated Messiah in her womb.

[46] And Mary said:
"My soul glorifies the Lord
[47] and my spirit rejoices in God my Savior,
[48] for he has been mindful
of the humble state of his servant.
From now on all generations will call me blessed,
[49] for the Mighty One has done great things for me –
holy is his name.
[50] His mercy extends to those who fear him,
from generation to generation.
[51] He has performed mighty deeds with his arm;
he has scattered those who are proud in their inmost thoughts.
[52] He has brought down rulers from their thrones
but has lifted up the humble.
[53] He has filled the hungry with good things
but has sent the rich away empty.
[54] He has helped his servant Israel,
remembering to be merciful
[55] to Abraham and his descendants forever,
just as he promised our ancestors."

In Eastern Orthodox Christianity, this pericope is called the Ode of the *Theotókos*, in other traditions it is called the Song of Mary, or the Canticle of Mary. It appears in liturgical services of Catholic, Eastern Orthodox, and Anglican churches around the world. Mary was an unmarried teenager with an illegitimate son yet spoke of God's favor upon her and God's judgment on the rich and powerful.

Women in World Christianity: Building and Sustaining a Global Movement, First Edition. Gina A. Zurlo.
© 2023 John Wiley & Sons Ltd. Published 2023 by John Wiley & Sons Ltd.

Her words are revolutionary, and she represents the poor, struggling, overlooked, and marginalized. The Magnificat was perceived to be so dangerous that it was banned during British imperial rule in India (1858–1947), the dictatorship in Guatemala (1980s), and the Argentine military junta (1974–1983) (Connelly 2014). It is a song of joy and pain, of victory over injustice, and of a faithful woman embracing God's plan. Mary does not ask for anything in her prayer; instead, she describes a prophetic vision of a world to come that promises justice. As Catholic theologian Nepolean James Raj concluded, "The knowledge of the hopes of Mary is an unquenchable spark which sustains hope in all who dream of an egalitarian society, justice, liberation, equality and full humanity" (Raj 2021, p. 136). Mary declares the inauguration of a new kingdom that rejects those of the past that relied on violence and exploitation (Evans and Chu 2021).

Mary has been a source of inspiration and veneration for women throughout Christian history. Women are the majority of the world's 2.5 billion Christians today, and many are demanding the justice, equality, and full humanity that Mary describes in her song. They are crying out against the violence in their societies, communities, and churches that relegate women to second-class status. Girded by their faith and encouraged by Mary and other women of the past, Christian women are increasingly breaking cultural barriers, becoming public figures, and participating in human flourishing. For example, consider Catholic sisters, who outnumber male priests and professed religious men on every continent. Consider the many women who persist despite indignities and threats of violence, notably sexual violence. In the Democratic Republic of the Congo (95% Christian) – once pronounced the "rape capital of the world" – women keenly realize that peacebuilding is part and parcel to Christian witness and must involve all spheres of life: social, political, and religious. Consider the many women who were the first at something previously unattainable for their sex: Lucia Okuthe was the first woman ordained an Anglican priest in Kenya (1983), Anne Burghardt was the first woman general secretary of the Lutheran World Federation (2021), and the first collection of writings from female theologians in the Pacific Islands was released in this century, *Weavings: Women Doing Theology in Oceania* (Johnson and Filemoni-Tofaeono 2003).

Yet, the centrality of women's contributions to the development of Christianity worldwide was not always recognized. Only since the 1970s have there been concerted efforts to uncover Christian women of the past and more seriously acknowledge women's activities as central, not marginal, to Christian life. Perhaps the most comprehensive analysis of global Christianity over time are the three editions of the *World Christian Encyclopedia* (1982, 2001, 2019). Each *Encyclopedia* features an entry for every country of the world, including small island nations in the Caribbean and the Pacific Islands that often get left off the map. Each entry includes quantitative data on religious and nonreligious adherence, as well as a list of every known denomination in the country and indicators of their growth or decline. These entries include photos of Christians in those countries, graphs illustrating the data, and a brief history of when different churches were formed and their contributions to Christian life. Despite all this information, the first two editions of the *Encyclopedia* included very few mentions of women, as if they had little to do with Christianity's spread or continuation. Women were barely counted at all – until now.

Gender and Quantitative Research on World Christianity

In the 1960s, David B. Barrett – a trained aeronautical engineer turned Anglican missionary priest – embarked on a novel idea. Using available technology in research for the social scientific study of religion, Barrett wanted to assess how many people in the world adhered to each religion. He compiled the most comprehensive global assessment of religious affiliation to date and published his results in the *World Christian Encyclopedia* (Barrett 1982), which contained an analysis of religious adherence down to the denominational level in each country. For the first time, the world's Christians were counted and included together in a single book, featuring new African Christian movements, among which Barrett lived and worked in Nairobi, Kenya. Yet, despite years of collecting and analyzing data and travel to 212 countries, Barrett overlooked variables that would have been critical for sociologists to uncover drivers of religious change. Sex and age distributions were omitted from Barrett's analyses, which was especially ironic since gender was a prominent factor in missionary statistics dating to the nineteenth century and at the height of the Western missionary movement (Dennis 1897; Student Volunteer Movement 1911). Barrett was a product of several male-dominated contexts: British and American elite universities, dominated by males; American professionalized, institutionalized sociology was largely male; the adherents of Christianity, though majority female, operated within male-oriented hierarchies and leadership structures; and engineering and the hard sciences were also essentially men's clubs. Data on the gender makeup of religious communities was admittedly difficult to obtain, but so was nearly all the data Barrett collected during the 13-year production of the *World Christian Encyclopedia* (Zurlo 2017, 2023).

The contemporary home of Barrett's research legacy, the Center for the Study of Global Christianity, sought to remedy the omission of gender in the third edition of the *World Christian Encyclopedia* from 2015 to 2019, which made extensive efforts to feature women in the narrative of World Christianity. The *Encyclopedia* includes examples of highly organized women's movements worldwide, such as the Young Women's Christian Association and Anglican Mothers' Unions. It describes women who provide education, combat HIV/AIDS, advocate for gender rights, and faithfully serve their congregations and local communities. The book included influential Christian women of the past, such as the female followers of Jesus who arrived in modern-day France in 49 CE, female founders of African Independent Churches such as Christiana Abiodun Emmanuel (1907–1994) in Nigeria, and the unnamed nineteenth-century Bible women in sub-Saharan Africa, East Asia, and Southeast Asia.

This research sparked increased interest in the role of women in churches around the world and the desire to include a gender variable in the *World Christian Database* (Johnson and Zurlo 2022). As a result, the Women in World Christianity Project (funded by the Louisville Institute and the Religious Research Association from 2019 to 2021) produced a dataset, for the first time, of the gender makeup of every Christian denomination in every country of the world. The project revealed that global church membership is 52% female, and that Mongolia reports the highest share of Christian women (63%). This study had severe limitations based on data availability, which is a major theme of the current volume. Many churches, denominations, and Christian networks that collect data on their members and affiliates either do not collect data on gender, or they do not publicly report it. The chronic lack of data related to women in World Christianity makes producing a global gender analysis of World Christianity extremely difficult. For example, significant discrepancies exist between data obtained from government censuses – the primary source for gender statistics that appear in this book – and data from religious communities themselves. While a census might report that Baptists are 52% female, data from the Baptists themselves (if available) are typically much higher, perhaps upward of 75%. A further discrepancy exists between membership versus attendance, where the former is typically equal between men and women, but the latter is dominated by women. The continental chapters in Part I provide examples of these discrepancies and gaps in data availability. The Women in World Christianity Project also included the Gender and Congregational Life Survey, which was administered online in English, Chinese, French, German, Korean, Mongolian, Portuguese, and Spanish from February 2021 to April 2021. The survey garnered over 1,000 responses from 72 countries. Select results from this survey are reported in Part I.

Christianity has always been majority female (e.g., Braude 1997) – after all, history shows that women were the last at the cross and the first at the tomb. In fact, demographers, social scientists, historians, and other scholars have stated for decades that women are more religious than men. The Pew Research Center's Gender Gap in Religion Around the World study (Pew Research Center 2016) claimed that, indeed, Christian women reported higher rates of church attendance, prayer, and religious self-identification than Christian men. Many sociological studies have also indicated this gender imbalance in religious identity, belief, and practice (Trzebiatowska and Bruce 2014). Estimating the nineteenth-century missionary movement from the United States as two-thirds female, mission historian Dana Robert even described World Christianity as a "women's movement" (Robert 1997, 2006). She asked, "What would the study of Christianity in Africa, Asia, and Latin America look like if scholars put women into the center of their research?" (Robert 2006, p. 180). What the Women in World Christianity Project began in attempting to answer that question, this book aims to carry through.

Women in the World Today

In the Western world, first-wave feminism of the late nineteenth and early twentieth centuries largely addressed legal obstacles to women's rights related to voting and property; that is, it was a movement about political power. Second-wave feminism emerged in the early 1960s with a much broader scope to address issues such as sexuality, reproductive rights, domesticity, domestic violence, marital rape, and divorce law. It also demanded change in patriarchal structures and cultural practices that deemed women less than men. Concentrated in Europe and North America, both first- and second-wave feminism were largely the initiatives of White, middle-class women, working under the assumption that women everywhere faced similar oppression to them. That is, they assumed all women suffered the same because of patriarchy and sexism. However, this approach ignored the intersectionality of oppression related to race, class, ethnicity, religion, colonialism, and politics (Herr 2013). In the 1980s and 1990s, women around the world challenged this narrow outlook and argued that their oppression was fundamentally different than that of White Western women; women suffer multiple and intersecting oppressions, not some "common condition" shared by all women worldwide (Herr 2013). The distinction between second-wave feminism and majority world feminist perspectives gave rise to so-called "third world" feminism (a term now largely out of vogue), transnational feminism (a popular term), and global feminism (or, feminisms); some use these terms interchangeably. Globally, women are not a monolith, their oppression is not the same everywhere (Mohanty 1987), and women's activism is not uniform around the world (see, for example, Campbell et al. 2010).

This book frequently points to the 1970s–1980s as a turning point for women, but it should not be read that White Western feminism was imported to Africa, Asia, Latin America and the Caribbean, and the Pacific Islands. Much like Black women in the West responding to the color blindness of second-wave feminism, women in the global South have claimed their agency to identify their own sources of oppression and advocate for their own rights separate from White Western women. For example, White female missionaries naïvely assumed that women's roles abroad should be reshaped according to Western gendered norms, and as a result indigenous women often lost agency and power with the arrival of Christianity, not gained it. Thus, use of the term "feminism" in the global South is not a reference to White Western second-wave feminism, but instead to how women in these places have created their own movements toward equality.

Social Norms and Power Imbalances

The 2019 Human Development Report of the United Nations was titled, "Beyond Income, Beyond Averages, Beyond Today: Inequalities in Human Development in the 21st Century." Chapter 4 was dedicated to gender inequalities in the world, with several striking findings (UNDHP 2019):

- Gender inequality is one of the most persistent inequalities across all countries.
- The world is not on track to achieve gender equality by 2030.
- If current trends continue, it will take 202 years for women to achieve complete economic equality with men.
- Gender equality in health, education, and economics has been *slowing* in recent years.
- Although substantial progress has been made in the last 25 years, there is no place in the world where women have complete equality with men.

These statements are not to erase the tremendous achievements women have made in recent years. Women today are the most qualified they have ever been in history. Fewer are dying in childbirth and more are obtaining secondary education. If this is the case, though, why is the gender gap so persistent? The UNHDP report highlights two underlying realities: social norms and power imbalances. Social norms dictate "men's roles" and "women's roles" in society, as well as set rules of behavior and attitudes that meld communities together. However, biases are widespread throughout social norms. The Multidimensional Gender Social Norms Index (Mukhopadhyay, Rivera, and Tapia 2019) reported that 86% of women and 90% of men held gender social norm biases. Power imbalances occur when these biased social norms expect men and women to perform certain duties, but women are excluded from the decision making that limits their opportunities and choices.

Social norms are extremely difficult to change. In many cases, people lack the information or knowledge to act or think differently. It is also an issue of what is at stake, particularly for those with more power: "A social norm will be stickiest when individuals have the most to gain from complying with it and the most to lose from challenging it" (UNHDP 2019, p. 158). In many places around the world, social norms are shifting away from traditional gendered expectations in both the public and private spheres. This is natural with increased women's education, political participation, and control over their own bodies and reproductive rights. These shifts typically push against prevailing beliefs and attitudes about how men and women should act in society. Indeed, it is beliefs about what people do and what people think other people should do that dictate what happens in the social sphere. At the same time, these beliefs and practices typically serve as active barriers that sustain gender inequalities now and likely in the future.

In the first few centuries of Christianity, women gained new opportunities for leadership and public activity by joining nascent churches, and their contributions helped grow Christianity from a fledgling movement into a world religion (Stark 1996). However, Christianity, Christians, churches, and Christian theology have also served as active barriers to women's opportunities, and this is difficult to change. While women make up the majority of church members worldwide, they are often prohibited from holding official leadership positions, are excluded from decision-making bodies, and their ministries are considered secondary to the main task of the Sunday morning worship service, where men are generally on public display. Church life, like everything else in the world, is gendered. Men and women experience life differently and they experience Christianity differently. This book aims to illustrate how, why, and in what ways those differences exist and how women respond to them.

Is World Christianity a Women's Movement?

Philip Jenkins's book, *The Next Christendom: The Coming of Global Christianity* (Jenkins 2002), is undoubtedly one of the most popular books on World Christianity. Although he did not discover it, he was the first to widely disseminate the finding that Christianity is no longer a majority White Western religion, but is in the hands of Africans, Asians, and Latin Americans. Originally published in 2002, *The Next Christendom* has been translated into other languages and has had multiple print runs. However, it was only in the third edition of the book (2011) that Jenkins realized the uniqueness of women's experiences, asking the question, "Does Christianity liberate women or introduce new scriptural bases for subjection?" (Jenkins 2011, p. 12). A comparison of the 2002 and 2011 editions reveals the addition of women in some chapters, such as the impact of female missionaries, Christian audiences mostly consisting of women, and a recognition that "women are critical to the growth of new churches across the global South" (Jenkins 2011, p. 211). However, women are not central to the story, they are additions to it in seemingly opportune places. This is common in many of the standard global Christianity texts, though improvements are being made, and of course there are exceptions. Sebastian Kim and Kirsteen Kim's *Christianity as a World Religion* (Kim and Kim 2016) is also a widely used text, helpful in its regional assessment of World Christianity combined with a deep description of Christianity as a world religion because of its countless local expressions linked by transnational ties. Christianity is primarily a movement of people, not institutions. Indeed, Kim and Kim communicate that by "people" they really do mean all people, with their inclusion of women's roles in their continental treatment of World Christianity, such as Bible women in Asia, Christian women's organizations in sub-Saharan Africa, women's ordination in North America, and *mujerista* theology in Latin America.

World Christianity is generally taught from historical or theological perspectives and overlaps with the field of mission studies. There are several excellent books on women in mission, such as Dana L. Robert, *Gospel Bearers, Gender Barriers: Missionary Women in the Twentieth Century* (Robert 2002); Dana L. Robert, *American Women in Mission: A Social History of Their Thought and Practice* (Robert 1997); Elizabeth Johnson, *The Strength of Her Witness: Jesus Christ in the Global Voices of Women* (Johnson 2016); and Christine Lienemann-Perrin et al., *Putting Names with Faces: Women's Impact in Mission History* (Lienemann-Perrin et al. 2012). Other texts are more biographical such as Anneke Companjen, *Hidden Sorrow, Lasting Joy: The Forgotten Women of the Persecuted Church* (Companjen 2005). These books have an important role in chronicling the countless contributions of the Western women's missionary movement and the expansion of Christianity in the global South by their efforts.

The many church history books specifically on women are helpful but are typically narrowly focused on Europe and North America, omitting the contributions of women from the global South. Examples include Elizabeth Clark, *Women in the Early Church* (Clark 1983); Barbara J. MacHaffie, *Her Story: Women in Christian Tradition* (MacHaffie 1992); and Elizabeth Gillan Muir, *A Women's History of the Christian Church* (Muir 2019). While these texts fill in the standard male narrative of Western church history, they generally do not contribute to scholarship on global Christian history. The body of literature on the histories and contributions of Christian women from continental, regional, country and/or ecclesiastical perspectives is growing. Works include Mercy Amba Oduyoye, *Beads and Strands: Reflections on an African Woman on Christianity in Africa* (Oduyoye 2004); Samuel Lee, *Japanese Women and Christianity* (Lee 2022); and Phyllis Martin, *Catholic Women of Congo-Brazzaville* (Martin 2009). Books with these narrower foci are well-suited for studies on Christianity by continent, region, or ecclesiastical tradition. Feminist theology from scholars such as Kwok Pui-lan, Ada María Isasi-Díaz, and Isabel Apawo Phiri have highlighted how the gendered experiences of women in the global South – now the center of World

Christianity – have influenced new kinds of theological thought. Non-male, non-Western scholarship should be moving from the periphery to the center of higher education curricula if schools want to provide more holistic and relevant theological perspectives for their students.

Women in World Christianity: Building and Sustaining a Global Movement aims to tie these strands together: mission and gendered church history, emerging scholarship from the global South, feminist theology, and the sociology of religion. It is the first textbook about women in World Christianity and aims to be transdisciplinary in combining history, theology, and the social sciences. This book directly answers Dana Robert's call from 2006: "What would the study of Christianity in Africa, Asia, and Latin America look like if scholars put women into the center of their research?" It would look something like this book, and it would show that, indeed, World Christianity *is* a women's movement.

Contents of This Book

By focusing on the twentieth and twenty-first centuries, this book highlights women's roles as Christianity continues its shift from a global North religion (Europe, North America) to a global South one (Africa, Asia, Latin America and the Caribbean, Oceania). This book is part history in describing Christian women from the past, but also part social science as it engages with what Christian women are doing around the world today. Furthermore, many chapters introduce readers to female theologians who produce scholarship that is largely marginalized in Western theological education.

This book is designed to be used in World Christianity courses on the undergraduate and graduate levels. By having a resource that calls attention to women's stories, instructors can be better equipped to provide a more balanced approach to how and why Christianity became a world religion, and how it is sustained. Although this is a book about women, its purpose is not to write men out of Christian history. The story of Christianity's development and global spread cannot be told without men, though it *has* been told without women. By noticing and prioritizing women's stories, experiences, and contributions, this book offers a corrective to our understanding of Christian history and Christian life today.

Parts I and II include, as much as possible, factors related to Christian women's historical, social, political, religious, and cultural contexts to help fully situate their experiences today. Part I (Chapters 1–7) is geographic in scope, covering major themes and trends in World Christianity, followed by Africa, Asia, Europe, Latin America and the Caribbean, North America, and Oceania. Each of these chapters includes history, quantitative data, results from the Gender and Congregational Life Survey, descriptions of Christian women's activities in the past and present, and female theologians from the continent. The history sections are not designed to be comprehensive, but rather introduce readers to important themes, movements, and contributions from key Christian women. These sections also include foreign female missionaries who planted churches and provided education for local women, as well as indigenous women who spread the Christian faith. These chapters address several specificities of women's activities in these places, such as women founders of African Independent Churches, Latina responses to *machismo*, and differences among Christian women's experiences in White, Black, Latino/a, and indigenous communities in North America. Each theology section calls attention to important female theologians, including major themes and the contextual nature of their scholarship.

Part II (Chapters 8–13) organizes World Christianity by major Christian tradition and movement: Catholic, Orthodox, Protestant, Independent, Pentecostal/Charismatic, and Evangelical. These chapters provide information to place women in these traditions in their historical contexts, quantitative data of how these traditions have changed over time, and discussions of the unique experiences of women across these different ecclesiological traditions today. Each chapter incorporates information on women in leadership, including in traditions where women are not permitted to hold formal leadership positions.

Many topics have been embedded in the continental and ecclesial chapters in Parts I and II, such as women's Christian history, ordination, mission, social service outreach, ecumenism, and theological contributions. It is not possible to comprehensively address all topics related to women in World Christianity. There is a long list of potential subjects that could have been included in Part III, such as Christian women in healthcare, interfaith relations, sex trafficking ministries, LGBTQ+ activism, family dynamics (marriage and motherhood), the arts, or political involvement. The inclusion of four chapters dedicated to gender-based violence, ecology, theological education, and peacebuilding is not to suggest these are the most pressing issues for Christian women, nor that they are the issues Christian women are most involved. Difficult subjects are discussed throughout this book, especially in Part III, such as sexual violence and discrimination against women. Readers are encouraged to engage cautiously with these sensitive subjects.

Gender-based violence (Chapter 14) has been included because nowhere in the world do women have complete physical safety. Compared to men, women are at a distinct disadvantage simply by nature of their birth – that is, if they are fortunate enough to be born, given rates of female infanticide. Women are in a state of constant heightened awareness of their physical surroundings and are not even completely safe from violence in churches. Any advocacy related to women, Christian or otherwise, must acknowledge that women's basic existence and safety are constantly under threat.

The climate crisis has been identified as one of – if not *the* – most pressing global issue of the twenty-first century (Chapter 15). Women around the world are heavily involved in faith-based ecological activism yet are consistently left out of discussions related to combatting climate change. Women are especially susceptible to severe impacts of rising sea waters, more intense weather events, and global temperature rise. Ecofeminist theologians have been addressing environmental issues for many decades, but much of this scholarship has been sidelined in some parts of the world as merely politically progressive, not central to a life of faith.

Education for women and girls is an ongoing goal of the United Nations Sustainable Development Goals, and there indeed has been much progress in this area. Yet, formal Christian theological education (Chapter 16) is still largely reserved for men, especially in the global South. Most global South women have little hope of receiving formal theological education due to cultural, theological, and ideological barriers. In some places, women are explicitly prohibited from enrolling in degree programs; in many others, they are discouraged from doing so. Nearly everywhere, there are comparatively few role models to inspire women in this area.

Peacebuilding (Chapter 17) is a major effort of women in World Christianity. While many Christian organizations consider peacebuilding to be core to their mission and identity, this topic is rarely even considered by many American missions organizations. Christian women have been on the forefront of peacebuilding activities to bring stability to their nations and ensure their survival. This chapter highlights several such movements and what women are doing to meld faith, activism, and politics to bring flourishing to their own lives and those of their families and communities.

Each chapter in this book includes reflection questions for group discussion and opportunities for self-theologizing. This book utilizes Harvard citation style with a slight modification: instead of only indicating the first initial of author/editor given names, the entire given name has been included. This way, the reader can observe that more than half of the scholarship cited in this book is authored by women, contributing to this book's aim of centering their perspectives. The goal is to understand how and in what ways World Christianity really is both a global movement and a women's movement. Ideally, readers can clearly see the countless ways women have contributed to Christianity becoming a world religion, and how women's acts of service continue to sustain it today and into the future.

Works Cited

Barrett, David B. (1982). *World Christian Encyclopedia*. Nairobi: Oxford University Press.

Barrett, David B., Kurian, George T., and Johnson, Todd M. ed. (2001). *World Christian Encyclopedia: A Comparative Survey of Churches and Religions in the Modern World*, 2nd edn. Oxford: Oxford University Press.

Student Volunteer Movement for Foreign Missions, and Bartholomew, John G. (1911). *World Atlas of Christian Missions: Containing a Directory of Missionary Societies, a Classified Summary of Statistics, an Index of Mission Stations, and Maps Showing the Location of Mission Stations Throughout the World*. New York: Student Volunteer Movement for Foreign Missions.

Braude, Ann (1997). Women's history *is* American religious history. In: *Retelling U.S. Religious History* (ed. Thomas Tweed), 87–107. Berkeley: University of California Press.

Campbell, Patricia J. et al. (2010). *An Introduction to Global Studies*. West Sussex: John Wiley & Sons.

Clark, Elizabeth A. (1983). *Women in the Early Church*. Wilmington, DE: M. Glazier.

Companjen, Anneke (2005). *Hidden Sorrow, Lasting Joy: The Forgotten Women of the Persecuted Church*. London: Hodder & Stoughton.

Connelly, Susan (2014). The Magnificat as social document. *Compass*, 8, 8–11.

Dennis, James S. (1897). *Christian Missions and Social Progress: A Sociological Study of Foreign Missions*. New York: Fleming H. Revell.

Dries, Angelyn (2016). Women in church, state, and society. In: *The Wiley Blackwell Companion to World Christianity* (ed. Lamin O. Sanneh, and Michael J. McClymond), 302–317. Hoboken, NJ: Wiley-Blackwell.

Evans, Rachel H. and Chu, Jeff (2021). *Wholehearted Faith*. New York: Harper One.

Herr, Ranjoo S. (2013). Transnational, third world, and global feminisms. In: *Encyclopedia of Race and Racism*, 2nd edn. (ed. Patrick L. Mason). Detroit, MI: Macmillan Reference USA.

Jenkins, Philip (2002). *The Next Christendom: The Coming of Global Christianity*. Oxford: Oxford University Press.

Jenkins, Philip (2011). *The Next Christendom: The Coming of Global Christianity*, 3rd edn. Oxford: Oxford University Press.

Johnson, Elizabeth (2016). *The Strength of Her Witness: Jesus Christ in the Global Voices of Women*. Maryknoll, NY: Orbis.

Johnson, Lydia and Filemoni-Tofaeono, Joan A. (2003). *Weavings: Women Doing Theology in Oceania*. Suva, Fiji: Weavers, South Pacific Association of Theological Schools and Institute of Pacific Studies, University of the South Pacific.

Johnson, Todd M. and Zurlo, Gina A. (2019). *World Christian Encyclopedia*, 3rd edn. Edinburgh: Edinburgh University Press.

Johnson, Todd M. and Zurlo, Gina A. ed. (2022). *World Christian Database*. Leiden/Boston: Brill.

Kim, Sebastian C.H. and Kim, Kirsteen (2016). *Christianity as a World Religion: An Introduction*, 2nd edn. London: Bloomsbury Academic.

Lee, Samuel (2022). *Japanese Women and Christianity*. Amsterdam: Academy Press of Amsterdam.

Lienemann-Perrin, Christine et al. (2012). *Putting Names with Faces: Women's Impact in Mission History*. Nashville, TN: Abingdon Press.

MacHaffie, Barbara J. (1992). *Readings in Her Story: Women in Christian Tradition*. Minneapolis, MN: Fortress Press.

Martin, Phyllis M. (2009). *Catholic Women of Congo-Brazzaville*. Bloomington: Indiana University Press.

Mohanty, Chandra (1987). Feminist encounters: locating the politics of experience. *Copyright*, 1(Fall), 30–44.

Muir, Elizabeth G. (2019). *A Women's History of the Christian Church: Two Thousand Years of Female Leadership*. Toronto: University of Toronto Press.

Mukhopadhyay, Tanni, Rivera, Carolina, and Tapia, Heriberto (2019). *Gender Inequality and Multidimensional Social Norms*. Working paper. United Nations Development Programme, Human Development Report Office, New York.

Oduyoye, Mercy A. (2004). *Beads and Strands: Reflections on an African Woman on Christianity in Africa*. Maryknoll, NY: Orbis Books.

Pew Research Center (2016). Gender Gap in Religion Around the World.

Raj, Nepolean J. (2021). The image of Mary in the Magnificat: mary's hope as spark, small but unquenchable. In: *Hope: Where Does Our Hope Lie?* (ed. Miloš Lichner), 123–139. Zurich: Lit Verlag.

Robert, Dana L. (1997). *American Women in Mission: A Social History of Their Thought and Practice*. Macon, GA: Mercer University Press.

Robert, Dana L. (2002). *Gospel Bearers, Gender Barriers: Missionary Women in the Twentieth Century*. Maryknoll, NY: Orbis.

Robert, Dana L. (2006). World Christianity as a women's movement. *International Bulletin of Missionary Research*, 30(4), 180–188.

Stark, Rodney (1996). *The Rise of Christianity: A Sociologist Reconsiders History*. Princeton, NJ: Princeton University Press.

Trzebiatowska, Marta and Bruce, Steve (2014). *Why are Women More Religious than Men?* Oxford: Oxford University Press.

United Nations Human Development Programme (UNHDP) (2019). *Human Development Report 2019: Beyond Income, beyond Averages, beyond Today: Inequalities in Human Development in the 21st Century*. New York: United Nations.

Zurlo, Gina A. (2017). 'A miracle from Nairobi': David B. Barrett and the quantification of World Christianity, 1957–1982. PhD dissertation. Boston University.

Zurlo, Gina A. (2023). *From Nairobi to the World: David B. Barrett and the Re-Imagining of World Christianity*. Leiden/Boston: Brill.

Part I

Women in World Christianity by Continent

1

Women in World Christianity

"When we put women in the center of the frame, then a different constellation of theology, cultural milieu, and social world will emerge. When woman is no longer simply the social and cultural background of the theological center, then a shift in historical method and a rethinking of theology are required."

Bernadette J. Brooten (Brooten 1985, p. 66)

Despite historians' assertions that Christianity has always been a majority female faith, uncovering the role of women behind its status as a world religion is only a recent phenomenon. World Christianity consists of 2.5 billion Christians, at least 52% of whom are women by membership, who speak a wide variety of languages, come from different cultural backgrounds, and express their faith in a multitude of ways. However, placing women at the center of historical, social scientific, and theological investigation demands new frameworks. Existing "gender-neutral" approaches to World Christianity paint with a broad brush that erase women's unique experiences and their contributions to the development and sustainment of the Christian faith. Spotlighting the experiences of women does not exclude those of men. As gender and religion scholar Bernadette Brooten describes, "To listen to women is not to refuse to hear men; it is to let those who have been mute speak" (Brooten 1985, p. 83). Focusing on women means moving their experiences and stories from the periphery to the center, from the margins of study to the core.

Endless examples illustrate women's deep involvement in global Christianity, both from regional and ecclesiological perspectives. Women are more likely to show up for church activities throughout the week, both at Sunday morning services and weeknight Bible studies. Catholic pilgrimage sites around the world are mostly visited by women. In Brazil, women are the majority of practitioners of popular Catholicism and many of its rituals are almost exclusively led by women. Membership in the Church of Christ in Congo, an ecumenical Protestant umbrella organization with at least 64 member denominations, is majority female. All congregations in Eswatini are majority female. Catholic sisters outnumber brothers on every continent and in most countries. There are more American female missionaries than male, especially among single people. Each chapter of this book illustrates women's crucial involvement in their faith communities and the importance of their commitment to the church.

Women in World Christianity: Building and Sustaining a Global Movement, First Edition. Gina A. Zurlo.
© 2023 John Wiley & Sons Ltd. Published 2023 by John Wiley & Sons Ltd.

World Christianity, 1900–2050

Christianity has been the world's largest religion over the last 120 years, representing 35% of the world's population in 1900 and 32% in 2020 (Table 1.1). By 2050, it is anticipated Christianity could increase to 34%, but that largely depends on birth rates and potential conversions to Christianity in India and China, the world's two largest countries. In this analysis, "Christian" refers to anyone who self-identifies as such or is in some way affiliated to a Christian congregation or denomination (see the Methodology section for more). By assessing membership, rather than belief or practice, it is possible to measure religion consistently across all six continents and all 234 countries. For example, it is widely observed that many Europeans self-identify as Christian or are baptized in Catholic or Orthodox churches as infants. Even if they do not believe in its core tenets or practice with any regularity, or at all, they are nevertheless counted as Christians because of their affiliation to a church. Comprehensive data do not exist for every country to measure and compare other indicators such as belief in God, frequency of prayer, and level of commitment to the Christian faith.

Global Christianity experienced a dramatic change in the twentieth century. In 1900, only 18% of all Christians lived in the global South (Asia, Africa, Latin America and the Caribbean, and Oceania) (Table 1.2; Figure 1.1). By 2020, this figure had grown to 67%, and it is expected to reach 77% by 2050. This is known as Christianity's shift to the global South, where the majority of its adherents live today. Africa is home to the most Christians (667 million; 49% Christian), followed by Latin America (612 million; 92% Christian), and Europe (565 million; 76% Christian). Official data, sourced largely from governmental censuses, reveals that in most places women claim only a slight majority of Christian affiliation over men. However, as this book illustrates, more localized studies reveal that women's share of congregations is much, much higher – in some cases, 90%!

Table 1.2 presents World Christianity by continent and United Nations regions, with its Christian population and its Christian gender makeup. Every continent has a female majority in its Christian population. North America reports the highest percentage of Christian women (54%), and Asia the lowest (51%). However, it is very likely that most of these percentages are in reality much higher due to a lack of available data (see Women in social scientific research section below). Historic longitudinal data for the gender makeup of world religions and Christian traditions are currently not available, so it is not possible to provide historical estimates or track trends over time.

Figure 1.1 Christianity in the global North and South, 1900 and 2020. *Source:* Data from Johnson and Zurlo 2022.

Table 1.1 World religions, 1900–2050.

Religion	Pop. 1900	% 1900	Pop. 2000	% 2000	Rate % p.a. 1900–2000	Pop. 2020	% 2020	Rate % p.a. 2000–2020	Pop. 2050	% 2050
Religious	1,616,370,000	99.8	5,342,790,000	87.0	1.20	6,893,141,000	88.4	0.85	8,885,011,000	91.3
Baha'is	205,000	0.0	6,050,000	0.1	3.45	8,482,000	0.1	1.76	14,328,000	0.1
Buddhists	126,946,000	7.8	453,685,000	7.4	1.28	532,657,000	6.8	0.29	580,708,000	6.0
Chinese folk-rel.	379,974,000	23.5	433,310,000	7.1	0.13	466,181,000	6.0	−0.05	459,195,000	4.7
Christians	558,346,000	34.5	1,981,177,000	32.2	1.27	2,506,426,000	32.2	0.96	3,334,019,000	34.2
Daoists	375,000	0.0	7,173,000	0.1	3.00	8,907,000	0.1	1.76	15,035,000	0.2
Confucianists	840,000	0.1	8,013,000	0.1	2.28	8,719,000	0.1	0.55	10,265,000	0.1
Ethnic rel.	117,313,000	7.2	223,863,000	3.6	0.65	284,527,000	3.7	−0.03	282,022,000	2.9
Hindus	202,976,000	12.5	824,760,000	13.4	1.41	1,058,245,000	13.6	0.44	1,206,856,000	12.4
Jains	1,324,000	0.1	4,809,000	0.1	1.30	6,317,000	0.1	0.76	7,919,000	0.1
Jews	11,725,000	0.7	12,813,000	0.2	0.09	14,817,000	0.2	0.49	17,137,000	0.2
Muslims	200,301,000	12.4	1,288,687,000	21.0	1.88	1,886,702,000	24.2	1.38	2,842,753,000	29.2
New rel.	5,986,000	0.4	62,899,000	1.0	2.38	66,614,000	0.9	−0.29	61,031,000	0.6
Shintoists	6,720,000	0.4	2,831,000	0.0	−0.86	2,823,000	0.0	0.03	2,845,000	0.0
Sikhs	2,962,000	0.2	20,033,000	0.3	1.93	26,743,000	0.3	0.89	34,914,000	0.4
Spiritists	269,000	0.0	12,500,000	0.2	3.92	14,779,000	0.2	0.23	15,820,000	0.2
Zoroastrians	109,000	0.0	186,000	0.0	0.54	201,000	0.0	−0.66	165,000	0.0
Nonreligious	3,255,000	0.2	800,704,000	13.0	5.66	901,657,000	11.6	−0.20	850,023,000	8.7
Agnostics	3,028,000	0.2	659,225,000	10.7	5.53	752,135,000	9.6	−0.21	707,144,000	7.3
Atheists	226,000	0.0	141,479,000	2.3	6.65	149,523,000	1.9	−0.15	142,879,000	1.5
Total	**1,619,625,000**	**100.0**	**6,143,494,000**	**100.0**	**2.46**	**7,794,799,000**	**100.0**	**1.21**	**9,735,034,000**	**100.0**

Source: Data from Johnson and Zurlo 2022.
Note: Names have been shortened for Chinese folk-religionists, Ethnic religionists, and New religionists. p.a. = percent change per annum, or each year.

Table 1.2 Christianity and percent Christian female by global North/South, 2020.

Continent and region	Christians 2020	% Christian 2020	% of all Christians 2020	% Christian female 2020	% region female 2020
Global North	**842,127,000**	**75.4**	**33.6**	**53.1**	**51.3**
Europe	572,603,000	76.6	22.8	52.6	51.7
Eastern Europe	245,905,000	83.9	9.8	53.1	53.0
Northern Europe	74,919,000	70.5	3.0	53.3	50.6
Southern Europe	122,688,000	80.6	4.9	51.5	51.1
Western Europe	129,091,000	65.8	5.2	52.4	50.9
North America	269,524,000	73.1	10.8	54.1	50.5
Global South	**1,664,299,000**	**24.9**	**66.4**	**51.7**	**49.3**
Africa	654,913,000	48.9	26.1	52.1	50.0
Eastern Africa	292,393,000	65.6	11.7	51.6	50.4
Middle Africa	148,998,000	83.0	5.9	52.0	50.1
Northern Africa	11,668,000	4.7	0.5	49.6	49.8
Southern Africa	55,465,000	82.2	2.2	54.1	50.8
Western Africa	146,389,000	36.4	5.8	52.6	49.7
Asia	377,842,000	8.1	15.1	51.0	48.9
Central Asia	5,658,000	7.6	0.2	53.6	50.5
Eastern Asia	128,446,000	7.7	5.1	52.6	49.0
South Asia	75,254,000	3.9	3.0	50.2	48.4
Southeastern Asia	152,878,000	22.9	6.1	49.8	50.1
West Asia	15,606,000	5.6	0.6	51.6	47.6
Latin America	602,892,000	92.2	24.1	51.6	50.8
Caribbean	36,616,000	84.1	1.5	51.9	50.6
Central America	171,979,000	95.7	6.9	51.7	51.0
South America	394,297,000	91.5	15.7	51.6	50.8
Oceania	28,652,000	67.1	1.1	51.7	49.9
Australia/New Zealand	17,244,000	56.9	0.7	53.4	50.3
Melanesia	10,239,000	92.1	0.4	48.9	49.0
Micronesia	511,000	93.1	0.0	51.0	49.7
Polynesia	657,000	96.1	0.0	51.2	49.0
Global total	**2,506,426,000**	**32.2**	**100.0**	**52.1**	**49.6**

Source: Data from Johnson and Zurlo 2022.

Table 1.3 Countries with the most Christians, 1900 and 2020.

Rank	Country	Christians 1900	Rank	Country	Christians 2020
1	United States	73,712,000	1	United States	245,457,000
2	Russia	62,545,000	2	Brazil	192,939,000
3	Germany	41,533,000	3	Mexico	123,370,000
4	France	40,731,000	4	Russia	119,945,000
5	United Kingdom	37,125,000	5	China	106,018,000
6	Italy	32,903,000	6	Philippines	99,307,000
7	Ukraine	28,501,000	7	Nigeria	95,186,000
8	Poland	22,040,000	8	DR Congo	85,061,000
9	Spain	18,795,000	9	Ethiopia	67,903,000
10	Brazil	17,319,000	10	India	66,316,000

Source: Data from Johnson and Zurlo 2022.

Table 1.4 Countries with the most Christians with percent Christian female, 2020.

Rank	Country	Christians 2020	% Christian 2020	% Christian female 2020	% Country female 2020
1	United States	245,457,000	74.2	54.3	50.5%
2	Brazil	192,939,000	90.8	51.6	50.9%
3	Mexico	123,370,000	95.7	51.7	51.1%
4	Russia	119,945,000	82.2	53.5	53.7%
5	China	106,018,000	7.4	52.6	48.7%
6	Philippines	99,307,000	90.6	49.5	49.8%
7	Nigeria	95,186,000	46.2	52.7	49.3%
8	DR Congo	85,061,000	94.9	51.9	50.1%
9	Ethiopia	67,903,000	59.1	50.0	50.0%
10	India	66,316,000	4.8	50.0	48.0%

Source: Data from Johnson and Zurlo 2022.

The countries with the most Christians in 1900 and 2020 reveal the twentieth-century shift of Christianity in more detail (Table 1.3). In 1900, only one country in the global South made the list (Brazil). However, in 2020, eight of the ten countries with the most Christians were in the global South. The United States remains an outlier, as the country with the most Christians in the world in 2020 (244 million, 74%), but located in the global North.

Table 1.4 compares the same top ten countries with the most Christians in 2020, with the addition of their gender makeup. One country is majority male (Italy), two countries are evenly split male/female (Spain, Brazil), and the remaining countries are majority female. The largest gap in this list is the United States: 54% female and 46% male.

Table 1.5 Countries with the highest and lowest percent Christian female, 2020.

Rank	Country	Christians 2020	% Christian 2020	% Christian female 2020	% Country female 2020
1	Mongolia	63,600	1.9	63.2	50.7%
2	Israel	188,000	2.2	63.0	50.2%
3	Estonia	495,000	37.3	62.8	52.6%
4	BES Islands	24,200	92.1	57.4	54.0%
5	Czechia	3,746,000	35.0	57.0	50.8%
6	Botswana	1,647,000	70.0	56.0	51.6%
7	Barbados	273,000	94.9	55.7	51.6%
8	Jamaica	2,504,000	84.5	55.4	50.4%
9	New Zealand	2,624,000	54.4	55.4	50.8%
10	Bermuda	55,200	88.7	55.2	51.4%
Rank	Country	Christians 2020	% Christian 2020	% Christian female 2020	% Country female 2020
225	Cambodia	426,000	2.5	49.0	49.4%
226	Bangladesh	915,000	0.6	49.0	51.2%
227	Saint Helena	5,800	95.8	48.7	50.6%
228	Palau	16,700	92.3	48.4	49.6%
229	Papua New Guinea	8,482,000	94.8	48.3	48.9%
230	Iran	579,000	0.7	47.0	49.5%
231	Bahrain	205,000	12.1	44.6	35.3%
232	Thailand	912,000	12.1	44.3	51.3%
233	Maldives	1,500	0.3	39.1	36.6%
234	Qatar	400,000	13.9	36.4	24.8%

Source: Data from Johnson and Zurlo 2022.

Table 1.5 lists the top ten countries with the highest and lowest female share of its Christian population. Mongolia ranks the highest, with Christianity at 63% female, and Qatar is at the bottom with 36% female.

It is difficult to make general observations about these data. There is no natural relationship, for example, between the size of a Christian population and its gender makeup, or the level of religious freedom in a country and the Christian gender makeup. Mongolia's Christian population is skewed female because of broader gender dynamics related to education rates, the country's unique rural–urban divide, and gender roles of the traditional herding lifestyle. Qatar is a majority Muslim country (80% in 2020), with its overall population only 24% female (76% male) due to migration patterns. Alongside a few indigenous adherents, Qatar's Christian population is largely an interdenominational expatriate community of Westerners, Indians, and Arabs. Most are men working in the oil industry, accounting for its low female percentage share in the Christian population. This could also be the explanation for low Christian female percentages in Bahrain and other Gulf States.

World Christianity by Major Tradition, Family, and Denomination

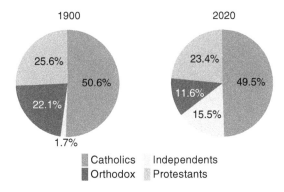

Figure 1.2 Christianity by major Christian tradition, 1900 and 2020. *Source:* Data from Johnson and Zurlo 2022.

Besides geography, another way to organize World Christianity is by major Christian tradition. It is important to consider women's involvement in churches from ecclesial perspectives because these traditions take different positions on women in leadership, the family, ministry, and society. These roles are shaped, among other factors, by scripture, theology, tradition, and culture. According to the taxonomy of the *World Christian Database* (Johnson and Zurlo 2022), World Christianity consists of four major traditions: Catholics, Orthodox, Protestants, and Independents, and two movements: Evangelicals and Pentecostals/Charismatics. An additional category is unaffiliated Christians, defined as persons who profess commitment to Christ but who have no church affiliation, which is different from affiliation with nondenominational churches. Major Christian traditions are mutually exclusive. A Christian cannot be considered both, for example, a Catholic and a Protestant. Yet, in countries with state churches, it is common for individuals to be baptized into one and later switch to another without being removed from the membership of the first. Such is the case in much of Europe, where people self-identify as Catholic but no longer practice, and in Latin America, where most people are baptized Catholic, but many now self-identify as *evangélicos* – Protestants, Evangelicals, and/or Pentecostals/Charismatics. In these contexts, a methodology of double-affiliation is employed to introduce a negative number to the calculations. Otherwise, there could be more Christians in a country than there are people as reported by the United Nations. Evangelicals and Pentecostals/Charismatics are found within each of the major Christian traditions. Thus, it is possible, for instance, to be a Catholic Charismatic, an Evangelical Protestant, or an Independent Charismatic Evangelical.

Independents are Christians who do-not self-identify as Catholic, Orthodox, or Protestant. They include Christians affiliated with African Independent Churches (AICs), the Church of Jesus Christ of Latter-day Saints (Mormons), Jehovah's Witnesses, as well as the majority of house churches and underground or secret communities of Christians, particularly in the global South (see Chapter 11). Many Christian traditions are not historically tied to the sixteenth-century Protestant Reformation in Europe, nor do they hold to certain aspects of traditional Protestant theology, whether by ascribing to additional sources of revelation or identifying as non-Trinitarian. In 2020, 49% of all Christians worldwide were Catholic, 23% Protestant, 16% Independent, and 12% Orthodox (Table 1.6; Figure 1.2).

Catholics have been, and are likely to remain, the largest tradition, though their share of all Christians worldwide dropped from its height of 52% in 1970 to 49% in 2020, with projected decline to 46% in 2050 (Table 1.6). Independent Christianity has experienced the fastest increase over this period, with a dramatic average annual growth rate of 3.2% between 1900 and 2020, and an estimated continued growth to 19% of all Christians in 2050 (up from less than 2% in 1900). Much of the increase in Independent Christianity was due to the expansion of house churches in China and African Independent Churches. Both Evangelicals and Pentecostals/Charismatics have increased their shares of World Christianity, the former growing from 14% of all Christians in 1900 to 15%, the latter growing from less than 1% in 1900 to 26%. As Christianity continues its shift to the global South, it is likely that Independent, Evangelical, and Pentecostal/Charismatic churches will grow as historic churches decline in the global North.

Table 1.6 Major Christian traditions, 1900–2050.

Tradition	Pop. 1900	1900 % of pop.	1900 % of Christians	Pop. 2020	2020 % of pop.	2020 % of Christians	Rate % p.a. 1900–2020	Pop. 2050	2050 % of pop.	2050 % of Christians
Catholics	265,756,000	16.4	47.6	1,239,271,000	15.9	49.4	1.29	1,518,441,000	15.6	45.5
Protestants	134,196,000	8.3	24.0	585,289,000	7.5	23.4	1.23	881,002,000	9.0	26.4
Independents	8,859,000	0.5	1.6	389,474,000	5.0	15.5	3.20	618,845,000	6.4	18.6
Orthodox	116,199,000	7.2	20.8	291,924,000	3.7	11.6	0.77	322,239,000	3.3	9.7
Doubly-affiliated	-2,569,000	-0.2	-0.5	-113,026,000	-1.5	-4.5	3.20	-113,528,000	-1.2	-3.4
Unaffiliated Christians	35,906,000	2.2	6.4	113,493,000	1.5	4.5	0.96	107,021,000	1.1	3.2
Evangelicals*	80,912,000	5.0	14.5	387,026,000	5.0	15.4	1.31	620,963,000	6.4	18.6
Pentecostals/ Charismatics*	981,000	0.1	0.2	644,260,000	8.3	25.7	5.55	1,031,500,000	10.6	30.9
Global total	**558,346,000**	**34.5**	–	**2,506,426,000**	**32.2**	–	**1.26**	**3,334,019,000**	**34.2**	–

Source: Data from Johnson and Zurlo 2022. p.a. = percent change per annum, or each year.
*These movements are found within Christian traditions listed above.

Table 1.7 displays the gender makeup of the major Christian traditions and movements. The highest proportion of women are among Independents (54%), followed by unaffiliated Christians, Evangelicals, Pentecostals/Charismatics, and Protestants (all rounded to 53%). Catholics and Orthodox report the lowest share of women (51% and 52%), though this is largely because Catholic and Orthodox populations closely mirror the populations of their regions and countries, especially in Europe and Latin America. The data on women in major Christian traditions would be much different – that is, there would be noticeably higher shares of women – if more data were available from churches and denominations themselves. The data in Table 1.7 represents reporting from governmental censuses, and it is assumed that churches have a greater knowledge of the size and demographic makeup of their communities than the government (see the Methodology section).

Table 1.7 Major Christian traditions with percent Christian female, 2020.

Tradition	Pop. 2020	% of global pop. 2020	% of Christians 2020	% Christian female 2020
Catholics	1,239,271,000	15.9	49.4	51.2
Protestants	585,289,000	7.5	23.4	52.7
Independents	389,474,000	5.0	15.5	53.8
Orthodox	291,924,000	3.7	11.6	52.2
Doubly-affiliated	–113,026,000	–1.5	–4.5	51.8
Unaffiliated Christians	113,493,000	1.5	4.5	53.2
Evangelicals*	387,026,000	5.0	15.4	52.8
Pentecostals/Charismatics*	644,260,000	8.3	25.7	52.8
Global total	**2,506,426,000**	**32.2**	**100**	**52.1**

Source: Data from Johnson and Zurlo 2022.
*Located within major traditions above.

Table 1.8 Christian families with percent Christian female, 2000 and 2015.

Family	Affiliated 2000	Affiliated 2015	% female 2015	Rate % p.a. 2000–2015
Latin-rite Catholic	1,009,659,000	1,170,521,000	51.2	0.99
Pentecostal/Charismatic*	188,072,000	264,163,000	53.9	2.29
Eastern Orthodox	207,569,000	221,319,000	52.9	0.43
Anglican	77,522,000	93,056,000	52.9	1.23
Baptist	70,223,000	81,520,000	53.5	1.00
United church or joint mission	53,331,000	72,942,000	52.0	2.11
Lutheran	58,613,000	66,370,000	52.6	0.83
Oriental and other Orthodox	49,423,000	63,927,000	50.2	1.73
Reformed, Presbyterian	55,353,000	62,900,000	52.2	0.86
Nontraditional, house, cell	49,499,000	54,666,000	53.6	0.66
Other Protestant/Independent	30,086,000	43,721,000	53.7	2.52
Methodist	28,511,000	30,978,000	54.0	0.55
Nondenominational	20,702,000	27,642,000	50.9	1.95
Adventist	16,401,000	25,721,000	52.4	3.05

(Continued)

Table 1.8 (Continued)

Family	Affiliated 2000	Affiliated 2015	% female 2015	Rate % p.a. 2000–2015
Jehovah's Witnesses	13,491,000	18,839,000	54.9	2.25
Eastern-rite Catholic	15,019,000	16,468,000	51.3	0.62
Latter-day Saints (Mormons)	11,279,000	16,109,000	54.2	2.40
Holiness	10,149,000	13,334,000	52.3	1.84
Restorationist, Disciple	9,225,000	10,934,000	52.9	1.14
Hidden believers in Christ	3,421,000	5,169,000	50.0	2.79
Old Catholic Church	5,015,000	5,110,000	49.6	0.13
Congregational	3,534,000	4,438,000	54.1	1.53
Christian Brethren	3,056,000	3,703,000	52.2	1.29
Mennonite	1,879,000	2,474,000	51.8	1.85
Salvationist	2,268,000	2,317,000	52.4	0.14
Friends (Quaker)	547,000	1,243,000	53.8	5.62
Moravian	816,000	962,000	52.8	1.10
Dunker	609,000	714,000	54.0	1.07

Source: Data from Johnson and Zurlo 2022. p.a. = percent change per annum, or each year.
*Excluding partially pentecostalized.
Note: 2015 is the latest data available for families and denominations. See the Methodology section for explanation.

Another way of viewing World Christianity from the perspective of traditions and movements is Christian families. These groupings (in Table 1.8) are recognizable names of denominations and networks that help answer questions such as, "How many Methodists are in the world?" To answer this, Protestant Methodists and Independent Methodists are added together to arrive at a global figure, which results in 31 million Methodists of all kinds. Sometimes these global figures differ from official statis of international bodies because the families include breakaway churches (see Chapter 11). For example, the United Methodist Church (UMC) reports 13 million members worldwide, a much smaller figure than 31 million, but the UMC does not include all kinds of Methodists in its calculations.

Among Christian families, the highest percent female is among Jehovah's Witnesses (55%), followed by Latter-day Saints, Congregationalists, Dunkers, Methodists, Friends (Quaker), house churches, and Baptists (each 54%). There does not appear to be any correlation nor causation between kinds of Christian families and the share of women in their global membership. It might be tempting to correlate gender equality with high female membership, but the data do not support such claims. For example, Holiness churches historically have been very inclusive of women in ministry and leadership, but they report 52% female, lower than many other groups. Similarly, Latter-day Saints wards (congregations) do not allow women to preach, and yet they have one of the highest shares of women in their membership.

Finally, the smallest unit of measurement in the *World Christian Database* taxonomy is denomination, defined as an organized Christian church, group, community of people, and/or aggregate of worship centers/congregations within a specific country who considers itself autonomous, distinct from other churches and traditions, and whose constituents are called by the same name. Denominations are defined and measured at the country level, creating a large number of separate denominations within Christian families and traditions. For example, the presence of the Catholic Church in the world's 234 countries results in 234 Catholic "denominations" even though there is

Table 1.9 Largest denominations with percent Christian female, 2015.

Rank	Country	Denomination	Affiliated 2015	% female 2015
1	Brazil	Igreja Católica no Brasil	148,550,000	50.0
2	Russia	Russian Orthodox Church	110,850,000	53.5
3	Mexico	Iglesia Católica en México	110,155,000	51.4
4	Philippines	Catholic Church in the Philippines	78,271,000	49.3
5	United States	Catholic Church in the USA	72,798,000	53.3
6	Italy	Chiesa Cattolica in Italia	45,563,000	51.4
7	DR Congo	Eglise Catholique au DR Congo	42,891,000	51.2
8	Colombia	Iglesia Católica en Colombia	42,206,000	51.2
9	Spain	Iglesia Católica en España	39,377,000	51.2
10	Ethiopia	Ethiopian Orthodox Church	39,200,000	50.0

Source: Data from Johnson and Zurlo 2022.

Table 1.10 Largest non-Catholic denominations with percent Christian female, 2015.

Rank	Country	Denomination	Affiliated 2015	% female 2015
1	Russia	Russian Orthodox Church	110,850,000	53.5
2	Ethiopia	Ethiopian Orthodox Church	39,200,000	50.0
3	China	Three-Self Patriotic Movement	30,000,000	51.5
4	Germany	Evangelische Kirche in Deutschland	24,450,000	55.0
5	United Kingdom	Church of England	23,000,000	53.8
6	Nigeria	Anglican Church of Nigeria	22,000,000	52.9
7	Brazil	Assembleias de Deus	20,987,000	55.0
8	China	Han traditional house churches	20,000,000	53.7
9	China	Han house churches Big Five (rural)	19,510,000	53.7
10	United States	Southern Baptist Convention	18,836,000	54.1

Source: Data from Johnson and Zurlo 2022.

one Roman Catholic Church. The typical way for Christians to count themselves is at the local con-gregational level and then aggregate these totals at the city, province, state, regional, and national level. Table 1.9 shows that Catholics represent the largest denominations (at the country level), such as in Brazil, Mexico, the Philippines, Italy, the Democratic Republic of the Congo, Colombia, and Spain. Catholic figures for percent female tend to closely mirror the gender makeup of the country, which is why Table 1.9 does not report significantly higher shares of women (that is, most are around 50% female). Unaffiliated Christians in the United States – Christians who are not members of or known to institutional churches – have a slightly higher than average share of women (54%). Table 1.10 removes Catholics from the analysis to illustrate a broader denominational diversity.

From the data that are available, two general trends appear to be true. First, surveys tend to report higher percent Christian female than government censuses. There are few surveys available for this kind of analysis, but some of the highest percent Christian female figures are from Argentina and the United States, both sourced from surveys, and neither country includes a reli-gion question on its national census for comparison. In Argentina, the religion survey by the

National Scientific and Technical Research Council reported 80% female for Evangelical Baptists and 62% for Pentecostals (Mallimaci et al. 2019). For the United States, the Pew Research Center reported 57% female for historically Black Protestants and 54% for Evangelical and mainline Protestants (Pew Research Center 2015). Second, denominations that fall under the Independent category tend to report higher shares of women in their memberships than other traditions, regardless of source. Examples include the Universal Church of the Kingdom of God (Brazil), 60% female; Jehovah's Witnesses (Brazil), 58% female; Church of the Lord (Prayer Fellowship) (Nigeria), 56% female; and the Assemblies of God (Zimbabwe), 56% female (Johnson and Zurlo 2022).

As Chapters 8–13 illustrate, a wide diversity of gendered expectations exists within these traditions, movements, families, and denominations. Some ordain women, others do not; some have substantial gender imbalances in their memberships, where others are more equal; some actively encourage women's public participation, others prefer women to have more supportive roles. Nevertheless, in all Christian traditions, women are finding ways to live out their vocational callings, make important contributions to the life of the church, and in many ecclesial contexts, are pushing boundaries for greater equality and public influence.

Dynamics of Religious Change

From a demographic perspective, there are a limited number of ways a religion can change on the national level. Growth of a religion requires high birth rates (natural growth), conversion, and/or immigration into the country. Factors that cause a religion to decline are death, conversion out, and emigration. All six dynamics of religious change had a role in the twentieth-century shift of Christianity to the global South.

Christianity declined in Europe during the twentieth century and continues to decline in the twenty-first century. Christians are leaving churches by either switching from Christianity to non-religion (atheism or agnosticism), choosing to be spiritual but not religious, or preferring to believe in Jesus but not belong to a Christian church. Most European countries also reported declining birth rates over the twentieth century, which meant Christians were not having enough children to replace losses from people leaving the faith. Furthermore, many Christians (Orthodox, in particular) were deported or killed in Central and Eastern Europe under Communism in the Soviet Union. State-imposed atheism drove many religious communities underground, forcing them to practice in private and at great risk to their own lives. In the twenty-first century, Europe has become more religiously diverse after receiving migrants from elsewhere in the world, such as Muslims from North Africa and the Middle East, as well as Christians from sub-Saharan Africa who are planting new churches. These churches tend to attract participants from immigrant communities, not locals.

North America is experiencing a confluence of several dynamics, the nature of which depend upon the group of people in question. Though White Christians are leaving churches, Christianity remains the continent's largest religion due to immigrants, both documented and undocumented, from Latin America and elsewhere in the global South. This movement of people is largely responsible for the United States having the most Christians of any nation now and likely into the future. Birth rates are declining across race and ethnicity, but are higher among Blacks, who tend to be more religious than Whites. At the same time, some churches still have higher than average birth rates, such as the Church of Jesus Christ of Latter-day Saints. The migration of persecuted Christians also factors significantly: Canada, for example, has received large numbers of migrants in recent years, many of whom are Christians fleeing religious persecution in the Middle East.

Over the twentieth century, the growth of Christianity in Africa was largely due to conversions from African Traditional Religions to Christianity, which were sustained by high birth rates. Conversion rates leveled off as the pool of potential converts declined; traditional religionists dropped from 58% of the continent in 1900, to 10% by 2000. Muslims also grew in Africa over the

Photo 1.1 Celebration of All Souls Day at Holy Rosary Catholic Church, Tejgaon, Bangladesh (2011). *Source:* Md Arifur Rahman/Flickr.

twentieth century, from 33% in 1900 to 42% in 2020, also due to conversions and high birth rates (Johnson and Zurlo 2022). Muslims in Africa do not tend to convert to Christianity, nor do African Christians tend to convert to Islam. In the twenty-first century, natural change (births and deaths) is the leading driver of religious change and is likely to remain so in the future.

Asia, the historical home to many religions, is the most religiously diverse place in the world, with large populations of Muslims, Hindus, Buddhists, nonreligious people, and Christians. Although Christianity originated in West Asia and first spread throughout Central Asia, it is a minority religion in Asia today (8% in 2020, up from 2% in 1900). Due to conversions from many different religions, Christianity in Asia grew twice as fast as the general population in the twentieth century. The fastest growth was among house churches, particularly in China. Because of China's one-child policy (1979–2015), birth rates were lower and so nearly all this growth can be attributed to conversions. However, in West Asia (part of the Middle East), Christians are under severe social and political pressure and have declined from 12% in 1900 to 4% in 2020, largely due to deaths and emigration.

Christianity has a long history in Latin America and the Caribbean, a region targeted by European Catholic colonialism and mission starting in the late fifteenth century. As a result, the population has been majority Catholic for hundreds of years, but with its own emphasis on popular devotion and a culturally appropriate blending with traditional beliefs and practices. In the twentieth and twenty-first centuries, Catholicism has been challenged by new expressions of Christianity via the introduction and growth of Protestantism, Pentecostalism, and Evangelicalism – followers of which are known in Spanish-speaking countries as *evangélicos*. Although Christianity in Latin America and the Caribbean represents a sizable majority of the continent (92% in 2020), its internal makeup is changing as Catholics switch to Protestant and Independent Christianity. Nevertheless, Latin America and the Caribbean are poised to remain majority Catholic in the future, an estimated 69% Catholic by 2050.

The continent of Oceania consists of Australia and New Zealand, plus dozens of Pacific Island nations in Melanesia, Micronesia, and Polynesia. It is a unique place in that Christianity arrived via British conquest in the late eighteenth century and took hold in Australia and New Zealand, but Australia/New Zealand rapidly secularized in the nineteenth and twentieth centuries, becoming far less Christian (together 54% in 2020, down from 97% in 1900). In the meantime, Pacific Islanders embraced Christianity and now most of those countries are at least 90% Christian, mostly Protestant with substantial populations of Latter-day Saints. The Pacific Islands are threatened due to rising sea levels caused by global climate change. It is likely that emigration will have a substantial role in the decline of Christianity in this region in the twenty-first century as people leave their ancestral homelands as environmental migrants or climate refugees.

Christianity in the twenty-first century is not expected to experience the kind of dramatic changes described above. Tracking births and deaths will always be the most important factor in studying future religious change, as religion is a strong predictor of marriage and childbearing trends. Studies have shown that, among religious people, fertility remains high, more traditional gender roles tend to be practiced, and women bear greater responsibility in child-rearing (Skirbekk 2022; Jenkins 2020; Schnabel et al. 2022). Religion is also positively correlated to gender inequality; that is, the nonreligious tend to be more egalitarian (Schnabel 2016). Understanding women's religiosity is crucial for predicting the future of faith, and religiosity is dependent on more than simply individual beliefs and convictions. Religion will be impacted by women's ability to choose when they marry and to whom, how much education they receive, what kind of family planning they use or not, essentially, what control they have over their own lives, bodies, and destinies. The religious future of Nigeria – a country evenly split between Muslims in the north and Christians in the south – will be largely dictated by how many babies are born to each religion, which is directly related to women's opportunities. The fertility gap between Christians and Muslims has widened, with Muslim women's fertility increasing from 6.4 to 6.8 children per woman between 1990 and 2013; that of Muslim women in states with Sharia law rose to 7.2 children. The Christian total fertility rate decreased over the same period, from 6.1 to 4.5 (Stonawski et al. 2016). The divergence is a result of the implementation of Sharia law in 1999 and differences in contraceptive use, sex education, general education for girls, mean age at marriage, and the prevalence of polygyny (when a man has more than one wife). Understanding the future involves tracking developments related to women's education, family planning, and a host of other social, cultural, and religious issues. In short, women are central to the future of faith.

Predicting the movement of people worldwide is a nearly impossible endeavor. Political upheavals, natural disasters, war, persecution, and other large-scale events all have consequences for religious populations as people move across borders without assurance of a return. Moreover, it is difficult to estimate potential conversions to Christianity, which are less common in this century than they were in the last, despite the global Christian missionary movement dedicated to that task. Nevertheless, it is suspected that some people are converting from Hinduism to Christianity in India, and from various religions and nonreligion to Christianity in China. Studies at the intersection of gender and conversion to Christianity are rare (Paris et al. 2012), but history suggests that women are more likely to switch religions than men (such as in Hodgson 2005). Known for sure is that women have their own reasons for converting to Christianity that are different from men (Kent 2004; Bauman 2008; Stark 1996; Yoo 2020). It is imperative to center women's experiences to truly comprehend changes that may occur in the religious and nonreligious worlds.

Women in Christian History

The contributions of women to the development of Christianity over time cannot be overemphasized. Jesus made deliberate decisions to challenge prevailing attitudes toward women in his time (Bailey 2008). He had women disciples (followers) and intentionally catered to women in his teaching, often using illustrations directed toward them. The accounts of Jesus's burial and resurrection both begin and end with women. In the early church, women made contributions to Christianity despite their social class and background: whether they were celibate or married, barren or mothering, in public or in private, with or without formal education. Throughout history, Christian women were apostles, martyrs, empresses, queens, sisters, nuns, mystics, preachers, social justice advocates, missionaries, and evangelists (Dzubinski and Stasson 2021; Muir 2019).

Facing both opportunities and obstacles in their ministries, women embraced challenges with radical obedience through sacrificial service to their churches and communities (Dzubinski and Stasson 2021). Historians as of late have made note of female majorities in churches and Christian movements around the world, documenting high women's involvement in church activities. As early as the first century, women were more likely than men to convert to Christianity. Churches prohibited infanticide and abortion, which helped reduce female mortality. Women enjoyed a higher status within Christian subcultures, and they had more children on average than pagans. All of these factors helped grow the nascent church (Stark 1996).

Beginning in the twelfth century, the Virgin Mary became an especially important Christian symbol for both women and men. Marian apparitions (visions) generated legends, such as that in December 1531 where a dark-skinned Mary appeared four times to Juan Diego in what is today Mexico. Our Lady of Guadalupe, now the Patroness of Mexico, the Americas, and Cebu, is the most-visited Catholic shrine in the world, with an estimated 12 million pilgrims a year. As the most powerful intercessor and a symbol of protection (Kupari and Vuola 2020), Mary is revered in Eastern Orthodoxy as the Mother of God, the All Holy, and above the angels. She is featured prominently alongside women saints in Eastern Orthodox iconography. Despite the veneration of women, Catholic women in the Medieval era were denied formal leadership in the church, leading them to form religious societies to worship God and serve the church outside of traditional ecclesiastical contexts.

Women have always made up the majority of congregations in North America, from the time of the British colonies to the present. Revivals of the Second Great Awakening (1790s–1840s) in the American colonies were mostly attended by women and children. Moreover, the American Protestant missionary movement in the nineteenth century was two-thirds female (Robert 1997). In Asia and sub-Saharan Africa, Bible women – indigenous evangelists – had the primary role in spreading Christianity throughout their communities. Such contributions by women have historically been marginalized. For instance, as the Catholic missionary work among the Maasai in Tanzania targeted men, it was deemed a failure when all the women converted (Hodgson 2005). Women have founded many large denominations: the Salvation Army (Catherine and William Booth), Seventh-day Adventist Church (Ellen G. White), Foursquare Gospel Church (Aimee Semple McPherson), and Yoido Full Gospel Church (Jashil Choi and David Yonggi Cho), among others. There would be no World Christianity to speak of today if it were not for women.

Despite all the women in church history, it was only recently that their stories began to be known and widely told. Since the 1960s, there have been two historiographical shifts in scholarship: (1) the inclusion of women's history alongside mainstream history; and (2) the inclusion of social and cultural history alongside institutional history. For generations, church history was the story of institutions founded and run by men, theological ideas penned by men, and movements built and sustained by men. While the rise of women's history in the 1960s and 1970s produced significant scholarship on women in church history, it has taken much longer for it to enter the mainstream (Brekus 2007). For example, reflecting on the history of American religion, historian Ann Braude observed: "The numerical dominance of women in all but a few religious groups constitutes one of the most consistent features of American religion, and one of the least explained" (Braude 1997, p. 88).

Women's history brings different questions and frameworks to the study of the past, requiring primary sources that are often more difficult to interpret, such as journals, diaries, and correspondence. These sources raise the question of agency, which most women of the past lacked. Centering women in the study of Christian history challenges previously held notions of how historical events unfolded, or what is most important in a historical account. For example, instead of analyzing the impact of a religious movement on a nation or politics, a women's history perspective might look at its impact on everyday lives, a vital perspective drawing on the experiences of those excluded from the political sphere. This is the core of including social history alongside institutional history. Instead of altering the historical narrative, social history aims to provide it with deeper interpretations that consider a wider cast of characters. Social history also includes popular religion and devotion – that is, religion beyond formal institutions – and diversifies traditional understandings of the past that only focus on the elite, and not the general populace. Beyond facts and figures of nations, governments, militaries, hierarchies, and leaders, social history provides windows into how people felt and thought, how they related to one another, and how they reacted to the events of their time.

These historiographical shifts are important for the study of women in World Christianity. The roles of women in the historical growth and development of Christianity in the global South have been made known thanks to the work of key female historians and theologians such as Dana Robert, Christine Lienemann-Perrin, Cathy Ross, Connie Shemo, Mercy Amba Oduyoye, Kwok Pui-lan, Philomena Mwaura, Dorothy Hodgson, Barbara Reeves-Ellington, Ada María Isasi-Díaz, Elizabeth Brusco, Ondina Gonzalez, Isabel Apawo Phiri, Rosemary Seton, and many others. It is becoming increasingly popular in World Christianity books and courses to highlight well-known Christian women such as Pandita Ramabai in India, the Virgin of Guadalupe in Mexico, and American and British missionaries like Ann Hasseltine Judson, Lottie Moon, Amy Carmichael, and Gladys Aylward. However, their presence is still relegated to the margins, a mere addition to an existing framework, rather than a much needed rewriting of the framework altogether. With women encompassing the majority of churches in the new centers of World Christianity, a more representative set of narratives would emerge if the experiences of women – especially women in the global South – were prioritized over those of men, and over "genderless" approaches.

Women in Social Scientific Research

In 2018, the Bill and Melinda Gates Foundation released their annual letter, reflecting on what surprised them in the previous year. The letter bluntly stated: "Data can be sexist." It continued, "There are huge gaps in the global data about women and girls. For example, we don't know how much income women in developing countries earned last year or how much property they own or how many more hours girls spend on household chores than boys do. Better data will help policymakers take action to improve women's and girls' lives." In *Invisible Women: Data Bias in a World Designed for Men*, Caroline Criado Perez (2019) investigated the lack of consideration of women in a wide variety of areas, including the

Photo 1.2 Christmas celebration at a secret meeting of Christians in Saudi Arabia (2017). *Source:* World Watch Monitor.

order of how snow is cleared off streets, the problems of ill-fitting police uniforms, inequalities in medicine, and crash test requirements for new automobiles. She uncovered numerous areas where research simply failed to account for the unique needs of women's bodies, activities, and lives. In some cases, decisions were made that resulted in structures that were merely inconvenient for women, like long lines in public bathrooms. In other cases, these decisions were downright deadly. For instance, women are 47% more likely than men to be seriously injured in a car crash because they do not sit in the "standard seating position;" that is, they do not sit the same way as men.

There is a serious lack of data in World Christianity studies as well. It is widely known that women are more likely than men to attend religious services, pray, and say that religion is important in their lives (Pew Research Center 2016). However, it was not known until very recently what percentage of the church in Africa, for example, is female (52% by membership, much higher by attendance and participation; see Chapter 2). Comprehensive data on women's activities in churches, their influences in congregational life, what kinds of leadership roles they have, and the extent of women's service to their churches and religious communities are not available.

Most Christian denominations collect data of all kinds, including church membership, detailed budgets, attendance, number of pastors, buildings, women's and children's ministries, tithes, and so on. However, precious few groups appear to collect data on the gender makeup of their membership. This is even the case for churches with robust statistical traditions, like the Roman Catholic Church and the Church of Jesus Christ of Latter-day Saints, both of whom produce annual statistical annals and have been collecting information on the demographic makeup and activities of their members for decades (or centuries!). Even for groups like these, gendered membership data are apparently unavailable to the public, and even unavailable by request. Two of the most globally spread Protestant denominations exhibit somewhat opposite trends: the Assemblies of God (AoG) and the Seventh-day Adventist Church (SDA), each present in nearly 200 countries and each with longstanding statistical initiatives. The AoG collected data on gender worldwide for many years but dropped the variable in the early 2020s to reduce the data collection burden on their member churches. On the other hand, the SDA added the gender variable, but only in 2021. With ministry roles so gendered, one would surmise that churches would collapse without women working behind the scenes. Without good data, good decisions cannot be made.

What do women *do* in churches? Women are preachers and evangelists, ordained or lay; teachers, deaconesses, elders, and missionaries; women run mother's groups, wives' clubs, ecumenical fellowships, and national chapters of the Young Women's Christian Association and other global entities. Women teach young girls life skills and ensure their education. They are involved in political activism and humanitarian work, speaking out for the oppressed and advocating for equal rights. Some women openly critique social norms in their churches and societies, while others quietly and effectively work within established systems. Women are increasingly elected to honored leadership positions within Christian organizations and denominations. Like in the first century of Christianity, women today are leaders of house churches and risk their lives to make disciples. Many have prominent roles in "hidden" Christian communities in North Africa, Central Asia, and the Middle East where it is illegal or dangerous to be a Christian.

The Gender and Congregational Life Survey (1,331 respondents) asked several questions regarding congregational ministries.[1] Half of respondents had been involved in their congregations over ten years. Congregational sizes varied, but the vast majority (77%) were under 500

---

1 The demographics of the respondents are important. Of the 1,331 responses, 81% were female and 19% were male. The survey title – Gender and Congregational Life – was interpreted by many potential respondents that it was a survey for women only, despite it being designed for both women and men. This is a problem in the wider field of gender studies, which is often interpreted narrowly as women's studies. Furthermore, the responses were skewed toward the global North, with 67% of respondents from the global North and 33% from the global South – the exact opposite of the actual demographics of World Christianity.

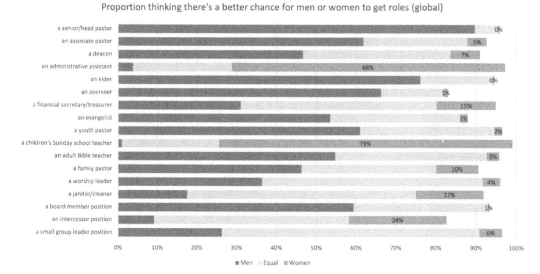

Figure 1.3 How do you think the chances of women and men compare when it comes to getting a ___ position in a congregation? (global). *Source:* Adapted from Gender and Congregational Life Survey (2021).

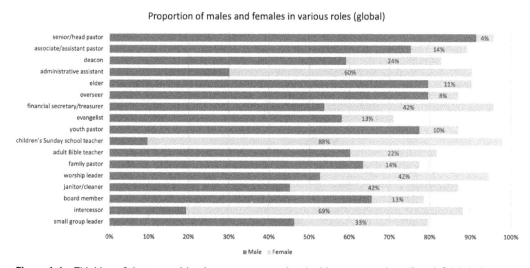

Figure 1.4 Thinking of the ___ position in your congregation, is this person male or female? (global). *Source:* Adapted from Gender and Congregational Life Survey (2021).

members. Most respondents (89%) indicated that the Sunday morning (or main) worship service was the most important ministry in their church, followed by small groups (44%) and community outreach (43%). The three least important ministries were men's ministry (72%), women's ministry (54%), and overseas missions (41%). Overall, respondents felt that women and men had generally equal chances to serve in a variety of church positions, such as financial secretary/treasurer, adult Bible teacher, family pastor, and small group leader (Figure 1.3).

However, when asked who actually holds these positions in their congregations, the gendered dynamics of church life became much more apparent. Even though, for instance, most respondents thought women and men had an equal chance of being an intercessor, most responded that position was held by a woman. Overall, women featured prominently in the roles of administrative assistant, children's Sunday school teacher, and intercessor. Just 4% responded that women were their senior/head pastor, 8% as overseer, and 14% as family pastor (Figure 1.4).

Regarding women pastors, 84% of respondents indicated that they strongly agreed or agreed that women should be allowed to serve as pastors, a sentiment most prominent for members of Methodist (98%), Anglican (95%), Holiness (91%), and Mennonite (93%) denominations. Yet, at the same time, only 15% of people reported that women had a better chance of getting a head pastor position over a man. Likewise, again, while most believed women can serve as pastors, only 23% indicated that the Bible places no restrictions on women's roles. These findings illustrate the imbalance that exists between theological and social scientific perspectives on women in congregational life. While many believe that women could be pastors, there are few women pastors to be found.

Women in Theology

Theology is typically divided into types such as biblical theology, historical theology, systematic theology, and practical theology. For most of church history, this kind of theologizing was done by cisgender White men in Europe and North America. However, over the twentieth century, different kinds of theologizing arose, together referred to as "contextual theology." The first wave of these theologies emerged due to the recognition that existing theology did not adequately address Christian experiences and perspectives from ethnic, social, gender, cultural, historical, and other contexts outside of cisgender White maleness. In response, feminist theology, womanist theology, and queer theology highlighted the perspectives of White women, Black women, and genderqueer people. Furthermore, with the shift of Christianity to the global South, the standard White Western theologies, again, did not fit the new cultural contexts of the faith. For example, the questions of White European men did not align with the needs of new and quickly growing churches in sub-Saharan Africa. Additional contextual theologies arose such as liberation theology (Latin America), *minjung* theology (South Korea), *mujerista* theology (Latina theology), *Dalit* theology (India), African theology, Asian feminist theology, and others. Reading biblical texts differently based on their social location, gender, history, language, and culture, these theologies approach Christianity as an incarnational faith, finding a home within every language, people, and culture in the world. In other words, the work of theology depends not only on the biblical text but the human experiences that engage it; as a result, all Christians can offer unique theological reflections based on their locations and experiences. However, a problem with the term "contextual theology" is its implication that plain "theology" (i.e., that of the West) is universal, while everything else is contextual. Because all theology is invariably contextual, the erroneous assumption that Western European male theology is universally valid (and not itself contextual) has hindered theological developments in the twentieth and twenty-first centuries, continuing the unsympathetic centering of White male experience above all else.

A core part of understanding World Christianity is listening to Christians from around the world. In general, women historically did not write books but the myth that they did not think theologically has been widely dismantled, with a still growing body of theological work by women for exploration. Yet, theology and biblical studies courses at many Christian colleges, seminaries, and universities – in both the global North and South – tragically neglect women's scholarship. There are numerous reasons for this, including theological convictions that women should not teach or lead men, a lack of awareness of gender diversity in the global Christian church, or the difficulty of moving past tradition into new areas of theologizing. But in neglecting women's theology from around the world, Christians reject a deeper level of understanding regarding the experiences, struggles, and joys of Christian women, who make up more than half the church. Knowing their stories and thoughts helps knit people of all genders together as a global Christian family.

Part of centering women theologically may require a recentering of biblical understanding, implementing the practice of historical imagination. For example, how different is the story of

David and Bathsheba (2 Samuel 11) if Bathsheba's thoughts and feelings were given equal attention to David's? What if there existed more information in the text about how Delilah felt in her relationship with Samson (Judges 16)? Did men and women in the upper room experience the Day of Pentecost and Christ's ascension differently (Acts 1 and 2)? What if the Christian scriptures were penned by women, instead of men? How might the perspectives differ? How do the experiences of women in the Bible influence how theology is understood today? These questions can be further extended by considering the differences between feminist and womanist approaches – that is, intersectional theology that considers the full spectrum of human experience.

Women are speaking and teaching, and Christians worldwide have the opportunity to listen, expand their horizons, and have their faith stretched. The Global Church Project, run by Australian Graham Joseph Hill, has made a tremendous contribution to uplifting women theologians through his coauthored (generally with women) series on "Women You Should Know About" (www.globalchurchproject.com). Organized regionally, Hill and colleagues – Jocabed Solano, Drew Jennings-Grisham, Stephanie A. Lowery, Emmanuella Carter, Juliany González Nieves, Grace Al-Zoughbi Arteen, Jessie Giyou Kim, Jen Barker, and Celucien L. Joseph – highlight the work of hundreds of female theologians: Africans, Latin Americans, Arabs, Australian/New Zealanders, Asians and Asian Americans, African Americans, and indigenous women. Other initiatives are less representative, such as *Majority World Theologies* (Yeh and Tienou 2018), where only three of 13 articles are authored by women. Five of the 32 articles in *The Routledge Handbook of African Theology* (Bongmba 2020) are by women, while *Christian Theology in Asia* (Kim 2008) contains only one female theologian (of 13 total) – writing about Asian feminist theology. Of the 47 articles in the 715-page volume *Majority World Theology* (Green, Pardue, and Yeo 2020), 10 are authored by women, though another 37 women are referenced in footnotes.

Ethnic diversity is an obvious demographic characteristic of World Christianity – when studying Christianity in the global South, one would expect to encounter the stories of Africans, Asians, Latin Americans, and Pacific Islanders. However, gender diversity is equally as important – especially since women make up more than half the church. If most of the theological scholarship is done by men and for a male or "genderless" audience, then over half the church is silenced. If more than half the church is silenced, the entire church is robbed of opportunities for growth and discipleship.

Conclusion

The study of Christianity around the world is indeed different when women are the focus. When properly centered, women are core to the history of Christianity, represent the status of the faith today, and are the hope of its future. Historically, Christian women were the driving force of local change in their communities – more likely to become Christian and influence their social circles toward the faith. Resilient in the face of challenges, global or local, women have made up the majority of congregational membership around the world and are actively preaching the gospel, ministering in a variety of capacities, and often doing so under significant strain. Theological writing from women is becoming more numerous and prominent, reflecting on what it means to be Christian from their unique social, cultural, and gendered perspectives. All of this activity points to an increased female future of World Christianity as its southward shift continues.

Reflection Questions

1) Characterize the current and projected global religious landscape and describe some demographic trends that have contributed to these realities. How might women's choices regarding employment, family planning, and religious involvement impact global trends in religious and nonreligious affiliation?

2) In what ways do you think congregational life is gendered? Describe from your personal experience gendered norms and roles within institutional Christian structures. How do these roles vary depending on theological tradition and geographic context?

3) Do you think it is necessary to recenter women theologically, and what role does rereading the Bible have in this process? How might the Bible have been received, interpreted, and understood differently if women were the main authors? How might our understanding of Christian history be different if women were the main interpreters of scripture?

Works Cited

Bailey, Kenneth E. (2008). *Jesus through Middle Eastern Eyes: Cultural Studies in the Gospels*. Downers Grove, IL: IVP Academic.

Bauman, Chad M. (2008). *Christian Identity and Dalit Religion in Hindu India, 1868–1947*. Grand Rapids, MI: William B. Eerdmans Pub.

Bongmba, Elias K. ed. (2020). *The Routledge Handbook of African Theology*. Abingdon: Routledge.

Braude, Ann (1997). Women's history is American religious history. In: *Retelling U.S. Religious History* (ed. Thomas Tweed), 87–107. Berkeley: University of California Press.

Brekus, Catherine (2007). Introduction: searching for women in narrative of American religious history. In: *The Religious History of American Women: Reimagining the Past* (ed. Catherine Brekus), 1–50. Chapel Hill: University of North Carolina Press.

Brooten, Bernadette J. (1985). Early Christian women and their cultural context: issues of method in historical reconstruction. In: *Feminist Perspectives on Biblical Scholarship* (ed. Adela Y. Collins), 65–92. Chico, CA: Scholars Press.

Chen, Carolyn (2002). Religious conversion as women's liberation from the family: the case of Taiwanese immigrant women. Working paper no. 54. Berkeley, CA: Center for Working Families, University of California, Berkeley.

Criado-Perez, Caroline (2019). *Invisible Women: Data Bias in a World Designed for Men*. New York: Abrams Press.

Dzubinski, Leanne M. and Stasson, Anneke H. (2021). *Women in the Mission of the Church: Their Opportunities and Obstacles Throughout Christian History*. Grand Rapids, MI: Baker Academic.

Green, Gene L., Pardue, Stephen T., and Yeo, Khiok-Khng (2020). *Majority World Theology*. Downers Grove, IL: InterVarsity Press.

Hodgson, Dorothy (2005). *The Church of Women: Gendered Encounters between Maasai and Missionaries*. Bloomington: Indiana University Press.

Jenkins, Philip (2020). *Fertility and Faith: The Demographic Revolution and the Transformation of World Religions*. Waco, TX: Baylor University Press.

Johnson, Todd M. and Zurlo, Gina A. (2019). *World Christian Encyclopedia*. 3rd edn. Edinburgh: Edinburgh University Press.

Johnson, Todd M. and Zurlo, Gina A. ed. (2022). *World Christian Database*. Leiden/Boston: Brill.

Kent, Eliza (2004). *Converting Women: Gender and Protestant Christianity in South India*. Oxford: Oxford University Press.

Kim, Sebastian C.H. (2008). *Christian Theology in Asia*. Cambridge: Cambridge University Press.

Kupari, Helena and Vuola, Elina (2020). *Introduction. In: Orthodox Christianity and Gender: Dynamics of Tradition, Culture and Lived Practice* (ed. Helena Kupari and Elina Vuola), 1–22. Abingdon: Routledge.

Mallimaci, Fortunato, Giménez Béliveau, Verónica, Esquivel, Juan C, and Irrazábal, Gabriela (2019). Society and religion in transformation. *Second National Survey on Religious Beliefs and Attitudes in Argentina*. Research Report No. 25. Buenos Aires: CEIL-CONICET.

Muir, Elizabeth G. (2019). *A Women's History of the Christian Church: Two Thousand Years of Female Leadership*. Toronto: University of Toronto Press.

Paris, Jenell, Jindra, Ines, Woods, Robert, and Badzinski, Diane (2012). Gender, religiosity, and the telling of Christian conversion narratives. *Sociology Educator Scholarship*, 2(1), 1–23.

Pew Research Center (2015). America's changing religious landscape.

Pew Research Center (2016). The gender gap in religion around the World.

Robert, Dana L. (1997). *American Women in Mission: A Social History of Their Thought and Practice*. Macon, GA: Mercer University Press.

Schnabel, Landon (2016). Religion and gender equality worldwide: a country-level analysis. *Social Indicators Research*, 129(2), 893–907.

Schnabel, Landon et al. (2022). Gender, sexuality, and religion: a critical integrative review and agenda for future research. *Journal for the Scientific Study of Religion*, 61(2), 271–292.

Skirbekk, Vegard (2022). *Decline and Prosper! Changing Global Birth Rates and the Advantages of Fewer Children*. Cham: Palgrave Macmillan.

Stark, Rodney (1996). *The Rise of Christianity: A Sociologist Reconsiders History*. Princeton, NJ: Princeton University Press.

Stonawski, Marcin et al. (2016). The changing religious composition of Nigeria: causes and implications of demographic divergence. *The Journal of Modern African Studies*, 54(3), 361–387.

Yeh, Allen L. and Tienou, Tite (2018). *Majority World Theologies: Theologizing from Africa, Asia, Latin America, and the Ends of the Earth*. Littleton: William Carey Publishing.

Yoo, Wonji (2020). Constructing soft masculinity: christian conversion and gendered experience among young Chinese Christian men in Beijing. *Chinese Sociological Review*, 52(5), 539–561.

2

Women in African Christianity

"The Church in Africa has a feminine face and owes much of its tremendous growth to the agency of women."

Philomena Mwaura (Mwaura 2009, p. 114)

One of the most common refrains of African Christianity is that it is majority female.[1] Women were among the first converts to Christianity and in most places, they are the drivers of church life, whether in official leadership positions or not. However, it is extremely difficult to obtain exact numbers for the gender makeup of African churches. The figures included in this book are largely extracted from governmental censuses that include a question about religion. Because these percentages only speak to self-identification as Christian or in a particular denomination on an official government census, they are not a measurement of women's participation, activities, commitment to church life, or other engagement. Consider, for example, the following statements about different churches in Africa:

- On the Catholic Church in Benin: "Women are very active in the Church, [she boasted]. For instance, women are the majority in Church attendance everywhere. Women do everything! .... Coming to the Church, you will find out that the population of women is greater. Women could be about 80%, while men would be something like 20% in attendance." (Uchem 2001, pp. 101–102)
- On the Church of Pentecost among the Birifor people of Western Africa: "A high percentage of the church members are women;" and, "We cannot know the number, but what we can say is that when you go to a place and there are five men, women would be more than 30. So women outnumber men. Everywhere women outnumber men. It is not even among the Birifor alone, but in the whole Church of Pentecost, women outnumber men." (Dah 2017, p. 122)
- On the Catholic Church in Cameroon: Sr. Anastasie Bekono of the Servants of the Holy Heart of Mary, "Yes. Women are part of the church. You can see that at the church services, all the contributions women make. As a matter of fact, at Sunday Mass you generally see many more women than men. They pray, they're very active in the church, they give their time and services to the church." (Allen 2009)

---

1 According to the United Nations, Africa consists of the following countries: Algeria, Angola, Benin, Botswana, Burkina Faso, Burundi, Cabo Verde, Cameroon, Central African Republic, Chad, Comoros, Congo, Cote d'Ivoire, Democratic Republic of the Congo, Djibouti, Egypt, Equatorial Guinea, Eritrea, Eswatini, Ethiopia, Gabon, Gambia, Ghana, Guinea, Guinea-Bissau, Kenya, Lesotho, Liberia, Libya, Madagascar, Malawi, Mali, Mauritania, Mauritius, Mayotte, Morocco, Mozambique, Namibia, Niger, Nigeria, Reunion, Rwanda, Saint Helena, São Tomé and Príncipe, Senegal, Seychelles, Sierra Leone, Somalia, South Africa, South Sudan, Sudan, Tanzania, Togo, Tunisia, Uganda, Western Sahara, Zambia, and Zimbabwe.

Women in World Christianity: Building and Sustaining a Global Movement, First Edition. Gina A. Zurlo.
© 2023 John Wiley & Sons Ltd. Published 2023 by John Wiley & Sons Ltd.

- On the International Centre for Evangelism, Burkina Faso: "Ouédraogo indicated that about 90 percent of their church members are women and they are far more dynamic than the men." (Dah 2017, p. 128)
- On Pentecostalism in Zambia: "When populism has to do with religion and politics, women often tend to be at the fore because women make up the majority of religious groups. Scholars have demonstrated that African Pentecostalism is populated by women who are involved in the redeeming work of God in the world within their societies." (van de Kamp 2018, p. 27).
- On African Protestantism in general: "Without question, women devotees [to traditional religion] outnumber men, as any Protestant congregation in Africa will demonstrate." (Oduyoye 1995, p. 120).

From a demographic perspective, Africa is the new center of World Christianity as the continent with the most Christians, and women are at the heart of African Christianity. Over the last 20 years, Christianity in Africa grew at a faster rate than the general population. Sub-Saharan Africa was the only region in the world where Christian births outnumbered Christian deaths between 2010 and 2015 – 64 million more births than deaths (Pew Research Center 2017). Africa is the home of Church Fathers Tertullian (present-day Tunisia), Origen (Egypt), and Augustine (present-day Algeria); desert Church Mothers in Egypt; historic Orthodox Christianity in Ethiopia and Eritrea; Protestant mission-founded churches from the nineteenth and twentieth centuries; African Independent Churches (AICs) founded by Africans, both women and men; neo-Pentecostal megachurches, and the list goes on. The historical subtexts of Christianity in Africa are the ongoing legacies of the transatlantic slave trade (sixteenth to nineteenth centuries), Western colonization (1880s–1970s), and decolonization (from South Africa in 1910 to Angola, Cabo Verde, Comoros, Mozambique, and São Tomé and Príncipe in 1975).

Catholicism grew quickly between 2000 and 2020 (on average 3% per year), faster than any other major Christian tradition (Johnson and Zurlo 2022). There are over 79,500 women religious (female Catholic workers) on the continent, more than the number of Catholic priests and brothers combined (see Chapter 8 for more on African women religious). A major feature of African Christianity is the development and sustainment of AICs – African Independent (or Initiated, or Indigenous) Churches – those that were founded in Africa, by Africans, and for Africans (Turner 1979).

The contemporary underlying context for African Christianity includes its booming population – expected to be over 2.5 billion people by 2050 – and its youth, with 60% of the population under 25 years of age. Furthermore, many African countries are consistently ranked lowest on measures related to health, education, and human development. The United Nations Human Development Index (HDI) is a composite index that measures achievement in three areas: a long and healthy life, knowledge, and a decent standard of living. It includes measurement of life expectancy, literacy, education, and Gross Domestic Product (GDP). Africa's HDI is the lowest in the world (50.4 out of 100), compared to North America (91.5), Europe (84.9), Oceania (78.4), Latin America (74.2), and Asia (69.4). Africa has fewer physicians, lower life expectancies, less access to safe drinking water, higher infant mortality rates, and higher rates of HIV and malaria. Women are disadvantaged in terms of political participation, access to secondary education, career opportunities, and the availability of proper health care. Consequently, African Christians are more vulnerable and less healthy compared to Christians elsewhere in the world. Conflict, war, violence, and displacement also disproportionately impact women. However, despite obstacles and deeply rooted gendered expectations, women have vital roles in African Christianity. African Christian women are agents of renewal, radical disciples, and subversive apostles imbued with spiritual power (Sigg 2014).

Christianity in Africa, 1900–2050

Africa experienced a profound change in its religious makeup over the twentieth century. In 1900, the continent was primarily followers of African Traditional Religions (Ethnic religionists, 58%), followed by Muslims (33%) and Christians (9%, see Table 2.1). By 2020, the African religious landscape had completely transformed: 49% Christian, 42% Muslim, and 8% traditional religionist. By 2050, it is estimated that Christians and Muslims together will represent 93% of Africa's population. Africa's religious future is largely in the hands of women, in the sense of how many children will be born to Christian versus Muslim families.

Other than data from government censuses, comprehensive statistics do not exist for the gender makeup of African churches; as a result, the figures in Tables 2.2–2.5 for percent Christian female are likely substantial undercounts. It can be reasonably estimated from on-the-ground observations that the female majority of most churches is likely closer to 75%, as opposed to the reported 52%. Part of the discrepancy lies in measurement of official church membership (closer to 52% female) and church attendance and participation (perhaps 75% female on average, and upward of 90% for some churches). Nevertheless, Table 2.2 reports that Christianity is more female than the general population of each African region, and equal in North Africa, where Christians are a minority.

Table 2.1 Religions in Africa over 1%, 1900–2050.

Religion	Pop. 1900	% 1900	Rate % p.a. 1900–2000	Pop. 2020	% 2020	Rate % p.a. 2020–2050	Pop. 2050	% 2050
Christians	9,640,000	8.9	3.74	654,913,000	48.9	2.26	1,280,641,000	51.4
Muslims	34,999,000	32.5	2.31	556,923,000	41.5	2.12	1,043,699,000	41.9
Ethnic religionists	62,472,000	57.9	0.22	112,403,000	8.4	0.60	134,611,000	5.4

Source: Data from Johnson and Zurlo 2022. p.a. = percent change per annum, or each year.

Table 2.2 Christianity in Africa by region, 2020.

Region	Majority religion	Pop. 2020	% Christian 2020	Christian pop. 2020	% Christian female 2020	% pop. female 2020
Africa	Christians	1,340,598,000	48.9	654,913,000	52.1	50.0
Eastern Africa	Christians	445,406,000	65.6	292,393,000	51.6	50.4
Middle Africa	Christians	179,595,000	83.0	148,998,000	52.0	50.1
Northern Africa	Muslims	246,233,000	4.7	11,668,000	49.6	49.8
Southern Africa	Christians	67,504,000	82.2	55,465,000	54.1	50.8
Western Africa	Muslims	401,861,000	36.4	146,389,000	52.6	49.7

Source: Data from Johnson and Zurlo 2022.

The countries with the most Christians in Africa (Table 2.3) are throughout sub-Saharan Africa, ranging from Nigeria in the west (95 million Christians) to Mozambique in the east (17 million). These countries also represent a range of Christian traditions: majority Protestant (Nigeria, Kenya, Tanzania, Ghana), Catholic (DR Congo, Uganda, Angola, Mozambique), and Independent (South Africa). Women make up the majority of church members in almost all of these countries.

Many countries with high shares of women are those where Independent Christianity is the largest Christian tradition. Indeed, it is globally the case that Independent churches tend to have higher proportions of women compared to Catholic, Protestant, and Orthodox churches. Table 2.4 shows this is the case for Botswana, South Africa, Eswatini, Zimbabwe, and Mayotte.

Table 2.3 Countries in Africa with the most Christians, 2020.

Rank	Country	Largest Christian tradition	Pop. 2020	% Christian 2020	Christian pop. 2020	% Christian female 2020	% pop. female 2020
1	Nigeria	Protestants	206,140,000	46.2	95,186,000	52.7	49.3
2	DR Congo	Catholics	89,561,000	95.0	85,061,000	51.9	50.1
3	Ethiopia	Orthodox	114,964,000	59.1	67,903,000	50.0	50.0
4	South Africa	Independents	59,309,000	81.8	48,520,000	54.3	50.7
5	Kenya	Protestants	53,771,000	81.0	43,554,000	52.3	50.3
6	Uganda	Catholics	45,741,000	84.4	38,624,000	51.4	50.7
7	Tanzania	Protestants	59,734,000	55.3	33,050,000	51.9	50.0
8	Angola	Catholics	32,866,000	92.9	30,517,000	52.0	50.5
9	Ghana	Protestants	31,073,000	71.1	22,097,000	53.0	49.3
10	Mozambique	Catholics	31,255,000	55.8	17,439,000	53.1	51.4

Source: Data from Johnson and Zurlo 2022.

Table 2.4 Countries in Africa with the highest percent Christian female, 2020.

Rank	Country	Largest Christian tradition	Pop. 2020	% Christian 2020	Christian pop. 2020	% Christian female 2020	% pop. female 2020
1	Botswana	Independents	2,352,000	70.0	1,647,000	56.0	51.6
2	South Africa	Independents	59,309,000	81.8	48,520,000	54.3	50.7
3	Eswatini	Independents	1,160,000	87.4	1,014,000	53.8	50.8
4	Zimbabwe	Independents	14,863,000	81.7	12,150,000	53.6	52.3
5	Mozambique	Catholics	31,255,000	55.8	17,439,000	53.1	51.4
6	Ghana	Protestants	31,073,000	71.1	22,097,000	53.0	49.3
7	Mayotte	Independents	273,000	0.5	1,400	52.9	50.8
8	Rwanda	Catholics	12,952,000	91.5	11,852,000	52.8	50.8
9	Nigeria	Protestants	206,140,000	46.2	95,186,000	52.7	49.3
10	Central African Republic	Catholics	4,830,000	73.2	3,535,000	52.6	50.4

Source: Data from Johnson and Zurlo 2022.

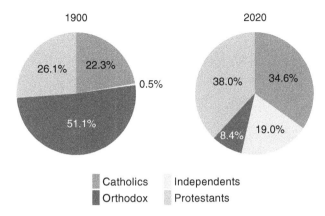

Figure 2.1 Christianity in Africa by major Christian tradition, 1900 and 2020. *Source:* Data from Johnson and Zurlo 2022.

Table 2.5 Christian families in Africa, 2000 and 2015.

Family	Affiliated 2000	Affiliated 2015	% female 2015	Rate % p.a. 2000–2015
Latin-rite Catholic	129,588,000	203,690,000	51.3	3.06
Pentecostal/Charismatic*	85,743,000	126,630,000	53.7	2.63
Anglican	41,428,000	58,865,000	52.4	2.37
Oriental and other Orthodox	35,073,000	49,144,000	49.8	2.27
Baptist	15,927,000	26,666,000	52.1	3.50
Reformed, Presbyterian	16,487,000	21,971,000	52.1	1.93
Other Protestant/Independent	11,990,000	19,790,000	54.2	3.40
United church or joint mission	10,995,000	17,388,000	51.0	3.10
Nondenominational	11,904,000	16,146,000	51.2	2.05
Lutheran	7,815,000	14,007,000	52.2	3.97
Methodist	9,296,000	11,566,000	53.2	1.47
Adventist	6,007,000	10,767,000	52.3	3.97
Restorationist, Disciple	2,971,000	4,405,000	53.3	2.66
Jehovah's Witnesses	2,571,000	4,318,000	53.7	3.52
Holiness	2,442,000	3,510,000	52.8	2.45
Congregational	2,179,000	2,913,000	54.1	1.95
Christian Brethren	1,124,000	1,445,000	52.3	1.69
Mennonite	718,000	1,202,000	51.2	3.50
Friends (Quaker)	299,000	1,004,000	53.8	8.41
Salvationist	853,000	969,000	52.5	0.85
Moravian	511,000	635,000	53.0	1.46
Latter-day Saints (Mormons)	156,000	553,000	52.9	8.78
Eastern Orthodox	458,000	547,000	50.8	1.18
Dunker	369,000	486,000	54.0	1.86
Eastern-rite Catholic	341,000	273,000	51.1	−1.48

(Continued)

Table 2.5 (Continued)

Family	Affiliated 2000	Affiliated 2015	% female 2015	Rate % p.a. 2000–2015
Old Catholic Church	119,000	266,000	49.5	5.51
Nontraditional, house, cell	106,000	144,000	51.8	2.08
Hidden believers in Christ	65,200	133,000	48.4	4.89

Source: Data from Johnson and Zurlo 2022. p.a. = percent change per annum, or each year.
*Excluding partially pentecostalized.

The diversity of Christianity in Africa is on full display when viewed from the perspective of Christian traditions (Figure 2.1) and families (Table 2.5). Catholicism is the largest family with over 200 million adherents (35% of all Christians), followed by Pentecostals/Charismatics, and Anglicans. Almost every Christian family experienced much higher than average growth rates between 2000 and 2015. However, this kind of growth is unsustainable and will level off in the twenty-first century as the pool of potential converts continues to shrink.

Most of the largest denominations in Africa are Catholic (DR Congo, Nigeria, Uganda, Angola, Tanzania, Kenya) and Anglican (Nigeria, Uganda), plus the Ethiopian Orthodox Church and the Church of Jesus Christ on Earth Through the Prophet Simon Kimbangu (Table 2.6).

Christianity gave African women new autonomy and a platform to challenge male dominance in society (Mwaura 2009). As a result, women's church organizations are a major feature of African Christianity today, called the "face of the African church" or "a church within a church" (Longwe 2016). Highly organized and very visible, women's groups make significant contributions to everyday church life. They range from small local Bible studies to groups that have grown nationally, like the Mothers' Unions of the Anglican Church. Most women's organizations are active in evangelization and church growth, hastening the spread and influence of Christianity across sub-Saharan Africa. At the same time, these groups provide safe spaces for women to be outside of

Table 2.6 Largest denominations in Africa, 2015.

Rank	Country	Denomination	Year begun	Affiliated 2015	% Christian female	Rate % p.a. 2000–2015
1	DR Congo	Eglise Catholique au DR Congo	1482	42,891,000	51.2	3.12
2	Ethiopia	Ethiopian Orthodox Church	332	39,200,000	50.0	2.54
3	Nigeria	Catholic Church in Nigeria	1487	23,125,000	51.2	2.74
4	Nigeria	Anglican Church of Nigeria	1842	22,000,000	52.9	1.94
5	Uganda	Catholic Church in Uganda	1879	16,282,000	51.4	3.23
6	Angola	Igreja Católica em Angola	1491	14,970,000	51.2	3.17
7	Uganda	Church of Uganda	1875	14,000,000	50.9	3.18
8	Tanzania	Catholic Church in Tanzania	1550	13,782,000	51.2	2.53
9	DR Congo	Église de Jésus Christ sur la Terre par son Envoyé Special Simon Kimbangu	1921	12,000,000	52.0	2.70
10	Kenya	Catholic Church in Kenya	1498	10,578,000	51.2	2.45

Source: Data from Johnson and Zurlo 2022. p.a. = percent change per annum, or each year.

patriarchal structures or gendered expectations of society and church. They serve as places for "women's self-expression, leadership skills development, spiritual development, and space for ecumenism" (Longwe 2016). In these spaces, women are free to discuss topics unique to their own experiences, such as gender-based violence, love, marriage, and family, and how the Bible speaks to their lives (Longwe 2017).

The Gender and Congregational Life Survey (2021) included 93 respondents from Africa, with the most from Nigeria, South Africa, Kenya, and Uganda. Respondents were majority female (55%), married (84%), well-educated (92% with bachelor's degree or higher), and employed full-time (72%). Christian families represented were Pentecostal (26%), nondenominational (24%), Baptist (14%), Anglican (8%), and Reformed/Presbyterian (5%), with 46% of respondents attending a church of 500 or more members. Women were reported to be extremely active participants, with 74% of respondents indicating more women than men in their main weekly worship service (voted the most important ministry of the church by 88% of respondents). Meanwhile, 63% stated that more women than men attend the midweek service.

While 78% of respondents agreed or strongly agreed that women should be allowed to serve as pastors (compared to 84% for all respondents worldwide), 85% agreed or strongly agreed that it is harder for women to be accepted into leadership roles in the church. Members of Anglican and Pentecostal/Holiness churches were more favorable toward women's pastoral roles and leadership than Baptist, Reformed/Presbyterian, and members of nondenominational churches. Indeed, the survey highlighted the gendered expectations and realities for men and women in African church life. The only positions that respondents felt were easier for women to obtain than men were administrative assistant and children's Sunday school teacher (see Figure 2.2).

When asked what roles women hold in their congregations, the most frequent responses were administrative assistant, children's Sunday school teacher, and intercessor (Figure 2.3). Four percent of respondents in Africa reported a female head or senior pastor, compared to 8% globally. Eight percent of African respondents had female overseers, with the global figure at 51%. For youth pastor, a reported 10% were women, compared to 55% globally.

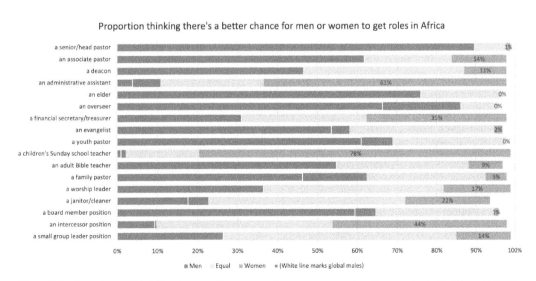

Proportion thinking there's a better chance for men or women to get roles in Africa

a senior/head pastor	1%
an associate pastor	14%
a deacon	11%
an administrative assistant	61%
an elder	0%
an overseer	0%
a financial secretary/treasurer	35%
an evangelist	2%
a youth pastor	0%
a children's Sunday school teacher	78%
an adult Bible teacher	9%
a family pastor	5%
a worship leader	17%
a janitor/cleaner	22%
a board member position	1%
an intercessor position	44%
a small group leader position	14%

■ Men   Equal   ■ Women   ■ (White line marks global males)

Figure 2.2 How do you think the chances of women and men compare when it comes to getting a ___ position in a congregation? (Africa). *Source:* Adapted from Gender and Congregational Life Survey (2021).

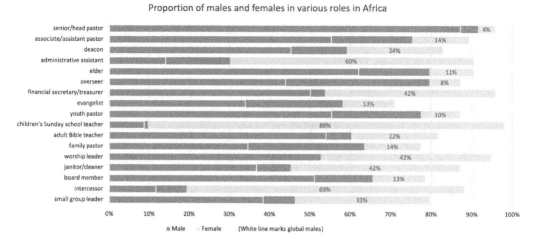

Figure 2.3 Thinking of the ___ position in your congregation, is this person male or female? (Africa). *Source:* Adapted from Gender and Congregational Life Survey (2021).

Women in African Christianity: Past and Present

From the third century BCE to the second century BC, the Kingdom of Kush was ruled by a series of independent queens. In the Book of Acts in the New Testament, the Apostle Philip converted to Christianity via the Ethiopian eunuch, an official of the queen of the Ethiopians (Acts 8:27–39). Catholicism and Orthodoxy have been present in Africa since the first century. Orthodox churches had been established in what is today Egypt, Ethiopia, Eritrea, Sudan, and South Sudan by the year 350. Women were prominent in Orthodox Christianity as Desert Mothers (see Chapter 9) and queens.

Catholicism began spreading in the thirteenth century and in earnest in the fifteenth century, with missions established in today's Senegal (1445), Guinea-Bissau (1462), Cabo Verde (1462), Ghana (1481), the Democratic Republic of the Congo (Kongo; 1482), Equatorial Guinea (1484), and Nigeria (1487), among others. The adoption of Christianity during this time was largely political, embraced by ruling elites for power and sometimes to enhance the well-being of their subjects – sometimes successfully, sometimes not (Ngong 2016). A major figure in the anti-Roman Catholic struggle was Walatta Petros (1592–1642), who became a nun in the Ethiopian Orthodox Tewahedo Church at age 25 after her three children died in infancy. She refused to convert to Catholicism and heavily protested foreign influence on Ethiopian culture, tradition, and religion. She formed several religious communities for others seeking to escape Catholicism.

The most well-known Christian woman of early African Christian history is Kimpa Vita (1682–1706), also known as Dona Beatrice, a popular prophetess in the Kongo Kingdom. Believing herself to be possessed by the spirit of St. Anthony of Padua, she taught her followers that Jesus, Mary, and other biblical figures were really Kongolese. She also used indigenous symbols to create a truly Africanized Christianity. Though the Portuguese burned her at the stake for heresy at the instigation of Capuchin Catholic missionaries, the Antonian Movement she founded outlasted her. Dona Beatrice is widely recognized as an early precursor of African Independent Christianity, which emerged two centuries later. Other influential Catholic women include Queen Nzinga of Ndongo and Matamba (1583–1663) (present-day Angola), a brilliant military leader who took over the empire after the death of her father and powerfully resisted Portuguese encroachment (Heywood 2017). Bakhita Kwashe (1841–1899) was the first Sudanese nun, captured by raiders, enslaved,

Photo 2.1 A Kenyan nun at a beatification ceremony of Italian Roman Catholic missionary nun Irene Stefani (1891–1930) (2015). *Source:* Stuart Price/Make It Kenya.

brought to Italy, and after she was emancipated returned to Africa for evangelization (see Chapter 8 for more on Catholic women in Africa).

Protestantism

The first Protestant presence on the continent was the Dutch Reformed Church in South Africa (1652), by way of Dutch colonization. Moravian missions began in the eighteenth century, as did British, resulting in the establishment of Anglicanism in Ghana (1752), Seychelles (1794), South Africa (1806), the Gambia (1816), and beyond. Other Protestant groups included Methodists, Congregationalists, Lutherans, and Presbyterians. One of the most prominent African Christian women of the nineteenth century was Queen Ranavalona II of Madagascar (1829–1883). During her reign, she transformed the traditional society of Madagascar into a Protestant one. Publicly baptized with her husband as Christians in 1869, she encouraged the arrival of foreign missionaries to the island, repealed traditional practices such as polygamy and idol worship, incorporated Christian symbolism throughout the kingdom, and mandated education for children, including girls.

Protestant missionaries established schools, translated the Bible into vernacular languages, and transplanted replicas of Western-style denominational churches, complete with Western theology, modes of worship, role expectations for women and men, and patriarchal church cultures. Western female missionaries were active in education and literacy (e.g., Florence Allshorn in Uganda), teaching the Bible (Isabella Lilias Trotter in Algeria), founding orphanages (Lillian Hunt Trasher in Egypt), Bible translation (Rosemary Guillebaud in Burundi), and care of children and the sick (Elizabeth Hall in the Congo). African American women participated in missions in Africa as well, such as Emma Bertha Delany (Malawi and Liberia), Eliza George (Liberia), Bessie McDowell (Angola), Amanda Berry Smith (Western Africa), and Althea Brown Edmiston (Belgian Congo). African women were typically among the first converts to Christianity and the most enthusiastic evangelists (Isichei 1995). Most missionaries did not remain long enough to properly learn African languages, and even when they did, most of the conversion activities were done by Africans themselves, in their own communities and in their own languages.

Vernacularization

Missionaries, both Catholic and Protestant, paid enormous "vernacular compliments" to Africans with the translation of scripture into their local languages, while simultaneously hastening modernization processes on the continent (Sanneh 1989). Ghanaian theologian Kwame Bediako stated, "There is probably no more important single explanation for the massive presence of Christianity on the African continent than the availability of the Scriptures in many African languages" (Bediako 1995, p. 62). Translators and missionaries used local names in African cultures for the "high god" as the God of the Bible, directly connecting the God of their ancestors with the God of Israel and the Father of Jesus Christ (Sanneh 1989). As a result, Africans had authentic encounters with Christianity because they heard the gospel message in their own languages. The availability of vernacular scriptures empowered local Christians to develop their own African questions of the faith and provide African answers (Bediako 1995). Africans responded to Christianity as they heard it, not as the missionaries experienced it; that is, they largely became Christians for religious reasons, not secular ones, such as financial or political gain (Walls 2002, 1996; Sanneh 1989). For example, Manche Masemola (1913–1928), a teenage girl from Transvaal (South Africa), was murdered by her non-Christian parents for becoming a Christian, though she died before receiving baptism. Her statue is featured in Westminster Abbey in London along with other prominent twentieth-century martyrs. Another example is Lydie Mengwelune (1886–1966), a former concubine of a powerful king in modern-day Cameroon who left behind riches and royalty to follow Jesus. She led her husband, children, and servants to faith in Christ, became a church elder, girls' schoolteacher, itinerant evangelist, and preacher (Pindzié 2008). These women exemplify Bediako's observation: "The phenomenon of African Christianity in the twentieth century, therefore, far from signifying an acute Westernisation of African life, may rather be the evidence of how much African peoples feel at home in the Gospel of Jesus Christ" (Bediako 1995, p. 62).

Colonization and Decolonization

In the nineteenth and twentieth centuries, indigenous African Christianity blossomed with the growth of religious movements that took seriously African cultural values, community, and spirituality (Mwaura 2004). Western missionaries contributed to the emergence of these movements, especially with the translation of scripture into local languages. However, despite the rumblings of indigenous Christianity at the end of the nineteenth century, the Western missionary movement thought very little of the potential conversion of the African continent in the twentieth century. Of the 1,215 delegates of the 1910 Edinburgh World Missionary Conference – seen as the culmination of the nineteenth-century missionary movement and the dawning hope for the twentieth century – only 18 were from what was called the "younger" churches in Asia. No African Christians were invited. Meanwhile, the 200 women delegates had no official voice. In attendance were some African American missionaries from the United States and one White American missionary serving in Liberia, plus one Indian missionary serving in Natal, South Africa (Stanley 2009); none were women. The delegates of Edinburgh 1910 believed there to be no preparation for Christianity in African animism and no hope for the "dark" and "backward" continent. The four million African Christians in Egypt and Ethiopia were dismissed as "lacking missionary character," and there was no consideration of indigenous Christian communities and their capacity for mission. Africans in general were perceived as "primitive, childlike, and at the bottom of the evolutionary hierarchy, relatively unimportant for the future of the world church" (Stanley 2009, p. 99). Furthermore, African Traditional Religion was seen as mere superstition, not actual religion. As a result, the churches in the West completely misdiagnosed the spread of Christianity and believed the future of the faith was in Asia, which they perceived to be more modern and sophisticated than Africa. The emergence of Christian Africa in the twentieth century came as a complete surprise to the modern missionary movement.

The so-called European Scramble for Africa heightened in the nineteenth century after the collapse of the global slave trade and the expansion of European power. The Berlin Conference in February 1885, attended by male representatives of Western nations with imperial interests in Africa, met to carve up the continent into "spheres of interest" for colonization and conquest. Representatives hailed from the United States, Germany, Portugal, Austria-Hungary, Belgium, Denmark, Spain, France, the United Kingdom, Italy, the Netherlands, Russia, Sweden-Norway, and the Ottoman Empire. Several countries that participated in the conference – Austria-Hungary, Denmark, the Netherlands, Sweden-Norway, and the United States – ultimately did not obtain any portion of the continent. Interests were political and social, but primarily economic. But as dramatic as such geopolitical consequences can get, so were the spiritual implications. The land grab sparked an organized quest for African souls, the establishment of commonwealths shaped by Christian denominations, and the inauguration of European languages on the continent. Belgium, Germany, Spain, France, Italy, and Portugal imported their own varieties of Catholicism; Germany reinforced strands of Protestantism; and the British spread Anglicanism throughout sub-Saharan Africa. The number of foreign missionaries increased tremendously, especially among Catholic missionary orders. Missionaries believed education was an open door to social and economic benefits and thus made young people in schools their main targets of evangelization, pairing Western education and Christian instruction. Millions of Africans became Christians between 1910 and 1960 because of missionary educational work.

Numerous factors contributed to the decolonization of the African continent, including two World Wars causing the deportation or withdrawal of many European missionaries, particularly British. The sudden lack of foreign Christian support heightened the role of African leaders in running their churches and Christian organizations. Nokutela Dube (1873–1917), for example, with her husband, was the first South African woman to establish a school; Ohlange High School was also the first school founded by Black teachers. A shrinking foreign Catholic priesthood also hastened the need to train indigenous African leadership – including sisters and brothers – an endeavor supported by reforms from the Second Vatican Council (1962–1965) regarding the use of vernacular languages in the Catholic Mass. The scramble *out* of Africa gave rise to independent African governments, with numerous leaders that had received education in missionary schools. Newly independent states took over many mission schools in the transition to African autonomy. As a result, by the last quarter of the twentieth century, Africa had been transformed as politically and religiously independent from Western powers. Although much of sub-Saharan Africa embraced Christianity in the twentieth century, they did so on African terms, not Western.

Ethiopian/Nationalist Churches

Africans had been responding to European Christianity since the nineteenth century with the Ethiopianist (Southern Africa), or Nationalist (Western Africa), movement, which represented the earliest stirring toward religious and political freedom at the start of the modern colonial period. In the 1880s, having been denied leadership in Western mission-founded churches, Africans began founding their own. Their desire for more relevant Christianity focused on the restoration of tribal life and political and cultural autonomy with the slogan, "Africa for Africans." Additionally, the term "Ethiopian" was historically important; in reference to the historical region from modern-day Egypt to Ethiopia, it pointed toward a return to a golden age of African civilization. Ethiopia was also biblical, as in Psalm 68:31b, "Let Ethiopia [Cush] stretch out her hands to God." The first of these churches was the Native Baptist Church founded by Mojola Agbebi (also known as David Vincent Brown) in Nigeria in 1888. In Southern Africa, Mangena Mokone was a former Wesleyan minister and the first to use the term "Ethiopian" when he founded the Ethiopian Church in 1892. Ethiopianist/Nationalist churches provided an ideal form of Christianity in the hands of Africans (see Chapter 11 on Independents for more).

Prophet-healing Movements

Another African response to Western Christianity came in the form of prophet-healing movements that became what is now known as African Independent Churches (AICs). Both prophets and prophetesses led these charismatic movements and were usually former members of Protestant or Catholic mission churches. Prophets and prophetesses typically called for the destruction of traditional idols, healed the sick, cast out demons, abstained from alcohol, observed the Sabbath, practiced believer's baptism, and included women more fully in church life. However, they were also all persecuted by colonial authorities. These movements typically began in the mission churches – Anglican, Methodist, Catholic, and others – and they were either expelled or voluntarily left after amassing large followings.

Prominent prophets at the turn of the twentieth century included William Wadé Harris (1860–1929, Western Africa), Garrick Sokari Braide (1882–1918, Niger Delta), Isaiah Shembe (1865–1935, Southern Africa), and Simon Kimbangu (1887–1951, Central Africa). Their movements became known as Spiritual churches (Southern Africa), Aladura churches (Western Africa), and Zionist churches (Southern Africa). Although most of these movements were led by men, women were active participants and, in some cases, charismatic leaders. Prophetess Sophia Odunlami (1900–1981) became a prominent leader in the Aladura movement in southwestern Nigeria after she experienced a miraculous healing during the 1918 influenza pandemic, where an estimated 3% of Nigeria's population died. She was integral to the divine healing ministries of the Precious Stone Society, where she became a well-known preacher, evangelist, and teacher. She also advocated for the full inclusion of women in ministry within Yoruba Christianity (Babatunde 2021). Another example is Lucy Adeoti (1900–1986) of Nigeria, denied leadership in her husband's church after his death because she was a woman. Undeterred, she began a prayer band, a mission, an orphanage, and her own Aladura church – emerging as a widely influential prophetess (Otesifan 2009).

African Independent Churches (AICs)

African women most acutely felt the disconnect between Western Christianity and African culture, especially regarding the missionary assault on the African family. Women held prominent positions in many African societies, with some matrilineal, others matriarchal, and yet others practicing polyandry. In fact, Africa has a higher proportion of matrilineal societies than any other continent

Photo 2.2 Anglican maternal healthcare workers on bicycles in Burundi (2013). *Source:* PWRDF/Flickr/CC BY 2.0.

(Mazrui 2014). Women oversaw agricultural duties and thus had economic control of tribal life. Although often denied access to the ancestor-cult rituals, women were largely identified with the earth mother and other spirits and deities. The arrival of Christianity, however, upended gender dynamics in traditional life, to the severe detriment of women. Polygamous families were torn apart, forcing the male head of the household to choose his favorite wife to the disgrace of the others. Women were denied leadership in the mission churches altogether, and the children of the dishonored women were considered illegitimate and unable to receive baptism (Barrett 1968). As observed by a male Anglican missionary in Kenya in the 1960s,

> At this point therefore the discrepancy between missions and scriptures crystallised out: the missions appeared to be practicing an unjustified form of social control, and in attacking the foundations of African society, focused on the family, they were attacking the status of African women and failing to offer them the full status accorded in the Bible.
>
> (Barrett 1968, p. 147)

Women faced further marginalization in many African Independent Churches, like that in wider African society, such as prohibitions from performing certain rituals, like baptism and communion, and denial of decision-making capacities. Women were also excluded from formal theological education. Yet, as the majority of church members, women wielded an incredible amount of corporate influence. Women, especially those with charisma, were widely recognized as prophetic leaders and healers; there are numerous examples of female founders, cofounders, and spiritual leaders of AICs, some of which still exist today. Several hundred of the 6,000 Christian movements in Africa were founded by women (Barrett 1968). Most female founders of AICs were in their late teens or early 20s when they became prominent charismatic leaders with tens of thousands of followers.

Grace Tani (1870s/1880s–1958), together with John Nackabah, founded the Church of the Twelve Apostles in Ghana in 1914. She was one of the initial converts – as well as the third wife – of the prophet William Wadé Harris. The church still exists today with roughly 320,000 members (Johnson and Zurlo 2022). There are also branches in Liberia and Côte d'Ivoire.

Christina Nku (1894–c.1980), formerly of the Apostolic Faith Mission, formed the St. John's Apostolic Faith Mission of South Africa in 1939. She survived severe illness as a child and consequently focused on a healing ministry, amassing thousands of followers in a male-dominated society. Most Zionist churches had strong female membership and organizations, and many were led by charismatic prophetesses (Kgatle 2019).

Christiana Abiodun Emmanuel (1907–1994), cofounder of the Cherubim and Seraphim Church of West Africa with Moses Orimolade Tunolase, experienced a 21-day trance, reportedly her celestial training to lead the movement. She was a healer, intercessor, preacher, and evangelist (Boniface 2004). After a schism between the two leaders, Emmanuel was granted leadership over what became known as the Cherubim and Seraphim Society, which has nearly one million members in Nigeria today, with branches throughout Western Africa.

Alice Lenshina Mulenga Mubisha (1924–1978) founded the Lumpa Church in Zambia after excommunication from the Presbyterian church. She received visions that resulted in her anti-witchcraft movement, which garnered upward of 100,000 former Presbyterians and Catholics. The Lumpa Church clashed with both colonial and national governments, with its anti-earthly-authority stance. Lenshina was arrested in the 1970s after violent and deadly skirmishes ended with her church being banned. Her movement died out soon after as members left for other churches (Brockman 1994).

Massan Koffigan (1947–1973) founded the Church of Deliverance and Complete Salvation in Jesus Christ in Togo, which had more female than male affiliates. She had twelve women as disciples and performed miracles, such as resurrecting two children from the dead. She had no successor, however, and her church died with her (Dah-Gbeto 2004).

Gaudencia Aoko (1943–2019) cofounded Legio Maria (Legion of Mary) with Simeo Ondetto in Kenya, a break-away group from the Roman Catholic Church. Aoko was a charismatic preacher and conducted mass baptisms. Legio Maria maintained many features of Catholicism, such as Latin Mass, liturgy, and hierarchies, but also features of African Christianity, such as healing, exorcism, spirit possession, and prohibition of dancing and pork (Kustenbauder 2009). The movement initially allowed women priests, though this was phased out by 1979 for an all-male leadership. Legio Maria was the largest schism from the Catholic Church in Africa and has over 600,000 affiliates in Kenya, Tanzania, and Uganda today (Johnson and Zurlo 2022).

Pentecostal/Charismatic Churches

The next major reorientation in African Christianity was the Independent Pentecostal/Charismatic movement, beginning in the 1970s and continuing today. African Christianity has always been of a *pneumatic* form: emphasizing the spiritual realm and the normative role of the Holy Spirit in Christian life (Asamoah-Gyadu 2013). However, twentieth- and twenty-first-century Pentecostalism (also sometimes called neo-Pentecostalism) is different from the charismatic nature of the AICs with biblical emphases on spirit-inspired worship, speaking in tongues, dynamic corporate worship, healing, exorcisms, and other spiritual gifts, all within a modern, globalized, and urbanized African context. African Pentecostalism has grown tremendously due to its rootedness in the African religious universe, its ability to adapt to African priorities, and its creative uses of contemporary media technology – all of this has attracted upwardly mobile young people. While Pentecostal/Charismatic churches have been growing – especially in Nigeria and Ghana – the older historic churches, such as Lutheran, Methodist, Reformed, and Catholic, are becoming increasingly pentecostalized or charismatic in worship and theology. African Pentecostal churches are also being planted elsewhere in the world due to diaspora movements.

Prosperity gospel theology, which teaches that God desires followers to flourish in both health and material wealth, has become associated with Pentecostal/Charismatic churches in Africa. While this emphasis is partly an export from American preachers such as Kenneth Hagin and Kenneth and Gloria Copeland, it is also home-grown with an ostensible omnipresence in Nigeria. Prosperity theology finds success in speaking into the economic challenges in much of sub-Saharan Africa, while providing spiritual explanations and solutions for economic problems (Kalu 2009). Benson Idahosa (1938–1998) is known as the "Father of Prosperity Theology" in Nigeria (Ayegboyin and Ogunewu 2017, p. 322). His wife, Margaret Idahosa, became the first archbishop of the Church of God Mission International, the first African woman to hold such a position. She is also the first African woman to serve as chancellor for a university, Benson Idahosa University, established in 2002.

However, expectations vary for men and women in Pentecostal churches throughout Africa. In theory, their focus on the empowerment by the Holy Spirit cuts across gender lines and affords women greater opportunities than in the historic churches and AICs. Women, known to each other as "sisters," can exercise their gifts in community and they are extremely active evangelists spreading the faith at home and abroad (Kalu 2008). The pastor's wife, sometimes known as the "first lady," is an extremely influential and important member of the congregation. Yet, at the same time, literal readings of scripture in some of these churches prevent women from preaching (Kalu 2008). In other cases, tradition underscores feminine identities as wives and mothers, and discourse still exists of women as the "weaker sex" in need of male guidance (Hackett 2017). Some Pentecostal churches tend to be more egalitarian and democratic. Several have established their own institutions of theological education, where women are encouraged to receive ministerial training. Women in Pentecostal churches also serve as healers, evangelists, and composers while having their dignity affirmed and gifts recognized, banding together to challenge male authority.

African Women in Theology

African theology has a different cultural starting place than Western theology. While Western students of the Enlightenment would say, "I think, therefore I am" – the statement made famous by French philosopher René Descartes (1596–1650) – African theologizing begins with the phrase, "I am, because we are," or "I belong, therefore I am." This *Ubuntu* conveys a broad concept of humanity's togetherness and corporate nature, as opposed to individualism. The spiritual, physical, and societal spheres are all interconnected. Africa's strong emphasis on community contradicts Western notions of individuality, upon which rests most of Western theology.

African theology is one of inculturation. It is the quest to engage Christianity from African perspectives, taking into consideration African culture and social issues. It is based on the premise that African Christians ask different questions that Western Christians; evidenced, for example, in the absence of theological content addressing polygamy in Western seminary curricula. African Christians need relevant answers to questions about divination, spirit possession, ancestor veneration, African Traditional Religion, colonialism and postcolonialism, spiritual power and deliverance, health and wealth (prosperity), and Christian–Muslim relations. Further questions arise about the theology of the Holy Spirit and spiritualistic views of reality, as well as issues concerning demons, witches, abuses of power, corruption, and exploitation.

Pioneers of African theology include Charles Nyamiti (1931–2020, Tanzania), John Mbiti (1931–2019, Kenya), Kwesi Dickson (1929–2005, Ghana), Kwame Bediako (1945–2008, Ghana), John Pobee (1937–2020, Ghana), and Kä Mana (1952–2021, Democratic Republic of the Congo). However, the first generation of African theologizing largely sidelined women's concerns, a result of theological influences from both Western and African contexts (Siwila 2016). The emergence of women African theologians in the 1970s was the catalyst for discussing gender in African Christianity. In 1988, Ghanaian theologian Mercy Amba Oduyoye (b.1934) formed the Circle of Concerned African Women Theologians, with the goal of raising the profile of gender issues in African Christianity, including women's leadership, theological education, and ordination. Oduyoye articulated a two-pronged approach of African women's theologizing that demanded male *and* female participation in the fight for gender justice (Siwila 2016). The Circle first focused on the significance of women's organizations, gender-based violence, the role of ministers' wives, the exclusion of women from institutions of theological education, and equipping ministers to properly handle issues related to gender (Phiri and Kaunda 2017). The Circle has also tackled head-on the patriarchy of African Christianity – rule by fathers or men – calling for gender justice and equality between men and women theologians.

African women are asking important theological questions relevant to their unique experiences related to polygamy, celibacy of the priesthood, liberation, sexuality, rituals, HIV/AIDS, and poverty. They, too, are facing the challenges of relating the Christian faith to their African cultural heritage but have the additional responsibility of adding gender to the equation. Further, African women's theology is "society sensitive" (Oduyoye 2001, p. 17) in that it is centered around communal relationships between men and women, between people and the divine, and between people and creation. As a result, African women's theologies are naturally ecologically sensitive. Several prominent theologians have emerged in this generation, such as Mercy Amba Oduyoye (Ghana), Musa W. Dube (Botswana), Philomena Njeri Mwaura (Kenya), Musimbi R.A. Kanyoro (Kenya), Isabel Apawo Phiri (Malawi), Elizabeth W. Mburu (Kenya), Rosinah Mmannana Gabaitse (Botswana), and Ruth Julian (Democratic Republic of the Congo).

Having inherited the Bible from Western colonialism, Africans were tasked with interpreting it as postcolonial subjects (Dube 2000). In many ways, African societies are closer to the biblical world than those of the West, a sentiment that created tension with Western missionaries who thought they had a monopoly on biblical interpretation. Musa Dube – elected as the President of the Society of Biblical Literature for 2023–2024 – outlines several important contextual aspects to postcolonial readings of scripture, based on the premise that the Bible is a postcolonial book:

- Land: The biblical texts were used to justify imperial purposes for White Christians to take Black African land.
- Race: Superiority of the White race and victimization of the Black race were bolstered by Western interpretations of scripture.
- Power: Unequal power distribution existed in the colonial era and persists into the postcolonial era, bolstered by biblical texts.
- Readers: The texts were written for people in specific times and places but have now traveled time and space beyond their original context and readers.
- International connection: Western interpretations of scripture had direct impacts on African realities, raising questions of the universality and particularities of the biblical text.
- Contemporary history and liberation: "To read the Bible as postcolonial subjects, therefore, is to participate in the long, uncompleted struggle for liberation of these countries and to seek liberation ways of interdependence." (Dube 2000, pp. 20–21)
- Gender: African Women were absent from the imperialist narrative and have been marginalized and oppressed by both the colonizer and African culture.

African women theologians take seriously both their gendered experiences and the realities of living in a postcolonial world. Considering women's perspectives requires different views and emphases of the Bible. For example, patriarchy in Africa suffocates women by prioritizing male interest. Although male dominance predates Christianity in Africa, it is reinforced by an interpretation of Genesis 1–3: the creation story read as God creating man first, then woman, and therefore subjugating the latter to the former and leaving women forever unequal to men (Chitando 2019). However, a different reading of the text as etiological, rather than historical, reveals the text not necessarily as God speaking gender roles into existence, but as men explaining the status quo and assigning a role to God (Gunda 2019). If this is the case, then the subjugation of women was done by men, not by God, and can therefore be undone. This kind of biblical interpretation reinforces the equality of men and women and avoids interpreting scripture in a way that does harm to women, the vulnerable, and the voiceless (Oduyoye 2001).

Conclusion

Africa holds a tremendously prominent place in World Christianity studies. In fact, World Christianity exists as a discipline because of the centrality of African Christian history and experience in the twentieth century. Sub-Saharan Africa became the demographic and geographic center of the Christian faith by the late twentieth century due to massive conversions to Christianity, sustained by high birth rates and the substantive contributions of women to teach, lead, pray, and evangelize. Most of the major themes in World Christianity studies were first explored in African Christian history – Bible translation and vernacularization, the missionary movement, contextualization, independency, colonization, gender roles, and racism.

Yet, African women's narratives have not been centered, to the detriment of our understanding of the establishment and spread of Christianity from this new epicenter of faith. In fact, as Kanyoro and Oduyoye state, "African women theologians have come to realize that as long as men and foreign researchers remain the authorities on culture, rituals, and religion, African women will continue to be spoken of as if they were dead" (Kanyoro and Oduyoye 2005, p. 1). But far from dead, African women live at the center of the story and will continue to do so in the future, as healers, prophets, evangelists, wives, mothers, and founders of churches and movements. They use their Christian faith as a catalyst for social renewal and justice in their countries and communities. Advocates for justice and peace, they theologize and innovate, making Africa a place of religious initiative, as well as one of revelation (Isichei 1995). The innovations and revelations for the future of African Christianity are in the hands of women.

Reflection Questions

1) Why did the emergence of Christianity in Africa in the twentieth century come as such a surprise to the modern Western missionary movement? Reflect on the encounters between Western missionaries and African people, especially African women, including the impact of vernacular Bible translations. How did women navigate changes inaugurated by Western missionaries to practice subversive authority?
2) A major feature of African Christianity is the development of AICs (African Independent Churches). Describe the unique characteristics of these churches including how they both support and limit women in their expression of Christian leadership. Name some female AIC leaders and their contributions to African Christianity despite their social and religious marginalization.
3) What does it mean for African theology to be contextual? What do you think are some differences between Western theology and African feminist theology?

Works Cited

Allen, John L. Jr. (2009). A quick pulse of women religious in Africa. 23 May. https://www.ncronline.org/news/quick-pulse-women-religious-africa (accessed 1 August 2021).

Asamoah-Gyadu, J. Kwabena (2013). *Contemporary Pentecostal Christianity: Interpretation from an African Context*. Eugene, OR: Wipf and Stock Publishers.

Ayegboyin, Isaac D. and Ogunewu, Michael A. (2017). Pentecostals/Charismatics. In: *Christianity in Sub-Saharan Africa* (ed. Kenneth R. Ross, J. Kwabena Asamoah-Gyadu, and Todd M. Johnson), 314–326. Edinburgh: Edinburgh University Press.

Babatunde, Timothy S. (2021). Odunlami, Sophia. *Dictionary of African Christian Biography*. https://dacb.org/stories/country/odunlami-sophia (accessed 2 August 2021).

Barrett, David B. (1968). *Schism and Renewal in Africa: An Analysis of Six Thousand Contemporary Religious Movements*. Nairobi: Oxford University Press.

Bediako, Kwame (1995). *Christianity in Africa: The Renewal of a Non-Western Religion*. Edinburgh: Edinburgh University Press.

Boniface, Ebeye (2004). Abiodun, Christiana. *Dictionary of African Christian Biography*. https://dacb.org/stories/nigeria/abiodun-christiana (accessed 4 August 2021).

Brockman, Norbert C. (1994). Lenshina Mulenga Mubishi, Alice. *Dictionary of African Christian Biography*. https://dacb.org/stories/zambia/lenshina1-alice (accessed 2 August 2021).

Chitando, Ezra (2019). Introduction. In: *The Bible and Gender Troubles in Africa* (ed. Rosinah Gabaitse, Johanna Stiebert, and Joachim Kügler), 13–24. Bamberg: Bamberg University Press.

Dah, Ini Dorcas (2017). *Women Do More Work than Men: Birifor Women as Change Agents in the Mission and Expansion of the Church in West Africa (Burkina Faso, Côte d'Ivoire and Ghana)*. Eugene, OR: Wipf & Stock Publishers.

Dah-Gbeto, Henri (2004). Koffigan, Massan. *Dictionary of African Christian Biography*. https://dacb.org/fr/stories/togo/massan-kofignan/ (accessed 2 August 2021).

Dube, Musa (2000). *Postcolonial Feminist Interpretation of the Bible.* Saint Louis, MO: Chalice Press-Christian Board.

Gunda, Masiiwa Ragies (2019). Genesis 1–3 and a gender-equal society. In: *The Bible and Gender Troubles in Africa* (ed. Rosinah Gabaitse, Johanna Stiebert, and Joachim Kügler), 25–47. Bamberg: Bamberg University Press.

Hackett, Rosalind I.J. (2017). Women, rights talk, and African Pentecostalism. *Religious Studies and Theology*, 36(2), 245–259.

Heywood, Linda (2017). *Njinga of Angola: Africa's warrior queen.* Cambridge: Cambridge University Press.

Isichei, Elizabeth (1995). *A History of Christianity in Africa: From Antiquity to the Present.* Grand Rapids, MI: Eerdmans.

Johnson, Todd M. and Zurlo, Gina A. ed. (2022). *World Christian Database.* Leiden: Brill.

Kalu, Ogbu (2008). *African Pentecostalism: An Introduction.* Oxford: Oxford University Press.

Kalu, Ogbu U. (2009). Christianity in Western Africa, 1910–2010. In: *Atlas of Global Christianity* (ed. Kenneth R. Ross and Todd M. Johnson), 130–131. Edinburgh: Edinburgh University Press.

Kanyoro, Musimbi R.A. and Oduyoye, Mercy A. (2005). Introduction. In: *The Will to Arise: Women, Tradition, and the Church in Africa* (ed. Musimbi R.A. Kanyoro and Mercy A. Oduyoye), 1–8. Eugene, OR: Wipf & Stock Publishers.

Kgatle, Mookgo S. (2019). A remarkable woman in African Independent Churches: examining Christina Nku's leadership in St John's apostolic faith mission. *Studia Historiae Ecclesiasticae*, 45(1), 1–14.

Kustenbauder, Matthew (2009). Believing in the black messiah: the Legio Maria church in an African Christian landscape. *Nova Religio: The Journal of Alternative and Emergent Religions*, 13(1), 11–40.

Longwe, Hany (2017). Zimbabwe, Zambia and Malawi. In: *Christianity in Sub-Saharan Africa* (ed. Kenneth R. Ross, J. Kwabena Asamoah-Gyadu, and Todd M. Johnson), 74–86. Edinburgh: Edinburgh University Press.

Longwe, Molly (2016). African church women's organisations. In: *Anthology of African Christianity* (ed. Isabel A. Phiri and Dietrich Werner), 944–948. Oxford: Regnum.

Mazrui, Ali A. (2014). *The Politics of Gender and the Culture of Sexuality: Western, Islamic, and African Perspectives.* Lanham, MD: University Press of America.

Mwaura, Philomena N. (2004). African instituted churches in East Africa. *Studies in World Christianity*, 10, 160–184.

Mwaura, Philomena N. (2009). Christianity in Eastern Africa, 1910–2010. In: *Atlas of Global Christianity* (ed. Kenneth R. Ross and Todd M. Johnson), 114–115. Edinburgh: Edinburgh University Press.

Ngong, David T. (2016). African Christianity in pre-colonial times. In: *Anthology of African Christianity* (ed. Isabel A. Phiri and Dietrich Werner), 23–30. Oxford: Regnum.

Oduyoye, Mercy A. (1995). *Daughters of Anowa: African Women and Patriarchy.* Maryknoll, NY: Orbis Books.

Oduyoye, Mercy A. (2001). *Introducing African Women's Theology.* Cleveland, OH: Pilgrim Press.

Oduyoye, Mercy A. (2017). The future of Christianity in Sub-Saharan Africa. In: *Christianity in Sub-Saharan Africa* (ed. Kenneth R. Ross, J. Kwabena Asamoah-Gyadu, and Todd M. Johnson), 461–480. Edinburgh: Edinburgh University Press.

Otefisan, Timothy Kennedy (2009). Adeoti, Lucy. Dictionary of African Christian Biography. https://dacb.org/stories/nigeria/adeoti-lucy (accessed 22 July 2022).

Pew Research Center (2017). The changing global religious landscape.

Phiri, Isabel A. and Kaunda, Chammah J. (2017). Gender. In: *Christianity in Sub-Saharan Africa* (ed. Kenneth R. Ross, J. Kwabena Asamoah-Gyadu, and Todd M. Johnson), 386–396. Edinburgh: Edinburgh University Press.

Pindzié, Robert A. (2008). Mengwelune, Lydia. Dictionary of African Christian biography. https://dacb.org/stories/cameroon/mengwelune-lydie (accessed 1 August 2021).

Sanneh, Lamin (1989). *Translating the Message: The Missionary Impact on Culture*. Maryknoll, NY: Orbis Books.

Sanneh, Lamin (2008). *Disciples of All Nations: Pillars of World Christianity*. Oxford: Oxford University Press.

Schroer, Silvia and Bietenhard, Sophia (2004). *Feminist Interpretation of the Bible and the Hermeneutics of Liberation*. London: A & C Black.

Sigg, Michèle M. (2014). Carrying living water for the healing of God's people: women leaders in the Fifohazana revival and the reformed church in Madagascar. *Studies in World Christianity*, 20(1), 19–38.

Siwila, Lilian C. (2016). Gender justice in African Christianity. In: *Anthology of African Christianity* (ed. Isabel A. Phiri and Dietrich Werner), 1061–1066. Oxford: Regnum.

Stanley, Brian (2009). *The World Missionary Conference, Edinburgh 1910*. Grand Rapids, MI: William B. Eerdmans Publishing Company.

Turner, Harold W. (1979). *Religious Innovation in Africa: Collected Essays on New Religious Movements*. Boston: G.K. Hall and Co.

Uchem, Rose N. (2001). Overcoming women's subordination in the Igbo African culture and in the Catholic Church: envisioning an inclusive theology with reference to women. Doctoral thesis. Indiana: Graduate Theological Foundation.

van de Kamp, Linda (2018). *Violent Conversion: Brazilian Pentecostalism and Urban Women in Mozambique*. Woodbridge: James Currey.

Walls, Andrew F. (1996). *The Missionary Movement in Christian History: Studies in the Transmission of Faith*. Maryknoll, NY: Orbis Books.

Walls, Andrew F. (2002). *The Cross-Cultural Process in Christian History: Studies in the Transmission and Appropriation of Faith*. Maryknoll, NY: Orbis Books.

3

Women in Asian Christianity

"Critiquing both the normative history of the West and the androcentric nationalistic Asian narratives, Asian women in divergent contexts have to plot pluralistic counter-histories and project new visions of their identities."

Kwok Pui-lan (Pui-lan 2000, p. 19)

Asia is a tremendously diverse continent, home to over 4.6 billion people in 51 countries, spanning from Türkiye in the West to Japan in the East, and to Malaysia in the southeast.[1] Asia has the lowest proportion of women in the world: 48.9% female. A minority religion, Christianity grew from 2% of the population in 1900 to 8% in 2020 (Table 3.1). The largest concentration of Christians is in Southeast Asia at 23% of the population, largely due to the long Catholic presence in the Philippines. Women are the majority of Christians in almost every region, with higher proportions in Central Asia (54%) and East Asia (53%). West Asia reports the lowest share of women in Christianity at 48% female, largely due to foreign workers in the oil industry, who are mostly men. However, the data on women in Asian Christianity are incomplete and weighted averages have been used in this analysis where more nuanced information is unavailable. For example, the Presbyterian Church in Korea (Tonghap) is one of the largest denominations in South Korea, with more than 2.7 million members (Johnson and Zurlo 2022). A study suggested that its membership is 70% female, much higher than the 52% reported in this chapter for all of South Korean Christianity (Cho 2011). Another example is the Chinese Catholic Church, which is reported 52% female here, but a more on-the-ground approach revealed 62% female (Yang 2018). It is likely the case that these higher figures are more representative of women's share of churches in Asia, but, unfortunately, this level of detail is not available for every denomination in every country.

The tremendous range of cultures and diversity in Asia includes more than 670 languages and 750 ethnic groups in Indonesia alone. The continent is also very diverse politically and ideologically, with the presence of communism (Vietnam, North Korea) and past and present military dictatorships (Myanmar, the Philippines, Indonesia, Timor-Leste, China, Japan, Korea), along with the forces of

---

1 According to the United Nations, Asia consists of the following countries: Afghanistan, Armenia, Azerbaijan, Bahrain, Bangladesh, Bhutan, Brunei, Cambodia, China, Cyprus, Georgia, Hong Kong, India, Indonesia, Iran, Iraq, Israel, Japan, Jordan, Kazakhstan, Kuwait, Kyrgyzstan, Laos, Lebanon, Macao, Malaysia, Maldives, Mongolia, Myanmar, Nepal, North Korea, Oman, Pakistan, Palestine, Philippines, Qatar, Saudi Arabia, Singapore, South Korea, Sri Lanka, Syria, Taiwan, Tajikistan, Thailand, Timor-Leste, Türkiye, Turkmenistan, United Arab Emirates, Uzbekistan, Vietnam, and Yemen.

Women in World Christianity: Building and Sustaining a Global Movement, First Edition. Gina A. Zurlo.
© 2023 John Wiley & Sons Ltd. Published 2023 by John Wiley & Sons Ltd.

Table 3.1   Religions over 1% in Asia, 1900–2050.

Religion	Pop. 1900	% 1900	Rate % p.a. 1900–2000	Pop. 2020	% 2020	Rate % p.a. 2020–2050	Pop. 2050	% 2050
Muslims	155,856,000	16.3	1.77	1,270,800,000	27.4	0.99	1,708,609,000	32.3
Hindus	202,516,000	21.2	1.41	1,049,702,000	22.6	0.43	1,194,647,000	22.6
Agnostics	47,100	0.0	9.72	547,520,000	11.8	−0.80	430,397,000	8.1
Buddhists	126,489,000	13.2	1.27	523,537,000	11.3	0.26	566,435,000	10.7
Chinese folk-religionists	379,883,000	39.7	0.13	464,135,000	10.0	−0.06	455,976,000	8.6
Christians	21,966,000	2.3	2.58	377,842,000	8.1	1.32	559,973,000	10.6
Ethnic religionists	50,532,000	5.3	1.02	165,126,000	3.6	−0.53	140,614,000	2.7
Atheists	7,000	0.0	10.19	118,157,000	2.5	−0.73	94,972,000	1.8
New religionists	5,946,000	0.6	2.33	62,222,000	1.3	−0.38	55,513,000	1.0

Source: Data from Johnson and Zurlo 2022. p.a. = percent change per annum, or each year.

Western colonization and decolonization (Portuguese, French, Spanish, British, Dutch, American). Asia is home to the two largest countries by population in the world, China (1.4 billion) and India (1.3 billion), plus the countries with the most Muslims (Indonesia), Hindus (India), Buddhists (China), agnostics (China), Baha'i (India), Jews (Israel), Sikhs (India), Confucianists (South Korea), Jains (India), Shinto (Japan), Daoists (China), Zoroastrians (India), and followers of new religions (Japan) (Johnson and Zurlo 2022).

Christianity was introduced throughout Asia at different times and locations. Orthodox Christianity and Catholicism in West Asia date to the time of Christ. Catholicism emerged in South and East Asia in the fifteenth and sixteenth centuries. The Western Protestant missionary movement boomed in the nineteenth century, spurring the establishment of many different denominations. The twentieth century was marked by indigenous forms of the faith and the massive growth of the Pentecostal/ Charismatic movement, including the founding of large megachurches. Some of the newest expressions of Christianity in the world are in Asia, particularly in Nepal and Mongolia. One major feature of Asian Christianity is the phenomenon of Muslim- and Hindu-background believers – people who choose to publicly identify with their family religion but secretly follow Christ, with large populations in Bangladesh and India. Although the future is difficult to predict, it appears that with continued conversions, Christianity is poised to grow, though likely not at the same pace as in the twentieth century. If current trends continue, Asia could be 10% Christian by 2050 – with many of those trends driven by women.

Socioeconomic inequality, partially a result of the considerable gap between rich and poor, marks the broader context for Christianity and other religions in Asia. Hundreds of millions of Asians have been lifted out of extreme poverty in the twenty-first century, yet the continent is still home to two-thirds of the world's poor. Asia's poverty is also related to educational access, where only 63% of the population has finished secondary education (compared to, for example, 97% in North America, 92% in Europe, and 72% in Oceania) (UN Development Programme 2022). Climate change is impacting large populations, with millions displaced in South Asia alone due to flooding, and Asian cities are some of the most polluted in the world. The gendered dynamics of Asia's inequalities are especially serious. Food insecurity is more prevalent among women, and rural women and girls have the lowest access to education as well as the lowest literacy rates. With 1.5 million girls already out of school, the COVID-19 pandemic beginning in 2020 only exacerbated existing gender inequalities. Women today also have less access to the Internet and they are restricted from upper-level employment. Gender-based violence, early marriage, and teenage pregnancies are also prevalent. Male domination and gender discrimination are widespread and most Asian societies are patriarchal, defined as the "gender-based allocation of power and roles in a given society" (Sechiyama 2013, p. 1).

Christianity in Asia, 1900–2050

Asia is the most religiously diverse continent, with nine religions (including atheism and agnosticism) each over 1% of the population in 2020. Profound regional differences exist related to the growth and decline of Asian Christianity (Table 3.1). The highest proportion of Christians is in Southeast Asia (23%), followed by East Asia (8%), Central Asia (8%), West Asia (6%), and South Asia (4%) (Table 3.2). Over the twentieth century, Christianity grew in four of the five regions. However, as the outlier of the story, Christians in West Asia have been under severe strain in the twenty-first century after over 400 years of living in relative peace with their Muslim neighbors. Christianity declined in West Asia from 23% of the population in 1900 to 6% in 2020, largely the result of emigration. Western military involvement has complicated life under religious extremism for Iraqi, Syrian, and Afghan Christians – many of whom are Orthodox and Catholic, with their lineages stretching to the first century. Women and children typically suffer disproportionately in these situations of conflict.

The general population of Central Asia – Kazakhstan, Kyrgyzstan, Tajikistan, Turkmenistan, Uzbekistan; together 8% Christian – is 51% female, revealing a greater proportion of women in the churches than in society overall at 54% (Table 3.2). Still, women in Central Asia, particularly in rural areas and small towns, do not have equal access as men to healthcare, employment, public decision-making, or economic opportunities (Jeyaraj and Anderson-Rajkumar 2019). Most Christian women in the region are either Russians or other European immigrants. The few indigenous Christians in the region live within Muslim-majority contexts and often read the Bible and listen to Christian broadcasts in secret. It is very common in small Central Asian house churches for women to have leadership roles as pastors and preachers.

East Asian Christianity is demographically dominated by China, home to 106 million Christians of all kinds (Table 3.3). It is difficult to pinpoint an exact figure, but China is home to roughly 55

Table 3.2 Christianity in Asia by region, 2020.

Region	Majority religion	Pop. 2020	% Christian 2020	Christian pop. 2020	% Christian female 2020	% pop. female 2020
Asia	Muslims	4,641,055,000	8.1	377,842,000	51.0	48.9
Central Asia	Muslims	74,339,000	7.6	5,658,000	53.6	50.5
East Asia	Agnostics	1,678,090,000	7.7	128,446,000	52.6	49.0
South Asia	Hindus	1,940,370,000	3.9	75,254,000	50.2	48.4
Southeast Asia	Muslims	668,620,000	22.9	152,878,000	49.8	50.1
West Asia	Muslims	279,637,000	5.6	15,606,000	51.6	47.6

Source: Data from Johnson and Zurlo 2022.

Table 3.3 Countries in Asia with the most Christians, 2020.

Rank	Country	Largest Christian tradition	Pop. 2020	% Christian 2020	Christian pop. 2020	% Christian female 2020	% pop. female 2020
1	China	Independents	1,439,324,000	7.4	106,018,000	52.6	48.7
2	Philippines	Catholics	109,581,000	90.6	99,307,000	49.5	49.8
3	India	Protestants	1,380,004,000	4.8	66,316,000	50.0	48.0
4	Indonesia	Protestants	273,524,000	12.2	33,409,000	50.0	49.7
5	South Korea	Independents	51,269,000	33.2	17,013,000	52.2	49.9
6	Vietnam	Catholics	97,339,000	9.2	8,927,000	51.2	50.1
7	Kazakhstan	Orthodox	18,777,000	26.0	4,891,000	53.6	51.5
8	Myanmar	Protestants	54,410,000	7.9	4,311,000	52.6	51.8
9	Pakistan	Protestants	220,892,000	1.9	4,188,000	51.8	48.5
10	Georgia	Orthodox	3,989,000	85.8	3,424,000	53.1	52.3

Source: Data from Johnson and Zurlo 2022.

million house church members. In the twentieth century, the house church movement was heavily populated by rural women, many of whom emerged as network leaders each with authority over tens of thousands of affiliates. In the early 2000s, women were an estimated 80% of house church leaders and evangelists (Wommack 2006) and 70%–80% of members (Aikman 2006). The gender ratio has evened out somewhat in the twenty-first century as the house church movement has become more urban and middle-class (see Independent and indigenous churches section below for more).

Mongolia and Israel have the highest Christian female percentages in Asia (Table 3.4). Mongolia has a reverse gender gap where female students disproportionately outnumber male students, a dynamic found in other spheres of society, like the churches. The country's gender gap is a

Table 3.4 Countries in Asia with the highest percent Christian female, 2020.

Rank	Country	Largest Christian tradition	Pop. 2020	% Christian 2020	Christian pop. 2020	% Christian female 2020	% pop. female 2020
1	Mongolia	Protestants	3,278,000	1.9	63,600	63.2	50.7
2	Israel	Catholics	8,656,000	2.2	188,000	63.0	50.2
3	Singapore	Unaffiliated Christians	5,850,000	20.7	1,209,000	54.7	47.7
4	Kazakhstan	Orthodox	18,777,000	26.0	4,891,000	53.6	51.5
5	Kyrgyzstan	Orthodox	6,524,000	4.4	286,000	53.4	50.5
6	Nepal	Independents	29,137,000	4.3	1,253,000	53.3	54.2
7	Tajikistan	Orthodox	9,538,000	0.7	65,900	53.2	49.6
8	Uzbekistan	Orthodox	33,469,000	1.0	348,000	53.2	50.1
9	Turkmenistan	Orthodox	6,031,000	1.1	68,000	53.2	50.8
10	Georgia	Orthodox	3,989,000	85.8	3,424,000	53.1	52.3

Source: Data from Johnson and Zurlo 2022.

consequence of the economic fallout at the end of the socialist state in the early 1990s, which resulted in a renewed emphasis on rural nomadic herding, a predominately male vocation. Despite their patriarchal society, Mongol women have historically had more responsibilities but enjoyed higher status than women in other Asian cultures. Nearly all Mongolian Protestant churches (98%) have women serving on their leadership boards, while women are permitted to preach in 83% of congregations and comprise 65% of church attendees (Visser, Byambatseren, and Stephens 2017).

The Israeli census revealed that Christians of all kinds were 63% female. The first nationally representative study of gender differences among religions in Israel found that Christian women were more likely than Christian men to attend church regularly (50% women vs. 35% men), pray daily (37% vs. 31%), and say that religion is very important in their lives (63% vs. 51%) (Schnabel, Hackett, and McClendon 2018). The gender imbalance could be due to increased opportunities for women in Christianity compared to Judaism and Islam, or a consequence of conversion or migration patterns.

Catholics are the largest Christian family in Asia (136 million affiliates and 38% of all Christians, Figure 3.1). The countries with the most Catholics are the Philippines (78 million), India (20 million), China (6 million Clandestine, 4 million Patriotic), Indonesia (7.5 million), Vietnam (6.5 million), and South Korea (6 million) (Table 3.6). When considered together, house churches are the second-largest Christian family in Asia with 53 million members (Table 3.5). The largest population of house church affiliates is in China, but they are also present in Saudi Arabia, North Korea, Bangladesh, and elsewhere throughout the region. Roughly a third of Asian Christians are Pentecostal/Charismatic, and nearly 20% of all Pentecostals/Charismatics in the world live in Asia.

Women in Asia experience discrimination in every context: political, social, economic, and religious (Lienemann-Perrin et al. 2012). There are at least 100 million missing Asian girls – girls who should have been born but were not due to selective abortions in male-preference societies. In India, the number of selective abortions of female fetuses rose from 0–2 million in the 1980s to 3–6 million in the 2000s, totaling an estimated 4.2–12.1 million aborted female fetuses from 1980–2010 (Jha et al. 2011). The Asian Christian woman's lower status is exacerbated due to her religious minority affiliation.

The historical interaction between Western female missionaries and indigenous women in the nineteenth century pushed up against the issue of Asian women's empowerment. While Western women recognized gendered oppression in Asian societies, they tried to address it with Western sensibilities, particularly, Victorian ideas of home and family. Apart from education for

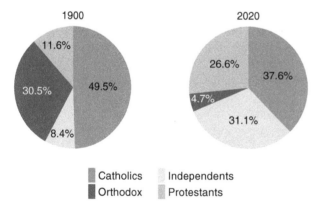

Figure 3.1 Christianity in Asia by major Christian tradition, 1900 and 2020. *Source:* Data from Johnson and Zurlo 2022.

Table 3.5 Christian families in Asia, 2000 and 2015.

Family	Affiliated 2000	Affiliated 2015	% female 2015	Rate % p.a. 2000–2015
Latin-rite Catholic	110,727,000	135,657,000	49.8	1.36
Nontraditional, house, cell	48,289,000	53,056,000	53.6	0.63
United church or joint mission	23,350,000	38,762,000	51.2	3.44
Pentecostal/Charismatic*	25,898,000	37,283,000	50.9	2.46
Reformed, Presbyterian	18,934,000	22,988,000	51.1	1.30
Lutheran	6,340,000	10,233,000	50.0	3.24
Eastern Orthodox	9,472,000	9,798,000	53.1	0.23
Oriental and other Orthodox	8,520,000	8,787,000	50.6	0.21
Baptist	7,532,000	8,464,000	51.1	0.78
Nondenominational	6,266,000	8,359,000	50.1	1.94
Eastern-rite Catholic	6,287,000	7,089,000	50.7	0.80
Other Protestant/Independent	4,834,000	6,409,000	51.0	1.90
Holiness	3,830,000	5,091,000	51.0	1.92
Hidden believers in Christ	3,290,000	4,955,000	49.9	2.77
Adventist	2,838,000	4,636,000	50.6	3.32
Methodist	3,642,000	4,268,000	51.8	1.06
Old Catholic Church	3,691,000	3,736,000	48.7	0.08
Restorationist, Disciple	1,800,000	2,365,000	50.1	1.84
Jehovah's Witnesses	1,101,000	1,467,000	53.5	1.93
Latter-day Saints (Mormons)	738,000	1,162,000	51.4	3.07
Anglican	1,014,000	1,160,000	51.1	0.90
Christian Brethren	581,000	778,000	50.5	1.96
Salvationist	548,000	619,000	50.5	0.81
Mennonite	309,000	356,000	50.2	0.95
Congregational	147,000	185,000	52.6	1.55
Friends (Quaker)	13,600	20,600	52.7	2.79

Source: Data from Johnson and Zurlo 2022. p.a. = percent change per annum, or each year.
*Excluding partially pentecostalized.

women and girls – which was generally (but not always) welcomed – Western notions of "women's liberation" did not align with Asian realities. This raised the question of whether Western Christianity provided emancipation for Asian women, or just another kind of patriarchy (Kim 2008). In other words, the contextualization of Christianity for Asian women should be in the hands of Asian, not Western, women.

Asian women's involvement in churches varies by geographic location and Christian tradition. Although women make up the majority of congregational membership, they are marginalized in church leadership and decision-making. Women are expected to fulfill traditional women's roles in religious life: cooking, cleaning, preparation of the altar, and secretarial work. In Catholic and

Table 3.6 Largest denominations in Asia, 2015.

Rank	Country	Denomination	Year begun	Affiliated 2015	% Christian female	Rate % p.a. 2000–2015
1	Philippines	Catholic Church in the Philippines	1521	78,271,000	49.3	1.50
2	China	Three-Self Patriotic Movement	1807	30,000,000	51.5	4.28
3	China	Han traditional house churches	1917	20,000,000	53.7	3.18
4	India	Catholic Church in India	1319	19,947,000	50.0	1.19
5	China	Han house churches Big Five (rural)	1979	19,510,000	53.7	−2.67
6	China	Han emerging urban church networks	1989	15,000,000	53.7	4.73
7	Indonesia	Catholic Church in Indonesia	650	7,577,000	50.0	1.25
8	Vietnam	Catholic Church in Vietnam	1533	6,546,000	51.0	1.42
9	China	Chinese Catholic Church (Clandestine)	1298	6,000,000	51.2	−0.53
10	South Korea	Catholic Church in Korea	1592	5,589,000	51.2	2.05

Source: Data from Johnson and Zurlo 2022. p.a. = percent change per annum, or each year.

Orthodox churches, women's leadership roles are not well integrated into the life of the churches, which operate with male-oriented hierarchies (Rizk 2018; see Chapters 8 and 9 for more on Catholic and Orthodox women). Male-only clergies are the norm for Catholics and Orthodox but not necessarily for some Protestant and Independent churches. For example, the first female priest was ordained in the Anglican Church in the Middle East in 2011 (Rizk 2018). Women must navigate the complexities of being both Asian and Christian and ascertain how to fulfill the obligations of both without offending either.

Women in Indonesia, for instance, are expected to be unassuming, accommodating to men, hardworking, and dedicated to family; they are generally considered less intelligent than men, more emotional, and better suited for nurturing roles (Adeney 2002). These expectations are challenged when a Christian woman receives a calling from God to minister in ways contrary to Indonesian gender ideologies. She cannot lay aside traditional gender roles entirely and must fulfill expected cultural roles while being obedient to her Christian calling. Indonesian women's leadership varies depending on geographic location and denomination. Indonesia is a Muslim-majority country and Christians are concentrated in Papua, West Papua, East Nusa Tenggara, and North Sulawesi. Among Reformed churches, women became ordained in the Minahasa churches in the 1950s, Chinese churches in the 1960s, Batak churches in the 1980s, and Javanese churches in the 1990s. Meanwhile, in Pentecostal churches, the pastor's wife may become a co-pastor, even without theological training. When the pastor dies, his wife will replace him until someone else can take over the role. Among Chinese churches – there are 2.4 million Chinese in Indonesia, around 40% of whom are Christian – female pastors are permitted, and most are single.[2]

The Gender and Congregational Life Survey (2021) included 163 respondents from Asia, with the most from Mongolia, Malaysia, Myanmar, South Korea, and Hong Kong. Respondents were majority female (73%), married (65%), well-educated (83% with bachelor's degree or higher), and employed full-time (66%). Christian families represented were Pentecostal (20%), nondenominational (16%), Reformed Presbyterian (12%), Baptist (4%), and Holiness (4%), with most respondents attending churches with fewer than 200 people (63%). Women are active participants in their churches, with 63% reporting more women than men in their main weekly worship service (the most important ministry of the church; 92%); 53% stated that more women than men attend the midweek service.

Most respondents (80%) agreed or strongly agreed that women should be allowed to serve as pastors (compared to 84% for all respondents worldwide), although only 54% agreed or strongly agreed that it is harder for women to be accepted in leadership roles in the church. Despite this, 54% also believed that the Bible places restrictions on women's roles in the church. Members of Holiness, Anglican, nondenominational, and Baptist churches were more favorable toward women's pastoral roles and leadership than Pentecostals and Reformed Presbyterians. The survey highlighted the gendered expectations and realities for men and women in Asian church life. The only positions that respondents felt were easier for women to obtain than men were children's Sunday school teacher, administrative assistant, and intercessor (Figure 3.2).

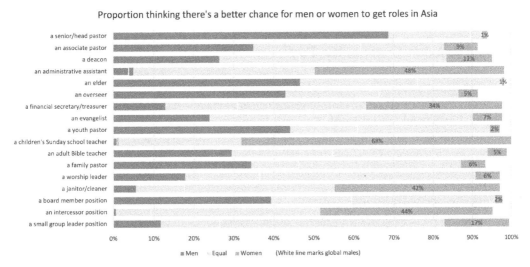

Figure 3.2 How do you think the chances of women and men compare when it comes to getting a ___ position in a congregation? (Asia). *Source:* Adapted from Gender and Congregational Life Survey (2021).

---

2 Thanks to David Dwi Chrisna for insight on Indonesian Christianity in this section.

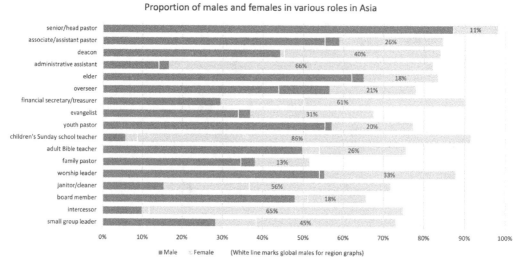

Figure 3.3 Thinking of the ___ in your congregation, is this person male or female? (Asia). *Source:* Adapted from Gender and Congregational Life Survey (2021).

The most frequently reported positions for women were children's Sunday school teacher (86%), administrative assistant (66%), and intercessor (65%) (Figure 3.3). Asian women were more likely than the global average to serve as financial secretaries/treasurers, children's Sunday school teachers, janitor/cleaners, intercessors, and small group leaders. Perhaps surprisingly, 11% of Asian respondents had a female senior or head pastor, which was more than the 8% global average.

Women in Asian Christianity: Past and Present

From the perspective of its founder (Jesus of Nazareth) and place of origin (Jerusalem), Christianity is an Asian religion (West Asia). Over time, the center of gravity of Christianity moved away from Asia into Europe and toward North America, Latin America, and in the twentieth century, to Africa. Despite its history, many Asians consider Christianity to be a foreign religion, a religion of outsiders, and a religion of Western imperialists. Vietnamese-born American Catholic theologian Peter Phan observed:

> If you visit the two largest cathedrals in Vietnam, Saint Joseph in Hanoi and Immaculate Conception in Saigon, the former in Gothic style and completed in 1186, the latter in neo-Romanesque style and completed in 1880, you will no doubt get a vivid sense that Christianity was and perhaps still remains to a significant degree a foreign religion...conversion to Christianity was much hindered by the fact that it was perceived as a religion that forbids the sacred duties of filial piety toward the ancestors.
>
> *(Phan 2012, pp. 132, 135)*

Christianity spread to both the West and East from Jerusalem. In going eastward, Christians encountered rival religions (Zoroastrians, Manicheans, Muslims, Buddhists) and spread to new languages (Syriac, Persian, Sogdian, Turkic, and others). Although Christianity grew, it was threatened by the Islamic conquest, the Crusades, Mongol invasions, plagues, and the reign of Tamerlane (1370–1405). By the fifteenth century, these forces had eclipsed Central Asian Christianity. Today, the themes of growth, persecution, minority status, restrictions, diversity, and struggle still embody Christianity in Asia. The arrival of Christianity in some ways made life worse for women by reinforcing a new kind of patriarchy; women in some Asian cultures had more freedom before missionaries arrived. As a result, Christianity in the modern period came to Asia as both liberator and oppressor (Lienemann-Perrin et al. 2012).

The Edinburgh 1910 World Missionary Conference included 18 delegates from Asia (of 1,215 total), invited as representatives of the "younger churches:" eight Indians, four Japanese, three Chinese, one Korean, one Burmese, and one Turk (Stanley 2009). None were women. The Asian delegates were meant to symbolize the changing composition of the world church and were regarded as representatives of the future of Christianity. Yet, while their presence was considered evidence of the success of the Western missionary movement, Western delegates did not expect the Asian delegates to have much influence on the outcome of the conference (Stanley 2009). However, a South Indian Anglican priest delivered perhaps two of the most widely remembered speeches from Edinburgh 1910. In his first speech, Bishop V.S. Azariah (1874–1945) identified India as the most underrepresented place in the world missionary movement because of the low proportion of Indians to missionaries. He estimated 100 million Indians were beyond the reach of any missionary, even though India was home to the highest number of missionaries at the time due to British colonization. In his second speech, Azariah pinpointed race relations as the most serious problem facing the church. Indians and Europeans were divided; they had little personal contact with each other, refusing to share meals or visit each other's homes. He concluded with a now famous quote, "Through all the ages to come the Indian Church will rise up in gratitude to attest the heroism and self-denying labors of the missionary body. You have given your goods to feed the poor. You have given your bodies to be burned. We ask for love. Give us FRIENDS" (World Missionary Conference 1910, p. 315). He urged delegates to imagine an Indian church that cut across caste, ethnicity, culture, and empire, a clarion call from 1910 that has largely gone unanswered.

Historic Churches

Christianity has a long history in Asia, with modern-day Israel and Palestine the birthplace of Jesus Christ, the spreading of the Church of the East along the Silk Roads in West and Central Asia, the alleged arrival of the Apostle Thomas in Kerala, India in 52 CE, and the famous Xi'an ("Nestorian") Steele in China from the year 781. Women have always had a role in the growth of Christianity in this region. The Christianization of Georgia, for example, is attributed to a young female slave, Nino of Cappadocia (d.338 CE), who healed Queen Nana, who, in turn, converted her pagan husband King Mirian III of Iberia. St. Nino is venerated in Eastern Orthodox, Oriental Orthodox, Roman Catholic, and Eastern Catholic churches with a feast day on 14 January. History also records notable female martyrs, such as those from Persia in the fifth to seventh centuries (Brock and Harvey 2008).

West Asia is home to historic Orthodox churches planted by the descendants of Jesus's disciples in the first century. These churches thrived until the Arab conquest in the seventh century, at which point they adopted a survival mentality that remains today. Christians from historic churches in West Asia have been under severe pressure in the twenty-first century with the advance of extremist Islamic groups, ongoing civil wars, and political and social upheaval. Christianity in the region declined from 23% of the population in 1900 to 6% in 2020, with an anticipated further drop to 4% by 2050, if current trends continue. In Iraq, for example, Christians were put at severe risk during and after the US-led invasion of the country in 2003, with the number of Christians dropping from nearly one million in 2000 to 175,000 in 2020 (Johnson and Zurlo 2022, 2019). Women in West Asian societies are typically considered inferior to men and are expected to be submissive to their fathers or husbands. Christian women and girls from Muslim backgrounds are at greater risk for physical and verbal abuse, discrimination, and rejection (Open Doors 2019). Those in Muslim-majority countries, such as under the Islamic State of Iraq and Syria (ISIS), have their vulnerabilities exacerbated in conflict situations, including increased domestic violence, forced confinement, rape, abduction, coerced marriage, and sexual slavery (Jackson and Watson 2018).

Women have been highly regarded in Armenian Orthodox churches since the earliest times. With Armenia the first country to adopt Christianity as its official religion in 301 CE, the Armenian Apostolic Church is the world's oldest national church, part of Oriental Orthodoxy and one of the most ancient Christian communities. Unlike other Orthodox churches, it is common for women to serve as chanters in liturgical services. The Armenian Apostolic Church is also one of the few Orthodox traditions to ordain women as deaconesses (see Chapter 9). Other historic churches in the region include Eastern Catholic churches (also known as Uniate churches), the Assyrian Church of the East, Oriental Catholics, and Eastern Orthodox.

Catholics

The great age of Catholic missions from the sixteenth to eighteenth centuries spread Catholic faith and practice – as well as European culture – throughout Asia, especially in China, Japan, India, and Southeast Asia. The only way to be a missionary was to join an order, so the first Catholic missionaries were single, celibate men. Notable Catholic missionaries in Asia include John of Montecorvino (1247–1328, India, China), Francis Xavier (1506–1552, India, Macao, China), Alessandro Valignano (1539–1606, India, Southeast Asia, Japan, China), Matteo Ricci (1552–1610, China), and Roberto de Nobili (1577–1656, India). To make Catholicism palatable in Asian contexts, Jesuits developed creative inculturation efforts such as adopting local dress, language, customs, and philosophies. However, male missionaries were unable to reach women in sex-segregated Asian societies. Nevertheless, indigenous women were important supporters of Catholic missions and had an essential role in spreading Christianity. In China, Candida Xu (1607–1680), granddaughter of a scholar and statesman, helped Jesuits in their missionary work, mediated between them and local officials, raised funds for missions and the poor, and facilitated printing Christian literature. Widely known as the Apostle of China, she helped spread Christianity among Chinese women (von Collani 2010). In Japan, female catechists Hosokawa Garasha (1563–1600, also known as Akechi Tama), Kiyohara Ito Maria (n.d.), and Kyōgoku Maria (1543–1618), and Naitō Julia (1566–1627) preached, baptized, and catechized fellow women (Ward 2016). Centuries later in Korea, early Catholic practice took place in homes, making it part of the woman's domain (Ledyard 2006). Twenty-nine women were among the 156 Korean Catholic martyrs in 1801, including Kollumba Kang Wansuk (1761–1801), known as the catechist of the Korean martyrs.

The Philippines is the largest majority Christian country in Asia, predominantly Catholic. Catholicism arrived via Spanish conquest and was reinforced by missionary orders, including the 14 female orders of *beatas* ("saintly" women) that formed over the 300 years of Spanish colonization (Santiago 1995). Catholicism grew substantially in the twentieth century, partly due to the Vatican's divestment of massive church estates and the encouragement of indigenous Filipino clergy and orders, both male and female. By the early 1990s, the clergy was predominantly Filipino, with all the diocesan hierarchy Filipino, while the church was supported by an extensive network of parochial schools. Catholic schools reinforced gendered expectations for women, emphasizing motherly sacrifice and virtue. Women in newly established orders ran most of the secondary and tertiary schools, many of which transformed into highly respected institutions of higher education (Barry 2018).

In China, Catholicism is translated as "Religion of the Lord of Heaven" after the term for "God" traditionally used in Chinese by Catholics. Christianity has existed in China in various forms since at least the Tang Dynasty in the eighth century. However, it was not until 1921 that the first non-cloistered Catholic missionary sisters arrived. The Maryknoll sisters were able to directly and widely evangelize Chinese society and thus hastened the development of Chinese Catholic families (Lutz 2010b).

Following the 1949 Communist takeover, Catholic and Protestant missionaries were expelled and religion was vilified as a manifestation of Western imperialism. In 1957, the Chinese government established the Chinese Patriotic Catholic Association, which rejects the authority of the Vatican and appoints its own bishops. As a result, China has millions of Catholics who are in contact with the Vatican and millions who are under the auspices of the government. Chinese Catholic women are widely known to be the mainstay of the church, with the most frequent and active attendance and service in Sunday schools, church maintenance, preparation of the altar, and visiting the sick (Lutz 2010a).

Veneration of the Virgin Mary has been a point of connection for Asian Catholic women. For example, in Vietnam, Mary reportedly appeared at La Vang (Quảng Trị province) to a group of persecuted Catholics under the rule of King Canh Thinh in 1798. With two angels beside her, holding the baby Jesus, and in traditional Vietnamese dress, she promised to protect them and all who visited that holy ground. First mistaken for a Buddha, a pagoda was built in her honor. She was later realized to be the Virgin Mary and the pagoda was donated to the Catholic Church. Hundreds of Catholics were martyred there in 1885 and the chapel from 1820 destroyed (Phan 2012).

Protestant Missionary Movement

Although Protestants had been in Asia since the early seventeenth century, formal missionary activities were often prohibited by colonial administrators. The first Protestant missionaries to Asia were Pietist German Lutherans Bartholomäus Ziegenbalg (1682–1719) and Heinrich Plütschau (1677–1752), beginning the Tranquebar Lutheran Mission in India (1706). There are countless examples of Western female missionaries to Asia from the eighteenth to twentieth centuries, including Harriet Winslow (Ceylon [Sri Lanka], 1796–1833), Sarah Smith (Syria, 1802–1836), Eliza Jones (Siam [Thailand], 1803–1838), Henrietta Shuck (Macao, Hong Kong 1817–1844), Fidelia Fiske (Palestine, 1816–1864), Mary Scranton (South Korea, 1832–1909), Lottie Moon (China, 1840–1912), Lillias Horton Underwood (South Korea, 1851–1921), Minnie Abrams (India, 1859–1912) Mildred Cable (China, 1878–1952), and sisters Evangeline French (China, 1869–1960) and Francesca French (China, 1871–1960). Baptist missionaries William and Dorothy Carey arrived in India in 1793. However, Dorothy was unable to make the adjustment from the English countryside to the difficulties of Indian society. While William was baptizing his first Indian convert, she was forcefully confined to her room, suffering from mental illness and unable to raise her children (Beck 1992; see Chapter 4).

Protestantism spread throughout Asia in the nineteenth and twentieth centuries. Ann and Adoniram Judson established the Baptist church in Myanmar (today the Burma Baptist Convention with 1.8 million members). British and American Baptists arrived in Thailand in the 1820s and 1830s and were particularly influential in medical missions. In Indonesia, German missionaries established the Batak Christian Protestant Church (Lutheran, 4.5 million members) in 1861. The emergence of twentieth-century indigenous Christianity in Asia was much different from that in Africa. In Africa, Christians broke free from Western colonialism and shaped their own forms of the faith; religious and political freedom were hand-in-hand. In Asia, indigenous Christianity was more in reaction against the Western Protestant missionary movement, and thus far less political than in Africa.

Protestant missionary women in the eighteenth and nineteenth centuries were expected to be assistants to their missionary husbands, reach otherwise unreachable women, and help raise the dignity of women abroad (Robert 1997). "Saving" foreign women from cultural and religious "oppression" was key to the Western women's missionary movement, though these missionaries were typically unable to untangle Western culture and the Christian gospel. As a result, they became oblivious agents of cultural imperialism on a grander scale than male missionaries since they worked more locally in "civilizing" families in the name of Christianity. American female missionaries in India, for example, advocated for Indian women's rights that they themselves did not have back in the United States (Khan 2010). By the early twentieth century, the Western Protestant missionary movement had replaced the language of "uplifting heathen women" with that of friendship and global sisterhood (Robert 1997).

Western missionaries prioritized Bible translation, medical missions, and education. Ann Hasseltine Judson (1789–1826), for example, was the first Protestant (woman or man) to translate scripture into Siamese with the book of Matthew in 1819. The first female Burmese convert, Ma Min Lay, was Ann's student. Moreover, women pioneered medical missions, with the first female missionary doctors sent to India, China, Japan, and Korea from the Women's Foreign Missionary Society of the American Methodist Episcopal Church (Robert 1997). Western missionaries became convinced that if Asians could be persuaded of the superiority of Western culture and the Western scientific method, then their religious cosmologies would collapse, ready to be replaced by Christianity. Women were needed to teach indigenous women and children in mission schools, out of reach from male missionaries. Education in Protestant missions became extremely important as the starting place for religious and social transformation, with both foreign and indigenous women at the fore. In India and Bengal, upper class women lived in *zenanas*, secluded areas of homes restricted to women, completely unreachable by men. British female missionaries established *zenana* missions to reach these women who otherwise would have no access to education, teaching them sewing, literacy, English, the Bible, and other subjects in aim of converting them to Christianity (Seton 2013; Semple 2018). In West Asia, early twentieth-century Evangelical Protestant schools provided women quality education that empowered them to gain the right to vote and obtain governmental positions (Wahba 2018). Some missionary schools turned into prestigious universities. A prominent example is Ewha Womans University in South Korea, formed as a mission school for girls by missionary Mary Scranton in 1886. It is now the largest women's-only school of higher education in the world (Kim 2008). The 1911 women's missionary jubilee launched an initiative to build seven women's colleges in India, China, and Japan; they raised three million dollars for the effort and some still exist today (Kohiyama 2010). Through education, Christianity provided new opportunities for Asian women's agency.

Photo 3.1 Women observe a moment of prayer at the 75th anniversary celebration of the Nepal Evangelical Lutheran Church in Laxmipur, with over 800 people in attendance (2018). *Source:* LWF/Albin Hillert.

Bible Women

Still, Asian women in general were noticeably absent from mission and church history, ignored in most historical records because of high illiteracy, low publication and scholarship, and due to the assumption that women were merely passive recipients of Christianity (Pui-lan 1992b). However, Protestantism could not have spread in the nineteenth century without the work of Bible women – indigenous traveling evangelists.[3] Trained and financially supported by foreign missionaries, these women were first-generation Christians engaging in frontier mission in their own cultures and contexts. They appear most often in mission history in China, India, and Korea with some examples in Myanmar and elsewhere in Southeast Asia. Bible women were cultural brokers, inter-mediaries, and translators, taking what they learned from foreign missionaries and spreading it largely among local communities of women. Many Bible women were middle-aged, having experienced personal tragedy (widowed, abandoned), physical impairments (e.g., blindness), or were otherwise considered unworthy by their families (Ling 2010). For example, in Chaoshan, China, most of the 30 Baptist Bible women were from the inland and were widows by death or economic migrant husbands on the move (Cai 2018). Being a Bible woman offered older women a way to utilize their trusted position as elders and cultural insiders to share a newfound faith as a liveli-hood – a rare opportunity for women, especially widows.

Bible women essentially did the work of male evangelists, pastors, and church planters but without overt foreign association. In some cases, Bible women exercised greater ministerial and financial freedom than Western female missionaries. Local female Christian leaders were essential due to societal gender divisions and the greater response to Christianity among women. Often forced into gender-divided meetings and discipleship, women found new ways to organize them-selves and gained experience leading other women. Bible women were trusted sources in the community, aided missionaries' evangelistic endeavors, and had the chance to earn income and literacy (Choi 2010). In China, the seclusion of women in traditional society gave female mission-aries a captive audience and the growing women's education movement in the West bolstered support for missions, including literacy efforts (Griffiths 2008). Their ministry of door-to-door evangelism was so effective in Korea, that the institutionalization of Christianity was seen as a det-riment to women's leadership (Hertig 2002). Protestant missionary work expanded in 1898 to the Philippines after the country became a possession of the United States at the end of the Spanish-American War. Bible women were essential in spreading Protestantism in the Catholic-majority territory; the role provided Filipinas the opportunity to become upwardly mobile (Prieto 2010). In 1910, American Baptist missionary Helen Barrett Montgomery (1861–1934) claimed, "The Bible woman has become an institution" (Montgomery 1910, p. 114).

Indigenous and Independent Churches

Part of the story of Asian Christianity in the twentieth and twenty-first centuries is the quest to frame Christianity as an authentic Asian religion. Many Independent churches in Asia arose either from Western-founded churches or reaction against those churches. Notable Asian evangelists in the nineteenth and twentieth centuries, such as Uchimura Kanzo (Japan, 1861–1930), contributed to the creation of indigenous expressions of the faith. Kanzo developed a non-sacramental, nonliturgical mode of church life as a direct critique of Western Christianity; his Non-Church Movement had a significant impact on formulating a distinctly Japanese Christianity. However, Kanzo did not support women in positions of ministry leadership in his adherence to traditional Japanese patriarchal

---

3 Thanks to Nadia Andrilenas for her insight on Asian Bible women.

traditions and a literal reading of Christian scripture (Lee 2022). In China, Dora Yü (Yu Cidu, 1873–1937) led the revival where later famous evangelist Watchman Nee's mother became a Christian (Lutz 2010a; Yü 1928). Watchman Nee (China, 1903–1972) founded the Church Assembly Hall (also known as The Little Flock), one of China's first independent churches that emerged separately from the missionary movement. Meanwhile, John Sung (1901–1944), known as China's John the Baptist, joined the Bethel Worldwide Evangelistic Band and preached in China and Southeast Asia, converting over 100,000 people to Christ. In India, Pandita Ramabai (1858–1922), a Sanskrit scholar and Hindu convert to Christianity, worked for the emancipation of women through exposing child marriage, child widows, and oppression of women in Hindu culture. She also translated the Bible from Hebrew and Greek into Marathi, and founded the Mukti Mission, an orphanage and school where one of the earliest Pentecostal revivals in the world occurred in 1905 (see Chapter 12).

The Philippines is home to the second-largest Independent population in Asia after China, with more than 500 denominations founded by Filipinos. The Philippine Independent Church is the largest, founded in 1901 by Catholic Filipino priest Gregorio Aglipay, who was excommunicated for speaking out against foreign domination of the church (Kim and Kim 2016). Now in communion with the Philippine Episcopal Church, it consecrated its first female bishop, Emelyn Dacuycuy, in 2019. Other large Independent movements formed by Filipinos are The Kingdom of Jesus Christ, the Church of Christ, the Jesus Miracle Crusade, and the Jesus is Lord Church – each with over 1.5 million members (Johnson and Zurlo 2022).

The most prominent expression of Independent and indigenous Christianity in Asia is the house church movement, found primarily, but not exclusively, in China. Known as "underground" churches, the Chinese house church movement consists of networks of unregistered assemblies that are separate from the government-sanctioned Three-Self Patriotic Movement (Protestant) and Chinese Patriotic Catholic Association. Most of these networks developed after 1949, when the Chinese Communist Party began requiring registration of all religious organizations. Especially after the Cultural Revolution (1966–1976) under Mao Zedong, religion of all kinds was attacked by the state and no communication from church leaders were received by the outside world from 1966 to 1969. While restrictions were loosened in the 1980s, the government's tolerance of these networks has waxed and waned. Sometimes they can operate peaceably; other times they experience extreme persecution by the state. Ironically, Christianity initially grew rapidly in China under Communism, which flattened traditional Confucian hierarchy and gave women new opportunities to lead. Most house churches today would not exist without the leadership of women.

Most Independent and indigenous forms of Asian Christianity are also Pentecostal/Charismatic, and the region is home to many megachurches. Jashil Choi (1915–1989), baptized in the Holy Spirit in a meeting led by evangelist Sung-Bong Lee, began a tent church with her Bible college colleague, Yonggi Cho (1936–2021), who later became her son-in-law and pastor of the largest church in the world, Yoido Full Gospel Church in Seoul, South Korea (Ma 2002). She also founded the well-known Osanri Jashil Memorial Fasting Prayer Mountain. Seven of the 10 largest congregations (by attendance) in the world are in Asia (the other three are in Nigeria): Yoido Full Gospel Church (Seoul, Korea; 480,000), Calvary Temple Church (Hyderabad, India; 225,000), Bethany Church of God (Surabaya, Indonesia; 140,000), Onnuri (All Nations) Community Church (Seoul, Korea; 75,000), New Life Church (Mumbai, India; 70,000), Victory Metro Manila (Manila, Philippines; 65,000), and Pyungkang Cheil Presbyterian Church (Seoul, Korea; 60,000) (Bird 2021). The Catholic Charismatic movement is also prominent in Asia, especially in the Philippines. El Shaddai, the movement founded by Brother Mike Velarde in 1981, has over 9 million members in the Philippines, 2 million in the Filipino diaspora, and hundreds of thousands of participants in its weekly prayer meetings in Manila. Most participants in El Shaddai services are women, often middle aged and older.

Photo 3.2 Baptism at Redemption Hill Church, an Evangelical congregation in central Singapore (2014). *Source:* Savio Sebastian/Flickr/CC BY 2.0.

Immigrant Churches

Asians are on the move due to many factors: economic opportunities, natural disasters, poverty, smuggling, violence, and persecution. In 2019, Asia was home to 40% of the world's international migrants (111 million); more than half (66 million) are Asians residing elsewhere in Asia (UN Migration 2019). Migrants make up 88% of the population of the United Arab Emirates, 72% of Kuwait, 79% of Qatar, and 45% of Bahrain. Lebanon has 156 refugees per 1,000 people (UN Migration 2019). Most migrants are from India, Pakistan, Bangladesh, Nepal, Indonesia, and the Philippines – with a substantial portion of them women. In 2015, for example, women were 49% of all intra-ASEAN (Association of Southeast Asian Nations) migrants, and 50% of migrants from Singapore and Thailand (UN Women 2017). Women work in a variety of industries abroad, including domestic service, healthcare, entertainment, agriculture, tourism, construction, and retail. Most are young (15–24) and have low levels of education.

Asian Christians are part of these migration patterns as they also pursue better work opportunities, seek finances to send home, and flee political unrest and religious persecution. Most churches in the Gulf States consist entirely of foreigners. In some cases, particular people groups are more Christian in diaspora than they are in their home countries, such as Han Chinese (Mandarin), who are 9% Christian in China but 27% Christian abroad; Palestinian Arabs are less than 2% Christian in Palestine but 3% Christian abroad (Johnson and Zurlo 2022). Christians fled Syria during its Civil War (2011–present) and fled Afghanistan during the end of the 20-year US occupation of the country and the subsequent takeover by the Taliban in August 2021. Christian women face double persecution in these scenarios as religious minorities and as the second-class sex. (See Chapter 14 for more on Christian women and gender-based violence.)

Indians in the United Arab Emirates are the largest Christian group in the country, representing many different denominations: Syrian Orthodox, Mar Thoma Syrian Church, Church of South India, and Indian Pentecostal Church (Jebejian 2018). Saudi Arabia is the only country in the Gulf that does not allow freedom of worship, yet there are 2 million Christians there, including Arabs, Filipinos, Indians, Koreans, and others. Due to the gendered dynamics of migration, churches in the Gulf States report some of the lowest proportions of women in all of World Christianity, such as Qatar (36% Christian female) and Bahrain (45% Christian female).

Asian Women in Theology

Asian Christians began seriously thinking about the theological contextualization of Christianity in the 1970s. Methodist Filipino Emerito Nacpil's "critical Asian principle" encouraged the development of indigenous theology in seeking what is unique in Asian experience and how that relates to Christian community, theology, and theological education (Nacpil 1976). Malaysian Methodist Bishop Hwa Yung pushed the contextualization conversation further with his book, *Mangoes or Bananas?*, arguing that Asian Christianity should not be yellow on the outside and white on the inside (like a banana), but instead be yellow on the inside *and* outside (like a mango) (Hwa 1997). Since the 1970s, there have been many developments in Asian theology, such as *Dalit* theology (India), *minjung* theology (South Korea), Anglican Bishop K.H. Ting's theology of accommodation (China), Kazoh Kitamori's "theology of the pain of God" (Japan), and Kosuke Koyama's water buffalo theology (Japan). However, these theologies – developed by men – reinforced homogeneous and patriarchal conceptions of Asian societies and histories and omitted the voices of women (Pui-lan 2000).

Asian feminist (or women's) theology has followed its own trajectory, not divided into various categories based on ethnicity, class, or geographic location, partly since there is no single language used across Asia. Both a kind of liberation theology (though not like that of Latin America) and a kind of feminist theology (but not like feminism in the West), Asian feminist theology began to emerge in the late 1970s with emphases on Asian women's experiences of colonialism, postcolonialism, neocolonialism, and oppression. It also emphasized the desire to contextualize the faith, develop new biblical hermeneutics, and envision new ways to address Asian women's struggles. Indonesian theologian and novelist Marianne Katoppo (1943–2007) critiqued the irrelevance of European theology and its denial of the Asian experience in 1979, emphasizing the specificity of her Asian, Christian, female identity (Katoppo 1979; Gnanadason 2017). The development of the Women's Commission of the Ecumenical Association of Third World Theologians (EATWOT) in New Delhi in 1981 boosted Asian women's theologizing as a response to the gender blindness of the emerging male theologians of the global South (Mananzan 1995).

The second phase of Asian feminist theology highlighted Asian women's unique experiences of neocolonialism, shining a light on Asian diversity. The work of Hong Kong-born theologian Kwok Pui-lan (b.1952) has brought to the fore the myriad interplay of gender, religion, and colonialism, and how Asian feminist theologians create dialogues between Christian faith, Asian religions, and social context (Pui-lan 2005). For instance, in the Indian *Dalit* context, feminist theologians are looking beyond traditional understanding of biblical texts considering their imperial and economic conditions, such as the work of Monica Jyotsna Melanchthon and Surekha Nelavala (see, for example, Melanchthon 1997, 2009; Nelavala 2014).

The third and current stage of Asian feminist theology has seen the field blossom tremendously, with the publication of numerous book-length treatises, the expansion of hyphenated Asian experiences (i.e., Asian American), and embrace of a wider range of topics including globalized theology and hybridization. Important organizations have emerged to help nurture, expand, and distribute Asian feminist theology, such as Pacific, Asian, and North American Asian Women in Theology and Ministry (PANAAWTM) and Innovative Space for Asian American Christianity (ISAAC).

The collective Asianness of the first phase is being challenged with new intersectional thinking. For example, Korean feminist theologian Namsoon Kang comments, "how many adjectives one needs to identify who one is reveals the multiple layers of discrimination and exclusion in a specific historical time and space. By using two adjectives, feminist and Asian, I reveal two layers of exclusion: *feminist* from the patriarchal world, and *Asian* from an Anglo-dominant world" (Kang 2012, p. 110). Common themes in Asian theology are storytelling, suffering/pain, and marginality. The communal nature of Asian society pushes back against the individuality of Western societies and is communicated theologically in the concepts of people-focused theology, neighborology, and a focus on horizontal relationships that bring Asians closer to Christ. The pain of Asia's past – colonization, warfare, strife – is seen in the suffering of Jesus on the cross, expressed in Japanese as *tsurasa* and in Korean as *han*. Eastern theology is generally shame–honor oriented. Jesus turned water into wine to save the couple from shame if they ran out of wine at their wedding and brought them honor by producing even better wine than the first (John 2:1–11). Jesus met the woman at the well at high noon when no other people would be around, restoring her honor and helping her avoid public shame (John 4:4–26).

Highlighting the hybridity of Asian culture, Namsoon Kang has called to move beyond the binary of West/Asia and other dichotomizing based on gender, sexuality, religion, and ethnicity (Kang and Ingram 2014). Speaking of women in East and Southeast Asia, Malaysian scholar Sharon Bong highlights the marginality of Asian feminist theologians:

> Feminist theologians risk being triply branded: as unfilial daughters (and sons, for men who identify as feminist), unpatriotic citizens and masculine women. They embody the socially marginal (insider–outsider) and socially marginalised identities of belonging but not quite within the home, church and nation. To find her place – after all, women hold up half the sky (as the Chinese proverb goes) – women paradoxically need to lose their place, to cross over and inevitably transgress boundaries, especially those steeped in gender binaries.
>
> *(Bong 2020, p. 419)*

The hybridity of Asian cultures – to be Asian is to be interreligious (Phan 2012) – makes it natural to cross gender and religious boundaries. This kind of theological hybridity is not new. Chinese women were attracted to Christianity in the nineteenth and twentieth centuries partly due to the feminization of Christian symbols. For example, the image of God as Father with no Mother did not align with Chinese values of honoring one's symmetrical parental unit and it challenged the authority of earthly fathers. As a result, some missionaries referred to, and the Chinese understood, God as both Father and Mother (Pui-lan 1992a). Asian Christian women are acknowledging what is important to them in their experiences of God, rather than what is dictated to them by Western theology. Kwok Pui-lan states,

> Christian feminists in Asia realize that they cannot be the gentle, passive and exotic females as portrayed in the global mass media; and neither can they be targets of Christian mission, nor eroticized objects in other people's theological imaginations. They must claim back the authority to be theological subjects, reflecting on God's liberating activities in Asia and articulating their own theology. Instead of passively consuming a male-oriented and Eurocentric theological tradition, they must challenge the past as they envision a new future.
>
> *(Pui-lan 2000, p. 31)*

Conclusion

The vastness of the Asian continent makes it impossible to speak of Asian Christianity as a unified whole. Christianity in Asia is expressed in a multitude of cultures, peoples, and languages, and Asian Christian women experience these contexts differently than men. They are part of patriarchies that render them second-class; many live in cycles of poverty and class/caste division. They gained agency in Christian networks and lost it, only to find their own ways to exert influence as spiritual leaders for themselves, their families, and their communities. Asian women pioneered the spread of Christianity among their own people, created Christian families, became evangelists, and are now theologizing in ways that align with their histories and religious and social contexts. They are nuancing Western feminist values and charting their own way to be Asian, female, and Christian. Despite the many obstacles, Asian Christian women find ways to integrate their culture and faith to live out their vocations. They both align and critique cultural expectations and serve one another in community. Absent from the historical record and theological opus for too long, Asian women have used their talents to express their faith in ways unique to their own experiences. Asian feminist theologians are democratizing theology and offering critical reflection and analytical frameworks that help them live out faith amid oppression.

Reflection Questions

1) Describe the role of women in Catholic and Protestant missions in Asia, and how they exacerbated intercultural tensions between Western missionaries and local communities. How did women's specific involvement in education impact these tensions? Reflect on the concept of "emancipation" of Asian women and how it was addressed by female foreign missionaries.
2) In the twentieth century, Western notions of "women's liberation" did not align with Asian realities. How did these Western ideals fail to address the discrimination faced by Asian women? How do women who feel called by God for public ministry clash with traditional cultural expectations of Asian societies?
3) Describe the various phases of Asian feminist theology and how it embodies a form of liberation theology. How does Asian feminist theology differ from Western feminist theology? As Hong Kong-born theologian Kwok Pui-lan states, Christian feminists in Asia must "challenge the past as they envision the future." What might this look like for women in Asian Christianity?

Works Cited

Adeney, Frances S. (2002). From the inside out: gender ideologies and Christian mission in Indonesia. In: *Gospel Bearers, Gender Barriers: Missionary Women in the Twentieth Century* (ed. Dana L. Robert), 171–184. Maryknoll, NY: Orbis Books.

Aikman, David (2006). *Jesus in Beijing: How Christianity Is Transforming China and Changing the Global Balance of Power*. Oxford: Monarch.

Andaya, Barbara W. (2012). Christianity in Southeast Asia. In: *Introducing World Christianity* (ed. Charles E. Farhadian), 108–121. Chichester, West Sussex: Blackwell.

Barry, Coeli (2018). Gender, nation, and Filipino Catholicism past and present. In: *The Routledge Handbook of the Contemporary Philippines* (ed. Mark R. Thompson and Eric V. Batalla), 330–340. London: Routledge.

Beck, James R. (1992). *Dorothy Carey: The Tragic and Untold Story of Mrs. William Carey*. Grand Rapids, MI: Baker Book House.

Bird, Warren (2021). 2021 Global megachurches. www.leadnet.org/world (accessed 31 August 2021).

Bong, Sharon A. (2020). Gender. In: *Christianity in East and Southeast Asia* (ed. Kenneth R. Ross, Francis D. Alvarez, and Todd M. Johnson), 413–424. Edinburgh: Edinburgh University Press.

Brock, Sebastian P. and Harvey, Susan A. (2008). *Holy Women of the Syrian Orient*. Berkeley, CA: University of California Press.

Cai, Ellen Xiang-Yu (2018). The first group of Chaoshan Biblewomen. In: *Christianizing South China: Mission, Development and Identity in Modern Chaoshan* (ed. Joseph Tse-Hei Lee), 15–36. Basingstoke, UK: Palgrave Macmillan.

Cho, Han Sang (2011). Equal discipleship in the Presbyterian Church of Korea (PCK). DMin dissertation. The Catholic Theological Union at Chicago.

Choi, Hyaeweol (2010). The visual embodiment of women in the Korea mission field. *Korean Studies*, 34(1), 90–126.

England, John (2013). Asian Ecumenism before the Ecumenical Movement. In: *Asian Handbook for Theological Education and Ecumenism* (ed. Dietrich Werner et al.), 3–11. Geneva: WCC Publications.

Gnanadason, Aruna (2017). Asian women in the ecumenical movement: voices of resistance and hope. *The Ecumenical Review*, 69(4), 516–526.

Griffiths, Valerie (2008). Biblewomen from London to China: the transnational appropriation of a female mission idea. *Women's History Review*, 17(4), 521–541.

Hertig, Young L. (2002). Without a face: the 19th century Bible woman and 20th century female Jeondosa. In: *Gospel Bearers, Gender Barriers: Missionary Women in the Twentieth Century* (ed. Dana L. Robert), 185–200. Maryknoll, NY: Orbis Books.

Hoefer, Herbert E. (2001). *Churchless Christianity*. Pasadena, CA: William Carey Library.

Hwa, Yung (1997). *Mangoes or Bananas? the Quest for an Authentic Asian Christian Theology*. Oxford: Regnum International.

Jackson, Olivia and Watson, Ruth (2018). *Iraq: compound structural vulnerabilities facing Christian women under pressure for their faith*. Open Doors International, World Watch Research Unit.

Jebejian, Hrayr (2018). Bahrain, Kuwait, Oman, Qatar, Saudi Arabia, United Arab Emirates (UAE), Yemen. In: *Christianity in North Africa and West Asia* (ed. Kenneth R. Ross, Mariz Tadros, and Todd M. Johnson), 177–189. Edinburgh: Edinburgh University Press.

Jennings, J. Nelson, Park, Yong Kyu, and Uy, Antolin V. (2016). Korea, Japan, the Philippines, and Southeast Asia. In: *The Wiley-Blackwell Companion to World Christianity* (ed. Lamin O. Sanneh and Michael McClymond), 561–574. Hoboken, NJ: Wiley-Blackwell.

Jeyaraj, Sheela and Anderson-Rajkumar, Evangeline (2019). Gender. In: *Christianity in South and Central Asia* (ed. Kenneth R. Ross, Daniel Jeyaraj, and Todd M. Johnson), 363–372. Edinburgh: Edinburgh University Press.

Jha, Prabhat et al. (2011). Trends in selective abortions of girls in India: analysis of nationally representative birth histories from 1990 to 2005 and census data from 1991 to 2011. *The Lancet*, 377(9781), 1921–1928.

Johnson, Todd M. and Zurlo, Gina A. (2019). *World Christian Encyclopedia*. 3rd edn. Edinburgh: Edinburgh University Press.

Johnson, Todd M. and Zurlo, Gina A. (2022). *World Religion Database*. Leiden/Boston: Brill.

Kang, Namsoon (2012). Transethnic feminist theology of Asia: globalization, identities, and solidarities. In: *The Oxford Handbook of Feminist Theology* (ed. Mary M. Fulkerson and Sheila Briggs), 109–125. Oxford: Oxford University Press.

Kang, Namsoon and Ingram, Laurie (2014). *Diasporic Feminist Theology: Asia and Theopolitical Imagination*. Minneapolis, MN: Fortress Press.

Katoppo, Marianne (1979). *Compassionate and Free: An Asian Woman's Theology*. Geneva: World Council of Churches.

Khan, Susan H. (2010). From redeemers to partners: American women missionaries and the 'Woman Question' in India, 1919–1939. In: *Competing Kingdoms: Women, Mission, Nation, and the American Protestant Empire, 1812–1960* (ed. Barbara Reeves-Ellington, Kathryn K. Sklar, and Connie A. Shemo), 141–163. Durham, NC: Duke University Press.

Kim, Chong-Bum (2008). For God and home: women's education in early Korean Protestantism. *Acta Koreana*, 11(3), 9–28.

Kim, Sebastian and Kim, Kirsteen (2016). *Christianity as a World Religion*. 2nd edn. London: Bloomsbury Academic.

Kohiyama, Rui (2010). No nation can rise higher than its women: the women's ecumenical missionary movement and Tokyo Woman's Christian College. In: *Competing Kingdoms: Women, Mission, Nation, and the American Protestant Empire, 1812–1960* (ed. Barbara Reeves-Ellington, Kathryn K. Sklar, and Connie A. Shemo), 218–239. Durham, NC: Duke University Press.

Ledyard, Gari (2006). Kollumba Kang Wansuk, an early Catholic activist and martyr. In: *Christianity in Korea* (ed. Robert E. Buswell and Timothy S. Lee), 38–71. Honolulu: University of Hawai'i.

Lee, Samuel (2022). *Japanese Women and Christianity*. Amsterdam: Academy Press of Amsterdam.

Lienemann-Perrin, Christine et al. (2012). Women's absence and presence in the history and records of Christian mission. In: *Putting Names with Faces: Women's Impact in Mission History* (ed. Christine Lienemann-Perrin, Atola Longkumer, and Afrie S. Joye), 45–98. Nashville: Abingdon Press.

Ling, Oi-Ki (2010). Bible women. In: *Pioneer Chinese Christian Women: Gender, Christianity and Social Mobility* (ed. Jessie G. Lutz), 246–266. Bethlehem: Lehigh University Press.

Lutz, Jessie G. (2010a). Introduction. In: *Pioneer Chinese Christian Women: Gender, Christianity, and Social Mobility* (ed. Jessie G. Lutz), 13–28. Bethlehem: Lehigh University Press.

Lutz, Jessie G. (2010b). Introduction. In: *Pioneer Chinese Christian Women: Gender, Christianity, and Social Mobility* (ed. Jessie G. Lutz), 51–54. Bethlehem: Lehigh University Press.

Ma, Julie C. (2002). Korean Pentecostal spirituality: a case study of Jashil Choi. *Asian Journal of Pentecostal Studies*, 5(2), 235–254.

Mananzan, Mary J. (1995). Feminist theology in Asia: a ten years' overview. *Feminist Theology*, 4(10), 21–32.

Melanchthon, Monica J. (1997). The Indian voice. *SEMEIA*, 78, 151–160.

Melanchthon, Monica J. (2009). Liberation hermeneutics and India's Dalits. In: *Bible and the Hermeneutics of Liberation* (ed. Alejandro F. Botta and Pablo R. Andinach), 199–211. Atlanta: Society of Biblical Literature.

Montgomery, Helen B. (1910). *Western Women in Eastern Lands: Fifty Years of Woman's Work in Foreign Missions*. New York: The Macmillan Company.

Nacpil, Emerito P. (1976). The critical Asian principle. In: *What Asian Christians are Thinking* (ed. Douglas J. Elwood), 3–6. Quezon City, Philippines: New Day.

Nelavala, Surekha (2014). Why make it a big deal! seeing the widow beyond her two coins (Mark 12: 41–44):a Dalit feminist perspective. In: *Mission at and from the Margins: Patterns, Protagonists and Perspectives* (ed. Peniel Rajkumar, Joseph Prabhakar Dayum, and I.P. Asheervadham), 173–178. Oxford: Regnum.

Open Doors (2019). Azerbaijan: country dossier. Open Doors, World Watch Research Unit.

Phan, Peter (2012). Vietnam, Cambodia, Laos, Thailand. In: *Christianities in Asia* (ed. Peter Phan), 129–172. Malden, MA: Wiley-Blackwell.

Prieto, Laurie R. (2010). Stepmother America: the woman's board of missions in the Philippines, 1902–1930. In: *Competing Kingdoms: Women, Mission, Nation, and the American Protestant Empire, 1812–1960* (ed. Barbara Reeves-Ellington, Kathryn K. Sklar, and Connie A. Shemo), 342–366. Durham, NC: Duke University Press.

Pui-lan, Kwok (1992a). *Chinese Women and Christianity, 1860–1927*. Atlanta: Scholars Press.

Pui-lan, Kwok (1992b). Claiming our heritage: chinese women and Christianity. *International Bulletin of Missionary Research*, 16(4), 150–154.

Pui-lan, Kwok (2000). *Introducing Asian Feminist Theology*. Sheffield: Sheffield Academic.

Pui-lan, Kwok (2005). *Postcolonial Imagination and Feminist Theology*. Louisville, KY: Westminster John Knox Press.

Rizk, Donna (2018). Gender. In: *Christianity in North Africa and West Asia* (ed. Kenneth R. Ross, Mariz Tadros, and Todd M. Johnson), 360–370. Edinburgh: Edinburgh University Press.

Robert, Dana L. (1997). *American Women in Mission: A Social History of Their Thought and Practice.* Macon, GA: Mercer University Press.

Santiago, Luciano P.R. (1995). To love and to suffer: the development of the religious congregations for women in the Philippines during the Spanish era (1565–1898). *Philippine Quarterly of Culture and Society*, 23(2), 151–195.

Schnabel, Landon, Hackett, Conrad, and McClendon, David (2018). Where men appear more religious than women: turning a gender lens on religion in Israel: gender lens on religion in Israel. *Journal for the Scientific Study of Religion*, 57(1), 80–94.

Sechiyama, Kaku (2013). *Patriarchy in East Asia: A Comparative Sociology of Gender.* Leiden: Brill.

Semple, Rhonda A. (2018). Bangladesh, People's Republic of. In: *Encyclopedia of Christianity in the Global South* (ed. Mark A. Lamport), 70. Lanham, MD: Rowman & Littlefield.

Seton, Rosemary E. (2013). *Western Daughters in Eastern Lands: British Missionary Women in Asia.* Santa Barbara, CA: Praeger.

Shan, Chuan Hang (2005). The role of the female Christian in the mainland China church. *Priscilla Papers.* CBE International.

Stanley, Brian (2009). *The World Missionary Conference, Edinburgh 1910.* Grand Rapids, MI: William B. Eerdmans Publishing Company.

United Nations Development Programme. 2022. Human Development Report 2021/2022: uncertain times, unsettled lives: shaping our future in a transforming World. New York.

United Nations Migration (2019). World migration report 2020. International Organization for Migration.

United Nations Women (2017). Women migrant workers in the ASEAN economic community.

Visser, Marten, Byambatseren, A., and Stephens, Kwai-Lin (2017). *Christian Church Growth in Mongolia: Conversion Growth of Protestant Churches in Mongolia.* London: OMF International.

von Collani, Claudia (2010). Lady Candida Xu: a widow between Chinese and Christian ideals. In: *Pioneer Chinese Christian Women: Gender, Christianity, and Social Mobility* (ed. Jesse G. Lutz), 224–245. Bethlehem: Lehigh University Press.

Wahba, Wafik (2018). Evangelicals. In: *Christianity in North Africa and West Asia* (ed. Kenneth R. Ross, Mariz Tadros, and Todd M. Johnson), 285–292. Edinburgh: Edinburgh University Press.

Ward, Haruko N. (2016). *Women Religious Leaders in Japan's Christian Century, 1549–1650.* London: Routledge.

Wommack, Timothy R. (2006). The women house church leaders of China: interviews with a muted group. Master's thesis. Liberty University.

World Missionary Conference (1910). *The History and Records of the Conference Together with Addresses Delivered at the Evening Meetings.* Edinburgh: Oliphant, Anderson, & Ferrier.

Yang, Fenggang (2018). *Atlas of Religion in China: Social and Geographical Contexts.* Leiden: Brill.

Yü, Dora (1928). *God's Dealings with Dora Yü. A Chinese Messenger of the Cross.* London: Morgan and Scott.

4

Women in European Christianity

"Analyses of secularization in the late twentieth and twenty-first centuries reveal very clearly the gendered nature of religious change: women are less ready than men to abandon their commitments to religion [in Europe], a finding which holds in almost all branches of the Christian Church."

Grace Davie and Lucian N. Leustean (Davie and Leustean 2022b, p. 13)

For much of European Christian history, women's stories were considered secondary to the narratives of men: their conversions (Constantine), theological innovations (Martin Luther, John Calvin), missionary activity (Dominicans, Franciscans, Jesuits), and historical preservation (Eusebius, Bede).[1] Institutional history is typically written from the perspective of the powerful, with women largely omitted since they were generally not political or military leaders, clergy, or authors of theological treatises. The advancement of social history in the 1960s and 1970s – the investigation of everyday people's lived experiences of the past – helped shed new light on European Christian women. The historiographical shift to social history put women's experiences in the center of the frame, not the periphery. Historical events previously told through an exclusive male lens have been revisited with new questions and sources to include the perspectives and activities of women – shifting the focus from the powerful to the powerless. More is now known about women of the past, including their participation in new Christian movements, ways of understanding the church in the world, and their theological contributions.

Europe has a long history as the continent with the largest number of Christians, from roughly the year 900 to 2015 (Johnson and Zurlo 2022). This is no longer the case, with only 22% of all Christians worldwide now living in Europe, down from 68% in 1900. European Christianity has been in proportional decline since the start of the twentieth century and has also internally changed in terms of its practice, theology, and importance in everyday life. European Christianity is by no means a monolith; it includes a wide range of theological beliefs and religious practices, even within the same tradition. Christianity in Europe is shaped by particular localities so that, for example, Catholicism is practiced differently in Italy than in Poland, and Orthodox Christianity

---

1 According to the United Nations, Europe consists of the following countries: Albania, Andorra, Austria, Belarus, Belgium, Bosnia-Herzegovina, Bulgaria, Channel Islands, Croatia, Czechia, Denmark, Estonia, Faroe Islands, Finland, France, Germany, Gibraltar, Greece, Holy See, Hungary, Iceland, Ireland, Isle of Man, Italy, Kosovo, Latvia, Liechtenstein, Lithuania, Luxembourg, Malta, Moldova, Monaco, Montenegro, Netherlands, North Macedonia, Norway, Poland, Portugal, Romania, Russia, San Marino, Serbia, Slovakia, Slovenia, Spain, Sweden, Switzerland, Ukraine, and United Kingdom.

Women in World Christianity: Building and Sustaining a Global Movement, First Edition. Gina A. Zurlo.
© 2023 John Wiley & Sons Ltd. Published 2023 by John Wiley & Sons Ltd.

differs from Greece to Ukraine. Immigration is also changing the Christian and religious landscape with the increased prominence of ethnic minority congregations, all adding to the complexity of religion in Europe (see Davie and Leustean 2022a).

The twentieth century was a tumultuous time for the European continent. The century began with great optimism for the human condition and the spread of Western civilization around the world. However, that optimism was quickly marred by war, genocide, political conflict, and social upheaval. The Balkan Wars (1912–1913), Bolshevik Revolution (1917–1923), World War I (1914–1918) and II (1939–1945), Communism, Nazism, Soviet expansion, the Cold War (1947–1991), the fall of the Berlin Wall (1989), nationalism, decolonization, massive technological innovation, second-wave feminism – all of these and more profoundly impacted Christian affiliation, which dwindled from 95% of Europe's population in 1900 to 77% in 2020 (Table 4.1). Widely considered a post-Christian continent, Christian belief and practice declined much more substantially (see section below). European Christianity – which, like elsewhere in the world, is majority women – is being redefined between its European and Christian identities, considering changing demographics.

The scholarship on European Christianity is immense. For generations, the historical arc of Christian history erroneously centered on Europe, recounting how the faith began in Jerusalem, spread through Paul's missionary journeys to the North and West, and transformed from a huddled persecuted sect to the prestigious religion of the Roman Empire. Church history itself was considered European at its core, chronicling the adaptation of the faith among the continent's noblemen (and sometimes noblewomen) via the so-called "barbarian conversion" from paganism (Fletcher 1998). Christianity initially spread first among the elite, the politically powerful, the kings and queens of diverse peoples, and then across constantly-shifting national boundaries. The conversion of these men and women and the subsequent diffusion of the faith among their dependents was critical in the creation of Christendom (Fletcher 1998), which then spread all over the world from the early modern period through colonization, commerce, and Christian mission. Adapting into European cultures, Christianity became intricately tied with aristocracies. Over time, "Christian culture" and "European culture" became synonymous, though questions remain on how Christian Europe really was in the past. The Christianity that triumphed across the continent could have been just a social movement imposed on the masses by powerful rulers, but nevertheless, from roughly the tenth century until the mid-twentieth century, Europe was Christian, and Christianity itself was considered a European faith.

In the twentieth and twenty-first centuries, European Christian women have been pioneering new ways of interpreting biblical texts, reimagining their roles in male-only church structures, and making unique contributions to the practice of Christianity. This chapter selectively addresses the women's missionary movement, ecumenism, Catholicism, Christianity in post-Christian Europe, post-Communist Eastern and Central Europe, and ethnic minority and immigrant Christianity.

Table 4.1 Religions in Europe over 1%, 1900–2050.

Religion	Pop. 1900	% 1900	Rate % p.a. 1900–2000	Pop. 2020	% 2020	Rate % p.a. 2020–2050	Pop. 2050	% 2050
Christians	380,647,000	94.5	0.39	572,603,000	76.6	−0.47	496,682,000	69.9
Agnostics	1,548,000	0.4	4.25	101,371,000	13.6	0.36	112,774,000	15.9
Muslims	9,365,000	2.3	1.47	50,647,000	6.8	1.26	73,792,000	10.4
Atheists	205,000	0.1	4.55	15,106,000	2.0	0.49	17,489,000	2.5

Source: Data from Johnson and Zurlo 2022. p.a. = percent change per annum, or each year.

Christianity in Europe, 1900–2050

The major story of Christianity in Europe over the twentieth century was its decline, coupled with an increase of the nonreligious (atheists and agnostics together), who were less than 1% in 1900 and grew to 16% in 2020 (Table 4.1). Islam also grew due to immigration and higher than average birth rates, and is now nearly 7% of Europe's population. The data on Christianity reported here represents membership or affiliation, not beliefs, attitudes, or practices. While Christian self-identification remains high (77%), it is widely observed that most European Christians are not practicing. Measures of religiosity are low in Western Europe in particular: 11% say religion is very important in their lives, 22% attend religious services at least monthly, 11% pray daily, and 15% believe in God with absolute certainty (Pew Research Center 2018a). Nonpracticing Christians outnumber practicing Christians everywhere in Western Europe except Italy, but at the same time, most nonpracticing Christians believe in a higher power, including God as described in the Bible (Pew Research Center 2018a). The dynamics are different for ethnic minority churches, which have experienced substantial growth in recent years due to continued arrival of Christians, particularly from sub-Saharan Africa, who are often Independent and Pentecostal/Charismatic.

In all regions of Europe, Christianity is more female than the general population (Table 4.2). Eastern Europe experienced a resurgence of Orthodox Christianity after the fall of the Soviet Union in 1991 – Eastern Europe was 84% Christian in 2020 (up from 57% in 1970) (Johnson and Zurlo 2022). A strong connection exists between religion and national identity in Eastern Europe – for instance, to be Russian is to be Orthodox – but rates of regular church attendance are still low. In Russia, the world's largest Orthodox country, only 5% of people attend religious services weekly (Haerpfer et al. 2022). While affiliation is higher in Eastern and Central Europe, levels of observance are still low: nearly everyone is baptized into a church, but only about 10% of people regularly attend worship services and just under a third pray daily (Pew Research Center 2017a). The theological differences between Western and Central/Eastern Europe are profound. For example, Catholics in Western Europe generally support legal same-sex marriage, but Catholics in Central and Eastern Europe overwhelmingly oppose it (Pew Research Center 2018b).

Christianity on the continent is 53% female and with only one exception (Russia), the countries with the most Christians all show higher female affiliation than male (Table 4.3). These countries also show a diversity of Christian tradition – Catholic, Orthodox, Protestant – and Orthodox churches tend to report lower female affiliation than Catholic and Protestant churches. In Moldova, for example, the 2014 census reported 52% female for Orthodox churches but 63% female for Jehovah's Witnesses, 58% for Seventh-day Adventists, 57% for Baptists, and 56% for Catholics and Pentecostals.

Table 4.2 Christianity in Europe by region, 2020.

Region	Majority religion	Pop. 2020	% Christian 2020	Christian pop. 2020	% Christian female 2020	% pop. female 2020
Europe	Christians	747,636,000	76.6	572,603,000	52.6	51.7
Eastern Europe	Christians	293,013,000	83.9	245,905,000	53.1	53.0
Northern Europe	Christians	106,261,000	70.5	74,919,000	53.3	50.6
Southern Europe	Christians	152,215,000	80.6	122,688,000	51.5	51.1
Western Europe	Christians	196,146,000	65.8	129,091,000	52.4	50.9

Source: Data from Johnson and Zurlo 2022.

Yet, at the same time, more nuanced and local studies reveal a much higher proportion of women in Russian Orthodox churches, such as in Russia (70–75% female, see Kizenko 2013) and in Iceland (61% female, see Statistics Iceland).

The highest Christian female percentage is in Estonia (63%) (Table 4.4). The largest denomination in the country is the Estonian Evangelical Lutheran Church, which operated underground during the Soviet period until 1988. It has ordained women clergy since 1967, one of the earliest denominations worldwide to do so. Women are far more likely than men in Estonia to believe in God, 53% versus 34% (Pew Research Center 2017a). In 2021, Estonian theologian Anne Burghardt

Table 4.3 Countries in Europe with the most Christians, 2020.

Rank	Country	Largest Christian tradition	Pop. 2020	% Christian 2020	Christian pop. 2020	% Christian female 2020	% pop. female 2020
1	Russia	Orthodox	145,934,000	82.2	119,945,000	53.5	53.7
2	Germany	Protestants	83,784,000	67.3	56,377,000	53.7	50.6
3	Italy	Catholics	60,462,000	77.5	46,863,000	51.4	51.3
4	United Kingdom	Protestants	67,886,000	67.4	45,742,000	53.8	50.6
5	France	Catholics	65,274,000	65.1	42,497,000	51.4	51.6
6	Spain	Catholics	46,755,000	86.7	40,526,000	51.2	50.9
7	Ukraine	Orthodox	43,734,000	84.6	37,005,000	52.9	53.7
8	Poland	Catholics	37,847,000	95.6	36,184,000	52.2	51.5
9	Romania	Orthodox	19,238,000	98.6	18,959,000	51.3	51.4
10	Netherlands	Catholics	17,135,000	55.5	9,515,000	51.7	50.2

Source: Data from Johnson and Zurlo 2022.

Table 4.4 Countries in Europe with the highest percent Christian female, 2020.

Rank	Country	Largest Christian tradition	Pop. 2020	% Christian 2020	Christian pop. 2020	% Christian female 2020	% pop. female 2020
1	Estonia	Protestants	1,327,000	37.3	495,000	62.8	52.6
2	Czechia	Catholics	10,709,000	35.0	3,746,000	57.0	50.8
3	Lithuania	Catholics	2,722,000	89.1	2,426,000	55.1	53.7
4	Hungary	Catholics	9,660,000	87.3	8,429,000	55.1	52.4
5	Portugal	Catholics	10,197,000	90.5	9,228,000	54.5	52.7
6	Slovenia	Catholics	2,079,000	83.3	1,732,000	53.8	50.2
7	United Kingdom	Protestants	67,886,000	67.4	45,742,000	53.8	50.6
8	Germany	Protestants	83,784,000	67.3	56,377,000	53.7	50.6
9	Russia	Orthodox	145,934,000	82.2	119,945,000	53.5	53.7
10	Bulgaria	Orthodox	6,948,000	82.7	5,749,000	53.1	51.4

Source: Data from Johnson and Zurlo 2022.

was elected the General Secretary of the Lutheran World Federation, the first woman and the first Central/Eastern European person to hold the position. In Czechia (formerly the Czech Republic), the Hussite Church, the country's second largest denomination, is 61% female and half of its priests are women. Notably, Czechia and Estonia have the two lowest percentages of Christians in post-Christian Europe, 37% and 35%, respectively (Kosovo is lower, but it is a Muslim majority country). In Czechia, however, people are not necessarily indifferent to religion and spirituality. Surveys over time have reported high rates of alternative spiritualities, such as fortune tellers, horoscopes, and supernatural powers, and these beliefs and practices are higher among people who grew up in Christian churches (Hamplová and Nešpor 2009). Throughout Europe, women outnumber men in alternative spiritualities, including New Age religion and neo-paganism, which in some cases are upward of 80% women (Heelas and Woodhead 2005).

European Christianity is very diverse, as the continent is home to majority Catholic, Orthodox, and Protestant countries. The shift of Christianity to the global South is evident in Europe's share of these traditions between 1900 and 2020 (Figure 4.1).

Although Catholicism is still the largest Christian family in Europe (Table 4.5), Europe's share of all Catholics worldwide dropped from 68% in 1900 to 20% in 2020 (Figure 4.1). This is the case for Orthodox Christianity as well, though it is still concentrated in Eastern Europe; 90% of all Orthodox

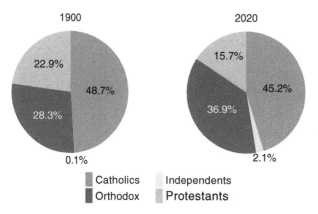

Figure 4.1 Christianity in Europe by major Christian tradition, 1900 and 2020. *Source:* Data from Johnson and Zurlo 2022.

Table 4.5 Christian families in Europe, 2000 and 2015.

Family	Affiliated 2000	Affiliated 2015	% female 2015	Rate % p.a. 2000–2015
Latin-rite Catholic	248,043,000	247,267,000	51.9	−0.02
Eastern Orthodox	190,756,000	202,678,000	52.8	0.40
Lutheran	33,621,000	32,453,000	53.5	−0.24
Anglican	26,281,000	24,946,000	53.7	−0.35
United church or joint mission	13,838,000	12,696,000	54.9	−0.57
Reformed, Presbyterian	11,065,000	10,340,000	53.3	−0.45
Pentecostal/Charismatic*	5,856,000	7,168,000	54.4	1.36

Table 4.5   (Continued)

Family	Affiliated 2000	Affiliated 2015	% female 2015	Rate % p.a. 2000–2015
Eastern-rite Catholic	5,360,000	5,327,000	51.8	−0.04
Oriental and other Orthodox	4,245,000	4,010,000	52.1	−0.38
Other Protestant/Independent	2,991,000	3,874,000	53.7	1.74
Jehovah's Witnesses	2,762,000	3,049,000	54.5	0.66
Baptist	979,000	911,000	54.2	−0.48
Methodist	1,018,000	612,000	53.9	−3.34
Christian Brethren	559,000	520,000	53.4	−0.48
Latter-day Saints (Mormons)	415,000	507,000	53.5	1.34
Adventist	447,000	438,000	53.9	−0.13
Old Catholic Church	370,000	328,000	56.2	−0.81
Nondenominational	264,000	283,000	53.1	0.48
Congregational	198,000	183,000	54.4	−0.54
Mennonite	147,000	139,000	53.4	−0.36
Holiness	103,000	121,000	52.9	1.07
Salvationist	147,000	107,000	53.3	−2.10
Restorationist, Disciple	48,200	69,100	52.8	2.43
Nontraditional, house, cell	51,900	68,300	56.5	1.85
Moravian	54,200	57,500	54.1	0.39
Hidden believers in Christ	27,500	37,800	55.6	2.14
Friends (Quaker)	26,100	21,100	53.8	−1.40

Source: Data from Johnson and Zurlo 2022. p.a. = percent change per annum, or each year.
*Excluding partially pentecostalized.

lived in Europe in 1900, today it is 70%. The same goes for Protestants, falling from 63% in 1900 to 12% in 2020. Even though the Pentecostal/Charismatic movement is growing everywhere around the world, Europe was less than 3% Pentecostal/Charismatic in 2020. Table 4.5 also shows the continued decline of Christianity across nearly all families. Very few churches appear to be keeping up with average annual population growth, which is roughly 2% per year.

Table 4.6 shows that the largest denominations in Europe are also in decline. The Ukrainian Orthodox Church is an outlier due to shifting allegiances between Kyiv and Moscow, not actual net growth in the number of Orthodox Christians. There is no apparent correlation between a denomination's female membership or activities and its decline over time.

Like elsewhere worldwide, trends related to European belief and practice are definitively gendered. Christianity is generally more prominent among women, older generations (over 55), people with less education, ethnic minorities, and immigrants. Although European women's commitments to religion have dropped substantially, especially since the 1960s, women are still more religious than men on a variety of measures. There are endless examples of women reporting higher rates of religiosity than men, and even more hypotheses as to why. Evidence on both sides illustrate the "nature vs. nurture" debate, where women are more religious because of biological factors, or because of certain kinds of religious socializations in childhood, or a combination of both. Education levels, employment, personality traits, psychological factors (like feelings of guilt

Table 4.6   Largest denominations in Europe, 2015.

Rank	Country	Denomination	Year begun	Affiliated 2015	% Christian female	Rate % p.a. 2000–2015
1	Russia	Russian Orthodox Church	988	110,850,000	53.5	0.97
2	Italy	Chiesa Cattolica in Italia	40	45,563,000	51.4	0.04
3	Spain	Iglesia Católica en España	63	39,377,000	51.2	0.56
4	France	Eglise Catholique de France	80	37,926,000	51.4	0.20
5	Poland	Catholic Church in Poland	966	34,462,000	52.1	−0.17
6	Germany	Evangelische Kirche in Deutschland	1517	24,450,000	55.0	−0.57
7	Germany	Katholische Kirche in Deutschland	90	24,246,000	53.0	−0.76
8	United Kingdom	Church of England	100	23,000,000	53.8	−0.37
9	Romania	Romanian Orthodox Church (Patriarchate Bucharest)	100	17,400,000	51.2	−0.58
10	Ukraine	Ukrainian Orthodox Church (Patriarchate Kyiv)	1991	16,000,000	53.2	9.68

Source: Data from Johnson and Zurlo 2022. p.a. = percent change per annum, or each year.

and risk aversion), women's social location, expected societal roles, workforce participation, and family values perhaps all have a role in explaining the phenomenon, which appears to be persisting (see, for example, Kregting et al. 2019; Hamplová 2011; Palmisano and Todesco 2019; Trzebiatowska and Bruce 2012).

Women attend church more frequently than men across the theological spectrum and among different age groups. They are more likely to donate funds to religious institutions, wear religious clothing and symbols, believe in God as described in the Bible, embrace spiritual ideas, pray, and have positive views of religion (Pew Research Center 2018a). Traditional gender roles are very common in Orthodox countries, such as women's responsibility to bear and raise children, obey their husbands, and defer to them to earn money (Pew Research Center 2017a, 2017b). Throughout the continent, more women than men say that religion is very important in their lives, with the largest gaps in Greece (62% of women and 48% of men) and Ukraine (28% vs. 14%) (Pew Research Center 2017a). Women pray more than men, such as in Armenia (55% of women pray daily compared to 32% of men), Poland (37% vs. 16%), and Ukraine (38% vs. 17%) (Pew Research Center 2017a). Women are also more likely to believe in God, the soul, miracles, and fate; believe in the evil eye, witchcraft, and reincarnation; take communion, fast, and share their faith (Pew Research Center 2017a).

The Gender and Congregational Life Survey (2021) included 270 respondents from Europe, with the most from Germany, Ireland, France, Austria, Russia, and Ukraine. Respondents were majority female (83%), married (71%), well-educated (78% with bachelor's degree or higher), and employed full-time (52%). The largest Christian families represented were Pentecostal (23%), nondenominational (15%), Baptist (14%), and Anglican (12%), with a wide range of church sizes (22% between 51–100 and 12% over 500). Women are active participants in their churches, though 60% reported about the same number of women and men in their main weekly worship service (the most important ministry of the church; 86%), and 38% of respondents stated there were more women than men in their congregations.

Most respondents (85%) agreed or strongly agreed that women should be allowed to serve as pastors (similar to the 84% for all respondents worldwide), and 86% agreed or strongly agreed that it is harder for women to be accepted in church leadership roles. Despite this, 73% also believed that the Bible places restrictions on women's roles in the church. Although all responses were high, members of Anglican (91%), Methodist (91%), Holiness (78%), and Reformed Presbyterian (77%) churches were more favorable toward women's pastoral roles and leadership than Congregational (67%) and nondenominational (68%) churches. The survey highlighted the gendered expectations and realities for men and women in European church life, where respondents felt it would be easier for women than men to only obtain the positions of administrative assistant and children's Sunday school teacher (see Figure 4.2).

When asked what roles women hold in their congregations, the most frequently reported were children's Sunday school teacher (81%), administrative assistant (63%), and intercessor (54%) (Figure 4.3). However, European women differed from women in the global South, as they were

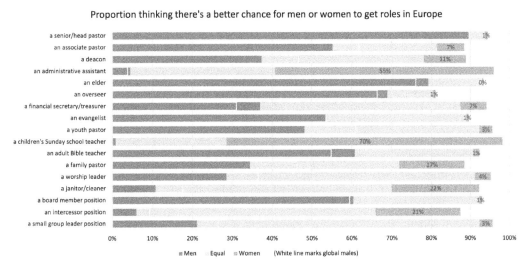

Figure 4.2 How do you think the chances of women and men compare when it comes to getting a ___ position in a congregation? (Europe). *Source:* Adapted from Gender and Congregational Life Survey (2021).

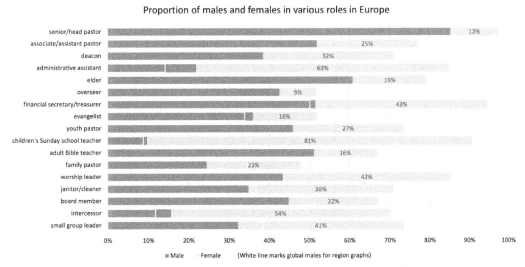

Figure 4.3 Thinking of the ___ in your congregation, is this person male or female? (Europe). *Source:* Adapted from Gender and Congregational Life Survey (2021).

more likely than the global average to serve in a variety of congregational positions: senior/head pastor, associate/assistant pastor, deacon, elder, overseer, youth pastor, adult Bible teacher, family pastor, worship leader, board member, and small group leader (Figure 4.3). This is a completely different scenario compared to women in Africa, Asia, and Latin America, who generally only rank higher than the global average for children's Sunday school teachers. Twelve percent of respondents from Europe reported having a woman senior/head pastor, higher than the 8% global average. The data indicate that, as expected, European women have more opportunities for congregational involvement than elsewhere in the world.

Women in European Christianity: Past and Present

The arrival of Christianity to Europe both empowered and subordinated women. They welcomed the teachings and actions of Jesus, who taught and ministered to both sexes and rejected the cultural assumption that women were inferior to men. Women were leaders in the early church, became venerated martyrs, and praised for their self-sacrifice and courage. They converted others to Christianity, and some rejected traditional feminine roles of wife and mother for a consecrated life. Yet, churches adopted a theological position that women were inferior to men, based on biblical passages in both the Hebrew Bible and Paul's letters that appeared to subordinate women. As Christianity became institutionalized, the relative gender equality of the early church disappeared, so much so that, "by the fifth century, the male leaders and theologians of Christianity had accepted and restated the most denigrating traditional views of women. All that was inferior or evil they associated with the female, all that was good and superior with the male" (Anderson and Zinsser 1988, p. 79). Any gains that women had achieved by affiliation with Christianity were nearly gone by the ninth century: "In the end, European women, like the women before them, would live in a culture whose values, laws, images, and institutions decreed their inferiority and enforced their subordination to men. Female subordination was the most powerful and enduring tradition inherited by European women" (Anderson and Zinsser 1988, pp. 83–84). Nevertheless, European church history is full of notable Christian women who made lasting impacts on the faith, such as:

- Clotilde, wife of Clovis I, who in the fourth century persuaded her husband to abandon paganism for Christianity, which became the religion of what is now France, Germany, the Netherlands, Belgium, and Luxembourg
- Queen Bertha and her daughter, Ethelberga, who converted King Ethelbert of Kent and King Edwin of Northumbria, leading to the Christianization of the Anglo-Saxons (England) (Anderson and Zinsser 1988)
- Medieval Catholic women and their vivid spirituality, such as the visions of Hildegard of Bingen (1141), Hadewijch of Brabant (c.1200s), and Bridget of Sweden (late 1300s) (Oden 1995)
- The Beguine Movement, begun around 1200 (Petroff 1986) and its radical female spiritual discipline of contemplative living and lay piety (which still exists in several dozen campuses in Belgium today)
- Argula von Grumbach, the first Protestant woman writer (Matheson 1995)
- Female lay theologians of the English Reformation: Anne Boleyn, Anne Askew, Katharine Parr, Jane Grey, and Catherine Willoughby (Zahl 2001)

These, and countless other women, eschewed the "preferred calling" of marriage and motherhood and the theology that required women to stay in the domestic sphere. In doing so, they laid a foundation for European Christian women to be creative, inventive, and pioneer new ways of being both female and Christian throughout European church history.

Women in Mission

Christianity is partly considered a world religion because of its spread across the globe (Kim and Kim 2008), and much of this spread is because of Europe's outward push beginning in the late fifteenth century. The first European missionaries were men in Catholic orders heading to sub-Saharan Africa, Latin America, and East/Southeast Asia. In convents and abbeys initially affiliated with a corresponding male order, Catholic women were active in ministry throughout Europe as nuns, such as those among the Dominicans in 1206. In the seventeenth century, women began to form their own separate orders for service, prayer, and consecrated life in Europe and abroad. For example, Clare of Assisi (1194–1253), one of the first followers of St. Francis of Assisi, founded the Order of Poor Ladies (now the Order of Saint Clare, or the Poor Clares) in the Franciscan tradition, and she was the first woman to write a religious Rule. Catholic female orders are either contemplative (cloistered), semi-contemplative, or active (Gallagher 2018). Of all the Catholic women religious in the world (619,546 in 2020), 34% minister in Europe (*Annuarium Statisticum Ecclesiae* 2020). There are numerous Catholic religious orders for women founded in Europe that work all over the world, such as the Institute of the Blessed Virgin Mary (Loreto Sisters; formed in England, 1609), Sisters of Mercy (Ireland, 1831), Little Sisters of the Poor (France, 1839), and Missionaries of Charity (founded by Mother Teresa in 1950). Women in religious orders minister in a wide variety of services, including healthcare, education, peacebuilding, orphan care, and support for other women and families. Chapter 8 provides more detail on Catholic women, especially those in orders.

The Protestant mission movement beyond Europe began in 1706, nearly 200 years after Martin Luther, with two Germans in India doing Bible translation and evangelization (see Chapter 3). Protestant women lost their previous agency in Catholic orders (Stjerna 2009) and were denied leadership in Catholic churches, so many turned to overseas missions to fulfill their ministerial callings. The first European woman to serve as an overseas missionary was likely Hannah Marshman (1767–1847), who arrived in India with her husband in 1799 (Seton 2013). Other prominent European women in mission include Mildred Cable (British, in China, 1878–1952), Francesca French (1871–1960) and her sister Evangeline French (British, in China, 1869–1960), Mary Slessor (Scottish, in Nigeria, 1848–1915), and Amy Carmichael (Irish, in India, 1867–1951).

Among other challenges, missionary wives struggled with culture shock, the death of their children, keeping a Christian home abroad, supporting their husbands, and differences in climate. William Carey (1761–1934), a British Baptist, is often called the "father of modern missions" for his theological arguments against Calvinist fatalism in relation to mission. He also authored a statistical survey of the religious adherents of the world and their access to Christianity, founded a Baptist missionary society that became the model for subsequent Protestant missionary sending, and engaged in 30 different Bible translations while serving in India for 41 years. However, his wife, Dorothy Carey (1756–1807), suffered horribly. She was an uneducated eighteenth-century English peasant involuntarily brought to India without the tools to make the cultural adjustment. She experienced a psychotic break that left her "stark mad," "quite insane," "often raving," and "deranged in her mind" (Beck 1992, pp. 152–160). Her famous missionary husband did not seek medical advice for her, and he forcefully confined her to a bedroom until she died.

Female missionaries were present, and well-represented, at the London 1888 and New York 1900 world missionary meetings (Seton 2013). However, women were sidelined at the important Edinburgh 1910 conference. Organizers made no distinction between men's and women's work overseas, despite the obvious differences, nor did they convene sessions to address women's work.

Women sat on six of the eight commissions addressing various aspects of world mission, but the most robust discussion regarding women in mission was about their organizational structure at home, not their work abroad. Even before Edinburgh 1910, male-run British and American boards both thought having separate women's boards for missionary sending was problematic and wanted to see them integrated with the general boards (Stanley 2009), even though women's boards were generally more successful, very well-run, and operated on leaner budgets. As women's boards were forcibly merged with general boards throughout the twentieth century, a process completed by the 1960s, women lost agency in missions and turned away from global activism to fight for their own rights at home. For example, women occupied a "somewhat uncertain place in joint administration" when the Church of England Zenana Missionary Society merged with the Church Missionary Society in 1957 (Seton 2013). Ultimately, Edinburgh 1910 contributed to the decline of women's autonomous missionary societies in Europe and America, with detrimental conse- quences for the entire Western missionary movement. Nevertheless, many missionaries are still sent from Europe today, perhaps upward of 38,000 a year. Exact figures are not available, but it is likely the majority are women. The Evangelical Lutheran Church of Finland, for example, sends over 400 missionaries abroad and 70% of them are women (Evangelical Lutheran Church of Finland, n.d.).

Ecumenism

The Edinburgh 1910 missionary conference also marked the beginning of the modern ecumenical movement, in which Christians across theological convictions came together for common wit- ness in a rapidly changing world. European Christians had a significant role in this movement after World War I and World War II, conflicts that involved "Christian nations" pulling their colonial subjects into a global conflict, resulting in mass devastation. Christians saw the need for a more unified voice, such as that of the World Council of Churches (WCC) in 1948, and advances toward full communion between Christian traditions, as demonstrated between the Anglican Communion and Old Catholic churches in Europe. Orthodox churches, including Orthodox women, were ecumenical partners from the start, and welcomed conversations with other Christian traditions. These ecumenical efforts provided Orthodox women opportunities for dia- logue otherwise unavailable to them (Kasselouri-Hatzivassiliadi, Moyo, and Pekridou 2010). From 1988 to 1998, the World Council of Churches held the Decade of the Churches in Solidarity with Women to specifically address the place of women in Christian theology, tradition, and culture in light of the United Nations Decade for Women (1975–1985). More recently, the WCC has been supporting other initiatives to advance gender justice, such as Thursdays in Black – the adornment of black on Thursdays to raise awareness of and support for victims of domestic and sexual violence worldwide. Furthermore, the White Ribbon project specifically encourages men and boys with the pledge, "I promise to never commit, excuse or remain silent about male vio- lence against women" (WhiteRibbon.org) (see Chapter 14 for more on Christianity and gender- based violence).

Catholicism

The Second Vatican Council of the Roman Catholic Church, opened by Pope John Paul XXIII in 1962 and closed by Pope Paul VI in 1965, was one of the most significant Christian events in the twentieth century. The first such council since 1869, Vatican II had huge implications for the growth of Catholicism around the world. Priests could celebrate Mass in languages other than

Latin for the first time, lay participation increased, new emphases began on religious freedom and interreligious relations, and a new spirit of collaboration ensued. In short, the initiatives of Vatican II signaled that the Catholic Church was going to be a part of the modern world. Second-wave feminism was beginning to emerge at this time, and the council also sparked new conversations about Catholic women, especially their role in the family and changes in their social, political, and cultural contexts. Twenty-four Catholic women (14 from Europe) participated in Vatican II as auditors, that is, invited guests alongside Protestant and Anglican observers (Madigan 2018). Ten were members of Catholic orders, 14 were lay women, and all but one was either single or widowed, and all were of older generations (Madigan 2018). Four additional women attended in part: Dorothy Day (of the Catholic Worker's Movement), Eileen Egan (Peace Movement), Barbara Ward (economist), and Patricia Crowley (expert on birth control). Catholic teachings on women had remained essentially unchanged since the times of Augustine of Hippo (354–430) and Thomas Aquinas (1225–1274), with themes of complementarity and women's subordinate place to men in the order of creation. These ideas began to shift with Vatican II as women advanced socially and became more outspoken concerning gender justice and equality with men.

Photo 4.1   A woman prays in front of Mary at St. Stephen's Basilica, Budapest, Hungary (2011). *Source:* Ramón Cutanda López/Flickr/CC BY 2.0.

The greatest changes in women's roles in the Catholic Church have come under Pope Francis, who, beginning in 2021, permitted women to read scripture, administer communion, and serve at the altar during Mass (but not become ordained priests). He appointed French Sister Nathalie Becquart as co-undersecretary of the Synod of Bishops, making her the first woman able to vote in the Catholic Synod of Bishops. Another woman, Catia Summaria (Italy), was appointed as the first female prosecutor in the Vatican's Court of Appeals (see Chapter 8 for more female firsts at the Vatican). It appears the door is opening for greater participation of women in the world's largest Christian tradition.

However, despite these changes, the Catholic Church is no longer considered the pillar of morality in most European societies. Marred by sex abuse scandals and unpopular positions on a range of social issues, Catholic conservatism has been increasingly pushed to the margins. There have been hundreds of thousands of child victims of sexual abuse by Catholic priests and other clerics, with 330,000 in France alone, according to a 2021 2,500-page report (Corbet 2021). With its posture toward women a determining factor of its decline, the Catholic Church has often been accused of misogyny because of male-only ordination and its theological stances on abortion and contraceptive use, all of which disproportionately impact women. In Ireland, for example, support for the Catholic Church declined sharply after the 2018 decision to repeal the constitutional amendment banning abortion. The Catholic Church did not participate in the referendum campaign, illustrating the loss of its societal clout. Catholic feminist theologians, such as Tina Beattie (b.1955), have realized the importance of moving beyond the political sphere to advocate for change in the church. She stated, "If feminists are to understand and challenge the misogyny that forms a dark undercurrent to the Catholic theological tradition, we must go beyond politics in order to ask why the Catholic hierarchy is so resistant to acknowledging the sacramentality of the female body in its capacity to reveal Christ" (Beattie 2006, p. 3).

Nevertheless, women are still active participants in European Catholicism. They are the majority of members in Catholic churches in nearly every country in Europe, with the highest female percentages in Estonia (58%), Czechia (57%), and Moldova (56%) (Johnson and Zurlo 2022). Catholic women have engaged in influential national women's movements including the Catholic Women's League (est. 1906 in England) and the European Alliance of Catholic Women's Organisations (est. 2006 in Budapest). Catholic women are also highly involved in global networks, such as the World Union of Catholic Women's Organizations (est. 1910). The church's largest humanitarian arm, Caritas, founded in Germany in 1897 (but officially recognized by the church in 1954), provides aid during conflict and disasters, as well as in response to food insecurity, development issues, health and HIV/AIDS work, human trafficking, and gender justice. Based in Brussels, Europe is home to 59 Caritas organizations with over 2.4 million staff members and volunteers.

Christianity in Post-Christian Europe

The story of Christianity in Europe is often told through the lens of "secularization theory," in which sociologist José Casanova outlined three primary characteristics: differentiation, decline, and privatization (Casanova 1994). Differentiation (or disestablishment) is when religion becomes just one of many social subsystems with a division between church and state, and ceases to be the most important organizing structure of society. The state churches of the United Kingdom, Greece, Denmark, Iceland, and some other European countries are more symbolic than politically powerful. Norway's Lutheran church was disestablished in 2017 – divorced from the state after 500 years – and now operates as an independent business. Nevertheless, the Evangelical Lutheran Church is still considered the national church of Norway.

The second characteristic of secularization is rather straightforward decline, where people become increasingly less likely to self-identify as religious and participate in religious rituals, either publicly or privately. This is evident across Europe, where church attendance, infant baptism, marriages in the church, and other important markers of Christian life are dropping every year. The third characteristic, privatization, is where religion and religious ideas and beliefs are marginalized in public life. One prominent example of privatization is sociologist Grace Davie's theories of "believing without belonging" and "vicarious religion" (Davie 1994, 2006). In Europe, she observes, one does not need to attend church to be a Christian; you can believe in the tenets of the faith without belonging to a faith community. She identifies this gray area in religion where people have a spiritual dimension but are less inclined to be told how to relate to it. Vicarious religion is uniquely European, where religion is performed by an active minority on behalf of a much larger majority. This is supported by the historic churches of Europe that, while largely disestablished with fewer and fewer members, have importance in European life even if people do not believe in the tenets of Christian faith. Here, too, religion is often replaced with spirituality. Another way of looking at religiosity in Europe is the concept of "fuzzy fidelity," where people are neither regular church goers nor self-consciously nonreligious (Voas 2009).

While all three of these secularization processes are happening (or have happened) in Europe, secularization is also gendered. The common narrative that modernization leads to secularization fits male experience, not female, because it was initially men who left village life for the urban jungle, not women (Woodhead 2008). Women started to enter the workforce in greater numbers in the 1960s but not as equals to men; they were stuck between expectations of paid labor outside the home and unpaid labor within the home. Women retained religion as the keepers of the home and were still affirmed in that gendered role. The 1960s and 1970s hastened secularization with second-wave feminism, new attitudes regarding sexuality and morality, postwar affluence, and widespread consumerism (Christie and Gauvreau 2013). Single women left churches to embrace permissiveness in youth culture, while married women left because of decreased time for church activities as more secular opportunities became available (Christie and Gauvreau 2013). Yet, while women were leaving the historic churches in Europe, some were joining Pentecostal, Independent, and newer churches that have formed since the 1960s (Chapman 2007). Women are also more likely than men to believe but not belong, a la Grace Davie (Storm 2009).

Christianity in Post-Communist Eastern and Central Europe

Christians, particularly the Orthodox, suffered horrifically in the twentieth century under Communist regimes (see Chapter 9 for more). Albania was home to 350 Orthodox priests before the ban on religion in 1976, and only 22 survived to see the end of Communism in 1990. In Poland, the Nazis executed six Catholic bishops, 2,030 priests, 127 seminarians, 173 brothers, and 243 sisters. The religious climate of many post-Communist states changed dramatically in the 1990s. Church buildings reopened, Sunday schools began, and membership grew. Some entire churches, such as the Romanian Orthodox Church, were identified as Communist regime sympathizers. In Poland, estimated 10% of priests were collaborators and provided information to the secret police on underground church activities. In much of Eastern Europe, Orthodox Christianity experienced a revival in terms of numbers, but also in societal influence, with a reconnection of national and Orthodox identity. Post-Communist states also received an influx of eager Protestant, Evangelical, and Pentecostal missionaries, though many underestimated the history and power of these nations' Orthodox heritages and newly reestablished national identities. However, the end of Communism did not stop the decline of Christianity everywhere; Czechia, for example, is 35% Christian today, down from 97% in 1900 (Johnson and Zurlo 2022).

Photo 4.2 Women wait for worship to begin at the Kronstadt Naval Orthodox Cathedral in St. Petersburg, Russia (2015). *Source:* Ninara/Flickr/CC BY 2.0.

"Women's issues" in Orthodox churches were largely ignored during Communist and Socialist regimes as these churches struggled to simply survive amidst oppression. Although public religion was banned by the state, religion operated underground, often with grandmothers performing rites such as infant baptisms and catechetical training in secret. Christian women experienced paradoxical circumstances under Communism. Communist ideology critiqued traditional gender roles ascribed by the churches, allowing women to gain literacy and employment in view of promoting their "equality" with men, even though these national power structures were run entirely by elite men. At the same time, Catholic and Orthodox legacies nourished traditional notions of patriarchy that regulated women's activities and conduct (Djurić Milovanović and Radić 2019). After the fall of Communism, Orthodox churches strove to regain their moral leadership in society, which included bringing back the family-oriented patriarchy of the past where women are to be self-sacrificing wives and mothers. This especially impacted women in poor and rural areas, inviting new forms of discrimination and social repression (Oprica 2008). The tension between secular and religious gendered expectations still exists; for example, "gender equality remains *to this day* a somewhat alien concept in practice for the majority of the Romanian population" (Oprica 2008, p. 29). The coming of religious freedom to Central and Eastern Europe after Communism – coupled with the women's movement beginning in the 1970s – opened the door for new conversations about women in Orthodox Christianity and theology.

Ethnic Minority and Immigrant Churches

In 2015, over one million asylum seekers arrived in Europe at the height of the early twenty-first century wave of immigration. Most arrivals were Muslims fleeing instability and violence in the Middle East, particularly in Iraq and Syria. The countries receiving the most migrants (by share of asylum seekers) were Germany (receiving 33.4% of all first-time applicant asylum seekers in 2015), Hungary (13.2%), Sweden (11.8%), Austria (6.5%), and Italy (6.5%) (Potančoková, Stonawski, and Krysińska 2017, p. 165). Their arrival raised many questions about European culture and the continent's "progressive" values. Most Europeans support restrictions on Muslim women's religious dress and opinions are divided on whether one must be born and have ancestors in a country to share that country's national identity (Pew Research Center 2018a). In the early 2020s, just over half of all migrants in European Union countries were women (OECD 2020), one-third of whom follow family connections. They face compounded disadvantages as both women and migrants with lower employment outcomes, lower levels of education, and more difficulty having their skills recognized by potential employers (European Commission 2018). Some Christian communities warmly welcomed their new neighbors. In 2015, Pope Francis encouraged "every parish, every religious community, every monastery, every sanctuary of Europe to take in one family" (Vatican Radio 2015). The Churches' Commission for Migrants in Europe – formed in 1964 and with Christian councils from 18 European countries – encourages Christians to take seriously the biblical message of offering dignity to all human beings, and does so by advocating for migrants and refugees.

Ethnic minority and immigrant churches defy the post-Christian characterization of Europe. Most of these churches are Independent Pentecostal/Charismatic and some have been planted by foreign missionaries from Latin America and sub-Saharan Africa. Among the fastest-growing churches in Europe, they have turned the continent from being primarily missionary-sending to one that is missionary-receiving. Africans, for example, are 20% of foreigners in Italy, arriving in the last 30–40 years. Their Pentecostal churches are not accepted by Italian society as legitimate churches, but they are expanding rapidly; there are at least 1,000 Nigerian and Ghanaian Pentecostal churches throughout Italy (Butticci 2016). The United Kingdom is home to over 600 congregations of the Redeemed Christian Church of God from Nigeria alone. Brazilian missionaries have been very active in Portugal due to their shared language. The second-largest denomination in Portugal, the Universal Church of the Kingdom of God, arrived in 1989 as the church's first European plant and grew among immigrants, particularly Brazilians and Black Africans, Roma people, and those with low incomes, less education, and middle-aged Portuguese women. Immigrant congregations are transnational, connecting the host and home culture, and perhaps other Christian influences from around the world. Like most churches, women make up the majority of many ethnic minority congregations. For example, they comprise between 65–95% of members of Black British congregations, despite patriarchal and hierarchical structures (Foster 1992). Tensions between traditional European churches and migrant-led churches have flared with clashing cultural expectations and theological perspectives. Many immigrant churches are more conservative – unlike broader European culture – where men are the leaders and women are their supporters. Delicate issues include the next generation of migrant church leadership, the practice of healing, the role of church leadership, gender expectations, and same-sex relations (Jackson and Passarelli 2020).

European Women in Theology

Feminist theology arose during second-wave feminism in the 1960s as part of a wider campaign to encourage men to take more seriously women's stories, experiences, and perspectives. The work of feminist theologians includes recognizing previously neglected voices in theological discourse, formulating different Christian symbols and values, and bringing to light the oppression and exploitation of women stemming from patriarchal systems in both society and the church.

Feminist theology in Europe was catalyzed by the creation of the World Council of Churches, Vatican II, the secular feminist movement, and the advent of feminist theology in the United States from Catholic women such as Rosemary Radford Ruether (1936–2022) and Mary Daly (1928–2010) (Grey 2012). The first phase (1960–1975) included reflections on women's roles in Catholicism during and after Vatican II, as well as an emphasis on gender relations in the World Council of Churches. The young WCC was committed to changing the role of women in the church by increasing their visibility, affirming their callings, and encouraging churches to act differently (Grey 2012). Notable women of this period included Gertrud Heinzelmann (1914–1999, Switzerland), Catharina Halkes (1920–2011, Netherlands), Kari Elisabeth Børresen (1932–2016, Norway), and Elisabeth Schüssler Fiorenza (b.1938, Romanian-born German). Fiorenza co-founded the *Journal of Feminist Studies in Religion* and became first female president of the Society of Biblical Literature (1987). Two of Fiorenza's major works, *In Memory of Her: A Feminist Theological Reconstruction of Christian Origins* (1983) and *But She Said: Feminist Practices of Biblical Interpretation* (1992), introduced feminist hermeneutics that reinterpreted Jesus, Paul, and the New Testament church as radically egalitarian, where men and women shared leadership responsibilities together. As a new discipline, early feminist theology was both grassroots and academic (Grey 2012).

The 1970s and 1980s saw the movement institutionally solidified with the first European Symposium on Women's Studies (1975) and the establishment of the European Ecumenical Forum of Christian Women (1982) and the European Society of Women in Theological Research (1986). European feminist theologians saw the connection of their movement to the wider theological world; however, realizing the limitations of their White, privileged feminist perspectives, they learned from trends among liberation theologians in Latin America and the Women's Commission of the Ecumenical Association of Third World Theologians (EATWOT). Over time, feminist theological scholarship drew closer to women's studies in academia more broadly and their work expanded to include contributions from Jewish and Muslim women (Grey 1996).

European Christian women have more opportunities than they did in the early years of feminist theology, as it is now generally acceptable and normal to see female professors, theologians, priests, and other high-ranking church leaders. Many Christian traditions in the West read scripture with at least some notion of gendered language or historical context of women at the time, however, a great divide still exists between "systematic theologians" and "feminist theologians" (Grey 2012). The decline of Christianity among young people in Europe poses a great challenge to feminist theology to push the discipline to be more inclusive of European women of color.

European feminist scholars are shifting theological thinking as a result of the intersection of spirituality, economics, and justice in an increasingly globalized world (Isherwood 2011). Other emerging themes in feminist theology include the relationship between feminism and transcendence, the climate crisis and ecofeminist theologies, and a refocus on the indigenous religions and spiritualities of Europe, which are growing in popularity, especially among women. Recent annual conference themes of the European Society of Women in Theological Research also illustrate current trends in feminist theology, such as the 2021 conference theme, "Against Gender Polarity and Nationalism," and for the Central and Eastern European conference, "Women's Voices and Actions: Inter-Religious Dialogue, Migrations, and Ecological Justice." European feminist theology has moved beyond advocating for nonpatriarchal readings of scripture and debating women's ordination into more nuanced intersections of faith, spirituality, gender, and society.

Conclusion

European Christian women have been charting their own path as the content, form, and practice of Christianity changes over time. From the New Testament to today, women are finding ways to exert influence in male-dominated structures. They are important in the past and future of European Christianity and World Christianity, from the first convert in Macedonia, Lydia of

Thyatira, a Greek Macedonian (the "woman of purple"), to the election of Ksenija Magda, a Croatian New Testament scholar, as the President of the Women's Department of the Baptist World Alliance in 2017. Migrant women have an important role as bridges between their communities and local churches in Europe (Jackson and Passarelli 2020), navigating between secular European culture and transnational, multilingual, passionate Pentecostal/Charismatic churches.

Europe is largely secular, but secularity is nuanced by continued women's involvement in the churches, increased immigration of highly religious people, and even growth of Evangelical and Pentecostal/Charismatic Christianity in ethnic minority and immigrant churches. Evangelical Protestantism in France, for example, increased sevenfold from the 1960s to the 2010s (Johnson and Zurlo 2022). The Catholic Church in some places is a church of immigrants, such as in Norway, mostly consisting of Polish and Vietnamese parishioners. These changes have challenged notions of what it means to be European, with a marked increase of anti-Muslim and anti-Semitic actions across the continent, with many believing that Islam in particular is incompatible with European values and norms.

Over the course of the twentieth century, Christianity lost political power throughout Europe and secularization processes hastened with increased scientific advancements and philosophical thinking that pushed Christianity to the private sphere (Kim and Kim 2008). Nevertheless, Europe is still home to the headquarters of major Christian bodies, such as the Roman Catholic Church (Vatican), Church of England (Canterbury), Lutherans (Geneva), and Eastern Orthodox (Moscow). Although Christianity continues its shift to the global South, Europe is still part of the global Christian family. As in most families worldwide, including in Europe, women are still the heartbeat – the pulse of the future, vitalizing the next generations of people of faith.

Reflection Questions

1) What opportunities did the European Protestant missionary movement provide women? Describe women's participation, or lack thereof, at the Edinburgh 1910 World Missionary Conference and how that meeting foreshadowed the fate of the women's missionary movement.
2) Consider the following quote from Tina Beattie (2006): "If feminists are to understand and challenge the misogyny that forms a dark undercurrent to the Catholic theological tradition, we must go beyond politics in order to ask why the Catholic hierarchy is so resistant to acknowledging the sacramentality of the female body in its capacity to reveal Christ." In your opinion, does the place of women in the Catholic Church disinherit, discriminate against, empower, or protect women? Why or why not?
3) Consider the following topics and trends that have impacted European Christianity in the twentieth and twenty-first centuries: Communism, secularization, ecumenism, and migration. How have European Christian women been impacted, responded to, and participated in each of these? How does one approach these subjects through a gendered lens to realize their full impact on European religiosity for all people, not just men?

Works Cited

Anderson, Bonnie S. and Zinsser, Judith P. (1988). *A History of Their Own: Women in Europe from Prehistory to the Present*. New York: Harper & Row.

Secretary Status, Rationarium Generale Ecclesiae (2020). *Annuarium Statisticum Ecclesiae: Statistical Yearbook of the Church*. Vatican City: Libreria Editrice Vatican.

Aune, Kristin (2016). The significance of gender for congregational studies. In: *Congregational Studies in the UK: Christianity in a Post-Christian Context* (ed. Mathew Guest, Karin Tusting, and Linda Woodhead), 185–202. New York: Routledge.

Beattie, Tina (2006). *New Catholic Feminism: Theology and Theory*. London: Routledge.

Beck, James R. (1992). *Dorothy Carey: The Tragic and Untold Story of Mrs. William Carey*. Grand Rapids, MI: Baker Book House.

Butticci, Annalisa (2016). African Pentecostal churches in Italy: a troubled presence in a Catholic country. In: *International Journal of Religion and Demography* (ed. Brian J. Grim, Todd M. Johnson, Vegard Skirbekk, and Gina A. Zurlo), 107–118. Leiden/Boston: Brill.

Casanova, José (1994). *Public Religions in the Modern World*. Chicago: University of Chicago Press.

Chapman, Diana (2007). *Searching the Source of the River: Forgotten Women of the Pentecostal Revival in Britain 1907–1914*. London: PUSH.

Christie, Nancy and Gauvreau, Michael (2013). 'Even the hippies were only very slowly going secular': dechristianization and the culture of individualism in North America and Western Europe. In: *Dechristianization in North America and Western Europe, 1945–2000* (ed. Nancy Christie and Michael Gauvreau), 3–38. Toronto: University of Toronto Press.

Corbet, Sylvie (2021). French report: 330,000 children victims of church sex abuse. October 5. *AP*. https://apnews.com/article/europe-france-child-abuse-sexual-abuse-by-clergy-religion-ab5da1ff10f9 05b1c338a6f3427a1c66 (accessed 15 October 2021).

Davie, Grace (1994). *Religion in Britain since 1945: Believing without Belonging*. Oxford: Blackwell.

Davie, Grace (2006). Vicarious religion: a methodological challenge. In: *Everyday Religion: Observing Modern Religious Lives* (ed. Nancy T. Ammerman), 21–35. New York: Oxford University Press.

Davie, Grace and Leustean, Lucian N. ed. (2022a). *The Oxford Handbook of Religion and Europe*. Oxford: Oxford University Press.

Davie, Grace and Leustean, Lucian N. (2022b). Religion and Europe: methods, theories, and approaches. In: *The Oxford Handbook of Religion and Europe* (ed. Grace Davie and Lucian N. Leustean), 1–16. Oxford: Oxford University Press.

Djurić Milovanović, Aleksandra and Radić, Radmila (2019). Women in the Serbian Orthodox Church: historical overview and contemporary situation. *Occasional Papers of Religion in Eastern Europe*, 39(6), 1–29. Article 2.

European Commission (2018). https://ec.europa.eu/migrant-integration/feature/integration-of-migrant-women (accessed 25 April 2022).

Evangelical Lutheran Church of Finland n.d. *Finns in mission*. http://notes.evl.fi/EVLen.nsf/Documents/C3C53EE1A948F2A5C2257C30004E8DDD?openDocument&lang=EN (accessed 25 April 2017).

Fletcher, Richard A. (1998). *The Barbarian Conversion: From Paganism to Christianity*. New York: H. Holt.

Foster, Elaine (1992). Women and the inverted pyramid of Black churches in Britain. In: *Refusing Holy Orders: Women and Fundamentalism in Britain* (ed. Gita Sahgal and Nira Yuval-Davis), 45–68. London: Virago.

Gallagher, Luisa J. (2018). Catholic female orders. In: *Encyclopedia of Christianity in the Global South* (ed. Mark A. Lamport), 125–127. Lanham, MD: Rowman & Littlefield.

Grey, Mary (2012). It all began with Miriam...Feminist Theology's Journey from Liberation to Reconciliation. *Feminist Theology*, 20(3), 222–229.

Grey, Mary C. (1996). Feminist theologies, European. In: *Dictionary of Feminist Theologies* (ed. Letty M. Russell and J. Shannon Clarkson), 102–104. Louisville, KY: Westminster John Knox Press.

Haerpfer, Christian et al. (2022). *World values survey: round seven – country-pooled datafile version 4.0.* Madrid, Spain and Vienna, Austria: JD Systems Institute and WVSA Secretariat.

Hamplová, Dana (2011). Religion and gender: why are women more religious than men? *Czech Sociological Review*, 47(2), 297–324.

Hamplová, Dana and Nešpor, Zdeněk R. (2009). Invisible religion in a 'non-believing' country: the case of the Czech Republic. *Social Compass*, 56(4), 581–597.

Heelas, Paul and Woodhead, Linda (2005). *The Spiritual Revolution: Why Religion Is Giving Way to Spirituality*. Oxford: Blackwell.

Isherwood, Lisa (2011). Feminist theologies and the European context. In: *The Oxford Handbook of Feminist Theology* (ed. Sheila Briggs and Mary M. Fulkerson), 280–291. Oxford: Oxford University Press.

Jackson, Darrell and Passarelli, Alessia (2020). *Mapping Migration: Mapping Churches' Responses in Europe, 'Being Church Together'*. 3rd edn. Geneva: World Council of Churches Publications.

Johnson, Todd M. and Zurlo, Gina A. ed. (2022). *World Christian Database*. Leiden/Boston: Brill.

Kasselouri-Hatzivassiliadi, Eleni, Moyo, Fulata L., and Pekridou, Aikaterini ed. (2010). *Many Women Were Also There: The Participation of Orthodox Women in the Ecumenical Movement*. Geneva: World Council of Churches Publications.

Kim, Sebastian and Kim, Kirsteen (2008). *Christianity as a World Religion*. London: Continuum.

Kizenko, Nadieszda (2013). Feminized patriarchy? orthodoxy and gender in post-Soviet Russia. *Signs*, 38(3), 595–621.

Kregting, Joris et al. (2019). Why Dutch women are still more religious than Dutch men: explaining the persistent religious gender gap in the Netherlands using a multifactorial approach. *Review of Religious Research*, 61(2), 1–28.

Madigan, Patricia (2018). Women during and after Vatican II. In: *Catholicism Opening to the World and Other Confessions: Vatican II and Its Impact 79–96* (ed. Vladimir Latinovic), 79–96. New York: Palgrave Macmillan.

Matheson, Peter (1995). *Argula von Grumbach: A Woman's Voice in the Reformation*. Edinburgh: T&T Clark.

Oden, Amy (1995). *In Her Words: Women's Writings in the History of Christian Thought*. London: SPCK.

Oprica, Vlad (2008). Gender equality and conflicting attitudes toward women in post-Communist Romania. *Human Rights Review*, 9, 29–40.

Organisation for Economic Co-operation and Development (OECD) (2020). https://www.oecd.org/migration/mig/migration-policy-debates-25.pdf (accessed 26 April 2022).

Palmisano, Stefania and Todesco, Lorenzo (2019). The gender gap in religiosity over time in Italy: are men and women really becoming more similar? *Social Compass*, 66(4), 543–560.

Petroff, Elizabeth (1986). *Medieval Women's Visionary Literature*. New York: Oxford University Press.

Pew Research Center (2017a). Religious belief and national belonging in Central and Eastern Europe.

Pew Research Center (2017b). Orthodox Christianity in the 21st Century.

Pew Research Center (2018a). Being Christian in Western Europe.

Pew Research Center (2018b). Facts about Catholics in Europe.

Potančoková, Michaela, Stonawski, Marcin, and Krysińska, Anna (2017). How many more Muslims? the effect of increased numbers of asylum seekers on the size of Muslim population in European countries. In: *Yearbook of International Religious Demography* (ed. Brian J. Grim, Todd M. Johnson, Vegard Skirbekk, and Gina A. Zurlo), 146–166. Leiden: Brill.

Schüssler Fiorenza, Elisabeth (1983). *In Memory of Her: A Feminist Theological Reconstruction of Christian Origins*. London: SCM Press.

Schüssler Fiorenza, Elisabeth (1992). *But She Said: Feminist Practices of Biblical Interpretation*. Boston: Beacon Press.

Seton, Rosemary E. (2013). *Western Daughters in Eastern Lands: British Missionary Women in Asia*. Santa Barbara, CA: Praeger.

Stanley, Brian (2009). *The World Missionary Conference, Edinburgh 1910*. Grand Rapids, MI: William B. Eerdmans Pub. Co.

Statistics Iceland (2014). Populations by religious organizations 1998–2014. Reykjavík, Iceland.

Stjerna, Kirsi I. (2009). *Women and the Reformation*. Malden, MA: Blackwell Pub.

Storm, Ingrid (2009). Halfway to heaven: four types of fuzzy fidelity in Europe. *Journal for the Scientific Study of Religion*, 48(4), 702–718.

Trzebiatowska, Marta and Bruce, Steve (2012). *Why are Women More Religious than Men?* Oxford: Oxford University Press.

Vatican Radio (2015). Pope asks all European parishes to take in a refugee family. http://www.archivioradiovaticana.va/storico/2015/09/06/pope_asks_all_european_parishes_to_take_in_a_refugee_family/en-1169953 (accessed 21 April 2022).

Voas, David (2009). The rise and fall of fuzzy fidelity in Europe. *European Sociological Review*, 25(2), 155–168.

Woodhead, Linda (2008). Gendering secularization theory. *Social Compass*, 55(2), 87–193.

Zahl, Paul F.M. (2001). *Five Women of the English Reformation*. Grand Rapids, MI: William B. Eerdmans.

5

Women in Latin American and Caribbean Christianity

"Women must vehemently reclaim and affirm their right to be considered created in the image and likeness of God."

Elsa Tamez (Tamez 1989, p. 6)

For women, Christianity in Latin America and the Caribbean is both a source of emancipation and oppression (Bartel 2018).[1] Patriarchy in the region is known as *machismo*, a term that encompasses male domination of women, chauvinism, and patriarchal privilege (Hurtado and Sinha 2016). Men are the heads of the family unit, and the family is the model of society. Although the home is the woman's domain, she lacks decision making power in both the private and public spheres. Inequality between men and women is profound, with Latin America ranking 39/100 on the Gender Inequality Index, which measures achievement between women and men in reproductive health, empowerment, and the labor market. The higher the value, the more inequality between women and men. For comparison, the rankings are 55 in Africa, 36 in Asia, 25 in Oceania, 17 in North America, and 12 in Europe (United Nations Development Programme 2022). Nevertheless, patriarchy is continuously challenged as Latinas enter different spheres of society and make strides outside the home, amplifying their voices to speak of their life experiences and their postures toward the Christian faith.

While it is common to make sweeping statements about Christianity in the global South versus the global North, such analyses tend to gloss over substantial differences in the histories, cultures, religions, beliefs, and practices of people around the world. Put simply, the history of Christianity in Latin America and the Caribbean is very different from that in Africa and Asia, even though they are all in the global South. With the introduction of Christianity via European conquest and colonization, followed by 400 years of Catholic hegemony on the continent, the region expresses a religious atmosphere much different than elsewhere in the world. While colonial Latin America (1492–1810) was Catholic, not everyone believed the same thing or practiced Catholicism in the same way. A tremendous amount of diversity in Christian belief and practice was influenced by gender, traditional cultures, class, and economics. The introduction of

---

1 According to the United Nations, Latin America and the Caribbean consists of the following countries: Anguilla, Antigua and Barbuda, Argentina, Aruba, Bahamas, Barbados, Belize, Bolivia, Brazil, British Virgin Islands, BES Islands (Bonaire, Sint Eustatius, and Saba), Cayman Islands, Chile, Colombia, Costa Rica, Cuba, Curacao, Dominica, Dominican Republic, Ecuador, El Salvador, Falkland Islands, French Guiana, Grenada, Guadeloupe, Guatemala, Guyana, Haiti, Honduras, Jamaica, Martinique, Mexico, Montserrat, Nicaragua, Panama, Paraguay, Peru, Puerto Rico, Saint Kitts and Nevis, Saint Lucia, Saint Vincent, Sint Maarten, Suriname, Trinidad and Tobago, Turks and Caicos Islands, United States Virgin Islands, Uruguay, and Venezuela.

Women in World Christianity: Building and Sustaining a Global Movement, First Edition. Gina A. Zurlo.
© 2023 John Wiley & Sons Ltd. Published 2023 by John Wiley & Sons Ltd.

Protestantism and Pentecostalism in the nineteenth and twentieth centuries raised discussions about the pentecostalization of Latin America and the future of Christianity on the continent.

Far from monolithic, the region composed of Latin America and the Caribbean is ethnically diverse, with a range of groups broadly categorized as *Mestizo* (combined European and indigenous ancestry), White (European descent), Amerindian (indigenous peoples), Black (or Afro-Latin, of African background), and Mulatto (mixed African and European ancestry) (Latinobarometer 2018). In many countries, especially in the Caribbean, descendants of enslaved Africans outnumber White settlers, such as in Anguilla, Antigua and Barbuda, and the Cayman Islands. While Spanish and Portuguese are the most widely spoken languages on the continent, there are at least 450 indigenous languages, such as Quechua (spoken in Argentina, Bolivia, Peru, Chile), Guarani (largely in Paraguay), and various Mayan languages in Central America. Other European languages are present due to the legacies of colonialism. French is an official language in Haiti, Guadeloupe, Martinique, Sint Maarten, and French Guiana; Dutch is the sole official language in Suriname and also spoken in Aruba, Curaçao, and Sint Maarten.

Catholicism is by far the largest Christian tradition in Latin America and the Caribbean; 76% of the region's population in 2020 was Catholic and 41% of all Catholics in the world live in this region (Johnson and Zurlo 2022). The term *evangélico* generally refers to all non-Catholic Christians: Protestants, Evangelicals, and Pentecostals/Charismatics (see López 2021; Schneider 2021). This chapter uses "Protestant" and "Evangelical/*evangélico*" interchangeably but uses "Pentecostal" or "Charismatic" to specifically refer to groups that emphasize prophecy, miraculous healing, speaking in tongues, and other gifts of the Spirit.

Christianity in Latin America and the Caribbean, 1900–2050

Latin America is home to only three religions over 1% of the population: Christians, agnostics, and Spiritists (Table 5.1). Spiritism is a broad term for religions that emphasize the interconnectivity between the physical and spiritual worlds, in particular, the communication between the two. Spiritism came to be through the mixing of African Traditional Religion brought by West African enslaved people, Catholicism brought by Europeans, and the traditional religions of indigenous peoples. Some religions include a vast pantheon of gods and goddess like Yoruba *orishas*, while others are monotheistic and theologically closer to Christianity. Spiritism also includes Afro-American spiritism, followers of Afro-Brazilian, Afro-Cuban, and other African religions in the Americas, often mixed with Amerindian beliefs and practices. Spiritism grew in Latin America from less than 1% of the population in 1900 to just over 2% in 2020 (Table 5.1).

Examples of Spiritist movements include Rastafarianism (from Jamaica), Obeah (a mixture of Christianity and African Traditional Religions), Santería (from Cuba), and Vodoo (Vodoun; throughout

Table 5.1 Religions in Latin America and the Caribbean over 1%, 1900–2050.

Religion	Pop. 1900	% 1900	Rate % p.a. 1900–2000	Pop. 2020	% 2020	Rate % p.a. 2020–2050	Pop. 2050	% 2050
Christians	62,002,000	95.2	2.07	602,892,000	92.2	0.43	685,870,000	90.0
Agnostics	372,000	0.6	3.83	22,594,000	3.5	2.18	43,154,000	5.7
Spiritists	257,000	0.4	3.93	14,352,000	2.2	0.20	15,235,000	2.0

Source: Data from Johnson and Zurlo 2022. p.a. = percent change per annum, or each year.

the Caribbean). The countries with the highest percentage of Spiritists are Cuba (17%), Cayman Islands (10%), and Jamaica (10%). Spiritism is largest in Brazil (10 million), with traditions such as Kardecism, Umbanda, and Candomblé. Although only 5% of Brazil's population self-identifies as Spiritist, an estimated 30% or more has engaged in organized Spiritist practices, and 15% are estimated to be actively engaged in organized Spiritism (Johnson and Zurlo 2019). Women typically have important roles in Spiritist religions, and, like Christianity, make up the majority of membership. In Brazil, 54% of Umbanda and Candomblé practitioners and 59% of Kardecists are female. Other groups are entirely female, such as the Sisterhood of Our Lady of the Good Death, an Afro-Catholic group in Bahia, Brazil. Spiritist religions provide women avenues for leadership not afforded to them in the male hierarchy of Catholicism, and where they can subvert patriarchal norms (Hucks 2006).

The numeric dominance of the Catholic Church in Latin America and the Caribbean skews the data, but Christianity is more female than the general population in every region by slight margins (Table 5.2). Women outnumber men in church membership in the countries with the most Christians, with the greatest disparity in Chile, where the country is 51% female, but Christianity is 54% female (Table 5.3). This is partly explained by high female membership in many Pentecostal denominations, which are reported as 55% female in Chile's most recent census. Women in Chile have a long record

Table 5.2 Christianity in Latin America and the Caribbean by region, 2020.

Region	Majority religion	Pop. 2020	% Christian 2020	Christian pop. 2020	% Christian female 2020	% pop. female 2020
Latin America	Christians	653,962,000	92.2	602,892,000	51.6	50.8
Caribbean	Christians	43,532,000	84.1	36,616,000	51.9	50.6
Central America	Christians	179,670,000	95.7	171,979,000	51.7	51.0
South America	Christians	430,760,000	91.5	394,297,000	51.6	50.8

Source: Data from Johnson and Zurlo 2022.

Table 5.3 Countries in Latin America and the Caribbean with the most Christians, 2020.

Rank	Country	Largest Christian tradition	Pop. 2020	% Christian 2020	Christian pop. 2020	% Christian female 2020	% pop. female 2020
1	Brazil	Catholics	212,559,000	90.8	192,939,000	51.6	50.9
2	Mexico	Catholics	128,933,000	95.7	123,370,000	51.7	51.1
3	Colombia	Catholics	50,883,000	95.4	48,543,000	51.3	50.9
4	Argentina	Catholics	45,196,000	88.8	40,118,000	51.6	51.2
5	Peru	Catholics	32,972,000	96.5	31,809,000	51.5	50.3
6	Venezuela	Catholics	28,436,000	92.6	26,343,000	51.4	50.8
7	Guatemala	Catholics	17,916,000	97.4	17,441,000	51.7	50.7
8	Chile	Catholics	19,116,000	88.2	16,869,000	53.6	50.7
9	Ecuador	Catholics	17,643,000	95.5	16,843,000	51.4	50.0
10	Bolivia	Catholics	11,673,000	92.8	10,836,000	49.9	49.8

Source: Data from Johnson and Zurlo 2022.

Table 5.4 Countries in Latin America and the Caribbean with the highest percent Christian female, 2020.

Rank	Country	Largest Christian tradition	Pop. 2020	% Christian 2020	Christian pop. 2020	% Christian female 2020	% pop. female 2020
1	BES Islands	Catholics	26,200	92.1	24,200	57.4	54.0
2	Barbados	Protestants	287,000	94.9	273,000	55.7	51.6
3	Jamaica	Unaffiliated Christians	2,961,000	84.5	2,504,000	55.4	50.4
4	Curacao	Catholics	164,000	93.5	153,000	54.7	54.0
5	Chile	Catholics	19,116,000	88.2	16,869,000	53.6	50.7
6	Antigua and Barbuda	Protestants	97,900	92.7	90,800	53.5	51.7
7	Sint Maarten	Catholics	42,900	89.3	38,300	53.4	54.0
8	Saint Lucia	Catholics	184,000	95.9	176,000	53.1	50.8
9	British Virgin Islands	Protestants	30,200	81.7	24,700	52.9	50.4
10	Nicaragua	Catholics	6,625,000	95.1	6,297,000	52.6	50.7

Source: Data from Johnson and Zurlo 2022.

of mobilization and public activism, as demonstrated in their resistance to the dictatorships of Salvador Allende (1970–1973) and Augusto Pinochet (1974–1990) (Baldez 2002). Like elsewhere in the world, data on the female share of Christians in Latin America and the Caribbean are limited. Nuanced information is not available for every denomination in every country, but for those that are available, a wider gender ratio appears to exist. For example, of a study of Catholic Charismatics in Haiti reported that women were 90% of church members (Rey 2010).

According to official census data, eight of the ten highest Christian female percentages in the region are in the Caribbean (Table 5.4). The BES Islands (Bonaire, Sint Eustatius, and Saba) have the highest at 57% female, compared to 54% female for the islands overall. Many denominations in the BES Islands report very high female affiliation, such as the Evangelical Church (69% female), the Baptist Association (61%), and Seventh-day Adventists (57%). At the same time, Protestant and Independent denominations in the country are also very small, with fewer than 1,000 members.

There is a great diversity of belief and practice within Latin American Christianity despite Catholicism's numerical weight. The continent was nearly entirely Christian in 1900 (95%), but the church has never been static, has always adapted to new political and social realities, and has consistently sought new ways to operate in the region. The Pentecostal/Charismatic movement swelled in the twentieth century, growing to 29% of the continent's population in 2020 (195 million). Table 5.5 shows the growth of many *evangélico* denominations in the twenty-first century, such as Baptist, nondenominational, and Pentecostal/Charismatic churches. Orthodox Christians have also increased, both Eastern and Oriental, though still less than 1% of all Christians (Figure 5.1).

The largest denominations in Latin America and the Caribbean are Catholic, with slightly higher than average rates of female membership (ranging from 51% to 55%; Table 5.6). However, removing Catholic denominations from the equation (Table 5.7) provides a more nuanced view of Christianity in the region as well as much higher levels of women's membership, ranging from 53% to 60%. Perhaps the most obvious explanation for higher female membership in Protestant groups is the increased opportunities for leadership and ministry compared to the male hierarchy of the Catholic Church. Such opportunities include the ordination of women in some Protestant denominations and the way Pentecostal and charismatic ministries cut across gender to allow men and women to functionally minister in the same roles (Suárez 2022).

Table 5.5 Christian families in Latin America and the Caribbean, 2000 and 2015.

Family	Affiliated 2000	Affiliated 2015	% female 2015	Rate % p.a. 2000–2015
Latin-rite Catholic	437,755,000	488,631,000	50.9	0.74
Pentecostal/Charismatic*	48,296,000	66,559,000	55.1	2.16
Adventist	5,468,000	7,848,000	53.5	2.44
Jehovah's Witnesses	4,376,000	6,754,000	55.9	2.94
Latter-day Saints (Mormons)	4,023,000	6,307,000	53.5	3.04
Other Protestant/Independent	3,965,000	5,612,000	54.8	2.34
Baptist	3,116,000	4,618,000	56.3	2.66
Reformed, Presbyterian	2,558,000	3,064,000	53.8	1.21
Eastern-rite Catholic	2,124,000	2,608,000	50.9	1.38
Holiness	1,574,000	2,027,000	52.9	1.70
Nondenominational	1,109,000	1,521,000	51.9	2.12
Nontraditional, house, cell	1,049,000	1,390,000	54.7	1.90
Methodist	1,022,000	1,262,000	54.5	1.42
Lutheran	1,118,000	1,204,000	52.1	0.50
Eastern Orthodox	845,000	1,143,000	50.4	2.04
Anglican	878,000	930,000	52.5	0.39
Christian Brethren	533,000	693,000	52.5	1.77
Old Catholic Church	641,000	600,000	50.1	−0.45
Restorationist, Disciple	298,000	485,000	53.4	3.31
Congregational	208,000	282,000	55.1	2.06
Moravian	195,000	224,000	51.7	0.92
Mennonite	159,000	199,000	53.0	1.51
Oriental and other Orthodox	76,600	140,000	51.3	4.08
United church or joint mission	145,000	139,000	52.9	−0.32
Friends (Quaker)	92,700	93,100	53.2	0.03
Salvationist	70,000	78,700	53.3	0.78
Dunker	4,200	4,800	51.4	0.89

Source: Data from Johnson and Zurlo 2022. p.a. = percent change per annum, or each year.
*Excluding partially pentecostalized.

Women in Latin America and the Caribbean are more involved in religious organizations than their male peers. Women typically bear the primary responsibility to raise children and pass on religious beliefs and practices. In addition, women who do not work outside the home generally have more flexible schedules than men, providing more time to participate in religious activities. Both Catholic and Protestant women attend worship services more regularly than men and report higher frequency of prayer. Women also report that religion is very important in their lives at higher rates than men; for example, in Paraguay, 63% of women vs. 48% of men, and in Colombia, 85% of women and 70% of men. On social issues, men and women generally agree on stances against same-sex marriage and abortion, though more women than men say that drinking alcohol

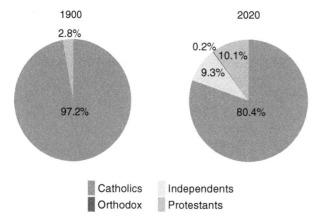

Figure 5.1 Christianity in Latin America and the Caribbean by major Christian tradition, 1900 and 2020. *Source:* Data from Johnson and Zurlo 2022.

Table 5.6 Largest denominations in Latin America and the Caribbean, 2015.

Rank	Country	Denomination	Year begun	Affiliated 2015	% Christian female	Rate % p.a. 2000–2015
1	Brazil	Igreja Católica no Brasil	1500	148,550,000	50.0	0.25
2	Mexico	Iglesia Católica en México	1518	110,155,000	51.4	1.13
3	Colombia	Iglesia Católica en Colombia	1512	42,206,000	51.2	0.91
4	Argentina	Iglesia Católica en Argentina	1539	34,323,000	51.7	0.56
5	Peru	Iglesia Católica en Perú	1533	27,005,000	51.2	0.82
6	Venezuela	Iglesia Católica en Venezuela	1513	24,820,000	51.2	1.05
7	Brazil	Assembleias de Deus	1910	20,978,000	55.0	1.12
8	Ecuador	Iglesia Católica en Ecuador	1534	13,805,000	51.2	1.33
9	Chile	Iglesia Católica en Chile	1541	12,611,000	53.0	0.47
10	Guatemala	Iglesia Católica en Guatemala	1524	11,535,000	51.2	1.69

Source: Data from Johnson and Zurlo 2022. p.a. = percent change per annum, or each year.

Table 5.7 Largest protestant and independent denominations in Latin America and the Caribbean, 2020.

Rank	Country	Denomination	Year begun	Affiliated 2015	% Christian female	Rate % p.a. 2000–2015
1	Brazil	Assembleias de Deus	1910	20,978,000	55.0	1.12
2	Brazil	Igreja Universal do Reino de Deus	1977	7,500,000	60.0	3.46
3	Brazil	Igreja Pentecostal Deus e Amor	1962	4,000,000	57.0	2.41
4	Brazil	Igreja do Evangelho Quadrangular	1951	3,100,000	57.0	4.09

Table 5.7 (Continued)

Rank	Country	Denomination	Year begun	Affiliated 2015	% Christian female	Rate % p.a. 2000–2015
5	Brazil	Congregação Cristã no Brasil	1910	2,500,000	54.0	2.33
6	Mexico	Testigos de Jehová	1893	2,149,000	56.1	3.23
7	Brazil	Convenção Batista Brasileira	1881	2,089,000	57.0	3.02
8	Brazil	Igreja Adventista do Sétimo Dia	1902	1,916,000	55.0	2.78
9	Brazil	Testemunhas de Jeová	1920	1,908,000	58.0	2.95
10	Mexico	Iglesia Nacional Presbiteriana de México	1872	1,800,000	53.4	2.46

Source: Data from Johnson and Zurlo 2022. p.a. = percent change per annum, or each year.

is wrong (Pew Research Center 2014). Women are divided on the question of wifely obedience to their husbands. In about half of countries surveyed, women completely or mostly agreed that wives should obey their husbands (with highest rates in Honduras, Guatemala, and the Dominican Republic), but elsewhere women disagreed (Chile, Uruguay, Argentina) (Pew Research Center 2014). This reveals mixed opinions of a women's place in Latin American society and the role of *machismo* – some women resist this while others accept it. Attitudes toward the Catholic priesthood are changing in Latin America and the Caribbean as well – 48% of Catholics think priests should be allowed to marry, and 42% reported that women should be allowed to become priests (Pew Research Center 2014).

The Gender and Congregational Life Survey (2021) included 39 respondents from Latin America and the Caribbean, with the most from Brazil, Mexico, Bolivia, and Suriname. Respondents were majority female (69%), married (51%), well-educated (79% with bachelor's degree or higher), and employed full-time (74%). The largest Christian families represented were Pentecostal (26%), Baptist (21%), Holiness (13%), nondenominational (13%), and Reformed Presbyterian (10%), with a wide range of church sizes (23% between 51–100 and 23% over 500). Women are active participants in their churches, with 51% reporting more women than men in their main weekly worship service (the most important ministry of the church at 90%), while 49% stated that more women than men attend the midweek service.

Most respondents (69%) agreed or strongly agreed that women should be allowed to serve as pastors (compared to 84% for all respondents worldwide), and 80% agreed or strongly agreed that it is harder for women to be accepted in leadership roles in the church. Despite this, 72% also believed that the Bible places restrictions on women's roles in the church. Members of Holiness (60%) and Pentecostal (50%) churches were more favorable toward women's pastoral roles and leadership than were Baptists (25%) and members of nondenominational churches (20%). The survey also highlighted the gendered expectations and realities for men and women in Latin American church life. The only position that respondents felt was easier for women to obtain than men was children's Sunday school teacher (Figure 5.2).

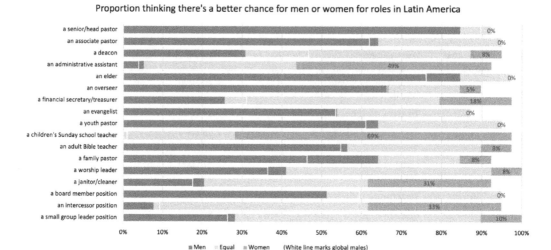

Figure 5.2 How do you think the chances of women and men compare when it comes to getting a ___ position? (Latin America and the Caribbean). *Source:* Adapted from Gender and Congregational Life Survey (2021).

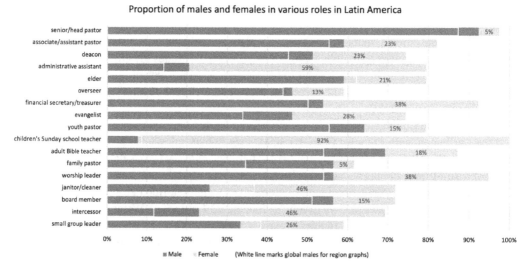

Figure 5.3 Thinking of the ___ in your congregation, is this person male or female? (Latin America and the Caribbean). *Source:* Adapted from Gender and Congregational Life Survey (2021).

The most frequently reported positions for women were children's Sunday school teacher (92%), administrative assistant (59%), intercessor (46%), and janitor/cleaner (46%) (Figure 5.3). The only position in which Latin American women were more likely than the global average to serve was children's Sunday school teacher. Only 5% of respondents from Latin America and the Caribbean reported having a woman as a head senior or head pastor, less than the 8% global average.

Women in Latin American and Caribbean Christianity: Past and Present

Christianity first arrived in Latin America and the Caribbean through European imperialism, conquest, and genocide. In fifteenth-century European Catholicism, Christian mission was transplantation – an uprooting of Catholicism to plant it religiously, culturally, and linguistically in a new geographic area. Spain and Portugal spread Catholicism beyond Europe, attempting to replicate its hierarchies, institutions, and practices elsewhere. The Inquisitions (eleventh to fifteenth centuries) combatted heresies of different kinds, ranging from Waldensians in France to the new European Protestant heresy starting in the 1510s. Inquisitions expanded European Catholicism beyond Spain and Portugal to their territories overseas, with Christians purposely going beyond Christendom for the first time. In colonial Latin America, many Inquisitions were lodged against indigenous women, especially those suspected of witchcraft, making pacts with the devil, or expressing their relationship to Jesus in sexual language. Those found guilty were jailed or exiled (Salinas 1992).

In 1493, Pope Alexander VI issued the papal bull, *Inter Caetera*, to prevent conflicts between Spain and Portugal in their overseas expansion. He drew a line down the map, allowing Spain to colonize to the West and Portugal to the East: the reason why Brazil speaks Portuguese and the rest of South America mostly speaks Spanish today. Empowered by the Doctrine of Discovery and assuming the role as the vicar of Christ on Earth, the pope had the authority to give foreign land to the Spanish and Portuguese crowns. The Spanish Requirement of 1513 (*Requerimiento*) declared Spain's divine right to invade, possess, exploit, and subjugate indigenous land and peoples. This legal document, enmeshed with Catholic theology, was read to indigenous peoples upon European entry and if locals refused its conditions, the Spanish could "justifiably" wage war and enslave them (Cook 2017). Furthermore, between 1501 and 1866, an estimated 10.7 million enslaved Africans survived the horrific Middle Passage of the Trans-Atlantic Slave Trade (of the total 12.5 million who embarked). Of those, five million alone landed in Brazil, compared to 252,000 in the United States (Gates 2011; Slave Voyages 2021). More Africans crossed the Atlantic than Europeans, and four of every five women who crossed the Atlantic were enslaved Africans (Eltis 2007).

The empires had dual goals: amass wealth and spread Spanish or Portuguese society. Christopher Columbus received permission from Queen Isabella of Castile and her husband King Ferdinand of Aragon to explore the "New World." Though he had both political and religious purposes in mind during his first encounter with indigenous people in 1493, his brutality against native populations led to the creation of the *encomienda* (plantation) system, along with slavery, genocide, new diseases (biological warfare), the burning of villages, the dismantling of ancient civilizations, and violent, coerced Christian "conversion." While Catholic missionary priests did the "converting," *conquistadores* did the conquering. Meanwhile, the hundreds of missionaries who ended up in the Americas were neither completely innocent nor completely guilty. Complicit in the slave trade, the Catholic Church initially did not consider slavery to be evil (Grimes 2017). Catholic priests lived with local women by the end of the colonial period and were widely known for their immorality; there are many accounts of clerical sexual abuse and rape (Salinas 1992). Yet, some priests protested: Dominican Bartolomé de las Casas (1484–1566) initially participated in the system of slavery but became convicted of its evils. Protesting for 50 years the abuse of indigenous peoples, he wrote one of the earliest exposés of slavery in 1542, *A Short Account of the Destruction of the Indies*. Though slavery was finally outlawed in Brazil in 1888, its legacy continues.

Intrinsic to the spread of Catholicism to Latin America was European-style patriarchy, complete with an unadorned, White, and pure image of the Virgin Mary as the expressed ideal of womanhood (Salinas 1992). This ideal was utterly unobtainable for indigenous women who were legally considered second-class to men and restricted to the private sphere. Indigenous women were generally considered dishonest, lustful, and even dangerous (Salinas 1992). They led largely sheltered lives and suffered from two categories of oppression: domestic strife and sexual abuse (Socolow 2015). Married women were subordinate to their husbands; men had a legal right to control and punish their wives. Physical abuse of wives was common especially in rural areas and among lower classes and Indian communities (Socolow 2015). Sexual violence against women was widespread, especially rape, and soldiers had numerous concubines, which led to the birth of *Mestizo* children. Nevertheless, to the best of their ability, women resisted, defended their land, and fought against invaders and European Catholicism. It was not uncommon to use magic and witchcraft to subvert male dominance.

While the adoption of Christianity among the indigenous population was largely forced, that did not preclude authentic expressions of Christian faith. One of the most prominent Christian women from the Spanish colonial period was Sor Juana Inés de la Cruz (1648–1695), born of Spanish descent near today's Mexico City. A child prodigy, she was fluent in Latin, Spanish, and Nahuatl, became a well-known philosopher, built her own library of 4,000 volumes, and became a nun in 1667. Now widely seen as a proto-feminist, she pushed back against seventeenth-century restrictions on women's activities and education, including those limiting Catholic leadership to men. She is perhaps most well-known for her defense of women as authoritative religious teachers, including women's ability to theologize and interpret scripture (Ahlgren 2005).

The throwing off of Spanish and Portuguese colonial rule began with the Haitian Revolution (1791–1804); by the early nineteenth century, independence from Spain had been achieved everywhere except Cuba and Puerto Rico. Brazil gained independence from Portugal in 1822. Other countries were not independent until the twentieth century, like those that broke from the United Kingdom in the 1960s to the 1980s in the Caribbean such as Jamaica, Barbados, Saint Lucia, and Saint Kitts and Nevis. Active in independence movements, women provided supplies, served as nurses to soldiers, and sometimes engaged in combat themselves (Earle 2000).

In 1910, the Edinburgh World Missionary Conference revealed the bias of the Western missionary movement toward Christianity in Latin America. Despite its name, the focus of the conference was not *world* mission but rather narrowly defined Christendom. A great debate ensued over the status of Christianity in the region (as well as in Türkiye, Persia, Syria, and Egypt), with some leaders considering Latin America "Christianized" and others demurring because of its Catholic majority. The tension was "resolved" by leaving discussions of mission in Latin America and the Caribbean out of the conference altogether (Stanley 2009). There were no delegates from Latin America or the Caribbean, and no discussion of the continent's Christian past, present, or future.

Twentieth-Century Catholicism

Latin America and the Caribbean in the twentieth century was marked by a series of economic troubles, urbanization, and social unrest. Military dictatorships were common – situations where governments were controlled by members of the military hierarchy, rather than democratically elected representatives. By the 1980s, most of the continent was under military regimes (Lowy, Sader, Gorman 1985). Under dictators like Juan Perón (Argentina), François Duvalier (Haiti), Rafael Trujillo (Dominican Republic), Anastasio Somoza (Nicaragua), Augusto Pinochet (Chile), and Alfredo Stroessner (Paraguay), tens of thousands of people were arrested or tortured, while many "disappeared" for their struggle against the state. Sexual violence against women, especially ethnic minority women, under these dictatorships was rampant. Four female Catholic American missionaries on a humanitarian mission in El Salvador – Maryknoll sisters Maura Clarke and Ita Ford; Ursuline sister Dorothy Kazel; and lay missionary Jean Donovan – were raped and murdered by five men of the El Salvador military in 1980, the same year Archbishop Óscar Romero (an outspoken critic of the military) was assassinated while performing Mass. During this time, women transformed from "simple housewives" into political organizers to locate relatives of the disappeared, challenge military regimes, and critique gender stereotypes (Arditti 1999). Times of conflict encouraged grassroots efforts to serve the tens of thousands of orphans and widows impacted by war. While women were victimized, they emerged as dignified survivors (Green 2000).

Photo 5.1   St. Peter Claver Catholic students in Gonaives, Haiti (2009). *Source:* Our Lady of Fatima International Pilgrim Statue/Flickr/CC BY-SA 2.0.

The Catholic Church had mixed responses to Latin American military dictatorships, sometimes referred to as the two faces of Latin American Christianity: both as the oppressor and as among those fighting against the oppressor (Hartch 2014; González and González 2008). Catholics, for example, were on both sides of Argentina's Dirty War (1974–1983), where tens of thousands of people were killed and/or disappeared for aligning with socialist values. Some bishops worked for the release of prisoners, while others were complicit. In the Dominican Republic, the church and government initially supported one another under Rafael Trujillo's regime (1934–1961), but after three decades the church began to formally oppose the dictator and support democracy. In Chile, Catholics created the ecumenical Committee for Peace to defend human rights and provide support for Pinochet's victims and their families, while excommunicating anyone who participated in his regime. In Nicaragua, the church wholly supported the corrupt Somoza family from 1934 to 1969, and only withdrew when the family lost popular support. Eventually, however, the Catholic Church became a defender of human rights.

In the twentieth century, with a dramatic increase in lay participation, especially among women, the Catholic Church was pressured by the lack of priests in Latin America and the Caribbean. The introduction of congregational-centered Protestantism made the Catholic Church think more seriously about the role of lay Catholics, bolstered by new teachings from the Second Vatican Council (1962–1965) and the development of liberation theology (see Theology section below). Every social class in Latin America and the Caribbean was touched by Catholic reforms in the second half of the twentieth century. Base Ecclesial Communities (*Comunidades Eclesiales de Base*, CEBs) reached the urban and rural poor with a new way of "being church" at the grassroots levels, in neighborhoods and villages. CEBs were small groups that emphasized church as community, paired with political engagement especially for the poor and needy – all in aim of social transformation. Women found new avenues for leadership in CEBs; formerly marginalized in traditional Catholic parishes, they made up the majority of members and were extraordinarily active (Lynch 2012). In Brazil, women were 70%–80% of CEB membership (Hayes 2017). New ecclesial movements served the working middle class and trained Catholics for evangelization, catechesis, and other ministries, while also emphasizing spiritual formation and friendship. One example is the *Focolare* (Italian for "hearth") movement, begun by Chiara Lubich (1920–2008) in Italy during World War II, which arrived in South America in 1958. Her companion, Italian nun Ginetta Calliari (1918–2001), began a branch in Brazil in 1959 and by 1999 the movement had over one million members in Latin America (Hartch 2014). New ecclesial movements provided new religious options within Catholicism, encouraging Catholics to find their vocations and callings within the church.

Latin American Christianity in the twenty-first century is marked by competition between Catholics and Protestants, the rapidly growing Pentecostal/Charismatic movement (including Catholic Charismatics), Christian involvement in politics, and responses to drug and gang violence that has contributed to the movement of peoples in the region and beyond, particularly to the US-Mexico border.

Popular Religion

Despite the brutality of Christianity's arrival in the fifteenth century, many people turned to Catholicism, but it was not the European Catholicism that missionaries expected. Local peoples mixed the new European faith with traditional customs and understandings, creating a new local/global version of Catholicism that better served their own needs. With never enough foreign priests on the continent to perform the rites of a hierarchical religion like Catholicism, the laity was forced to create their own forms of the faith less reliant on clergy. These expressions are often described as "popular" or "folk" religion, defined as religion that "accepts the dogmas and rites of the church but in actual practice assigns them a secondary role" (González and González 2008, p. 7). As a result, Christianity in this region was never confined to its orthodox forms and institutional structures. A common point of connection between Catholicism and local religion were the saints, associated with local gods and worshipped with practices passed down from ancestors. Enslaved Africans also brought their own worldviews, gods, and traditions and placed them alongside Christianity. Protestant missionaries condemned popular religion as pure syncretism, but over time Latin American Protestantism came to embrace elements of it. While many Catholics attempted to work against these religious expressions, they became increasingly convinced that most popular religion, rather than contradicting the Catholic faith, vitally expressed it. The great diversity of Christianity in Latin America and the Caribbean goes beyond the official limits of either Catholicism or Protestantism.

The Virgin Mary had a tremendous role in the indigenization of Catholicism in Latin America and the Caribbean. The local theologizing of Mary in the colonial period is often cited as the first truly indigenous expression of Christianity in the modern era: "the oppressed peoples of Latin America developed an extraordinary theology. By mixing together Euro-mediterranean folk traditions about Mary with cults of pre-Columbian and African divinities, they achieved a religious formulation highly resistant to imperial Christianity. Thus, the image of women was being radically transformed" (Salinas 1992, p. 536). The Virgin Mary appeared to Cuauhtlatoatzin (Juan Diego, his Christian name) in what is now Mexico in 1531. She was dressed like an Aztec princess and spoke to him in Nahuatl, requesting a shrine to be built in her honor for her to protect the indigenous people. The Virgin of Guadalupe, as she became known, became a symbol of Latin American Catholicism and remains so today. She goes by many names, such as Our Lady of Luján (Argentina), Our Lady of Copacabana (Bolivia), Our Lady of Aparecida (Brazil, after a 1717 apparition), and Our Lady of Carmel of the Maipú (Chile, after a 1785 apparition).

Nuestra Señora de la Santa Muerte is another popular expression of Catholicism in Latin America, a female deity or folk saint among Mexicans and Mexican Americans. She is the personification of death and is associated with healing, protection, and safe delivery to the afterlife (Chesnut 2018). Although not approved by the Vatican, Santa Muerte's popularity has been growing since 2000, with perhaps upward of 20 million devotees today, rivaling the Virgin of Guadalupe. Her image evolved as a mixture of pre-Columbian Mesoamerican religion and Spanish culture, reflecting the reverence of death that exists in Latin America. Another prominent folk saint is María Lionza in Venezuela, which represents a mixture of veneration of the Virgin Mary with Amerindian and African rituals. She supports many women in their struggles against patriarchy in Latin America and the Caribbean (Hurbon 2021).

Photo 5.2　The Sisterhood of Our Lady of the Good Death, an Afro-Catholic religious group in Bahia, Brazil (2011). *Source:* Rosino/Flickr/CC BY-SA 2.0.

Protestantism

The combination of nineteenth-century Latin American political independence, anti-clericalism against the Catholic Church, and new religious liberties opened the door for novel foreign influence from England and the United States – mainly, Protestantism and economic investors. Protestants had been present since the seventeenth century with their strongest presence via Dutch, French, and English imperial interests, including the slave trade, in the Guianas, Jamaica, and the Antilles (Moreno 2021). In their home country of Antigua, sisters Anne Hart Gilbert (1768–1833) and Elizabeth Hart Thwaites (1772–1833) were inspired by their Methodist faith and Moravian influences to challenge slavery and raise the status of Black women in the church and society (Francis 2021). The first permanent Protestant missionaries arrived in the 1870s under the influence of politically liberal Latin American governments that wanted to undermine the Catholic hierarchy (Dove 2016). Missionaries – Presbyterian, Methodist, Lutheran, and Baptist – arrived mainly from the United States and engaged in evangelistic campaigns (Moreno 2021).

The Monroe Doctrine (1823) was the new version of the *Inter Caetera*, which prohibited further European colonization in the Americas but demanded unrestricted United States influence in its place. This policy prepared the region for a massive influx of Protestant missionaries (González and González 2008) who believed the continent to be nominally Catholic at best and pagan at worst. Protestant missionaries translated the Bible, built schools, and targeted marginalized ethnic minority groups who felt treated as outsiders by the reign of Catholicism. In turn, influential organizations like the American Bible Society, Wycliffe Bible Translators, South American Indian Mission, and New Tribes Mission helped spread Protestantism throughout the continent. Many workers were faith missionaries who relied totally on God for protection, finances, and sustenance, often at risk to their lives. Bible translation was initially a male endeavor; however, by the 1930s women were taking up the task (Tucker 1988). Bible translator Marianna Slocum (1918–2017) and her colleague Florence Gerdel (1921–2019) worked in Mexico and Colombia for 65 years. Slocum translated the New Testament into Highland Tzeltal, Bachajón Tzeltal, and Páez, and Gerdel operated health clinics with hundreds of visitors a month (Wycliffe 2017). Other female translators include Loretta "Lorrie" Doris Anderson (1922–2020) and Doris Cox (1921–2018) in Peru, and Eunice Pike (1913–2011) and Florence Hansen (1915–1997) in Mexico. These women were single female missionaries at a time when many thought it too dangerous for them to be engaged in such work. However, in villages, foreign women were typically perceived as less threatening than foreign men. Women are now 85% of Wycliffe Bible Translators (Shellnutt 2017).

Marginalized people – women, ethnic minorities, rural and urban migrants – were particularly responsive to Protestantism, finding a new faith home in a Christian tradition that promised a closer relationship with God and a strong social safety net. The theology of the priesthood of all believers was attractive to both men and women who welcomed the opportunity to have new official roles in church life (Prien and Buckwalter 2013). Leadership of Protestant churches was quickly passed to local converts, who were successful in growing their congregations. Though periods of the most rapid expansion of Protestantism often coincided with conflict and violence, such as military dictatorships in the mid-to-late twentieth century, the arrival of Protestantism to Latin America and the Caribbean provided religious choice: either self-define as more vigorously Catholic or convert to Protestantism (Hartch 2014). The spread of Protestantism created, for the first time in the modern era, a religious marketplace in Latin America.

Pentecostal/Charismatic Churches

One of the earliest movements of Pentecostalism in Latin America is the Methodist Pentecostal Church of Chile. Faith missionaries Willis and May Hoover arrived in Valparaiso, Chile in 1889. May was a roommate of Minnie Abrams at the Methodist training school in Chicago, and Abrams became a helper at Pandita Ramabai's Mukti Mission in India for widows and orphans. A Pentecostal revival broke out at the Mukti Mission in 1905, an event relayed to May via Abrams's book that described the events. The Hoovers began to pray for a similar revival, which came in 1909. Though the Hoovers were eventually expelled from the Methodist church, an Independent Chilean church emerged, still strongly tied to its Methodist roots and thus very different from classical Pentecostalism in North America. Today, roughly 95% of all Protestants in Chile trace their roots to the original Methodist Pentecostal Church. A Pentecostal movement subsequently emerged in Brazil (via Italian American Presbyterians and Swedish American Baptists), and then throughout the rest of the continent.

By the 1950s, the Pentecostal/Charismatic movement was core to the fabric of Latin American society and its religious landscape. Exceeding non-Pentecostal Protestants (63 million) in numbers and influence, Pentecostals (195 million) have grown for many reasons, including their emphasis on the Holy Spirit and experience of transformed lives, promises of physical healing, vibrant and passionate music and worship, effective community outreach, and a different approach to leadership. Pentecostal pastors generally have the same level of education as their congregants, thus reducing the gap between clergy and lay. They are considered leaders among the people and more accessible and practical than those with formal theological education. Spirit-filled expressions of Christianity were also particularly popular among youth, helping fill the spiritual vacuum in urban areas for those who had left their families and religious traditions behind in rural areas. In the 1970s, Pentecostalism spread from the poor to the middle class, and today they are found throughout all social strata, including the political arena. Most Protestant denominations have experienced a pentecostalization of worship, doctrine, and practice (Moreno 2021).

Responses to Pentecostalism are gendered. In Latin America, Pentecostalism provided a new kind of feminism, one in which both women and men changed their behavior to the degree that roles for both slowly became counter cultural (DeBorst 2012). Conversion to Pentecostalism (and Protestantism more broadly), required substantial commitment to separate themselves from the societal mainstream. In Brazil, women are more attracted to Pentecostalism for healing of a physical ailment or illness for themselves or their children (Chesnut 1997). Meanwhile, men explore Pentecostalism out of pressure from their wives or due to personal problems like alcoholism or unemployment (Hayes 2017). In Colombia, women found that Pentecostalism elevated women's domesticity and transformed gender roles, bringing men back into the family (Brusco 1995). Women's commitment to Pentecostalism was also part of their effort to combat the "demons of *machismo*," including drinking, gambling, adultery, and negligence of family life (Hayes 2017).

In theory, the Holy Spirit cuts across gender lines, providing both women and men the same access to spiritual power and giftings. Yet, in practice, it is more complicated. While women can minister in services, Pentecostal reading of scripture retains "theoretical and practical belief in men's superiority" (Suárez 2022, p. 405). Many Pentecostal churches operate within their own hierarchies, placing women subordinate to men. Even though women can, for example, prophesy in church and participate in healing services, their spiritual power is considered marginal to male power. Pentecostal women live in a paradox of being simultaneously included and excluded (Suárez 2022). While some women have established Pentecostal movements, leadership is often transferred to men (especially their husbands) when it becomes institutionalized. In El Salvador, for instance, Guatemalan Carmen Mena Fuentes (1911–1961) was the principal leader among indigenous Guatemalans of the Prince of Peace Church (Martin 1993), which is one of the largest denominations today but is now under male leadership. At the same time, Pentecostalism is more democratic than Catholicism, providing women opportunities for leadership in home gatherings and small group meetings (Bartel 2018). Throughout Latin America and the Caribbean, Pentecostalism has grown more quickly among people of lower levels of education and income.

The growth of Pentecostalism was a shock to the Catholic hierarchy, provoking the question, "How could such unorganized, undisciplined, impoverished churches pose a serious challenge to an institution that had made Latin America?" (Hartch 2014, p. 125). Pentecostalism offered something that Catholicism did not; it helped spark the Catholic Charismatic Renewal (CCR) movement, begun in the 1960s and now the largest such movements in the world (of the 195 million Catholic Charismatics worldwide, 59% live in Latin America) (Johnson and Zurlo 2022). However, while millions of Latin Americans were intrigued by the Pentecostal experience, they were unwilling to leave their religious traditions behind. Consequently, spurred by Vatican II's deeper recognition of the Holy Spirit and charismatic gifts, and coupled with the challenge of Pentecostal church growth, Catholicism entered a period of revival that mirrored some of the characteristics of Protestant Pentecostalism: passionate worship, small group learning, and community involvement. In the CCR, women especially found new opportunities for service and spiritual growth. Being denied leadership in the Catholic hierarchy, women had new access to authority in the CCR through the power of the Holy Spirit.

The neo-Pentecostal movement emerged in the 1980s, often known as Independent Charismatics. While most of these churches have roots in historic Protestantism or classical Pentecostal churches, some have different theological beliefs that set them apart. Sometimes seen as "post-denominational," most emphasize the prosperity gospel, physical healing, and political involvement (Moreno 2021), while attacking traditional or folk religions under the guise of "spiritual warfare" (da Silva 2017). The largest of these is the Universal Church of the Kingdom of God (UCKG; Brazil), which is present in over 120 countries. The UCKG is notoriously patriarchal in its leadership and hierarchy, with all male bishops (also typically White and wealthy) and perhaps fewer than 1% women pastors (Doran 2013). However, there are three to four times as many unpaid church laborers (*obreiros*) in the UCKG than pastors. These *obreiros*, typically elderly women, are "indispensable to the ritual functioning of the church" (Doran 2013, p. 28).

Latin American and Caribbean Women in Theology

Liberation theology is by far the most well-known Latin American expression and interpretation of the Christian faith. Catalyzed by Vatican II and in response to the social, economic, and political trials of twentieth-century Latin America, theologians such as Gustavo Gutiérrez (Peru; b.1928), Leonardo Boff (Brazil; b.1938), and Pedro Arrupe (Spain; 1907–1991) centered their theology around God's "preferential option for the poor." Reading the Bible through the lens of the poor and oppressed, they emphasized orthopraxis over orthodoxy and the important reality of structural sin in the lives of Christians and in society. Inherent to liberation theology is a critique of Latin America's economic and social inequalities, and an emphasis on political activism to combat human rights abuses. As a bottom–up movement, liberation theology provided the theological support for CEBs, new ecclesial movements, and other twentieth-century reforms. Its exportation around the world birthed new schools of theology – such as Black theology in the United States, *minjung* theology in South Korea, and *Dalit* theology in India – that helped inspire socio-economic-political liberation from different forms of poverty and oppression.

However, like other twentieth-century theological innovations, the first wave of liberation theologians overlooked the unique needs of Christian women in Latin America and the Caribbean. Catholic theologian María Pilar Aquino (Mexico; b.1956) argued that the "liberation of the poor cannot be fully achieved without women's liberation" (Aquino 1993, p. 21). She asks several questions of liberation theology:

- "What does it mean to be a Christian in a world of poor people struggling for liberation?
- In what language can those who have been denied human wholeness be told that they are daughters and sons of God?
- How can the fullness of life in God be proclaimed to those who live at the edge of survival?
- What does it mean to be a woman in a continent conquered and then colonized by aggressive patriarchal capitalism?" (Aquino 1993, p. 10)
- How do we construct new ways of living together, more human ways, as people of Christian faith?

The term *mujerista* theology – Hispanic feminist theology – was coined by Catholic theologian Ada María Isasi-Díaz (Cuban American; 1943–2012) in response to the sexism, racism, and economic oppression that uniquely impacted women in Latin America and Latinas in diaspora in the United States. She stated, "*Mujerista* theology is about creating a voice for Latinas, not the only one but a valid one; and *mujerista* theology is also about capturing public spaces for the voices of Latinas" (Isasi-Díaz 1996, p. 1). In offering a corrective to liberation theology, Isasi-Díaz gave Latinas a way to theologically identify with the church from the perspective of their own experiences and concerns. Lived experience is the foundation of *mujerista* theology, grounded in contemplation, prayer, word, and commitment, helping to challenge women's subjugation, poverty, and exclusion in church and society. *Mujerista* theology provides women space to tackle what Isasi-Díaz identified as their five areas of oppression (*lo cotidiano*, "the condition"): exploitation, marginalization, powerlessness, cultural imperialism, and systemic violence. Within this are two important aspects: *la lucha*, "the struggle" of Latinas to fight against the extant social order, and *la comunidad*, "the community" as central to Latina experience.

Newer to theological discourse among Latin American women are *evangélicas* – Evangelical Protestant women. Prominent among them is Ruth Padilla DeBorst (Colombia/Costa Rica), daughter of theologian C. René Padilla (1932–2021) who coined the term "integral mission." Sometimes considered the Evangelical version of liberation theology, integral mission is best understood as a holistic approach to Christian mission that fully integrates both evangelism and social justice – that is, both the proclamation of the gospel and its demonstration (Padilla 2010). DeBorst in turn describes Latin American theologians as liberationist and holistic, those who provide hope and develop local praxis that resists definition by the outside. Hope comes from God who entered history in the form of Jesus Christ, who exalted women and children and whose proclamation of the good news is just as applicable to the twenty-first century as the first. There is no social, political, or religious context where God's presence in word and spirit is not able to take on flesh and walk among God's people for the sake of God's peacemaking purposes (DeBorst 2018). In exploring the marginalization of Latin American women and the interrelationship of faith and family, Cuban American theologian Katrina Armas theologizes from the margins, asking the question, "What if some of our greatest theologians wouldn't be considered theologians at all?" In doing so, she identifies the theological contributions of mothers, grandmothers, sisters, and daughters in their everyday lives (Armas 2021).

Conclusion

Women's experiences in Latin America and the Caribbean are not monolithic. Race, class, and geography historically had important roles in determining a woman's fate, and this is still true today. Both Protestant and Catholic churches have been paradoxical places for women in this part of the world. Christianity arrived with violence, conquest, and a new kind of foreign patriarchy imposed on women that remains in some Christian circles today. Combined with *machismo* and socioeconomic oppression, these lasting effects have made life for women extraordinarily difficult. Yet, in some cases, Christianity provided women new spheres of influence previously unavailable to them in the wider society. They emerged as leaders in CEBs, prophetic voices in charismatic services, and as advocates for other women in the domestic sphere, elevating their importance and value in both home and society. In the twentieth century, feminist theologians found a platform to speak their truths into the church, to deconstruct stereotypes about their sex, and to engage in practical theological reflection to improve their lives, along with those within their communities. Finding mutual support, Latinas have gained strength to resist and reform *machismo* within a new kind of feminism that goes beyond Western debates of "complementarian" vs. "egalitarian." The future of Christianity in Latin America and the Caribbean is dependent on the continuing witness of these women, who are now challenging Western notions of what it means to be a woman of faith.

Reflection Questions

1) Reflect on the following statement from this chapter: "The hundreds of missionaries who ended up in the Americas were neither completely innocent nor completely guilty." Elaborate on the dynamic between the Catholic Church and the *conquistadores*. How did the attempted export of Catholicism by the Spanish and Portuguese frame the advent of European imperialism, conquest, and genocide, and how did this impact women in particular?

2) How have military dictatorships in Latin America and the Caribbean shaped the spirit of Christianity on the continent, and what are the "two faces" of Latin American Christianity? Explain how both Protestant and Catholic churches responded to political and social unrest and the ways women participated in these movements through grassroots activism.

3) Explain the role of patriarchy and *machismo* in forming public opinion on women's roles in Latin American society. How do these ideas extend to the role of women in the churches? How have women responded to these ideas via liberation theology and *mujerista* theology? How does lived experience influence these theological expressions?

Works Cited

Ahlgren, Gillian T.W. (2005). Preface. In: *Sor Juana Inés de la Cruz: Selected Writings* (trans. Juana I. de la Cruz and Pamela K. Rappaport), 1–4. New York: Paulist Press.

Aquino, Maria P. (1993). *Our Cry for Life: Feminist Theology from Latin America*. Maryknoll, NY: Orbis Books.

Arditti, Rita (1999). *Searching for Life: The Grandmothers of the Plaza de Mayo and the Disappeared Children of Argentina*. Berkeley: University of California Press.

Armas, Katrina (2021). *Abuelita Faith: What Women on the Margins Teach Us about Wisdom, Persistence, and Strength*. Grand Rapids, MI: Brazos Press.

Baldez, Lisa (2002). *Why Women Protest: Women's Movements in Chile*. Cambridge: Cambridge University Press.

Bartel, Rebecca C. (2018). Women and Christianity in Latin America. In: *Encyclopedia of Women in World Religions: Faith and Culture across History* (ed. Susan de Gaia), 180–185. Santa Barbara, CA: ABC-CLIO Publishing.

Brusco, Elizabeth E. (1995). *The Reformation of Machismo: Evangelical Conversion and Gender in Colombia*. Austin: University of Texas Press.

Chesnut, R. Andrew (1997). *Born Again in Brazil: The Pentecostal Boom and the Pathogens of Poverty*. New Brunswick, NJ: Rutgers University Press.

Chesnut, R. Andrew (2018). *Devoted to Death: Santa Muerte, the Skeleton Saint*. 2nd edn. New York: Oxford University Press.

Cook, Karoline P. (2017). Requerimiento. In: *Latin American History and Culture: Encyclopedia of Pre-Colonial Latin America: (prehistory to 1550s)* (ed. J. Michael Francis and Thomas M. Leonard). New York: Credo Reference.

da Silva, Vagner G. (2017). Crossroads: conflicts between neo-Pentecostalism and Afro-Brazilian religions. In: *Handbook of Contemporary Religions in Brazil* (ed. Steven Engler and Bettina Schmidt), 489–507. Leiden/Boston: Brill.

DeBorst, Ruth Padilla (2012). Songs of hope out of a crying land: an overview of contemporary Latin American theology. In: *Global Theology in Evangelical Perspective: Exploring the Contextual Nature of Theology and Mission* (ed. Jeffrey P. Greenman and Gene L. Green), 86–101. Downers Grove, IL: IVP Academic.

DeBorst, Ruth Padilla (2018). Sermon, christ at the checkpoint conference in Bethlehem. Palestine. https://christatthecheckpoint.bethbc.edu/blog/2018/10/03/christ-at-the-checkpoint-2018-jesus-christ-at-the-center (accessed 14 September 2021).

Doran, Justin M. (2013). Demon-haunted worlds: enchantment, disenchantment, and the Universal Church of the Kingdom of God. Master's thesis. The University of Texas at Austin.

Dove, Steven (2016). Latin America and the Caribbean. In: *The Wiley Blackwell Companion to World Christianity* (ed. Lamin O. Sanneh and Michael J. McClymond), 511–522. Hoboken, NJ: John Wiley & Sons, Ltd.

Earle, Rebecca (2000). Rape and the anxious republic, revolutionary Colombia, 1810–1830. In: *Hidden Histories of Gender and the State in Latin America* (ed. Elizabeth Dore and Maxine Molyneuz), 127–146. Durham, NC: Duke University Press.

Eltis, David (2007). A brief overview of the Trans-Atlantic slave trade. Slave Voyages. https://www.slavevoyages.org/voyage/essays#interpretation/a-brief-overview-of-the-trans-atlantic-slave-trade/introduction/0/en (accessed 14 September 2021).

Francis, JoDeanne (2021). Gilbert, Anne Hart (1768–1833). Caribbean Methodist Pioneer. https://www.bu.edu/missiology/gilbert-anne-hart-1768-1833 (accessed 22 September 2021).

Gates, Henry L. (2011). *Black in Latin America*. New York: New York University Press.

González, Ondina E. and González, Justo L. (2008). *Christianity in Latin America: A History*. Cambridge: Cambridge University Press.

Green, Linda (2000). *Fear as a Way of Life: Mayan Widows in Rural Guatemala*. New York: Columbia University Press.

Grimes, Katie W. (2017). *Fugitive Saints: Catholicism and the Politics of Slavery*. Minneapolis: Fortress Press.

Hartch, Todd (2014). *The Rebirth of Latin American Christianity*. Oxford: Oxford University Press.

Hayes, Kelly E. (2017). Women and religion in contemporary Brazil. In: *Handbook of Contemporary Religion in Brazil* (ed. Bettina Schmidt and Steven Engler), 395–430. Leiden/Boston: Brill.

Hucks, Tracey E. (2006). 'I smoothed the way, I opened doors': women in the Yoruba-Orisha tradition of Trinidad. In: *Women and Religion in the African Diaspora: Knowledge, Power, and Performance* (ed. R. Marie Griffith and Barbara D. Savage), 19–36. Baltimore: Johns Hopkins University Press.

Hurbon, Laënnec (2021). Afro-descendant populations. In: *Christianity in Latin America and the Caribbean* (ed. Kenneth R. Ross, Ana María Bidegain, and Todd M. Johnson), 453–463. Edinburgh: Edinburgh University Press.

Hurtado, Aída and Sinha, Mrinal (2016). *Beyond Machismo: Intersectional Latino Masculinities*. Austin: University of Texas Press.

Isasi-Díaz, Ada María (1996). *Mujerista Theology: A Theology for the Twenty-First Century*. Westminster: John Knox.

Johnson, Todd M. and Zurlo, Gina A. (2019). *World Christian Encyclopedia*. 3rd edn. Edinburgh: Edinburgh University Press.

Johnson, Todd M. and Zurlo, Gina A. ed. (2022). *World Christian Database*. Leiden/Boston: Brill.

Latinbarometer (2018). Informe 2018. https://www.latinobarometro.org/lat.jsp (accessed 20 September 2021).

López, Dario (2021). Evangelicals. In: *Christianity in Latin America and the Caribbean* (ed. Kenneth R. Ross, Ana María Bidegain, and Todd M. Johnson), 311–321. Edinburgh: Edinburgh University Press.

Lowy, Michael, Sader, Eder, and Gorman, Stephen (1985). The militarization of the state in Latin America. *Latin American Perspectives*, 12(4), 7–40.

Lynch, John (2012). *New Worlds: A Religious History of Latin America*. New Haven: Yale University Press.

Martin, David (1993). *Tongues of Fire: The Explosion of Protestantism in Latin America*. Oxford, UK: Blackwell.

Moreno, Pablo (2021). Protestants. In: *Christianity in Latin America and the Caribbean* (ed. Kenneth R. Ross, Ana María Bidegain, and Todd M. Johnson), 285–297. Edinburgh: Edinburgh University Press.

Padilla, C. René (2010). *Mission between the Times*. Revised and expanded edition. Carlisle: Langham Monographs.

Pew Research Center (2014). Religion in Latin America: widespread change in a historically catholic region.

Prien, Hans-Jürgen and Buckwalter, Stephen E. (2013). *Christianity in Latin America*. Revised and expanded edition. Leiden: Brill.

Rey, Terry (2010). Catholic Pentecostalism in Haiti: spirit, politics, and gender. *Pneuma*, 32(1), 80–106.

Salinas, Maximiliano (1992). Christianity, colonialism and women in Latin America in the 16th, 17th and 18th centuries. *Social Compass*, 39(4), 525–542.

Schneider, Nicolas I. (2021). Pentecostals/Charismatics. In: *Christianity in Latin America and the Caribbean* (ed. Kenneth R. Ross, Ana María Bidegain, and Todd M. Johnson), 322–334. Edinburgh: Edinburgh University Press.

Shellnutt, Kate (2017). How single women became an unstoppable force in Bible translation. *Christianity Today*. https://www.christianitytoday.com/ct/2017/april-web-only/how-single-women-became-unstoppable-force-in-bible-translat.html (accessed 19 July 2022).

Slave Voyages (2021). Trans-Atlantic slave trade – estimates. https://www.slavevoyages.org/assessment/estimates (accessed 14 September 2021).

Stanley, Brian (2009). *The World Missionary Conference, Edinburgh 1910*. Grand Rapids, MI: William B. Eerdmans Pub. Co.

Socolow, Susan M. (2015). *The Women of Colonial Latin America*. 2nd edn. New York: Cambridge University Press.

Suárez, Ana Lourdes (2022). Gender. In: *Christianity in Latin America and the Caribbean* (ed. Kenneth R. Ross, Ana María Bidegain, and Todd M. Johnson), 397–407. Edinburgh: Edinburgh University Press.

Tamez, Elsa (1989). Introduction: the power of the naked. In: *Through Her Eyes: Women's Theology from Latin America* (ed. Elsa Tamez). Maryknoll, NY: Orbis Books.

Tucker, Ruth (1988). *Guardians of the Great Commission: The Story of Women in Modern Missions*. Grand Rapids, MI: Academie Books.

United Nations Development Programme (2022). *Human development report 2021/2022: uncertain times, unsettled lives: shaping our future in a transforming World*. New York.

Wycliffe Bible Translators (2017). Three-time pioneers. November 30. https://www.wycliffe.org/blog/posts/threetime-pioneers (accessed 21 September 2021).

6

Women in North American Christianity

"The numerical dominance of women in all but a few religious groups constitutes one of the most consistent features of American religion, and one of the least explained."

Ann Braude (Braude 1997, p. 88)

From the start of the twentieth century until second-wave feminism in the 1960s, women in North American Christianity were generally expected to be obedient wives and mothers, faithful in service to their husbands, and submissive to men. The notion of domesticity emphasized women's sacrificial ministry of keeping a well-run home and raising proper children. This idealistic picture of women was challenged over time, from Progressive Era (1890s–1910s) activists advocating for suffrage and temperance, to feminists in the 1960s and 1970s, to twenty-first century women pushing the boundaries of passed-down orthodoxy regarding gender, sexuality, purity, and Christian subcultures. Having made tremendous strides, North American Christian women verge on many opportunities and challenges. Several Protestant denominations ordain women (see Chapter 10 for more detail), Catholic women have emerged as prominent theologians, biblical scholars, and activists, and women across race and denomination are charting their own authentic ways of being both female and authentically Christian.

The shift of Christianity to the global South has raised many questions about what role Christianity in North America and Europe will have in the future of the world's largest religion.[1] North America represents a decreasing share of all Christians worldwide, dropping from 14% of all Christians in 1900 to 11% of all Christians in 2020 (Johnson and Zurlo 2022). The United States (331 million) and Canada (38 million) dominate the region demographically, and the United States still has a prominent place in World Christianity as the country with the most Christians in the past (74 million in 1900), present (244 million in 2020), and likely future (262 million in 2050) (Johnson and Zurlo 2022). The dynamics between the global North and South are further compounded when viewed from the perspective of socioeconomic indicators. North America is highly developed, with strong rankings on the United Nations Development Index (92.4/100) and in education (96%), adult literacy (100%), Internet access (78%), and gender gap (0.9%). This is unlike the socioeconomic context of the global South, which is home to a greater share of Christians but not nearly as much Christian wealth and stability. A substantial amount of theology, scholarship, historical writing,

---

1 According to the United Nations, North America consists of the following countries: Bermuda, Canada, Greenland, Saint Pierre and Miquelon, and the United States.

Women in World Christianity: Building and Sustaining a Global Movement, First Edition. Gina A. Zurlo.
© 2023 John Wiley & Sons Ltd. Published 2023 by John Wiley & Sons Ltd.

and other facets of Christianity continue to be exported from North America, raising questions about new forms of Western colonization imposed on the practice of Christianity around the world.

Immigration is a major force of religious change in North America, which contributes to both increased religious and Christian diversity. Immigrants from Latin America, documented or otherwise, help sustain the United States as the country with the most Christians, despite Christianity's slow proportional decline (97% in 1900, 74% in 2020, expected 67% in 2050). Canadian society has also been considerably changed because of immigration. From 98% Christian in 1900, Canada is now 64% Christian with substantial populations of Muslims (3%), Buddhists (2%), Chinese folk-religionists (2%), and Sikhs, Hindus, and Jews (1% each) (Johnson and Zurlo 2022). Sikhs have a particular prominence in Canadian society; there are more Sikh members of parliament (MPs) in Canada then there are in India. From this perspective, North America is becoming more ethnically, culturally, and theologically diverse. Historians have shown that America was never a "melting pot." From nineteenth-century sectarian groups to the arrival of new religions in the twentieth century, North America has always been marked by plurality of religious practice, both within and outside Christianity. Religious studies scholar Yvonne Haddad calls ethnic diversity and cultural (including religious) pluralism the twin successors of the melting pot theory (Haddad 2006). A significant amount of scholarship has emerged along these lines, continuing trend started by Laurence Moore (1994) and others of studying so-called religious "outsiders" (Catholics, Latter-day Saints, Jews) and, of course, women's religious experiences. This scholarship all points not only to a diversity of North American culture, but also a lack of conformity among the immigrant experiences that continue to propel diversity.

Christianity in North America, 1900–2050

Most people who have left Christianity in North America have become nonreligious (atheists and agnostics together), a group that expanded from 1% of the population in 1900 to 20% by 2020 (Table 6.1). The number of Muslims and Jews have increased, now each over 1% of the continent's population. The decline of Christianity in North America is part of secularization processes that are different from those in Europe (see Chapter 4), and the United States in particular remains a very religious nation compared to other Western societies. Nevertheless, church membership in the US declined from 73% in the 1940s to 47% in 2020 (Jones 2021). Monthly religious service attendance is now around 34%–43%, down from 54% in 2007 (Pew Research Center 2019, 2021b).

Table 6.1 Religions in North America over 1%, 1900–2050.

Religion	Pop. 1900	% 1900	Rate % p.a. 1900–2000	Pop. 2020	% 2020	Rate % p.a. 2020–2050	Pop. 2050	% 2050
Christians	79,254,000	97.1	1.17	269,524,000	73.1	0.08	276,078,000	64.9
Agnostics	1,010,000	1.2	3.57	64,155,000	17.4	1.17	91,007,000	21.4
Atheists	2,000	0.0	8.17	10,587,000	2.9	2.37	21,351,000	5.0
Jews	1,074,000	1.3	1.68	5,940,000	1.6	−0.32	5,390,000	1.3
Muslims	10,100	0.0	6.20	5,671,000	1.5	2.68	12,551,000	3.0
Buddhists	40,400	0.0	4.69	4,953,000	1.3	1.59	7,951,000	1.9

Source: Data from Johnson and Zurlo 2022. p.a. = percent change per annum, or each year.

Table 6.2   Countries in North America with the most Christians, 2020.

Rank	Country	Largest Christian tradition	Pop. 2020	% Christian 2020	Christian pop. 2020	% Christian female 2020	% pop. female % 2020
1	United States	Catholics	331,003,000	74.2	245,457,000	54.3	50.5
2	Canada	Catholics	37,742,000	63.5	23,952,000	52.3	50.4
3	Bermuda	Protestants	62,300	88.7	55,200	55.2	51.4
4	Greenland	Protestants	56,800	95.9	54,400	52.3	50.3
5	Saint Pierre and Miquelon	Catholics	5,800	94.4	5,500	51.2	51.6

Source: Data from Johnson and Zurlo 2022.

Women make up the majority of Christians in each of the continent's five countries (Table 6.2). The highest figure is in Bermuda (55% female), a British Overseas Territory in the Atlantic Ocean, where the largest denominations are the Anglican Church (55% female), Catholic Church (50%), the African Methodist Episcopal Church (57%), and the New Testament Church of God (59%) (Johnson and Zurlo 2022). Lutherans are the largest denomination in Greenland and report 52% female. Saint Pierre and Miquelon has fewer than 6,000 inhabitants, 95% of whom are Catholic (51% female). The French territorial collectivity is served by three Catholic priests and six women religious (*Annuarium Statisticum Ecclesiae* 2020).

Christianity has always been very diverse in North America, a region where religious experimentation and fragmentation are common. While Catholics are the largest family (86 million and 40% of all Christians; Figure 6.1), many other Christian families number well into the tens of millions, such as Baptists, Pentecostals/Charismatics, and Methodists (Table 6.3). However, Table 6.3 reveals the decline of these traditions over time; between 2000 and 2015, nearly every major Christian family experienced decline or below replacement fertility rates.

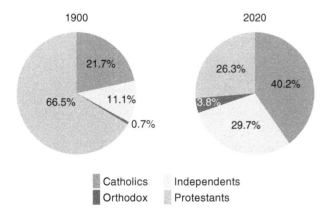

Figure 6.1   Christianity in North America by major Christian tradition, 1900 and 2020. *Source:* Data from Johnson and Zurlo 2022.

Table 6.3 Christian families in North America, 2000 and 2015.

Family	Affiliated 2000	Affiliated 2015	% female 2015	Rate % p.a. 2000–2015
Latin-rite Catholic	75,757,000	85,978,000	53.1	0.85
Baptist	42,378,000	40,473,000	54.7	−0.31
Pentecostal/Charismatic*	21,149,000	24,320,000	55.7	0.94
Methodist	12,945,000	12,686,000	55.5	−0.13
Other Protestant/Independent	5,913,000	7,528,000	53.9	1.62
Lutheran	8,520,000	7,091,000	54.1	−1.22
Latter-day Saints (Mormons)	5,561,000	7,019,000	55.5	1.56
Eastern Orthodox	5,330,000	6,236,000	53.6	1.05
Reformed, Presbyterian	5,621,000	3,941,000	54.0	−2.34
Restorationist, Disciple	3,986,000	3,475,000	54.1	−0.91
Jehovah's Witnesses	2,532,000	3,077,000	55.5	1.31
Anglican	3,030,000	2,614,000	54.1	−0.98
Holiness	2,098,000	2,449,000	54.0	1.04
United church or joint mission	2,928,000	1,996,000	54.6	−2.52
Oriental and other Orthodox	1,434,000	1,741,000	53.6	1.30
Adventist	1,152,000	1,433,000	54.2	1.46
Nondenominational	863,000	964,000	52.2	0.74
Eastern-rite Catholic	675,000	850,000	53.0	1.54
Congregational	645,000	713,000	54.1	0.67
Mennonite	547,000	578,000	53.4	0.37
Salvationist	552,000	465,000	53.8	−1.14
Dunker	237,000	223,000	54.1	−0.38
Old Catholic Church	193,000	181,000	55.5	−0.43
Christian Brethren	172,000	173,000	53.8	0.05
Friends (Quaker)	113,000	102,000	54.1	−0.73
Moravian	56,200	45,900	53.9	−1.34
Hidden believers in Christ	37,500	42,500	54.1	0.84
Nontraditional, house, cell	4,000	7,000	54.1	3.80

Source: Data from Johnson and Zurlo 2022. p.a. = percent change per annum, or each year.
*Excluding partially pentecostalized.

In the twenty-first century, numerous Christian denominations are struggling and splintering over differences related to women's rights in the church, abortion, same-sex relations, racism, and the relationship between Christianity and politics. The figures for the female share of Christian families and denominations presented in this chapter are likely undercounts due to a lack of data. More nuanced information, which is not available for every denomination, reveals, for example:

- Jehovah's Witnesses, 56% female, elsewhere reported 65% female (Lipka 2016)
- American Baptist Churches, 54% female, elsewhere reported 60% female (ABC 2019)
- Christian Churches and Churches of Christ, 54% female, elsewhere estimated 60% female (personal communication)

Table 6.4 Largest denominations in North America, 2015.

Rank	Country	Denomination	Year begun	Affiliated 2015	% Christian female	Rate % p.a. 2000–2015
1	United States	Catholic Church in the USA	1526	72,798,000	53.3	0.97
2	United States	Southern Baptist Convention	1845	18,836,000	54.1	−0.51
3	Canada	Catholic Church of Canada	1608	14,015,000	52.0	0.28
4	United States	National Baptist Convention, USA	1773	9,200,000	57.4	−0.26
5	United States	Church of God in Christ	1895	8,046,000	57.4	0.93
6	United States	United Methodist Church	1766	7,067,000	54.1	−1.06
7	United States	Church of Jesus Christ of Latter-day Saints	1830	6,642,000	55.6	1.63
8	United States	Evangelical Lutheran Church in America	1623	4,300,000	54.1	−1.13
9	United States	National Baptist Convention of America	1880	4,250,000	57.4	0.40
10	United States	Assemblies of God USA	1906	3,522,000	54.1	2.10

Source: Data from Johnson and Zurlo 2022. p.a. = percent change per annum, or each year.

Given the demographic weight of the United States, nine of the top ten largest denominations are in the US, and each is majority female (Table 6.4). Of these ten denominations, three are historically Black: National Baptist Convention, USA, Church of God in Christ, and the National Baptist Convention of America. Black denominations tend to have higher Christian female percentages than White denominations. Historian Estrelda Alexander observed this dynamic the following way in relationship to Pentecostalism:

> As Cheryl Townsend Gilkes's title, *If It Wasn't for the Women*, highlights, black Pentecostalism would be considerably poorer without their contribution. Despite generally being locked out of higher levels of denominational leadership, women not only filled the pews but also established and pastored congregations, served as missionaries and developed the numerous auxiliaries that helped fuel Pentecostalism's phenomenal growth. Their involvement helped move a marginalized movement into the center of the contemporary American and global religious scenes. However, as Jane Sims astutely contends, "The absence of women's stories and particularly those of women of color, from official historiographies … creates the perception that women's role was minimal or non-existent."
>
> (Alexander 2011, pp. 293–294)

Women in North America are widely known to be more religious than men. In the United States, women believe in the God of the Bible more than men (61% vs. 50%), are more likely to say that God loves all people despite their faults (82% vs. 76%), and more likely to believe that God is all-knowing (76% vs. 65%) (Pew Research Center 2018). Women also talk to God more (81% vs. 66%) and believe that God talks back to them (32% vs. 24%). However, the intensities of religious belief and identification vary by denomination and race. According to longitudinal analyses of the General Social Survey from 1994 to 2012, Black Protestant women showed stronger religious affiliation, more daily prayer, belief in God with no doubts, and more likely to have a "born-again" experience compared to Evangelical Protestant women, mainline Protestant women, and Catholic women (Schnabel 2015). The same study also suggested that Evangelical Protestant women have greater belief in the afterlife and more frequent weekly church attendance.

Generally, women in American churches have more opportunities for leadership than women in Africa, Asia, and Latin America. This is evident in the rise of female clergy in the US, growing from virtually zero in the 1960s to nearly 16% of American clergy by 2018, leading 10% of congregations (Campbell-Reed 2018). The 2016 American Communities Survey reported women were 21% of clergy; in addition, 79% of congregations allow women to volunteer in any positions that men can hold (Chaves and Eagle 2015). However, some immigrant or ethnic communities place greater restrictions on women's roles. For example, Korean American women operating within the male-centeredness of Korean ethnic churches are caught between the traditional values of their communities and those of larger US society (Park 2001). Female Korean elders are rare, even in egalitarian contexts. In the Korean United Methodist Church, 23% of active ministers are female, and no women serve as bishops (Han 2016).

Canada is sometimes seen as a prime example of secularization (Brown 2012) and looks more like Europe than the United States in its posture toward religion. Between 1957 and 1990, women in Canada reported a 47% decline in church attendance and a 61% decline in church membership, though the figures are nearly the same for men (Brown 2012, cf. Bibby 1993). Wave 7 of the World Values Survey (2017–2020) reported the following for Canada: women reported greater importance of religion in their lives (37% for women and 34% for men), higher rates of prayer (11% of women and 8% of men responded "several times a day"), but men attended religious services at least weekly at a slightly higher rate than women (12% for women and 13% for men).

The Gender and Congregational Life Survey (2021) included 620 respondents from North America, of which all were in the United States and Canada. Respondents were majority female (85%), married (72%), well-educated (77% with bachelor's degree or higher), and employed full-time (59%). The largest Christian families represented were Pentecostal (16%), Baptist (14%), and Anglican (11%), with a wide range of church sizes (22% between 101–200 and 26% over 500). Though women are active participants, 76% of respondents said the main worship service of church is attended roughly equally by men and women, though 18% stated there were more women than men in their congregations.

Most respondents (84%) agreed or strongly agreed that women should be allowed to serve as pastors and 90% agreed or strongly agreed that it is harder for women to be accepted in leadership roles in the church. Despite this, 74% also believed that the Bible places restrictions on women's roles in the church (much lower than respondents in Africa, Asia, and Latin America). Members of Mennonite (90%), Holiness (83%), and Anglican (73%) churches were highly favorable toward women's pastoral roles and leadership than those in Disciple (62%), Christian Brethren (60%), and Catholic (40%) churches. The survey highlighted the gendered expectations and realities for men and women in North America church life, where respondents felt it would be easier for women than men to only obtain the positions of administrative assistant and children's Sunday school teacher (Figure 6.2).

   The most frequently reported roles for women were children's Sunday school teacher (86%), and administrative assistant (79%), and intercessor where such a position existed (38%) (Figure 6.3). However, North American women differed from women in the global South, as women in North America were more likely than the global average to serve in a variety of congregational positions: associate/assistant pastor, administrative assistant, elder, financial secretary/treasurer, evangelist, children's Sunday school teacher, and intercessor (Figure 6.3). Ten percent of respondents from North America reported having a woman as a senior or head pastor, higher than the 8% global average, and in line with other surveys on the subject. The data indicate that, as expected, North American women have more opportunities for congregational involvement.

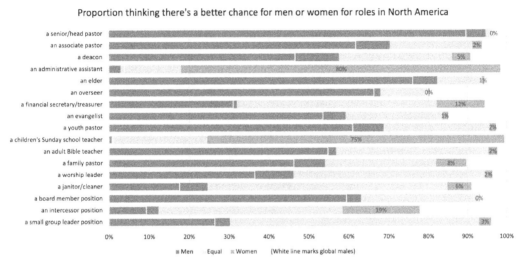

Figure 6.2 How do you think the chances of women and men compare when it comes to getting a ___ position? (North America). *Source:* Adapted from Gender and Congregational Life Survey (2021).

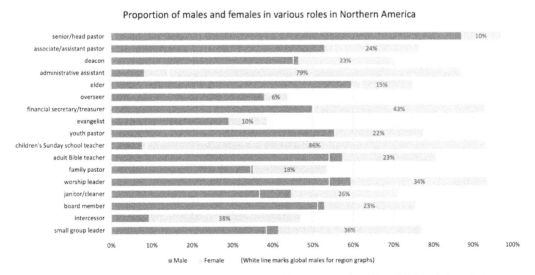

Figure 6.3 Thinking of the ___ in your congregation, is this person male or female? (North America). *Source:* Adapted from Gender and Congregational Life Survey (2021).

Women in North American Christianity: Past and Present

From Robert Baird's *Religion in America* (1844) to the pinnacle of consensus history, Sydney Ahlstrom's *A Religious History of the American People* (1972), American religious historians assumed their main task was to explain how religion – typically defined as White, male Protestantism – had influenced American politics and civic culture. Much of this scholarship attempted to identify a single, unifying thread throughout American religious history, while noting – some more than others – the stubborn persistence of what was deemed "sectarian" groups like Catholics, the Church of Jesus Christ of Latter-day Saints (Mormons), and a host of nineteenth-century restoration movements like Seventh-day Adventists and the Stone-Campbell movement. In writing institutional history over social history, generations of historians overlooked the importance of women, immigrants, adherents of other religions, and the vast diversity of race, ethnicity, and language.

The rise of women's history in the 1960s and 1970s was catalyst for an entirely new area of historical scholarship on North American religion. The coupling of feminist history alongside mainstream history, with that of social history alongside institutional history, made it possible to "reimagine the past" and uncover the important contributions of women to religious life and theological thought (Brekus 2007). Early women's histories primarily focused on White, Protestant women who contributed to civic life, such as Catherine Beecher (1800–1878, education activist), Harriett Beecher Stowe (1811–1896, abolitionist), and Elizabeth Cady Stanton (1815–1902, women's rights activist). However, by the mid-1980s historians realized this was limited and began including women of color and women outside of Protestantism. Nevertheless, questions remain on how well-integrated "women's history" is with "mainstream" history on North American religion.

Ann Braude's landmark 1997 essay, "Women's History *Is* American Religious History" was a watershed moment for understanding America's gendered religious past. She argued that it is more accurate to understand religious history from the perspective of women's presence, not men's absence. She debunked three several dominant historiographical frameworks to support her thesis: (1) declension (that religion declined in the colonial period); (2) feminization in the Victorian Era (1837–1901); and (3) secularization in the twentieth century. Simply put, churches did not decline in Puritan New England, they did not experience a new female majority in the nineteenth century, and they did not disappear in the twentieth century. She suggested that declension, feminization, and secularization are "narrative fictions" because the processes they describe cannot be discerned from empirical data about church membership. All three fictions result from the assumption that the public influence of Protestant clergy is the most important measure of the role of religion in American society. She stated, "Perhaps it is not women who have sentimentalized American Protestantism, but rather the male clergy who have cherished a romantic notion of a patriarchal past" (Braude 1997, p. 96). To understand the history of American women, one must examine the beliefs and activities of women in religion; also, to understand American religious history, one must study women (Braude 2008). This description can be stretched to the contemporary period, as well; one must understand the role of women in North American Christianity to understand it at all.

Early Christianity on Turtle Island

The fifteenth-century Doctrine of Discovery was the European legal, political, and religious justification for taking lands that did not belong to them in the area known to its original inhabitants as Turtle Island (the Native American name for North America). In one of the earliest examples of international law, it explicitly considered European and Caucasian identity as superior to other cultures, religions, and races (Miller 2008). Christianity was central to the Doctrine, which did not consider non-Christians to have the same rights to land, sovereignty, and self-determination. France,

Britain, and Spain used the Doctrine of Discovery to sweep First Nations and Native Americans from their lands, cultures, ancestors, languages, and livelihoods. The population of North America – roughly two million people before 1492 – dropped to 500,000 by the start of the twentieth century, mostly due to the spread of foreign diseases but also because of conflict, war, and genocide (Klein 2004). Indigenous populations were reduced by 89%–95% in the northwest and California.

By the early eighteenth century, Native populations began to engage with Christianity, first affiliating with colonial churches and then establishing their own indigenous separatist churches and schools. Indigenous women were more likely than men to affiliate, be baptized in, and serve in both kinds of churches. For example, more women than men were involved in the First, Second, and Third East Congregational churches in Stonington, Connecticut, and twice as many native women than men were affiliated with churches in Long Island, New York; the Narragansett Indian Church in Rhode Island and the Mohegan Church in Connecticut, two native churches, were also majority women (Fisher 2012). Native American families typically joined churches together, with mothers and grandmothers bringing their children for baptism because it ensured the children would receive an education. In many cases, indigenous women leveraged their dual identities as Christian and native for increased recognition and authority in their communities by becoming "exemplary Christians." In doing so, they both impressed colonial authorities and advocated for their own people's survival (Criales 2019).

The creation of Indian Residential Schools – run by Catholic, Anglican, Presbyterian, and Uniting churches – was the Canadian government's solution to turn native children into "useful Christian Canadian men and women" that, in reality, were homes of neglect and abuse (Milloy 2017, p. xxxvi). While young girls were taught how to properly execute the domestic arts with skills such as sewing, cooking, and cleaning, they were also subject to rape and sexual abuse. From 1879 to the closing of the last such school in 1997, upward of 150,000 indigenous children were subjected to removal from their families, punishment for using their mother tongue, and untold emotional and physical abuse. In 2021, more than a thousand unmarked graves were discovered on the grounds of former residential schools in Kamloops, Saskatchewan, and Cranbrook. In July 2022, Pope Francis visited Canada and apologized for the Catholic Church's role in residential school abuse. It was the first apology on Canadian soil from a pope.

Catholicism

Early French and Spanish settlements were staffed with priests, nuns, and brothers to carry out missionary work in Canada. The first female missionary in the "New World" was Marie Guyart (Marie of the Incarnation, 1599–1672), a French widow in the Ursuline order who founded the first school for indigenous girls in North America to shape them into "good Christians," complete with French culture. She was canonized in 2014 and the Anglican Church of Canada also has a feast day in her honor. Other early female Catholic saints include Marguerite Bourgeoys (1620–1700), a French-born nun who became the first female saint of Canada (canonized in 1982), and Kateri Tekakwitha (1656–1690), the first among Native Americans to be canonized (Algonquin-Mohawk, canonized in 2012). The first North American citizen canonized female saint (1946) was Maria Francesca Cabrini (also known as Frances Xavier Cabrini, 1850–1917), an Italian-born nun called by Pope Leo XIII to help Italian immigrants in America. She founded the Missionary Sisters of the Sacred Heart in 1880.

The Vatican considered the United States a mission field until 1908. The first American Catholic missionary organization – the Catholic Foreign Mission Society of America (Maryknoll Fathers and Brothers) – sent their first missionaries in 1918. Mostly wives and mothers, Catholic women were not officially considered missionaries proper until the mid-twentieth century (Robert 1997). Nevertheless, Mary Josephine Rogers (1882–1955) founded the Foreign Mission Sisters of St. Dominic (Maryknoll Sisters) in 1912, the first American women religious committed to cross-cultural work. They sent their first missionaries abroad in 1921 to China (Robert 1997). The Oblate Sisters of Providence was the first Catholic religious order for Black and Native American women, founded in 1829. Women were attracted to Catholicism partly due to the community of saints that resonated with their traditional religions and Catholicism's willingness to reformulate indigenous religious rites. Catholicism provided the option of a religious vocation where single women could pursue orders and engage in meaningful work to help improve society. After Vatican II (1962–1965), Catholic missionary sisters were more fully considered agents of evangelization; no longer deemed auxiliary to the work of men, they refocused their work on addressing the roots of poverty and oppression in line with liberation theology.

Catholicism challenged American identity as a nation of English-speaking Protestants. Despite its long presence, modern Catholicism in North America is linked to immigration history of the nineteenth and twentieth centuries with the arrival of millions of Irish, Italians, Poles, and others. Catholics had to constantly defend their faith against Protestants, who generally perceived Catholics as did their English Protestant forebearers, as "papists" who could not possibly be loyal to both America and the pope in Rome. Catholics found their way by making substantial contributions to public life. They became known for their wide network of parochial schools, hospitals, orphanages, elder homes, and settlement houses. Catholic women were crucial in the acceptance of Catholicism to North American culture through their work in these social services, especially nursing, day care centers, and teaching. Women were generally far more effective than bishops or priests in addressing the challenges faced by immigrant communities (Ewens 1981). Elizabeth Anne Seton (1774–1821), for example, a widowed Catholic convert from the Episcopal church, opened a school for girls and established the Sisters of Charity in 1809 for work among the poor. She was the first American-born Catholic to reach sainthood (1975). By the year 1900, there were 40,000 Catholic sisters in the United States and nearly 4,000 parochial schools, all run by women. Catholic sisters enjoyed a huge amount of freedom compared to other women and

Photo 6.1 A young girl receives Catholic baptism during an Easter Vigil in Monrovia, California, US (2014). *Source:* Prayitno/Flickr/CC BY 2.0.

helped ensure their church's survival: "Though barred from the priesthood, they exercised a sacramental and educational ministry that was essential for Catholicism's continued existence" (Ewens 1981, p. 107). Nevertheless, the number of Catholic sisters in the US has dropped dramatically, from 181,421 in 1962 to 39,912 in 2020 (Berrelleza, Gautier, and Gray 2014; *Annuarium Statisticum Ecclesiae* 2020). Furthermore, roughly a quarter of sisters in the United States are foreign born (Johnson et al. 2019). There are an additional 9,628 women religious in Canada, Bermuda, and Saint Pierre and Miquelon (Greenland has no sisters, just one diocesan priest).

Catholic social action was an important contributor to twentieth-century civic life. Dorothy Day (1897–1980) established the Catholic Worker Movement in 1931 to combine socialist political thought with Catholic spirituality. She represented the paradox of many Catholic women of that century: influenced by conservative Catholic tradition but radical in social praxis. She and other Catholic women advocated for the dignity of all, including the right to procreate on their own terms, and worked against child labor laws and unsafe factory conditions. Yet, Pope Paul VI's encyclical, *Humanae Vitae* (1968), forbade any form of artificial birth control, which marked the first time in American Catholic history where the majority of Catholics deliberately ignored a major teaching of the church as they continued to engage in family planning (Noll 2019). Care for the unborn was always part of Catholic Social Teaching, but the 1973 *Roe v. Wade* landmark court decision legalizing abortion aligned conservative Catholics, Protestants, Latter-day Saints, and Jews like never before. Catholics in North America have moved well beyond their nineteenth- and twentieth-century marginalized status to full inclusion in national life. They did so partly due to their contributions to civil society and their political prowess, symbolized by the election of the US's first Catholic president in 1961, John F. Kennedy. In 2022, Catholics made up seven of the nine justices on the US Supreme Court (the remaining two were Jewish and Protestant), and two of those seven Catholics were women (Sonia Sotomayor and Amy Coney Barrett).

White Protestant Evangelicalism

Women were always the majority of White American churches, from the colonial period throughout the nineteenth century and to present day. While some women achieved prominence in the colonial period (Anne Hutchinson, Mary Dyer, Sarah Osborn), women were generally limited to the domestic sphere and to motherhood: "Mothers, it was thought, were the ones who could most effectively inculcate the virtues of public-spiritedness and self-sacrifice that were essential to the life of the republic" (Noll 2019, p. 165). The Second Great Awakening (1790s–1840s) was the first national event to encourage women – primarily White, middle- and upper-class women – to have identities outside of the home, and the church became the location of women's extra-domestic activity. Two-thirds of participants at the Cane Ridge revival that sparked the Second Great Awakening were women and children (Westerkamp 1999), and Methodist and Baptist churches made the most gains from the 1790s–1840s. Women had important roles in Methodist churches, with a role model in John Wesley's mother, Susanna Wesley (1669–1742), well known for her piety, wisdom, and spiritual leadership (Westerkamp 1999). As a result, women were active in Methodist ministry in the eighteenth century; the first Methodist woman licensed to preach was Sarah Crosby in 1791 (in England). Women exercised spiritual authority in new Evangelical networks, but that authority did not translate to the churches: "Evangelicalism gave women a voice, but when they exercised that voice many were judged the founders of scandal and divisions" (Westerkamp 1999, p. 169). While Baptist churches experienced tremendous growth during this time, women lost their agency as Baptist movements institutionalized. Both seventeenth-century Puritans and nineteenth-century post-revival Evangelicals saw women by nature as fundamentally different from men, and thus inferior.

Many women turned to overseas missions as the place to exercise not only spiritual influence, but also their talents in teaching, medicine, evangelism, partnership, and prayer. They founded their own separate women's mission boards from the general denominational boards to oversee their ministerial affairs separate from men – and they were highly effective. The Boston Female Society for Missionary Purposes formed in 1800 for mission among Native Americans; the next year, the Boston Female Society for Promoting the Diffusion of Christian Knowledge was founded. Several more women's organizations followed in Massachusetts, Connecticut, Pennsylvania, New York, New Jersey, and Maryland (Montgomery 1910); many of these formed before the well-known American Board of Commissioners for Foreign Mission (ABCFM) in 1810. The ABCFM became one of the most influential sending agencies in American Protestantism and sent its first missionaries to Asia in 1812: five married couples including Ann and Adoniram Judson in Burma, as well as Roxana Nott and Harriet Newell (the first American martyr to mission). The Progressive Era (1890s–1910s) marked height of the American foreign mission enterprise with women at the fore, and by 1890, women were 60% of the American missionary movement (Robert 1997). The Woman's Foreign Missionary Society of the Methodist Episcopal Church (WFMS, founded in 1869) was the most powerful mission organization of the late nineteenth and early twentieth centuries. By 1910, the WFMS had the largest budget, most teachers, most Bible women, largest number of schools and colleges, and most contributing members of any women's missionary organization in the United States, all founded and run by women (Robert 1997). Although women were highly influential in mission, female missionaries were not cultural radicals; they would not jeopardize their independence by challenging the male monopoly over the pulpit.

The twentieth century was a time of great change for American Evangelical Protestantism, including the start of American Pentecostalism, the optimism of the 1910 Edinburgh World Missionary Conference, the Fundamentalist-Modernist controversy, the massive decline of mainline Christianity in the United States and Canada, the tremendous impact of second-wave feminism, and the rise of politically motivated White Evangelicalism in the 1970s. The White Evangelicalism that has dominated American public discourse since the 1970s is arguably a movement more about culture than theology, characterized by a "militarized masculinity," complementarian theology, the rights of the unborn, and conservative Republic politics (Du Mez 2020) – all of which disproportionally impact women. The entanglement of national politics, economics, culture, religion, gender, and American identity has made Evangelicalism in the United States prone to strife and divisiveness, often with "women's issues" like leadership, healthcare, and sexuality front and center. This enmeshment led historian Mark Noll to declare in 1994, "Much of what is *distinctive* about American evangelicalism is not *essential* to Christianity" (Noll 1994, p. 243). While there are certainly many White women who retain conservative theological positions – such as the belief that women should not be pastors or preachers and the defense of so-called traditional family values – there is also a growing progressive Evangelical movement among women advocating for increased inclusion in the churches, challenging racist and sexist policies and structures, and pushing for LGBTQ+ rights. For example, the public theology and activism of Rachel Held Evans (1981–2019, American), Sarah Bessey (b.1979, Canadian), and Nadia Bolz-Weber (b.1969, American) have galvanized many "Exvangelical" women and like-minded progressive men to promote greater diversity, equality, and inclusion in Protestant churches, and specifically Evangelicalism.

Black Christianity

One of the most immediate consequences of the Doctrine of Discovery was the slave trade, with the first enslaved Africans arriving in 1502, and the direct passage of slave ships from Africa to the Americas beginning in 1525, all justified by fifteenth-century papal bulls of the Catholic Church. Between the first attack on West African villages in 1441 until the 1830s, more Africans than Europeans crossed the Atlantic to North and Latin America (Noll 2019). Between 1626 and 1875, an estimated one million enslaved people arrived in North America (Slave Voyages 2021). In Spanish, Portuguese, and French colonies, enslaved Africans mixed their traditional gods and spirits with Catholic saints to create new forms of popular Catholicism. Throughout the American colonies, enslaved Africans adopted Christianity on their own terms and in doing so, they challenged the legitimacy of slavery and engaged in abolitionist activities against their masters: men and women who also professed Christianity.

Blacks joined the new Evangelical movement in the First Great Awakening under the influence of prominent preachers like George Whitefield (1714–1770) and Jonathan Edwards (1703–1758). They became Christians in even greater numbers in the late eighteenth century (Harvey 2011), even though Whitefield promoted slavery in Georgia and South Carolina and Edwards owned enslaved Black people. The Independent African church movement began in the 1730s with the founding of Silver Bluff Church in South Carolina by David George (Noll 2019), followed by, among others, the First African Baptist Church of Savannah (1790, Andrew Bryan), Bethel African Methodist Episcopal Church (1794, Philadelphia, the first to ordain women), and the African Methodist Episcopal Church (1816, Richard Allen). Proclaiming a message of equality, the Awakenings were successful in attracting enslaved people, including Black women, to this new kind of Christianity (Raboteau 2001). The emphasis on a personal experience of God resonated equally with Blacks and Whites, but the many specific parallels between Evangelical faith and African spirituality included the de-emphasis of written language in favor of storytelling and oral Bible learning, extemporaneous prayer, preaching and testimony, and the emotional, experience-centered nature of revivals (Westerkamp 1999). Numerous Black women became evangelists and itinerant preachers, including Jarena Lee (1783–1864, who openly challenged Richard Allen to allow women preachers), Julia Foote (1823–1900, first female deacon of the African Methodist Episcopal Zion Church), Amanda Berry Smith (1837–1915, Wesleyan-Holiness preacher), Rebecca Cox Jackson (1795–1871, minister in a Shaker community), Zilpha Elaw (1790–1873, Methodist preacher), and Old Elizabeth (d.1866, itinerant preacher). Many of these women were freed Blacks preaching in southern slave-holding states at great risk to their own lives and freedom. Though Black women could not serve in church in all the capacities of men, they were respected for their spiritual power and gifts and helped overturn expectations for Black women of their time (Westerkamp 1999). Black women continued to be advocates, pioneers, and activists, as shown in their instrumental roles in the abolition movement (Harriet Tubman, Sojourner Truth), the birth of Pentecostalism (Jennie Evans Moore), and the 1960s Civil Rights Movement (Rosa Parks, Ella Baker).

Photo 6.2   Celebrating the Eucharist at the Episcopal Church of Southwest Florida, US (2014). *Source:* Episcopal Diocese of Southwest Florida/Flickr/CC BY 2.0.

Today, the term "Black Church" in the United States is generally used as an umbrella term for the historically Black denominations: National Baptist Convention USA, Church of God in Christ, African Methodist Episcopal, National Baptist Convention of America, Progressive National Baptist Convention, African Methodist Episcopal Zion, Christian Methodist Episcopal, and Full Gospel Baptist. The majority of Black Christians identify with these denominations (70% of women and 60% of men), with about 6% identifying as Catholic (Pew Research Center 2021a). Sociologists C. Eric Lincoln and Lawrence Mamiya observed in their landmark study of the Black Church that, "All of the seven mainline black denominations are characterized by a predominantly female membership and a largely male leadership, even though the major programs of the Black Church in politics, economics, or music depend heavily upon women for their promotion and success. However, although the public figures have usually been men, black women in each of the seven denominations have carved out their own space for leadership and power in the women's conventions in their denominations" (Lincoln and Mamiya 1990, p. 275). This is still the case today. Although the majority agree that women should be allowed to serve as senior church leaders (87% of Black women and 84% of Black men), only 16% of Black churches have female leaders (Pew Research Center 2021a; National Congregations Study 2019). However, this is up from the 4% reported by Lincoln and Mamiya in 1990.

Honored as "mothers of the church," Black women are involved in nearly every ministry imaginable. Again, Lincoln and Mamiya stated that, "The phenomenon of 'church mother' has no parallel in white churches; it is derived from the kinship network found within black churches and black communities" (Lincoln and Mamiya 1990, p. 275). Like elsewhere in the region and the world, Black women are more likely to believe in God (specifically the God of the Bible), pray daily, attend religious services, believe that prayer can heal illnesses, and say religion is very important in their lives (Pew Research Center 2021a). Black churches would hardly survive without the same women who are denied official leadership in their ranks.

Black Christian women face double discrimination for their race and their sex. Law professor Kimberlé Crenshaw coined the term "intersectionality" to describe the sexism and racism faced by Black women, which has now been widely adopted to describe the interconnectedness of race, class, and gender in light of discriminatory practices and systems. As Crenshaw has argued, "Because the intersectional experience is greater than the sum of racism and sexism, any analysis that does not take intersectionality into account cannot sufficiently address the particular manner in which Black women are subordinated" (Crenshaw 1998, p. 315). While both Black men (72%) and women (71%) say that opposing sexism is essential to their faith, only 28% of Black congregants had heard a sermon preached on sexism in their churches in the past year (Pew Research Center 2021a). Of those who had, they were more likely to hear that message from a Black church than a White or multiracial church. Although there are egalitarian leanings in Black communities, especially regarding equality in parenting, the common perception that men are leaders and women are followers still prevails and reduces women's opportunities to excel in congregational leadership.

Latino/a Christianity

While often considered the newest phenomenon of American religious diversity, Latino/as are indigenous to North America. Mexicans are among both the oldest and newest inhabitants of the US, living in the south, west, and southwest since before the US was the US (Noll 2019). The Treaty of Guadalupe Hidalgo (1846) and the Gadsden Purchase (1854) expanded the US's borders and made tens of thousands of Mexicans instant US citizens. With waves of immigrants arriving after the Mexican Revolution (1910–1920), hundreds of thousands were then deported during the Great Depression (1930s), before new labor programs encouraged them to come back in droves (1940s).

Latino/as are the largest immigrant group in the country, although they are by no means mono-lithic. In 2020, Latino/as were 18.5% of the total US population and 50.8% female (US Census Bureau 2020). Most migrants from Mexico and Central America are men seeking work opportu-nities across the US-Mexico border, whereas immigrants from the Caribbean, South America, Asia, and Europe are more likely to be women (Migration Policy Institute 2020).

Most Latino/as are Catholic but not in the same way as European-descended Catholics in the United States and Canada. There are more Hispanics in the United States than any other country in Latin America except Brazil and Mexico (Pew Research Center 2014). Roughly 55% of US Hispanics are Catholic, 22% are Protestant (*evangélicos*; most of which are converts from Catholicism), and 18% are unaffiliated (Pew Research Center 2014). Hispanic Christianity has a more Pentecostal/Charismatic flair, with, for example, 69% of Protestants and 49% of Catholics having witnessed speaking in tongues, prayer for miraculous healing, and prophesying in church. Though Latino/as were part of the Pentecostal movement in North America from its beginning, their participation was overshadowed by the story of Black-White integration in the early Pentecostal movement (Espinosa 2014). Indigenous Latino/as, especially women, helped spread Charles Parham's and William Seymour's Pentecostal message throughout the southwest, Puerto Rico, and Mexico (see Chapter 12). As is the typical pattern, Latinas are more religious than Latinos, with US Hispanic Catholic women, for example, reporting more regular Mass attendance, daily prayer, and that religion is very important in their lives (Pew Research Center 2014).

Church of Jesus Christ of Latter-day Saints

The headquarters of the Church of Jesus Christ of Latter-day Saints (Mormons) is in Salt Lake City, Utah, the hub for the world's 16.5 million Mormons. More than 5 million Latter-day Saints (LDS) live in the United States and 193,000 in Canada (Johnson and Zurlo 2022). In many ways, LDS rep-resent a quintessential American religion, where faith in God and democracy go hand-in-hand (Bowman 2012). Joseph Smith Jr. (1805–1844) observed fervent revivals in the so-called burned-over district of upstate New York during the Second Great Awakening but sensed God leading him to start a new church rather than join an existing one. As a self-declared prophet, Smith preached the coming millennium, the judgment of Christ, and exclusive salvation in the new Latter-day Saint church (Bowman 2012). The LDS canon consists of four books: the Bible, Book of Mormon, Doctrine and Covenants, and the Pearl of Great Price.

Smith's first wife, Emma Hale Smith (1804–1879), compiled a hymnbook and taught scriptures, but that was the closest any woman came to having revelations like men. Women were excluded from LDS priesthood and leadership but had distinct roles as wives and mothers, with marriage primarily sought as a divine purpose, not necessarily for love. Nineteenth-century Mormon polygamy encouraged men to take on additional wives as they moved higher in church rank. The historical record is unclear on how many wives Joseph Smith had, but it is estimated 30 in total, ranging between 14 and 56 in age (Bowman 2012). Mainstream Mormons practiced polygamy until it was outlawed in 1890. Many women defended the practice publicly but suffered silently from it; Emma despised it. Some small Mormon schisms continue to illegally practice polygamy today, such as the Fundamentalist Church of Jesus Christ of Latter-day Saints.

Initially, LDS did not encourage women to be missionaries like in other nineteenth- century churches: "The gendered particularities of Mormon organization were one thing the Mormons had in common with the mainstream of American society. American women in the 1840s had little access to government, little independence under the law, and few opportunities to gain power. But one route that stood open to them was the voluntary association" (Bowman 2012, p. 72). Mormon women were extremely active in what became the Mormon Relief Society, with notable women such as Sarah Kimball (1818–1898) and Eliza Snow (1804–1887). In 1898, single LDS women were permitted to serve on missions at age 21, with the first two women sent to England, Jennie Brimhall (1875–1957) and Inez Knight (1876–1937). In 2012, the minimum age was lowered to 19, which resulted in a massive spike in the number of female missionaries. In 2020, there were 51,800 full-time Mormon missionaries serving worldwide (Church of Jesus Christ of Latter-day Saints 2021). The statistics of gender in mission by generation reveals the increased prominence of women over time: 44.5% of female Mormon millennials have served on a mission (66% of men), 28% of female Gen X Mormons (53% of men), and 13% of Boomer Mormons (49% of men) (Riess 2019).

A small Mormon feminist movement dating to the 1970s critiques the church's emphasis on gendered submission, advocates for greater recognition of a Mother in heaven, the ordination of women to the priesthood, and increased gender equality. Though small, the movement has helped enact some changes in policy, such as the ability of women to wear pants in LDS church work (2017) and on the mission field (2018), and the unveiling of women's faces in temple endowment and burial services (2019). In 2020, the LDS church issued a new statement on feminism. While emphasizing the fundamental differences between men and women, especially their different roles in the family, the document supported "basic human rights" and "basic fairness" for women and encouraged them to be educated and serve society. Yet, it also cautioned against philosophies or ideologies that "distracted from (or even work against) the ideals of marriage and family" (Church of Jesus Christ of Latter-day Saints 2020).

North American Women in Theology

While there are earlier examples of female Christian theologians working in North America – such as Mildred Bangs Wynkoop (1905–1997, Nazarene) and Georgia Harkness (1891–1974, Methodist) – the women's movement of the 1960s and 1970s dramatically altered women's perceptions of themselves in North American society and powerfully impacted the churches.[2] Women in large numbers began to question the roles placed upon them by male-centered institutions: "While for generations women had seemingly accepted their subordination in church and synagogue as simply given, in the course of the 1960s they were increasingly aware of and angry at their marginalization" (Plaskow 2014, p. 22). Mary Daly's (1928–2010, post-Catholic) *The Church and the Second Sex* (1968) was a watershed moment for feminist theology in its call for the Catholic Church to enact real change for women. The 1970s gave rise to a new generation of female theologians, such as Rosemary Radford Reuther (1936–2022, Catholic), Monika Hellwig (1929–2005, Catholic), Sallie McFague (1933–2019, Anglican), and Mary Stewart Van Leeuwen (b.1943, Reformed Protestant).

The 1970s also saw the institutionalization of feminist studies of religion (not just Christian, but also Jewish) with the formation of the Working Group on Women and Religion at the joint meeting of the American Academy of Religion (AAR) and the Society of Biblical Literature in 1971, followed by the first female president of the AAR, Christine Downing (Plaskow 2014). Feminist biblical studies developed next, encouraged by Leonard Swidler's, "Jesus was a Feminist" (1971) and Phyllis Trible's, "Depatriarchalizing in Biblical Interpretation" (1973). Feminists of this period were keenly aware of the Bible's role in subordinating women and saw the need for women's liberation, its connection with liberation theology from Latin America, and wanted to sternly address Christian patriarchy. Because of these feminist scholars in the 1970s and 1980s, it

---

2 This section largely covers feminist and womanist theologies. Discussions of *mujerista*, African, and Asian feminist theologies are in their respective continental chapters.

is now widely known that women in the New Testament and church history were founders of congregations, prophetesses, leaders, missionaries, and apostles.

Second-wave feminism, however, was also deeply divisive for American Christianity, with a large sector eschewing feminism and its calls for abortion rights, freely available birth control, and the Equal Rights Amendment (the proposed amendment to the US constitution that would provide equal rights regardless of sex; it was introduced in Congress in 1923, approved in 1971, but never ratified). Perceived by many as an assault on traditional Christian family values, conservatives rejected the notions espoused by feminist theologians of the time, contributing to the growing chasm between "conservative" and "liberal" theologians that continues today.

Feminist theology largely overlooked the experiences of Black women and failed to take into consideration the wider context of race and class and how racism uniquely impacts Black women's lives. Similarly, Black liberation theology was authored by Black men, also leaving Black women out of the conversation. The emergence of womanist theology, centered around the experiences and perspectives of Black women, offered a corrective to the narratives of White Western feminism. Novelist Alice Walker (b.1944) coined the term "womanist" in the 1980s and theologian Delores S. Williams (1937–2022, Presbyterian) was the first to use the term "womanist theology" in 1987 (see Walker 1984; Williams 1993). Other early pioneers included Katie Cannon (1950–2018), the first Black woman ordained in the United Presbyterian Church (see Cannon 1988), and Methodist minister Jacquelyn Grant (b.1948) (see Grant 1989). Womanist theology is not centered merely around intellectual concepts, but also incorporates the richness of lived experience and a powerful belief in prayer and one's relationship with God. It celebrates the meaning that already exists in Black women's lives and is fundamentally communal (Mitchem 2002). Delores Williams's description of womanist theology called for radical subjectivity, traditional communalism, redemptive self-love, and critical engagement. Womanist theology seriously considers how race, class, gender, and all other forms of oppression informs theological reflection, enriches Black women's lives, and empowers them to enact change.

Theology is not only present in the ivory towers of academia, and North American Christianity has a strong outward-facing public theology as well. Among some conservative Evangelicals, the term "feminist" is gaining traction, perhaps defined differently than progressives but nevertheless points to the importance of viewing scripture, tradition, and history from women's perspectives for a more holistic understanding. Examples include the works of Beth Felker Jones (Northern Seminary), Kristen Deede Johnson (Western Theological Seminary), and Grace Ji-Sun Kim (Earlham School of Religion). On the other hand, many conservative churches do not believe that women should be theologically trained nor hold authority over men in church or the academy. Theologically conservative schools – even egalitarian ones – tend to have low women's enrollment because the congregations of potential female students are typically led by men and women do not have role models to suggest that theological education is a viable option for them (see Chapter 16).

Among the most prominent of public theologians is American Evangelical Beth Moore (b.1957, Baptist-turned-Anglican), the Bible teacher, evangelist, and founder of Living Proof Ministries. Since 1978, Moore has encouraged tens of thousands of women to follow Jesus and engage more deeply with scripture. She publicly and dramatically left the Southern Baptist Convention (SBC) in 2020 after years of critique over its support of Donald Trump for US president and calling out church leaders for objectifying women and dismissing sexual abuse claims. She also apologized for her former support of complementarian theology and critiqued the SBC for upholding White supremacy.

The #MeToo movement began in 2006 and went viral in 2017 after the sex abuse allegations against American film producer Harvey Weinstein. The movement expanded to Christianity with the hashtag #ChurchToo, begun by Emily Joy and Hannah Paasch on Twitter, to draw attention to sexual misconduct and other abuses of power in churches. While the clergy sex abuse scandals in the Catholic Church had been publicly known since at least 2001, the #ChurchToo movement helped shed light on abuse in Evangelical Protestant circles, such as the revelation in 2019 of hundreds of cases of sexual abuse in Southern Baptist churches in the prior 20 years. Furthermore, in 2022, a report by an outside firm hired by the SBC Executive Committee revealed that for nearly two decades, male leaders of the denomination lied to its members, covered up sexual scandals, and vilified victims of abuse. It also kept a database of all accused sex offenders in its ranks, with over 700 names of known and accused abusers. Many women see the #ChurchToo movement as an opportunity to push back against Evangelical teachings on gender and sexuality, in particular, "patriarchy, male leadership coupled with female submission, purity culture, evangelical personality cult culture, lack of sex-positive and medically accurate sex education, homophobia, and white supremacy" (Joy n.d.). The #ChurchToo movement is an example of the intersection between public theology and social media in North American Christianity, where women – with or without formal theological education – are using their voices in the digital sphere to draw attention to how Christianity as a whole, but especially American Evangelical subculture, has negatively impacted women.

Conclusion

Christianity in North America has been described as "feminine," but this is not typically considered a compliment. Although Christianity in this region has always been majority female, women have not historically been the primary decision-makers, theologians, historians, or even administrators of the churches. Up until the 1960s – and in some areas continuing to today – Christian women were expected to be silent submissive wives and mothers. The opening of possibilities to women more broadly in North American societies quickly expanded to the churches, with varying impacts. On the one hand, women have greater agency in North American churches than elsewhere in the world, with increasing numbers of theologically trained women, female pastors and clergy, and scholars. On the other hand, prominent conservative Evangelical thought still abounds where complementarian theology teaches that men and women are different but "complement" each other in marriage, family life, and the church. North American churches, such as the United Methodist Church and the Episcopal Church, are divided over the inclusion of LGBTQ+ people in their church communities. Women in North American churches often find themselves at the fault lines of splintering denominations, public scandals, and theological debates. Yet, like women elsewhere in the world, they continue in their callings, ministries, families, and communities to make important contributions to the life of the church.

Reflection Questions

1) Historian Ann Braude suggested that American religious history should be studied from the perspective of women's presence, and not men's absence. Describe the three aspects of this perspectival shift, and how they enhance our understanding of American Christian history. How does prioritizing social history over institutional history help uncover the contributions of women in the past?

2) Modern Catholicism in North America is linked to immigration patterns in the nineteenth and twentieth centuries that challenged American identity as a Protestant nation. How did the experiences of immigrant Catholics catalyze social action in the twentieth century, and who were some key figures of these movements? How did women contribute to the social acceptance of Catholicism in America?

3) In the 1960s and 1970s, feminist and womanist theologies developed in North America as part of broader second-wave feminism. Describe the progression of the feminist and womanist theological movement to the present day, noting key figures, events, and trends. What are some legacies of the theological innovations from this era?

Works Cited

Ahlstrom, Sydney E. (1972). *A Religious History of the American People*. New Haven: Yale University Press.

Alexander, Estrelda (2011). *Black Fire: One Hundred Years of African American Pentecostalism*. Downers Grove, IL: IVP Academic.

American Baptist Church (ABC) (2019). Women word. American Baptist women in ministry. Volume 7.

Secretaria Status, Rationarium Generale Ecclesiae (2020). *Annuarium Statisticum Ecclesiae: Statistical Yearbook of the Church*. Vatican City: Libreria Editrice Vatican.

Badillo, David A. (2006). *Latinos and the New Immigrant Church*. Baltimore, MD: Johns Hopkins University Press.

Baird, Robert (1844). *Religion in America, Or, an Account of the Origin, Progress, Relation to the State and Present Condition of the Evangelical Churches in the United States: With Notices of the Unevangelical Denominations*. New York: Harper & Bros.

Berrelleza, Erick, Gautier, Mary L., and Gray, Mark M. (2014). Population trends among religious institutes of women. Center for Applied Research in the Apostolate, Georgetown University.

Bibby, Reginald W. (1993). *Unknown Gods: The Ongoing Story of Religion in Canada*. Toronto: Stoddart.

Bowman, Matthew B. (2012). *The Mormon People: The Making of an American Faith*. New York: Random House.

Braude, Ann (1997). Women's history *Is* American religious history. In: *Retelling U.S. Religious History* (ed. Thomas Tweed), 87–107. Berkeley: University of California Press.

Braude, Ann (2008). *Sisters and Saints: Women and American Religion*. New York: Oxford University Press.

Brekus, Catherine A. (2007). Introduction: searching for women in narratives of American religious history. In: *The Religious History of American Women: Reimagining the Past* (ed. Catherine A. Brekus), 1–50. Chapel Hill: University of North Carolina Press.

Brown, Callum G. (2012). *Religion and the Demographic Revolution: Women and Secularization in Canada, Ireland, UK and USA since the 1960s*. Woodbridge: Boydell Press.

Campbell-Reed, Eileen (2018). State of clergywomen in the U.S.: a statistical update.

Cannon, Katie G. (1988). *Black Womanist Ethics*. Atlanta: Scholars Press.

Chaves, Mark and Eagle, Alison (2015). Religious congregations in 21st century America. National Congregations Study.

Church of Jesus Christ of Latter-day Saints (2020). What is the church's stance on feminism? https://www.churchofjesuschrist.org/study/new-era/2020/01/q-a/what-is-the-churchs-stance-on-feminism?lang=eng&fbclid=IwAR0lTT8kJtW34xNNuFhV02fYsRxU6D7_5LubUW9XRPGeGG40jVTPpNANFi8 (accessed 26 October 2021).

Church of Jesus Christ of Latter-day Saints (2021). 2020 statistical report for the April 2021 conference. April 3. https://newsroom.churchofjesuschrist.org/article/april-2021-general-conference-statistical-report (accessed 26 October 2021).

Crenshaw, Kimberlé (1998). Demarginalizing the intersection of race and sex: a black feminist critique of antidiscrimination doctrine, feminist theory, and antiracist politics. In: *Feminism and Politics* (ed. Anne Phillips), 314–343. New York: Oxford University Press.

Criales, Jessica (2019). 'Women of our nation': gender and Christian Indian communities in the United States and Mexico, 1753–1837. *Early American Studies*, 17(4), 415–442.

Du Mez, Kristin K. (2020). *Jesus and John Wayne: How White Evangelicals Corrupted a Faith and Fractured a Nation*. New York: Liveright.

Espinosa, Gastón (2014). *William J. Seymour and the Origins of Global Pentecostalism: A Biography and Documentary History*. Durham, NC: Duke University Press.

Ewens, Mary (1981). The leadership of nuns in immigrant Catholicism. In: *Women and Religion in America, Volume 1: The Nineteenth Century* (ed. Rosemary R. Ruether and Rosemary S. Keller), 101–149. San Francisco: Harper and Row.

Fisher, Linford D. (2012). *The Indian Great Awakening: Religion and the Shaping of Native Cultures in Early America*. New York: Oxford University Press.

Grant, Jacquelyn (1989). *White Women's Christ and Black Women's Jesus: Feminist Christology and Womanist Response*. Atlanta: Scholars Press.

Haddad, Yvonne (2006). Introduction: becoming American—religion, identity, and institution building in the American mosaic. In: *Religion and Immigration: Christian, Jewish, and Muslim Experiences in the United States* (ed. Yvonne Y. Haddad, Jane I. Smith, and John L. Esposito), 1–18. Lanham, MD: Altamira Press.

Han, Sang Shin. ed. (2016). *Han-In Chong-hwe 40Nyun: HweKoWa ChunMang*. The Association of Korean Churches in The United Methodist Church.

Harvey, Paul (2011). *Through the Storm, through the Night: A History of African American Christianity*. Lanham, MD: Rowman & Littlefield Publishers, Inc.

Johnson, Mary et al. (2019). *Migration for Mission: international Catholic Sisters in the United States*. New York: Oxford University Press.

Johnson, Todd M. and Zurlo, Gina A. ed. (2022). *World Christian Database*. Leiden/Boston: Brill.

Jones, Jeffrey (2021). U.S. Church membership falls below majority for first time. Gallup. March 29. https://news.gallup.com/poll/341963/church-membership-falls-below-majority-first-time.aspx (accessed 28 October 2021).

Joy, Emily (n.d.) "#ChurchToo" emily joy poet: blog. http://emilyjoypoetry.com/churchtoo (accessed 28 October 2021).

Klein, Herbert S. (2004). *A Population History of the United States*. Cambridge, UK: Cambridge University Press.

Lincoln, C. Eric and Mamiya, Lawrence H. (1990). *The Black Church in the African American Experience*. Durham, NC: Duke University Press.

Lipka, Michael (2016). A closer look at jehovah's witnesses living in the U.S. Pew Research Center. https://www.pewresearch.org/fact-tank/2016/04/26/a-closer-look-at-jehovahs-witnesses-living-in-the-u-s (accessed 12 July 2022).

Migration Policy Institute (2020). Immigrant women and girls in the United States. March 4. https://www.migrationpolicy.org/article/immigrant-women-and-girls-united-states-2018 (accessed 21 October 2021).

Miller, Robert J. (2008). *Native America, Discovered and Conquered: Thomas Jefferson, Lewis & Clark, and Manifest Destiny*. Lincoln, NE: University of Nebraska Press.

Milloy, John S. (2017). *A National Crime: The Canadian Government and the Residential School System*. 2nd edn. Winnipeg: University of Manitoba Press.

Mitchem, Stephanie Y. (2002). *Introducing Womanist Theology*. Maryknoll, NY: Orbis Books.

Montgomery, Helen Barrett (1910). *Western Women in Eastern Lands: Fifty Years of Woman's Work in Foreign Missions*. New York: The Macmillan Company.

Moore, Robert L. (1994). *Selling God: American Religion in the Marketplace of Culture*. New York: Oxford University Press.

National Congregations Study (2019). https://www.norc.org/Research/Projects/Pages/national-congregations-study.aspx (accessed 21 October 2021).

Noll, Mark A. (1994). *The Scandal of the Evangelical Mind*. Grand Rapids, MI: W.B. Eerdmans.

Noll, Mark A. (2019). *A History of Christianity in the United States and Canada*. 2nd edn. Grand Rapids, MI: William B. Eerdmans Publishing Company.

Park, Soyoung (2001). The intersection of religion, race, gender, and ethnicity in the identity formation of Korean American evangelical women. In: *Korean Americans and Their Religions: Pilgrims and Missionaries from a Different Shore* (ed. Ho-Youn Kwon, Kwang-Chung Kim, and R. Stephen Warner), 193–208. University Park: Pennsylvania State University Press.

Pew Research Center (2014). Religion in Latin America: widespread change in a historically catholic region.

Pew Research Center (2018). When Americans say they believe in god, what do they mean?

Pew Research Center (2019). In U.S., decline of christianity continues at rapid pace.

Pew Research Center (2021a). Faith among Black Americans.

Pew Research Center (2021b). Measuring religion in Pew Research Center's American trends panel.

Plaskow, Judith (2014). Movement and emerging scholarship: feminist biblical scholarship in the 1970s in the United States. In: *Feminist Biblical Studies in the Twentieth Century: Scholarship and Movement* (ed. Elisabeth S. Fiorenza), 21–34. Atlanta: Society of Biblical Literature.

Raboteau, Albert J. (2001). *Canaan Land: A Religious History of African Americans*. New York: Oxford University Press.

Riess, Jana (2019). *The Next Mormons: How Millennials are Changing the LDS Church*. New York: Oxford University Press.

Robert, Dana L. (1997). *American Women in Mission: A Social History of Their Thought and Practice*. Macon, GA: Mercer University Press.

Schnabel, Landon (2015). How religious are American women and men? gender differences and similarities. *Journal for the Scientific Study of Religion*, 54(3), 616–622.

Slave Voyages (2021). Trans-Atlantic slave trade – estimates. https://www.slavevoyages.org/assessment/estimates (accessed 14 September 2021).

US Census Bureau (2020). QuickFacts: United States. https://www.census.gov/quickfacts/fact/table/US/RHI725219 (accessed: 21 October 2021).

Walker, Alice (1984). *In Search of Our Mothers' Gardens: Womanist Prose*. San Diego: Harcourt Brace Jovanovich.

Westerkamp, Marilyn J. (1999). *Women in Early American Religion 1600–1850: The Puritan and Evangelical Traditions*. Taylor and Francis.

Williams, Delores S. (1993). *Sisters in the Wilderness: The Challenge of Womanist God-Talk*. Maryknoll, NY: Orbis Books.

7

Women in Oceanic Christianity

"The goal is not reverse discrimination, women dominating men, but a new heaven and a new earth taking hold, with no one being dominated or subordinated, each participating according to their gifts in genuine mutuality."

Emi Frances Oh (Oh 2003, p. 148)

As is the case nearly everywhere in the world, Christian congregations in Oceania are majority female but most churches and Christian organizations in the region are run by men (Bouma, Ling, and Pratt 2010).[1] The women's liberation movement beginning in the 1960s helped spur women into new areas of educational advancement and leadership, providing additional freedoms in employment, pay, and reproductive rights that continue to increase in the twenty-first century. New Zealanders, for example, have elected two women as prime ministers, Helen Clark (1999–2008) and Jacinda Ardern (2017–2023), and Australians have elected one, Julia Gillard (2010–2013). In the Pacific Islands (Melanesia, Micronesia, and Polynesia), more women are becoming politicians, clergy, and theological educators, though inequalities persist. For instance, Vanuatu remains one of the few countries in the world with no women in parliament (Prior 2021). In the islands, "feminism" and "gender equality" are widely considered Western ideologies and a poor fit for island culture. These concepts are perceived as attempts to devalue the contributions of men to raise women above them (Kavafolau 2021). Women in the Pacific Islands are generally expected to be subservient to men and be primarily active in the domestic sphere. Regional differences exist, such as in Polynesia, where Tahitian women have decision-making capabilities in society alongside men, and in Tonga, where women can achieve higher positions similar to men. However, in Melanesia it is culturally acceptable for women to be dominated by men and as a result, gender-based violence is a significant problem (covered in more depth in Chapter 14) (Kavafolau 2021).

The geography of Oceania – the "liquid continent" – is unlike that of anywhere else in the world: nearly every country in the region is an island, ranging in size from Australia (three million square miles, 26 million people) to Tokelau (four square miles, 1,350 people). The Pacific Islands were the last reached by European and American colonization and thus the most recent region to decolonize (Williams 2021), beginning with Samoa in 1962. There are still some countries that have yet to achieve full independence, such as French Polynesia and American Samoa. Oceania is

---

1 According to the United Nations, Oceania consists of the following countries: American Samoa, Australia, Cook Islands, Fiji, French Polynesia, Guam, Kiribati, Marshall Islands, Micronesia, Nauru, New Caledonia, New Zealand, Niue, Northern Mariana Islands, Palau, Papua New Guinea, Samoa, Solomon Islands, Tokelau, Tonga, Tuvalu, Vanuatu, and Wallis and Futuna Islands.

Women in World Christianity: Building and Sustaining a Global Movement, First Edition. Gina A. Zurlo.

frequently left off the map in discussions of Christianity's shift to the global South. Part of the reason is geographic, given that much of the population lives in small island nations that are technically difficult to include from a cartographic perspective. However, it is also historical, given that the arrival of Christianity to the region was first via the British, using Australia as a penal colony for convicted felons (both male and female). Oceania is technically in the global South, but it encountered Christianity before many places in Africa and Asia. Australia and New Zealand are experiencing secularization processes similar to Western Europe, but the Pacific Islands are retaining their deeply held Christian identities that are now completely intertwined with local cultures and societies (Ernst 1994). The region is also overlooked because of its small population size compared to the dramatic growth and size of Christianity in, for example, sub-Saharan Africa.

At the same time, Oceania can be considered a microcosm of World Christianity. Like the global North, Australia and New Zealand are widely considered to be post-Christian contexts; Australia is 35% nonreligious (atheists and agnostics together) and New Zealand is 36% (Johnson and Zurlo 2022). However, religion in the Pacific Islands more closely mirrors trends in sub-Saharan Africa and Asia, where Christianity arrived comparatively later, grew quickly, and has been sustained by local leaders, evangelists, and theologians.

Oceania is marked by a wide socioeconomic gap, ranging from stable and wealthy Australia (Gross Domestic Product [GDP] $1.3 trillion) and New Zealand (GDP $212.5 billion) to Tuvalu (GDP $48.9 million), which, with the lowest GDP in the world, is one of its least developed countries. Many of the Pacific Islands have virtually no exports and poverty and unemployment are high. Pasifika peoples – the term that connects Pacific Islanders at home and in the diaspora in Australia and New Zealand – are also highly mobile, frequently on the move in search of work and education (Williams 2021). New Zealand is home to larger populations of people from the Cook Islands, Niue, and Tokelau than on the respective islands themselves, with also many large communities of Samoans, Tongans, and Fijians. Migration to the United States is also common via Hawai'i and USA-administered American Samoa, as in the case of Tongan and Samoan Latter-day Saints migrating to Utah. Pacific Islander diasporic churches tend to flourish with their strong cultural emphases on faith, family, and community (Williams 2021).

Christianity in Oceania, 1900–2050

Between 1900 and 2020, Oceania reported a decline in its Christian population from 77% to 67% (Table 7.1), but this masks intricacies in the data that make this region unique. Australia and New Zealand carry the continent's demographic weight, with 26 million and 5 million people, respectively; between 1900 and 2020, Christianity declined in those two countries from 97% to 57% (Johnson and Zurlo 2022). The religious demographics of Australia/New Zealand resemble those in Western Europe: a declining Christianity replaced with increased nonreligious (less than 1% in 1900 to 33% in 2020) and more religious diversity. Buddhists, Muslims, and Hindus are each around 2% of the continent's population and growing.

Melanesia, Micronesia, and Polynesia have a different trajectory for their religious demographics since many of these island nations became Christian in the nineteenth and twentieth centuries and have not experienced nearly the same level of decline as Australia/New Zealand – or any decline at all. Melanesia grew from 15% Christian in 1900 to 92% in 2020; Micronesia grew from 76% to 93%, and Polynesia dropped only slightly from 99% to 96% (Johnson and Zurlo 2022). For this reason, it is difficult to speak about Christian trends in Oceania as a whole, given the tremendous historical, religious, and demographic differences between Australia/New Zealand and the Pacific Islands.

Table 7.1 Religions in Oceania over 1%, 1900–2050.

Religion	Pop. 1900	% 1900	Rate % p.a. 1900–2000	Pop. 2020	% 2020	Rate % p.a. 2020–2050	Pop. 2050	% 2050
Christians	4,837,000	77.4	1.64	28,652,000	67.1	0.65	34,776,000	60.6
Agnostics	43,800	0.7	4.61	8,281,000	19.4	1.59	13,303,000	23.2
Atheists	900	0.0	7.13	1,732,000	4.1	2.24	3,365,000	5.9
Buddhists	6,500	0.1	4.34	980,000	2.3	1.42	1,497,000	2.6
Muslims	12,600	0.2	3.52	888,000	2.1	1.54	1,403,000	2.4
Hindus	15,400	0.2	3.26	815,000	1.9	1.12	1,137,000	2.0
Ethnic religionists	1,299,000	20.8	−1.43	462,000	1.1	0.36	514,000	0.9

Source: Data from Johnson and Zurlo 2022. p.a. = percent change per annum, or each year.

Table 7.2 Christianity in Oceania by region, 2020.

Region	Majority religion	Pop. 2020	% Christian 2020	Christian pop. 2020	% Christian female 2020	% pop. female 2020
Oceania	Christians	42,678,000	67.1	28,652,000	51.7	49.9
Australia/New Zealand	Christians	30,322,000	56.9	17,244,000	53.4	50.3
Melanesia	Christians	11,123,000	92.1	10,239,000	48.9	49.0
Micronesia	Christians	549,000	93.1	511,000	51.0	49.7
Polynesia	Christians	684,000	96.1	657,000	51.2	49.0

Source: Data from Johnson and Zurlo 2022.

Table 7.3 Countries in Oceania with the most Christians, 2020.

Rank	Country	Largest Christian tradition	Pop. 2020	% Christian 2020	Christian pop. 2020	% Christian female 2020	% pop. female 2020
1	Australia	Catholics	25,500,000	57.3	14,620,000	53.1	50.2
2	Papua New Guinea	Protestants	8,947,000	94.8	8,482,000	48.3	48.9
3	New Zealand	Protestants	4,822,000	54.4	2,624,000	55.4	50.8
4	Solomon Islands	Protestants	687,000	95.3	654,000	52.1	49.2
5	Fiji	Protestants	896,000	63.9	573,000	52.7	49.4
6	Vanuatu	Protestants	307,000	93.4	287,000	49.9	49.3
7	French Polynesia	Catholics	281,000	93.8	264,000	52.0	49.4
8	New Caledonia	Catholics	285,000	85.1	243,000	51.6	49.7
9	Samoa	Protestants	198,000	98.8	196,000	50.6	48.2
10	Guam	Catholics	169,000	94.0	159,000	51.4	49.6

Source: Data from Johnson and Zurlo 2022.

Table 7.4 Countries in Oceania with the highest percent Christian female, 2020.

Rank	Country	Largest Christian tradition	Pop. 2020	% Christian 2020	Christian pop. 2020	% Christian female 2020	% pop. female 2020
1	New Zealand	Protestants	4,822,000	54.4	2,624,000	55.4	50.8
2	Niue	Protestants	1,600	96.7	1,600	53.6	48.2
3	Australia	Catholics	25,500,000	57.3	14,620,000	53.1	50.2
4	American Samoa	Protestants	55,200	98.0	54,100	53.0	48.2
5	Nauru	Protestants	10,800	75.0	8,100	52.9	49.6
6	Marshall Islands	Protestants	59,200	95.0	56,300	52.8	49.6
7	Fiji	Protestants	896,000	63.9	573,000	52.7	49.4
8	Solomon Islands	Protestants	687,000	95.3	654,000	52.1	49.2
9	French Polynesia	Catholics	281,000	93.8	264,000	52.0	49.4
10	Northern Mariana Islands	Catholics	57,600	81.2	46,700	51.7	49.6

Source: Data from Johnson and Zurlo 2022.

Women are the majority of Christians in Oceania by a slight majority according to official census data. The lower share of Christian women in Melanesia (49%, Table 7.2) is due to Papua New Guinea, where the most recent census reported 48% female for all Christian traditions.

Australia is the country with the most Christians in Oceania (Table 7.3), followed by Papua New Guinea and New Zealand. Among these countries, New Zealand reports the highest Christian female percent at 55%, largely due to the 2013 census report of 57% female for the Anglican Church of Aotearoa, New Zealand, and Polynesia, the largest denomination in the country. Even Catholics in New Zealand report 54% female, higher than Catholics elsewhere in the world. In fact, the lowest percent Christian female in New Zealand is still 52%, indicating higher female membership rates across Christian traditions.

The list of countries with the highest percent Christian female in Oceania (Table 7.4) brings some of the smaller island nations to the fore. Niue reports the second highest percent Christian female at 54%, a country with 1,600 people in 100 square miles. Other higher percentages (53% each) are reported in American Samoa, Nauru, Marshall Islands, and Fiji.

There are many different Christian families in Oceania, but Catholics and Anglicans are the vast majority given their long presence in the region (Table 7.5; Protestants are 49% of all Christians, Figure 7.1). Although Australia was a majority Anglican country from its beginning, Catholicism grew tremendously via immigration such that by 2015, Protestants (which includes Anglicans) and Catholics were nearly equal in size. While Anglicanism is declining due to secularizing factors, the arrival of Catholic immigrants continues from such places as the Philippines. In 2020, Australia was 26% Catholic and 23% Protestant (Johnson and Zurlo 2022). Although according to census data, it does not look like women represent a large share of churches in the region (Table 7.2), surveys have reported that women make up the majority of church attenders in Australia and New Zealand by a much wider margin:

- Anglican Church of Australia, 61% female (Powell, Pepper, and Hancock 2016)
- Uniting Church in Australia, 63% female (Powell, Pepper, and Hancock 2016)
- Presbyterian Church of New Zealand, 62% female (Presbyterian Church of Aotearoa New Zealand 2016).

Table 7.5   Christian families in Oceania, 2000 and 2015.

Family	Affiliated 2000	Affiliated 2015	% female 2015	Rate % p.a. 2000–2015
Latin-rite Catholic	7,788,000	9,297,000	51.1	1.19
Anglican	4,891,000	4,541,000	54.0	−0.49
Pentecostal/Charismatic*	1,130,000	2,203,000	50.4	4.55
United church or joint mission	2,075,000	1,962,000	53.2	−0.37
Lutheran	1,197,000	1,382,000	49.4	0.96
Eastern Orthodox	707,000	918,000	52.2	1.75
Adventist	488,000	599,000	50.0	1.37
Reformed, Presbyterian	688,000	596,000	53.4	−0.95
Methodist	588,000	585,000	53.1	−0.04
Latter-day Saints (Mormons)	387,000	561,000	51.7	2.50
Other Protestant/Independent	393,000	508,000	53.0	1.72
Baptist	292,000	389,000	50.9	1.93
Nondenominational	296,000	369,000	49.6	1.49
Eastern-rite Catholic	232,000	322,000	52.0	2.23
Jehovah's Witnesses	150,000	173,000	55.2	0.97
Congregational	156,000	161,000	54.3	0.21
Holiness	103,000	135,000	48.8	1.83
Restorationist, Disciple	122,000	135,000	52.5	0.64
Oriental and other Orthodox	75,000	105,000	50.3	2.27
Christian Brethren	87,400	93,800	51.7	0.47
Salvationist	97,100	78,900	55.0	−1.37
Friends (Quaker)	2,500	2,500	61.5	0.00
Nontraditional, house, cell	500	800	55.0	3.18

Source: Data from Johnson and Zurlo 2022. p.a. = percent change per annum, or each year.
*Excluding partially pentecostalized.

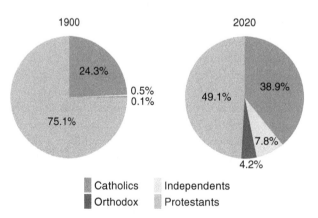

Figure 7.1   Christianity in Oceania by major Christian tradition, 1900 and 2020. *Source:* Data from Johnson and Zurlo 2022.

The Pentecostal/Charismatic movement has experienced the most growth in the last few decades, now representing 11% of the continent's population (Johnson and Zurlo 2022). In the 1980s and 1990s, renewal movements spread and new Pentecostal, Charismatic, and Evangelical churches, part of increased globalization, helped to link Oceania to the rest of the world (Ernst 2006). The Assemblies of God (AoG) is the oldest Pentecostal denomination in the region and in many countries – such as American Samoa, Samoa, Fiji, and Vanuatu – schisms from the AoG have led to the creation of new Pentecostal groups. Other increases include Oriental and other Orthodox (via immigration), Eastern-rite Catholics (immigration), and Latter-day Saints (conversion in the Pacific Islands). Latter-day Saints grew tremendously through missionary activity; as a result, Tonga and Samoa are the only majority-Mormon countries in the world, 64% and 41%, respectively (Johnson and Zurlo 2022).

The largest denominations in Oceania are, naturally, in the largest countries: Australia, New Zealand, and Papua New Guinea (Table 7.6). The fastest growth rate in these denominations was among the Assemblies of God in Papua New Guinea, with an astounding increase of over 9% per year between 2000 and 2015. Many of these new Pentecostals are Christians from historic denominations.

The World Values Survey, the most widely used global survey with questions on religion, only includes Australia and New Zealand from Oceania in its dataset. Wave 7 (2017–2020) reported very low levels of religiosity in these two countries. Together, 55% of respondents in Australia/New Zealand reported "never" or "practically never" attending religious services, 48% "never" or "practically never" pray, and 41% reported that religion was "not at all important" in their lives. There was little difference between men and women on these measures (Haerpfer et al. 2020). Yet, the 2016 National Church Life Survey (NCLS) in Australia reported that church attenders were 60% female and 40% male, a constant figure since 2006. According to the NCLS, women outnumber

Table 7.6 Largest denominations in Oceania, 2015.

Rank	Country	Denomination	Year begun	Affiliated 2015	% Christian female	Rate % p.a. 2000–2015
1	Australia	Catholic Church in Australia	1803	5,158,000	52.0	1.00
2	Australia	Anglican Church of Australia	1788	3,500,000	54.0	−0.68
3	Papua New Guinea	Catholic Church in Papua New Guinea	1847	2,200,000	48.3	2.02
4	Australia	Uniting Church in Australia	1809	1,200,000	56.0	−0.73
5	Papua New Guinea	Evangelical Lutheran Church of Papua New Guinea	1886	950,000	48.3	1.03
6	Papua New Guinea	United Church in Papua New Guinea	1871	630,000	48.3	0.25
7	New Zealand	Anglican Church in Aotearoa, New Zealand, and Polynesia	1814	600,000	56.9	−0.63
8	Papua New Guinea	Assemblies of God	1948	562,000	48.3	9.21
9	Australia	Greek Orthodox Church (Archdiocese of Australia)	1896	550,000	51.0	2.04
10	New Zealand	Catholic Church in New Zealand	1838	521,000	54.1	0.85

Source: Data from Johnson and Zurlo 2022. p.a. = percent change per annum, or each year.

men in all denominations and age groups (Powell, Pepper, and Kerr 2018). Ruth Powell, director of NCLS research, has suggested that the imbalance is related to differences in socialization of boys (independent, self-reliant) versus girls (interdependent, responsible for others), Australian male rejection of authority structures, greater emotional capacities for women, and increased status for women's roles in the churches (Powell 2017). Pre-NCLS, an analysis of the Australian Values Study Survey in 1987 suggested that Australian men prefer "mateship" over religious authority, found more so in the pub across the street from the church, a central place for Australian male identity (Kaldor 1987).

The Gender and Congregational Life Survey (2021) included 146 responses (11% of all respondents worldwide) from Oceania, including Australia, New Zealand, and from Papua New Guinea. Respondents were majority female (88%), married (74%), and well-educated (84% with bachelor's degree or higher). The largest Christian families represented were Anglican (35%), Baptist (26%), and Pentecostal (13%), with a wide range of church sizes (29% between 101 and 200 and 16% over 500). Sixty-one percent reported about the same number of women and men in their main weekly worship service (the most important ministry of the church at 92%).

Most respondents (93%) agreed or strongly agreed that women should be allowed to serve as pastors (higher than the 84% of all respondents worldwide), and 92% agreed or strongly agreed that it is harder for women to be accepted in leadership roles in the church. Slightly more than half (54%) believed that the Bible places restrictions on women's roles in the church (much lower than respondents in Asia, Africa, and Latin America). All respondents from Holiness, Congregational, and Lutheran denominations were highly favorable toward women's pastoral roles and leadership; the lowest support was among members of Reformed Presbyterian and nondenominational churches. The survey illustrated the gendered expectations and realities for men and women in church life, where respondents felt it would be easier for women than men to only obtain the positions of administrative assistant and children's Sunday school teacher (Figure 7.2).

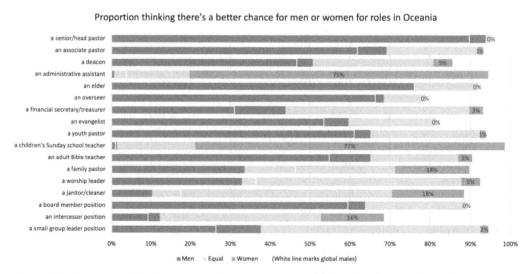

Figure 7.2 How do you think the chances of women and men compare when it comes to getting a ___ position? (Oceania). *Source:* Adapted from Gender and Congregational Life Survey (2021).

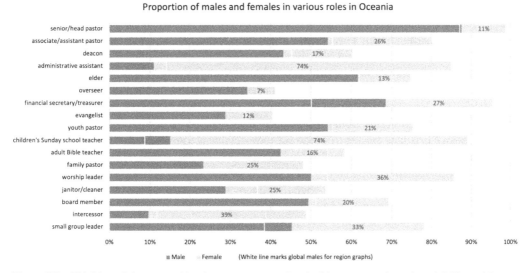

Figure 7.3 Thinking of the ___ position in your congregation, is this person male or female? (Oceania). *Source:* Adapted from Gender and Congregational Life Survey (2021).

The most frequently reported roles for women were children's Sunday school teacher (74%) and administrative assistant (74%) (Figure 7.3). Women in Oceania were more likely than the global average to serve in a variety of congregational positions: associate/assistant pastor, deacon, administrative assistant, elder, evangelist, youth pastor, adult Bible teacher, family pastor, worship leader, janitor/cleaner, board member, and intercessor (Figure 7.3). Eleven percent of respondents from Oceania had a female head or senior pastor, higher than the 8% global average.

Women in Oceanic Christianity: Past and Present

The histories, cultures, and encounters with Christianity in Australia/New Zealand are so different from those in Melanesia, Micronesia, and Polynesia that they are treated separately here. Oceania's "left off the map" theme rang true at the Edinburgh 1910 World Missionary Conference, where the region was already considered part of Christendom and thus not a priority for the conference (Stanley 2009). The apparent greatest missiological minds of the North Atlantic considered the task of evangelization in the Pacific Islands nearly complete, except New Guinea (indeed, Melanesia was only 15% Christian in 1900, of which New Guinea represented its largest population). With no participants from the Pacific Islands at the event, the region did not attract attention in any of the conference commissions though its inhabitants were considered a "mixture of fully Christianised and heathen" (Stanley 2009, p. 255). The evangelization of the Pacific Islands happened both in partnership between European and indigenous missionaries, as well as by natural contact between Islanders on the move throughout the region (Williams 2021). This vibrant indigenous missionary movement was completely overlooked by Christian leaders in Europe and North America.

Australia/New Zealand

Christianity came to Australia in 1788 by way of Anglican chaplains to what is now Sydney, to minister to the convict population; the first Catholic priests (also convicts) arrived in 1800. In New Zealand, Protestantism (Church Missionary Society, CMS) arrived in 1814 and Catholicism (Marists) in 1838. British forces dispossessed indigenous Aboriginal and Torres Strait Islanders in Australia and Māori in New Zealand, forcing upon them British sovereignty as they replaced indigenous lands, languages, cultures, and religions. Though British colonization of the indigenous Māori population began 25 years after the missionaries' arrival, CMS missionaries failed to protect the local population from British political and land interests before the signing of the Treaty of Waitangi in 1840 (signed by 13 female Māori leaders alongside hundreds of male Māori leaders). The Aboriginal population in Australia declined from 300,000 in 1770 to 80,000 by 1900; meanwhile, the Māori population dropped from 80,000 in 1840 to 46,000 in 1900. Most deaths were due to lack of immunity from European diseases. Distrust between indigenous populations and European Christians existed from the start, especially as transplanted Christianity grew.

Among the arriving convicts in the first two decades of Australian settlement were White women. A total of 9,422 women (compared to 78,077 men convicts) arrived in New South Wales between 1788 and 1841 when transportation ended (Summers 2016, p. 410). Many of these women were sexually abused on the journey and had little recourse to support themselves upon arrival other than prostitution, a reputation that was nearly impossible to shed. In colonial Australia (1788–1901), Aboriginal women faced a double burden as indigenous people and female, subject to the whims of powerful White men in addition to the range of hostilities against indigenous populations. Christian Aboriginal women became leaders in grassroots activism for indigenous peoples liberation, especially among other women, such as Emma Timbery ("Queen of la Perouse" or "Granny Timbery," c.1842–1916, Mulgoa), Gladys Nicholls (1906–1981, Djadjawurrung, Baraparapa, and Punjabi Indian), and Margaret Lilardia Tucker ("Auntie Marge," 1904–1996, Yorta Yorta and Wiradjuri) (see Grimshaw 2011). European missionary women ministered via education, nursing, and evangelization while colonial settler governments separated Aboriginal children from their families and attempted to destroy Aboriginal culture (Cruickshank and Grimshaw 2019). While tasked with "protecting" Aboriginal girls and supporting missionary men's endeavors, missionary women were caught between the expectations of settler governments and their own understanding of the missionary task. Settler governments looked to missionaries to "manage" Aboriginal people, and for women, this often took the form of running residential children's homes that devastated indigenous families (Cruickshank and Grimshaw 2019, p. 176). All of this is while missionary women were supposed to be modeling ideal Christian familial relationships.

Catholicism and Anglicanism are the two largest denominations in Australia and New Zealand, though Anglicans in both countries have experienced greater decline than Catholics. Catholics

Table 7.7 Catholics and Anglicans in Australia and New Zealand, 1901 and 2013/2016.

	% Catholic	% female in Catholic tradition	% Anglican	% female in Anglican tradition
Australia				
1901	23.1	49.1	40.3	47.7
2016	22.6	52.5	13.3	53.7
New Zealand				
1901	14.2	48.2	41.8	47.7
2013	11.6	53.6	10.8	58.0

Source: Census data, reported in Johnson and Zurlo 2019.

have been able to offset shrinkage with immigration from Europe and Southeast Asia, especially among Filipinos. Between 1901 and 2016, the percent female of both Catholics and Anglicans remained rather stable in Australia, whereas the proportion of women in these churches increased in New Zealand (Table 7.7).

Anglican women have had prominent roles in Australia and New Zealand, pioneering new areas of leadership and advocating for gender justice. In 1992, Barbara Darling (1948–2015) was among the first female priests in the Anglican Church of Australia (ordained in 1992), and then became the first female bishop in the Diocese of Melbourne in 2008. Sarah Macneil (b.1955) was the first female diocesan bishop (Diocese of Grafton) in 2014, and in 2017, Kay Goldsworthy (b.1956) became the first Australian Anglican female archbishop (Reed 2021). Yet, the Anglican Church in Australia is split on the issue of women's ordination, as the dioceses of Ballarat, North West Australia, Sydney, and The Murray do not ordain women as priests. In 1995, 4% of Australian Anglican priests were women, and this increased to 19% by 2013 (Anglican Church of Australia 1995; Scarfe 2014).

In 1893, New Zealand became the first self-governing country in the world to allow women to vote in national elections, a true trendsetter in first-wave feminism. In 1977, the Anglican Church of Aotearoa, New Zealand, and Polynesia became one of the first Anglican churches in the world to ordain women to the priesthood. The first female diocesan bishop was Penelope Jamieson (b.1942), consecrated as Bishop of Dunedin in 1990. Māori women are an important part of the church: the first Māori priest, Puti Murray (1922–2005), was ordained in Te Kao in 1978 (Honoré 2013); the first female Māori bishop, Waitohiariki Quayle (b.1950), was ordained a deacon in 2013 a priest in 2014, and archdeacon of Wairarapa from 2015 to 2019.

Indigenous peoples also pioneered their own forms of Christianity. The Ratana Church (est. 1918) and Ringatu Church (est. 1860s) among Māori in New Zealand both attempted to retain elements of traditional culture while adopting Christian beliefs and practices. In Australia, the government has made efforts to restore relationships with Aboriginal and Torres Strait Islanders through apologies for forced assimilation, child separation policies, and restoration of land sovereignty. Aboriginal women have made strides to heal Aboriginal/non-Aboriginal relations: Anne Pattel-Gray, the first Aboriginal person to obtain a PhD from the University of Sydney, has worked to hold churches and governments accountable to racial equity. In August 2022, she was appointed Professor of Indigenous Studies and the inaugural Head of the School of Indigenous Studies at the University of Divinity, Australia. From a liberation theology perspective, she has identified racism as the original sin of Australian culture (Pattel-Gray 1998) while also highlighting the underlying racism of the feminist movement that claimed to represent all women but sidelined Aboriginal voices (Pattel-Gray 1999).

Melanesia, Micronesia, and Polynesia

Christianity came to the Pacific islands via Western exploration and colonialism, by missionaries searching both for natural resources to exploit and "lost souls" to "save" (Ernst and Anisi 2016). The first to the region were Catholics, such as Jesuits in the Northern Mariana Islands (1668) and Marist priests in the Solomon Islands (1845). Early Catholic missions failed due to their lack of robust inculturation efforts and the hostility of local populations. Many missionaries, Catholic and Protestant, in introducing Christianity to the region, were killed by local populations. The London Missionary Society (LMS) pioneered Protestant work, first in Tahiti (1797). Indigenous populations eventually adopted Christianity for spiritual reasons, but also for pragmatic opportunities to gain literacy, weapons, and education. As local chiefs served as the gatekeepers of their communities, missionaries quickly learned that the conversion of a chief led to the conversion of a people. All Tongans, for example, became Christian within eight years after the consecration of

Photo 7.1 Local pastor offers remembrance for the deceased during a funeral in Yap, Federated States of Micronesia (2008). *Source:* E W/Flickr.

Tāufaʻāhau I as king in 1845 (George Tupou I, baptized in 1831). Christianity spread throughout the islands by foreign missionaries but in collaboration with local evangelists. For example, the Cook Islands Christian Church – the country's largest denomination with nearly 52% of the population – was established via the LMS beginning in 1821. From 1872 to 1896, the church sent 70 indigenous missionaries to introduce Christianity to Papua. Christianity arrived in New Caledonia first via a native Tongan in 1834. Among Protestants, the most active missionary societies were Anglican, Methodist, Congregationalist, and Presbyterian. Most churches today can trace their roots to these early missions.

Early colonial authorities sidelined women in favor of providing new positions of authority for men (Mowbray 2014). However, the arrival of Christianity transformed gender relations in Melanesian societies. Where traditional ritual life was led exclusively by men, Christianity provided women opportunities for public spirituality and functionally moved them from the margins to the center of communal religious life (Robbins 2012). With gender differences sometimes downplayed to avoid blasphemous taboos, a new kind of individualism was introduced that gave men and women equal access to the divine. Formerly subordinated women gained a new venue for action through the church, and in doing so, made themselves central to communal life (Robbins 2012).

By the end of the nineteenth century the entire Pacific region was colonized by European powers, mostly British, but also French, Spanish, Dutch, German, and American. Christianity became intricately tied to tribal life and, like elsewhere in the world throughout the twentieth century, decolonization brought great change to Christianity. In many places, Christians supported decolonization efforts and served as peace negotiators, such as in the Solomons in the 1990s. The Maasina Ruru nationalist movement in the Solomons de-emphasized White missionary authority in favor of local evangelists and leaders to move the country toward independence (Akin 2013).

Beginning in the 1950s, ecumenical efforts encouraged more cooperation between churches, and two influential groups formed in 1966: the Pacific Conference of Churches (PCC, with over 30 denominations represented) and the Pacific Theological College (PTC) in Fiji. The dawning ecumenical movement was one indication that the Pacific region was responding to globalization amidst the sweeping changes of the mid-twentieth century (Nokise 2021). The PCC's three core initiatives relate to ecumenism, stewardship, and self-determination, with women and gender issues imperatives within each initiative (Kavafolau 2021). Although the PCC is still important for the life of churches in the region, the ecumenical movement appears to have peaked. Newer Pentecostal/Charismatic churches have emerged, sometimes causing tension with older established churches impacted by pentecostalization. Despite arriving on the wings of colonization and globalization, Christianity has become increasingly contextualized in the region as Christians seek to adopt faith and practice to Pacific ways of life (Kavafolau 2021).

Papua New Guinea (PNG) experienced one of the most profound changes in its religious composition over the twentieth century, rising from 4% Christian in 1900 to 95% by 2000 (Johnson and Zurlo 2022). From the 1840s to the 1950s, PNG received many kinds of missionaries, including Anglicans, Methodists, Lutherans, Seventh-day Adventists, and Catholics. Numerous Evangelical groups such as New Tribes Mission, the Church of the Foursquare Gospel, and the Christian Revival Crusade arrived after World War II. Churches came under indigenous leadership beginning in the 1960s, and today the historic churches are losing members to newer Pentecostal/Charismatic groups such as the Christian Life Centre, Christian Mission Fellowship, and Christian Revival Crusade (Bouma, Ling, and Pratt 2010). Women's grassroots movements are important in Papua New Guinea; their public organizing first revolved around traditional women's activities of motherhood, cooking, and welfare, but has since expanded to address reproductive health, domestic violence, human rights, and women's political empowerment (Dickson-Waiko 2003). For example, in the conflict over the island of Bougainville (1988–1998), women brought warring sides together for peace talks and were effective in reconciliation ministries and the promotion of dignity. With members from Catholic, Seventh-day Adventist, Pentecostal, and United churches, they formed the Bougainville Inter-Church Women's Forum, which encouraged women to aspire beyond their traditional gendered roles (Bouma, Ling, and Pratt 2010). Women's church fellowships have been described as the missing link in the growth of indigenous feminism in Papua New Guinea, and in Melanesia more broadly, as well as the primary catalyst for potential social change (Dickson-Waiko 2003).

Church of Jesus Christ of Latter-day Saints

Latter-day Saints (LDS) experienced tremendous growth in the Pacific Islands due to missionary activity. The first Mormon missionary, Addison Pratt (1802–1872), was commissioned by LDS founder Joseph Smith Jr. and arrived in French Polynesia in 1844 (Ernst 1994). Growth was rapid until World War II and has since leveled off. Mormonism's success in the region can be partly contributed to the Book of Mormon, which teaches that Pacific Islanders are descendants of the Lost Tribes of Israel. While not able to hold positions in the LDS priesthood, women often serve in the Church Relief Society, on ward governing councils, in missions, as prayer leaders, and in administrative and teaching positions (Ernst 1994).

Environment

The United States conducted nuclear testing on the Marshall Islands from 1946 to 1958, prompting increased cancer diagnoses and the migration of tens of thousands of Marshallese to the US. The French conducted tests in French Polynesia from 1966 to 1974. Women have been at the forefront of the Movement for the Nuclear Free and Independent Pacific, formed in Fiji in 1975. The Fiji Young Women's Christian Association (YWCA) was a key supporter of the antinuclear movement along with

Photo 7.2 Nuns of the Christian Care Centre in the Solomon Islands (2013). *Source:* Department of Foreign Affairs and Trade/Flickr/CC BY 2.0.

major Christian denominations (Bouma, Ling, and Pratt 2010). Ruth Lechte (1932–2012) and Anne Walker (b.1937) were key antinuclear, feminist, and independence activists serving via the Fiji YWCA. Lechte went on to serve the World YWCA, and Walker at the International Women's Tribune Centre in New York.

Many of the Pacific Islands lie just above sea level – like Kiribati, only six feet – and are in grave danger from environmental changes due to global climate change. Rising sea levels are caused mostly by actions from industrial practices of large countries like the United States, China, and India. In the Pacific Islands, daily floods are common, threatening crops and drinking water supplies amidst rising food insecurity. Many islands are projected to be completely uninhabitable by the mid-twenty-first century if current trends continue. In some places, governments and churches are at odds, with some Christians torn between the reality of climate change and the biblical promise that God will not destroy the Earth again with a flood. But elsewhere, Christians are on the forefront of developing ecotheologies and practical action to combat rising sea waters (see Theology section below, as well as Chapter 15). Christian women are active participants in climate change activism. In Kiribati, for example, two young women – Tinaai Teaua and Vasiti Tebamare – serve as youth leaders of their local Seventh-day Adventist Church and are representatives of the Kiribati Climate Action Network.

Oceanic Women in Theology

Contextual theology from the Pacific Islands became more pronounced at the 1976 Pacific Conference of Churches Third Assembly in Port Moresby, Papua New Guinea. Prominent Tongan theologian Sione 'Amanaki Havea (1922–2000) stated that the conference was considering "whether the time had come that we look to a Pacific Christ: instead of a figure with white face and firm lips with blue eyes, that we start to visualize a figure with brown eyes and fuzzy-wuzzy hair" (Havea 1987, p. 7). More broadly, the gathering represented the shift from missionary, imperial, Western, and Eurocentric theology to more relevant ideas closer to home (Vaka'uta and Jackson

2021). Havea further stated, "Pacific theology is an effort to put faith and the Gospel in the local soil and context so that they can exist in a local climate," and further described Pacific theology as "a theology of celebration" with emphases on community, extended family, and elder care (Havea 1987, pp. 11, 13). Most famously, his "coconut theology" – theology that is white on the inside but brown on the outside – rippled across the region and the conference was a watershed moment for the development of Pacific contextual theology. However, the conference booklet listed 30 participants, of which only one was a woman, Akisi Rakadrudru (other women listed were identified only as wives of male participants). Unlike male attenders, Rakadrudru did not have a biography in the book. None of the chapters in the conference volume were authored by women.

Gender was not a prominent theme among Christian leaders in Oceania due to traditional norms that dictated gender hierarchies. The regional feminist movement of the 1970s introduced new ideas of equality and relationships between men and women both in society and church, ideas that became more widespread in the 1990s (Kavafolau 2021). Women had been achieving ordination in many Protestant churches for some time in Australia and New Zealand before women's identity in the church became an important topic to theologize. Rose Kara Ninkama (Papua New Guinea) was one of the first Pacific women to theologically argue for women's equality in the church with her 1987 article, "A Plea for Female Ministers in Melanesia" (Ninkama 1987; Hill 2010).

A pioneering publication for female theologians of the region was *Weavings: Women Doing Theology in Oceania* (Johnson and Filemoni-Tofaeono 2003), which included, for the first time, a collection of writings from Oceanic women. The volume helped set the stage for theologizing about gender justice (Vaka'uta and Jackson 2021). In emphasizing women's theologizing "from below," female theologians critiqued the received wisdom of male church authorities "from above" (Johnson 2003). Patriarchy is widespread in Pacific cultures, with Christian women caught between the gendered expectations of both traditional culture and Christianity. Patriarchy is in "stark contrast to many Indigenous Pacific views of matriarchy, and many traditional means of leadership, such as *Ariki tepaeru* (female leader) roles in society, became subservient roles due to patriarchal ideologies. The Christian God, known as Father and Son, perpetuates and supports this dominant patriarchal ideology, especially in religious institutions whose leaders were expected to be male" (Kavafolau 2021, p. 345).

The arrival of Christianity to Oceania has been described as a "missiology of colonialism" (Skye 2016, p. 162). Aboriginals in Australia and Māori in New Zealand were considered less than human and first encountered Christianity in the context of violence. Today, Indigenous Christians are making unique theological contributions to their understanding of God and the role of the church in the world, especially as it pertains to theologies of creation. The lack of separation between the physical and spiritual worlds, combined with reverence for the land and sea, makes the Indigenous peoples of Oceania uniquely poised to theologically address arguably the most important global issue of the twentieth-first century: the climate crisis.

Feminist theology from this region is ecowomanist, contextual, ecumenical, egalitarian, and inclusive. Indigenous female theologians align with womanist theologians around the world with intersectional views on race, class, and sex – each important aspects to their understanding of God and the church. But their emphasis on the sacredness of all life, and especially the sacredness of land, sets Indigenous women apart. Their Christology is in context with the land, where Christ has become one with creation and thus unites spirit and nature, thus destroying the Western dualism that has led to environmental degradation (Skye 2016). The linking of both Earth as mother and Christ in the form of a man represents the linking of the feminine and the masculine. The relationality of God in the Trinity is paralleled to the relationality among God, creation, and people (Vaai 2021). Fijian theologian Seforosa Carroll has also stressed the importance of "place, space, home, power," travel, and geography as they relate to Pacific theology, and how men and women approach place and space differently (Carroll 2004, p. 75). Women begin their theologizing from experience, such as connecting the process of birthing to participating in God's liberation in the world.

A major area of women's contributions to Pacific life and the church is by addressing domestic violence and abuse. Samoan theologian Mercy Ah Sui-Maliko is a pioneer in this area, using her doctoral dissertation to discuss domestic violence from a Christian perspective, considering half of all Samoan women have experienced abuse by intimate partners or parents (Siu-Maliko 2016). In theory, Christianity can positively contribute to combatting women's second-class status in society with biblical teachings of dignity for all people and equal creation in the image of God. Among Catholics, women look to the Virgin Mary for help and solace, as well as empowerment to resist and endure violence (Hermkens 2008). Women are often targets for accusations of witchcraft, which provides rationale for violence. Female theologians from the region have emphasized Christianity's ability to combat oppressive social and cultural structures (Kavafolau 2021) and many Christian organizations have taken up the marginalization of women and children as a core part of their outreach efforts.

Conclusion

The number of women Christian leaders in Oceania is growing. In 2020, Graham Joseph Hill and Jen Barker of the Global Church Project constructed a list of "160+ Australian and New Zealander Women in Theology You Should Know About," which includes women from different ethnic and ecclesial backgrounds (see Hill 2021). In the last 50 years, women in this region have made tremendous strides to live into their vocational callings despite varying interpretations of gender equality between Australia/New Zealand and the Pacific Islands, and despite challenging economic and ecological issues. From women's ordination to highly relevant contextual theologizing, women are making an impact on the micro and macro levels. As Tongan-Australian theologian Katalina Tahaafe-Williams stated, "Culturally appropriate approaches are necessary precisely because solutions that are contextually sensitive, relevant and sustainable are critical for the participation of women and youth in the future story of Oceanian Christianity" (Tahaafe-Williams 2021, p. 371). Like many places around the world, the future vitality of Christianity in Oceania is dependent on its women and youth, as they navigate what it means to be authentically Christian and true to their histories, cultures, and traditions.

Reflection Questions

1) Compare the development of Christianity in Australia/New Zealand and the Pacific Islands (Melanesia, Micronesia, and Polynesia). How were women impacted by the arrival of Christianity in each region, and how did Indigenous communities pioneer their own forms of the faith? How does Oceania's unique geography as the "liquid continent" impact life and faith there?

2) Describe the clash between Western missionaries and Indigenous peoples, especially in relation to gender roles in Pacific societies. Why has the vibrancy of the Indigenous missionary movement from Oceania been overlooked, perpetuating the trend of Oceania being "left off the map"?

3) Many countries in the Pacific Islands are nearly entirely Christian, yet gender-based violence is endemic. How can Christianity positively contribute to combatting women's second-class status in society and the church? Describe how feminist theology from the region addressed this problem, especially as a result of the 1976 Pacific Conference of Churches Third Assembly.

Works Cited

Akin, David (2013). *Colonialism, Maasina Rule, and the Origins of Malaitan Kastom*. Honolulu: Center for Pacific Islands Studies, School of Pacific and Asian Studies, University of Hawai'i, Mānoa.

Anglican Church of Australia General Synod (1995). Proceedings of the tenth general synod 1995: official report. New South Wales: The Anglican Church of Australia Trust Corporation.

Bouma, Gary D., Ling, Rod, and Pratt, Douglas (2010). *Religious Diversity in Southeast Asia and the Pacific: National Case Studies*. Dordrecht, the Netherlands: Springer.

Carroll, Seforosa (2004). Weaving new spaces: christological perspectives from Oceania (pacific) and the Oceanic diaspora. *Studies in World Christianity*, 10(1), 72–92.

Cruickshank, Joanna and Grimshaw, Patricia (2019). *White Women, Aboriginal Missions and Australian Settler Governments: Maternal Contradictions*. Leiden: Brill.

Dickson-Waiko, Anne (2003). The missing rib: mobilizing church women for change in Papua New Guinea. *Oceania*, 74(1/2), 98–119.

Ernst, Manfred (1994). *Winds of Change: Rapidly Growing Religious Groups in the Pacific Islands*. Suva, Fiji: Pacific Conference of Churches.

Ernst, Manfred (2006). *Globalization and the Re-shaping of Christianity in the Pacific Islands*. Suva, Fiji: Pacific Theological College.

Ernst, Manfred and Anisi, Anna (2016). The historical development of Christianity in Oceania. In: *The Wiley Blackwell Companion to World Christianity* (ed. Lamin O. Sanneh and Michael J. McClymond), 588–604. Hoboken, NJ: Wiley-Blackwell.

Grimshaw, Patricia (2011). Gladys Nicholls: an urban Aboriginal leader in post-war Victoria. In: *Founders, Firsts and Feminists: Women Leaders in Twentieth-Century Australia* (ed. Fiona Davis, Nell Musgrove, and Judith Smart), 64–74. Melbourne: eScholarship Research Centre.

Haerpfer, Christian, Inglehart, Ronald, Moreno, Alejandro, Welzel, Christian, Kizilova, Kseniya, Diez-Medrano, Jaime, Lagos, Marta, Norris, Pippa, Ponarin, Eduard, Puranen, Bi et al. ed. (2020). World values survey: round seven – country-pooled datafile. Madrid, Spain and Vienna, Austria: JD Systems Institute & WVSA Secretariat. doi: 10.14281/18241.13 (accessed 1 November 2021).

Havea, Sione 'Amanaki (1987). Christianity in the Pacific context. *In: South Pacific Theology: Papers from the Consultation on Pacific Theology, Papua New Guinea, January 1986*, 11–15. Paramatta, Australia: World Vision International South Pacific.

Hermkens, Anna-Karina (2008). Josephine's journey: gender-based violence and marian devotion in urban Papua New Guinea. *Oceania*, 78(2), 151–167.

Hill, Graham Joseph (2021). Protestants. In: *Christianity in Oceania* (ed. Kenneth R. Ross, Katalina Tahaafe-Williams, and Todd M. Johnson), 177–189. Edinburgh: Edinburgh University Press.

Hill, Helen (2010). Women and religious diversity. In: *Religious Diversity in Southeast Asia and the Pacific: National Case Studies* (ed. Gary D. Bouma, Rod Ling, and Douglas Pratt), 247–254. Dordrecht, the Netherlands: Springer.

Honoré, Christopher (2013). The Anglican Church in Aotearoa, New Zealand, and Polynesia. In: *The Wiley-Blackwell Companion to the Anglican Communion* (ed. Ian S. Markham, J. Barney Hawkins IV, Justyn Terry, and Leslie N. Steffensen), 373–386. Chichester: John Wiley & Sons.

Johnson, Lydia (2003). 'Weaving the mat' of Pacific women's theology: a case study in women's theological method. In: *Weavings: Women Doing Theology in Oceania* (ed. Lydia Johnson and Joan A. Filemoni-Tofaeono), 10–22. Suva, Fiji: Weavers, South Pacific Association of Theological Schools and Institute of Pacific Studies, University of the South Pacific.

Johnson, Lydia and Filemoni-Tofaeono, Joan A. (2003). *Weavings: Women Doing Theology in Oceania* (ed. Lydia Johnson and Joan A. Filemoni-Tofaeono). Suva, Fiji: Weavers, South Pacific Association of Theological Schools and Institute of Pacific Studies, University of the South Pacific.

Johnson, Todd M. and Zurlo, Gina A. (2019). *World Christian Encyclopedia*. 3rd edn. Edinburgh: Edinburgh University Press.

Johnson, Todd M. and Zurlo, Gina A. ed. (2022). *World Christian Database*. Leiden/Boston: Brill.

Kaldor, Peter (1987). *Who Goes Where? Who Doesn't Care?* New South Wales: Lancer Books.

Kavafolau, Victoria (2021). Gender. In: *Christianity in Oceania* (ed. Kenneth R. Ross, Katalina Tahaafe-Williams, and Todd M. Johnson), 298–308. Edinburgh: Edinburgh University Press.

Mowbray, Jemima (2014). 'Ol Meri bilong wok' (Hard-working women): women, work and domesticity in Papua New Guinea. In: *Divine Domesticities: Christian Paradoxes in Asia and the Pacific* (ed. Hyaeweol Choi and Margaret Jolly), 167–198. Acton: ANU press.

Ninkama, Rose K. (1987). A plea for female ministers in Melanesia. In: *The Gospel Is Not Western: Black Theologies from the Southwest Pacific* (ed. Garry W. Trompf), 128–138. Maryknoll, NY: Orbis Books.

Nokise, Feleterika (2021). Pacific conference of churches. In: *Christianity in Oceania* (ed. Kenneth R. Ross, Katalina Tahaafe-Williams, and Todd M. Johnson), 226–234. Edinburgh: Edinburgh University Press.

Oh, Emi Frances (2003). A dream as metaphor for a new vision of church in the Pacific. In: *Weavings: Women Doing Theology in Oceania* (ed. Lydia Johnson and Joan A. Filemoni-Tofaeono), 141–149. Suva, Fiji: Weavers, South Pacific Association of Theological Schools and Institute of Pacific Studies, University of the South Pacific.

Pattel-Gray, Anne (1998). *The Great White Flood: Racism in Australia*. Atlanta: Scholars.

Pattel-Gray, Anne (1999). The hard truth: white secrets, black realities. *Australian Feminist Studies*, 14(30), 259–266.

Powell, Ruth (2017). *Why are Women More Religious than Men?* https://www.ncls.org.au/articles/why-are-women-more-religious-than-men/ (accessed 29 October 2021).

Powell, Ruth, Pepper, Miriam, and Hancock, Nicole (2016). *2011 NCLS Research Collection*. Revised edition. North Sydney, Australia: NCLS Research.

Powell, Ruth, Pepper, Miriam, and Kerr, Kathy J. (2018). *Gender Mix in Australian Churches*. https://www.ncls.org.au/articles/gender-mix-in-australian-church-attenders/ (accessed 29 October 2021).

Presbyterian Church of Aotearoa New Zealand (2016). Parish membership statistics.

Prior, Randall A. (2021). Vanuatu. In: *Christianity in Oceania* (ed. Kenneth R. Ross, Katalina Tahaafe-Williams, and Todd M. Johnson), 100–107. Edinburgh: Edinburgh University Press.

Reed, Brenda (2021). Anglicans. In: *Christianity in Oceania* (ed. Kenneth R. Ross, Katalina Tahaafe-Williams, and Todd M. Johnson), 153–165. Edinburgh: Edinburgh University Press.

Robbins, Joel (2012). Spirit women, church women, and passenger women: Christianity, gender, and cultural change in Melanesia. *Archives de Sciences Sociales des Religions*, 157, 113–133.

Scarfe, Janet (2014). Changed ruled, changing culture? The ordination of women. *St. Mark's Review* 229(2), 51–57.

Siu-Maliko, Mercy A. (2016). A public theology response to domestic violence in Samoa. *International Journal of Public Theology*, 10(1), 54–67.

Skye, Lee M. (2016). Australian Aboriginal women's Christologies. In: *The Strength of Her Witness: Jesus Christ in the Global Voices of Women* (ed. Elizabeth A. Johnson), 162–171. Maryknoll, NY: Orbis Books.

Stanley, Brian (2009). *The World Missionary Conference, Edinburgh 1910*. Grand Rapids, MI: William B. Eerdmans Pub.

Summers, Anne (2016). *Damned Whores and God's Police: The Colonisation of Women in Australia*. Revised edition. University of New South Wales Press.

Tahaafe-Williams, Katalina (2021). The future of Christianity in Oceania. In: *Christianity in Oceania* (ed. Kenneth R. Ross, Katalina Tahaafe-Williams, and Todd M. Johnson), 367–376. Edinburgh: Edinburgh University Press.

Vaai, Upolu L. (2021). Faith and culture. In: *Christianity in Oceania* (ed. Kenneth R. Ross, Katalina Tahaafe-Williams, and Todd M. Johnson), 235–246. Edinburgh: Edinburgh University Press.

Vaka'uta, Nāsili and Jackson, Darrell (2021). Theology. In: *Christianity in Oceania* (ed. Kenneth R. Ross, Katalina Tahaafe-Williams, and Todd M. Johnson), 259–271. Edinburgh: Edinburgh University Press.

Williams, Andrew (2021). Migration and diaspora. In: *Christianity in Oceania* (ed. Kenneth R. Ross, Katalina Tahaafe-Williams, and Todd M. Johnson), 352–383. Edinburgh: Edinburgh University Press.

Part II

Women in World Christianity by Tradition and Movement

8

Women in Catholicism

"If the Church is to be relevant in the world, it must pay serious attention to the status of its women."

Margaret J. Mealey (1966, in Henold 2020)

Mary, the mother of Jesus, is known to Catholics by many names, epithets, and titles: the Mother of God, the Queen of Heaven, Blessed Mother, Virgin Mary, Our Lady, Star of the Sea, Mother of Mercy. Four dogmas are key to Mariology: (1) Mary's perpetual virginity before, during, and after giving birth (second century); (2) Mary as the Mother of God (third century); (3) Mary's bodily assumption into heaven (fifth century); and (4) Mary's immaculate conception (conceived without original sin; an official teaching in 1854) (Muir 2019; Perry and Kendall 2013). Marian devotion has been a long-standing tradition of the Catholic Church. It remains so today, though on a spectrum from minimalism and maximalism as Catholic leaders and theologians aim to articulate what Mary's role and symbolism should be in modern Catholic thought (Perry and Kendall 2013). Marian pilgrimages are wildly popular, with shrines to the Virgin Mary all over the world receiving millions of visitors a year. One of the most prominent sites is the Basilica of the National Shrine of Our Lady of Aparecida in Brazil, which is the largest cathedral and the second largest Catholic church in the world after St. Peter's Basilica at the Vatican. It receives more than 12 million annual visitors.

Catholicism is the largest Christian family in the world, with its 1.2 billion members representing 16% of the world's population and 49% of all Christians in 2020 (Table 8.1; Johnson and Zurlo 2022). It is also among the world's oldest and continuously operating Christian churches, tracing its hierarchy to Jesus Christ as the head of the church, its bishops as successors to the 12 apostles in the New Testament, and the pope as the successor of the Apostle Peter, upon whom Christ built the church (Matthew 16:18). The Catholic Church is headquartered in the Holy See, which is also a fully functional country (one of the smallest in the world by land and population) with the pope as the head of state. The Holy See also has full ownership of Vatican City, an independent city-state within Rome and the episcopal see of the Catholic Church headed by the pope. It is home to the Roman Curia, which consists of the numerous administrative bodies of the Catholic Church: two Secretariats (State; Economy), three Dicasteries (Laity, Family and Life; Promoting Integral Human Development; Communications), nine congregations (Doctrine of the Faith; Oriental Churches; Divine Worship and the Discipline of the Sacraments; Causes of Saints; Evangelization of Peoples; Clergy; Institutes of Consecrated Life and Societies of Apostolic Life; Catholic Education; Bishops), three tribunals (Apostolic Penitentiary; Rota Romana; Apostolic Signature); and five Pontifical Councils (Promoting Christian Unity; Legislative Texts; Interreligious Dialogue; Culture; Promoting the New Evangelization). The papacy, the college of cardinals (direct council to the pope), and bishops are reserved for men only. In recent years, an increasing

Women in World Christianity: Building and Sustaining a Global Movement, First Edition. Gina A. Zurlo.
© 2023 John Wiley & Sons Ltd. Published 2023 by John Wiley & Sons Ltd.

number of women have been appointed to positions within the Roman Curia, indicating a decisive step forward for more women in leadership. Catholic women are tremendously active in the life of the church through mission (religious sisters), social services (charitable work in schools, hospitals, orphanages), the media (newspapers and magazines), and other avenues of the church. The Catholic Church operates more than 72,000 kindergartens, 99,000 primary/elementary schools, and 49,000 secondary schools totaling more than 61 million students; plus, the Catholic Church runs over 5,000 hospitals, 9,000 orphanages, 10,000 nurseries, and other kinds of welfare services (*Annuarium Statisticum Ecclesiae* 2020). Most of these figures have increased substantially since 1970, and women are prominent in leadership and service in these institutions.

Catholics, 1900–2050

In this volume, Catholics are defined as all Christians in communion with the Church of Rome (also known as Roman Catholics), and members include all baptized Catholics plus catechumens. This includes Eastern-rite Catholics, who are in communion with Rome but practice rites other than Latin. Latin-rite Catholics are the largest Christian family in the world, with nearly 1.2 billion members in 2020. The center of gravity of global Catholicism has shifted dramatically over the last century. Catholicism was a religion of the global North for much of its history, with most Catholics living primarily in Europe until the Age of Discovery beginning in the late fifteenth century. At that time, Catholicism – along with European culture and civilization – began to move outward from Europe to Latin America, Asia, and sub-Saharan Africa. At the start of the twentieth century, 73% of Catholics lived in the global North and 27% in the global South; by the year 2020, Catholicism's center of gravity had completely flipped, with 27% living in the North and 73% in the South (Table 8.1); 41% of Catholics worldwide live in Latin America alone (Figure 8.1). Looking to 2050, it is anticipated that Catholicism will continue to decline in the North and grow in the South, with over 1.2 billion Catholics in the global South alone and overall, just 20% of Catholics in the North and 80% in the South.

The gender makeup of Catholic church members is generally more evenly distributed than other Christian traditions, with women comprising just over 51% of all members (Table 8.2). The reason for this is that the demographic makeup of a region or country generally tracks closely with that of its largest religion. There are slight regional variations, such as higher proportions of women in the global North (52%) vs. the global South (51%); the highest percent Catholic female is in North America (53%) and the lowest is in Asia (50%) (Table 8.2). Yet, it is widely known that women are more active in churches than men.

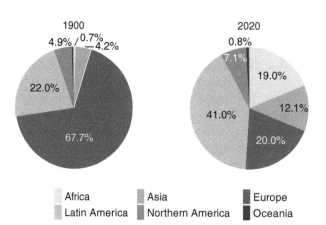

Figure 8.1 Catholics by continent, 1900 and 2020. *Source:* Data from Johnson and Zurlo 2022.

Table 8.1 Catholics by continent, 1900–2050.

Region	Catholics 1900	% of pop. 1900	% of Catholics 1900	Rate % p.a. 1900–2020	Catholics 2020	% of pop. 2020	% of Catholics 2020	Catholics 2050	% of pop. 2050	% of Catholics 2050
Global North	193,055,000	39.9	72.6	0.47	340,011,000	30.5	27.4	306,377,000	27.0	20.2
Europe	180,044,000	44.7	67.7	0.28	251,997,000	33.7	20.3	211,164,000	29.7	13.9
North America	13,011,000	15.9	4.9	1.61	88,015,000	23.9	7.1	95,213,000	22.4	6.3
Global South	72,701,000	6.4	27.4	2.12	899,260,000	13.5	72.6	1,212,064,000	14.1	79.8
Africa	1,890,000	1.8	0.7	4.10	234,373,000	17.5	18.9	470,882,000	18.9	31.0
Asia	11,192,000	1.2	4.2	2.19	150,293,000	3.2	12.1	200,406,000	3.8	13.2
Latin America	58,567,000	89.9	22.0	1.81	504,199,000	77.1	40.7	528,678,000	69.3	34.8
Oceania	1,052,000	16.8	0.4	1.93	10,395,000	24.4	0.8	12,098,000	21.1	0.8
Global total	**265,756,000**	**16.4**	**100.0**	**1.29**	**1,239,271,000**	**15.9**	**100.0**	**1,518,441,000**	**15.6**	**100.0**

Source: Johnson and Zurlo 2022. p.a. = percent change per annum, or each year.

Table 8.2 Catholics by continent with percent female, 2020.

Region	Catholics 2020	Catholic % of pop. 2020	% of Catholics 2020	% Catholic female 2020	% region female 2020
Global North	340,011,000	30.5	27.4	52.2	51.3
Europe	251,997,000	33.7	20.3	51.9	51.7
North America	88,015,000	23.9	7.1	53.1	50.5
Global South	899,260,000	13.5	72.6	50.8	49.3
Africa	234,373,000	17.5	18.9	51.3	50.0
Asia	150,293,000	3.2	12.1	49.9	48.9
Latin America	504,199,000	77.1	40.7	50.9	50.8
Oceania	10,395,000	24.4	0.8	51.1	49.9
Global total	**1,239,271,000**	**15.9**	**100.0**	**51.2**	**49.6**

Source: Data from Johnson and Zurlo 2022.

Table 8.3 Countries with the most Catholics, 2020.

Rank	Country	Country pop. 2020	Catholics 2020	Catholics % of pop. 2020	% Catholic female 2020	% country female 2020
1	Brazil	212,559,000	150,000,000	70.6	50.0	50.9
2	Mexico	128,933,000	115,574,000	89.6	51.4	51.1
3	Philippines	109,581,000	83,000,000	75.7	49.3	49.8
4	United States	331,003,000	73,900,000	22.3	53.3	50.5
5	DR Congo	89,561,000	49,200,000	54.9	51.2	50.1
6	Italy	60,462,000	45,100,000	74.6	51.4	51.3
7	Colombia	50,883,000	43,800,000	86.1	51.2	50.9
8	Spain	46,755,000	39,170,000	83.8	51.2	50.9
9	France	65,274,000	38,540,000	59.0	51.4	51.6
10	Argentina	45,196,000	35,500,000	78.5	51.7	51.2

Source: Data from Johnson and Zurlo 2022.

Six of the top ten countries with the most Catholics are in the global South (Table 8.3) and, according to census data, there are not substantial differences between the country's female share of the population and women's share of the Catholic population. The countries with the highest percent of Catholics, except for Mexico, Poland, and Paraguay, are small in population and have little variation in their Catholic female percentages due to the close connection between the overall country's population and its religious makeup (Table 8.4).

Growth rates can be misleading because a country with a very small Catholic population can exhibit large growth rates with only a small number of converts or immigrants. The countries with the fastest Catholic growth rates worldwide (Table 8.5) generally make the list because of migration. Qatar, the United Arab Emirates, and Kuwait receive large numbers of foreign workers from around the world, particularly Southeast Asia. These Gulf States have imbalanced gender ratios due to a higher proportion of men working in the oil industry compared to women working in retail, domestic service, and other industries. Qatar is only 25% female, the United Arab Emirates is 41%, and Kuwait is 29%. In each of these countries, however, Catholics report a higher proportion of women: Qatar's Catholics are 36% female, and United Arab Emirates and Kuwait's are both 51%.

Table 8.4 Countries with the highest percent of Catholics, 2020.

Rank	Country	Country pop. 2020	Catholics 2020	Catholics % of pop. 2020	% Catholic female 2020	% country female 2020
1	Martinique	375,000	360,000	95.9	51.2	54.0
2	Wallis and Futuna Islands	11,200	10,600	94.6	51.2	48.2
3	Saint Pierre and Miquelon	5,800	5,300	91.6	51.2	51.6
4	Poland	37,847,000	34,100,000	90.1	52.1	51.5
5	Mexico	128,933,000	115,574,000	89.6	51.4	51.1
6	Cabo Verde	556,000	498,000	89.6	51.2	49.8
7	Guadeloupe	449,000	400,000	89.2	51.2	53.9
8	Malta	442,000	390,000	88.3	51.2	49.9
9	Paraguay	7,133,000	6,237,000	87.4	49.7	49.2
10	Colombia	50,883,000	43,800,000	86.1	51.2	50.9

Source: Data from Johnson and Zurlo 2022.

Table 8.5 Countries with the fastest growth of Catholics, 2020.

Rank	Country	Country pop. 2020	Catholics 2020	Catholics % of pop. 2020	% Catholic female 2020	% country female 2020	Catholic rate % p.a. 2000–2020
1	Qatar	2,881,000	353,000	12.2	36.4	24.8	10.49
2	Azerbaijan	10,139,000	650	0.0	51.2	50.0	8.81
3	Turkmenistan	6,031,000	200	0.0	51.4	50.8	7.18
4	Sierra Leone	7,977,000	280,000	3.5	50.4	50.1	7.05
5	Norway	5,421,000	180,000	3.3	51.2	49.5	6.38
6	United Arab Emirates	9,890,000	977,000	9.9	51.2	30.9	6.08
7	Mongolia	3,278,000	1,300	0.0	63.2	50.7	6.07
8	Kuwait	4,271,000	400,000	9.4	51.4	38.8	5.90
9	Iceland	341,000	13,000	3.8	51.2	49.8	5.68
10	Liberia	5,058,000	400,000	7.9	50.3	49.7	5.33

Source: Data from Johnson and Zurlo 2022. p.a. = percent change per annum, or each year.

Table 8.6 illustrates the varieties of Catholicism worldwide, where in some countries it is a very old tradition (Italy, Spain, and France) and in others, it dates to the spread of Catholicism in the sixteenth century beyond Europe (Brazil, Mexico, the Philippines, United States, Democratic Republic of the Congo, and Colombia). In each of these Catholic churches, women do not make up a substantially higher proportion of membership than men, with the range only between 49% (Philippines) and 53% (US). This table also shows the proportional decline or relative statis of Catholicism not only in the global North, but also in the global South. The Democratic Republic of

Table 8.6 Largest Catholic denominations, 2015.

Rank	Country	Denomination	Year begun	Affiliated 2015	% female	Rate % p.a. 2000–2015
1	Brazil	Igreja Católica no Brasil	1500	148,550,000	50.0	0.25
2	Mexico	Iglesia Católica en México	1518	110,155,000	51.4	1.13
3	Philippines	Catholic Church in the Philippines	1521	78,271,000	49.3	1.50
4	United States	Catholic Church in the USA	1526	72,798,000	53.3	0.97
5	Italy	Chiesa Cattolica in Italia	40	45,563,000	51.4	0.04
6	DR Congo	Eglise Catholique au DR Congo	1482	42,891,000	51.2	3.12
7	Colombia	Iglesia Católica en Colombia	1512	42,206,000	51.2	0.91
8	Spain	Iglesia Católica en España	63	39,377,000	51.2	0.56
9	France	Eglise Catholique de France	80	37,926,000	51.4	0.20
10	Poland	Catholic Church in Poland	966	34,462,000	52.1	−0.17

Source: Data from Johnson and Zurlo 2022. p.a. = percent change per annum, or each year.

the Congo is the only country to report growth in the last five years (3.12% average annual growth rate; Table 8.6).

Women in Catholic History

Although most historians today believe her to be a myth, the legend of Pope Joan still looms large in popular oral Catholic history. Somewhere between the eighth and eleventh centuries, Pope Joan wielded the power of the pope until it was discovered that she was indeed a woman, evidenced by her pregnant belly after she had taken a secret lover. She remains a popular character in fictional work and cultural lore. In the sixteenth century, a woman became acting pope when Lucrezia Borgia (1480–1519), the 21-year-old daughter of Pope Alexander VI and his mistress Vannozza dei Cattanei, was briefly in charge of the Vatican while her father traveled throughout Europe (Hofmann 2002).

From the late twelfth century to the end of the Middle Ages, holy women gained substantial notoriety for their asceticism, deep devotion, visions, and revelations (Coakley 2006). Although living under the authority of men and excluded from the priesthood, women were perceived as exemplars of the faith with remarkable private devotional lives and closeness to Christ, as communicated via the hagiographies written about them by male clerics. Among female saints are queens and abbesses, members of convents and royal families; some poor, others not; some lay, others cloistered nuns.

Founded in 1588, the Congregation for the Causes of Saints has overseen the process of canonizing saints, which includes identifying heroic virtues, beatification, approving miracles, and presenting cases to the pope. All members of this congregation are men. The Catholic Church has recognized more than 10,000 saints. At the start of the twentieth century, 13% of canonized saints were women, a figure that rose to 20% by 1990 and 25% by 2020 (Espín 2020). Many female saints were nuns, founders of religious orders, or virgins. Female saints are encouragements to women, with many having a particular appeal to women's roles in both the church and the world. Some popular and notable female saints include:

- St. Elizabeth Seton (1774–1821), patron saint of Catholic schools, founder of the United States system of parochial schools, the first American congregation of sisters (Sisters of Charity), and the first Catholic girls' schools; the first American female saint.
- St. Josephine Bakhita (1869–1947), patron saint of Sudan, South Sudan, and human trafficking survivors, who was enslaved by Arab traders, emancipated, became a Canossian Sister, and lived the rest of her life in Italy.
- St. Alphonsa (born as Anna Muttathupadathu, 1910–1946), patron saint against illnesses and diseases related to feet, first Indian woman canonized as a saint, a member of the Syro-Malabar Church (Eastern Catholic), with many physical healings attributed to her.
- St. Teresa of Calcutta (1910–1997), patron saint of World Youth Day, Missionaries of Charity, and the Archdiocese of Calcutta; Albanian nun and founder of the Missionaries of Charity; winner of the 1979 Nobel Peace Prize for her work among the poor of India.
- St. Gianna Beretta Molla (1922–1962), patron saint of working mothers, wives, families, and unborn children, an Italian pediatrician who refused an abortion and hysterectomy during a difficult pregnancy, dying after the birth of her fourth child.

There are four women among the 37 renowned Doctors of the Church, an honorific bestowed upon specific saints for their significant contributions to Catholic life, theology, spirituality, and study (see Malone 2017):

- St. Teresa of Avila (1515–1582), patron saint of sick people and those of religious orders, a Spanish mystic, writer, and theologian; her reforming work led to the establishment of the Discalced Carmelites.
- St. Catherine of Siena (1347–1380), patron saint of bodily ills and sick people, an Italian mystic known for her deep devotional discipline that she passed onto her followers, having nursed victims of the Black Death.
- St. Thérèse of Lisieux (1873–1897), patron saint of, among other things, missionaries, HIV/AIDS survivors, florists, France, and Russia; a French Discalced Carmelite nun widely known for the simplicity of her deep inner spiritual life.
- St. Hildegard of Bingen (c.1098–1179), patron saint of musicians and writers, a German Benedictine abbess as well as writer, composer of both lyrics and melodies, mystic, visionary, and medical writer.

Women at the Second Vatican Council

The Second Vatican Council was arguably the most important Christian meeting in the twentieth century. Opened in 1962 by Pope John Paul XXIII and closed by Pope Paul VI in 1965, Vatican II communicated that the Catholic Church was ready to enter the modern world. The council was very ecumenical and welcoming of non-Catholics, took new positions on Catholic–Protestant and Catholic–Jewish relations, and had massive implications for the growth of Catholicism worldwide. Priests were permitted to celebrate Mass in languages other than Latin for the first time in history. They faced the congregation during Mass instead of having their backs to them, signaling they were worshipping alongside them, not merely performing on their behalf. Girls were permitted to serve at the altar beginning in 1965, and now there are more altar girls than boys in service in many

European countries (Magyar 2019). Without Vatican II, the Catholic Church perhaps would not have made such tremendous gains in sub-Saharan Africa, nor been able to strengthen Catholics in Latin America against dictatorships and the emerging threat of Protestantism.

The encyclical *Pacem in Terris* (1963) of Pope John XXIII acknowledged the growing role of women in political life and recognized that "Women are gaining an increasing awareness of their natural dignity" and "are demanding both in domestic and public life the rights and duties which belong to them as human persons" (John XXIII 1963). Overall, Vatican II helped make the issue of women's dignity more visible, including a confirmation of their right to serve and their increased recognition as important actors for the renewal of the Catholic Church (Gyarmathy-Amherd 2008). Vatican II spurred the creation of the International Union of Superiors General (IUSG) in 1965, the organization that promotes deeper connections among women religious worldwide. The IUSG helped advocate for the founding of Regina Mundi Pontifical Institute in 1955, the first place where women could study theology in Rome. However, it closed in 2005 with the increased presence of female students at Catholic institutions all over the world, including in Rome. According to the IUSG website, its members today are from Africa (166), Asia (184), Europe (1,046), the Americas (479), and Oceania (28).

Vignettes: Catholic Women Worldwide

Mass attendance is an important part of Catholic life, and frequency of attendance is often used in social scientific studies to gauge levels of religiosity in a community. Attendance is generally lower in the global North and higher in the South, and it is on the decline in many countries. Catholicism is the largest religion in Latin America and has been so for hundreds of years, but Chile, Mexico, and Peru, for instance, have all experienced declines in attendance. Argentina reported the lowest weekly Catholic attendance in the latest World Values Survey at 16%; the highest was Colombia (42%) (Haerpfer et al. 2022). In Europe, weekly Mass attendance has been declining for much longer and is very low in some countries, such as the Netherlands (6%), Bulgaria (9%), and Andorra (8%). Weekly attendance remains comparatively high in North Macedonia (56%) and Georgia (53%) (Haerpfer et al. 2022).

Although census data does not report high proportions of women in Catholic church membership (Table 8.6), it is widely observed in qualitative research and in an abundance of case studies that Catholic churches worldwide are majority female. Furthermore, women report high levels of participation in many aspects of Catholic life. In 2021, Pope Francis changed canon law to allow women to serve as lectors (those who recite prayers and sacred texts but not the gospel) and acolytes (assistants to the priests or deacons, including during communion) during Mass. This was the first official recognition of women's service during Mass – changing the language from "lay men" to "lay persons." Some examples of women's prominence in Catholic churches include:

- The Belgian Catholic Bishops' Conference reported a "feminization of the Church," where women represented 55% of people serving at various levels. They concluded that "women play a key role in the future of the Church and the transmission of the faith" (Belgian Bishops' Conference 2020).
- In the Netherlands, young men have soured on the priesthood and religion of all kinds since the nineteenth century. Catholicism especially, "has become feminized" as images of God have become more feminine and religious domains provide women opportunities to develop their own agency (Knibbe 2013, pp. 13–14).

- In the United States, many Catholic women feel called to the diaconate, or could imagine themselves discerning such a call if it were open to them. Nevertheless, Catholic women live out this call as "de facto deacons" with a "do it anyway" mentality, without official titles (Bruce, Masso-Rivetti, and Sherman 2021, p. 29).

Catholic Women in Mission

For much of Catholic history, mission was considered transplantation: take the Catholic faith of Europe and replant it elsewhere in the world to grow. While there were extraordinary efforts by some Catholic missionaries, notably the Jesuits, to spread contextual forms of Catholicism, it was not until the twentieth century that the church officially abandoned the transplantation model of mission for more culturally sensitive and appropriate methods. What followed was a reinvigoration of Catholic mission through the founding of new mission societies, the ordination of indigenous clergy, and the rehabilitation of the missiology of the Jesuits, now known as "inculturation." The Second Vatican Council released the apostolic decree *Ad Gentes* (on the missionary activity of the church) in 1965, which defined mission as proclamation, presence, and dialogue; envisioned the Catholic Church as a sacrament of salvation sent to the nations; and placed mission activity in the center of church life, naming it the "greatest and holiest task of the Church" (Ad Gentes 1965).

Women religious, also referred to as sisters, are female members of religious institutes or orders. They take vows of poverty, chastity, and obedience as do religious men (brothers) and work on behalf of the Catholic Church in the world in numerous capacities, such as in education and social services. Nuns, also called sisters, are different from women religious in that they live in cloistered or semi-cloistered contemplative monastic communities. Nuns take an additional vow – the perpetual solemn vow – and serve the world in prayer and communal religious life within the monastery or convent. The number of religious sisters in the world has been slowly declining; from over one million in 1970 to 619,546 in 2020 (Table 8.7). There are regional differences: between 2015 and 2020, the number of women religious *increased* in Africa (up nearly 8,000) and Asia (up 3,800). Women religious occupy a special kind of "sacred space" where they can transcend boundaries, access typically inaccessible places, and are considered "paragons of virtue" in their work among the poor, abused, and disenfranchised (Behrens 2004, p. 190).

Despite a numeric decline, women religious outnumber total priests and professed religious men in every region of the world, and there are nearly 159,000 more women religious than priests and religious men combined. Globally, the number of Catholic elementary schools, secondary schools, and orphanages are on the rise, and most of these institutions are staffed by Catholic women.

Catholic Women in Leadership

Most Catholic women have come to terms with a male-only hierarchy, where only men can become priests, bishops, cardinals, and popes. The rationale for women's exclusion begins with the 12 named male apostles of Jesus in the gospels. Catholic Church leaders are in apostolic succession with the original 12, and thus priestly ordination is reserved for men (Bieringer 2008). In 1976, Pope Paul VI issued the apostolic letter *Inter Insigniores* (Declaration on the Question of the Admission of Women to the Ministerial Priesthood) in response to the Episcopal Church USA's

Table 8.7 Catholic workers, 2020.

Region	Total priests*	Professed religious men	Total priests and religious men	Women religious
Africa	50,465	9,188	59,653	79,557
Asia	71,032	12,604	83,636	175,128
Europe	163,954	14,466	178,420	207,994
Latin America	76,608	8,346	84,954	100,851
North America	43,664	4,852	48,516	49,540
Oceania	4,496	1,113	5,609	6,476
World	**410,219**	**50,569**	**460,788**	**619,546**

Source: Annuarium Statisticum Ecclesiae 2020/Libreria Editrice Vaticana. Reprinted with the kind permission of Dicastero per la Comunicazione – Libreria Editrice Vaticana.
*Both diocesan (secular) and religious priests.

decision to ordain women. The letter opened with the line, "The Catholic Church has never felt that priestly or episcopal ordination can be validly conferred on women" (Paul VI 1976). Spurred by second-wave feminism of the 1960s and 1970s, a small women's ordination movement continued, but was quashed by John Paul II's apostolic letter in 1994, *Ordinatio Sacerdotalis*, which assumed that God could only be incarnate in a man, and that only men can continue Jesus's mission. He made clear, "I declare that the Church has no authority whatsoever to confer priestly ordination on women and ... this judgment is to be definitively held by all the Church's faithful" (John Paul II 1994).

The women's ordination movement is not prominent in the global South, home to more Catholics in the world and where gender roles tend more conservative. African women religious see no need for women to be ordained to the priesthood, given ample opportunities for women elsewhere in the church, such as in holding offices in dioceses and the episcopal conference (Allen 2009). Some women feel the debate over women's ordination has taken up too much space, recognizing the opportunities for them that not only already exist in the church, but have expanded under Pope Francis.

Despite the ongoing debate over women's ordination, Catholic women – nuns, scholars, and other professionals – have been increasingly promoted to prominent church positions since Vatican II. In 1970, the first woman was appointed undersecretary to a Vatican congregation: Sr. Enrica Rosanna (Italy). In 2002, 10% of the Vatican workforce were women (Hofmann 2002), and in 2019, it was 22% (Sailer 2019). Pope Francis has been particularly active in appointing women to higher levels of leadership. In March 2022, his new constitution of the Roman Curia expanded the potential role of laypeople in any office to serve in management positions with greater responsibilities, opening the possibility for even more women in leadership. In July 2022, he announced the appointment of three women to the previously all-male Dicastery for Bishops, which oversees nominations for bishops: Sr. Raffaella Petrini (Italy), Sr. Yvonne Reungoat (France), and Maria Lía Zervino (Argentina). Other notable women at the Vatican include:

- Sr. Luzia Premoli (Brazil), the second woman appointed to a Vatican congregation, the Congregation for the Evangelization of Peoples (2014)
- Barbara Jatta (Italy), the first female director of the Vatican Museums (2016)
- Francesca Di Giovanni (Italy), appointed Undersecretary for Multilateral Affairs in the Section for Relations with States (2020)
- Catia Summaria (Italy), the first woman appointed Promoter of Justice in the Vatican's Court of Appeals (2021)
- Sr. Nathalie Becquart (France), the first female undersecretary of the Synod of Bishops (2021)
- Sr. Alessandra Smerilli (Italy), appointed undersecretary for the Faith and Development Sector of the Dicastery for Promoting Integral Human Development of the Roman Curia (2021)
- Sr. Núria Calduch i Benages (Spain), secretary of the Pontifical Biblical Commission (2021)

Social Activism

Catholic Social Teaching dates to the nineteenth century, most notably to Wilhelm-Emmanuel von Ketteler (1811–1877), bishop of Mainz in Germany (Aubert and Boileau 2003). Ketteler, in his ministry to factory workers, realized deep structural economic problems and class tensions, leading him to advocate for economic and social reform to improve workers' conditions. He preached on practical aspects of reform, such as higher wages, shorter working days, Sunday rest, and outlawing labor of women and young girls (Aubert and Boileau 2003). His social teachings became widespread and influenced Pope Leo XIII, who wrote about labor, political power, human liberty, and the conditions of the working class in his encyclical *Rerum Novarum* (1891), helping to shape what would become Catholic Social Teaching (CST). Over the nineteenth and into the twentieth century, Catholic social consciousness gradually moved from charity to justice. CST took on a new importance under Pope John Paul II, who "prioritized labor over capital with the belief that capital is meant to serve labor and those that make up the labor force" (Boileau 1998, p. 17). In a rebuke of capitalism and individualism, he placed the worker above the work, and laborer over economic gain. CST is concerned with the social aspects of life like economic justice, human rights, war and peace, and centers around the idea of "integral development," which prioritizes the well-being of the whole person, not just economic growth (Sniegocki 2009). With a holistic view of human wellness, CST realizes the importance of the social, cultural, and ecological aspects of religious and spiritual life. There are numerous Catholic nonprofits, ministries, charities, orders, and other organizations that advocate for CST throughout the world, many of which are staffed by women and serve women.

Catholic Social Teaching has empowered Catholic women around the world to participate in the alleviation of suffering, advocate for social justice, and care for God's creation. Grounded in belief of the sanctity of all human life, CST is oriented toward the common good. Caritas Internationalis, for example, is a confederation of more than 160 Catholic relief and development agencies, present in over 200 countries. It is one of the main Catholic arms promoting charity and justice through faith in action, emergency response, and life transformation. Women are prominent throughout the organization; in Algeria, for instance, 90% of Caritas staff are women (Caritas 2018). Many extraordinary Catholic women are human rights advocates. Perhaps one of the most famous is Dorothy Day (1897–1980), a Catholic laywoman and cofounder with Peter Maurin of the Catholic Worker Movement, which espouses civil disobedience and nonviolence to provide aid for people experiencing poverty and homelessness. There are numerous influential and inspirational female Catholic activists today, such as:

- Sr. Mary John Mananzan (Philippines), founder of GABRIELA, a political party and federation of women's activist organizations
- Sr. Ephigenia Gachiri (Kenya), campaigner against female genital mutilation
- Léonie Kandolo (DR Congo), human rights activist, raising awareness of HIV/AIDS and an advocate for women in politics
- Sr. Brigid Arthur (Australia), cofounder of the Brigidine Asylum Seekers Project
- Sr. Helen Prejean (US), campaigner against the death penalty
- Thea Ormerod (Australia), president of Australian Religious Response to Climate Change
- Dr. María Cristina Grela Melluso (Uruguay), women's healthcare advocate, founder of the Montevideo office of Catholics for Choice
- Sr. Norma Pimentel (Mexico-US), advocate for migrants along the US-Mexico border
- Sr. Mary Haddad (US), president of the Catholic Health Association of the United States, among the nation's largest nonprofit healthcare providers
- Carolyn Woo (Hong Kong-US), from 2012 to 2016, president and CEO of Catholic Relief Services, which offers aid in more than 100 countries with an annual budget of $900 million

Catholic Social Teaching advocates for women's rights around the world, ranging from access to education and healthcare to addressing climate and environmental justice. At the same time, Catholic teaching affirms women's special and irreplaceable role in the family while also recognizing and respecting women's work, that is, that "roles and professions should be harmoniously combined, but with respect for the primary and inalienable right to work for home and raising children" (Wilczek-Karczewska, Pawlus, and Waleszczyński 2021, p. 81). The combination of affirming both work and domestic life provides a model for Catholic women in traditional global South cultures.

Slavery and Human Trafficking

Women religious have been active in combatting slavery and human trafficking for centuries. Talitha Kum, based in Rome and in 92 countries, is a global network of religious sisters that has assisted trafficked persons since the 1990s. The name is derived from Mark 5:41, where Jesus raises a girl from the dead: "Young girl, I say to you, get up!" Currently under the direction of Sr. Gabriella Bottani, SMC, Talitha Kum lives "in solidarity with our brothers and sisters who suffer the consequences of the evil of human trafficking" by offering prevention efforts, protection, social reintegration programs, rehabilitation, and political lobbying (Talitha Kum, n.d.). The Migrants and Refugees Section of the Vatican has several women serving as regional coordinators for Western Europe, the Middle East, East Asia, and Oceania, as well as female researchers, communication managers, and administrators. Their research highlights the unique precarity of socioeconomic hardship and unequal gender relations for women and girls, making them the most susceptible to trafficking.

HIV/AIDS

Catholic theologians have been outspoken on the global HIV/AIDS pandemic, a health situation where "women disproportionately bear the weight of infection, care, and stigma" of the disease, and are recognized as "key for the relief of many contemporary social, political and ecclesial ills" (Iozzio 2008, p. xiii). Primary contributors to infection rates include poverty, gender inequalities, traditional gender roles, the low status of women, and women's biological vulnerability (Tran 2008). More than 25% of global AIDS care services are provided by Catholic organizations, making the Catholic Church both an institutional support as well as a moral authority. Tensions exist between the deadly reality of HIV/AIDS and the church's teachings against contraceptive use since condoms are one of the most highly effective tools for stopping the spread of HIV/AIDS but officially banned by the Vatican.

Women religious in Africa are important providers of healthcare, education, and spiritual support to their communities. In sub-Saharan Africa, 59% of new HIV/AIDS infections are among women ages 15 and older. In 2019, young women were 24% of new AIDS infections, even though they are only 10% of the region's population (UNAIDS 2020). Many Catholic organizations have been formed to provide relief and support against HIV/AIDS. For example, in 2002, the All-Africa Conference: Sister to Sister organization formed in partnership with Yale Divinity School in New Haven, Connecticut, comprised of Catholic women religious and lay workers responding to HIV/AIDS. In partnership with African women, including the Circle of Concerned African Women Theologians, 6,500 sisters have helped half a million people combat HIV/AIDS, COVID-19, and poverty.

Abortion

Abortion was prohibited in 1869 by Pope Pius IX and became a priority for the Catholic Church under John Paul II. The antiabortion movement in the United States was the largest moral reform movement of the late twentieth century, with Catholic women at the fore such as Juli Loesch (b.1951) and Joan Andrews (b.1939) (Haugeberg 2017). Though the Catholic Church was initially the only large institution against the legalization of abortion, it gradually inspired Evangelical Protestants and other conservative religious groups to join the antiabortion movement. Groups such as the National Council of Catholic Women blocked the Equal Rights Amendment, fought against the legalization of abortion, and reaffirmed what was considered traditional family values. Many Catholic women in the 1970s questioned whether second-wave feminism was good for women, with wider contraceptive use, delayed marriage, smaller family sizes, and new opportunities for women outside the home.

The prohibition on abortion has consistently clashed with secular movements around the world, which consider access to safe abortion part of women's overall healthcare. In Catholic-majority countries in Europe and Latin America, feminist activists have redefined abortion as a public health and women's rights issue. Secular activists in these places are up against powerful Catholic organizations that lobby politicians against legal abortion, which have been generally – but not always – more successful than grassroots feminist organizations (Blofield 2008). The prohibition on contraceptive use is likely the least adhered law in contemporary Catholicism. In the United States, a study found that just 15% of American Catholics think using contraceptives is wrong; 41% said it is morally acceptable and 36% say it is not a moral issue at all (Pew Research Center 2012). Despite the diversity of attitudes in Latin America, comparatively lower proportions of Catholics think using contraceptives is morally wrong, such as 46% in El Salvador and Honduras (the highest) to 6% in Uruguay and 5% in Chile (the lowest) (Pew Research Center 2014).

Child Sex Abuse

Among the most serious problems in the twenty-first century Catholic Church is rampant sexual abuse of children and the networks of clerics involved in decades-long coverups. Most victims are between 11 and 14 years old, mainly boys, but some girls; global totals are unknown, but there have been hundreds of thousands of victims abused by thousands of priests all over the world. Lucetta Scaraffia, a prominent Italian Catholic reporter, stated that having a greater number of women at the Vatican could have helped prevent abuse as well as address the "veil of secrecy" surrounding it, since women are more likely than men to defend victims of abuse (Butt 2010). Marie Collins, an Irish Catholic survivor of clergy sexual abuse, is another outspoken advocate for child safety in the church.

Anne Barrett Doyle, a long-time Catholic crusader against clergy sex abuse, operates BishopAccountability.org, established in 2003. The website documents cases of abuse in the Catholic Church in the United States, Argentina, Italy, Ireland, and beyond. In February 2022, Pope Benedict XVI (1927–2022) offered a formal statement on his failures in handling the abuse crisis. He largely claimed ignorance, not responsibility, and denied any wrongdoing despite ample evidence that he covered up abuse while Archbishop of Munich (1977–1982). Pope Francis established the Pontifical Commission for the Protection of Minors in 2014 specifically to deal with abuse and to protect children from pedophiles in the church. Led by Boston's Cardinal Archbishop Seán O'Malley, the commission consists of 18 members, eight of whom are women from the United Kingdom, Tonga, India, the United States, South Africa, Zambia, Poland, and the Netherlands/Germany.

Catholic Women in Africa

One of the most well-known instances of gendered conversion to Catholicism in Africa is Dorothy Hodgson's ethnographic fieldwork among the Maasai in Tanzania (Hodgson 2005). In the 1950s, Spiritan missionaries (the Congregation of the Holy Spirit) attempted to convert men but deemed the mission a frustrated failure when Maasai women converted in droves to create a "church of women." Between 1900 and 2000, Catholicism grew in Africa at an average of 4.32% per year, only dropping to 3.02% per year between 2000 and 2020 – still growing faster than the general population. In 2020, Africa is home to 236 million Catholics, representing 19% of all Catholics worldwide. Several African nations are majority Catholic: Cabo Verde (90%), Seychelles (81%), Reunion (79%), São Tomé and Príncipe (73%), Equatorial Guinea (71%), Burundi (63%), the Republic of the Congo (61%), the Democratic Republic of the Congo (55%), Lesotho (55%), Angola (51%), and South Sudan (51%) (Johnson and Zurlo 2022). The Catholic Church has been extremely active in institution-building in Africa, such as in education, healthcare, politics, and peacebuilding. Women have been at the fore of these initiatives as teachers, nurses, and activists of all kinds. For example, in the political turmoil of the 1990s in Congo-Brazzaville (Republic of the Congo), the Catholic Church was seen as the one of the few legitimate national institutions able to fill the void left by a broken governmental system. Catholic sisters, the majority of whom were Congolese, were heavily involved in peace work, refugee shelters, peace marches, prayer vigils, aid distribution, and assistance in postwar recovery efforts (Martin 2009).

Of the nearly 80,000 women religious in Africa, the largest populations are in Tanzania (12,730), the Democratic Republic of the Congo (10,186), and Kenya (7,982) (*Annuarium Statisticum Ecclesiae* 2020). The first female order to arrive in Africa was the Missionary Sisters of Our Lady of Africa, or White Sisters, which was founded in 1878 in Algeria and then spread out across the continent. The first African congregation was formed in Tanzania. African sisters were initially denied places in European convents, but this changed in 1949 (Hahn 2019). Since the 1960s and 1970s, religious vocations have been growing among women, even though the initial thought of "losing" women to religious life was difficult to comprehend: "If resistance to giving up girls for baptism and church marriage was strong, the loss of a young woman to a religious vocation was unthinkable: the vow of celibacy unnatural and a denial of social obligations, the vow of poverty incomprehensible, and the vow of obedience an irreparable loss" (Martin 2009, p. 93). Nevertheless, Africans are the majority of sisters today as European missionaries have retired, died, and not been replaced. Women see the Catholic Church as a place to work toward emancipation, with opportunities there not afforded in wider society; African women religious are more involved in apostolic works than in contemplative life (Ngundo and Wiggins 2017). While some young girls join to escape village poverty, they sign up for a different kind of sacrificial poverty in the order and a life of ministering to others. Some young women face hostility from their families when joining an order, since it represents a departure from their expected role of wife and mother. Yet, upon joining an order, women are provided education and leadership training to engage in a wide variety of callings, including fundraising, counseling, financial planning, and other occupational training. African women religious engage in holistic ministry to care for the spirit, body, land, and community.

Catholic Women in Asia

Catholics comprise less than 5% of the population in most Asian countries – the major exceptions are Timor-Leste and the Philippines – but Catholicism has had a substantial influence in the region, especially through institution-building (Brown and Chambon 2022). Catholic schools and hospitals are important in the social fabric of many Asian communities. Female Catholic orders are a critical part of this history, where women formed social and religious networks for service. India is home to more than 99,500 women religious, although Catholics are only 1.5% of the country's population. Most of these sisters are under 35 years old. According to the Catholic Bishops' Conference of India, there are 285 religious sister congregations, 13 women's contemplative communities, and 35 women's secular institutes. Women religious in India face discrimination on numerous fronts, as religious minorities and as women, and face constant pressure from the Hindu nationalist government and new restrictions on missionary work. For example, the Missionaries of Charity, the order founded by Mother Teresa, shut down its adoption services in 2015 after the country implemented new international adoption rules that did not align with Catholic religious views on relationships and family (Catholic News Agency 2015).

China is home to 10 million Catholics, four million in government-sanctioned churches and six million "underground" but in contact with the Vatican (Johnson and Zurlo 2022). Many religious congregations in China have roots in the late nineteenth and early twentieth centuries, initially working very closely with foreign missionaries. They virtually disappeared from the public with the rise of Mao Zedong in 1949 and the Cultural Revolution (1966–1976). By 1957, no foreign sisters were in the country except for a single school in Beijing that taught children of foreign diplomats (Leung and Wittberg 2004). Some sisters married and entered public secular service, while

Photo 8.1 South Korean women pray at the mass for peace and reconciliation at the Myeongdong Cathedral in Seoul during a papal visit of Pope Francis (2014). *Source:* Jeon Han/Flickr/CC BY-SA 2.0.

others continued in secret prayer and service until orders were re-recognized in the late 1970s. Official Vatican surveys do not include mainland China, but a 2015 study reported 3,170 women religious in 87 registered religious congregations and 1,400 women religious in 37 unregistered religious congregations (Chambon 2019). Cultural anthropologist Michel Chambon's extensive study of women religious in Fujian, China concluded that

> Despite a whole range of efforts and a strong desire to belong to the universal Catholic Church, Chinese nuns do not simply follow the standardized Catholic forms of religious life that encourages a collective pursuit of a unique "charism" either within apostolic or contemplative congregations. Instead, Chinese nuns organize their religious commitment along a wide and evolving spectrum of practices that borrows from two traditional Catholic models, the *beatas* [Latin term referring to consecrated women] and the missionary congregations. Thus, their religious life fosters a multidimensional and changing apostolate combined with a search for autonomy from social and ecclesial institutions.
>
> *(Chambon 2019, p. 2)*

Chinese women religious are in a precarious position with limited training in education and healthcare, financial difficulties, lack of autonomy due to the country's political situation, and no access to the international network of religious orders and Catholic Church officials (Leung and Wittberg 2004).

Catholic Women in Latin America

Latin America is home to over 102,000 women religious, with the largest numbers in Brazil (25,842), Mexico (25,561), and Colombia (12,776). The number of women religious in the region has been declining. In 1980, South America was home to 89,936 sisters (Greenwood and Gautier 2018); in 2020, the figure was 63,340. Argentina's number dropped by more than half: 12,446 in 1980 and 6,695 in 2020 (*Annuarium Statisticum Ecclesiae* 2020).

The first women's organizations in Latin America – where politics, culture, and faith are interconnected – were linked to the Catholic Church in their advocacy for the poor, service in education, and in the church (Stein 2001). Their advocacy expanded in the 1970s and 1980s into land reform, reproductive health services, human rights organizations, and other social movements demanding for political change during harsh dictatorships. By the end of the century, Catholic women in Latin America and the Caribbean were more vocal for women's empowerment, publicly debating on issues such as sexuality, abortion, and availability of contraceptives (Stein 2001). Much of their advocacy was catalyzed by liberation theology, which despite encouraging working class women to take up more space in church and society, did not specifically address the unique needs of women. However, liberation theology also helped shape mission as accompaniment of the poor, which became a major focus of Catholic missionary identity (Robert 1997).

Catholic Women in Europe

Catholic sisters in Eastern Europe suffered tremendously during and after World War II, when communist governments tried to reduce the public influence of the church in society. In some countries, like Romania, Poland, Hungary, and Czechoslovakia (Czechia), orders were banned, their houses confiscated, and many sisters and brothers sent to labor camps, imprisoned, or killed. More than men, women withstood the pressure from secret police to bribe religious workers to serve as agents of the state. In Poland, under communism from 1947 to 1989, only 30 of the country's 27,000 sisters informed for the police, compared to thousands of priests who did so (Catholic News Service 2007).

Photo 8.2 Women religious pray during mass officiated by Pope Francis at the Shrine of Our Lady of Charity in Santiago de Cuba (2015). *Source:* Calixto N. Llanes/Flickr Public Domain.

In Slovakia, Sr. Florina Boenighová was arrested by secret police in 1951 at the hospital she worked at, accused of running a secret seminary and shielding priests. She was tortured, tried, and served 15 years in prison where she died and was buried in an unmarked grave. In Russia, most Catholic priests and nuns were killed within 20 years of the 1917 Russian Revolution (Luxmoore 2016). Catholics were greatly persecuted in Georgia, Kazakhstan, Latvia, Ukraine, and Lithuania, but many sisters secretly worked to encourage Catholics underground. After the fall of the Berlin Wall in 1989 and bolstered by the election of Polish Karol Józef Wojtyła as pope (John Paul II), female orders were quickly revived in Eastern Europe.

Europe has experienced a profound decline in the number of sisters, from 537,046 in 1976 to 207,994 in 2020 (*Annuarium Statisticum Ecclesiae* 1976; *Annuarium Statisticum Ecclesiae* 2020). The number of vocations in Italy, the country with the highest number of sisters, dropped precipitously from 145,083 in 1976 to 70,020 in 2020. The decline can be attributed to several factors. The gradual secularization of most European countries has been impacting women's religious life on the continent, as did the feminist movement of the 1970s, which provided new opportunities for women outside of home and the church. Other potential reasons for decline include the sexual scandals among Catholic clergy and burnout, trauma, and exploitation of sisters.

Catholic Women in North America

The Maryknoll Sisters was the first Catholic religious congregation established in the United States, founded in 1912 by Sr. Josephine Rogers (1882–1955). First an auxiliary to the Maryknoll Fathers, women soon became missionaries in their own right (though not formally recognized until 1937), as the first sisters were sent to China in 1921 (Robert 1997). The Maryknoll Sisters grew rapidly during the World War II era and just after it, when the number of sisters more than doubled between 1940 and 1960 to 1,430 (Behrens 2004, p. 193). It was around this time that the church entered the modern world and redefined itself as the people of God and not simply a hierarchy of priests, bishops, and laity (Robert 1997). Becoming a religious sister provided Catholic women an alternative to traditional domestic life and affirmed their independence as women: "By becoming a Maryknoll sister, a woman could have the best of all possible worlds. She would fulfill her 'spiritual nature' as a woman, yet also enjoy new opportunities and the chance to go abroad and work in the world" (Behrens 2004, p. 193).

The number of sisters dropped dramatically in the United States from 179,954 in 1965 to just 39,912 in 2020 (*Annuarium Statisticum Ecclesiae* 2020). The fastest period of decline was after Vatican II in the late 1960s and 1970s, when leaders were encouraged with the difficult task to bring renewal to religious orders. Many sisters broke from existing orders to found new ones, while others left institutes altogether. Perhaps the single greatest challenge to growing the number of vocations is ageing; there are more sisters over age 90 than under age 60 (Berrelleza, Gautier, and Gray 2014). The decline of vocations in the United States might be staved off by the increasing diversity of religious orders, with mission becoming tightly intertwined with migration. Nearly a quarter of all sisters in the country involved in formation, studies, or ministry are foreign-born (Johnson et al. 2019). Many sisters are from Vietnam, the Philippines, Mexico, Canada, and Australia (Do, Wiggins, and Gaunt 2021). The largest – and one of the oldest (1843) – women's institute in the United States is the Sisters of Mercy of the Americas, with over 2,000 members.

Catholic Women in Oceania

The largest Catholic populations in Oceania are in Australia (26% Catholic; 4,330 sisters), Papua New Guinea (26% Catholic; 827 sisters), New Zealand (11% Catholic; 601 sisters), and New Caledonia (50% Catholic; 57 sisters). The countries with the highest percent Catholic are Wallis and Futuna Islands (95% Catholic; 41 sisters), Guam (82% Catholic; 64 sisters), and Northern Mariana Islands (72% Catholic; 13 sisters) (Johnson and Zurlo 2022; *Annuarium Statisticum Ecclesiae* 2020).

Women have been central to the Australian Catholic Church since the arrival of five Sisters of Charity in Sydney in 1838 from Ireland. Australia's first women's religious orer formed in 1857, the Sisters of the Good Samaritan. Women have been particularly active in education, nursing, immigrant support, orphanages, and other charitable works. The first and only Aboriginal women's order existed between 1938 and 1951, the Daughters of Our Lady, Queen of the Apostle. Established in the northwest in Beagle Bay for Indigenous women to work among their own people, the order closed after eleven years (Choo 2001, 2019). Indigenous women had status within the mission, but were regarded lower than the European priests, brothers, and nuns; they were also geographically and culturally isolated. All the women left the order before they became professed sisters. The only Catholic saint from Australia is a woman, Mary MacKillop (1842–1909), dedicated to education for the poor and canonized in 2010. The 2016 National Church Life Survey reported that attendance in the Catholic Church in Australia is 62% female, 93% of Catholics attend Mass at least monthly, and the average age was 59 years old (NCLS Research 2017). The Catholic Women's League of Australia has been long engaged in activism related to bioethics (antiabortion, reproductive technologies, euthanasia, stem cell research) and in living out Catholic Social Teaching in society.

Conclusion

Though the Catholic Church is well-known for its prohibition on female clergy, the debate over women's ordination does not frame the picture of gender roles within Catholic parishes and communities worldwide. Church tradition holds women in high regard. Marian devotion encourages millions of spiritual pilgrimages a year, countless numbers of laywomen in local parishes are involved in nearly every aspect of church life, and more than 619,000 Catholic sisters worldwide are engaged in contemplative prayer and apostolic works, as well as political, social, and ecological activism (see Chapter 15).

Catholic women religious are extraordinary, taking vows of chastity, poverty, and obedience to work as selfless servants of Jesus Christ all around the world. Yet, as recent research has revealed, one of the most hidden issues within the church is that sisters experience mental and physical abuse, oppression, and racism (Cernuzio 2021). In 2019, Pope Francis called the abuse of sisters an "ongoing problem" and a "scandal." That year he also released a decree, "Vos Estis Lux Mundi" ("You Are the Light of the World") making it mandatory for priests and nuns to report cases of abuse (Giangravé 2021). However, just 4% of religious congregations are under investigation by the Vatican due to abuse allegations. In 2019, Lucetta Scaraffia and her team resigned from the Vatican's women's magazine *Woman Church World*, claiming that church leaders had consistently tried to censor their reporting of sexual abuse of nuns, secret abortions, and misogyny in the church. Catholic theologian Tina Beattie, a long-standing advocate for women's prominence in the church, stated, "If the [Catholic] Church has any hope of being listened to by modern women, it needs to go beyond its present anachronistic sexual stereotypes and authoritarian structures, to present the Gospel in a way that is attentive to the questions, needs and values of the age, without surrendering the central truths of the Christian faith" (Beattie 2006, p. 13). While there is a strong tradition of female reverence and respect in the Catholic Church, women from within its ranks are speaking out on abuse, neglect, and exploitation to awaken the male clergy and move toward healing, restoration, and reconciliation.

Reflection Questions

1) Describe the historical development of Catholic Social Teaching (CST) and reflect on its role in empowering Catholic women worldwide. In what ways does CST encourage Catholic engagement in the world, and on what kinds of issues?
2) Reflect upon the ways in which the Catholic Church has spoken out on various social issues that specifically relate to women, such as sexuality, healthcare, and sex trafficking. How have Catholic women used their agency to alleviate human suffering on these, and other, pressing social issues?
3) Catholic sisters outnumber professed men on every continent and in most countries. What, do you think, is appealing about the life of women religious? What challenges and opportunities do they face in living out their Christian calling in their various cultural contexts worldwide?

Works Cited

Ad Gentes (1965). Decree *Ad Gentes* on the mission activity of the church. https://www.vatican.va/archive/hist_councils/ii_vatican_council/documents/vat-ii_decree_19651207_ad-gentes_en.html (accessed 8 February 2022).

Allen, Jr., John L. (2009). A quick pulse of women religious in Africa. National Catholic Reporter. https://www.ncronline.org/news/quick-pulse-women-religious-africa (accessed 8 February 2022).

Secretaria Status, Rationarium Generale Ecclesiae (1976). *Annuarium Statisticum Ecclesiae: Statistical Yearbook of the Church*. Vatican City: Libreria Editrice Vatican.

Secretaria Status, Rationarium Generale Ecclesiae (2020). *Annuarium Statisticum Ecclesiae: Statistical Yearbook of the Church*. Vatican City: Libreria Editrice Vatican.

Aubert, Robert and Boileau, David A. (2003). *Catholic Social Teaching: An Historical Perspective*. Milwaukee: Marquette University Press.

Beattie, Tina (2006). *New Catholic Feminism: Theology and Theory*. London: Routledge.

Behrens, Susan F. (2004). From symbols of the sacred to symbols of subversion to simply obscure: maryknoll women religious in Guatemala, 1953 to 1967. *The Americas*, 61(2), 189–216.

Belgian Bishops' Conference (2020). L'Église Catholique en Belgique.

Berrelleza, Erick, Gautier, Mary L., and Gray, Mark M. (2014). *Population trends among religious institutes of women*. Center for Applied Research in the Apostolate Special Report, Georgetown University, Washington DC.

Bieringer, Reimund (2008). The scriptural argument in *Ordinatio Sacerdotalis*. In: *World Christianity in the Twentieth Century: A Reader* (ed. Noel Davies and Martin Conway), 251–253. London: SCM Press.

Blofield, Merike (2008). Women's choices in comparative perspective: abortion policies in late-developing Catholic countries. *Comparative Politics*, 40(4), 399–419.

Boileau, David A. (1998). *Principles of Catholic Social Teaching*. Milwaukee, WI: Marquette University Press.

Brown, Bernardo and Chambon, Michel (2022). Catholicism's overlooked importance in Asia. *The Diplomat*, February 4. https://thediplomat.com/2022/02/catholicisms-overlooked-importance-in-asia (accessed 8 February 2022).

Bruce, Tricia C., Masso-Rivetti, Cella, and Sherman, Jennifer (2021). Called to contribute: findings from an in-depth interview study of US Catholic women and diaconate.

Butt, Riazat (2010). Archbishop links priestly celibacy and Catholic sex abuse scandals. *The Guardian*. March 11. https://www.theguardian.com/world/2010/mar/11/priestly-celibacy-catholic-sex-scandals (accessed 11 February 2022).

Caritas (2018). Caritas women leaders. https://www.caritas.org/2018/03/women-2018 (accessed 11 February 2022).

Catholic News Agency (2015). New policy forces missionaries of charity to end adoption services in India. October 14. https://www.catholicnewsagency.com/news/32815/new-policy-forces-missionaries-of-charity-to-end-adoption-services-in-india (accessed 14 February 2022).

Catholic News Service (2007). Polish Catholic nuns withstood secret police. https://historynewsnetwork.org/article/35175 (accessed 14 February 2022).

Center for the Applied Research in the Apostolate (2020). Frequently requested church statistics. https://cara.georgetown.edu/frequently-requested-church-statistics (accessed 11 February 2022).

Cernuzio, Salvatore (2021). *Il Velo del Silenzio: Abusi, Violenze, Frustrazioni Nella Vita Religiosa Femminile*. Cinisello Balsamo, Milano: San Paolo.

Chambon, Michel (2019). Chinese Catholic nuns and the organization of religious life in contemporary China. *Religions*, 10(447), 1–17.

Choo, Christine (2001). *Mission Girls: Aboriginal Women on Catholic Missions in Kimberley, Western Australia, 1900–1950*. Crawley: University of Western Australia Press.

Choo, Christine (2019). Daughters of our lady, queen of the apostles—the first and only order of Aboriginal sisters in Australia, 1938–1951: history, context and outcomes. *Journal of the Australian Catholic Historical Society*, 40, 103–130.

Coakley, John W. (2006). *Women, Men, and Spiritual Power: Female Saints and Their Male Collaborators*. New York: Columbia University Press.

Do, Thu T., Wiggins, Jonathon L., and Gaunt, Thomas P. (2021). Cultural diversity in vocations to religious life in the United States: a national study of new religious members. Center for Applied Research in the Apostolate, Georgetown University, Washington DC.

Espín, Oliva M. (2020). *Women, Sainthood, and Power: A Feminist Psychology of Cultural Constructions*. Lanham: Lexington Books.

Fuszara, Małgorzata (2005). Between feminism and the Catholic Church: the women's movement in Poland. *Sociologický Časopis/Czech Sociological Review*, 41(6), 1057–1075.

Giangravé, Claire (2021). New book shines light on abuse and racist discrimination on Catholic nun. *Religion News Service*, November 29, https://religionnews.com/2021/11/29/new-book-shines-light-on-abuse-and-racist-discrimination-of-catholic-nuns (accessed 9 February 2022).

Greenwood, Julia and Gautier, Mary (2018). Trends in the life and ministry of religious sisters in Latin America. CARA Special Report.

Gyarmathy-Amherd, Catherine (2008). The ordination of women in the Roman Catholic Church. In: *Women and Ordination in the Christian Churches: International Perspectives* (ed. Ian Jones, Kirsty Thorpe, and Janet Wooten), 40–53. London: T&T Clark.

Haerpfer, Christian et al. (2022). *World values survey: round seven – country-pooled datafile version 4.0.* Madrid, Spain and Vienna, Austria: JD Systems Institute and WVSA Secretariat.

Hahn, Allison (2019). Christianity in Africa. In: *Encyclopedia of Women in World Religions: Faith and Culture Across History* (ed. Susan J. De Gaia), 176–178. Santa Barbara: ABC-CLIO.

Haugeberg, Karissa (2017). *Women Against Abortion: Inside the Largest Moral Reform Movement of the Twentieth Century*. Urbana: University of Illinois Press.

Henold, Mary J. (2020). *The Laywoman Project: Remaking Catholic Womanhood in the Vatican II Era.* Chapel Hill: University of North Carolina Press.

Hodgson, Dorothy L. (2005). *The Church of Women: Gendered Encounters between Maasai and Missionaries*. Bloomington, IN: Indiana University Press.

Hofmann, Paul (2002). *The Vatican's Women: Female Influence at the Holy See*. New York: St. Martin's Press.

Iozzio, Mary Jo (2008). Preface: a companion to Catholic ethicists on HIV/AIDS prevention. In: *Calling for Justice Throughout the World: Catholic Women Theologians on the HIV/AIDS Pandemic* (ed. Mary Jo Iozzio), xi–xvi. New York: Continuum.

John Paul II (1994). Apostolic letter *Ordinatio Sacerdotalis* of John Paul II to the bishops of the Catholic Church on reserving priestly ordination to men alone. https://www.vatican.va/content/john-paul-ii/en/apost_letters/1994/documents/hf_jp-ii_apl_19940522_ordinatio-sacerdotalis.html (accessed 8 February 2022).

John XXIII (1963). Pacem in terris: encyclical of Pope John XXIII on establishing universal peace in truth, justice, charity, and liberty. April 11. https://www.vatican.va/content/john-xxiii/en/encyclicals/documents/hf_j-xxiii_enc_11041963_pacem.html (accessed 9 February 2022).

Johnson, Mary et al. (2019). *Migration for Mission: International Catholic Sisters in the United States.* New York: Oxford University Press.

Johnson, Todd M. and Zurlo, Gina A. ed. (2022). *World Christian Database*. Leiden/Boston: Brill.

Knibbe, Kim E. (2013). *Faith in the Familiar: Religion, Spirituality and Place in the South of the Netherlands*. Leiden/Boston: Brill.

Kum, Talitha (n.d.) About us: mission. https://www.talithakum.info/en/about-us/mission (accessed 9 February 2022).

Leo XIII (1891). Rerum novarum: encyclical of Pope Leo XIII on capital and labor. https://www.vatican.va/content/leo-xiii/en/encyclicals/documents/hf_l-xiii_enc_15051891_rerum-novarum.html (accessed 10 February 2022).

Leung, Beatrice and Wittberg, Patricia (2004). Catholic religious orders of women in China: adaptation and power. *Journal for the Scientific Study of Religion*, 43(1), 67–82.

Luxmoore, Jonathan (2016). *The God of the Gulag*. 2 vols. Leominster, UK: Gracewing Publishing.

Magyar, Judit E. (2019). Christianity in Europe. In: *Encyclopedia of Women in World Religions: Faith and Culture Across History* (ed. Susan J. De Gaia), 178–180. Santa Barbara: ABC-CLIO.

Malone, Mary T. (2017). *Four Women Doctors of the Church*. Maryknoll, NY: Orbis Books.

Martin, Phyllis M. (2009). *Catholic Women of Congo-Brazzaville*. Bloomington: Indiana University Press.

Muir, Elizabeth G. (2019). *A Women's History of the Christian Church*. Toronto: University of Toronto Press.

NCLS Research (2017). Church life profile for the Catholic Church in Australia. National Church Life Survey.

Ngundo, Bibiana M. and Wiggins, Jonathan (2017). Women religious in Africa. CARA Special Report.

Paul VI (1976). Declaration *Inter Insigniores* on the question of admission of women to the ministerial priesthood. https://www.vatican.va/roman_curia/congregations/cfaith/documents/rc_con_cfaith_doc_19761015_inter-insigniores_en.html (accessed 8 February 2022).

Perry, Tim S. and Kendall, Daniel (2013). *The Blessed Virgin Mary*. Grand Rapids, MI: William B. Eerdmans Pub.

Pew Research Center (2012). Public divided over birth control insurance mandate. https://www.pewresearch.org/politics/2012/02/14/public-divided-over-birth-control-insurance-mandate (accessed 11 February 2022).

Pew Research Center (2014). Religion in Latin America: widespread change in a historically Catholic Religion.

Robert, Dana L. (1997). *American Women in Mission: A Social History of Their Thought and Practice*. Macon, GA: Mercer University Press.

Sailer, Gudrun (2019). Number of women employees in the Vatican on the rise. *Vatican News*. https://www.vaticannews.va/en/vatican-city/news/2020-03/number-of-women-employees-in-the-vatican-on-the-rise.html (accessed 10 February 2022).

Sniegocki, John (2009). *Catholic Social Teaching and Economic Globalization: The Quest for Alternatives*. Milwaukee, WI: Marquette University Press.

Stein, Laura G. (2001). The politics of implementing women's rights in Catholic countries of Latin America. In: *Globalization, Gender and Religion: The Politics of Women's Rights in Catholic and Muslim Contexts* (ed. Jane H. Bayes and Nayareh Tohidi), 127–156. New York: Palgrave.

Tran, Y-Lan (2008). HIV/AIDS in Vietnam: calling for dignity, justice, and care. In: *Calling for Justice Throughout the World: Catholic Women Theologians on the HIV/AIDS Pandemic* (ed. Mary Jo Iozzio), 31–37. New York: Continuum.

UNAIDS (2020). Seizing the moment: tackling entrenched inequalities to end epidemics. Geneva: Joint United Nations Programme on HIV/AIDS.

Wilczek-Karczewska, Magdalena, Pawlus, Małgorzata, and Waleszczyński, Andrzej (2021). Combatting legal and cultural forms of discrimination against women from the point of view of Catholic Social Teaching. In: *Sustainable Development Goals and the Catholic Church: Catholic Social Teaching and the UN's Agenda 2030* (ed. Katarzyna Cichos), 72–86. Abingdon, Oxon: Routledge.

9

Women in Orthodox Christianity

"The greatest of souls in the ancient Church recognized that the hierarchy of spiritual gifts had nothing at all to do with sex."

Elisabeth Behr-Sigel (Behr-Sigel 2000, p. 43)

Orthodox churches emphasize the passing of traditions that keep the faithful linked to the early church and the apostles of Jesus Christ. However, the emphasis on tradition can make it difficult to reimagine Orthodox beliefs and practices in subsequent generations; the "living tradition" of Orthodoxy requires reconceptualizing the faith in different times and places, while still respecting the faith that came before (Tamer 2018). This reconceptualization directly impacts gender roles, both in broader society and the church. Women are held to traditional gendered expectations of their participation in the Sunday Divine Liturgy, if they can receive formal theological education, and if they are encouraged toward leadership in their communities. Yet, at the same time, Orthodox history lauds women for passing on tradition to their children, recognizing numerous faithful women of the past as saints and exemplars of the faith.

The term "Orthodox" originates from Greek: *ortho*, meaning "straight," and *doxa*, meaning "opinion." Orthodox history can be divided into four eras: prehistory (time of Christ to 500), early Byzantine Era (500–1000), late Byzantine Era (1000–1500), and the national church period (1500 to today) (Jacobsen 2021). Orthodoxy traces its roots to Greek-speaking Christians in the Eastern Roman Empire (as opposed to Latin speakers in the West). There was no "Orthodoxy" nor "Catholicism" in Christianity's first few hundred years; what is now known as Eastern Orthodox Christianity began to form at the First Council of Nicaea (325) in Türkiye. Tensions between Eastern and Western Christians over matters of culture, language, and theology eventually culminated in the "Great Schism," which divided Catholicism and Orthodoxy in 1054 and pit the popes of each tradition against each other. The Byzantine Empire, coined as such in reference to the Eastern half of the old Roman Empire (today's Greece and Türkiye) lasted until 1453.

The rise of Islam beginning in the seventh century eventually captured much of the territory where Orthodoxy had previously flourished throughout the Middle East. There were four patriarchs of Orthodox Christianity until the Islamic conquest: Constantinople, Antioch, Alexandria, and Jerusalem, and these cities represented one of the earliest forms of Christian self-organization (McGuckin 2016). Only Constantinople remained after the conquest. Orthodoxy moved eastward with conversions in Russia, Syria, and northern Iraq until the rise of the Turks in the early 1000s, which began the long and slow decline of the Byzantine Empire and the Eastern Orthodox Church.

Catholic–Orthodox relations were never the same after the fourth crusade in 1204, where Catholics destroyed any remnants of the Byzantine Empire. Ottoman Turks in the 1400s proved an

Women in World Christianity: Building and Sustaining a Global Movement, First Edition. Gina A. Zurlo.

extensive threat to Orthodox Christianity, and Constantinople – the last patriarch – fell to the Turks in 1439. Following the collapse of the Byzantine Empire, the church became increasingly fragmented; individual Orthodox churches became more closely associated with specific countries and languages, rather than empires. Therefore, Orthodox Christianity today takes the form along national or ethnic lines: Russian Orthodox Church, Romanian Orthodox Church, Greek Orthodox Church, Coptic Orthodox Church, etc. Orthodox Christian belief and practice are informed by the seven ecumenical councils: First Council of Nicaea (325), First Council of Constantinople (381), Council of Ephesus (431), Council of Chalcedon (451), Second Council of Constantinople (553), Third Council of Constantinople (680–681), and Second Council of Nicaea (787).

This historical preamble is important because the histories, structures, and cultures of Orthodox Christianity are markedly different from other Christian traditions – differences that impact expectations for women in Orthodox communities. Rome remains an important center for Roman Catholic identity and belonging, Protestant churches tend to form along theological lines, and Independent Christianity emerges from a mixture of theology, charismatic leadership, and postcolonial politics. Yet, Orthodox Christianity is tied to its history of empire, persecution, fragmentation, and ethnolinguistic identity. Church history also illustrates that no other Christians have suffered like the Orthodox. From its start until the fifteenth century, Orthodox Christians were under threat from Catholics, Arabs, Turks, and Mongols; in the twentieth century, they were severely persecuted by Soviets, Nazis, and Communists. In the twenty-first century, they face several new pressures – socially from Muslims in North Africa and the Middle East, religiously from missionary-minded Evangelical Protestants, and politically and militarily from Russia. Consequently, survival is an integral part of Orthodox identity. This chapter will discuss the tension of Orthodox tradition as it relates to women's roles, including debates over the female diaconate and ordination, women's monasticism, women in the ecumenical movement, and the unique challenges women faced in the severity of twentieth-century persecutions.

Orthodox, 1900–2050

Orthodox Christianity includes four traditions: Eastern (Chalcedonian), Oriental (Pre-Chalcedonian, Non-Chalcedonian, Monophysite), Assyrian, and nonhistorical Orthodox. The largest of these is Eastern Orthodox (Russian, Ukrainian, Romanian, etc.) with 221 million affiliates (Johnson and Zurlo 2022). Oriental Orthodox are in five major types: Armenian, Coptic, Ethiopian, Syrian, and Syro-Malabarese, totaling nearly 64 million. Eastern and Oriental Orthodox are not in eucharistic communion with one another (Ionita and Glazer 2009). Orthodox Christianity consists of 11 autocephalous churches (self-governing in ecclesiastical and political life though in communion with one another), three autonomous churches that are not entirely self-governing, and various diaspora churches worldwide composed of people living outside their historic homeland (McGuckin 2016).

The demographic trajectory of Orthodox Christianity in the twentieth century was unlike all other Christian traditions. Orthodox Christians represented 7% of the world's population in 1900, but this dropped to less than 4% by 1970 due to persecution under atheistic regimes in Europe (Table 9.1; Johnson and Zurlo 2022). Although Orthodoxy has rebounded slightly, it has not reclaimed its former share of the world's population. In 1900, Orthodox were 21% of all Christians, but in 2020, they were 12%. Orthodox Christianity is also different from other traditions in its North/South distribution. Whereas Protestantism, Catholicism, and Independent Christianity shifted to the global South between 1900 and 2000, Orthodox Christianity was majority global South from its origins until around the year 1300, when it became majority North as it was pushed

Table 9.1 Orthodox by continent, 1900–2050.

Region	Orthodox Christians 1900	% of pop. 1900	% of Orthodox 1900	Rate % p.a. 1900–2020	Orthodox Christians 2020	% of pop. 2020	% of Orthodox 2020	Orthodox Christians 2050	% of pop. 2050	% of Orthodox 2050
Global North	104,972,000	21.7	90.3	0.60	213,978,000	19.2	73.3	193,276,000	17.0	60.0
Europe	104,557,000	26.0	90.0	0.57	205,608,000	27.5	70.4	183,176,000	25.8	56.8
North America	415,000	0.5	0.4	2.54	8,370,000	2.3	2.9	10,100,000	2.4	3.1
Global South	11,227,000	1.0	9.7	1.63	77,947,000	1.2	26.7	128,962,000	1.5	40.0
Africa	4,324,000	4.0	3.7	2.17	56,564,000	4.2	19.4	106,062,000	4.3	32.9
Asia	6,892,000	0.7	5.9	0.84	18,903,000	0.4	6.5	19,215,000	0.4	6.0
Latin America	6,400	0.0	0.0	4.57	1,365,000	0.2	0.5	2,212,000	0.3	0.7
Oceania	4,200	0.1	0.0	4.76	1,115,000	2.6	0.4	1,473,000	2.6	0.5
Global total	**116,199,000**	**7.2**	**100.0**	**0.77**	**291,924,000**	**3.7**	**100.0**	**322,239,000**	**3.3**	**100.0**

Source: Data from Johnson and Zurlo 2022. p.a. = percent change per annum, or each year.

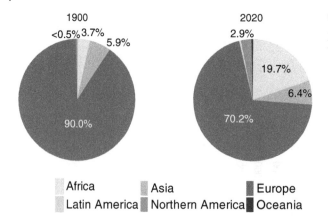

Figure 9.1 Orthodox by continent, 1900 and 2020. *Source:* Data from Johnson and Zurlo 2022.

Table 9.2 Orthodox by continent with percent female, 2020.

Region	Orthodox 2020	% of pop. 2020	% of Orthodox 2020	% Orthodox female 2020	% region female 2020
Global North	213,978,000	19.2	73.3	52.9	51.3
Europe	205,608,000	27.5	70.4	52.8	51.7
North America	8,370,000	2.3	2.9	53.6	50.5
Global South	77,947,000	1.2	26.7	50.4	49.3
Africa	56,564,000	4.2	19.4	49.8	50.0
Asia	18,903,000	0.4	6.5	51.9	48.9
Latin America	1,365,000	0.2	0.5	50.5	50.8
Oceania	1,115,000	2.6	0.4	52.0	49.9
Global total	**291,924,000**	**3.7**	**100.0**	**52.2**	**49.6**

Source: Data from Johnson and Zurlo 2022.

out of the Middle East and became more concentrated in Eastern and Southern Europe. Although Orthodoxy is growing slightly in the global South, such as in Guatemala and Kenya, it looks like its future will remain in the global North (in 2050, projected 60% in the North, 40% in the South). In 2020, 70% of Orthodox lived in Europe (Figure 9.1).

In 2020, the highest concentration of Orthodox Christians was in Europe (28% Orthodox), followed by Africa (4%; Table 9.2). Official data from government censuses report that women's share of Orthodox churches closely mirrors that of the general population, especially in places with larger populations of Orthodox Christians. The highest share of women among Orthodox is in North America (54%).

Eight of the ten countries with the most Orthodox are in the global North, with the largest population in Russia (79% of the population; Table 9.3). The highest proportion of women is in the United States, where Orthodoxy is 54% female. This is the case for most countries, where women's share of Orthodox is nearly the same or only one percent higher. Studies of individual Orthodox congregations would likely reveal a greater gender imbalance than in data from official government censuses.

Table 9.3 Countries with the most Orthodox, 2020.

Rank	Country	Country pop. 2020	Orthodox % of pop. 2020	Orthodox 2020	% Orthodox female 2020	% country female 2020
1	Russia	145,934,000	79.3	115,700,000	53.5	53.7
2	Ethiopia	114,964,000	39.7	45,600,000	50.0	50.0
3	Ukraine	43,734,000	70.9	31,000,000	53.2	53.7
4	Romania	19,238,000	88.9	17,100,000	51.2	51.4
5	Greece	10,423,000	88.0	9,170,000	50.4	50.9
6	Egypt	102,334,000	8.6	8,800,000	48.8	49.5
7	United States	331,003,000	2.2	7,150,000	54.2	50.5
8	Belarus	9,449,000	59.8	5,650,000	53.4	53.4
9	Bulgaria	6,948,000	80.9	5,620,000	53.0	51.4
10	Serbia	6,641,000	83.5	5,545,000	51.3	51.0

Source: Data from Johnson and Zurlo 2022.

Table 9.4 Countries with the highest percent of Orthodox, 2020.

Rank	Country	Country pop. 2020	Orthodox % of pop. 2020	Orthodox 2020	% Orthodox female 2020	% country female 2020
1	Moldova	4,034,000	94.7	3,821,000	51.8	52.1
2	Romania	19,238,000	88.9	17,100,000	51.2	51.4
3	Greece	10,423,000	88.0	9,170,000	50.4	50.9
4	Georgia	3,989,000	84.2	3,357,000	53.0	52.3
5	Armenia	2,963,000	83.6	2,477,000	52.2	53.0
6	Serbia	6,641,000	83.5	5,545,000	51.3	51.0
7	Bulgaria	6,948,000	80.9	5,620,000	53.0	51.4
8	Russia	145,934,000	79.3	115,700,000	53.5	53.7
9	Montenegro	628,000	71.2	447,000	50.9	50.6
10	Ukraine	43,734,000	70.9	31,000,000	53.2	53.7

Source: Data from Johnson and Zurlo 2022.

The ten countries with the highest percentage share of Orthodox are in Eastern and Southern Europe, ranging from 95% in Moldova and 71% in Ukraine (Table 9.4). Beyond these ten countries, an additional three countries have high shares of Orthodox: Cyprus (66%), North Macedonia (63%), and Belarus (60%) (Johnson and Zurlo 2022).

The main driver of change in Orthodox populations is typically migration, though growth rates can be deceiving because of slight changes in very small populations. For example, Orthodox in Iceland reported an average annual growth rate of 26% between 2000 and 2020 (Table 9.5), but there are only 1,000 Orthodox Christians in the country, roughly half Russian and half Serbian. Guatemala is the only country on this list where conversion had a major role in Orthodox growth. Fr. Andres Giron, a Catholic priest working among indigenous populations (primarily Maya) in Guatemala and southern Mexico, converted to Orthodoxy in 2010 and many followed. He died in 2014 but the tradition continues.

Table 9.5 Countries with the fastest growth of Orthodox, 2020.

Rank	Country	Country pop. 2020	Orthodox % of pop. 2020	Orthodox 2020	% Orthodox female 2020	% country female 2020	Orthodox rate % p.a. 2000–2020
1	Iceland	341,000	0.3	1,000	52.8	49.8	25.89
2	Malta	442,000	1.0	4,500	52.6	49.9	19.87
3	Norway	5,421,000	0.4	20,000	53.5	49.5	11.38
4	Italy	60,462,000	2.0	1,233,000	50.9	51.3	9.77
5	Guatemala	17,916,000	1.1	200,000	50.3	50.7	7.18
6	Nepal	29,137,000	0.0	5,400	53.3	54.2	3.93
7	Denmark	5,792,000	0.6	36,000	51.1	50.3	3.53
8	Qatar	2,881,000	0.2	7,000	36.4	24.8	3.38
9	Ireland	4,938,000	0.2	10,000	51.0	50.4	3.13
10	Madagascar	27,691,000	0.1	28,000	51.0	50.1	3.10

Source: Data from Johnson and Zurlo 2022. p.a. = percent change per annum, or each year.

Table 9.6 Largest Orthodox denominations, 2015.

Rank	Country	Denomination	Year begun	Affiliated 2015	% female	Rate % p.a. 2000–2015
1	Russia	Russian Orthodox Church	988	110,850,000	53.5	0.97
2	Ethiopia	Ethiopian Orthodox Church	332	39,200,000	50.0	2.54
3	Romania	Romanian Orthodox Church (Patriarchate Bucharest)	100	17,400,000	51.2	−0.58
4	Ukraine	Ukrainian Orthodox Church (Patriarchate Kyiv)	1991	16,000,000	53.2	9.68
5	Ukraine	Ukrainian Orthodox Church (Patriarchate Moscow)	991	13,500,000	53.2	−4.62
6	Greece	Church of Greece	50	8,460,000	50.3	−0.63
7	Egypt	Coptic Orthodox Church	33	8,400,000	48.8	1.22
8	Bulgaria	Bulgarian Orthodox Church	150	5,800,000	53.0	−0.76
9	Serbia	Serbian Orthodox Church	150	5,611,000	51.3	−0.83
10	Belarus	Belarusian Orthodox Church	988	5,400,000	53.4	0.38

Source: Data from Johnson and Zurlo 2022. p.a. = percent change per annum, or each year.

In Table 9.6, "denomination" is used as shorthand for rites, which is slightly different than the usage of the term "denomination" in Protestant and Independent traditions, since Orthodox Christianity is much more intertwined with national, ethnic, and cultural identities. As such, the largest Orthodox "denomination" is the Russian Orthodox Church in Russia (111 million members), and Russian Orthodox churches in other countries are considered separate denominations. Ukraine is unique in that it is home to four major Eastern Orthodox bodies, split by history and politics: Ukrainian Orthodox Church (Kyiv), the Ukrainian Orthodox Church (Moscow), the Ukrainian Autocephalous Orthodox Church, and the Orthodox Church of Ukraine. The long-term impact of the 2022 Russian invasion of Ukraine on Orthodox Christianity remains to be seen but will most certainly impact the demographic makeup of the Ukrainian churches, especially in light of the millions of women and children who have fled the country. Even before the war, conflict in the Russian-controlled Donetsk and Luhansk regions had already displaced 1.6 million Ukrainians, 60% of whom were women (Zorgdrager 2020).

Women in Orthodox History

Both Eastern and Oriental Orthodox churches consider themselves in apostolic succession to Jesus Christ. Mary, the Mother of Jesus, has a central place in Orthodox theology as "she who begot God" (*Theotókos*), "blessed among women," and the "new Eve." As the closest person to God, Mary's obedience ushered Christ into the world. Women were considered disciples of Jesus, but not appointed apostles.

The early Church Fathers had some choice words about women, such as Tertullian ("Woman is the gate to hell") and Clement of Alexandria ("Every woman ought to be weighed down with shame at the thought she is a woman") (cited in Kollontai 2000, p. 166). Yet, the Church Fathers were supported by women, many of whom did the same things as men: dwell in the desert, live monastically, and offer wisdom for a life of faith (Swan 2001). The first Christian monastics practiced this lifestyle in their homes, with communal prayer times, scripture study, and service to the poor; some were called to lives of solitude. Although sparse, evidence for female monks began to emerge in the 1970s (Brakke 2020). Desert Mothers (*ammas*, "spiritual mothers") were mature ascetic Christian women, exemplars in faith, study, prayer, and service in the deserts of Egypt, Palestine, and Syria. Among the most well-known Desert Mothers are Theodora of Alexandria, Sarah of the Desert, and Syncletica of Alexandria, all of whom had sayings attributed to them in the *Sayings of the Desert Fathers* from the fourth and fifth centuries. At least 47 of the nearly 800 sayings (the exact figure varies on the translation) were from Desert Mothers, not Fathers. For example, Amma Syncletica stated, "There are many who live in the mountains and behave as if they were in the town; they are wasting their time. It is possible to be a solitary in one's mind while living in a crowd; and it is possible for those who are solitaries to live in the crowd of their own thoughts." The contributions of Desert Mothers are becoming increasingly well-known (see Earle 2007; Keller 2005).

Although its history has been largely told through the stories of powerful men, the Christianization of Europe – including now Orthodox-majority areas in Southern and Eastern Europe – was accomplished also because of women. Historian Jehu Hanciles has suggested that women's contributions come into focus when viewed through the lens of migration, as women were on the move throughout the region as slaves, captives, migrants, and royal brides – all bringing their faith with them (Hanciles 2021). Many female captives became missionaries in the lands of their captors; women also founded monastic communities and converted other women to the faith. Hanciles highlights missionary and aristocratic women in the Byzantine Empire who were keenly able to make political alliances and Christianize pagan peoples. For instance, the reluctant marriage of Anna Porphyrogenita (963–c.1011), the daughter of Emperor Romanos II of Byzantium, to the Grand Prince of Kyiv Volodymyr I (c.958–1015), led to the conversion of her husband to Eastern Christianity in 988 and the Christianization of the Kievan Rus' (modern-day Belarus, Russia, and Ukraine). Ironically, Volodymyr I became the patron saint of Ukraine and Russia while Anna – his wife who led him to the faith and his very influential religious advisor – did not achieve sainthood. However, his grandmother, Olga of Kiev (c.890–969) is a saint in Eastern Orthodoxy and considered "Equal to the Apostles" for her efforts to Christianize the Kievan Rus' even though her son, Sviatoslav I, would not convert.

In Georgia, one of the earliest Christian kingdoms, a female Christian captive named Nino (c.280–c.332) led to the healing of Queen Nana. King Mirian III was initially reluctant to adopt Christianity but did so after calling on the name of Christ while lost in the forest (Hanciles 2021). Because of Nino's witness, the Georgian people became Christian, and remain Christian today

(86% Christian in 2020). A venerated saint in Eastern and Oriental Orthodoxy (in addition to Roman and Eastern Catholicism), Nino is an important symbol for the Georgian Orthodox Church, the church represented by the grapevine cross.

Female Saints

Reverence of and prayers to saints are extremely important in Orthodox faith, as saints "occupy a significant place within the life of the Orthodox Church and form an integral part of the religious practice and piety of Orthodox Christians" (Skedros 2012, p. 442). The lives of saints offer examples of Christian behavior such as service, prayer, or giving one's life for the faith. The church calendar is replete with feast days in honor of saints and Orthodox parents often name their children after them. Popular devotion to saints can be observed in everyday Orthodox life, especially through icons and intercessory prayer. There are hundreds of female saints, beginning with the *Theotókos* herself and including but not limited to:

- Patron saints of countries, such as St. Devota (third century), the patron saint of Monaco, killed during the persecutions of Roman emperors Diocletian and Maximian.
- Martyrs such as St. Tatiana of Rome (third century), the patron saint of students, blinded and tortured for her faith and beheaded; St. Apollonia of Alexandria (third century), patron saint of dentists and tooth problems, an elderly virgin woman struck until her teeth fell out and then burned by a mob for not renouncing her faith; and St. Marina the Great Martyr (third century), patron saint of pregnant women, disowned by her father as a teenager for becoming a Christian, tortured, and decapitated.
- Evangelists such as St. Photini (first century), the Samaritan woman who immediately told her community about meeting Jesus and his offer of living water.
- Mothers like St. Emmelia of Caesarea (fourth century), the patron saint of mothers. Five of her 10 children became saints, including Sts. Basil and Gregory, warranting her the name, "Mother of the Saints."

Women were clearly important contributors to the consolidation of the early church through their witness, teaching, martyrdom, and other kinds of support (Kontouma 2012). Before its institutionalization, Christianity was a home-based movement in which women could naturally serve as evangelists, apostles, and teachers. The mainstreaming of Christianity led to the marginalization of women, who were not permitted to have such roles in public.

Women in Congregational Life

Orthodox theology holds that men and women are created in the image of God but are fundamentally distinct. Because of the natural created order, women are subordinated to men and thus each should hold different roles in the church and the family. Women are not to have spiritual authority over men, especially clerical functions. They are encouraged in secular life to have parity with men, and the notion of "different but complementary" roles apply only to church and family life. Thus, Orthodox authority and theology do not allow for ordained female priests and there is essentially no movement advocating for women's ordination. A study reported that 89% of respondents from Ethiopia, 77% from Georgia, 74% from Romania, and 72% from Armenia expressed overwhelming agreement with the church's prohibition on female priests (Pew Research Center 2017a). Of the 19 countries in the study, none offered broad support for women's ordination, nor same-sex marriage, and women were just as likely as men to oppose women's ordination. Prohibitions on women's activities continue, extending beyond ordination. Following the tradition of Byzantine times, women are still not allowed to step foot on Mount Athos, Greece, home to one of the most holy sites of Greek Orthodox Christianity.

The most notable theological arguments against the prohibition on female priests came from Orthodox theologians Eva Catafygiotu Topping (1920–2011) and Elisabeth Behr-Sigel (1907–2005) in the late twentieth century. Behr-Sigel remains one of the most prominent female Orthodox theologians in recent years. She was a leading voice to guide the Orthodox church through the end of the twentieth century and into the twenty-first. Famous for her support of female priests, defending her position from biblical and theological reasons, she also addressed the celebrated Orthodox "tradition" argument. She convinced notable Orthodox theologians Kallistos Ware and Olivier Clément that the prohibition on female priests was not so straightforward (see Wilson 2020; Ware 2020). Fundamentally, she refused to acknowledge women as second-class citizens in her church (McGuckin 2020).

An unresolved issue in Orthodox churches is whether a woman is ritually unclean during her menstrual cycle and 40 days after giving birth. During these times – menstrual cycles generally occur monthly and last seven days – women are prohibited from taking Holy Communion and other sacraments, from reading scripture, lighting candles, baking the offering bread, or anything else related to worship. Estonian folklorist Andreas Kalkun's fieldwork among the Seto people in Estonia and Russia revealed that their reverence for Mary, the Mother of God, was related to this issue, where legend holds that Mary was the first woman to have a period. The Seto learned ritual taboos from their mothers and grandmothers who tied ritual restrictions to Mother of God theology, thus making the restrictions a normal part of Orthodox women's lives (Kalkun 2020). Aside from raising the question whether a woman's "cleanness" is linked to her spiritual ability in any way (Rizk 2018), the issue illustrates that the Orthodox church is in a difficult spot to address women's issues. The church strives to be relevant and alive, while also firm in its beliefs and practices. At the same time, it relies heavily on tradition yet must adjust to the pastoral needs of its people.

Orthodox women are active in congregational life as supportive diaconia, administration, and educational ministries of the church such as priests' wives, nuns, and increasingly, theologians (Kollontai 2000). They are often the most active members of Orthodox parishes. Such women help keep Orthodox faith alive, connect their families to ecclesiastical life, and prepare the sacraments (Korkala-Zorba 2012). Their ministry of motherhood means they are usually the first to introduce their children to faith and guide them through their early spiritual lives. They are their children's first theological teachers long before they ever talk to an ordained male priest (Liveris 2007).

The Female Diaconate

Phoebe is considered the first female deacon of the church, mentioned by Paul in his letter to the Romans. Women were deaconesses in Orthodox churches from the second century, especially in Greece, Asia Minor, and Syria. Deaconesses appeared to be considered clergy in their own right (though this is debated) and ministered among women, children, the sick, and the elderly (Kollontai 2000). They were also educators, evangelists, and spiritual mothers (Chryssavgis 2009). However, the office of the diaconate fell into disuse by the twelfth century. Women in the Armenian Apostolic Church have always held leadership positions as chanters and readers during liturgical services. This church is also one of the few to ordain deaconesses, as does the Alexandrian Patriarchate of the Greek Orthodox Church. In February 2017, the Eastern Orthodox Patriarch of Alexandria ordained to the order of the diaconate five African women in the Congo (Tadros 2018).

The female diaconate is controversial because some believe that allowing for women deacons will lead to other changes in Orthodox Christianity, like ordaining women to the priesthood or more progressive stances on contemporary issues like same-sex relations. However, this overlooks many hundreds of years of history where women served in this capacity without the possibility of priesthood. The female diaconate provides women opportunities to exercise their gifts in church, unique to their sex.

Monasticism

In Orthodox Christianity there are no orders akin to those in Catholicism, such as the Sisters of Mercy or the Sisters of Charity. Instead, men and women are members of single fellowships attached to a particular male or female monastery. Historically, convents were places for women who were unwilling or unable to be married (both young women and widows). They learned a

Photo 9.1 A woman prays inside the Eastern Orthodox Church in Tashkent, Uzbekistan (2012). *Source:* Adam Jones/Flickr/CC BY-SA 2.0.

variety of skills such as needlework, artistry, and, sometimes, how to read and write. They engaged in all aspects of caring for the monastery, ranging from its finances and property to caring for liturgical objects (Kontouma 2012). Monasticism proved to be liberative and affirming for women, offering them opportunities alternatives to marriage and motherhood.

Monasticism suffered under the Ottoman Empire and again under twentieth-century genocides, wars, and atheistic ideologies (see section below). Clergy and monastics suffered for their overt connection to the church. Since the 1990s, women's monasteries have become more common, but are still scarce since many were abandoned, destroyed, or repurposed during times of persecution. With no centralized body keeping statistics on monasteries in Orthodoxy, it is difficult to estimate the size of the women's monastic movement. A 1996 study found there were 706 nuns and 74 novices in 32 eparchies (provinces) of the Serbian Orthodox Church, both in former Yugoslavia states and in the diaspora; this was far higher than the number of monks, which was under 300 (Bakić-Hayden 2003, 2021). A 2016 survey of Eastern Orthodox communities in the United States reported 40 monastic communities for men and 39 for women, with 308 male monastics and 265 female (Krindatch 2016).

Between 1861 and 1914 the number of officially registered convents in Russia increased from 137 to 475, and the number of nuns and novices grew to 80,000 (Beliakova 2020). They were critical for meeting societal needs, especially in rural areas, and provided healthcare, childcare, and education. Severely reduced by Communism, Russian Orthodoxy today is dominated by sisterhoods providing aid, and women are beginning to receive formal theological training. In 2015, there were 482 nunneries in Russia, compared to 462 monasteries (Johnson and Zurlo 2019).

Women in Ecumenism

Orthodox churches have participated in the ecumenical movement since its inception in the early twentieth century, when in 1920 the Ecumenical Patriarchate of the Church of Constantinople sent a letter to "all the churches of Christ everywhere" for the formation of a "league of churches." Apart from Georgia, Bulgaria, and Estonia, all Eastern Orthodox churches are members of the World Council of Churches, founded in 1948. All Oriental Orthodox Churches are also members. Willem Visser 't Hooft – Dutch theologian and first secretary of the World Council of Churches – recognized the importance of women in the ecumenical movement, stating, "Unless women are given more responsibility in the life of their local churches, the renewal cannot be achieved" (cited in Webb 2002).

Ecumenical dialogue within the World Council of Churches, followed by second-wave feminism in the 1960s, ushered in new debates of women's roles in Orthodox Christianity. The first inter-Orthodox gathering on women's roles was in 1976 in Agapia, Romania, with the theme, "The Role of Orthodox Women in Church and Society." This meeting was a watershed moment for Orthodox women, galvanized by wider changes in society (feminism, civil rights, violence) to advocate for new roles in their churches, instead of leaving such decisions solely to men. On the consultation, historian Leonie B. Liveris observed, "For the first time in Christian history, women were called upon to reflect together, in dialogue with bishops and theologians, on their vocation and specific ministry" (Liveris 2007, p. 66). The consultation highlighted the need for more access to theological education for women, the importance of family life, the affirmation of female monastic life, and support for women's special gifts in addressing issues of social justice (Karkala-Zorba 2012). However, while women spoke out, they were hesitant to do anything to threaten their authority as homemakers and matriarchs of the family (Liveris 2007).

The next meeting – the 1988 Inter-Orthodox Symposium in Rhodes, Greece – placed the women's ordination issue front and center with the title, "The Place of Woman in the Orthodox Church and the Question of the Ordination of Women." It concluded that the apostolic order of deaconesses should be revived, stating that "the revival of women deacons of the Orthodox Church would emphasize in a special way the dignity of woman and give recognition to her contribution to the work of the Church as a whole" (Ecumenical Patriarchate 1988). The symposium reaffirmed the impossibility of women becoming priests and that feminism should be only cautiously considered (Kollontai 2000). Several meetings have since occurred, all of which underlined the importance of women, but not their priestly ordination. The broader culture is very important in the gender parity discussion, since customs and traditions influence the extent to which churches lean into the equality espoused by Orthodox theology. Others see the whole issue of women's equality as purely a "feminist" or "women's lib" matter, and not one that belongs in Orthodox dialogue at all.

A leading voice in women's ecumenical dialogue is Aruna Gnanadason of the Church of South India, coordinator of the World Council of Churches Women in Church and Society program on Justice, Peace and Creation from 1991 to 2009. She authored a history of women's involvement in the World Council of Churches from its founding in 1948 (Gnanadason 2020). In it, she addressed two major issues for women in ecumenical dialogue: violence against women and the question of women's ordination to the priesthood. The ambiguity that exists within Orthodoxy about women's issues – ritual uncleanness, ordination, Western feminism, gender roles, theological education – pushes women to engage seriously in ecumenical dialogue with women in other Christian traditions. Orthodox women's participation in ecumenism has helped bring their concerns more profoundly to the fore.

Vignettes: Orthodox Women Worldwide

The twentieth century was a tumultuous time for Orthodox Christians due to numerous catastrophic events and oppressive ideologies throughout the century, such as the Armenian Genocide (1915–1917), Russian Revolution (1917), World War I (1914–1918), World War II (1939–1945), and the Cold War (1947–1989). Communist influence was not just in Europe; Ethiopian Orthodox Christians also suffered during the Communist revolution of 1974, in which the church was disestablished, its land confiscated, and Patriarch Abuna Theophilos was executed (1979). Despite debates over women's issues described above in the 1970s, Orthodox churches were more concerned with survival for most of the century and did not have the luxury of discussing topics like gender roles (Rizk 2018). Communist and socialist governments imposed atheism throughout Eastern, Central, and Southern Europe, with detrimental results for Orthodox belief, practice, and identity in Russia, Ukraine, Belarus, Uzbekistan, Kazakhstan, Poland, Lithuania, Latvia, Estonia, and Czechia. Europe was 26% Orthodox in 1900 and 16% in 1970 (Johnson and Zurlo 2022). The most dramatic losses occurred in Russia (77% Orthodox in 1900, 30% in 1970); Moldova (89% to 43%), Montenegro (88% to 43%), Serbia (77% to 54%), Estonia (43% to 21%), and Romania (88% to 67%). Albania was declared an officially atheistic state in 1967, and the Orthodox share of the population dropped from 20% in 1900 to less than 5% by 1970. The number of Orthodox priests plummeted from 350 to 22. In Russia, dozens of bishops and perhaps upward of 100,000 priests were killed, often by firing squads, with many more Orthodox Christians killed or sent to labor camps. The first Russian concentration camp was in a former monastery in the Solovki (Solovetsky) Islands in 1922. Russian Orthodoxy was nearly eradicated by the time of Adolf Hitler's invasion of the Soviet Union in 1941, and pressure against religion waxed and waned until the late 1980s/early 1990s. Following the breakup of the Soviet Union in 1991 and the disintegration of Yugoslavia, Orthodox Christianity rebounded in most places, especially by the year 2000, with Europe's overall share back at 27% and many countries back at over 80% Orthodox. Yet, some did not follow suit. Montenegro's share rebounded to just 65% Orthodox, and Orthodox populations (by percentage) in other countries remain lower than they were in 1900, as in Estonia (11%), Albania (12%), and Poland (2%) (Johnson and Zurlo 2022). The revival of Orthodox Christianity in post-Soviet states has more to do with the retrieval of traditional life and national, political, and ideological factors than it does with personal faith and practice (Milovanović and Radić 2019).

Women were among the faithful keeping Orthodox Christianity alive in times of severe persecution, faced with the task of preserving as much of church life as possible. With religious life forced underground, churches and priests were sparse and women took on religious and quasi-clerical roles to fill the gap (Romashko 2020). The home was a woman's domain, and in many places the home was the only place to fulfill Orthodox rituals and traditions; for those under persecution, it was imperative to keep pre-Communist religious traditions alive (see Young 2013). Women received conflicting messages during and after Communism. "Gender equality" was generally a foreign concept in Central, Southern, and Eastern European societies, introduced primarily by Communist ideology. Communist

Photo 9.2 An Orthodox nun walks past the day of judgment fresco at the medieval Voroneț monastery in Romania (2007). *Source:* Alastair Rae/Flickr/CC BY-SA 2.0.

governments espoused equality between the sexes in terms of employment, voting rights, and political participation, though these governments were nearly entirely run by small groups of powerful men. Women were still expected to fulfill traditional roles of wife, mother, and keeper of the home. The double burden became, and still is, the norm. Under the regime of Nicolae Ceaușescu in Romania, childbearing became an important part of nationalist policy. Abortions were outlawed and women were pressured to have many children. Couples over age 25 without children were fined monthly by the state, and women were subjected to monthly mandatory gynecological exams (Oprica 2007). In 1986, the target number was five children per family and by 1989, Romania had the highest maternal mortality rate in Europe due to secret abortions. Although these policies are no longer in place, the renewed position of the Orthodox Church in society – with its moral compass and social influence – has complicated expectations of women by teaching traditional, patriarchal gender roles, complete with the ideas of female servility and self-sacrifice. Women are further caught between the interests of liberal politics, women's NGOs, and Western-style feminism.

Africa Spotlight: Ethiopian Orthodox Tewahedo Church

The largest Orthodox churches in Africa are the Ethiopian Orthodox Tewahedo (meaning "united as one" in Ge'ez) Church (39 million), the Coptic Orthodox Church (Egypt; 8.4 million), and the Eritrean Orthodox Church (1.4 million) (Johnson and Zurlo 2022). The Ethiopian Orthodox Tewahedo Church is the second largest Orthodox church in the world, after Russian Orthodox, and the largest Oriental Orthodox church. Ethiopia was one of the earliest Christian nations, with Christianity adopted as the state religion in the year 334. It has a unique connection to Judaism and the Hebrew Bible and traces its roots to the time of King Solomon (r.970–931 BCE) when the Ark of the Covenant was allegedly brought to Aksum from Jerusalem; the Ark remains an important part of Ethiopian identity today (Lee and Siefemichael 2017). Ethiopian Orthodox keep Saturday and Sunday Sabbath, practice circumcision, and observe Levitical food practices; the liturgical language is Ge'ez. Based on standard measures of religiosity, Ethiopian Orthodox tend to be more religious than Orthodox in Europe. For example, in a 2017 study, 98% of Ethiopian Orthodox respondents stated that religion was "very important" in their lives (the highest figure in Europe was Greece at 59%), 78% reported attending church weekly or more, and 65% said they prayed daily (Pew Research Center 2017a). Ethiopia also ranked the highest in favoring the church's prohibition of female priests: 89% (Pew Research Center 2017a).

Ethiopian Orthodox history includes many high-ranking noble women, including queens who patronized churches and monasteries. Women have never served as deacons, priests, or other kinds of spiritual teachers and there is a strict separation of sexes. Women are prohibited from entering churches while menstruating, men and women sit separately during worship services, and women also cover their heads in church. They are forbidden access to the Debre Damo Monastery, founded in the sixth century in Tigray, and must remain at the base of the cliffs to pray (Liveris 2007). There are notable convents, such as the Sabata Convent, Dire Dawa, and Asebi Maryam Convent, which care for orphaned girls and house hundreds of nuns who produce handicrafts and other fine arts. Women outnumber men in Ethiopian Orthodox Sunday schools and youth movements. Despite substantial women's activities in the church, most men and women believe in women's subordination, especially in rural areas and among the less educated (Berhane-Selassie and Müller 2015).

Some traditional cultural practices in Ethiopia can be particularly harmful for women, with many unaware of laws that prevent gender-based violence. For example, two-thirds of Ethiopian women believe that wife-beating can be justified. Female genital mutilation is an ongoing problem, with around 23% of girls countrywide undergoing the procedure, though it could be as high as 47% in the Amhara region (UN Women 2013). An estimated 40% of women are married before age 18. Most of these practices perhaps technically have little to do with religion but are traditions that keep women and girls subjected to violence and discrimination. The Ethiopian Orthodox Tewahedo Church Development and Inter-Church Aid Commission works on a wide range of social issues including building roads, providing rural water supply, teaching HIV/AIDS prevention, and working to prevent child marriage and female genital mutilation. The church offers vocational training for women to help lift them from poverty and raise awareness of gender-based violence. However, the protection and education of women in Ethiopia will not progress unless Orthodox priests choose to advocate on their behalf.

Conclusion

Although Orthodox Christianity is geographically centered in Central and Eastern Europe, the faith has been spreading around the world through migration, and in some cases, conversion. In 2020, 70% of the world's Orthodox lived in Europe, but this is anticipated to drop to 59% by 2050 (Table 9.1). Growth is anticipated in sub-Saharan Africa, where conversion movements to Eastern Orthodox churches have occurred in Kenya, Uganda, Burundi, Rwanda, and northern Tanzania. Women around the world are considered keepers of Orthodox tradition, but are also restricted by those traditions either culturally, religiously, or a mixture of both. History has proven that Orthodox women are resilient in facing obstacles of persecution, war, and political conflict. Most Orthodox churches consider marriage and motherhood the chief responsibility of women; for a woman to care for her husband and children serves God and society. Orthodox-majority countries in Central and Eastern Europe, for example, generally uphold traditional gender roles regarding wifely obedience to her husband (42% overall; the highest reported was 82% in Armenia), a woman's social responsibility to bear children (70%), and greater employment rights for men than women (46%) (Pew Research Center 2017b). Nevertheless, women are living into their calling as transmitters of faith to the next generation. They are charting their own paths to define what it means to be Orthodox while nuancing Western-style debates of feminism and gender equality that make sense in their own cultural, ethnic, religious, and geographic contexts.

Reflection Questions

1) Describe the ways in which Orthodox women contributed to the Christianization of Europe and the formation of European Orthodox identity. How do history, politics, and culture help define and sustain Orthodox life today, and how do women participate in Orthodox identity formation?
2) Tradition is both a defining characteristic of Orthodox Christianity as well as a limiting factor for women's involvement in the church. How have women, in particular, female Orthodox theologians, navigated the tension between sacred tradition and contemporary women's rights? Reflect especially on Orthodox women in the ecumenical movement.
3) Women received conflicting messages about gender roles during twentieth-century Communist governments in Europe. Describe these tensions and gendered expectations. What changed for women in post-Communist majority Orthodox societies, and what stayed the same?

Works Cited

Bakić-Hayden, Milica (2003). *Women Monastics in Orthodox Christianity: The Case of the Serbian Orthodox Church*. Washington, DC: The National Council for Eurasian and East European Research.
Bakić-Hayden, Milica (2021). Doubly neglected: histories of women monastics in the Serbian Orthodox Church. In: *Women and Religiosity in Orthodox Christianity* (ed. Ina Merdjanova), 176–205. New York: Fordham University Press.

Behr-Sigel, Elisabeth (2000). The ordination of women: also a question for the Orthodox churches. In: *The Ordination of Women in the Orthodox Church* (ed. Elisabeth Behr-Sigel and Kallistos Ware), 11–48. Geneva: World Council of Churches.

Beliakova, Nadezhda (2020). Women in the church: conceptions of Orthodox theologians in early twentieth-century Russia. In: *Orthodox Christianity and Gender: Dynamics of Tradition, Culture and Lived Practice* (ed. Helena Kupari and Elina Vuola), 48–62. Abingdon, Oxon: Routledge.

Berhane-Selassie, Tsehai and Müller, Angela M. (2015). Women in the Ethiopian Orthodox Täwaḥǝdo church: gender and irregularities at holy water sites. *Annales d'Éthiopie*, 30, 119–151.

Brakke, David (2020). Holy men and women of the desert. In: *The Oxford Handbook of Christian Monasticism* (ed. Bernice M. Kaczynski), 35–50. New York: Oxford University Press.

Chryssavgis, John (2009). *Remembering and Reclaiming Diakonia: The Diaconate Yesterday and Today.* Brookline, MA: Holy Cross Orthodox Press.

Dries, Angelyn (2016). Women in church, state, and society. In: *The Wiley Blackwell Companion to World Christianity* (ed. Lamin O. Sanneh and Michael J. McClymond), 302–317. Hoboken, NJ: Wiley-Blackwell.

Earle, Mary C. (2007). *The Desert Mothers: Spiritual Practices from the Women of the Wilderness.* Harrisburg, PA: Morehouse Pub.

Ecumenical Patriarchate (1988). Inter-orthodox theological consultation, the place of woman in the Orthodox Church and the question of the ordination of women, Rhodes, Greece, 30 October–7 November. Istanbul, Türkiye: The Ecumenical Patriarchate.

Gnanadason, Aruna (2020). *With Courage and Compassion: Women and the Ecumenical Movement.* Minneapolis: Fortress Press.

Hanciles, Jehu (2021). *Migration and the Making of Global Christianity.* Grand Rapids, MI: Wm. B. Eerdmans Publishing.

Ionita, Viorel and Glazer, Hacik R. (2009). Orthodox, 1910–2010. In: *Atlas of Global Christianity* (ed. Kenneth R. Ross and Todd M. Johnson), 84–95. Edinburgh: Edinburgh University Press.

Jacobsen, Douglas G. (2021). *The World's Christians: Who They Are, Where They Are, and How They Got There.* 2nd edn. Chichester, West Sussex: Wiley-Blackwell.

Johnson, Todd M. and Zurlo, Gina A. (2019). *World Christian Encyclopedia.* 3rd edn. Edinburgh: Edinburgh University Press.

Johnson, Todd M. and Zurlo, Gina A. ed. (2022). *World Christian Database.* Leiden/Boston: Brill.

Kalkun, Andreas (2020). How to ask embarrassing questions about women's religion: menstruating Mother of God, ritual impurity, and fieldwork among Seto women in Estonia and Russia. In: *Orthodox Christianity and Gender: Dynamics of Tradition, Culture and Lived Practice* (ed. Helena Kupari and Elina Vuola), 97–114. Abingdon, Oxon: Routledge.

Karkala-Zorba, Katerina (2012). The Ordination of Women from an Orthodox Perspective. In: *Women and Ordination in the Christian Churches: International Perspectives* (ed. Ian Jones, Janet Wootton, and Kirsty Thorpe), 54–63. London: T&T Clark.

Kasselouri-Hatzivassiliadi, Eleni, Moyo, Fulata M., and Pekridou, Aikaterini ed. (2010). *Many Women Were Also There: The Participation of Orthodox Women in the Ecumenical Movement.* Geneva: World Council of Churches Publications.

Keller, David G.R. (2005). *Oasis of Wisdom: The Worlds of the Desert Fathers and Mothers.* Collegeville, MN: Liturgical Press.

Kollontai, Pauline (2000). Contemporary thinking on the role and ministry of women in the Orthodox Church. *Journal of Contemporary Religion*, 15(2), 165–179.

Kontouma, Vassa (2012). Women in Orthodox. In: *The Orthodox Christian World* (ed. Augustine Casiday), 432–441. New York: Routledge.

Krindatch, Alexei ed. (2016). *Atlas of American Orthodox Christian Monasteries.* Brookline, MA: Holy Cross Orthodox Press.

Lee, Ralph and Siefemichael, Daniel (2017). Orthodox. In: *Christianity in Sub-Saharan Africa* (ed. Kenneth R. Ross, J.Kwabena Asamoah-Gyadu, and Todd M. Johnson), 264–276. Edinburgh: Edinburgh University Press.

Liveris, Leonie B. (2007). *Ancient Taboos and Gender Prejudice: Challenges for Orthodox Women and the Church*. Farnham: Ashgate Pub.

McGuckin, John A. (2016). Orthodoxy and Eastern Christianity. In: *The Wiley Blackwell Companion to World Christianity* (ed. Lamin O. Sanneh and Michael J. McClymond), 617–627. Hoboken, NJ: Wiley-Blackwell.

McGuckin, John A. (2020). *The Eastern Orthodox Church: A New History*. New Haven: Yale University Press.

Metso, Pekka, Maskulin, Nina, and Laitila, Teuvo (2020). Tradition, gender, and empowerment: the Birth of Theotokos Society in Helsinki, Finland. In: *Orthodox Christianity and Gender: Dynamics of Tradition, Culture and Lived Practice* (ed. Helena Kupari and Elina Vuola), 32–79. Abingdon, Oxon: Routledge.

Milovanović, Aleksandra D. and Radić, Radmila (2019). Women in the Serbian Orthodox Church: historical overview and contemporary situation. *Occasional Papers on Religion in Eastern Europe*, 39(6), article 2, 1–29.

Oprica, Vlad (2007). Gender equality and conflicting attitudes toward women in post-Communist Romania. *Human Rights Review*, 9, 29–40.

Pew Research Center (2017a). Orthodox Christianity in the 21st century.

Pew Research Center (2017b). Religious belief and national belonging in Central and Eastern Europe.

Rizk, Donna (2018). Gender. In: *Christianity in North Africa and West Asia* (ed. Kenneth R. Ross, Mariz Tadros, and Todd M. Johnson), 360–370. Edinburgh: Edinburgh University Press.

Romashko, Elena (2020). Russian Orthodox icons of Chernobyl as visual narratives about women at the center of nuclear disaster. In: *Orthodox Christianity and Gender: Dynamics of Tradition, Culture and Lived Practice* (ed. Helena Kupari and Elina Vuola), 191–209. Abingdon, Oxon: Routledge.

Skedros, James (2012). Hagiography and devotion to the saints. In: *The Orthodox Christian World* (ed. Augustine Casiday), 442–452. New York: Routledge.

Swan, Laura (2001). *The Forgotten Desert Mothers: Sayings, Lives, and Stories of Early Christian Women*. New York: Paulist Press.

Tadros, Mariz (2018). Christianity in North Africa and West Asia. In: *Christianity in North Africa and West Asia* (ed. Kenneth R. Ross, Mariz Tadros, and Todd M. Johnson), 15–38. Edinburgh: Edinburgh University Press.

Tamer, Georges (2018). Eastern Orthodox. In: *Christianity in North Africa and West Asia* (ed. Kenneth R. Ross, Mariz Tadros, and Todd M. Johnson), 235–246. Edinburgh: Edinburgh University Press.

UN Women (2013). In Ethiopia, church bells ring for women and girls. https://www.unwomen.org/en/news/stories/2013/10/in-ethiopia-church-bells-ring-for-women-and-girls (accessed 16 March 2022).

Ware, Kallistos (2020). 'Why I have changed my mind': revisiting the ordination of women. In: *Women and Ordination in the Orthodox Church: Explorations in Theology and Practice* (ed. Gabrielle Thomas and Elena Narinskaya), 79–84. Eugene, OR: Cascade Books.

Webb, Pauline (2002). Women in church and society. In: *Dictionary of the Ecumenical Movement* (ed. Nicholas Lossky), 1208–1211. Geneva: World Council of Churches Publications.

Wilson, Sarah H. (2020). Elisabeth Behr-Sigel's Trinitarian case for the ordination of women. In: *Women and Ordination in the Orthodox Church: Explorations in Theology and Practice* (ed. Gabrielle Thomas and Elena Narinskaya), 99–113. Eugene, OR: Cascade Books.

Young, Hilary (2013). 'God can wait': composing non-religious narratives in secular and post-Communist societies. In: *Ageing, Ritual and Social Change: Comparing the Secular and Religious in Eastern and Western Europe* (ed. Peter G. Coleman, Daniela Koleva, and Joanna Bornat), 67–87. Farnham: Ashgate Publishing.

Zorgdrager, Heleen (2020). Shaping public Orthodoxy: women's peace activism and the Orthodox Churches in the Ukrainian crisis. In: *Orthodox Christianity and Gender: Dynamics of Tradition, Culture and Lived Practice* (ed. Helena Kupari and Elina Vuola), 150–170. Abingdon, Oxon: Routledge.

10

Women in Protestant Christianity

"One of the most striking features of modern Protestant mission work is the liberation of women."

Werner Ustorf (Ustorf 2004, p. 397)

At six years old, Katharina (Katy) von Bora (1499–1552) was sent to a Benedictine cloister by her father for education in 1504; she moved to a Cistercian monastery at nine years old. After many years of cloistered religious life, she and several other nuns became interested in the growing reform movement within the Catholic Church. They escaped the monastery with help from the famous reformer Martin Luther, whom von Bora married in 1525. Katharina and Martin Luther became an important symbol for families in the nascent Protestant movement: ordered Martin first, Katy second (Tucker 2017).

Inklings of Protestantism began in the fourteenth century. Reformers such as Englishman John Wycliffe (1320s–1384) and Czech Jan Hus (1372–1415) questioned core doctrines of the Catholic Church, such as privileged clergy status and Latin-only Mass and scriptures. By the sixteenth century, numerous reformers contributed to what became known as the Protestant Reformation, sparking massive political, social, and religious upheavals throughout Europe. The Protestant missionary movement beyond Europe began nearly 200 years later, with Pietist German Lutherans Bartholomäus Ziegenbalg (1682–1719) and Heinrich Plütschau (1677–1752) arriving in India in 1706. In this book, all denominations and networks that trace their historical roots to the sixteenth-century Protestant Reformation are considered Protestant, which encompasses a wide variety of Christian belief and practices, especially regarding the role of women. There are many commonalities between Protestant and Independent denominations, as numerous Independent groups were formed via schism from Protestant denominations. This is the case for most Black churches in the United States, who are considered Independent in this book, rather than Protestant, even though they might theologically resemble Protestants. Black churches are discussed in Chapter 6 (North America). Likewise, many Independent churches or networks might theologically look like Protestants, such as Chinese house churches, but are considered Independent for historical, sociological, and cultural reasons (see Chapter 11).

Some Protestant churches baptize infants while others practice believer's baptism; some Protestants have a high view of scripture, while others do not; and many Protestant denominations are split over the inclusion of LGBTQ+ people in their congregations. The great diversity of Protestant history, theology, and practice lends itself to varying opportunities for women. This is true even within denominations. The Southern Baptist Convention (SBC), the largest Baptist denomination in the world, does not permit women to be pastors. Some SBC churches have allowed it regardless, such as the very large and prominent Saddleback Church, which appointed three women pastors in

Women in World Christianity: Building and Sustaining a Global Movement, First Edition. Gina A. Zurlo.
© 2023 John Wiley & Sons Ltd. Published 2023 by John Wiley & Sons Ltd.

2021. However, in 2023, the SBC disfellowshipped Saddleback for the decision. Other kinds of Baptists do permit female pastors, such as the American Baptist Church, the Bund Evangelisch-Freikirchlicher Gemeinden (Union of Free Evangelical Churches in Germany), the Baptist Union of Great Britain, and the Baptist Federation of Canada. In the Anglican Communion, some provinces ordain women (such as Aotearoa, New Zealand, and Polynesia; Brazil; and the Episcopal Church USA) while others do not (such as Central Africa; Melanesia; and Papua New Guinea).

This chapter discusses women in the Protestant Reformation, especially what they both lost and gained in leaving Catholicism to join the emerging Protestant movement. The following sections include brief discussions of female founders of Protestant denominations and Protestant women in mission. This chapter features vignettes of women's activities, priorities, and experiences in Protestant churches and organizations as well as within movements in Africa, Asia, Latin America, Europe, North America, and Oceania.

Protestants, 1900–2050

Like World Christianity as a whole, Protestantism experienced a substantial shift to the South during the twentieth century. In 1900, 93% of all Protestants lived in Europe and North America; by 2020, this had dropped dramatically to 25% (Table 10.1). Africa, Asia, Latin America, and Oceania are now together home to 75% of all Protestants in the world – a reality that surely could not have been imagined by the original sixteenth-century reformers (Figure 10.1). Africa's population jumped from just 2% Protestant in 1900 to 19% in 2020, while Latin America's grew from 3% to 11%. In 2050, Africa will likely be home to 54% of the world's Protestants; Europe, the historic home of the tradition, could be home to just 9%. The largest Protestant Christian families are Anglicans (93 million), Uniting churches (85 million), Baptists (81 million), Reformed Presbyterians (63 million), and Lutherans (54 million) (Johnson and Zurlo 2022).

Table 10.1 Protestants by continent, 1900–2050.

Region	Protestants 1900	% of pop. 1900	% of Protestants 1900	Rate % p.a. 1900–2020	Protestants 2020	% of pop. 2020	% of Protestants 2020	Protestants 2050	% of pop. 2050	% of Protestants 2050
Global North	124,453,000	25.7	92.7	0.13	145,091,000	13.0	24.8	140,340,000	12.4	15.9
Europe	84,540,000	21.0	63.0	0.03	87,516,000	11.7	15.0	76,981,000	10.8	8.7
North America	39,914,000	48.9	29.7	0.31	57,575,000	15.6	9.8	63,359,000	14.9	7.2
Global South	9,743,000	0.9	7.3	3.23	440,197,000	6.6	75.2	740,661,000	8.6	84.1
Africa	2,204,000	2.0	1.6	4.05	257,484,000	19.2	44.0	477,087,000	19.2	54.2
Asia	2,635,000	0.3	2.0	3.13	106,211,000	2.3	18.1	158,632,000	3.0	18.0
Latin America	1,659,000	2.5	1.2	3.08	63,398,000	9.7	10.8	88,332,000	11.6	10.0
Oceania	3,244,000	51.9	2.4	1.17	13,104,000	30.7	2.2	16,611,000	29.0	1.9
Global total	**134,196,000**	**8.3**	**100.0**	**1.23**	**585,289,000**	**7.5**	**100.0**	**881,002,000**	**9.1**	**100.0**

Source: Data from Johnson and Zurlo 2022. p.a. = percent change per annum, or each year.

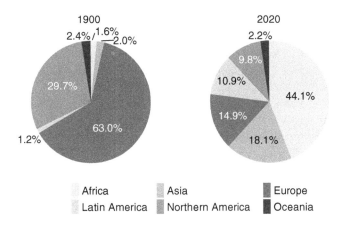

Figure 10.1 Protestants by continent, 1900 and 2020. *Source:* Johnson and Zurlo 2022.

Table 10.2 Protestants by continent with percent female, 2020.

Region	Protestants 2020	% of pop. 2020	% of Protestants 2020	% Protestant female 2020	% region female 2020
Global North	145,091,000	13.0	24.8	53.9	51.3
Europe	87,516,000	11.7	15.0	53.8	51.7
North America	57,575,000	15.6	9.8	54.1	50.5
Global South	440,197,000	6.6	75.2	52.3	49.3
Africa	257,484,000	19.2	44.0	52.5	50.0
Asia	106,211,000	2.3	18.1	51.0	48.9
Latin America	63,398,000	9.7	10.8	53.9	50.8
Oceania	13,104,000	30.7	2.2	52.2	49.9
Global total	**585,289,000**	**7.5**	**100.0**	**52.7**	**49.6**

Source: Data from Johnson and Zurlo 2022.

Table 10.3 Countries with the most Protestants, 2020.

Rank	Country	Country pop. 2020	Protestant % of pop. 2020	Protestants 2020	% Protestant female 2020	% country female 2020
1	Nigeria	206,140,000	30.1	62,059,000	52.8	49.3
2	United States	331,003,000	16.3	54,035,000	54.1	50.5
3	China	1,439,324,000	2.4	34,000,000	51.5	48.7
4	Brazil	212,559,000	15.1	32,140,000	55.4	50.9
5	United Kingdom	67,886,000	39.8	27,000,000	53.8	50.6
6	Kenya	53,771,000	48.4	26,000,000	52.6	50.3
7	Germany	83,784,000	29.9	25,031,000	55.0	50.6
8	India	1,380,004,000	1.7	23,000,000	50.0	48.0
9	Indonesia	273,524,000	7.4	20,204,000	50.0	49.7
10	Uganda	45,741,000	42.2	19,300,000	51.3	50.7

Source: Data from Johnson and Zurlo 2022.

In 2020, the largest population of Protestants in the world was in Africa (257 million), representing 44% of all Protestants (Table 10.2). On all continents, women make up the majority of Protestants, ranging from 51% (Asia) to 54% (North America). In reality, these figures are likely much higher, as it is consistently reported that women make up the majority of Protestant congregations around the world (see continent section below for more details).

In 1900 and up until 2014, the United States was home to the most Protestants in the world. However, Nigeria's Protestant population grew quickly and now claims the top spot (Table 10.3). Nigeria has many Protestant denominations over one million in size, such as the Anglican Church, Nigerian Baptist Convention, Evangelical Church Winning All, the Assemblies of God, and the Apostolic Church of Nigeria. Nigeria's Protestants are 53% female, higher than the country's overall population, which is 49% female.

Table 10.4 Countries with the highest percent of Protestants, 2020.

Rank	Country	Country pop. 2020	Protestant % of pop. 2020	Protestants 2020	% Protestant female 2020	% country female 2020
1	Faroe Islands	48,900	97.5	47,700	52.2	50.3
2	Marshall Islands	59,200	84.5	50,000	53.1	49.6
3	Montserrat	5,000	84.0	4,200	49.4	53.9
4	Tuvalu	11,800	83.1	9,800	50.7	48.2
5	Saint Kitts and Nevis	53,200	81.3	43,200	51.9	53.9
6	Iceland	341,000	79.4	271,000	52.1	49.8
7	Denmark	5,792,000	77.7	4,500,000	52.1	50.3
8	American Samoa	55,200	76.0	42,000	53.7	48.2
9	Bahamas	393,000	75.1	296,000	52.2	51.4
10	Vanuatu	307,000	75.1	231,000	49.6	49.3

Source: Data from Johnson and Zurlo 2022.

Table 10.5 Countries with the fastest growth of Protestants, 2020.

Rank	Country	Country pop. 2020	Protestant % of pop. 2020	Protestants 2020	% Protestant female 2020	% country female 2020	Rate % p.a. 2000–2020
1	Kosovo	2,096,000	0.6	12,700	51.8	51.0	8.25
2	Bhutan	772,000	0.9	7,200	53.0	46.9	7.51
3	São Tomé and Príncipe	219,000	8.0	17,500	49.5	50.0	6.20
4	Cambodia	16,719,000	1.7	280,000	49.0	51.2	5.66
5	Nepal	29,137,000	0.9	270,000	53.3	54.2	5.28
6	Mongolia	3,278,000	1.1	36,200	63.2	50.7	5.04
7	Albania	2,878,000	0.5	13,000	53.2	49.1	5.01
8	Guinea-Bissau	1,968,000	1.7	33,300	52.0	51.1	5.00
9	Benin	12,123,000	10.3	1,250,000	53.1	50.1	4.85
10	Wallis and Futuna Islands	11,200	1.8	200	52.5	48.2	4.69

Source: Data from Johnson and Zurlo 2022. p.a. = percent change per annum, or each year.

Seven of the ten countries with the highest percentages of Protestants are in the global South and they all have populations under 300,000 (Table 10.4). Denmark ranks seventh at 78% Protestant, 52% of whom are female; the Faroe Islands is the country with the highest percentage of Protestants in the world (98%), also 52% female.

The countries with the fastest Protestant growth are generally very small. Except for Benin (10% Protestant and 1.3 million adherents), they all have fewer than 300,000 Protestants (Table 10.5). Kosovo, for example, reports the highest growth of Protestantism but there are only 12,700 adherents in the country. Mongolia is the only country on the list with a wide gap between its Protestant percent female and country percent female, 63% vs. 51%.

Six of the ten largest Protestant denominations in the world are in the global South, and two of those are in Ethiopia, a majority Orthodox country (Table 10.6). China tops the list with the Three-Self Patriotic Movement, which is the state-sanctioned Protestant church with an estimated 30 million affiliates (52% female). Three of the top ten denominations are Anglican – in the United Kingdom, Nigeria, and Uganda, ranking third, fourth, and seventh, respectively. Two are in the United States, the Southern Baptist Convention and the United Methodist Church, each of which report 54% female. All global North denominations in Table 10.6 are on the decline, while those in the global South report remarkably high growth rates, such as the Evangelical Church Mekane Yesus in Ethiopia, which grew nearly 6% per year between 2000 and 2015.

Table 10.6   Largest Protestant denominations, 2020.

Rank	Country	Denomination	Year begun	Affiliated 2015	% female	Rate % p.a. 2000–2015
1	China	Three-Self Patriotic Movement	1807	30,000,000	51.5	4.28
2	Germany	Evangelische Kirche in Deutschland	1517	24,450,000	55.0	−0.57
3	United Kingdom	Church of England	100	23,000,000	53.8	−0.37
4	Nigeria	Anglican Church of Nigeria	1842	22,000,000	52.9	1.94
5	Brazil	Assembleias de Deus	1910	20,978,000	55.0	1.12
6	United States	Southern Baptist Convention	1845	18,836,000	54.1	−0.51
7	Uganda	Church of Uganda	1875	14,000,000	50.9	3.18
8	Ethiopia	Word of Life Evangelical Church	1927	8,500,000	50.0	2.82
9	Ethiopia	Evangelical Church Mekane Yesus	1859	7,887,000	50.0	5.85
10	United States	United Methodist Church	1766	7,067,000	54.1	−1.06

Source: Data from Johnson and Zurlo 2022. p.a. = percent change per annum, or each year.

Women in Protestant History

Reformation teaching on the "order of creation" held that while women were created in the image of God, they were subordinate to men because Eve was created after Adam. John Calvin and Martin Luther argued that these gender dynamics were a result of the Fall – Eve violated the order by giving Adam the fruit – and relations between men and women have been thus forever strained (Rigby 2004). Protestant women have been pushing back against this theology since the sixteenth century. The priesthood of all believers supports women's full participation in the church, and the *sola scriptura* Reformation refrain allows women to access and interpret the biblical text for themselves. Among the first generation of Protestant reformers, Katharina Schütz Zell (1498–1562) reinterpreted the call of housewives from powerlessness to active service to Jesus. Her first public text (1524) encouraged women left behind by fleeing men in Catholic–Protestant conflicts in Kenzingen, Germany. She praised persecuted Protestant women for their witness and provides a very Protestant reading of biblical texts, such as their "gift of faith" for "women in the world" (as opposed to a convent) (Zell and McKee 2006, p. 47–48).

The Protestant Reformation set in motion major changes for women in vocation and marriage. In Catholicism, women had the opportunity to serve God and community through a religious order, or through commitment to a contemplative life of prayer in a convent. However, Protestants upheld marriage as a vocation itself with male ministers able and encouraged to marry. As a result, the highest calling for Protestant women became that of wife and mother in support of men. Nevertheless, numerous notable Protestant women exercised their felt callings from God to preach, minister, evangelize, and interpret scripture. Women fought fiercely alongside men for the right to theologize for themselves. Among Anabaptists, for instance – one of the most persecuted Protestant groups of the sixteenth century – one-third of all martyrs were women. Their crime was the practice of believers' baptism and pacifism (Muir 2019). Women in seventeenth-century Baptist churches in the Netherlands and England made up at least 60% of church membership and served as deaconesses, prophetesses, and authors, though their public ministries were not always welcomed by men (Muir 2019).

Female Founders

Women became integral to the growing Protestant movement in Europe and North America. Quakers welcomed women ministers: 12 of the first 66 Quaker preachers (18%) in England were women, and between 1649 and 1660, 220 of 300 ministers were women (73%; Muir 2019). Many died for their faith, such as Mary Dyer (1611–1660), hung in Boston Common in Massachusetts Bay Colony for defying Puritan law that banned Quakers from the commonwealth. Former Quaker Jane Wardley and her husband, James, founded the Shaker community around 1747 after receiving visions from God that Jesus was coming back soon, this time as a woman. Ellen G. White (1827–1915) cofounded the Seventh-day Adventist Church in 1863 from the Millerite movement, which believed Jesus would return in the year 1844. After this "Great Disappointment," White received thousands of visions from God, often in public settings. The Seventh-day Adventist Church is one of the most global denominations today, present in nearly every country and with over 20 million members. Other notable female founders of Protestant denominations include Mary Baker Eddy (1821–1910), founder of the Church of Christ, Scientist; Mary Lee Cagle (1864–1955), cofounder of the Church of the Nazarene; Aimee Semple McPherson (1890–1944), founder of the International Church of the Foursquare Gospel; and Catherine Booth (1829–1890), cofounder of the Salvation Army.

Women in Mission

Protestantism spread around the world through the imperial outreach of Western European nations and the United States, coupled with the Western missionary movement of which Protestant women became the driving force. The Progressive Era (1890s–1910s) missionary movement was rooted in Christian nationalistic zeal, where Americans believed they were under a special obligation to save and renovate the world (Hutchison 1987). Missionaries held to only broad indictments of their own cultures, though some spoke out against the superiority of Western civilization, such as Sarah Smith (1802–1836), missionary wife in Syria, who was keenly aware of the problems in American culture and their negative impact on mission work. Western missionaries were always caught between cultures and ideologies. If they preached Christ only, they were accused of ignoring the need for social and material amelioration. If they focused too much on social issues, they were criticized for promoting Western technology and ideology above the gospel.

The nineteenth-century "cult of domesticity" stressed virtues of humility, cleanliness, purity, order, and harmony, with women expected to serve as homemakers and mothers. Initially, the only way for women to serve overseas was to marry a missionary, but missionary wives were considered mere assistants to their husbands and restricted to work only with women and children (Robert 1997). Their priority was to their households and to prop up their husbands, and their ministry largely consisted of teaching women and girls who had no access to male missionaries, especially in sex-segregated societies. Yet, women were also considered "civilizing" agents, sent with their husbands to raise the dignity of "heathen" women trapped in non-Christian religions abroad. As a result, female missionaries focused on human need, education for women and children, and prayer. In addition to education and evangelization efforts, Western women abroad combatted perceived social evils like foot binding in China, infanticide, suicide, witchcraft, polygamy, and child marriage.

The women's missionary movement was truly remarkable in its size, scope, dedication, and long-lasting impact (see Chapter 6 for more detail). Britain sent the most missionaries in the late nineteenth century and by the turn of the century, well over half were women (Seton 2013). Women made up 60% of the American missionary force of this time and they participated in the creation of both distinctly American and uniquely female mission theories (Robert 1997). Women worked within unpredictable ecclesiastical contexts as subordinates in male-dominated churches. Yet, they rejected mission theories developed by men that separated the physical and spiritual realms, instead engaging in holistic service aimed at mind, body, and spirit. Protestant female missionaries wanted to make the world a better place through education, women's empowerment, and healthcare, as well as save souls and build the church. However, they contributed to the prevailing "mission as civilization" theme by linking Christianity with proper Western culture such as dress, child-rearing, family values, and gender roles (Robert 1997). At the same time, women missionaries were not a homogenous group of cultural imperialists, but people who reinvented the meanings of nationalism and imperialism as they encountered competing versions of these ideologies in varying colonial settings (Reeves-Ellington, Sklar, and Shemo 2010).

The first missionary teachers faced two hurdles: convincing locals that Western education was worthwhile and then persuading them that their girls were capable of learning. Initially, education for girls was not for knowledge's sake, not for women's rights, nor for women's flourishing; girls should be educated so that indigenous Christian men could find wives and women could raise children in the faith. Helen Barrett Montgomery (1861–1934), the first female president of the Northern Baptist Convention in the USA, observed, "The education of girls is the quickest method of elevating the home life of the East. These educated girls make better mothers, better wives, better housekeepers, than their untrained sisters, so that American school-teachers, whether they wish or not, often find themselves running very flourishing matrimonial agencies, as they train the new kind of wife to go with the new Christian home" (Montgomery 1910, pp. 105–106). Girls' education was primarily for the establishment and continuation of Christian homes.

Women educating women led to an increase of their rights abroad, but it was complicated by the exportation of Western gender ideologies to other cultures. In some cases, the connection between women's education and empowerment had unintended consequences. In Maharashtra, India, for example, American missionary efforts to promote women's literacy contributed to a revitalization of Hinduism, not mass conversions to Christianity (Porterfield 1997). Nevertheless, despite the interconnectedness of the Western missionary movement, colonization, and cultural imperialism in the nineteenth and twentieth centuries, the education of women and girls is routinely considered one of the greatest benefits of mission.

Despite their massive contributions to the Western missionary movement, women were noticeably absent from the Edinburgh 1910 World Missionary Conference. Historian Brian Stanley found that conference convener John Mott, "drew the conference's attention to the paucity of women offering to speak; he complained that on this occasion he had received only one card from a woman desiring to speak, compared with seventy or eighty from men. The gender imbalance improved a little as the conference proceeded, and women's voices came briefly into their own on the penultimate morning devoted to the discussion of the Commission V report on The Preparation of Missionaries, when six women addressed the conference in succession, out of a total of fifteen speakers from the floor" (Stanley 2009, p. 87). There were no official women delegates.

Famous British Protestant missionary women include Mary Slessor (1848–1915, Nigeria), Amy Carmichael (1867–1951, India), and Gladys Aylward (1902–1970, China), with many more whose names will never be known. British women were involved in *zenana* ministry in India, serving otherwise unreachable secluded Hindu women and girls. They also engaged in healthcare, providing services and evangelizing women in sex-segregated societies, especially in Asia. Despite the wide range of female missionary influence around the world, their work teaching girls, training female evangelists, and providing medical care was generally considered marginal, not essential, to mission (Seton 2013).

Notable American Protestant women in mission include Ann Hasseltine Judson (1789–1826, Myanmar), Sarah Smith (1802–1836, Syria), Elizabeth Fisher (1862–1955, China), Amanda Berry Smith (1837–1915, India, England, Africa), and Charlotte "Lottie" Moon (1840–1912, China). Separate British and American women's mission boards were extremely successful but were nearly extinct by the mid-twentieth century. Discussions had begun in the late nineteenth century about combining women's boards with general boards – run by men – and these conversations intensified at the Edinburgh 1910 conference (Stanley 2009). Overseas missions, one of Protestant women's most important endeavors, intersected with debates over biblical literalism, new respect for non-Christian peoples and culture, and the crushed optimism after global conflict, wars, and genocide. The loss of distinct women's organizations caused many Protestant women to turn their attention from global needs to local ones; the first women in mainline Protestant churches to seek ordination were former overseas missionaries. The loss of women's missionary boards also contributed to the overall decline in Western Protestant missions in the mid-twentieth century (Robert 1997).

Vignettes: Protestant Women Worldwide

As in all other Christian traditions, Protestant women around the world are engaged in many activities ranging from pastoral ministry, social work, political activism, and education. Protestantism's theological and geographic diversity means that women have inconsistent opportunities for leadership, even within the same denomination in the same country. While achieving formal ordained ministry positions is not the chief goal of many Protestant women, the women's ordination debate dominates conversations about their roles in the church. In fact, the issue is so divisive that some Protestant denominations have split over women's ordination, such as the Presbyterian Church USA and the Presbyterian Church in America, and the Lutheran Church Missouri Synod and the Evangelical Lutheran Church in America. Women's ordination sparks deeper debates about biblical interpretation, inerrancy, and the relationship between Christian faith and changes in the broader culture. The following section is organized by continent to introduce dynamics related to women's ordination in select Protestant denominations. While not intended to be exhaustive, it aims to provide a window into both the opportunities and challenges women face within Protestantism.

Africa

Women constitute the majority of Protestant congregations in Africa even though they are often left out of decision-making processes (Nyomi 2017). There are numerous women's groups on the continent that come together for support, education, and empowerment, and most major denominations have a separate women's fellowship. Women maintain both formally recognized and unrecognized leadership positions. Though many Protestant denominations ordain women, there is not uniformity across the continent; for instance, the Presbyterian Church of East Africa ordains women, but the Reformed Church of East Africa does not (Mombo 2012). Local context, culture, and history factor significantly. Lack of access to

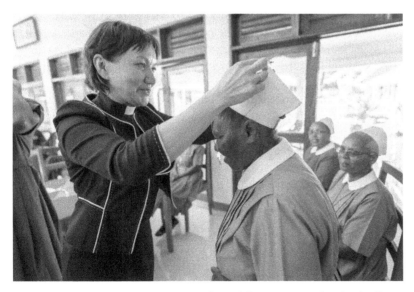

Photo 10.1   Lutheran World Federation General Secretary Anne Burghardt offers a replica of the Lund Cross to a member of the Lutheran Sisters' Convent of the Evangelical Lutheran Church in Moshi, Tanzania (2022). *Source:* LWF/Albin Hillert.

education, never mind theological education, is a major barrier for obtaining official leadership positions (see Chapter 16).

Nevertheless, Protestant women are advancing into leadership in some denominations. In 2020, the United Methodist Church elected its first African female bishop, Joaquina Filipe Nhanala (Mozambique). The Methodist Church of Southern Africa elected Purity Nomthandazo Malinga as Presiding Bishop in 2019, and 25% of the church's 12 districts are led by female regional bishops (Scott 2020). In 2020, the Methodist Church in Togo had both a female President and General Secretary, the top two leaders of the denomination. The Circle of Concerned African Women Theologians is a leading voice for the continued empowerment and uplifting of women on the continent.

Some of the largest Protestant denominations in Africa are Anglican, such as in Nigeria (22 million), Uganda (14 million), Kenya (6 million), and Tanzania (4 million) (Johnson and Zurlo 2022). As mentioned above, provinces of the Anglican Communion have differing views on women's leadership in the church. There are 14 Anglican provinces in Africa: Alexandria, Burundi, Central Africa, Congo, Kenya, Mozambique and Angola, Nigeria, Rwanda, Southern Africa, South Sudan, Sudan, Tanzania, Uganda, and West Africa. Of these, women can serve as:

- Deacons only – Congo, Nigeria
- Deacons and priests only – Burundi, Kenya, Rwanda, West Africa
- Deacons, priests, and bishops – Southern Africa, South Sudan, Sudan, Tanzania, Uganda, Mozambique, Angola
- No higher levels of leadership – Central Africa, Alexandria

Lucia Okuthe was the first ordained Anglican female priest in Kenya in 1983, and in the same year three women were ordained in Uganda: Monica Sebidega, Deborah Micungwa Rukara, and Margaret Kizanye Byekwaso. In 2012, Ellinah Ntombi Wamukoya became the first female Anglican bishop in Africa. Her consecration came on the twentieth anniversary of women's ordination to the priesthood in the Anglican Church of Southern Africa.

British Anglican Mary Sumner founded the first Mothers' Union in 1876, inspired by the birth of her first grandchild. The movement spread rapidly through the British Empire and by 1940, Africa was home to more Union members of any continent (Moyse 2009). There are 30 Mothers' Unions in Africa, ranging in size from Seychelles (69 members) to Nigeria (60,000 members) (Mothers' Union 2021). Although initially founded to support women in their identities as mothers and to uphold traditional marriage and family values, their activities today touch nearly every aspect of society. In Nigeria, members are active in hospital visitations, health clinics, support for widows and orphans, day cares, nursery schools, marriage preparation, vocational training, prison ministry, and parenting. Even in a smaller country like Lesotho (2 million people), the 3,500 members of the Mothers' Union campaign against gender-based violence and participate in projects such as sewing, pig-rearing, environmental protection, and elder and orphan care. Mothers' Unions and other similar Christian women's groups tend to reinforce traditional roles for women that exclude them from leadership and decision-making bodies (Trisk 2013).

Asia

Protestant churches in Asia are influenced by prevailing cultural attitudes toward women's roles, often relegating women to acts of private, not public, service. At the same time, many communities still face pressure from Western Protestant missionaries to exclude women from the pulpit. While some Protestant churches critique patriarchy in Asian societies, recent appointments and permissions for women's ordination and leadership do not equate to gender parity.

The push for women's ordination in the global Anglican Communion began in Asia, when Florence Li Tim-Oi (1907–1992) was ordained in Hong Kong in 1944. Subsequently, British women began to advocate for their own full participation in the church (Pui-lan 2018), as did Canadian and American women. In the Middle East, the Evangelical Lutheran Church in Jordan and the Holy Land (ELCJHL) was the first church in the region to permit women's ordination in 2015. Gender equality is one of five main areas for the ELCJHL, among education, contextual theology, ecumenism, and interreligious dialogue (Raheb 2018). The ELCJHL ordained its first Palestinian woman in 2023, Sally Azar.

The arrival of Protestantism to Korea in the late nineteenth century was coupled with Western Victorian ideals of womanhood, primarily domesticity in marriage and motherhood (Kim 2008). At the same time, Korean women had access to education and career opportunities never available to them before. The Ewha Girls School was the most prominent of women's schools, founded by Mary Scranton (1832–1909) in 1886, which grew into Ewha Womans University, Korea's first university and now the world's largest female university. Protestantism in Korea is majority female; for example, the Presbyterian Church in Korea (Tonghap), the fourth largest denomination in the country and the second largest Protestant denomination, is 70% female (Cho 2011).

Protestant Christianity in late-twentieth-century China was majority female; in some areas, Protestant communities were comprised of 94% women (Kao 2013, citing Guo 2007). The 2007 Spiritual Life Study of Chinese Residents – regarded one of the most reliable surveys on religion in a country notoriously difficult to do survey work – reported 72% female Protestants and 27% male. Women experienced a new kind of community in Protestantism, with the ability to make their own religious choices separate from their husbands or other men and achieve personal transformation unavailable in traditional culture (Kao 2013).

In Japan, women are known for being the majority of churchgoers, but they represent a minority of decision-makers. Many original translations of biblical texts affirm traditional Japanese patriarchy, making women feel like second-class citizens in the church (Lee 2022). Women are expected to have supportive roles to their husbands, not be leaders. Yet, Japan's largest Protestant denomination, the United Church of Christ in Japan (UCCJ, 197,000 members), ordained its first female pastor as early as 1930, and ordained more than 240 women by the year 2000, one-fifth of all UCCJ pastors (Lee 2022).

Women have increasing opportunities for church leadership throughout East and Southeast Asia. The Lutheran World Federation reports that 41 of its 54 member churches (76%) in the region ordain women, and other Protestant groups with many women in leadership include the World Communion of Reformed Churches, Three-Self Patriotic Movement (China), several Indonesian denominations (Javanese Christian Church, Batak Christian Protestant Church, Christian and Missionary Alliance), the Methodist and Lutheran churches in Taiwan, and the Church of Christ in Thailand (Lim 2020).

Europe

The Ecumenical Forum of European Christian Women (EFECW) formed in 1982 with participants from 33 European countries and aims to create safe places for Christian women across the theological spectrum in public life. Emphasizing the dignity of all Christian women, Nicole Fisher, EFECW's second president, stated at the second general assembly in Järvenpää, Finland (1986), "We demand the right to be represented at all levels in church and society, and we must bring to this demand our perspectives as women, our abilities as women, our feelings and hopes as women. And we will only succeed in this, if we are in the world. For we must emphasize that we are all God's children, who are made completely in his image, just like everyone else. Because God has promised it, we long to be fully human" (cited in Schintlmeister 2010). After Eastern Orthodoxy and Latin-rite Catholicism, Lutheranism is the third largest Christian family and the largest Protestant family in Europe, with 4% of the continent's population (Johnson and Zurlo 2022). Lutherans are the largest denomination in Denmark, Finland, Norway, Latvia, Hungary, and Slovakia. Women are the of majority members in each of these, at least upward of 56%. The Lutheran World Federation elected their first female general secretary, Anne Burghardt from Estonia, in 2021. She was also the first general secretary from Central and Eastern Europe to lead the global organization. Yet, the Lutheran church in some countries has taken different approaches to women's roles in the church. More than 80% of the Lutheran World Federation's 148 member churches worldwide ordain women, though women can serve everywhere as evangelists. In Latvia, the Evangelical Lutheran Church began ordaining women in 1975, but stopped in 1994. In 2016, the church officially ruled that women could not be ordained ministers. Lutheranism has been the state religion since 1550 in Iceland, and one-third of Lutheran pastors there are women. Agnes M. Sigurðardóttir became the church's first female bishop in 2012. Over half the population of Sweden has membership in the Church of Sweden (Lutheran), where the first woman was ordained in 1960 and today more than 40% of priests are women; anyone who does not recognize female priests in the Church of Sweden is barred from ordination (Lande 2004). The Église Protestante Unie de France (United Protestant Church of France) was formed in 2012 from a merger of the Reformed Church and the Evangelical Lutheran Church; one-third of its 500 pastors are women.

The largest Protestant denomination in Europe is the Evangelische Kirche in Deutschland (EKD, Evangelical Church in Germany), which is more like a federation of autonomous churches than a single united church, and contains United, Lutheran, and Reformed churches. All 20 member churches ordain women and the EKD had a female council chair in 2009–2010, Lutheran theologian Margot Käßmann, having served only one year before stepping down. In 2021, theologian Annette Kurchus was elected president.

Latin America

In Latin America, most non-Catholic churches are known as *evangélico*, which encompasses historic Protestant, Independent, and Pentecostal/Charismatic denominations. "Protestant" and "Evangelical" are synonymous in the region. On most measures of religious belief and practice, Protestant women are widely considered more religious than men. Most churches are still led by men even though in some contexts, as in Chile, society is more open to greater participation from women (Gumucio 2022).

Women's leadership remains a contentious issue in ecumenical relations, considering the relative lack of women in Catholic leadership vis-à-vis the numerous Protestant denominations, and mixed messaging on women's roles from Pentecostal groups (Suárez 2022). Women make up the majority of members of historic Protestant churches in Latin America and have achieved leadership roles in the face of *machismo* (Moreno 2022). In the Caribbean, women have long been leaders in African-derived churches; the European-derived churches such as Methodists and Reformed only began ordaining women in the 1980s and 1990s (Vernon 2012). The Anglican Episcopal Church began ordaining women in 1984, with Carmen Etel Alves Gomes its first female priest. Reformed/Presbyterian, Methodist, and Lutheran churches followed. Pentecostal women are caught between the messages that the Holy Spirit empowers Christians regardless of gender, and messages distilled from literal readings of the Bible that promote male headship and women's submission to men. The Assemblies of God (AoG) is the largest Protestant denomination in Brazil, Argentina, Venezuela, and Nicaragua, but the status of women's leadership in each of these is unclear. Generally, Pentecostal women can become pastors in Venezuela and

Nicaragua, but not in Argentina. The AoG in Brazil ordained its first female pastor in 2020, but there is not much movement in that direction.

Among Anglicans, Mexico ordained its first female priest in 1982, Brazil in 1985, and the Province of the West Indies in 1996. The Anglican Church in Central America voted to ordain women in 2008, but there have been female priests only in Costa Rica and Nicaragua. There are not yet any female bishops in these countries even though, for example, in Brazil, women make up 30% of Anglican clergy (Burity 2022). The Anglican Church of South America did not allow for women's ordination until 2015, when women were ordained in Bolivia and Uruguay. There are 25 female priests in the diocese of Jamaica and several others throughout the Caribbean (Vernon 2012).

North America

Historian Ann Braude famously stated, "In America, women go to church" (Braude 1997, p. 87). Yet, North American Christianity has a long history of tensions over the women's rights movement. Women's ordination predated second-wave feminism; the United Church of Canada ordained women in 1930, and Presbyterians and Methodists in the United States did so in 1956 (Bendroth 2023). In the 1970s, most mainline churches supported women's rights, and women represented upward of two-thirds of their churches, operating as a kind of special interest group within their denominations, able to maintain some power and influence (Bendroth 2023). Other Protestant denominations, however, have consistently clashed with the women's movement, such as the Southern Baptist Convention (SBC). The SBC has participated in an ongoing debate over women's status in the church since the 1960s. It was observed in the mid-1970s that "Women, who are strongly assumed to be a statistical majority in the SBC membership, are an obvious minority in local church and convention-wide decision-making positions" (Anders 1975, pp. 38–39). The denomination officially banned female ministers in 1984, violating the Baptist principle of congregational autonomy (Braude 2007). There has neither been a female president nor executive secretary of the denomination, though women have served on the executive committee.

According to the long-standing National Congregations Study, women constitute 13.5% of Protestant clergy in the United States, up from 5% in the 1990s, despite that 72% of people believe that women should be allowed to preach and 56% believe that women can be religious leaders (Chaves 2021). According to American church historian Margaret Bendroth, "Female clergy still contend with a 'stained-glass ceiling' that has kept them in smaller, often failing churches rather than major pulpits" (Bendroth 2023). Part of the gap between perception and reality is due to biblical interpretation, but also because of vocal complementarian organizations such as the Council on Biblical Manhood and Womanhood and preachers like John Piper, Wayne Grudem, John MacArthur, and Tim Keller who have popularized this theology since the 1980s.

The Reformed/Presbyterian family of denominations (3.7 million in 2020) embodies a broad spectrum of attitudes toward women's leadership. The largest of these, the Presbyterian Church USA (PC(USA), 1.7 million), ordained its first female minister in 1956, Margaret Towner (Hunter 2016). PC(USA) membership is 58% female, and despite strong support for female pastors, gender discrimination is still prevalent, with a study reporting that 80% of female teaching elders had experienced harassment, discrimination, or prejudicial comments due to their gender (Androit and Coe 2016). Women make up 38% of all teaching elders and only 29% of all elders in the denomination. Women in ministry has long been a controversial subject in Reformed/ Presbyterian churches, with several denominations prohibiting women's ordination, such as the Presbyterian Church in America, Reformed Church in the United States (not to be confused with the Reformed Church in America, which does ordain women), Free Reformed Churches, and the Orthodox Presbyterian Church. Others leave the decision to individual congregations, such as the Evangelical Presbyterian Church.

Nevertheless, women are at the helm of major denominations in North America. The presiding bishop of the largest Lutheran body in the US, the Evangelical Lutheran Church in America, is Elizabeth Eaton. The first female bishop in the global Anglican Communion was Barbara Harris, when she became Suffragan Bishop of Massachusetts in the Episcopal Church USA (Trisk 2013), and the Episcopal Church had a female presiding bishop from 2006 to 2015, Katharine Jefferts Schori. Rosemarie Wenner served as president of the United Methodist Church council of bishops, and the first women outside of the United States to do so. Other women have exerted tremendous influence in North American Christianity without formal ordination, such as Bible teacher Beth Moore, women's advocate Carolyn Custis James, disability activist Joni Eareckson Tada, and evangelist Anne Graham Lotz (second daughter of Billy and Ruth Graham).

Oceania

Women have been preachers in mainline Protestant churches in Australia since the turn of the twentieth century. In North Melbourne, Pentecostal Sarah Jane Lancaster (1858–1934) began preaching and faith healing in 1909, in what became the country's first Pentecostal congregation. Winifred Kiek (1884–1974) was ordained in the Congregational Church in Adelaide in 1927, the first ordained woman in the country. Doreen Rita Allen (c.1906–1993), a lay Methodist preacher, led the way for the approval of Methodist women's ordination in 1932, though the first women were not ordained until 1969, Margaret Sanders and Coralie Ling (Handasyde 2021).

The Anglican Church in Aotearoa, New Zealand and Polynesia ordained five women in 1977 and to date, over 500 women have become priests in the denomination. In the Anglican Church of Australia, women were permitted to be deacons in the 1980s, priests in the 1990s, and bishops in the 2000s. Kay Goldsworthy became the country's first female archbishop in 2018. Yet, there is a great diversity within the church concerning women's opportunities. The dioceses of Sydney, North West Australia, and The Murray do not ordain women at all, but the other 21 dioceses do.

Photo 10.2 Women dance and sing at the Women and Men's pre-assembly to the World Council of Churches 11th General Assembly in Karlsruhe, Germany (2022). *Source:* Albin Hillert/World Council of Churches.

The churches in Melanesia and Polynesia have been resistant to changes in gender roles to allow for women clergy (Breward 2004). Nevertheless, the Anglican Diocese of Polynesia ordained its first female priest in 1985 (an English missionary nurse) and appointed its first Indigenous Anglican female minister in 1995. Most women clergy in the region are considered "worker priests" not directly responsible for parishes and spend most of their time assisting male priests (Reed 2021). In Kiribati, women could attend Tangintebu Theological College beginning in the 1970s and the Kiribati Uniting Church began ordaining women in 1984. The Nauru Congregational Church was founded in 1888 and ordained the first female ministers in 2015, Wanda Joleen Hiram and Ruth Omodien Garabwan.

The Maohi Protestant Church is the largest Protestant body in French Polynesia, with 95,000 members and 35% of the country's population (Johnson and Zurlo 2022). Its roots trace to the London Missionary Society in the late eighteenth century and the Paris Society for Evangelical Missions in the nineteenth. The arrival of Protestantism sent mixed messages to women: "on the one hand emancipation through equal access to instruction and baptism; on the other reinforced control of sexuality and family norms" (Malogne-Fer 2012, p. 177). The church became autonomous from Western missionaries in 1963 and women could become ministers in 1995, with the first female ordination in 2003 after six years of training. Women's ordination pushed against the prevailing "pastoral couple" concept where male ministers must be married and their wives are required to oversee women's activities – though unpaid (Malogne-Fer 2012).

Women in Protestant leadership goes beyond pastoral ministry. For example, Anglican Deaconess Ministries in Australia, begun in 1891 by Mervyn and Martha Archdall, is quite robust in training women. It founded Mary Andrews College and maintains a Mental Health and Pastoral Care Institute, mercy and justice programs, and other programming for Christian women. The Methodist Women's Fellowship is very active in Fiji, with specific programs advocating for gender equality theology and encouraging women to understand their self-worth and dignity. In the Solomon Islands, the Christian Care Centre is the only institution dedicated to serving women and girls who have been victims of violence; it is staffed by Anglican nuns from Sisters of the Church and the Sisters of Melanesia.

Conclusion

The expectations placed upon women since the advent of Protestantism simultaneously held them up as spiritually pious while denying them opportunities to serve the church and community previously afforded to them in Catholicism. Nevertheless, like women throughout Christian history, Protestant women found ways to exert spiritual influence, establish churches, run mission organizations, and push for equal opportunities. Although women are achieving greater recognition in Protestant churches and organizations, challenges still abound. Cultural factors keep women relegated to certain societal spheres, theological interpretations of scripture keep women from pursuing their felt calls into ministry, and societal expectations keep women from fulfilling their ambition in the church. As Protestantism continues to shift to the global South, the experiences and voices of women in Africa, Asia, Latin America, and the Pacific Islands will be increasingly important. Africa could be home to 54% of the world's Protestants by 2050, and women already make up the majority of these congregations. As current trends continue, women should constitute an increasing proportion of Protestant decision-making bodies and leadership roles. Women's fellowships, prayer groups, and groups like the Mothers' Union continue to be the backbone of women's communities around the world, providing mutual support, encouragement, and friendship.

Reflection Questions

1) Consider the differences between women's roles in Catholic and Protestant churches. What changed for women with the advent of Protestantism? What were the new gender norms for Protestant women and families? What did women lose and gain in switching from Catholicism to Protestantism?

2) Describe Protestant women's involvement in the Western missionary movement. What opportunities did women have as overseas missionaries that were not available to them at home? In what ways did women's ministry and missionary activity represent holistic approaches to life, faith, and service, and how did indigenous women respond to their message?

3) Women in ordained pastoral leadership remains a contentious issue, with significant variation by Protestant denomination and geographical context. With more Protestants in Africa than any other continent, what is the future of women's roles in African Christianity? How do Protestant women gain influence beyond just pastoral ministry in settings that restrict their advancement?

Works Cited

Anders, Sarah F. (1975). Woman's role in the Southern Baptist Convention and its churches. *Review and Expositor*, 72(1) 31–39.

Androit, Angie and Coe, Deb (2016). Gender and leadership in the PC(USA). PCUSA Research Services.

Bendroth, Margaret (2023). Protestants. In: *Christianity in North America* (ed. Kenneth R. Ross, Grace J-S. Kim, and Todd M. Johnson), Edinburgh: Edinburgh University Press.

Braude, Ann (1997). Women's history *is* American religious history. In: *Retelling US Religious History* (ed. Thomas Tweed), 87–107. Berkeley: University of California Press.

Braude, Ann (2007). *Sisters and Saints: Women and American Religion.* New York: Oxford University Press.

Breward, Ian (2004). Australia, New Zealand, and Oceania. In: *The Blackwell Companion to Protestantism* (ed. Alister E. McGrath and Darren C. Marks), 232–238. Malden, MA: Blackwell Pub.

Burity, Joanildo (2022). Anglicans. In: *Christianity in Latin America and the Caribbean* (ed. Kenneth R. Ross, Ana María Bidegain, and Todd M. Johnson), 253–261. Edinburgh: Edinburgh University Press.

Chaves, Mark (2021). National congregations study, cumulative dataset (1998, 2006–2007, 2012, and 2018–2019).

Cho, Han Sang (2011). Equal discipleship in the Presbyterian Church of Korea. DMin dissertation. The Catholic Theological Union at Chicago.

Fleming, Jody B. (2015). Christian renewal and the Pentecostal-Charismatic movement in Venezuela. In: *Pentecostals and Charismatics in Latin America and Latino Communities* (ed. Néstor Medina and Sammy Alfaro), 35–48. New York: Palgrave Macmillan.

Gumucio, Cristián Parker (2022). Chile. In: *Christianity in Latin America and the Caribbean* (ed. Kenneth R. Ross, Ana María Bidegain, and Todd M. Johnson), 37–48. Edinburgh: Edinburgh University Press.

Guo, Chao (2007). Christianity and Chinese Society: a religious vitality perspective. Paper presented at the biannual conference of International Society for the Sociology of Religion 29th Conference, Leipzig, Germany. July 24.

Handasyde, Kerrie (2021). Mother, preacher, press: women ministers and the negotiation of authority, 1910–1933. In: *Contemporary Feminist Theologies: Power, Authority, Love* (ed. Kerrie Handasyde,

Cathryn McKinney, and Rebekah Pryor), 88–99. Abingdon, Oxon: Routledge, Taylor & Francis Group.

Hunter, Rhashell (2016). PC (USA) celebrates 60 years of women clergy. Presbyterian Church (USA). https://www.pcusa.org/news/2016/5/24/pcusa-celebrates-60-years-womens-ordination (accessed 25 February 2022).

Hutchison, William R. (1987). *Errand to the World: American Protestant Thought and Foreign Missions*. Chicago: University of Chicago Press.

Johnson, Todd M. and Zurlo, Gina A. (2019). *World Christian Encyclopedia*. 3rd edn. Edinburgh: Edinburgh University Press.

Johnson, Todd M. and Zurlo, Gina A. ed. (2022). *World Christian Database*. Leiden/Boston: Brill.

Kao, Chen-Yang (2013). Church as 'women's community': the feminization of Protestantism in contemporary China. *Journal of Archaeology and Anthropology*, 78, 107–140.

Kim, Chong Bum (2008). For God and home: women's education in early Korean Protestantism. *Acta Koreana*, 11(3),9–28.

King, Ursula (1994). Introduction. In: *Feminist Theology from the Third World: A Reader*. (ed. Ursula King), 1–22. Eugene, OR: Wipf & Stock.

Lande, Aasulv (2004). Nordic Protestantism to the present day. In: *The Blackwell Companion to Protestantism* (ed. Alister E. McGrath and Darren C. Marks), 130–146. Malden, MA: Blackwell Publishing.

Lee, Samuel (2022). *Japanese Women and Christianity*. Amsterdam: Academy Press of Amsterdam.

Lim, Timothy (2020). Protestants. In: *Christianity in East and Southeast Asia* (ed. Kenneth R. Ross, Francis Alvarez, and Todd M. Johnson), 295–309. Edinburgh: Edinburgh University Press.

Malogne-Fer, Gwendoline (2012). The feminization and professionalization of ordained ministry within the Ma'ohi Protestant Church in French Polynesia. In: *Women and Ordination in the Christian Churches: International Perspectives* (ed. Ian Jones et al.), 177–188. London: T&T Clark Bloomsbury.

Mombo, Esther (2012). The ordination of women in Africa: an historical perspective. In: *Women and Ordination in the Christian Churches: International Perspectives* (ed. Ian Jones et al.), 123–143. London: T&T Clark Bloomsbury.

Montgomery, Helen Barrett (1910). *Western Women in Eastern Lands: Fifty Years of Woman's Work in Foreign Missions*. New York: The Macmillan Company.

Moreno, Pablo (2022). Protestants. In: *Christianity in Latin America and the Caribbean* (ed. Kenneth R. Ross, Ana María Bidegain, and Todd M. Johnson), 285–297. Edinburgh: Edinburgh University Press.

Mothers' Union (2021). Where we work. https://www.mothersunion.org/what-we-do/where-we-work (accessed 24 February 2022).

Moyse, Cordelia (2009). *A History of the Mothers' Union: Women, Anglicanism and Globalisation, 1876-2008*. Woodbridge: Boydell & Brewer.

Muir, Elizabeth G. (2019). *A Women's History of the Christian Church: Two Thousand Years of Female Leadership*. Toronto: University of Toronto Press.

Nyomi, Setri (2017). Protestants. In: *Christianity in Sub-Saharan Africa* (ed. Kenneth R. Ross, J. Kwabena Asamoah-Gyadu, and Todd M. Johnson), 277–288. Edinburgh: Edinburgh University Press.

Porterfield, Amanda (1997). *Mary Lyon and the Mount Holyoke Missionaries*. New York: Oxford University Press.

Pui-lan, Kwok (2018). The study of Chinese women and the Anglican Church in cross-cultural perspective. In: *Christian Women in Chinese Society: The Anglican Story*. (ed. Wai-Ching Angela Wong and Patricia P.K. Chiu), 19–36. Hong Kong: Hong Kong University Press.

Raheb, Mitri (2018). Protestants. In: *Christianity in North Africa and West Asia* (ed. Kenneth R. Ross, Mariz Tadros, and Todd M. Johnson), 259–270. Edinburgh: Edinburgh University Press.

Reed, Brenda (2021). Anglicans. In: *Christianity in Oceania* (ed. Kenneth R. Ross, Katalina Tahaafe-Williams, and Todd M. Johnson), 153–165. Edinburgh: Edinburgh University Press.

Reeves-Ellington, Barbara, Sklar, Kathryn K., and Shemo, Connie A. ed. (2010). *Competing Kingdoms: Women, Mission, Nation, and the American Protestant Empire, 1812–1960*. Durham, NC: Duke University Press.

Rigby, Cynthia (2004). Protestantism and feminism. In: *The Blackwell Companion to Protestantism* (ed. Alister E. McGrath and Darren C. Marks), 332–343. Malden, MA: Blackwell Publishing.

Robert, Dana L. (1997). *American Women in Mission: A Social History of Their Thought and Practice*. Macon, GA: Mercer University Press.

Schintlmeister, Inge (2010). Spirituality – reconciliation – hope for life – vision for the future: ecumenical forum of European Christian Women from 1982 to 2010. Ecumenical Forum of European Christian Women.

Scott, David W. (2020). Methodist women leaders in Africa. https://um-insight.net/in-the-church/umc-global-nature/methodist-women-in-leaders-in-africa (accessed 24 February 2022).

Seton, Rosemary E. (2013). *Western Daughters in Eastern Lands: British Missionary Women in Asia*. Santa Barbara, CA: Praeger.

Stanley, Brian (2009). *The World Missionary Conference, Edinburgh 1910*. Grand Rapids, MI: William B. Eerdmans Publishing Company.

Suárez, Ana Lourdes (2022). Gender. In: *Christianity in Latin America and the Caribbean*. (ed. Kenneth R. Ross, Ana María Bidegain, and Todd M. Johnson), 397–407. Edinburgh: Edinburgh University Press.

Trisk, Janet (2013). Women in the Anglican Communion. In: *The Wiley-Blackwell Companion to the Anglican Communion* (ed. Ian S. Markham, J. Barney Hawkins IV, Justyn Terry, and Leslie Nuñez Steffensen), 617–626. Chichester: John Wiley and Sons.

Tucker, Ruth (2017). *Katie Luther, First Lady of the Reformation: The Unconventional Life of Katharina von Bora*. Grand Rapids, MI: Zondervan.

Ustorf, Werner (2004). Protestantism and missions. In: *The Blackwell Companion to Protestantism* (ed. Alister E. McGrath and Darren C. Marks), 392–402. Malden, MA: Blackwell Publishing.

Vernon, Rachel E. (2012). Daughters of Jerusalem, Mothers of Salem: caribbean women in the ministry of the Anglican church. In: *Women and Ordination in the Christian Churches: International Perspectives* (ed. Ian Jones et al.), 215–224. London: Bloomsbury.

Zell, Katharina and McKee, Elsie Anne (2006). *Church Mother: The Writings of a Protestant Reformer in Sixteenth-Century Germany*. Chicago: University of Chicago Press.

11

Women in Independent Christianity

"The main concern of women is not merely a demand for more positions and equal opportunity in decision-making bodies of the church; it is more than that. It is a struggle to recognize women's theological and spiritual contribution as an integral part of the church's prophetic ministry in the world."

Emelyn Dacuycuy (Vergara 2019)

Mai Chaza (1914–1960) formed an Independent church movement in Rhodesia (Zimbabwe) after experiencing illness, death, a vision from God, and a bodily resurrection. Upon returning from some time in the mountains, she began to heal the sick, preach, eradicate witchcraft, and famously pray for barren women to conceive. Her movement, the Guta ra Jehovah (City of God), began in 1955 after she was no longer accepted by the Methodist church (Mwaura 2007; Martin 1971). Her messianic leadership led to the development of a very popular charismatic movement. However, like many such movements, she failed to name a successor and after her death in 1960 the movement began to dwindle. Nevertheless, it still exists today, and her followers call her "Matenga" – "the heavens."

While perhaps the most misunderstood tradition worldwide, Independent Christianity is having a significant impact in World Christianity in terms of its size, growth, and uniqueness. This is also an extremely diverse category with many representations of Christian history, theology, culture, and rituals around the world. Independent Christians are those who do not self-identify with Catholic, Protestant, or Orthodox churches and denominations. As such, this is naturally a very broad category, consisting of numerous Christian denominations that might not otherwise be associated with each other. For example, placing African Independent Churches in the same category as the Church of Jesus Christ of Latter-day Saints does not suggest that these two movements are historically or theologically related. Rather, placing them in the same category makes an overarching sociological statement that members of these denominations self-identify separately from Catholic, Orthodox, and Protestant Christianity. Though many Independent groups might resemble Protestantism in terms of their theology, ecclesiology, ritual, or worship, they do not trace their lineage to the Protestant Reformation and thus are not considered Protestant.

There are two ways for a Christian denomination to be Independent. The first is by splintering from an existing, usually mainline, historic, or mission-founded denomination. There are numerous historical examples of this, such as the Stone-Campbell Movement. All emerging from the Stone-Campbell Movement, the Disciples of Christ are Protestants, but the Christian Churches and Churches of Christ are Independents because they broke from the Disciples of Christ. The Churches of Christ self-identifies outside of historic, mainstream Protestantism. Another example

Women in World Christianity: Building and Sustaining a Global Movement, First Edition. Gina A. Zurlo.
© 2023 John Wiley & Sons Ltd. Published 2023 by John Wiley & Sons Ltd.

is the Methodist Pentecostal Church of Chile, which split from the Methodist church in 1909. Subsequently, in 1947, the Pentecostal Church of Chile broke from the Methodist Pentecostal Church and in 1952, the Pentecostal Mission Church split from the Evangelical Pentecostal Church. There are more contemporary examples as well, such as the Anglican Church of North America (ACNA), which split from the Episcopal Church USA in 2009. The Episcopal Church USA is Protestant and the ACNA is Independent.

The second kind of Independents are those that began disconnected from Catholic, Orthodox, and Protestant Christianity. Often these movements originate from revivals or are centered around charismatic leadership, growing into legitimate denominations in their own right. Examples include the Church of Jesus Christ of Latter-day Saints, Jehovah's Witnesses, and the numerous African Independent Churches (see Chapter 2) that sprouted and grew in the second half of the twentieth century. Independent churches have been growing rapidly and represent a new era of World Christianity. This chapter features different Independent movements around the globe and the challenges and opportunities that women face within them.

Independents, 1900–2050

Independent Christianity grew substantially in the twentieth century, from less than 1% of the global population in 1900 to 5% in 2020, with anticipated continued increase to at least 6% by 2050 (Table 11.1). However, more striking is the growth of Independents' share of all Christians, starting from less than 2% of all Christians in 1900, growing to over 15% in 2020, and to an anticipated 19% by 2050 (Johnson and Zurlo 2022). In 1900, 77% of all Independents lived in the global North, but this dropped dramatically to 20% by 2020 (Table 11.1). The largest share is in Africa, home to 33% of all Independents, though North America is close with 32% (Figure 11.1). African Independent Christianity in sub-Saharan Africa, the Church of Jesus Christ of Latter-day Saints in the Pacific Islands, and networked Charismatic movements like Vineyard churches grew over the century, especially since 1970, and have contributed to the increasing Independent share of World Christianity.

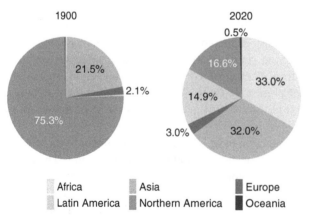

Figure 11.1 Independents by continent, 1900 and 2020. *Source:* Data from Johnson and Zurlo 2022.

Table 11.1 Independents by continent, 1900–2050.

Region	Independents 1900	% of pop. 1900	% of Independents 1900	Rate % p.a. 1900–2020	Independents 2020	% of pop. 2020	% of Independents 2020	Independents 2050	% of pop. 2050	% of Independents 2050
Global North	6,857,000	1.4%	77.4	2.03	76,907,000	6.9	19.7	90,134,000	7.9	14.6
Europe	185,000	0.0	2.1	3.52	11,792,000	1.6	3.0	15,624,000	2.2	2.5
North America	6,672,000	8.2	75.3	1.92	65,115,000	17.7	16.7	74,510,000	17.5	12.0
Global South	2,002,000	0.2	22.6	4.30	312,567,000	4.7	80.3	528,711,000	6.1	85.4
Africa	40,000	0.0	0.5	6.96	128,346,000	9.6	33.0	233,986,000	9.4	37.8
Asia	1,906,000	0.2	21.5	3.54	124,080,000	2.7	31.9	207,370,000	3.9	33.5
Latin America	33,200	0.1	0.4	6.42	58,045,000	8.9	14.9	84,463,000	11.1	13.6
Oceania	21,900	0.4	0.2	3.88	2,096,000	4.9	0.5	2,892,000	5.0	0.5
Global total	**8,859,000**	**0.5**	**100.0**	**3.20**	**389,474,000**	**5.0**	**100.0**	**618,845,000**	**6.4**	**100.0**

Source: Data from Johnson and Zurlo 2022. p.a. = percent change per annum, or each year.

Table 11.2   Independents by continent with percent female, 2020.

Region	Independents 2020	% of pop. 2020	% of Independents 2020	% Independent female 2020	% region female 2020
Global North	76,907,000	6.9	19.7	55.4	51.3
Europe	11,792,000	1.6	3.0	54.5	51.7
North America	65,115,000	17.7	16.7	55.5	50.5
Global South	312,567,000	4.7	80.3	53.4	49.3
Africa	128,346,000	9.6	33.0	53.7	50.0
Asia	124,080,000	2.7	31.9	52.0	48.9
Latin America	58,045,000	8.9	14.9	55.8	50.8
Oceania	2,096,000	4.9	0.5	52.2	49.9
Global total	**389,474,000**	**5.0**	**100.0**	**53.8**	**49.6**

Source: Data from Johnson and Zurlo 2022.

Table 11.3   Countries with the most Independents, 2020.

Rank	Country	Country pop. 2020	Independent % of pop. 2020	Independents 2020	% Independent female 2020	% country female 2020
1	United States	331,003,000	19.3	63,800,000	55.6	50.5
2	China	1,439,324,000	4.3	62,000,000	53.5	48.7
3	Nigeria	206,140,000	13.7	28,285,000	54.1	49.3
4	Brazil	212,559,000	12.2	26,000,000	57.1	50.9
5	South Africa	59,309,000	41.0	24,325,000	55.0	50.7
6	DR Congo	89,561,000	26.7	23,930,000	52.8	50.1
7	Philippines	109,581,000	17.6	19,300,000	49.9	49.8
8	India	1,380,004,000	1.3	18,130,000	50.0	48.0
9	South Korea	51,269,000	22.1	11,330,000	52.0	49.9
10	Kenya	53,771,000	16.7	9,000,000	53.0	50.3

Source: Data from Johnson and Zurlo 2022.

Independent Christianity is found all over the world, though more profoundly in the global South. In 2020, Africa was home to the largest population of Independents: 128 million total, 10% of the continent's population, and 33% of all Independents in the world (Table 11.2). Asians represent 32% of all Independents globally, mostly due to the Chinese house church movement and networks of Muslim, Hindu, and Buddhist background believers. Women make up the majority of all Independent populations on every continent, ranging from 52% in Oceania to 56% in North America.

Nine of the ten countries with the most Independents are in the global South, except for the United States at number one (Table 11.3). Four countries with the most Independents are in Asia, four are in Africa, and one in Latin America. Independents do not make up the majority of any of these countries – the largest is 27% in South Africa – but in all of them, women comprise a higher proportion of Independents than the country, and by some of the widest margins (e.g., Brazil is 51% female, but Independents are 57% female). Worldwide, Independent churches tend to report higher shares of female affiliation than historic or mainline churches.

Table 11.4 Countries with the highest percent of Independents, 2020.

Rank	Country	Country pop. 2020	Independent % of pop. 2020	Independents 2020	% Independent female 2020	% country female 2020
1	Tonga	106,000	79.9	84,500	49.3	49.9
2	Eswatini	1,160,000	54.4	631,000	54.4	50.8
3	Zimbabwe	14,863,000	42.7	6,350,000	54.9	52.3
4	Samoa	198,000	42.3	84,000	48.6	48.2
5	South Africa	59,309,000	41.0	24,325,000	55.0	50.7
6	American Samoa	55,200	39.0	21,500	53.0	48.2
7	Botswana	2,352,000	34.2	805,000	56.0	51.6
8	Niue	1,600	28.2	460	53.4	48.2
9	DR Congo	89,561,000	26.7	23,930,000	52.8	50.1
10	Saint Vincent	111,000	26.6	29,500	56.1	49.3

Source: Data from Johnson and Zurlo 2022.

Table 11.5 Countries with the fastest growth of Independents, 2020.

Rank	Country	Country pop. 2020	Independent % of pop. 2020	Independents 2020	% Independent female 2020	% country female 2020	Rate % p.a. 2000–2020
1	Iran	83,993,000	0.4	342,000	47.0	49.5	7.13
2	Mozambique	31,255,000	14.4	4,500,000	53.9	51.4	6.10
3	Bhutan	772,000	1.2	9,000	52.9	46.9	6.01
4	Chad	16,426,000	4.0	652,000	54.2	50.1	5.95
5	Algeria	43,851,000	0.3	110,000	48.7	49.5	5.16
6	Saint Kitts and Nevis	53,200	8.7	4,600	54.9	53.9	4.66
7	Albania	2,878,000	1.0	28,000	54.1	49.1	4.54
8	South Sudan	11,194,000	1.6	180,000	56.0	49.9	4.48
9	Mauritania	4,650,000	0.1	2,700	53.2	49.8	4.19
10	Tajikistan	9,538,000	0.0	4,500	53.2	49.6	4.19

Source: Data from Johnson and Zurlo 2022. p.a. = percent change per annum, or each year.

The countries with the highest percent of Independents span the world: five are in Africa, four are in the Pacific Islands, and one is in the Caribbean (Table 11.4). The high proportions of Independents in Tonga, Samoa, American Samoa, and Niue are due to large populations of Latter-day Saints. Women's share of Independents in these countries vary; in Saint Vincent and American Samoa, they make up a much larger proportion (56% and 53%), but elsewhere the figures are much closer (Tonga, Samoa).

The countries with the fastest growth of Independents are often those where people are converting to Christianity from non-Christian religions (Iran, Bhutan, Algeria, Mauritania, Tajikistan) and places where Christians are switching from one church to another (Mozambique, Chad, Saint Kitts and Nevis, Albania, South Sudan). A large proportion of converts to Independent Christianity is within underground house church networks in countries where it is illegal or very difficult to be a Christian, such as Iran (7.13% growth between 2000 and 2020, see Table 11.5). Women are initially

Table 11.6   Largest Independent denominations, 2015.

Rank	Country	Denomination	Year begun	Affiliated 2015	% female	Rate % p.a. 2000–2015
1	China	Han traditional house churches	1917	20,000,000	53.7	3.18
2	China	Han house churches Big Five (rural)	1979	19,510,000	53.7	−2.67
3	China	Han emerging urban church networks	1989	15,000,000	53.7	4.73
4	DR Congo	Eglise de Jésus-Christ sur la Terre par le Prophète Simon Kimbangu	1921	12,000,000	52.0	2.70
5	United States	National Baptist Convention, USA	1773	9,200,000	57.4	−0.26
6	United States	Church of God in Christ	1895	8,046,000	57.4	0.93
7	Brazil	Igreja Universal do Reino de Deus	1977	7,500,000	60.0	3.46
8	United States	Church of Jesus Christ of Latter-day Saints	1830	6,642,000	55.6	1.63
9	South Africa	Zion Christian Church, South Africa	1924	5,000,000	55.2	1.17
10	United States	National Baptist Convention of America	1880	4,250,000	57.4	0.40

Source: Data from Johnson and Zurlo 2022. p.a. = percent change per annum, or each year.

more likely to join these churches than men, and after converting they tend to encourage their husbands and family members to join. Many such underground house churches are also led by women.

Naturally, the largest Independent denominations are in countries with very large Christian populations, such as the United States, China, and Brazil (Table 11.6). The top three largest Independent groups are networks of Chinese house churches: traditional, rural, and urban. In the United States, the largest Independent denominations include majority Black churches and Latter-day Saints. All of the top ten largest Independent denominations are majority female, and by wider margins compared to Catholic, Orthodox, and Protestant churches. The Universal Church of the Kingdom of God in Brazil has one of the highest reported proportions of female adherents in the world, at 60%.

Women in Independent Christian History

The concept of Independent Christianity is rooted in mid-twentieth century research on newly forming churches in sub-Saharan Africa by missionary-researchers Bengt Sundkler, Harold Turner, Marthinus Daneel, Andrew Walls, and David B. Barrett. In fact, the identification and investigation of Independent Christianity was a precursor for the entire academic discipline of World Christianity as it exists today. As researchers encountered new kinds of Christian faith, they embedded themselves within these groups and shared their findings with the Western world. In doing so, these researchers not only helped identify the newest forms of Christianity in the world, but they also helped legitimize these expressions to Western observers, many of whom were skeptical of African-led churches. Even though all these early researchers were men, they did include analyses of women in African Independent Churches (AICs) in their research. Having recognized that mission churches prohibited women's leadership and attempted to suppress women's influence, these men reported on how women gained access to the social, political, and spiritual realms in AICs.

Bengt Sundkler (1908–1995) was a missionary with the Lutheran Church of Sweden in Zululand, specifically, Natal, and authored *Bantu Prophets in South Africa* in 1948. Written for a White, Western audience, this book was the first to record the massive growth of Christianity among what would be known as AICs. An authoritative work, it included a 20-page list of Independent churches in South Africa in the 1940s. Sundkler described women's roles in traditional Zulu religion, such as the uNomdede cult where women are central. For example, they dance in honor of the Queen of Heaven to solicit a good harvest. Becoming a traditional diviner was one way for women to obtain social prestige otherwise unattainable to them. Mission churches in Zululand were mostly composed of women and girls, with ministers calling their congregations "a women's church" (Sundkler 1948, p. 140). Sundkler reported that women had even greater opportunities in new Zulu Independent churches as local leaders. Women had ranking positions in the hierarchic system, mirroring women's advancement in Zulu society at the time. Sundkler even compared Zulu Christian women to prominent Western female founders Mary Baker Eddy (Christian Science), Ellen G. White (Seventh-day Adventists), and Aimee Semple McPherson (International Church of the Foursquare Gospel).

Sundkler's typology of African Independent Churches – Zionist/spiritual churches and Ethiopian/African churches – became the standard. Wesleyan minister Mangena M. Mokone (1851–1931), motivated by the racial segregation he experienced in the church, with one conference for Europeans and another for Africans, founded the first Ethiopian church in 1892. It was named after Psalm 68:31, "Ethiopia shall soon stretch out her hands unto God." While women could not be official leaders in Ethiopian churches, they still held significant influence as leaders' wives, paralleled to their husbands'. Sundkler reported, "As local leaders, especially in Zululand, women generally show more initiative than men" (Sundkler 1948, p. 142).

Zionist churches began with the Christian Catholic Apostolic Church in Zion, founded in the United States in 1896 by Scottish-Australian faith healer John Alexander Dowie (1847–1907). The church focused on divine healing and the impending second coming of Jesus Christ. Dowie's colleague Daniel Bryant brought the movement to South Africa. After encountering Pentecostal/Apostolic faith missionaries, Bryant received the baptism of the Holy Spirit and renamed their church the Zion Apostolic Church, from which numerous Zionist churches emerged. Zionist churches were led by charismatic leaders who emphasized faith healing, received revelation through dreams, and practiced full immersion baptism in South African congregations that were majority female. In Zionist churches, top positions of leadership could be occupied by women, such as "Sister Ministress" Lucy S. Mofokeng, founder of the Holy Apostle Mission Church of South Africa in 1943. Female leaders in Zionist churches received pushback from men, but women tended to be more self-reliant in the absence of the strict hierarchy found in Ethiopian churches.

New Zealand-born Presbyterian minister Harold Turner (1911–2002) continued the academic study of AICs. After arriving in Sierra Leone in 1954, Turner encountered both African Independent Christianity and the work of renowned mission historian Andrew Walls (Hitchen 2002). Turner's two-volume work, *History of an African Independent Church*, was published in 1967. He made a further distinction between Ethiopian AICs and prophet-healing AICs. Ethiopian churches were like Sundkler's – orthodox in doctrine, worship, and polity, imitative of Western churches but spiritually independent from them. Prophet-healing type churches were united in certain theological criteria such as belief in the one supreme God who worked through the power of the Holy Spirit and baptism of the Holy Spirit. They also emphasized visions, dreams, the gifts of tongues, and other expressions of the Spirit. Ethiopian churches rejected the spiritual pantheism of traditional African religion and embraced a "this-worldly" view of salvation. These churches were known as Zionist in southern Africa (Sundkler), but as Aladura among the Yoruba in Western Africa.

Turner documented the presence of women in the Church of the Lord (Aladura) throughout his two-volume series. Josiah Olunowo Ositelu (1900–1966) was the church's founder and first Primate. His mother was an early adherent of her son's movement and became the first female president of the organization. Upon her death, she was succeeded by a daughter, Dorcas Oyetola Sodipo (Turner 1967:I). Ositelu also had seven wives, many of whom became prophetesses in the movement: Orebo; Agnes Odutayo, Juliana Olufunlayo, Comfort Omobola, Victoria Yetunde Bamtefa, and Ester Oludoyin (Turner 1967:I). Donned with the honorific "Spiritual Mother" or "Church Mother" (Turner 1967:II), minister's wives had special privileges and duties. Turner recognized the disregard of women in mission churches and thus detailed some teachings regarding women, such as their ritual uncleanness during menstruation and Eve's blame for Adam's fall. Yet, attitudes varied widely on gender relations in marriage and a women's place in society. After all, women served as gifted prophetesses and preachers and received training for evangelism, pastoral care, and conducting meetings for other women (Turner 1967:II). Compared to mission churches, women in the Church of the Lord had ample opportunities for learning and service, though many did not take them because of existing child-rearing responsibilities. Of the 21 schismatic groups from the Church of the Lord, five were established by women (Turner 1967:I).

Women were among the first members of the Celestial Church of Christ (CCC), established in 1947, and were instrumental in establishing parishes in Nigeria and beyond (Crumbley 1992). Women with visions contributed to the founding of Christ Apostolic Church (CAC). However, the received oral history of both churches relegated women as passive followers of their husbands or removed them from the historical record altogether. In reality, women were central in ensuring the success of these movements. The Church of the Lord (Aladura) recognized the role of women from the beginning as deaconesses and Reverend Mothers. Aladura churches typically have many rules and regulations for women: prohibition on women's ordination, allowing men and boys to be leaders above them, and refusing them entry to church while menstruating. Women can nevertheless have prominent and successful ministries, and in the Church of the Lord, for example, there exists parallel egalitarian leadership structures to men (for instance, roles such as Apostle General and Reverend Mother General) (Crumbley 1992).

David B. Barrett (1927–2011), a Welsh-British missionary in Western Nyanza Province, Kenya, documented Independent Christianity among the Luo people. Africans had played a significant role in the growth of Christianity in the region as catechists, clergy, and administrators. By the mid-1960s, most of the Protestant churches were under Luo leadership. Despite the growth of Christianity among the Luo, religious protest movements began almost immediately. By the 1940s, the East African Revival had spread from Ruanda to Luo Christians in Kenya, and the first Christian Luo separatist movement began in 1914, led by Johana Owalo (Nomiya Luo Mission). Upon Barrett's arrival in 1957, the largest schism from the Anglican church was underway among the Luo, the Johera (People of Love) movement, led by Abednego Matthew Ajuoga (Zurlo 2017). Barrett considered AICs to be authentic renewal movements within the mission churches as they were rooted in vernacular scripture, infused with African culture, and emphasized traditional African values such as brotherly love. From these areas emerged uniquely African theology, centered on communal life.

As discussed in Chapter 2, Barrett identified the assault on the African family – especially women's roles – as one of the major contributing factors to breakaway African Independent Churches. Women lost their traditional religious status with the arrival of Western Christianity. In the breakup of polygamous families, wives other than the favorite were separated from their husbands and suffered under the rigidity of institutionalized churches (Barrett 1968). Women embraced the availability of the Bible in local languages, but realized they had more to lose than men, noticing the stark contrast between the missionary stance on gender roles and Jesus's own interactions with women in the New Testament. At the time of Barrett's research in the 1960s, women comprised the majority of members of AICs, many of which had only recently formed.

Vignettes: Independent Women Worldwide

Independent Christianity is perhaps the most diverse of the major Christian traditions, given the wide theological spectrum that exists among denominations under this umbrella. Just as the emergence of Independent Christianity was highly influenced by nationalism, colonization, ethnicity, identity, and theology, these factors continue to shape women's experiences and opportunities in these churches.

Africa

The Organization of African Instituted Churches (OAIC) formed in 1978 when AIC leaders from across Africa gathered in Cairo at the invitation of Pope Shenouda III of the Coptic Orthodox Church. The OAIC serves as a forum to share concerns, hopes, and plans for addressing challenges such as poverty, health, and the breakdown of African cultural and social systems (OAIC 2015). It is based in Nairobi, Kenya, and represents 30 million members of AICs across the continent.

The debate on women's roles in AICs is ongoing. Women have served as founders of these movements and have helped lay the foundation for future women in leadership (see Chapter 2 for examples). These women were also focused on holistic mission that included the transformation of society, not just spiritual transformation. The OAIC's statement on women in leadership names the promotion of female leaders "an integral part of visioning for a better world" (Awinoh 2019). Though women's ordination and participation in the priesthood of AICs is common (Lubaale 2017), women remain only a small proportion. They have a much larger influence in these churches as the majority of members, in prayer ministries, and by participation through other gifts of the Spirit such as prophecy and healing.

The Church of Jesus Christ on Earth Through the Prophet Simon Kimbangu (Église de Jésus-Christ sur la Terre par le Prophète Simon Kimbangu, EJCSK) in the Democratic Republic of the Congo (DRC) is the largest AIC in Africa, with an estimated 12 million members (Johnson and Zurlo 2022). Simon Kimbangu (1887–1951) was a Baptist catechist who began a healing ministry in 1921, attracting many followers and alarming Belgian colonial authorities. His first miracle was healing a young woman named N'Kiantondo (Gampiot 2014). He was convicted to life imprisonment but eventually exiled to the city of Lubumbashi. His movement went underground during the leadership of his wife, Marie Muilu Kiawanga Nzitani (1880–1959), but it also spread throughout the Congo, splintering into different factions. Kimbanguism has always had female leaders: "The matrilineal nature of Kimbangu's ethnic background made his church receptive to female church leaders almost from the start. In that respect the Kimbanguist church was ahead of the mainstream Christian denominations in the Western world" (Mazrui 2014, p. 189). Three of Marie Muilu Kiawanga Nzitani and Simon Kimbangu's sons reorganized the church in 1959, when it was officially recognized by Belgian authorities. The church grew rapidly following the DRC's independence in 1960, and the EJCSK became the first AIC to join the World Council of Churches in 1969, although it was expelled in 2021 for theological reasons (see Vähäkangas 2021). The church believes that Simon Kimbangu was the embodiment of the Holy Spirit; it avoids politics, rejects violence, polygamy, witchcraft, alcohol, tobacco, and dancing.

Asia

The largest expression of Independent Christianity in the world is the Chinese house church movement, the rise of which is briefly discussed in Chapter 3. Chinese house churches consist of tens of millions of Christians who worship without legal status, and the movement has grown rapidly since the 1970s (Ro 2020). In the nineteenth century, much of China was evangelized by Bible women – local evangelists trained by female foreign missionaries to spread the Christian message throughout their communities. In the 1970s and 1980s, the house church movement was primarily rural and upward of 80% female. In the 1990s and early 2000s, the movement emerged in the cities and among the middle class, and the gender dynamic began to change with more men joining the churches. Pastor's wives, who have authority and leadership as coworkers alongside their husbands, often receive formal theological and leadership training, but bear a double burden of expectation as church leaders related to matters of filial piety – such as caring for one's parents, elders, and ancestors (Nation 2017). Women bear much of the stress related to running understaffed and underfunded house church networks and congregations.

Hidden believers in Christ from Muslim and Hindu backgrounds represent another form of Independent Christianity in Asia. These are individuals who are followers of Jesus, yet self-identify publicly as Muslim or Hindu, often doing so for safety reasons. It is difficult to estimate the size of these movements, but they are found in large numbers in India (an estimated four million), Iran (315,000), Bangladesh (178,000), Nepal (140,000), and Indonesia (120,000) (Johnson and Zurlo 2022) – places where conversion to Christianity is illegal or considered socially undesirable. In many Muslim- and Hindu-majority contexts, women generally have fewer political and social freedoms than men, making it more difficult to learn about Christianity. Nevertheless, they are often more likely than men to convert to Christianity and join Muslim or Hindu background Christian networks. They are attracted to Christianity because of a personal relationship with a Christian, or because of learning about Jesus's positive interactions with women as recorded in the New Testament (Miller 2018). New Christian converts tend to face extreme pressure from their families to revert to Islam or Hinduism. For young women or girls, it would not be uncommon for them to be prohibited from leaving the house until they reconvert. Furthermore, conversion has ramifications for marriage and family. Sharia law prohibits interreligious marriage, and "if a male BMB [background Muslim believer] marries a Christian woman, then according to sharia their children must be Muslims and will be so designated legally" (Miller 2018, p. 229). This creates a confusing situation for children who are raised Christian at home but are considered Muslim in public.

Photo 11.1 Worship service of rural house church members in China, most of whom were women (1990s). *Source:* Love China International HC.

The Philippine Independent Church (PIC) is an indigenous church formed 1902 in under the leadership of Isabelo de los Reyes (1864–1938), as a schism from the Roman Catholic Church during a wave of anti-Spanish colonial nationalism. Gregorio Aglipay (1860–1940) was the PICs first bishop (Chow 2020). It has suffered numerous breakaway groups since its founding, but still claims 3.5 million members and is among the largest Independent denominations in Asia (Johnson and Zurlo 2022). Since 1960, the PIC has been in full communion with the Episcopal Church in the United States and is thus part of the global Anglican Communion. The PIC permits women's ordination, marriage of priests, and support for contraceptives and same-sex rights. Yet, despite over 20 years of permitting women's ordination (Rosalina Rabaria was the first female priest, ordained in 1997), the PIC has mirrored the patriarchy of wider Filipino society, with women noticeably absent from higher ranking positions in the church. However, in 2019, the first female bishop of the PIC was appointed, Emelyn Dacuycuy. The organization, Women of the Philippine Independent Church, formed in 1957 and today is a very active and highly visible arm of the PIC.

Latin America

Independent Christianity in Latin America is derivative of the Pentecostal/Charismatic movement; indeed, "most of the independent churches that are born and prosper in Latin America have their origin in evangelical Protestantism and, particularly, in the Pentecostal movement" (Beltrán 2022, p. 263). Independent Charismatic churches in Latin America place significant authority on the pastor, who is believed to be called by God and entrusted with power and charisma from the Holy Spirit. Healing, words of wisdom, and other miracles are common. Many of these churches are considered heretical by traditional Protestant and Catholic churches because of the creative biblical interpretation sometimes performed by Independent pastors, the vast majority of whom are men. Many megachurches in Latin America are also a part of the New Apostolic Reformation (see North America and Europe section below), dating to the 1980s, a movement in which leaders consider themselves apostles, not pastors; that is, they receive their call to ministry directly from Jesus Christ (like the Apostle Paul) instead of from any particular denomination or Christian organization. They are the "elite of post-denominational Christianity" and have little oversight or accountability, except to other self-styled apostles (Beltrán 2022, p. 274).

The largest Independent denomination in Latin America is the Universal Church of the Kingdom of God (Igreja Universal do Reino de Deus, IURD), founded in 1977 by Edir Macedo (b.1945) in Rio de Janeiro, Brazil. The IURD has spread around the world, now present in at least 180 countries. Its headquarters is Solomon's Temple in São Paulo, a replica of Solomon's Temple in the Hebrew Bible – but bigger. The church is "Evangelical/Pentecostal in theology and worship and holds traditional views of spirit baptism, water baptism, supernatural gifts, and the Lord's Supper. However, the church has been accused of numerous illegal activities, both in Brazil and abroad, ranging from money laundering, financial fraud, overly aggressive evangelistic techniques and illegal adoption" (Johnson and Zurlo 2019, p. 136). Gender relations in Brazil are quite conservative, hierarchical, and patriarchal, dynamics that are mirrored in the IURD. Extreme male headship theology is prominent, in which women are expected to be completely submissive to their fathers and then husbands. IURD bishop Renato Cardoso and his wife Cristiane Cardoso – the daughter of Edir Macedo – began The Love School in 2011, designed to portray the ideal marriage via television, books, and other media. Women are expected to value family, relational morality, and be obedient wives; men are expected to value hierarchy and should be winners and providers (Januário 2017, pp. 281, 283). Cristiane Cardoso formed the IURD's women's group, Godllywood, in 2008, designed to combat what the IURD considers ungodly values from Hollywood and to encourage women toward a more "biblical" womanhood. It is particularly active on Facebook, Instagram, and Twitter in bringing together IURD women from around the world.

The second largest Independent church in Latin America is also in Brazil – the God is Love Pentecostal Church (IPDA, Igreja Pentecostal Deus é Amor). It formed in 1962 as a church of three: David Miranda, his mother Anália Miranda, and his sister Araci Miranda. Having grown to over 4 million members and present in more than 130 countries, it is known for authoritarianism and a high level of expectation for its members, proof of church membership and attendance, along with strict dress codes that include a prohibition on cutting women's hair and wearing makeup. Women cannot be ordained pastors, deaconesses, or elders in the IPDA, though they can be formal evangelists. Yet, at Miranda's passing in 2015, rather than his eldest son, as expected, his wife, Ereni Oliveira de Miranda, became the head of the IPDA.

North America and Europe

Independent Christianity in North America is numerically dominated by the United States, which is home to a huge diversity of denominations in this category. These churches are prolific in the US for several reasons: historical support for Christian pluralism, religious disestablishment (i.e., separation of church and state), the democratization of American Christianity in the nineteenth century, and an emphasis on popular religion and voluntarism (Hegi 2023). Chapter 6 on North America contains substantial coverage of Black churches in the United States, which comprise many of the largest Independent denominations – National Baptist Convention, USA (9 million), the Church of God in Christ (8 million), and the National Baptist Convention of America (4 million) (Johnson and Zurlo 2022). The Church of Jesus Christ of Latter-day Saints is also one of the largest Independent denominations in the US, with nearly 7 million members (Johnson and Zurlo 2022), also covered in Chapter 6.

Jehovah's Witnesses (JW) trace their history to the Millenarian and restorationist movement of the nineteenth century, in which many Christians were seeking the return of Christ and to first-century Christianity. Charles Taze Russell (1852–1916) joined the Bible Student Movement in the 1870s to gain a better understanding of scripture but ended up disagreeing with several core Christian doctrines: immortality of the soul, hellfire, predestination, the bodily return of Jesus Christ, and the Trinity. In 1881, Russell founded Zion Watch Tower Tract Society and by 1912 he was the most distributed Christian author in the United States. Jehovah's Witnesses have been persecuted worldwide for their refusal of military service and salutation of secular bodies/powers (such as the Pledge of Allegiance), prohibition of blood transfusions, and aversion of holidays and birthdays. Two thousand JWs were killed in Nazi Germany during the Holocaust and 9,300 were deported to Serbia during Soviet rule in the USSR. Jehovah's Witnesses are banned in Singapore, China, Vietnam, Russia, and elsewhere worldwide. In the United States, JWs are one of the most ethnically diverse religious groups, with 36% White, 32% Latino/a, 27% Black, and 5% other ethnicities; furthermore, 65% of its membership is female. It is unlike many other religious groups in that nearly 65% of their converts are adults, not children. JWs are extremely religious, with 94% believing in the Bible as the word of God, 90% believing in God with certainty, 90% praying daily, and 85% attending weekly services (Lipka 2016). While women cannot hold leadership positions (elders and ministerial servants) in JW congregations, all members are considered ministers and are urged to participate in public ministry, such as door-to-door evangelism. JW women are encouraged to cover their hair in public and dress modestly. Jehovah's Witnesses have spread around the world, with the three largest populations outside of the US in Mexico (2 million), Brazil (2 million), and Nigeria (918,000) (Johnson and Zurlo 2022). Most of the largest Independent denominations in Europe are also Jehovah's Witnesses, such as in Russia (432,000), Italy (425,000), and Ukraine (283,000). Germany is home to at least three different JW groups. The original has roughly 279,000 members, and there are two smaller offshoots: the Free Bible Congregation (8,200 members) and the Kingdom of God (4,500) (Johnson and Zurlo 2022).

The New Apostolic Reformation (NAR) represents one of the newest Independent Christian movements in North America, and with 369 million members worldwide, the NAR is also one of the fastest growing in the world (Johnson and Zurlo 2022). Although it traces its roots to the Pentecostal revivals of the early twentieth century and third wave charismatic Christianity of the 1960s, C. Peter Wagner identified the year 2001 as the beginning of the second apostolic age, which included the restoration of the offices of prophet and apostle (Wagner 2000). The NAR is not a denomination, but rather a network of autonomous ministries and churches tied together by their belief in the five modern-day offices – apostle, prophet, evangelist, pastor, and teacher – which distinguishes the NAR from other kinds of Independent movements. Many affiliates are also deeply politically connected and motivated to use the gift of prophecy in the political realm, as in prophesying winners of presidential elections. The NAR tends to be very theologically conservative, though its belief in the active work of the Holy Spirit leads to a kind of egalitarianism in which women can serve in positions of leadership alongside their husbands while still maintaining a theology of male headship. Women leaders of the NAR include Cindy Jacobs (Generals International in Red Oak, Texas), Kim Clement (Kim Clement Center in Tulsa, Oklahoma), and Jane Hansen Hoyt (Aglow International, headquartered in Edmonds, Washington).

Oceania

The most prominent Independent denomination in Oceania is the Church of Jesus Christ of Latter-day Saints (LDS), which makes up the majority of the population in Samoa (41%) and Tonga (64%), as well as in relatively large populations in Australia (148,000), New Zealand (112,000), French Polynesia (27,000), and Papua New Guinea (25,000) (Johnson and Zurlo 2022). Twentieth-century LDS mission work was extremely successful in the Pacific Islands. David O. McKay, ninth president of the LDS church (1951–1970), traveled widely to visit LDS communities around the world and coined the phrase "Every member a missionary" to encourage such activity among its members. Going on a mission is considered a rite of passage for young Mormons, both men and women. Men can serve at age 18 for two years, and women at 19 for 18 months. Women were expected to wear knee-length skirts; in 2018, dress slacks became permitted except in the temple and Sunday morning services. A missionary's daily schedule is very precise, with at least eight hours of proselytizing a day.

Photo 11.2 A latter-day Saint volunteer dances with a student at Atlele Primary School in Tonga (2013). *Source:* Jeon Han/Flickr/CC BY-SA 2.0.

Conversion to the LDS church in the Pacific Islands typically correlates with higher health outcomes, education, employment opportunities, and spiritual benefits of fellowship and enhanced family bonds (Morris 2015). Early Mormon missionaries equated Polynesian peoples with the ancient Israelites. They also noted many similarities between Polynesian cultures and Mormonism, such as prophetic traditions and interest in family lineages and ancestry (Morris 2015). The Mormon doctrine of "forever family" – that family is not separated at death – was attractive to multigenerational households in the Pacific Islands. The first LDS missionaries in Samoa were John Kimo Pelio (1813–1976) and Samuela Manoa (1836–1884) from Hawai'i in 1863, but the Samoan mission did not open until 1888 with the arrival of Joseph Dean (1857–1937) and Florence Dean (1866–1942). Florence served as president of the first Relief Society on the island, and the first Indigenous Samoan LDS missionary, Pologa, was called in 1888. Brigham Smoot (1869–1946) and Alva Butler (1845–1909), the first LDS missionaries in Tonga, arrived in 1891. The mission closed after six years due to a lack of converts but reopened in 1907. Mormons established many schools, which became central in the spread of the LDS message on the islands. Missionary sisters Malia and Lillie Josephs organized the first Primary and Relief Society in Tongatapu in 1912. The first member of the Tongan royal family to join the church was the niece of King Tāufa'āhau Tupou IV, Princess 'Elisiva Fusipala Vaha'i (1949–2014), baptized in 1989.

Religious movements unique to the Pacific Islands are cargo cults, which are based on prophecies that God will send ships and aircraft filled with goods (like those delivered by American military personnel during World War II) if certain religious rites are performed. Many of these movements have adopted enough Christian symbolism and beliefs to be included in the Independent category, such as those in Papua New Guinea, Vanuatu, and New Caledonia. Vanuatu is home to three distinct factions of John Frum cargo cults that began on the island Tanna in 1935. John Frum ("frum" sounding like "broom" in Tannese) revealed himself to a group of men drinking *kava* (ceremonial and medicinal sedative depressant) to encourage a return to traditional practices that foreign missionaries had outlawed, like dancing, polygamy, communication with ancestral spirits, and drinking *kava*. Like patriarchal Melanesian society, a lineage of male leaders in spiritual contact with John Frum emerged. These leaders excluded both White people and women from their meetings. These movements were reactions against foreign imperialism, the Western missionary movement in Melanesia, and consumerist desire as these societies entered the modern world. Yet, followers of John Frum believed that a White-skinned foreigner would sweep away all Whites from their island to restore traditional life. On Tanna, John Frum is celebrated on 15 February and many hope he will return with goods to share with islanders.

Conclusion

Independent Christianity is perhaps the most historically, sociologically, and theologically diverse segment of World Christianity. It represents older Western antiestablishment forms of Christianity, such as the Church of Jesus Christ of Latter-day Saints, newer Pentecostal/Charismatic forms of the faith emerging in Africa and Latin America, and hidden networks of Christians in places where it is extremely difficult to live out the faith. Women have important roles in each of these diverse expressions of Christianity, but debates loom large over their "proper" roles in church, marriage, and society. Many Independent denominations are theologically conservative and as such, practice strict forms of complementarianism that prohibit women from top levels of leadership. However, in these cases, women have found themselves exerting substantial influence in the role of pastor's wives or heads of important auxiliaries. On the other hand, Independent churches in the global South are mostly Pentecostal/Charismatic and place a high priority on the work of the Holy Spirit, which in theory empowers women just as much as men. However, tensions persist in these churches between the inspiration of the Spirit and cultural gender norms. Furthermore, the Bible is very important in Independent Christianity and is interpreted in a wide variety of ways, sometimes in support of women's formal leadership in church, and in other times against it. Yet, women have found deep inspiration in the biblical text to convert to Christianity and join Independent churches. Jesus's ministry among women – the dignity he offered them, the closeness he had with them – continues to encourage women around the world to take seriously the Christian message and model Jesus's example of women's empowerment.

Reflection Questions

1) What challenges and opportunities did women face with the modern arrival of Christianity to Africa? What were women's roles in early Independent movements in Africa, and how do African women participate in Independent Christianity today?
2) In what ways do Independent churches provide women spaces to exercise their spiritual gifts and ministerial callings? Reflect on, for example, Asian women critiquing traditional cultural norms and how they overcome these obstacles.
3) Describe the establishment of the Church of Jesus Christ of Latter-day Saints (LDS) in Oceania. Compare the church's views on women with traditional cultural norms in the region, especially the Pacific Islands. What opportunities do LDS women have for leadership and service?

Works Cited

Awinoh, Martha (2019). Honouring the role of women within African Independent Churches. Organization of African Independent Churches. http://www.oaic.org/?p=1962 (accessed 2 February 2022).

Barrett, David B. (1968). *Schism and Renewal in Africa: An Analysis of Six Thousand Contemporary Religious Movements*. Nairobi: Oxford University Press.

Beltrán, William M. (2022). Independents. In: *Christianity in Latin America* (ed. Kenneth R. Ross, Ana María Bidegain, and Todd M. Johnson), 262–274. Edinburgh: Edinburgh University Press.

Chow, Alexander (2020). Theology. In: *Christianity in East and Southeast Asia* (ed. Kenneth R. Ross, Francis D. Alvarez, and Todd M. Johnson), 375–386. Edinburgh: Edinburgh University Press.

Crumbley, Deidre H. (1992). Impurity and power: women in Aladura churches. *Africa: Journal of the International African Institute*, 62(4), 505–522.

Gampiot, Aurelien M. (2014). Kimbanguism: an African initiated church. *Scriptura*, 113(1), 1–11.

Hedlund, Roger E. (2019). Independents. In: *Christianity in South and Central Asia* (ed. Kenneth R. Ross, Daniel Jeyaraj, and Todd M. Johnson), 261–273. Edinburgh: Edinburgh University Press.

Hegi, Jeremy P. (2023). Independents. In: *Christianity in North America* (ed. Kenneth R. Ross, Grace Ji-Sun Kim, and Todd M. Johnson). Edinburgh: Edinburgh University Press.

Hitchen, John M. (2002). Harold W. Turner remembered. *International Bulletin of Missionary Research*, 26(3), 112–113.

Januário, Soraya B. (2017). A hegemonic masculinity: ethos and consumption in the Universal Church of the Kingdom of God. In: *Annual Review of the Sociology of Religion* (ed. Michael Wilkinson and Peter Althouse), 274–290. Leiden: Brill.

Johnson, Todd M. and Zurlo, Gina A. (2019). *World Christian Encyclopedia*. 3rd edn. Edinburgh: Edinburgh University Press.

Johnson, Todd M. and Zurlo, Gina A. ed. (2022). *World Christian Database*. Leiden/Boston: Brill.

Lindstrom, Lamont (2018). Cargo cults. *The Cambridge Encyclopedia of Anthropology*. https://www. anthroencyclopedia.com/entry/cargo-cults (accessed 2 February 2022).

Lipka, Michael (2016). A closer look at Jehovah's witnesses living in the U.S. Pew Research Center. April 26. https://www.pewresearch.org/fact-tank/2016/04/26/a-closer-look-at-jehovahs-witnesses-living-in-the-u-s (accessed 2 February 2022).

Lubaale, Nicta (2017). Independents. In: *Christianity in Sub-Saharan Africa* (ed. Kenneth R. Ross, J. Kwabena Asamoah-Gyadu, and Todd M. Johnson), 252–263. Edinburgh: Edinburgh University Press.

Martin, Marie-Louise (1971). The Mai Chaza church in Rhodesia. In: *African Initiatives in Religion: 21 Studies from Eastern and Central Africa* (ed. David B. Barrett), 109–121. Nairobi: East African Publishing House.

Mazrui, Ali A. (2014). *The Politics of Gender and the Culture of Sexuality: Western, Islamic, and African Perspectives*. Lanham: University Press of America.

Miller, Duane A. (2018). Independents. In: *Christianity in North Africa and West Asia* (ed. Kenneth R. Ross, Mariz Tadros, and Todd M. Johnson), 227–234. Edinburgh: Edinburgh University Press.

Morris, Paul (2015). Polynesians and mormonism: the church of jesus christ of latter-day saints in the 'Islands of the Sea'. *Nova Religio*, 18(4), 83–101.

Mwaura, Philomena N. (2007). Gender and power in African Christianity: african instituted churches and Pentecostal churches. In: *African Christianity: An African Story* (ed. Ogbu Kalu). Trenton, NJ: Africa World Press. 410–445.

Nation, Hannah (2017). Women in China's house church movement face a hidden challenge. *Christianity Today*. November 6. https://www.christianitytoday.com/ct/2017/november-web-only/ women-in-chinas-house-church-movement-face-hidden-challenge.html (accessed 2 February 2022).

Organization of African Instituted Churches (2015). About us. https://www.oaic.org/?page_id=51 (accessed 2 February 2022).

Ro, David (2020). Mainland China (house churches). In: *Christianity in East and Southeast Asia* (ed. Kenneth R. Ross, Francis D. Alvarez, and Todd M. Johnson), 63–73. Edinburgh: Edinburgh University Press.

Ross, Kenneth R. (2021). Independents. In: *Christianity in Oceania* (ed. Kenneth R. Ross, Katalina Tahaafe-Williams, and Todd M. Johnson), 166–170. Edinburgh: Edinburgh University Press.

Sundkler, Bengt (1948). *Bantu Prophets in South Africa*. London: Lutterworth.

Turner, Harold W. (1967). *History of an African Independent Church: The Church of the Lord (Aladura)*. 2 vols. Oxford: Clarendon Press.

Vähäkangas, Mika (2021). The Kimbanguist Church as a test-case for the World Council of Churches. In: *'Ökumene ist Keine Häresie': Theologische Beiträge zu Einer Ökumenischen Kultur* (ed. Daniel Munteanu), 397–413. Paderborn: Brill: Ferdinand Schöningh.

Vergara, Winfred (2019). First woman bishop makes history in Philippine Independent Church. *Episcopal News Service*. May 29. https://www.episcopalnewsservice.org/2019/05/29/first-woman-bishop-makes-history-in-philippine-independent-church (accessed 2 February 2022).

Wagner, C. Peter (2000). *Apostles & Prophets: The Foundation of the Church*. Ventura, CA: Regal.

Zurlo, Gina A. (2017). 'A miracle from Nairobi': David B. Barrett and the quantification of world Christianity, 1957–1982. PhD dissertation. Boston University School of Theology.

12

Women in Pentecostal/Charismatic Christianity

"If there's a women's movement among the poor of the developing world, Pentecostalism has a good claim to the title."

Brendan Thornton (Thornton 2016, p. 170)

Pentecostal and Charismatic Christianity is the fastest-growing religious movement in the world. Between 2000 and 2020, it grew faster than the global population, than any world religion, and faster than any other Christian tradition or movement. Sometimes referred to as Spirit-empowered Christianity, it is certainly the most prominent form of Christianity today and represents the future of World Christianity. Part of its increase in size and influence is due to its missionary spirit, of which women have had a tremendous role. Pentecostalism also has a keen ability to adapt to any culture, especially those that do not strictly differentiate between the spiritual and physical worlds.

The Pentecostal/Charismatic movement can be considered as a unified whole consisting of three types: Pentecostals (Type 1), Charismatics (Type 2), and Independent Charismatics (Type 3) (see Johnson 2014; Johnson and Zurlo 2022a). This three-part typology is based on history, theology, geography, and ecclesiology. Pentecostals (Type 1; 18% of the Pentecostal/Charismatic movement) are Protestant denominations most directly linked to the Azusa Street Revival (1906), also known as Classical Pentecostals, such as the Assemblies of God and the International Church of the Foursquare Gospel. Pentecostals are characterized by a post-conversion experience of the baptism of the Holy Spirit, typically accompanied by receiving spiritual gifts such as divine healing through prayer, speaking and interpreting tongues, dancing in the Spirit, dreams, visions, and words of wisdom or knowledge. For some time, speaking in tongues, also known as *glossolalia*, was considered the initial evidence of salvation and known as the baptism of the Holy Spirit, but this is becoming less of an emphasis in these churches. Charismatics (Type 2; 43% of all Pentecostals/Charismatics) are Christians in mainline or historic churches – Anglican, Catholic, Lutheran, Baptist, Orthodox, and so on – who have been baptized in the Holy Spirit and emphasize spiritual gifts as described in the New Testament. They typically remain within their home churches rather than establish separate ones. This movement became more pronounced during the 1960s charismatic renewal and grew tremendously until the twenty-first century. The largest Type 2 movement is Catholic Charismatics, with a large presence in Brazil, the Philippines, and the United States. Independent Charismatics (Type 3; 39% of all Pentecostals/Charismatics) are located within Independent denominations (see Chapter 11) worldwide, mostly in the global South. They typically do not consider baptism in the Holy Spirit a separate experience from Christian conversion. Though without an emphasis on tongues, they exercise the gifts of the spirit and practice power encounters, signs and wonders, and other supernatural miracles. Type 3 churches are sometimes

Women in World Christianity: Building and Sustaining a Global Movement, First Edition. Gina A. Zurlo.
© 2023 John Wiley & Sons Ltd. Published 2023 by John Wiley & Sons Ltd.

referred to as post-denominational, restorationist, neo-Apostolic, or Third Wave. The largest Independent Charismatic movements are in China, the Democratic Republic of the Congo, the United States, Brazil, and South Africa.

The great diversity within the movement has had profound implications for the role of women in Pentecostal/Charismatic Christianity. Women were active from the start in revivals all around the world, as missionaries spreading the Spirit-empowered message, and as founders of new Pentecostal/Charismatic movements. In theory, the Pentecostal message cuts across gender barriers with its message of accessibility to the Spirit for all believers in Jesus Christ. On the day of Pentecost as recorded in the Acts of the Apostles, both men and women experienced the power of the Holy Spirit, the tongues of fire, and could understand different languages. The prophet Joel (2:28–29) was explicit in his inclusion of women: "And afterward, I will pour out my Spirit on all people. Your sons and daughters will prophesy, your old men will dream dreams, your young men will see visions. Even on my servants, both men and women, I will pour out my Spirit in those days." The biblical narrative suggests that women have just as much access to spiritual power as men, and this has indeed been the perception among many Pentecostal movements throughout history. However, while widely recognized as having spiritual power, women in these movements are often denied institutional authority (Stephenson 2011).

One of the most cited characteristics of Pentecostal/Charismatic movements is equality between men and women, but this equality is not found everywhere, not in all denominations, and not in all contexts. Despite women's significant contributions to Pentecostal churches, prominent women who helped shape church leadership are often overlooked, with credit for their labors given to men. Many female-founded movements have been turned over to male leadership once they became institutionalized, often to a husband or son. Pentecostalism has grown so quickly over the last 100 years in part because of its ability to adapt to local cultures. However, in doing so, it can also adapt to prevailing gender norms that contradict one of Pentecostalism's core tenets: universal access to the power of the Holy Spirit, regardless of gender (Johnson and Zurlo 2022a).

Pentecostals/Charismatics, 1900–2050

The nascent Pentecostal/Charismatic movement at the start of the twentieth century was mostly concentrated in North America and Africa after the Azusa Street Revival in Los Angeles, California and charismatic missions in South Africa. Over the twentieth century, the movement spread from its polycentric origins (see history section below) throughout the world, so that by 2020, 8% of the world's population and 26% of all Christians were Pentecostal/Charismatic (Table 12.1; Johnson and Zurlo 2022b). Furthermore, 86% of all Pentecostals/Charismatics worldwide now live in the global South. By 2050, it is anticipated that this movement will represent 11% of the world's population, 31% of all Christians, and 89% will live in Africa, Asia, Latin America, and Oceania.

The highest concentration is in Africa, home to 36% of all Pentecostals/Charismatics (Figure 12.1) in 2020 and likely 53% by 2050. The lowest concentration is in Europe, just 3% (Table 12.2). Women make up the majority of the movement everywhere in the world, ranging from 51% in Oceania to 55% in North America (Table 12.2). However, like all other data on the gender makeup of Christian denominations and traditions, it is likely these figures undercount women's share of the movement. For example, Pentecostalism scholar Allan Anderson stated, "Most Pentecostals worldwide are women – there are around three Pentecostal women to every two men, and in some countries the proportion of women is even higher" (Anderson 2013, p. 265). Likewise, Donald Miller observed, "In my own observations of Pentecostalism, it is not unusual for two-thirds of the seats in worship services to be occupied by women" (Miller 2016, p. 91). He

Table 12.1 Pentecostals/Charismatics by continent, 1900–2050.

Region	Pentecostals/ Charismatics 1900	% of pop. 1900	% of Pentecostal/ Charismatic 1900	Rate % p.a. 1900– 2020	Pentecostals/ Charismatics 2020	% of pop. 2020	% of Pentecostal/ Charismatic 2020	Pentecostals/ Charismatics 2050	% of pop. 2050	% of Pentecostal/ Charismatic 2050
Global North	66,100	0.0	6.7	6.19	88,887,000	8.0	13.8	116,462,000	10.3	11.3
Europe	20,000	0.0	2.0	5.97	21,116,000	2.8	3.3	27,436,000	3.9	2.7
North America	46,100	0.1	4.7	6.27	67,771,000	18.4	10.5	89,025,000	20.9	8.6
Global South	915,000	0.1	93.3	5.49	555,373,000	8.3	86.2	915,038,000	10.6	88.7
Africa	901,000	0.8	91.8	4.73	230,220,000	17.2	35.7	450,689,000	18.1	43.7
Asia	4,300	0.0	0.4	8.94	125,395,000	2.7	19.5	214,497,000	4.1	20.8
Latin America	10,000	0.0	1.0	8.58	195,222,000	29.9	30.3	243,225,000	31.9	23.6
Oceania	0	0.0	0.0	11.47	4,536,000	10.6	0.7	6,627,000	11.6	0.6
Global total	**981,000**	**0.1**	**100.0**	**5.55**	**644,260,000**	**8.3**	**100.0**	**1,031,500,000**	**10.6**	**100.0**

Source: Data from Johnson and Zurlo 2022b. p.a. = percent change per annum, or each year.

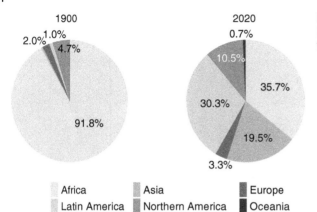

Figure 12.1 Pentecostals/Charismatics by continent, 1900 and 2020. *Source:* Data from Johnson and Zurlo 2022b.

Table 12.2 Pentecostals/Charismatics by continent with percent female, 2020.

Region	Pentecostals/ Charismatics 2020	% of pop. 2020	% of Pentecostals/ Charismatics 2020	% Pentecostal/ Charismatic female 2020	% region female 2020
Global North	88,887,000	8.0	13.8	54.5	51.3
Europe	21,116,000	2.8	3.3	53.4	51.7
North America	67,771,000	18.4	10.5	54.9	50.5
Global South	555,373,000	8.3	86.2	52.4	49.3
Africa	230,220,000	17.2	35.7	53.1	50.0
Asia	125,395,000	2.7	19.5	51.1	48.9
Latin America	195,222,000	29.9	30.3	52.5	50.8
Oceania	4,536,000	10.6	0.7	51.3	49.9
Global total	**644,260,000**	**8.3**	**100.0**	**52.7**	**49.6**

Source: Data from Johnson and Zurlo 2022b.

furthermore stated that women are more likely to first convert to Pentecostalism and lead her family likewise. More localized research also supports a higher proportion of women in Pentecostal churches. Brazilian Pentecostalism in Mozambique, for example, is perhaps upward of 75% female: "Based on fieldwork it is possible to affirm that nearly 75 per cent of the visitors and converts at Brazilian Pentecostal churches in Maputo are women of varying age... In general, women outnumber men in Christian churches... but in Mozambique Brazilian Pentecostalism appears to be a very 'female-oriented' religion as compared to Catholic and Protestant mission churches where I often counted that women made up about 60 per cent of the visitors and men 40 per cent" (van de Kamp 2018, p. 21).

Table 12.3 Countries with the most Pentecostals/Charismatics, 2020.

Rank	Country	Country pop. 2020	Pentecostals/ Charismatics 2020	Pentecostal/ Charismatic % of pop. 2020	% Pentecostal/ Charismatic female 2020	% country female 2020
1	Brazil	212,559,000	108,000,000	50.8	52.8	50.9
2	United States	331,003,000	65,000,000	19.6	55.0	50.5
3	Nigeria	206,140,000	60,000,000	29.1	53.4	49.3
4	Philippines	109,581,000	38,000,000	34.7	49.6	49.8
5	China	1,439,324,000	37,000,000	2.6	53.0	48.7
6	DR Congo	89,561,000	28,000,000	31.3	52.7	50.1
7	South Africa	59,309,000	27,700,000	46.7	54.8	50.7
8	India	1,380,004,000	21,000,000	1.5	50.0	48.0
9	Mexico	128,933,000	17,450,000	13.5	52.0	51.1
10	Kenya	53,771,000	17,300,000	32.2	53.0	50.3

Source: Data from Johnson and Zurlo 2022b.

Table 12.4 Countries with the highest percent of Pentecostals/Charismatics, 2020.

Rank	Country	Country pop. 2020	Pentecostals/ Charismatics 2020	Pentecostal/ Charismatic % of pop. 2020	% Pentecostal/ Charismatic female 2020	% country female 2020
1	Marshall Islands	59,200	37,500	63.4	53.4	49.6
2	Zimbabwe	14,863,000	9,250,000	62.2	54.5	52.3
3	Puerto Rico	2,861,000	1,650,000	57.7	52.1	52.6
4	Eswatini	1,160,000	595,000	51.3	54.3	50.8
5	Brazil	212,559,000	108,000,000	50.8	52.8	50.9
6	Guatemala	17,916,000	8,980,000	50.1	52.0	50.7
7	South Africa	59,309,000	27,700,000	46.7	54.8	50.7
8	American Samoa	55,200	23,500	42.6	53.2	48.2
9	Ghana	31,073,000	11,500,000	37.0	53.5	49.3
10	Vanuatu	307,000	110,000	35.8	50.5	49.3

Source: Data from Johnson and Zurlo 2022b.

The countries with the most Pentecostals/Charismatics are in the global South, except for the United States, which is ranked second (Table 12.3). Women make up the majority of affiliates, ranging from 50% (Philippines) to 55% (South Africa).

The countries with the highest percentages of Pentecostals/Charismatics are found all over the world, from in small island nations (Marshall Islands, where Pentecostals are 63% of the population) to some of the largest countries in the world (Brazil, 51%) (Table 12.4).

The countries with the fastest growth of Pentecostals/Charismatics are in the Gulf States – Qatar, United Arab Emirates, Kuwait, Saudi Arabia, and Oman – due to the arrival of foreign workers from majority Christian countries such as the Philippines and from sub-Saharan Africa (Table 12.5). Most of these workers are men in the oil industry, which accounts for the very low proportions of women. Other countries on the list, such as Iran, Cambodia, and Algeria, are countries

Table 12.5 Countries with the fastest growth of Pentecostals/Charismatics, 2020.

Rank	Country	Country pop. 2020	P/C 2020	P/C % of pop. 2020	% P/C female 2020	% country female 2020	Rate % p.a. 2000–2020
1	Qatar	2,881,000	98,500	3.4	36.4	24.8	8.96
2	Bhutan	772,000	11,300	1.5	53.0	46.9	7.17
3	Iran	83,993,000	300,000	0.4	47.0	49.5	7.05
4	United Arab Emirates	9,890,000	270,000	2.7	51.4	30.9	5.50
5	Cambodia	16,719,000	365,000	2.2	49.0	51.2	5.34
6	Kuwait	4,271,000	105,000	2.5	51.4	38.8	5.15
7	Burkina Faso	20,903,000	2,048,000	9.8	52.0	50.0	4.88
8	Algeria	43,851,000	40,000	0.1	49.1	49.5	4.79
9	Saudi Arabia	34,814,000	550,000	1.6	51.4	42.2	4.44
10	Oman	5,107,000	36,000	0.7	52.5	34.0	4.28

Source: Data from Johnson and Zurlo 2022b. p.a. = percent change per annum, or each year.

Table 12.6 Largest Pentecostal/Charismatic denominations, 2020.

Rank	Country	Denomination	Year begun	Affiliated 2015	% female	Rate % p.a. 2000–2015
1	Brazil	Igreja Católica no Brasil	1500	59,420,000	50.0	0.25
2	Philippines	Catholic Church in the Philippines	1521	23,481,000	49.3	1.50
3	Brazil	Assembleias de Deus	1910	20,978,000	55.0	1.12
4	United States	Catholic Church in the USA	1526	18,199,000	53.3	0.97
5	China	Han house churches Big Five (rural)	1979	17,619,000	53.7	-2.67
6	Colombia	Iglesia Católica en Colombia	1512	12,820,000	51.2	0.91
7	DR Congo	Eglise de Jésus-Christ sur la Terre par le Prophète Simon Kimbangu	1921	12,000,000	52.0	2.70
8	Mexico	Iglesia Católica en México	1518	10,923,000	51.4	1.13
9	United States	Church of God in Christ	1895	8,046,000	57.4	0.93
10	Brazil	Igreja Universal do Reino de Deus	1977	7,500,000	60.0	3.46

Source: Data from Johnson and Zurlo 2022b. p.a. = percent change per annum, or each year.

where Christianity is comparatively smaller and younger, often found in house church or underground movements that tend to be Charismatic in nature and with higher female participation.

The largest Pentecostal/Charismatic denominations represent a mixture of Type 1, Type 2, and Type 3 groups (Table 12.6). The Assemblies of God in Brazil (ranked third) is the largest Classical Pentecostal denomination, with 21 million members. The most prominent Type 2 (Charismatic) denominations are Catholic Charismatics, found in large numbers in Brazil, the Philippines, the United States, Colombia, and Mexico. Independent Charismatics (Type 3) are represented in China (Han house churches), the Democratic Republic of the Congo (Kimbanguists), the United States (Church of God in Christ), and Brazil (Igreja Universal do Reino de Deus) – the latter two with high female affiliation, 57% and 60%, respectively.

Women in Pentecostal/Charismatic History

The origins of the Pentecostal/Charismatic movement are polycentric and global. Revivals in the nineteenth century helped pave the way for the beginning of what has arguably become one of global Christianity's most powerful expression of the faith. American Methodist evangelist Phoebe Palmer (1807–1874) is considered one of the founders of the Holiness movement within Methodism, which emphasized John Wesley's "Christian perfection" and Charles Finney's "perfect love" or "entire sanctification" (Noll 2019). After Palmer received the so-called second blessing (the baptism of the Holy Spirit), she began her Tuesday Meeting for the Promotion of Holiness in 1835 for both men and women. A Pentecostal-like movement had been known in South India beginning around 1860 that reported speaking in tongues and other manifestations of the Spirit. In 1895, independent preacher Charles Fox Parham (1873–1929) resigned from the Methodist Church in the United States after experiencing physical healing and began a healing ministry and school in Topeka, Kansas, where he encouraged students to receive the baptism of the Holy Spirit. On 1 January 1901, Agnes Ozman (1870–1937) was the first to speak in tongues (Synan n.d.). The Welsh Revival in 1904–1905 emphasized the presence and power of the Holy Spirit under the leadership of Methodist minister Evan Roberts (1878–1951), with meetings marked by spontaneous prayer and testimonies of personal encounters with God. At Pandita Ramabai's (1858–1922) Mukti Mission near Bombay, India, young widows and orphans under her care experienced a two-year revival beginning in 1905, where participants experienced various ecstatic phenomena, including speaking in tongues. The Azusa Street Revival in Los Angeles, California, began in 1906 under the leadership of a blind-in-one-eye Black preacher named William Seymour (1870–1922). Azusa Street dramatically caught the attention of the American public with its egalitarian movement that transcended race, gender, and class. The Korean Pentecost in Pyongyang (modern day North Korea) broke out in 1907–1908, characterized by public emotional repentance, loud weeping, and prayer. American Methodist missionary Minnie Abrams (1859–1912) was an assistant to Pandita Ramabai in India and spread the news of the revival to her former missionary training school roommate May Hoover, serving in Chile with her husband, Willis. The Hoovers prayed for revival, which began in 1909 and catalyzed the entire Pentecostal movement in Chile, from which 95% of Chilean Pentecostal denominations today trace their roots. The first Pentecostal church in Australia was founded by a woman in 1909, Sarah Jane Lancaster (1858–1934), known as "Mother" to her congregation (Handasyde 2021, p. 90).

Although Pentecostal/Charismatic Christianity did not begin at the Azusa Street Revival, it is particularly important for the history and identity of the movement. This revival represented several key characteristics, such as the development of Pentecostal theology, its inclusion of White, Black, and Latino/a Christians, its egalitarian leadership, and its missionary impulse (Johnson and Zurlo 2022a). William J. Seymour attended one of Charles Parham's Bible schools in 1906, where Parham encouraged Seymour to preach the new Pentecostal theology to Blacks in Texas. While

Parham was a controversial figure – he was unwelcoming of mixed-race gatherings and experienced a same-sex scandal toward the end of his life – he made significant theological contributions, such as the doctrine of initial evidence (tongues as evidence of the baptism of the Holy Spirit). His work led to the eventual founding of the Assemblies of God, the largest Classical Pentecostal denomination today, as well as every other major Classical Pentecostal denomination (Church of God in Christ, Church of God (Cleveland), the United Pentecostal Church, and others). Seymour moved to Los Angeles to pastor a Holiness mission founded by Julia Hutchins, a Black minister who had left to serve as a missionary in Liberia. Seymour's meetings featured elements that have become standard in many Pentecostal churches: Black church style and leadership, oral liturgy, narrative theology and witness, and whole community participation. Fourteen years before women received the right to vote in the United States and at the height of the Jim Crow era of racial segregation, Seymour's meetings began with 15 Blacks (men and women, including five children) and grew to 1,500 people packed into the building seven days a week, all day long. The egalitarianism of the early meetings consisted of Blacks, Whites, and Latinos/as all worshipping together, and featured the full participation of women. Women were just as instrumental as men in initiating the revival, ensuring its success, and spreading its message around the world (Alexander 2005). For example, Black Holiness pastor Lucy Farrow, the first Black woman known to speak in tongues, introduced Seymour to Parham and the doctrine of the baptism of the Holy Spirit. Six of the 12 elders of the Azusa Street Mission were women (Jennie Evans Moore, May Evans, Phoebe Sergeant, Ophelia Wiley, Clara Lum, and Florence Crawford); and among the first to push the message outward were women, such as Ivy Campbell (Ohio), Mabel Smith (Chicago), and Lillian Anderson Garr (India, China) (Alexander 2005).

These origin stories illustrate that there was no one single Pentecostal beginning and point to a radical equality between men and women centered on the work of the Holy Spirit. Wherever Christianity grew in the twentieth century, so did the Pentecostal/Charismatic movement. Its expansion in the twentieth century was not solely the fruit of Western missionaries from North America and Europe, but rather, the result of spontaneous contextualization of the Pentecostal message by indigenous preachers who brought the message to their own people in their own contexts (Anderson 2005). While there are many similarities among Pentecostal/Charismatic worship services, expressions, and theologies around the world, it is deeply shaped by its social audience, leading to many regional variations. In Latin America and Africa, many people of lower classes embraced the Pentecostal message to help enter the modern world; but in Southeast Asia, most converts were among the middle class, especially in the Chinese diaspora. For Latin Americans, Pentecostalism is a religion of the oppressed that offers hope for mobility, social membership, and welfare, welcoming those who felt overlooked by the Catholic Church. In North America and Europe, the Charismatic movement grew within existing mainline churches and denominations (Martin 2002).[1]

Pentecostalism transcends ethnicity and place and responds to the needs of the marginalized and the mobile, especially those who have migrated away from their traditional contexts to urban settings (Martin 2002). Many who embrace Pentecostalism find there are economic, political, educational, and health benefits associated with these churches, in addition to the emphasis on spiritual power that aligns with traditional religious beliefs and practices. Reminiscent of traditional cultures and religions, the accessibility of the spiritual realm fills a gap left by Western missionaries who typically preached a secessionist form of the faith. Corporate, energetic, and emotional worship is also attractive, especially for youth. Pentecostal movements have always

---

1 Portions of this section are reproduced from Johnson and Zurlo 2022a with permission from Oral Roberts University Press.

been keen to adapt the latest media technology for evangelistic purposes, beginning with radio ministries in the early twentieth century, television in the mid-twentieth century, and today in the form of billboards, social media, and live streaming. The growth of Pentecostalism has been particularly spectacular among the poor and marginalized, since it encourages participants to see their most important identity as children of God, not members of a particular class, race, or caste (Robbins 2004). It would be mistaken to attribute the growth of Pentecostalism among the poor to economic drivers alone. Throughout the global South, conversions to Pentecostalism among the poor, especially women, have been multifaceted. For instance, women *Dalit* converts in India receive multiple forms of empowerment, such as increased dignity, new forms of agency, social advancement, educational opportunities, and spiritual support (Shah 2016).

Pentecostal/Charismatic Women in Mission

The Pentecostal/Charismatic movement has always had a strong missionary impulse and outward facing vision, and women were at the forefront of the movement's expansion from the beginning. Many missionaries from Azusa Street believed they had the gift of *xenolalia*, the ability to speak and interpret foreign languages, which would help them more efficiently serve on foreign mission fields. The majority of missionaries sent from Azusa Street were self-supporting women, and two-thirds of missionaries from the American Assemblies of God after its formation in 1914 were also women (Anderson 2013). In Sri Lanka, Pentecostalism traces its roots to a Danish woman, Anna Lewini (1876–1951), who dedicated three decades of service to the country (Satyavrata 2019). However, throughout the twentieth century, Pentecostal churches and mission became increasingly formalized and institutionalized, providing women less autonomy and fewer leadership opportunities.

The faith mission movement of the twentieth century was in line with the Spirit-empowered ethos, where individual Christians felt moved to serve overseas regardless of their educational status or connection with a denominational sending board. Faith missionaries depended wholly on God's grace for financial support and sustenance overseas. Part of the change from old denominational structures to faith mission and new parachurch mission organizations was a shift from postmillennial to premillennial theology. Instead of working to improve the conditions of the world to hasten Christ's second coming, Christians anticipated Christ coming like a "thief in the night" (1 Thessalonians 5:2), encouraging them to save as many souls as possible before the last days. There was no time for formal education or support-raising. No data are available on the number of Pentecostal/Charismatic missionaries in the world today, and especially not on the gender makeup of those missionaries. Well-known is that the growth of the Pentecostal/Charismatic movement would not have been possible without the "vast number of ordinary and virtually forgotten women and men who networked across regional and even national boundaries," proclaiming the Spirit-empowered message (Anderson 2013, p. 213).

Vignettes: Pentecostal/Charismatic Women Worldwide

Like other Christian traditions around the world, women make up the majority of members of Pentecostal/Charismatic churches. Across the world, women display higher levels of religious commitment than men in religious service attendance, prayer, and importance of religion in their lives, and this trend applies to women in the Pentecostal movement as well. In some congregations, women can be ordained for pastoral leadership, while in others, they serve in nearly every other function except lead pastor. However, Pentecostal groups are more likely than other Protestants to allow women to serve as pastors and leaders. In the United States, a study found that

74% of Pentecostals and 70% of Charismatics agreed that women should be allowed to serve as pastors, compared to 66% of other Christians (Pew Forum on Religion and Public Life 2006). Yet, there are significant regional variations. In India, only 39% of Pentecostals and 36% of Charismatics supported female pastors, compared to 34% of other Christians, which overall illustrates less acceptance for female leaders. In Nigeria, 70% of Pentecostals supported female pastors, compared to just 47% of other Christians (Pew Forum on Religion and Public Life 2006). Although female leadership is more common in Pentecostal/Charismatic churches, cultural norms restrict women's roles outside of the church as well. Survey research has shown, for instance, that many Pentecostals/Charismatics believe that wives should obey their husbands and that men make better political leaders than women (Pew Forum on Religion and Public Life 2006).

Where women are denied formal leadership opportunities in Pentecostal/Charismatic churches, they often turn to alternative avenues such as women's ministries and as church mothers (Isgrigg 2023). These associations typically become the core of church social and religious life, given the great influence and larger proportion of women in these churches (Blanes and Zawiejska 2020). Yet, it is common in Independent Charismatic churches for men and women to lead together, such as a husband and wife serving as co-pastors. Female Pentecostal influence has expressed itself in a variety of ways throughout history and within the movement today, such as missionaries (especially single missionaries), as pastor's wives (who often have more influence within congregations than their husbands), as evangelists (historically, often unnamed), and as everyday stewards of faith and tradition. The following sections highlight some Pentecostal/Charismatic women who have been founders of movements and denominations, sparked revivals, and notably served as pastor's wives.

Africa

A wide variety of Pentecostal/Charismatic Christianity exists in Africa, in particular, African Independent Churches (AICs). AICs represent a spectrum of charismatic beliefs, practices, and relationships with African Traditional Religion. Women were founders of AICs, such as Agnes Okoh (1905–1995), an illiterate Igbo woman, who founded the Christ Holy Church International in 1947. She preached, evangelized, healed, and prophesized and stressed repentance, righteousness, and holiness (Oduro 2007). Her church is now present throughout Western Africa. Pentecostalism in Africa is primarily an indigenous movement led by African preachers and prophets (Ogunewe and Ayegboyin 2017). Some AICs are patriarchal in structure, whereas others are more egalitarian. Female originators of Pentecostal churches are common and include Bishop Margaret Wangari, Anointed Christian Fellowship (Kenya); Bishop Margaret Wanjiru, Jesus is Alive Ministries (Kenya); Teresia Wairimu, Faith Evangelistic Ministry (Kenya); Christie Doe Tetteh, Solid Rock Chapel International (Ghana); Archbishop Dorcas Siyanbola Olaniyi, Agbala Daniel Church (Nigeria); Stella Ajisebutu, Water from the Rock Church (Nigeria); and Bishop Mercy Yami, The Love of God Church (Malawi).

"Ma" Christinah Nku (1894–c.1980) founded St. John's Apostolic Faith Mission of South Africa after receiving baptism in the Apostolic Faith Mission in 1924. She experienced many vivid revelations from God, in particular, a dream during a serious illness where God told her she would not die. Although women had always held prominent positions of spiritual leadership and healing in South Africa, her mystical visions and personal healing helped legitimize her call to leadership in a male-oriented religious society. After receiving a vision of a church with 12 doors, she founded a new church in 1939, called the Temple. Her iconic healing rituals and use of blessed water was considered radical and led to a rift between her church and White-led Pentecostal denominations. She also established schools and programs for youth and adults. However, after a long-standing power struggle with Nku, Petros John Masango was lawfully elected bishop, after which he broke ties with the Nku family and established himself as the founder of the church as prophesied by Nku. More conflict ensued and now the original church founded by Nku is divided into three larger factions and several smaller groups.

For 12 years, Christie Doe Tetteh (b.1956) served as the personal secretary to Pentecostal/ Charismatic Archbishop Benson Idahosa, known as the "father of Pentecostalism" in Nigeria. In Ghana, she began a small home-based fellowship in 1993 that grew into the very large and influential Solid Rock Chapel International, marked by healing and prayer ministries. She is one of the few women in Ghana with this level of influential spiritual and ministerial leadership independent of men. While possessing a deep femininity and a motherly style of leadership (Soothill 2007), her religious authority is innovative in how she is both the general overseer and main head of her church while not operating as a "stand-in male." Her experience points to a gender-neutral shift within Charismatic movements in Ghana as well as a departure from earlier models of women's religious leadership in the country (Soothill 2007).

Margaret Wanjiru (b.1961) worked as a house cleaner, hawker, and other odd jobs before she became a sales and marketing executive and eventually, a politician in Kenya. After her conversion to Christianity, she founded Jesus is Alive Ministries (JIAM), of which she serves as bishop. JIAM has 20,000 members and a popular television program, *The Glory Is Here*. Her ministry focuses on freedom from demonic powers as well as physical prosperity. Public scrutiny of her personal life and family relationships in 2007–2008 did not taint her ministry; instead, she emerged as a strong female leader, overcoming a deliberate attempt to tarnish her reputation and spiritual power. Bishop Wanjiru remains both a spiritually and politically respectable force in Kenya.

Archbishop Nicholas Duncan-Williams (b.1957) and his then-wife "Mama" Francisca Duncan-Williams (b.1960) founded Action Chapel International in Accra in 1979. Nicholas is credited with founding the charismatic movement in Ghana, while Francisca organized women's activities in the church and founded the Pastors, Wives and Women in Ministry Association. In many Independent Charismatic churches, pastor's wives tend to have a dual leadership role alongside the head male pastor. Many wives become archbishops and pastors alongside their husbands to lead large congregations. Though Francisca's role highlighted the male–female dual headship of the church, behind the initial front of equality between the Duncan-Williams duo was also a quasi-political role of women only as wives of influential pastors, which then perpetuates conservative cultural gender norms. In other words, Francisca's spiritual leadership was only in relation to her husband. After their public divorce in 2001 (and again in 2007), Nicholas continued to be extremely influential while Francisca lost much of her power in the church.

Archbishop Margaret Idahosa (b.1943) was born into a royal family in Edo State, Nigeria, and entered ministry in 1983. She took over the Church of God Mission International in Benin City, Nigeria, after her husband, Archbishop Benson Idahosa (1938–1998) passed away, making her the first African female archbishop of any denomination. While her husband was instrumental in the spread of Pentecostalism in the region, she has become one of the most prominent female Pentecostal figures in Africa and became an archbishop in 2009. Her church has several weekly services, a private university (of which she serves as chancellor, the first woman in Africa to do so), and oversees Christian schools and hospitals. Unlike Francisca Duncan-Williams, Margaret Idahosa was able to transcend the role of pastor's wife to become a prominent leader in her own right.

Photo 12.1 A Nigerian woman worships in a church hosted by Mission Africa (2011).
Source: Aalborg Stift/Flickr/CC BY 2.0.

Asia

Pandita Ramabai Sarasvati (1858–1922) was born into a Brahmin family and converted to Christianity while in England. A brilliant scholar, she earned the titles of "Pandita" and "Sarasvati" as a Sanskrit scholar by the University of Calcutta – the first woman to be awarded such distinction. She founded the Mukti Mission in Kedgaon for orphans and widows in the late 1890s, which still operates today to provide housing and education for women and children in need. Her organization's Charismatic spirituality and the powerful 1905 Mukti Revival influenced many Indian women to become Christians and pursue lives dedicated to spreading Christianity. Though Ramabai's ministry was met with criticism from men, she persisted and endlessly advocated for women. She is known for her role in not only sparking an influential Pentecostal revival but defending women's rights and supporting the development of truly indigenous Indian churches. The Episcopal Church honors Ramabai with a feast day on 5 April and the Church of England on 30 April.

Jashil Choi (1915–1989) became a Christian at a tent revival meeting in 1927 led by a popular Holiness preacher. After escaping Japanese-occupied North Korea for the South, Choi attended the Assemblies of God Bible School in Seoul and started a small congregation in her house. She heavily emphasized prayer and fasting as the foundation to Christian life. Later taken over by her son-in-law, David Yonggi Cho, her small congregation by the 1980s had become the largest church in the world. Though Cho frequently referred to Jashil Choi as his spiritual mentor and mother, her influence on the founding of Yoido Full Gospel Church is often overlooked. Choi also began a prayer center by the Korean demilitarized zone (DMZ) associated with Yoido. While Choi did not have the nearly the influence or recognition of Cho during her life, she defied odds and pioneered innovations in Charismatic Korean Christianity in a conservative, male-oriented society.

Kong Duen Yee (1923–1966) was born in Beijing, China and became a prominent actress, known as Mui Yee, in Hong Kong. She converted to Christianity at a Pentecostal revival in 1963 and led many revival meetings throughout Hong Kong, Singapore, Taiwan, and Malaysia. She established the Christian Charismatic Evangelistic Team, which became the New Testament Church in Hong Kong. Her theology included speaking in tongues as evidence of salvation. Yee was succeeded by her daughter, Zhang Lude (Ruth Chang), but Chang renounced the extremities of her mother's Pentecostal theology and moved to California, US, to become an Assemblies of God pastor. Leadership of Yee's New Testament Church was turned over to Elijah Hong (b.1927), who changed the name to the Taiwan Apostles Faith Church, where he is considered the modern-day Elijah and his followers modern-day Israelites.

Europe

The Pentecostal/Charismatic presence in Europe primarily consists of migrant churches and the Roma movement. The Vie et Lumière (Light and Life) Pentecostal movement began in the 1950s in France with pastor Clément Le Cossec (1921–2001), who evangelized Roma peoples, believing them to be chosen alongside Jews because of their persecution during the Holocaust. A revival began in Leskovac, Serbia, in the late 1980s when a Roma woman first experienced physical healing. Roma Pentecostal movements keep the Romany language, joyfulness, loudness, and dancing of their culture while forbidding fortune-telling, drinking, smoking, arranged marriages, and illegal activities like tax evasion. They are Pentecostal in their belief in miracles, full-immersion baptism, and literal interpretation of scripture, but unlike other Pentecostal/Charismatic movements they do not allow women to preach or be pastors. Domestic violence is a problem in many Roma communities where traditional gender roles prevail alongside high poverty rates, social exclusion of women, and a lack of social services in their communities.

Latin America

In Latin America, the introduction of Pentecostalism (here simply referring to non-Catholic Christianity) fundamentally changed the continent's religious landscape, causing many people to either to convert, to become more ardently Catholic, or to join a Catholic Charismatic movement. Pentecostal/Charismatic Christianity grew to 30% of the population by 2020 (Table 12.1). Across the continent, women sought out this new form of Christianity as a religion that improved the quality of life for themselves and their families. Many women have joined Pentecostal faith

Photo 12.2   Catholic nuns at the arrival of Pope Francis at Copacabana Beach, Brazil (2013).
Source: GABRIEL BOUYS/AFP/Getty Images.

communities because of abandonment by husbands or fathers, domestic strife, or feelings of powerlessness. Today, women make up 70% of Catholic Charismatic participants in Brazil, which is the largest CCR movement in the world (Hayes 2017; Johnson and Zurlo 2022b).

Bishop Sônia Hernandes (b.1958) received a call to Christian ministry at a youth camp. She and her husband (Estevam Hernandes) founded Igreja Renascer em Cristo, an Independent Apostolic church, in 1986, which claims over 2 million members in Brazil and around the world. Bishop Sônia is the fifth wealthiest pastor in the country and Igreja Renascer em Cristo is one of the wealthiest Independent Apostolic churches in Brazil. Bishop Sônia is also a television figure, radio host, and choral musician. In 2009, she and her husband served five months in an American prison for smuggling cash into the United States. This led to significant controversy surrounding their leadership, with many suspecting fraud and money laundering under the guise of religion, even as the church continues to grow.

North America

Born of a Salvation Army mother and a Methodist father, Aimee Semple McPherson (1890–1944) was imprinted with a "Wesleyan view of sanctification, the Calvinist distinction between the visible and invisible church, the Lutheran view of civil government, and the Puritan goal of being a 'city set upon a hill'" (Ray 2010, p. 158). McPherson (Sister Aimee) returned from a mission in China in 1910 as a widow and single mother of a newborn baby girl (see Blumhofer 1993). After a visit to Los Angeles in 1917 and several years of cross-country evangelism, she began a healing ministry in 1921 and founded the Angelus Temple in Los Angeles in 1923. The Temple became the largest congregation at the start of the twentieth century, was valued at $1.5 million (the equivalent of nearly $15 million today), and held services in five languages. Sister Aimee pioneered radio ministries and was a media sensation. She imbued the Pentecostal movement with a personality that championed healing, the power of the Holy Spirit, and a theology that combined Arminianism and Calvinism. Her focus on the work of the Holy Spirit contrasted with the fire-and-brimstone preaching of prominent male evangelists. She placed an emphasis on the Spirit in relationship to God's love, not "bombastic, untactful preaching" (Ray 2010, p. 160). While the growth of Sister Aimee's organization dovetailed with that of the Pentecostal movement, it faced criticism as an Evangelical institution that became led mostly by White middle-class men, a far cry from the example set by Sister Aimee. Despite its early commitment to female ministers, the denomination grew rapidly while male leaders filled the ranks of the institutionalizing movement. After her death in 1944, Aimee's son, Rolf McPherson, took over as president of the denomination, leading for 44 years. There have been no female presidents of The Foursquare Church since Sister Aimee, yet the denomination – with 5 million members – is proud of its history of strong women's leadership and innovation.

In 1901, Pillar of Fire International was founded in Denver, Colorado, by Alma White (1862–1946), the first female bishop of an American denomination. Originally the Pentecostal Union, it changed names to differentiate itself from the Pentecostal movement in 1915. Though sharing the same doctrine, the Pillar of Fire Church distanced itself from the Methodist tradition, believing it to be corrupt, though it retained a focus on holiness in the Wesleyan tradition. Members were called "holy rollers" and "holy jumpers" because of their frenzy in worship. Under White's leadership from the 1920s to the 1940s, the Pillar of Fire Church developed a close partnership with the Ku Klux Klan, and she unashamedly attacked racial and religious minorities in her ministry and writings. Her son led the church after her death, and the branches in the US fell from 52 to 6. The church today focuses its work in three main areas: radio, education, and missions.

Bishop Ida Robinson (1891–1946) became a Christian as a teen through a Church of God street meeting in Pensacola, Florida, and after moving to Philadelphia with her family, became a seasoned preacher. She believed that God would use her as an instrument to bring godly women to serve alongside men in the church, with full clergy rights. When her congregation, the United Holy Church, announced they would not publicly ordain women, she received a prophetic vision from God to establish Mount Sinai Holy Church of America in 1924, with her first Board of Elders staffed mostly by women (Trulear 1989). Despite its Independent nature, the church identified as part of historic Christianity, and open to engage with other churches, especially those of the Holiness/Pentecostal tradition. Robinson was a dynamic leader, alternating between teaching, preaching, and singing at intervals of two to three hours. Mount Sinai Holy Church of America continues to be a predominately Black denomination, with a presence in 14 states and six countries. It is the only denomination founded by a Black woman that retained consistent female leadership from its founding and its emphasis on gender equality.

Oceania

Perhaps the most well-known Pentecostal movement in Oceania – though certainly not the most representative (see, for example, Riches 2019 for a study on Aboriginal Pentecostalism) – is Hillsong Church, a megachurch in Australia founded as Sydney Christian Life Center by Frank Houston (1922–2004) in 1983. Frank's son, Brian (b.1954) and his wife Bobbie (b.1957) Houston, took over the church in 1999 and together held the title of Global Senior Pastors. They have been credited with a centralization of the Assemblies of God in the country (known as the Australian Christian Churches), as well as reframing Pentecostalism by de-emphasizing premillennial eschatology, promoting a modified version of prosperity theology, and increasing Pentecostal social and political involvement. Hillsong's influence is all over Pentecostal and Evangelical churches worldwide through its very popular worship bands and albums, which represent a large portion of the church's roughly $87 million annual revenue. Bobbie founded Hillsong Sisterhood to unite women in faith and activism; her Colour Conference first met in 1997, and the 2020 meeting had nearly 15,000 in-person and 5,000 online attendees from 62 countries. Hillsong's women's group has a focus on combatting domestic violence and raising awareness of endometriosis. Hillsong came under scrutiny with revelations of Frank Houston's deathbed admission of sexual abuse of a young boy in the 1970s and Brian Houston's cover-up of the incident in 1999. Brian Houston stepped down from church leadership in 2022 after allegations of mistreating two women in the church. Bobbie remains affiliated with the church, but her future appears uncertain.

Conclusion

The challenges and opportunities for women in Pentecostal/Charismatic churches vary considerably by geographic and cultural context. Pentecostalism's literal reading of scripture often leads to the subordination of women to men in all spheres of life, both within and outside the church. Yet, at the same time, women are believed to have access to spiritual power and Christians are neither "male nor female" in Christ (Galatians 3:28). In some Pentecostal churches women can be ordained and become bishops, while in others they cannot; some have prominent women's organizations that encourage women's participation while also promoting women's subordination to men (Anderson 2013). In short, Pentecostal women receive mixed messages. Yet, the nature of Pentecostalism is to be Spirit-led in all aspects of life, which has been demonstrated by women across Christian traditions for generations. New Independent Charismatic churches are being formed seemingly daily while older historic mainline churches are becoming pentecostalized worldwide, as exemplified in the Catholic Charismatic Movement. As Christianity continues to grow in the global South and recede in Europe and North America, an increasingly greater proportion of the faith is female and Pentecostal/Charismatic, which should urge the rest of the world church to reckon with not only the female majority of World Christianity, but also its increasingly charismatic face.

Reflection Questions

1) Although not the sole origin of the Pentecostal movement, the Azusa Street Revival was a pivotal moment for Pentecostalism. Describe the revival's importance in the history and identity of the movement, as well as its theological contributions, especially considering its racial and gendered dynamics. In what ways does Pentecostalism continue to operate as a boundary-crossing movement within Christianity?
2) How has diversity within the Pentecostal/Charismatic movement influenced potential opportunities for Pentecostal women? Reflect on the radical egalitarianism of the early Pentecostal movement and the development of women's roles in Pentecostal churches over time.
3) Reflect on the contributions of three women presented in this chapter who adopted visionary leadership within the Pentecostal/Charismatic movement. What are some unifying characteristics among these women?

Works Cited

Alexander, Estrelda (2005). *The Women of Azusa Street*. Cleveland, OH: Pilgrim Press.

Anderson, Allan H. (2005). The origins of Pentecostalism and its global spread in the early twentieth century. *Transformation*, 22(3), 175–185.

Anderson, Allan H. (2013). *An Introduction to Pentecostalism*. 2nd edn. Cambridge: Cambridge University Press.

Blanes, Ruy L. and Zawiejska, Natalia (2020). The Pentecostal antirevolution: reflections from Angola. *Journal of Religion in Africa*, 28(1), 217–258.

Blumhofer, Edith L. (1993). *Aimee Semple McPherson: Everybody's Sister*. Grand Rapids, MI: Eerdmans.

Handasyde, Kerrie (2021). Mother, preacher, press: women ministers and the negotiation of authority, 1910–1933. In: *Contemporary Feminist Theologies: Power, Authority, Love* (ed. Kerrie Handasyde, Cathryn McKinney, and Rebekah Pryor), 88–99. Abingdon, Oxon: Routledge, Taylor & Francis Group.

Hayes, Kelly E. (2017). Women and religion in contemporary Brazil. In: *Handbook of Contemporary Religion in Brazil* (ed. Bettina Schmidt and Steven Engler), 395–430. Leiden; Boston, MA: Brill.

Isgrigg, Daniel D. (2023). Pentecostals and Charismatics. In: *Christianity in North America* (ed. Kenneth R. Ross, Grace Ji-Sun Kim, and Todd M. Johnson). Edinburgh: Edinburgh University Press.

Johnson, Todd M. (2014). Counting Pentecostals worldwide. *Pneuma*, 36, 265–288.

Johnson, Todd M. and Zurlo, Gina A. (2019). *World Christian Encyclopedia*. 3rd edn. Edinburgh: Edinburgh University Press.

Johnson, Todd M. and Zurlo, Gina A. (2022a). *Introducing Spirit-Empowered Christianity: The Global Pentecostal and Charismatic Movement in the 21st Century*. Tulsa, OK: Oral Roberts University Press.

Johnson, Todd M. and Zurlo, Gina A. ed. (2022b). *World Christian Database*. Leiden/Boston: Brill.

Martin, David (2001). *Pentecostalism: The World Their Parish*. Oxford: Blackwell.

Miller, Donald E. (2016). Where the Spirit leads: pentecostalism and freedom. In: *Christianity and Freedom: Vol. 2* (ed. Timothy S. Shah and Allen D. Hertzke), 87–106. New York: Cambridge University Press.

Noll, Mark A. (2019). *A History of Christianity in the United States and Canada*. 2nd edn. Grand Rapids, MI: William B. Eerdmans Publishing Company.

Oduro, Thomas (2007). Okoh, Agnes. Dictionary of African Christian Biography. https://dacb.org/stories/nigeria/okoh-agnes (accessed 3 August 2021).

Ogunewe, Michael A. and Ayegboyin, Isaac D (2017). Pentecostals and Charismatics. In: *Christianity in Sub-Saharan Africa* (ed. Kenneth R. Ross, J.Kwabena Asamoah-Gyadu, and Todd M. Johnson), 314–326. Edinburgh: Edinburgh University Press.

Pew Forum on Religion and Public Life. (2006). Spirit and power: a 10-country survey of Pentecostals.

Ray, Donna E. (2010). Aimee Semple McPherson and her seriously exciting gospel. *Journal of Pentecostal Theology*, 19, 155–169.

Riches, Tanya (2019). *Worship and Social Engagement in Urban Aboriginal-led Australian Pentecostal Congregations: (Re)imagining Identity in the Spirit*. Leiden: Brill.

Robbins, Joel (2004). The globalization of Pentecostal and Charismatic Christianity. *Annual Review of Anthropology*, 33, 117–143.

Satyavrata, Ivan (2019). Pentecostals and Charismatics. In: *Christianity in South and Central Asia* (ed. Kenneth R. Ross, Daniel Jeyaraj, and Todd M. Johnson), 287–300. Edinburgh: Edinburgh University Press.

Shah, Rebecca S. (2016). Christianity among the marginalized: empowering poor women in India. In: *Christianity and Freedom* (ed. Timothy S. Shah and Allen D. Hertzke), 107–132. New York: Cambridge University Press.

Soothill, Jane E. (2007). *Gender, Social Change and Spiritual Power: Charismatic Christianity in Ghana*. 170. Leiden: Brill.

Stephenson, Lisa P. (2011). Prophesying women and ruling men: women's religious authority in North American Pentecostalism. *Religions*, 2(3), 410–426.

Synan, Vinson (n.d.) *The origins of the Pentecostal movement*. Holy Spirit Research Center.

Thornton, Brendan J. (2016). *Negotiating Respect: Pentecostalism, Masculinity, and the Politics of Spiritual Authority in the Dominican Republic*. Tampa, FL: University Press of Florida.

Trulear, Harold D. (1989). Reshaping black pastoral theology: the vision of Bishop Ida B. Robinson. *The Journal of Religious Thought*, 46(1), 20.

van de Kamp, Linda (2018). *Violent Conversion: Brazilian Pentecostalism and Urban Women in Mozambique*. Woodbridge: James Currey.

13

Women in Evangelicalism

"If the man may preach, because the Saviour died for him, why not the woman? seeing he died for her also. Is he not a whole Saviour, instead of a half one? as those who hold it wrong for a woman to preach, would seem to make it appear."

Jarena Lee (Lee 1849, p. 11)

Women in Evangelicalism have a complicated history. They are enthusiastic supporters of their churches and the majority of members, but they are not generally the head pastors. More women than men serve as missionaries, but they are not usually leaders of mission organizations. Women are the main supporters of Evangelical parachurch organizations but are not typically running them. Evangelical women called to ministerial leadership are consistently caught between competing expectations of their roles in church life. Many Evangelical church historians, theologians, and biblical scholars – both male and female – believe that the sexes have different, but equal, gifts and callings. Yet, history is peppered with women of strong conviction fighting for their right to be heard and respected as leaders in church settings. Today, Evangelical women worldwide are navigating the expectations of conservative theology and traditional cultures, both privately and publicly.

The Evangelical movement began in Britain but there are now far more Evangelicals in Africa (162 million) than in Europe (16 million; Table 13.1). The United States is the country with the most Evangelicals (69 million), but when ranked by size, most majority Christian countries in the global South have more Evangelicals than in the global North (Table 13.3). Historian David Bebbington's work on Evangelicals in modern Britain from the 1730s to the 1980s produced the most cited description of the movement (Bebbington 1992; see also Fisher 2016). Bebbington described Evangelicals of this time with four primary characteristics: "*conversionism*, the belief that lives need to be changed; *activism*, the expression of the gospel in effort; *biblicism*, a particular regard for the Bible; and what may be called *crucicentrism*, a stress on the sacrifice of Christ on the cross" (Bebbington 1992, p. 16, emphasis original). Although the Bebbington quadrilateral is ubiquitous, it was designed to identify Evangelicals in a particular time and place in history – modern Britain – and was not meant to serve as a rubric for identifying Evangelicals in *all* times and places.

The term "Evangelical" is not a primary Christian identity in the global South, nor is it something that people explicitly convert to as they did in modern Britain (Hutchinson and Wolffe 2012). Evangelicals are united in "fellowship in a spiritual bond based upon personal faith in the Lord Jesus Christ, a desire to be shaped by the Scriptures and a commitment to obedience to Christ's missionary mandate" (Dowsett and Escobar 2009, p. 97). In the global South, the contours of

Women in World Christianity: Building and Sustaining a Global Movement, First Edition. Gina A. Zurlo.
© 2023 John Wiley & Sons Ltd. Published 2023 by John Wiley & Sons Ltd.

Evangelicalism parallel those of Protestantism more broadly, with the introduction of Christianity via Western colonization and mission, the passing of leadership to local Christians, and the continued contextualization of the faith. Worldwide, Evangelicals share concerns about the availability of scripture in local languages, literacy, education, missions, and evangelism. They are rooted in the importance of the Bible (*sola scriptura*), local and global outreach, and a shared theology of the centrality of Christ. There are significant regional differences in how Evangelical faith is practiced. In the United States, although Evangelicalism began as a theological movement, in the mid-to-late twentieth century it became centered around certain sociological characteristics – in particular, among White, middle-class, suburban men – after which it eventually morphed into a political movement aligned with conservative Republicanism (Rah 2023). By contrast, in Latin America, *evangélico* faith (non-Catholic Christianity) concerns "structural justice, political repression, Marxism, exploitation of the poor by the powerful (who are often associated with church structures), and the acute suffering engendered by rapid urbanization and industrialization" (Dowsett and Escobar 2009, p. 97).

In this book, Evangelicals are identified by their self-identification with a denomination or network affiliated with a national, regional, or global Evangelical organization. For example, if a denomination in Thailand is a member of the Asia Evangelical Alliance, then all members of that denomination are considered Evangelical. Such Evangelical alliances also exist nationally, such as the Evangelical Fellowship of Botswana, the Barbados Evangelical Association, and the Cyprus Evangelical Alliance. For groups not affiliated with a national, regional, or global body, a percent Evangelical is assigned to the denomination based on survey data and expert estimates (see Zurlo 2015 for a more detailed methodology of counting Evangelicals).

Evangelicals, 1900–2050

Over the twentieth century, the center of gravity of global Evangelicalism shifted even more dramatically than global Christianity as a whole. Africa by far leads as the continent with the most Evangelicals (162 million); North America is second with 71 million (Table 13.1). In 1900, 92% of all Evangelicals lived in Europe and North America; by 2020, this had dropped to just 23% (Figure 13.1). Africa grew from just under 2% Evangelical in 1900 to 12% by 2020, and Latin American Evangelicalism increased from 1% to 13% over the same period. The smallest (by percentage) Evangelical population is in Europe, just under 3%. Looking toward 2050, it is estimated that 82% of all Evangelicals will live in Africa, Asia, Latin America, and Oceania, compared to just 18% in Europe and North America.

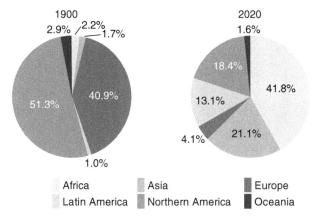

Figure 13.1 Evangelicals by continent, 1900 and 2020. *Source:* Data from Johnson and Zurlo 2022.

Table 13.1 Evangelicals by continent, 1900–2050.

Region	Evangelicals 1900	% of pop.1900	% of Evangelicals 1900	Rate % p.a. 1900–2020	Evangelicals 2020	% of pop.2020	% of Evangelicals 2020	Evangelicals 2050	% of pop.2050	% of Evangelicals 2050
Global North	74,593,000	15.4	92.2	0.13	87,009,000	7.8	22.5	110,164,000	9.7	17.7
Europe	33,062,000	8.2	40.9	−0.61	15,907,000	2.1	4.1	17,844,000	2.5	2.9
North America	41,531,000	50.9	51.3	0.45	71,102,000	19.3	18.4	92,321,000	21.7	14.9
Global South	6,319,000	0.6	7.8	3.27	300,017,000	4.5	77.5	510,799,000	5.9	82.3
Africa	1,789,000	1.7	2.2	3.83	161,716,000	12.1	41.8	315,304,000	12.7	50.8
Asia	1,336,000	0.1	1.7	3.49	81,642,000	1.8	21.1	114,968,000	2.2	18.5
Latin America	825,000	1.3	1.0	3.49	50,595,000	7.7	13.1	72,559,000	9.5	11.7
Oceania	2,370,000	37.9	2.9	0.79	6,063,000	14.2	1.6	7,967,000	13.9	1.3
Global total	**80,912,000**	**5.0**	**100.0**	**1.31**	**387,026,000**	**5.0**	**100.0**	**620,963,000**	**6.4**	**100.0**

Source: Data from Johnson and Zurlo 2022. p.a. = percent change per annum, or each year.

Evangelical churches generally report higher shares of women than in other Christian traditions, such as Catholic and Orthodox churches. Regionally, the highest percent Evangelical female is in Latin America (54%, Table 13.2), followed by North America (53.9%) and Europe (53.6%). As is the case among other Christian traditions, these figures are likely undercounts given a lack of data reporting from Evangelical denominations and networks.

Nine of the ten countries with the most Evangelicals are in the global South, with the lone exception, the United States, ranking number one (Table 13.3). The highest share of Evangelical women in these countries in is Brazil, with 55%.

Table 13.2 Evangelicals by continent with percent female, 2020.

Region	Evangelicals 2020	% of pop. 2020	% of Evangelicals 2020	% Evangelical female 2020	% region female 2020
Global North	87,009,000	7.8	22.5	53.9	51.3
Europe	15,907,000	2.1	4.1	53.6	51.7
North America	71,102,000	19.3	18.4	53.9	50.5
Global South	300,017,000	4.5	77.5	52.6	49.3
Africa	161,716,000	12.1	41.8	52.5	50.0
Asia	81,642,000	1.8	21.1	52.1	48.9
Latin America	50,595,000	7.7	13.1	54.0	50.8
Oceania	6,063,000	14.2	1.6	51.6	49.9
Global total	**387,026,000**	**5.0**	**100.0**	**52.9**	**49.6**

Source: Data from Johnson and Zurlo 2022.

Table 13.3 Countries with the most Evangelicals, 2020.

Rank	Country	Country pop. 2020	Evangelicals 2020	Evangelical % of pop. 2020	% Evangelical female 2020	% country female 2020
1	United States	331,003,000	69,000,000	20.8	53.9	50.5
2	Nigeria	206,140,000	45,500,000	22.1	52.8	49.3
3	China	1,439,324,000	35,000,000	2.4	53.5	48.7
4	Brazil	212,559,000	29,000,000	13.6	55.4	50.9
5	Ethiopia	114,964,000	21,500,000	18.7	50.0	50.0
6	Kenya	53,771,000	16,500,000	30.7	52.5	50.3
7	South Korea	51,269,000	12,855,000	25.1	52.5	49.9
8	India	1,380,004,000	12,200,000	0.9	50.0	48.0
9	Indonesia	273,524,000	9,414,000	3.4	50.0	49.7
10	Tanzania	59,734,000	9,400,000	15.7	52.7	50.0

Source: Data from Johnson and Zurlo 2022.

The countries with the highest percentage share of Evangelicals are spread around the world (Table 13.4). Apart from Kenya and the Central African Republic, most of these countries are relatively small, such as the top ranked country, the Marshall Islands, with only 35,600 people (60% Evangelical). Several are in the Pacific Islands: Marshall Islands, Vanuatu, and Palau; and in the Caribbean: Barbados, Bahamas, and Dominica.

Table 13.4 Countries with the highest percent of Evangelicals, 2020.

Rank	Country	Country pop. 2020	Evangelicals 2020	Evangelical % of pop. 2020	% Evangelical female 2020	% country female 2020
1	Marshall Islands	59,200	35,600	60.1	53.5	49.6
2	Barbados	287,000	114,000	39.7	57.3	51.6
3	Vanuatu	307,000	111,000	36.1	49.9	49.3
4	Bahamas	393,000	136,000	34.6	52.3	51.4
5	Palau	18,100	5,700	31.5	50.6	49.6
6	Dominica	72,000	22,100	30.7	54.8	53.9
7	Kenya	53,771,000	16,500,000	30.7	52.5	50.3
8	Central African Republic	4,830,000	1,450,000	30.0	54.1	50.4
9	Isle of Man	85,000	25,000	29.4	52.9	50.6
10	British Virgin Islands	30,200	8,500	28.1	52.7	50.4

Source: Data from Johnson and Zurlo 2022.

Table 13.5 Countries with the fastest growth of Evangelicals, 2020.

Rank	Country	Country pop. 2020	Evangelicals 2020	Evangelical % of pop. 2020	% Evangelical female 2020	% country female 2020	Rate % p.a. 2000–2020
1	Bhutan	772,000	3,300	0.4	53.4	46.9	8.01
2	Kosovo	2,096,000	4,700	0.2	52.3	51.0	6.85
3	Cambodia	16,719,000	320,000	1.9	49.0	51.2	6.45
4	Iran	83,993,000	85,000	0.1	47.0	49.5	5.95
5	Azerbaijan	10,139,000	9,000	0.1	53.2	50.0	5.57
6	Guinea-Bissau	1,968,000	30,000	1.5	52.0	51.1	5.15
7	Belgium	11,590,000	90,000	0.8	53.4	50.4	4.98
8	Bangladesh	164,689,000	300,000	0.2	49.0	49.4	4.97
9	Algeria	43,851,000	55,000	0.1	48.5	49.5	4.84
10	Burkina Faso	20,903,000	1,877,000	9.0	52.0	50.0	4.81

Source: Data from Johnson and Zurlo 2022. p.a. = percent change per annum, or each year.

Table 13.6   Largest Evangelical denominations, 2015.

Rank	Country	Denomination	Year begun	Affiliated 2015	% female	Rate % p.a. 2000–2015
1	Brazil	Assembleias de Deus	1910	20,978,000	55.0	1.12
2	United States	Southern Baptist Convention	1845	18,836,000	54.1	−0.51
3	China	Han emerging urban church networks	1989	15,000,000	53.7	4.73
4	China	Han house churches Big Five (rural)	1979	12,505,000	53.7	−2.67
5	Nigeria	Anglican Church of Nigeria	1842	11,000,000	52.9	1.94
6	Ethiopia	Word of Life Evangelical Church	1927	8,500,000	50.0	2.82
7	Ethiopia	Evangelical Church Mekane Yesus	1859	7,887,000	50.0	5.85
8	Nigeria	Evangelical Church Winning All	1893	6,800,000	51.1	2.64
9	Nigeria	Assemblies of God in Nigeria	1939	5,964,000	53.5	7.87
10	Uganda	Church of Uganda	1875	5,600,000	50.9	3.18

Source: Data from Johnson and Zurlo 2022. p.a. = percent change per annum, or each year.

Evangelicalism, like any other religious traditions, grows at the national level due to births, conversions, and immigration. Of the countries with the fastest growth of Evangelicals (Table 13.5), several are growing because of conversion, such as in Bhutan, Cambodia, Iran, and Algeria. In these countries, Christians converting from Islam, Buddhism, Hinduism gather in underground or illegal house church networks and wish to remain unknown to official authorities. This kind of Independent Christianity tends to be more Evangelical in faith and practice as converts take serious risks to leave their family religion behind for Christianity. In addition, these secret networks of Christians typically have more women than men, as women are generally more likely than men to switch religions because of relational bonds formed with Christians. Most of the countries with the fastest growth of Evangelicals have a higher proportion of women in Evangelicalism than in the country overall.

Evangelicals are found across a wide range of denominations, from historic or mainline churches such as Anglicans, Baptists, and Methodists. There is also substantial overlap with the Pentecostal/Charismatic movement, many of which are also Evangelical in faith, practice, and self-identification. The Assemblies of God, for example, is in many countries both the largest Evangelical and the largest Pentecostal/Charismatic denomination (Table 13.6). The denominations with the most Evangelicals are found all over the world and, except for the Southern Baptist Convention in the United States, are all in the global South. China is home to two of the largest Evangelical networks in the world: urban house churches and rural house churches, both of which average roughly 54% female, though that figure is likely much higher. In the twentieth century, more women than men joined Chinese house churches as they emerged in rural areas. Nigeria is home to three of the largest denominations with the most Evangelicals worldwide, the Anglican Church, the Evangelical Church Winning All, and the Assemblies of God.

Women in Evangelical History

The Evangelical movement began with a series of renewal movements that emphasized a new kind of spirituality within Protestantism, first in Europe and then throughout the British Empire. As a movement within the Lutheran church, late seventeenth-century Pietism stressed a high moral standard for Christians, a revival of piety and devotion, and an emphasis on the Bible to inform faith and practice (Noll 2019). Other initiatives include Charles (1707–1788) and John Wesley's (1703–1791) Methodist movement within the Church of England, the Welsh revival influenced by Howell Harris (1714–1773) and Daniel Rowland (1713–1790), and the First Great Awakening (1730s–1750s) in the American colonies and Britain. Women were always active and enthusiastic participants in these movements. With new opportunities for public leadership in prayer, praise, and exhortation (Bebbington 1992), women were numerous in the early Evangelical movement within British Methodism; more women, many of them single, converted to early Evangelical movements than men.

Early Evangelical revivals were marked by heightened emotion, a deep individual commitment to accept Jesus Christ as savior, and a commitment to a renewed standard of Christian morality (Noll 2019). Newport, Rhode Island resident Sarah Osborn represented the tens of thousands of ordinary people who responded to the Evangelical message of the First Great Awakening in the American colonies in the transition between Puritanism and Evangelicalism. Her memoir, interpreted by historian Catherine Brekus, reveals the inner torture of a woman struggling to trust God in difficult conditions, including the death of her son, suicidal thoughts, and chronic illness (Brekus 2013; Osborn 2017). Her story also illustrates how revivalism and the Evangelical movement provided women otherwise unattainable public opportunities for ministry and service. Osborn essentially turned her home into a church and used her private space for public ministry, thereby blurring the prevailing rule that the home is the woman's domain, and the church is run by men. Early Evangelicalism was both liberating and oppressive for women. They were encouraged to publish books, hold meetings in their homes, and in more radical cases speak publicly about their beliefs. However, while emphases on personal experience and individualism became tools of women's liberation, women were still confined within a male-dominated religious structure that saw them as the weaker sex, restricted from public leadership and civic life.

During the Second Great Awakening (1790s–1840s), women and children outnumbered men at revivals and women created strong female Evangelical networks to exercise their spiritual authority outside of official church structures (Westerkamp 2016). Women began to question the prohibition against them speaking in church, but as historian Marilyn Westerkamp observes, "evangelicalism often gave women a voice, but when they exercised that voice many were judged the founders of scandal and divisions" (Westerkamp 2016, p. 169). The revivals also provided new spiritual opportunities for former enslaved women and free Black women, such as famous preachers Jarena Lee (1783–1864), Zilpha Elaw (1790–1873), Rebecca Cox Jackson (1795–1871), Julia Foote (1823–1900), and Amanda Berry Smith (1837–1915). At the same time, Black women could not enjoy the same freedoms that Evangelicalism brought White women. Slavery made it impossible for African American women to follow the moral code they were taught in Evangelical churches. They were told to be faithful wives and mothers yet were divided from their husbands and children by sale; they were told to be chaste, yet were subject to the sexual whims of their masters. Black women did not benefit from Evangelical individualism the way that White women did, nor were many able to benefit from other features of Evangelical Protestantism like the ability to read scripture for themselves, since many were illiterate (Braude 2007). The spiritual authority women achieved in early Evangelicalism largely disappeared upon the movement's institutionalization. In new Evangelical churches, women were not allowed to preach, teach, pray aloud, or vote in congregational affairs. Women lost their agency in the transition from sect to church.

Evangelical Women in Leadership

Historically, women have had difficulty obtaining leadership positions in Evangelical churches, mission organizations, and parachurch organizations. Part of the reason is due to particular interpretations of scripture. Passages like 1 Timothy 2:11–12 are often used to prevent women from holding leadership over men, both within and outside of the church: "a woman should learn in quietness and full submission. I do not permit a woman to teach or to assume authority over a man; she must be quiet" (NIV). Generally, an Evangelical worldview does not encourage women to see themselves as leaders of men. Despite affirming the equality of men and women, most Evangelical organizations are patriarchal in practice and separation of gender roles remains an important feature of Evangelical history and subculture (Dahlvig and Longman 2016). There are exceptions, the most notable of which is perhaps the Evangelical Covenant Church (ECC), founded in 1885 in Chicago, Illinois, which elected its first female president in 2022: Tammy Swanson-Draheim. Most members are in the United States and Canada, but there are also ECC congregations in South Sudan and Mexico, with missionaries serving all around the world. In mission, it is widely perceived that women, especially single women, make up the majority of missionaries, but there are very few female leaders of mission organizations. Exceptions include Bev Upton Williams, Chief Executive Officer of Haggai International, and Mary Ho, Executive Director of All Nations International.

Gendered approaches to mentoring and discipleship prevent women from access to male leaders for support, encouragement, and leadership development. Famous Evangelical revivalist Billy Graham (1918–2018), for example, would not travel, meet, or eat alone with any woman who was not his wife, Ruth, to avoid perceived sexual impropriety. The "Billy Graham rule" (or the "Modesto Manifesto") has become somewhat ubiquitous in Evangelical circles, where male leaders will not spend one-on-one time with any woman who is not his wife. A strict separation of sexes severely limits women's access to obtaining the skills, knowledge, and experience necessary for leadership. It also prohibits male leaders from acknowledging the talents of young women and identifying their potential for advancement.

The World Evangelical Alliance (WEA) was founded in London in 1846 to unite Evangelicals around the world. Now the world's largest Evangelical body, the WEA has had 15 General Secretaries, all men, though Singaporean Peirong Lin was appointed Deputy General Secretary in 2021. Only two General Secretaries have been from the global South, both from the Philippines. One of the nine regional Evangelical alliance directors is a woman (as of 2022): Rachel Afeaki-Taumoepeau of the South Pacific Evangelical Alliance. Women do lead in other capacities, such as directors of various departments (church engagement, global advocacy, and global theology, among others). For example, Esmé Bowers serves as the chairperson of the Evangelical Alliance of South Africa, established the African Women in Mission Network in 2012, founded and served as president for 12 years of the Women's Ministry of the Full Gospel Church of God in South Africa, and was chair of the Pan African Christian Women's Alliance for three terms. The WEA and most of its regional alliances have a women's commission that is run by a woman and exclusively dedicated to serving Evangelical women.

Another major global Evangelical organization is the Lausanne Movement, which grew out of the 1974 International Congress on World Evangelization held in Lausanne, Switzerland under the leadership of Billy Graham. Like the WEA, Lausanne has never had a female global Executive Director, though women serve on the board of directors and as catalysts for different interest groups such as health, children, integral mission, disability concerns, and as regional leaders. The 1989 Manila Manifesto included the following on gender equality:

> God created men and women as equal bearers of his image, accepts them equally in Christ, and poured out his Spirit on all flesh, sons and daughters alike. In addition, because the Holy Spirit distributes his gifts to women as well as to men, they must be given opportunities to exercise their gifts. We celebrate their distinguished record in the history of missions and are convinced that God calls women to similar roles today. Even though we are not fully agreed what forms their leadership should take, we do agree about the partnership

in world evangelization which God intends men and women to enjoy. Suitable training must therefore be made available to both.

(Lausanne Movement 1989)

Evangelical organizations tend to emphasize men and women serving together in ministry, in contrast to progressive or mainline Christian organizations that more overtly advocate for feminism, Christian feminism, and women's empowerment. The 2010 Lausanne gathering in Cape Town, South Africa, produced the Cape Town Commitment with an entire section dedicated to "men and women in partnership." Expanding on the Manila Manifesto, the Commitment encourages Evangelicals to see the equality of men and women "in creation, in sin, in salvation, and in the Spirit" and to "not quench the Spirit by despising the ministry of any" (Lausanne Movement 2010). The statement furthermore encourages dialogue on the issue of women in leadership, recognizing differences in biblical interpretation among today's cultures and contexts.

Vignettes: Evangelical Women Worldwide

In places where Christians are a minority, especially a persecuted minority, Evangelical churches are typically newer and tend to theologically align with historic Evangelical characteristics on the importance of the Bible, a personal conversion narrative, and a desire to spread the faith. For example, in North Africa and West Asia more than half of contemporary Evangelicals from a non-Christian background have become Christian in the last decade (Wahba 2018). Women are often prominent in these movements as those more likely to convert to Christianity and pass the faith to their children. Elsewhere in the world, Evangelicalism is organized in formal bodies affiliated to national, regional, or global organizations. While women might not feature prominently in the leadership of these associations, they are extremely active members and run women's-only spaces within them to advocate for their own spiritual needs.

Asia is home to many secret networks of hidden believers in Christ, people who publicly follow Jesus within their family religion (Hinduism, Buddhism, or Islam) but inwardly profess faith in Christ. These individuals do not leave their cultural heritage behind to join a Christian community or church. Among the largest of these movements is in Bangladesh, where *Isai imandars* ("those faithful to Jesus") in the Jamaat movement number over 115,000, with some worshiping in messianic mosques (Johnson and Zurlo 2022). While retaining cultural elements of Islamic worship and practice, they have adopted core Christian theology and faith; many are also charismatic. Communities of *Isai imandars* follow the wider patriarchal culture, though women can participate in public prayer and Bible study (Jørgensen 2009). Similar communities exist in Nepal, Myanmar, Sri Lanka, India, Iran, and Afghanistan. One of the most renowned examples of hidden believers in Christ were among upper-class Nadar women of Sivakasi, Tamil Nadu, India. Hundreds of women kept their Christianity private for over 50 years (1917–1970s), secretly practicing Christianity while outwardly participating in Hindu rituals and cultural expectations (Kent 2011). These women had received the Christian gospel through female Anglican *zenana* missionaries in the late nineteenth century.

In the twentieth century, the rural Chinese house church movement was majority female (80%). As Christianity grew, it became more urbanized and attractive to the middle class, as well as to men. Women had tremendous leadership roles in Chinese house churches and up until recently, they made up the majority of leaders. However, since the turn of the twenty-first century, the influence of Calvinist theology has led to the rise of complementarianism and the increased subordination of women. Chinese women and men have together been involved in missions, from first reaching ethnic minorities in China to working cross-culturally. Formal Chinese house church missionary movements began in the 1990s and have gained significant momentum. The most famous is the Back to Jerusalem Movement, which dates to the 1920s and aims to send Chinese missionaries everywhere between China and Jerusalem, returning Christianity to its historic origin along the Silk Roads.

Evangelical women often create their own separate organizations to address issues relevant to them. Formed in 1989, for example, the Alliance des Femmes Évangéliques (Alliance of Evangelical Women) in Burkina Faso coordinates spiritual, social, and economic projects for women. In Croatia, Evangelical women have formed several different groups to promote connections between women and offer support for their ministries, such as Daughters of the King (a nondenominational organization), women's work within the Baptist Union (est. 1936), and two newsletters exclusively for Evangelical women, *Bilken* and *The Sisters Newsletters*. The Association Feminine des Eglises Protestantes Evangéliques de Côte d'Ivoire (AFEPCI, Women's Association of Evangelical Protestant Churches of Ivory Coast) gathers women from at least ten different Evangelical denominations for unity, prayer, support, and evangelization. The AFEPCI has also organized conferences combatting HIV/AIDS and advocating for peace in Côte d'Ivoire and across Africa. The Pan African Christian Women Alliance (PACWA), a commission of the Association of Evangelicals in Africa, is present in 23 African countries (plus a chapter in the United States). With the mission to "empower women to be all that God made them to be, wherever they are," women of the PACWA meet regularly for prayer, missions mobilization, community development training, rural women's empowerment, aid to women in crisis, and encouragement of women in leadership.

Evangelical women also confront patriarchal structures where they are expected to submit to male leadership and authority. In Eswatini, single female missionaries Malla Moe (1863–1953) and Laura Strand (1879–?) founded the Swazi Evangelical Church and the Free Evangelical Assemblies. They also laid a foundation for educating girls, and as a result, women are now represented throughout Swazi society, including in government and the private sector. Eswatini also has the second-highest proportion of Christian women in Africa at 54% (after Botswana, 56%).

Despite being the country with the most Evangelicals in the world, the United States does not resemble the rest of the world in its Evangelicalism. Historically, American Evangelicals held to characteristics such as the centrality of the Bible and upright morality, but the Evangelicalism that

Photo 13.1 A woman emerges from her baptism at the Bobo Dioulasso congregation of Eglise Evangélique Mennonite du Burkina Faso (Evangelical Mennonite Church of Burkina Faso) (2014). *Source:* Frank Nacanabo, Mennonite Mission Network.

has dominated American society since the 1970s is more of a cultural movement than a theological one, with militant masculinity one of its defining features (Du Mez 2020). The development of complementarian theology in 1987 by conservative theologians John Piper and Wayne Grudem led to the founding of the Council on Biblical Manhood and Womanhood. Complementarian theology reduced women's authority and capacity to lead in Evangelical circles and has also contributed to abusive behavior and sexual misconduct in some denominations, such as the Southern Baptist Convention (see Chapter 6). The 2016 election of Donald J. Trump as president – a thrice-married former pro-choice Democrat with a record of alleged sexual abuse of women – was supported by 81% of White Evangelical voters, including 20% of White female Evangelical voters (12.6 million votes). While some thought Evangelicals had betrayed their values, historian Kristen Kobes Du Mez suggested that "Evangelical support for Trump was no aberration, nor was it merely a pragmatic choice. It was, rather, the culmination of evangelicals' embrace of militant masculinity, an ideology that enshrines patriarchal authority and condones the callous display of power, at home and abroad" (Du Mez 2020, p. 3). The rise of masculine Evangelicalism has been detrimental for women, who, as stereotyped, are reduced to merely needing love, not respect like men (Eggerichs 2006), ridiculed for "radical feminism" (Dobson 2004), told they need saving by their husbands and fathers (Eldredge 2001), encouraged to choose husbands who are more devoted to Jesus than their families (Elliot 2002; Dorsett 2008), and are repeatedly pushed to reaffirm their perceived traditional roles in church and society (MacArthur 1987). Furthermore, Evangelicalism in the United States is primarily a White movement, with Christians of color – even those who are theologically similar – marginalized by the waves of the White cultural movement and its association with conservative Republican politics. As theologian Soong-Chan Rah observed,

> Non-white evangelicals who held a high view of Scripture, a high Christology and a conversionist revivalist fervour were not seen as part of the Evangelical mainstream as those theological categories no longer defined US Evangelicalism. As non-white evangelicals often pursued a different social and political agenda that included racial justice, care for the immigrant, and the rights of women, the gulf between the theologically-akin non-white evangelicals with their sociologically and politically defined white Evangelical cousins increased. US Evangelicalism as currently defined along non-theological boundaries may have excluded the actual heirs of evangelical orthodoxy by embracing a social and political identity over their theological and ecclesial identity.
>
> *(Rah 2023)*

While Evangelicalism in the global South bears some resemblance to that in the United States – such as the emphasis on personal conversion, literal reading of scripture, and evangelistic zeal – concerns of Evangelicals in the global South are generally broader, as adherents use their faith to work for positive social action related to immigration, women's rights, peacebuilding, serving the poor, and standing up against injustice. For example, the adaptation of Evangelicalism among *Dalits* in India allowed for access and social mobility that significantly improved their lives and empowered them to spread that message to other groups (Shah and Samuel 2019). Furthermore, Evangelicals in the global South tend to be more Pentecostal/Charismatic than those in the North. Healing and exorcisms are common methods for evangelization, with an emphasis on spiritual power and personal experience of God.

Another similarity between Evangelicals in the United States and those in the global South is political engagement. In sub-Saharan Africa, Evangelicals intentionally enter the political sphere based on Paul's teaching that political powers are ordained by God, and they can use political power to influence countries to adopt Christianity (Balcomb 2017). Evangelicals in South Asia also attempt to influence politics with protests, preaching on political issues from the pulpit, and endorsing particular politicians (Shah and Samuel 2019).

Photo 13.2   Performance by the Yetsedik Tsehay choir of the Ethiopian Evangelical Church Mekane Yesus in Addis Ababa, Ethiopia (2019). *Source:* LWF/Albin Hillert.

Conclusion

Evangelicalism is home to a wide spectrum of belief and practice concerning gender roles, though Evangelicals appear to agree on some core ideals. Because Jesus lifted the status of women, Christians are expected to do so today, thus giving them a responsibility to promote the dignity of women. Evangelicals uniformly support the education of girls, the equal spiritual authority of women and men, and the importance of women's presence in the church, no matter what role they serve. Evangelicals also believe in heeding women's callings and spiritual gifts in service of the church and the world (Spencer 2015), though, in some circles, it is widely held that women cannot be called as preachers and pastors. Though biblical authority is important for Evangelical faith, women are often caught between literal readings of scripture and their calling to higher levels of leadership in Evangelical churches and organizations. Evangelicals are united in their desire to ground their beliefs and practices in the Bible, although there remains disagreement on how exactly that is done (Wilson 2018). The status of women in Evangelicalism is in many ways a battle over biblical interpretation, and this is not new. The Bible has been used throughout history to gain insight into relevant issues of the time, such as whether to abolish slavery, or whether women should be granted the right to vote (Bendroth 1993).

Evangelical women – and some men – are reengaging with the Bible to highlight the important contributions of women, to recognize the cultural and historical context of the Bible more deeply in relationship to women's roles and to critique patriarchal structures. Popular Christian teacher Carolyn Custis James, for example, interprets the Garden of Eden as a battleground, with Eve as Adam's cowarrior, not his "helpmeet" (James 2021). Furthermore, patriarchy – "Your desire will be for your husband, and he will rule over you" (Genesis 3:16) – was not a part of God's original plan in Genesis 1 and 2, but instead a consequence of Adam and Eve's sin. Throughout the biblical accounts, God consistently subverts patriarchal structures by not choosing the first-born male (e.g., God chose Abel over Cain and chose Moses over Aaron); by providing women rights not typically afforded to them (e.g., giving Mahlah, Noah, Hoglah, Milkah, and Tirzah their deceased father's land inheritance, Numbers 27:1–8); and by including women in the genealogy of Christ

(Matthew 1:1–17). Medieval historian Beth Allison Barr suggests that Paul's commentary on women in the church should be read as "resistance narratives to Roman patriarchy" (Barr 2021, p. 32). According to Barr, Paul was teaching Christians to live *differently* than Rome:

> Instead of endowing authority to a man who speaks and acts for those within his household, the Christian household codes offer each member of the shared community—knit together by their faith in Christ—the right to hear and act for themselves. This is radically different from the Roman patriarchal structure. The Christian structure of the house church resists the patriarchal world of the Roman Empire.
>
> *(Barr 2021, p. 34)*

Evangelical egalitarianism certainly does exist in the United States, the country with the most Evangelicals. In fact, the "evangelical left" existed before the rise of the Religious Right in the 1970s (Swartz 2012), but it has been marginalized in most Evangelical circles, partly because complementarian views – perceived as more traditional – are espoused, preached, and spread far and wide by powerful Evangelical organizations with substantial resources (see Gallagher 2004). This may be changing, with the rise of progressive Evangelicalism under the leadership of popular theologians Sarah Bessey (b.1979), Jeff Chu, and Rachel Held Evans (1981–2019). However, most progressive Evangelicals extend their support to the LGBTQ+ movement, which is an anathema to conservative Evangelicals in both the global North and South. If women's empowerment and egalitarian views are connected to support for same-sex marriage and LGBTQ+ rights, then progressive Evangelicalism, and its egalitarianism, will likely remain marginalized and a minority position in the broader Evangelical movement. Historian Brian Stanley has commented that the fate of Evangelicalism is in the hands of the global South, but the context of Evangelicalism there is drastically different from the Enlightenment backdrop of Europe and North America (Stanley 2013). The tensions in the global Evangelical movement, of which gender roles are among the most important, are likely to continue in the future.

Reflection Questions

1) Consider how the term "Evangelical" is understood in different contexts around the world, and the variety of roles for women that exist in these contexts. What are David Bebbington's four descriptors of Evangelicalism, and in what ways does global Evangelicalism transcend these characteristics?
2) How did the emphases of early Evangelical revivals contribute to the liberation of women? Describe how women's roles changed in relationship to both the church and home as a result of the revivals. How did Black women's experiences in American revivalism differ from White women? How do White and Black women continue to experience Evangelicalism differently today?
3) In what ways have Evangelical women critiqued patriarchal structures, in both church and society, around the world? What are their primary motivations and tools for doing so?

Works Cited

Balcomb, Anthony (2017). Evangelicals. In: *Christianity in Sub-Saharan Africa* (ed. Kenneth R. Ross, J. Kwabena Asamoah-Gyadu, and Todd M. Johnson), 302–313. Edinburgh: Edinburgh University Press.

Barr, Beth A. (2021). *The Making of Biblical Womanhood: How the Subjugation of Women Became Gospel Truth*. Grand Rapids, MI: Brazos Press.

Bebbington, David (1992). *Evangelicalism in Modern Britain: A History from the 1730s to the 1980s*. Grand Rapids, MI: Baker Book House.

Bendroth, Margaret L. (1993). *Fundamentalism and Gender, 1875 to the Present*. New Haven: Yale University Press.

Braude, Ann (2007). *Sisters and Saints: Women and American Religion*. Oxford: Oxford University Press.

Brekus, Catherine A. (2013). *Sarah Osborn's World: The Rise of Evangelical Christianity in Early America*. New Haven: Yale University Press.

Dahlvig, Jolyn E. and Longman, Karen A. (2016). Influences of an Evangelical Christian worldview on women's leadership development. *Advances in Developing Human Resources*, 18(2), 243–259.

Dobson, James C. (2004). *Marriage Under Fire: Why We Must Win This War*. Sisters, OR: Multnomah.

Dorsett, Lyle W. (2008). *A Passion for God: The Spiritual Journey of A.W. Tozer*. Chicago: Moody.

Dowsett, Rosemary and Escobar, Samuel (2009). Evangelicals. In: *Atlas of Global Christianity* (ed. Kenneth R. Ross and Todd M. Johnson), 96–97. Edinburgh: Edinburgh University Press.

Du Mez, Kristin K. (2020). *Jesus and John Wayne: How White Evangelicals Corrupted a Faith and Fractured a Nation*. New York: Liveright.

Eggerichs, Emerson (2006). *Love & Respect: The Love She Most Desires, the Respect He Desperately Needs*. Nashville, TN: Thomas Nelson.

Eldredge, John (2001). *Wild at Heart: Discovering the Secret of a Man's Soul*. Nashville, TN.: Thomas Nelson.

Elliot, Elisabeth (2002). *Passion and Purity: Learning to Bring Your Love Life under Christ's Control*. 2nd edn. Grand Rapids, MI: Fleming H.Revell.

Fisher, Linford (2016). Evangelicals and Unevangelicals: the contested history of a word, 1500–1950. *Religion and American Culture: A Journal of Interpretation*, 26(2), 184–226.

Gallagher, Sally K. (2004). The marginalization of Evangelical feminism. *Sociology of Religion*, 65(3), 215–237.

Hutchinson, Mark and Wolffe, John (2012). *A Short History of Global Evangelicalism*. Cambridge England: Cambridge University Press.

James, Carolyn Custis (2021). Affirmation of women's stories. Rise in Strength Virtual Consultation. October 30–November 1.

Johnson, Todd M. and Zurlo, Gina A. ed. (2022). *World Christian Database*. Leiden/Boston: Brill.

Jørgensen, Jonas A. (2009). Jesus Imandars and Christ Bhaktas: report from two field studies of interreligious hermeneutics and identity in globalized Christianity. *International Bulletin of Missionary Research*, 33(4), 171–176.

Kent, Eliza F. (2011). Secret Christians of Sivakasi: gender, syncretism, and crypto-religion in early twentieth-century South India. *Journal of the American Academy of Religion*, 79(3), 676–705.

Lausanne Movement (1989). The manila manifesto. https://lausanne.org/content/manifesto/the-manila-manifesto (accessed 8 December 2021).

Lausanne Movement (2010). The cape town commitment. https://lausanne.org/content/ctc/ctcommitment (accessed 8 December 2021).

Lee, Jarena (1849). *Religious Experience and Journal of Mrs. Jarena Lee, Giving an Account of Her Call to Preach the Gospel, Revised and Corrected from the Original Manuscript Written by Herself*. Philadelphia: Printed and published for the author.

MacArthur, John (1987). *God's High Calling for Women*. Chicago, IL: Moody Press.

Noll, Mark A. (2019). *A History of Christianity in the United States and Canada*. 2nd edn. Grand Rapids, MI: William B. Eerdmans Publishing Company.

Osborn, Sarah (2017). *Sarah Osborn's Collected Writings* (ed. Catherine A. Brekus). New Haven: Yale University Press.

Rah, Soong-Chan (2023). Evangelicals. In: *Christianity in North America* (ed. Kenneth R. Ross, Grace Ji-Sun Kim, and Todd M. Johnson). Edinburgh: Edinburgh University Press.

Seton, Rosemary E. (2013). *Western Daughters in Eastern Lands: British Missionary Women in Asia*. Santa Barbara, CA: Praeger.

Shah, Rebecca S. and Samuel, Vinay (2019). Evangelicals. In: *Christianity in South and Central Asia* (ed. Kenneth R. Ross, Daniel Jeyaraj, and Todd M. Johnson), 274–280. Edinburgh: Edinburgh University Press.

Spencer, Aída B. (2015). Evangelicals and gender. In: *Evangelicals around the World: A Global Handbook for the 21*[st] *Century* (ed. Brian C. Stiller, Todd M. Johnson, Karen Stiller, and Mark Hutchinson), 112–119. Nashville, TN: Thomas Nelson.

Stanley, Brian (2013). *The Global Diffusion of Evangelicalism: The Age of Billy Graham and John Stott*. Downers Grove, IL: IVP Academic.

Swartz, David R. (2012). *Moral Minority: The Evangelical Left in an Age of Conservatism*. Philadelphia: University of Pennsylvania Press.

Wahba, Wafik (2018). Evangelicals. In: *Christianity in North Africa and West Asia* (ed. Kenneth R. Ross, Mariz Tadros, and Todd M. Johnson), 285–292. Edinburgh: Edinburgh University Press.

Westerkamp, Marilyn J. (2016). *Women and Religion in Early America, 1600–1850: The Puritan and Evangelical Traditions*. Abingdon, Oxon: Routledge, Taylor & Francis Group.

Wilson, Linda (2018). Evangelicals and gender. In: *The Routledge Research Companion to the History of Evangelicalism* (ed. Andrew Atherstone), 217–231. New York: Routledge.

Zurlo, Gina A. (2015). Demographics of global Evangelicalism. In: *Evangelicals around the World: A Global Handbook for the 21*[st] *Century* (ed. Brian C. Stiller, Todd M. Johnson, Karen Stiller, and Mark Hutchinson), 34–47. Nashville, TN: Thomas Nelson.

Part III

Women in World Christianity by Select Topics

14

Christianity and Gender-based Violence

"The womb, which is hidden inside the body of a woman, swells up when bearing a child, as if to remind the entire world that the power to give life, to produce and reproduce life still lies with the female of the species. It seems that the womb might as well as be outside for all the violence and discrimination it faces in society, within a patriarchal world."
Evangeline Anderson-Rajkumar (Jeyaraj and Anderson-Rajkumar 2019, p. 371)

Violence, harassment, and discrimination are common occurrences for women everywhere in the world. Sexual violence is a tool of warfare and exceedingly common among intimate partners, as well as nonpartners. Violence is often unreported or underreported because of the shame associated with being violated. It happens across all ages, all educational levels, and in all contexts; it occurs in public, in the workplace, and in homes, schools, and places of worship. These behaviors continue despite numerous programs from governments, public campaigns, NGOs, and faith-based organizations on the importance of protecting women and girls; around the world, social norms and individual beliefs and behaviors perpetuate discrimination against women (Conceição 2019). The stark reality is that women are simply not safe anywhere in the world. Addressing women's safety requires the creation of "positive gender norms and an absence of gender discrimination, with laws preventing unequal treatment, harassment and violence against women" (Conceição 2019, p. 167). Achieving this is a mammoth task, requiring advancements in education, reproductive rights, political participation, and a fundamental shift in cultural and religious norms. Psychological, emotional, sexual, and physical violence against women are poised to continue without substantial interventions on the international, national, and local levels.

Though religious communities must also be a part of the solution, they are often part of the problem. In many contexts, gender norms are heavily influenced by particular readings of scripture and long-held traditions that are difficult to discuss, never mind change. Women often suffer silently, instructed to submit to their husbands as if to God. Some women are abused, including spiritually abused, without even knowing they are victims. Many Christian communities have developed a culture of self-silencing, where women who have experienced forms of gender-based violence (GBV) in their marriages justify their own abuse with passages such as Proverbs 21:9, "Better to live on a corner of the roof than share a house with a quarrelsome wife" (NIV) (Chisale 2018). Often, religious communities stand in the way of governments trying to ratify laws toward ending discrimination against women, especially on the issue of marital rape (King and Sifaki 2019; Nazneen 2019).

This chapter discusses the global situation concerning violence, harassment, and discrimination of women, including gender-specific persecution in some of the world's most difficult places to be a Christian. It follows with examples of Christian communities, churches, and organizations responding to gender-based violence.

Gender-based Violence and Discrimination Worldwide

Violence and discrimination against women come in a variety of forms and are only partially documented by international agencies such as the United Nations, World Bank, and the World Health Organization. The United Nations defines violence against women as "any act of gender-based violence that results in, or is likely to result in, physical, sexual or psychological harm or suffering to women, including threats of such acts, coercion or arbitrary deprivation of liberty, whether occurring in public or in private life" (General Assembly Resolution 48/104 Declaration on the Elimination of Violence against Women 1993). The Global Database on Violence Against Women from United Nations Women includes, among other measures, statistical data on physical and sexual intimate partner violence, lifetime non-partner sexual violence, child marriage, and gender equality indexes. The United Nations Development Programme Gender Inequality Index (GII) is a composite measure that reflects inequality between men and women in three dimensions: reproductive health, empowerment, and the labor market. Sustainable Development Goal number five of the United Nations aims to achieve gender equality and empower all women and girls, with the following targets (United Nations 2022):

- End all forms of discrimination against all women and girls everywhere.
- Eliminate all forms of violence against all women and girls in the public and private spheres, including trafficking and sexual and other types of exploitation.
- Eliminate all harmful practices, such as child, early, and forced marriage and female genital mutilation.
- Recognize and value unpaid care and domestic work through the provision of public services, infrastructure, and social protection policies and the promotion of shared responsibility within the household and the family as nationally appropriate.
- Ensure women's full and effective participation and equal opportunities for leadership at all levels of decision-making in political, economic, and public life.
- Ensure universal access to sexual and reproductive health and reproductive rights as agreed in accordance with the Programme of Action of the International Conference on Population and Development and the Beijing Platform for Action and the outcome documents of their review conferences.
- Undertake reforms to give women equal rights to economic resources, as well as access to ownership and control over land and other forms of property, financial services, inheritance, and natural resources, in accordance with national laws.
- Enhance the use of enabling technology, in particular information and communications technology, to promote the empowerment of women.
- Adopt and strengthen sound policies and enforceable legislation for the promotion of gender equality and the empowerment of all women and girls at all levels.

Progress toward achieving these goals has been extremely slow, further hampered by the global COVID-19 pandemic beginning in 2020 that exacerbated existing inequalities. As violence against women has increased, women also have greater burdens of work and family care and have been under stress as the majority of frontline healthcare workers. The consequences of GBV are vast and include serious physical injury, unplanned pregnancies, and sexually transmitted diseases such as HIV. In addition, GBV also results in deep mental and emotional trauma that is always carried by the victim and can be manifested in deep anger and hatred, eating disorders, substance abuse, and depression.

There is not a single country in the world where women have complete physical security (WomenStats Project 2019a).[1] Women generally lack the ability to freely move in public spaces without harassment. In some countries – Somalia, Saudi Arabia, Afghanistan, and Nepal – governmental law regulates women's public movement, whereas in others, women often need male escorts to move freely and safely (Mali, India, and Pakistan). Harassment of women is common everywhere around the world.

Sexual violence is one of the most common forms of violence against women and girls. Rape is a problem everywhere in the world but is endemic in the Democratic Republic of the Congo, Central African Republic, Chad, Mali, Tunisia, and Afghanistan; it is a major problem in at least another 50 countries (WomenStats Project 2018).[2] Underreporting of rape is so common that officially reported statistics are widely known to be completely unreliable indicators of the actual prevalence of rape in a society.

An estimated 117 million girls go "missing" every year due to female infanticide (sex-selective abortion in utero or killing baby girls upon birth). Half of the world's missing girls are in India. A study of 2.1 million birth histories in India between 1987 and 2016 found that 13.5 million female births were missing, resulting in a natural sex ratio of 950 girls per 1,000 boys (Saikia et al. 2021; the 2011 Indian census revealed a ratio of 943 females to 1,000 males in the country). In 2019, of the 200 births reported in 132 villages over a three-month period in Uttarkashi district (Uttarakhand state), none were girls. Although infanticide is illegal in India, male preference is driven by poverty, marriage dowries, and lack of social support for women and girls.

Global maternal mortality rates have been dropping; in 1900, there were 360 maternal deaths due to pregnancy-related causes per 100,000 live births worldwide, and this dropped to 204 deaths by 2017. Sustainable Development Goal number three is to reduce the global maternal mortality ratio to less than 70 deaths per 100,000 live births. Despite some progress, maternal mortality is still high (defined as more than 301 maternal deaths per 100,000 live births) in much of Africa, South Asia, and Southeast Asia. The highest rates are in South Sudan (1,150 deaths per 100,000 live births), Chad (1,140 deaths), Sierra Leone (1,120 deaths), and Nigeria (917 deaths) (United Nations Statistics Division 2020). In comparison, the lowest rates are only two maternal deaths per 100,000 live births in Poland, Norway, Italy, and Belarus. Italy's population is five times larger than South Sudan's (60 million vs. 11 million) but its maternal mortality rate is 0.2% of South Sudan's.

Female genital mutilation (FGM) is practiced across the African Sahel and in Southeast Asia, particularly Indonesia. Between 2004 and 2018, the highest rates of FGM were reported in Somalia (98% of girls and women were cut between ages 15 and 49), Guinea (95%), Djibouti (94%), Mali (89%), and Egypt (87%) (United Nations Statistics Division 2020). Although it is not routinely practiced everywhere, nearly all countries in Latin America, Asia, and North Africa have no laws against FGM. It is only technically unlawful in North America, Australia, New Zealand, and Western, Northern, and Southern Europe.

---

1 Physical security measures domestic violence, rape and sexual assault, martial rape, incest, murder, military service, governmental exploitation, suicide, and other unspecified violence.

2 The comprehensive scale of rape combines officially reported rape prevalence, strength of taboos against reporting rape, scope of laws concerning rape, estimate of similarity between rape victimization and reported rape prevalence (estimate of underreporting), estimate of martial rape victimization, legal exemption for rapists if marriage is offered, and existence of enclaves of higher rape rates.

It is very common for girls to be married at age 16 or younger in parts of North Africa, sub-Saharan Africa, the Arabian Peninsula, Brazil, and Papua New Guinea; in some of these places it is culturally encouraged for girls to marry this young. Between 2005 and 2019, the highest rates of child marriage (defined by the United Nations as percent of women ages 20–24 married by age 18) were reported in Niger (76%), Central African Republic (68%), Chad (67%), Bangladesh (59%), and Mali (54%) (United Nations Statistics Division 2020).

Governmental participation by women varies widely. Several countries, such as New Zealand, Zimbabwe, Tanzania, Spain, and Canada report that women make up 40% or more of their national parliaments/governments. Yet, many countries have between zero and 20% female parliamentarians, including in the world's largest countries: China, India, Brazil, and the Democratic Republic of the Congo (WomenStats Project 2019b).

Trafficking of women and young girls is very common and even legal in some countries such as Russia, Venezuela, Iran, Libya, Mauritania, and Turkmenistan (WomenStats Project 2019c).[3] Roughly 70% of trafficking victims worldwide are women and girls, most of them targeted for being young, undocumented, unemployed, poor, or otherwise marginalized (UNODC 2020). Additional discrimination against women exists in the practice of family law, property rights, bride price/dowry practices, domestic violence, education (especially secondary education), and is reported in other measures of safety, health, wellness, and human flourishing. It is dangerous to be a woman in the world today.

Christianity and Gender-based Violence

Women have a place of prominence in the Bible as mothers, judges, prophetesses, disciples, and witnesses to the resurrection of Jesus. Yet, the Bible is also rife with stories of physical and sexual violence against women, some overt, some subtle. Feminist biblical scholar Phyllis Trible's *Texts of Terror* (1984) was the first major work to systematically address violence against women in the Hebrew Bible. She detailed the horrific stories of Hagar (a used, abused, and rejected slave), Tamar (a raped and discarded princess), the unnamed concubine of Judges (raped, murdered, and dismembered), and the daughter of Jephthah (a slain and sacrificed virgin) (Trible 1984). Other examples include the rape of Dinah (Genesis 34), the gift of 400 virgins to the warriors of Benjamin after the massacre of their communities (Judges 21), and the jealous husband who made his wife drink poison to prove her fidelity (Numbers 5). The scrutinization of biblical texts through the lens of violence against women has since expanded to encompass the entire Bible, interpretations from both women and men, and from scholars worldwide (see, most prominently, Melanchthon and Whitaker 2021).

The legal text of the Torah (Genesis, Exodus, Leviticus, Numbers, and Deuteronomy) also includes laws that blame female victims and even promote violence against them. For example, only female sorcerers are to receive the death penalty (Exodus 22:18) and a woman raped in a town should be put to death with her rapist (Deuteronomy 22:22–23). The wisdom literature often portrays God as a faithful husband, while Israel or Jerusalem is the sexually promiscuous wife, with many texts supporting violence against her (Hosea 1–3, Ezekiel 16 and 23, and Lamentations 1:8–10). Jewish biblical scholar Tamar Kamionkowski stated, "These texts suggest that women are generally the property of men, and as such, may be controlled, manipulated, and brutalized" (Kamionkowski 2021). These passages have been interpreted throughout history to support male domination, control, and violence against women. Bolstered by text and tradition, Christianity has a historical track record of overlooking at best, and condoning at worst, violence against women.

---

3 Trafficking can be within countries or across borders and does not include prostitution. This indicator includes sex trafficking, mail order brides, procreative trafficking, and slavery.

Churches have not been shielded from this issue. Recently revealed sexual abuse scandals in the Catholic Church, Southern Baptist Convention, and others have put pressure on patriarchal structures to change. Unfortunately, churches have often been part of the problem, not the solution, and the spread of Christianity to the global South has not appeared to slow rates of violence against women. Intimate partner violence and family and domestic violence is just as prevalent in wider society as they are in the church (see, for example, Pepper and Powell 2022 and Nason-Clark 1996). Furthermore, victims have little confidence in their churches to respond appropriately to abuse disclosures (McPhillips and Page 2021).

The Democratic Republic of the Congo is 95% Christian, yet at least 51% of women have experienced physical and/or sexual violence in their lifetimes, and 37% have experienced it in the last year (see Table 14.1). The United States, the country with the most Christians, ranks low on the Gender Inequality Index (19/100, meaning women and men are relatively equal), yet one out of every five women in America has been the victim of an attempted or completed rape in her lifetime; 81% of women report experiencing some form of sexual harassment or assault in her lifetime (Smith et al. 2018; see also Morgan and Thompson 2021). The situation is worse for Native American women, who are twice as likely to experience rape or sexual assault compared to women of other ethnicities.

The countries with the greatest gender inequality (Table 14.2) are mostly in Central Asia and Africa, except for Papua New Guinea in Melanesia. Papua New Guinea and the DR Congo are majority Christian, both 95%. PNG ranks 74/100 on the Gender Inequality Index and the DR Congo ranks 65/100, meaning high inequality between men and women. However, there are a lot of gaps in Tables 14.1 and 14.2. The most comprehensive data collection mechanism on this subject, the United Nations, does not report data on lifetime physical/sexual partner violence nor non-partner

Table 14.1 Gender-based violence in countries with the most Christians.

Rank	Country	Christians	% Christian	% lifetime physical/ sexual partner violence	% physical/ sexual partner violence last 12 months	% lifetime non- partner sexual violence	Gender Inequality Index*(max 100)
1	United States	245,457,098	74.2	N/A	6.0 **	N/A	18
2	Brazil	192,938,521	90.8	16.7	3.1	N/A	39
3	Mexico	123,370,089	95.7	24.6	9.5	38.8	31
4	Russia	119,945,103	82.2	N/A	6.0 **	N/A	20
5	China	106,018,155	7.4	N/A	8.0 **	N/A	19
6	Philippines	99,307,046	90.6	14.8	5.5	N/A	42
7	Nigeria	95,186,337	46.2	17.4	11.0	1.5	68
8	DR Congo	85,061,043	95.0	51.0	37.0	N/A	60
9	Ethiopia	67,902,667	59.1	28.0	20.0	N/A	52
10	India	66,315,897	4.8	28.8	22.0	N/A	49

Sources: UN Women Global Database on Violence against Women; Johnson and Zurlo 2022.
*UN Development Programme: Human Development Report 2022. A lower value indicates low inequality between women and men based on a combination of factors: maternal mortality, adolescent birth rate, share of parliamentary seats, share of secondary education, and participation in the labor force. Regional averages were calculated for countries not reported.
**Georgetown Institute for Women, Peace and Security (2022) Women, Peace and Security Index 2021/2022. Extracted from UN Women Global Database on Violence against Women 2021. Index captures the percentage of women who experienced physical or sexual violence committed by their intimate partner in the previous 12 months.

Table 14.2 Countries with the highest Gender Inequality Index scores.

Rank	Country	Christians	% Christian	% lifetime physical/ sexual partner violence	% physicalsexual partner violence last 12 months	% lifetime non-partner sexual violence	Gender Inequality Index*(max 100)
1	Yemen	16,500	0.1	N/A	18.2 **	N/A	82
2	Papua New Guinea	8,482,000	94.8	59.0	48.0	N/A	73
3	Nigeria	95,186,000	46.2	22.0	14.0	N/A	68
4	Afghanistan	7,500	0.0	51.0	46.0	N/A	68
5	Central African Republic	3,535,000	73.2	30.0	26.0	N/A	67
6	Chad	5,780,000	35.2	29.0	18.0	N/A	65
7	Liberia	2,085,000	41.2	50.0	35.0	2.6	65
8	Haiti	10,748,000	94.3	26.0	14.0	N/A	64
9	Sierra Leone	933,000	11.7	53.0	40.0	N/A	63
10	Mauritania	10,900	0.2	9.0	6.0	N/A	63

Sources: UN Women Global Database on Violence against Women; Johnson and Zurlo 2022.
*UN Development Programme: Human Development Report 2022. A lower value indicates low inequality between women and men based on a combination of factors: maternal mortality, adolescent birth rate, share of parliamentary seats, share of secondary education, and participation in the labor force. Regional averages were calculated for countries not reported.
**Georgetown Institute for Women, Peace and Security (2022) Women, Peace and Security Index 2021/2022. Extracted from UN Women Global Database on Violence against Women 2021. Index captures the percentage of women who experienced physical or sexual violence committed by their intimate partner in the previous 12 months.

violence in many countries, even where it is a known problem. These tables reveal a gaping chasm in our knowledge of violence against women, which raises the question: How can violence against women and girls be eliminated if the full extent of the problem is essentially unknown? A lack of data and knowledge naturally leads to a lack of power to enact change.

Routine denunciation of violence against women by Christian organizations is critical because such violence cannot be curbed without the help of religious institutions. Religious leaders help shape public opinion, moral values, and behavior expectations in society. As such, they have a responsibility to educate people on what constitutes GBV, how to prevent it, and how to help victims of abuse. Church leaders can begin with recognizing religious beliefs, texts, and teachings that perpetuate violence against women, as well as those that help women, while exploring new interpretations of scripture and tradition that eliminate roadblocks for victims and maximize the resources available to them (Fortune and Enger 2005). Faith-based interventions should happen not only in places of worship but across all levels of society, including among politicians, families, and community leaders.

Gender-specific Religious Persecution

Since the 1960s, Open Doors International has produced the World Watch List, which provides information about the top 50 most difficult countries to be a Christian. It is the most-cited resource for learning how to pray for and support Christians under persecution (Table 14.3).

It was only in 2018 that Open Doors International began reporting on the gendered realities of Christian persecution, focusing more explicitly on the experiences of Christian women. Christian men and women experience persecution very differently: "Persecution against Christian men is focused, severe and visible. Persecution against Christian women is violent, hidden and complex" (Miller et al. 2022, p. 2). Researchers have consistently found that Christian communities are weakened when persecutors exploit the social–cultural norms surrounding gender roles. In situations of persecution, men and boys are at risk for (in order of frequency) physical violence, psychological violence, economic harassment, imprisonment, and forced enlistment in the military or militia – all usually to remove them from positions of influence as financial providers and

Table 14.3 World Watch List 2022: 50 most difficult countries to be a Christian.

Rank	Country	Rank	Country
1	Afghanistan	26	Laos
2	North Korea	27	Morocco
3	Somalia	28	Indonesia
4	Libya	29	Bangladesh
5	Yemen	30	Colombia
6	Eritrea	31	Central African Republic
7	Nigeria	32	Burkina Faso
8	Pakistan	33	Niger
9	Iran	34	Bhutan
10	India	35	Tunisia
11	Saudi Arabia	36	Oman
12	Myanmar	37	Cuba
13	Sudan	38	Ethiopia
14	Iraq	39	Jordan
15	Syria	40	Democratic Republic of the Congo
16	Maldives	41	Mozambique
17	China	42	Türkiye
18	Qatar	43	Mexico
19	Vietnam	44	Cameroon
20	Egypt	45	Tajikistan
21	Uzbekistan	46	Brunei
22	Algeria	47	Kazakhstan
23	Mauritania	48	Nepal
24	Mali	49	Kuwait
25	Turkmenistan	50	Malaysia

Source: Open Doors International 2022a/Open Doors.

protectors. However, for women, persecution comes in the form of (in order of frequency) sexual violence, forced marriage, physical violence, psychological violence, and house arrest – all of which brings shame not only upon them, but their entire family and community. Women are widely perceived as being worth less than men, and the violence they experience is typically longer lasting (Miller et al. 2022).

Violence against women in the global South is often linked to accusations of witchcraft, a difficult problem to address because of differing understandings of witches and witchcraft across cultures. There is no comprehensive data available on the number of people accused, persecuted, or killed due to witchcraft, though it is widely observed that the majority are women and children. The lack of attention given to the subject in human rights discussions means there is also little information on the patterns of killings and how they can be prevented (UN General Assembly 2009). While the killing of witches is not uncommon in the Pacific Islands, where Christianity has grown quickly, it is not uncommon for Christians to continue consulting witchdoctors to handle challenges related to evil spirits, curses, and sorcery, such as in Papua New Guinea (Gallagher and Gallagher 2019). The killing of witches has also been observed in Central African Republic, Gabon, Burkina Faso, India, Ghana, Tanzania, South Africa, Angola, Mali, the Democratic Republic of the Congo, Nepal, Nigeria, Mexico, and Saudi Arabia (UN General Assembly 2009). In some of these cases, witchcraft is punishable in accordance with the nation's criminal code: women accused of witchcraft often face psychological trauma, physical harm, social exclusion, and other forms of violence.

Christian Responses to Gender-based Violence

International Christian organizations have launched campaigns denouncing gender-based violence and have provided resources to combat this issue, especially through education and support. Many do so in concert with UN Women's 16 Days of Activism Against Gender-Based Violence, which is an annual international campaign that runs from 25 November (the International Day for the Elimination of Violence Against Women) to 10 December (Human Rights Day). This tradition began in 1991 and is organized by the Center for Women's Global Leadership based at Rutgers University (New Jersey, US).

The World Council of Churches (WCC) inaugurated the Thursdays in Black campaign from its Decade of Solidarity with Women (1988–1998), which was the WCC's response to the United Nations Decade for Women (1976–1985). During this decade, stories of gender-based violence worldwide became more visible to the global church. Inspired by women's movements in Argentina, Israel, Palestine, Rwanda, Bosnia-Herzegovina, and South Africa, the WCC encourages Christian communities worldwide to wear black on Thursdays in support of victims of violence and has also released a Thursdays in Black Bible study series. Ambassadors for Thursdays in Black include both men and women from faith communities worldwide and is observed in partnership with the United Church of Christ, Lutheran World Federation, Religions for Peace, United Methodist Women, Finn Church Aid, Christian Aid, Presbyterian Women, the Anglican Communion, and the American Baptist Church.

While these global initiatives help bring awareness to pressing issues for women worldwide, they are limited, with responses more often coming from women, rather than the men that need to hear the message. In a response to the WCC's Decade of Solidarity with Women, a group of women acknowledged that "the Decade of Solidarity with Women became a decade of women in solidarity with women" (Decade Festival 1998). Finding faith-based solutions to problems impacting women requires commitment from the whole church, not only part of it.

Photo 14.1 Ecumenical women church leaders of the World Council of Churches observe Thursdays in Black toward a world without rape and violence (2022). *Source:* Albin Hillert used with permission from the WCC.

Africa

Despite the massive growth of Christianity in Africa over the twentieth century (9% Christian in 1900, 49% Christian in 2020; Johnson and Zurlo 2022), gender-based violence continues to be a serious problem on the continent. In many contexts, it continues to be culturally normative for women to be inferior to men, bolstered by biblical stories. Domestic violence is often linked to socioeconomic struggles, patriarchy that informs marriage relationships, as well as to the legacy of Western missionaries who imported new understandings of gender relations, drawing from biblical texts that subjugate women (Chisale 2018). For example, in an analysis of Christianity, gender-based violence, and the Bible in Botswana, biblical scholar Sidney K. Berman found that Christians uphold oppressive biblical teachings and patriarchal texts because they appear to be in line with traditional Tswana culture. The Setswana proverb, for instance, "cattle are never led by a cow, otherwise they will fall into a gorge" supports male leadership over women and suggests a convergence between traditional culture and violent biblical texts, such as the relationship between the prophet Hosea and his apparently unfaithful wife, Gomer (Berman 2015, p. 125). Berman states that "in both the Setswana traditional and Biblical contexts... seniority, authority and discipline often merge with abuse" (Berman 2015, p. 126). Findings from prominent African feminist theologians such as Isabel Phiri (2002), Philomena Mwaura (2010), and Lilian Cheelo Siwila (2012) support the conclusion that though churches are aware of the problem of domestic violence, women often choose silence to avoid further victimization. Fulata Moyo is a systematic feminist theologian from Malawi and a fierce advocate for gender justice. A survivor of sexual violence, she is a member of the Circle of Concerned African Women Theologians, was a visiting researcher at Harvard Divinity School, and has worked with the World Council of Churches and UNAIDS. Her study of matrilineal societies in Malawi revealed that instead of traditional strong matriarchies, pervasive patriarchies resulted from the presence of Christianity (Moyo 2016).

In Zimbabwe, more than one in three women suffer physical violence before the age of 15, and in general, violence against women – beatings, rape, child neglect, domestic violence – is increasing throughout the country (Magezi and Manzanga 2019). Although the government has

Photo 14.2 Liberian Nobel laureate Leymah Gbowee speaks at the Global Summit to End Sexual Violence in Conflict (2014). *Source:* Foreign, Commonwealth & Development Office/Flickr/CC BY 2.0.

made concerted efforts to curb GBV, its presence is complex and difficult to combat due to cultural, social, and religious norms. Although the country is majority Christian (82%; Johnson and Zurlo 2022), Christians are complicit in GBV, whether they are aware of it or not. Sexual abuse by pastors notwithstanding, women are marginalized in church settings, even though they make up the majority of congregants. Christian initiatives include the Tamar Campaign of the Anglican Diocese of Manicaland, which aims to reinterpret passages of scripture that appear to support male domination over women. The World Council of Churches launched the Ecumenical HIV and AIDS Initiative in Africa, which seeks to equip men to be more aware of the connection between GBV and HIV. Yet, much of the onus of change is on pastors of churches – who are typically male – to be outspoken against GBV and seek improved gender relations in their congregations and communities (Magezi and Manzanga 2019).

Asia

Christianity is a minority religion in Asia (8% of the population), a continent where most societies are patriarchal and proscribe women roles that typically expect them to be submissive, virtuous, soft-spoken, well-mannered, and faithful. Women experience discrimination and abuse in child marriage, lack of legal protections, unjust divorce laws, and human trafficking. With emphases on honor and shame in Asian cultures, sexual violence in the region, despite its prevalence, brings ignominy on a woman's family and community. In addition, female converts to Christianity often keep their faith a secret for fear of bringing shame to their families, thus reducing possibilities for interaction with other Christians for support.

While patriarchy in Islam is a hotly debated subject, in most North African and West Asian countries, women are considered second class to men and have severely restricted rights. For example, women are discriminated against in Islamic courts, where female testimony is worth less than that of males. In some Muslim-majority contexts, women are forced to wear the *hijab* or other face or full-body veil; in Sudan, Saudi Arabia, and Afghanistan, women have a required dress code and will face violence and/or legal prosecution if these laws are violated. In Afghanistan, women have chronically low education and employment rates, and suffer due to patrilineal inheritance traditions (Open Doors International 2022a). The Taliban takeover of the country in August 2021 meant the closure of girls' schools and the removal of women from most public areas. Female converts to Christianity have little social protection, common among them forced marriage, rape, abduction, and sex slavery.

Human trafficking, as defined by the United Nations, is "the recruitment, transport, transfer, harbouring or receipt of a person by such means as threat or use of force or other forms of coercion, abduction, fraud or deception for the purpose of exploitation" (UNODC 2022). Half of trafficked victims worldwide are adult women, and another one-third are girls. Women and girls are targeted for their economic vulnerability, often exacerbated by intimate partners, immigration status, limited language knowledge, and/or dysfunctional families. Half of all victims are trafficked for sexual exploitation, and another 38% for forced labor (for women, particularly domestic servitude). Among victims in Western and Southern Europe, 9% are from East Asia and the Pacific, 5% are from South Asia, and 8% are from North Africa and the Middle East; among victims in Central and Southeastern Europe, 10% are from Eastern Europe and Central Asia, and 24% from East Asia and the Pacific; among trafficking victims in North America, 18% are from East Asia, South Asia, and the Pacific. Most trafficked persons in the Middle East are from East Asia and the Pacific (28%), South Asia (14%), and elsewhere in the Middle East (38%). Men are two-thirds of those convicted of human trafficking (UNODC 2021).

China's former one-child policy created a gender imbalance in the country that is still impacting Christian communities in neighboring countries, where Christian women are being trafficked as brides. According to World Watch Research, using US State Department data, "traffickers have increasingly targeted impoverished Christian communities. For instance, 629 Pakistani girls, many of whom were Christian, were reportedly trafficked to China between 2018 and 2019. In Myanmar, women from the Christian-majority Kachin State have been trafficked, married and raped until they become pregnant" (Open Doors International (2022b)., p. 30). Thailand is a major hub for sex tourism and trafficking; although data are difficult to obtain, an estimated 2.3 million people are engaged in sex work. Sex tourism is 10% of all tourist money spent in Thailand, and the country is home to around 610,000 modern-day slaves (Langteau and Dunham 2021).

Trafficking is a global phenomenon, but there are numerous Christian initiatives in Asia to combat it. Chiang Mai, Thailand, is a destination for foreign mission organizations addressing the problem, such as the Connecting for Freedom Network, which unites 70 anti-trafficking organizations in northern Thailand (nearly 60 in Chiang Mai alone) (see Miles et al. 2014). The Faith Alliance Against Slavery and Trafficking (FAAST) also unites Christian organizations in solidarity against the issue. Members include Christian faith-based organizations, universities, mission organizations, and denominations. In Asia, FAAST members can be found in Indonesia, Cambodia, Bangladesh, India, Iraq, Kuwait, Nepal, the Philippines, and Tajikistan.

Latin America

Most countries in Latin America have laws and policies to combat, curb, and address gender-based violence, yet one-third of women in the region have experienced physical or sexual violence in their lifetime; 12% of women and girls between ages 15 and 49 experienced violence at the hands of their intimate partner in a 12-month period. Femicide is an ongoing problem, with at least 3,800 deaths of female fetuses in 2019 alone. During the COVID-19 pandemic, violence against women surged in Latin America and the Caribbean, dubbing GBV the "shadow pandemic." Reports of domestic violence against women rose by 51% in Colombia, 50% in Brazil, 39% in Argentina, and 30% in Mexico (United Nations Women 2020). In this region, GBV is compounded by armed conflict, structural racism, and lack of women's financial independence. Laws designed to protect women are irregularly enforced. Research has found that 24 of the 33 countries rely on what is called "first generation" laws from the 1990s that only protect the rights of survivors of domestic violence, that is, only protect the rights of women abused in their own home, not elsewhere (Essayag 2017). Between 2013 and 2016, "second generation" laws emerged in nine countries that take a more wholistic and comprehensive approach to protecting women and, depending on the country, cover issues such as feminicide, justice for abuse victims, and child protection. Bolivia was the first country in the region (2012) to have a specific law to punish acts committed against female political candidates and elected officials, including political harassment and violence.

Common themes among Latina theologians – whether Catholic or Protestant, conservative or liberal – include female responses to *machismo* culture, the discrimination, violence, and oppression of women in Latin American culture, and the agreement that traditional theology has historically overlooked women (Tamez 1989). Mexican theologian Elsa Tamez (b.1951) stated, "Liberation theology, when done from women's perspective, not only deals concretely with daily experience, but it is the basis, the point of departure for their theological work. Thus, not only is daily experience integral to their theology, but theology is transformed by the incorporation of women's life experience, especially that of poor women" (Tamez 1989, p. 4.). Moreover, among Catholic theologians, the Virgin Mary is an important symbol of liberation and action (Bidegain 1989) and is known as the mother of the poor (Gebara and Bingemer 2004). For Latina theologians, investigating their experiences and the struggle for liberation is essential for understanding God and how Latin American realities reveal God at work in the world. Overall, Latina theologians are making contributions so that "those who have been silenced are making themselves loudly heard" (de Rocchietti 1989, p. 109).

Churches are trusted institutions, and their leaders serve not only as spiritual guides, but also moral ones. Leaders have an important role to raise awareness of GBV and provide a platform for healing, though many remain silent on the issue. Some have been proactive, such as leaders in the Jamaica Council of Churches, an organization that has participated in the World Council of Churches Thursdays in Black campaign since 2017 and has publicly advocated for the rights of women and girls. Other examples include the Evangelical Lutheran Church of Brazil creating a "For a home without violence" campaign in 2020 to encourage churches to promote safe homes for women, and the Evangelical Church of the River Plate (Argentina, Uruguay, Paraguay) creating a "Pastoral Listening Guard" team of women volunteers to provide phone-based support for fellow women. In addition, the #ProtestantesActivandoDerechos campaign brought together Protestants in the region to advocate for the rights of women and girls.

Europe

The European Institute for Gender Equality has been measuring gender equality in the European Union (EU) roughly every two years since 2013. The index measures variables related to work, money, knowledge, time, power, health, violence against women, and intersecting inequalities. In 2020, the EU was ranked 67.9/100, indicating that it has a long way to go until achieving equality. The index has increased just 4.1 points since 2010 and 0.5 points since 2017. At this rate, it will take an additional 60 years for men and women to achieve gender parity in the EU. Women are making gains in full-time employment, parliamentary representation, and economic decision-making; yet women continue to do most of the unpaid care work, and women with disabilities continue to struggle to have their health needs met. The Istanbul Convention, a human rights treaty of the Council of Europe Convention, was intended to combat violence against women on the continent (2011, effective in 2014). Türkiye was the first country to ratify the agreement (although it withdrew in 2021), and another 45 European countries have joined. However, this legal framework, focused on preventing domestic violence and protecting victims of violence, has been critiqued by some Christian groups for not going far enough, such as the European Evangelical Alliance, which has called for nations to also address pornography and prostitution and their connection to GBV. Pope Francis has been outspoken against GBV, especially after upticks in violence during the COVID-19 lockdowns beginning in 2020, calling violence against women "almost satanic" (Pullella 2022).

The most comprehensive, and most recent, survey on violence against women in Europe was the 2012 survey by the Fundamental Rights Agency consisting of interviews with 42,000 women across the 28 member states of the European Union (European Union Agency for Fundamental Rights 2014; a new study is forthcoming in 2023). The study found that 33% of women had experienced physical and/or sexual violence since they were 15 years old; 8% of women had experienced it in the year prior to the survey; and 31% of women had experienced physical violence since the age of 15. Women in Latvia, Finland, and Denmark reported the highest rates of physical and sexual violence.

Roma communities in Europe maintain traditional gender roles, where men are economic providers and women are responsible for keeping the home and caring for children. However, Roma women experience intersectional discrimination and social exclusion based on their sex, ethnicity/race, class, and education (Milenković 2018). In these communities, people tend to trust their family networks more than the government, resulting in very low reporting rates of violence, especially domestic violence, against Roma women. In Albania, Montenegro, and North Macedonia, Roma women report lower literacy across all levels of education, and low employment. Arranged marriages are common, and it is culturally acceptable for husbands to be violent toward their wives. The growth of Pentecostalism among Roma people has been positively linked with decreases in crime and domestic violence, as well as improvements in the status of women (Wachsmuth 2017).

The Sophia Network – a UK-based group that advocates for gender equality and women in church leadership – issued their Minding the Gap survey of women in UK churches in 2017. Two-thirds of respondents had experienced sexism in the church, such as having their calling into ministry questioned and being limited to traditional church roles; 42% said that a lack of theological understanding of women and men working together was a barrier to women in leadership (Sophia Network 2018). A survey by the World Evangelical Alliance and the Lausanne Movement of 500 Evangelical Christian women worldwide identified gender-based violence and sexism as two of the church's biggest obstacles. As a result, the Europe-based Rise in Strength network met in 2019 in Amsterdam to recognize the struggle of women in Christian contexts and issued a call: "We call on men and women of the global Church to act so that women, men, girls and boys can all embrace their spiritual giftings to strengthen the work of the Church, and Her witness to the glory of God" (Global Consultation for Women 2019).

North America

In the United States, one in five women have experienced rape (attempted or completed) during her lifetime (Smith et al. 2018). Forty-four percent of women have experienced some form of contact sexual violence in their lifetime, with 43% reporting it happened before age 18. Nearly one in six women is a victim of stalking, and a quarter of women have experienced intimate partner violence. Native American and Alaska Native women experience assault and domestic violence at rates higher than any other ethnic group; over 84% of Native women have experienced violence in their lifetime and 67% have experienced psychological abuse (Rosay 2016). Indigenous women and girls are also murdered at 10 times the rates of other ethnicities and there are over 9,500 missing indigenous American Indian and Alaska Native women and girls, most of whom under the age of 18 (Operation Lady Justice 2021). Forty-five percent of Black women have experienced intimate partner physical/sexual violence or stalking, many of whom develop symptoms of posttraumatic stress disorder (Smith et al. 2017; Breiding et al. 2014).

Sociologist Nancy Nason-Clark pioneered the intersection of gender-based violence and Christianity in the North American context, identifying how churches fail to respond adequately to disclosures of sexual, physical, and psychological abuse (McPhillips and Page 2021; Nason-Clark 2000, 2003). Women in North American congregations, especially Evangelical ones, are more likely to endure abusive marriages, keep silent, and downplay abuse under the banner of "family values." This is particularly the case for women abused by husbands who are church leaders. Nason-Clark's study of Evangelical Protestant churches in Canada revealed that leaders were reluctant to look outside of their faith perspective for solutions to domestic violence, nor were they likely to partner with secular organizations to help prevent or respond to it (Nason-Clark 1996).

The United States is home to more guns than people, and firearms are routinely used to control and intimidate victims and survivors of domestic violence, mainly women. The combination of domestic violence and guns is deadly – most murders of women by male intimate partners are killed with firearms (Violence Policy Center 2021). Black women are twice as likely to die from gun violence than White women; 91% of Black victims knew their murderer. Prior domestic violence against women was a warning sign in most recent cases of mass shootings in the US (Claiborne and Martin 2019). Most religious groups in the United States support some form of gun control, but there is a wide spectrum. Catholics (both White and of color), Evangelicals of color, and mainline Protestants generally support background checks for all gun sales (ranging from 90% to 92% in favor) and assault weapon bans (62%–73% in favor). However, White Evangelicals are the outlier in both cases: 84% of White Evangelicals support universal background checks and just 47% support a ban on assault weapons (Burge 2018). White Evangelicals also believe that it should be easier for people to obtain a concealed-carry gun permit, not harder (54%, compared to non-White Evangelicals at 34%). Among both men and women in White Evangelical communities, there is a connection between spirituality and gun ownership, as well as a felt need to protect and defend their communities (Vegter and Kelley 2020). Many religious leaders are involved in gun control advocacy, such as Clergy for Safe Cities, which has trained more than 500 faith leaders on best practices to reduce gun violence in their communities. Other groups include the LIFE FREE Campaign (California), Chester Community Coalition (Pennsylvania), ENGAGE: Lutherans for Gun Violence Prevention (Minnesota), and Bishops United Against Gun Violence (Episcopal; nationwide).

Oceania

The cultural expectations of men and women in the Pacific Islands provide a foundation for potential abuse and exploitation of women (Prior 2021; Carroll 2021). Violence against women is especially severe in Papua New Guinea, Solomon Islands, Vanuatu, New Caledonia, and Fiji – even though these countries are majority Christian. Two-thirds of women in Papua New Guinea have experienced domestic violence; in March 2019 alone, 23 murders of women were attributed to domestic violence (Human Rights Watch 2020). The Catholic Church has been on the forefront of combatting violence against women in Papua New Guinea beginning with the Catholics' Bishops Conference declaring in 1987 that marriages should be violence-free (Eves 2012). One important strategy is to make women's medical clinics more accessible throughout the country. Churches have an important role to combat violence as the central institution in many Pacific societies with a great deal of authority, a strong value system, and a message of equality (Eves 2012).

Women in Fiji experience one of the highest rates of violence in the world, with upward of 74% of women having experienced physical, sexual and/or emotional violence in their lifetimes (UN Women 2021). Many churches support programs to combat gender-based violence. For example, the Anglican Diocese of Polynesia has adopted a zero-tolerance policy concerning violence against women and children in the church and at home. The House of Sarah runs 21 Sarah Centers in Anglican, Methodist, Catholic, Seventh-day Adventist, and Salvation Army churches, providing counseling services, workshops for preventing GBV, and other services for victims and vulnerable populations in Fiji and throughout the South Pacific. The House of Sarah works closely with the government on the Fiji National Plan of Action of Prevention of Violence Against Women and Girls.

Despite efforts by Christians to address violence against women in Oceania, the problem has not been adequately addressed by the region's churches. Oceanic patriarchy is directly linked to forms of violence, especially violence against women (Filemoni-Tofaeono and Johnson 2016). Theological justifications for violence are common, such as the "men of God" who lead churches without being challenged for their beliefs and behaviors toward women. Pacific Island culture values hospitality, generosity, and respect for authority, but women bear the burden of upholding these cultural responsibilities, even in societies with more matriarchal tendencies.

Conclusion

Part of addressing gender-based violence is care for victims: listening, healing, and reconciling. Practical resources are available, written from biblical and theological perspectives, to help churches, their leaders, and their congregations take seriously domestic violence and other forms of gender-based violence (see, for example, Reed 2009; Pellauer 1987; Murphy 2003; Nason-Clark 2000; Nason-Clark, Fisher-Townsend, and Fahlberg 2013). Fulata Moyo has contributed significantly to this area, drawing upon a holistic notion of mission as healing and wholeness, prioritizing victims' stories, and building on the communitarian concept of *Ubuntu* found across Africa (Moyo 2020). *Ubuntu* holds "I am because you are, and since we are, therefore I am." This kind of togetherness upholds victims as they seek restoration from their trauma. From her experience of working with women in Nigeria, Sierra Leone, and South Sudan, Moyo observes that churches in these countries include trauma healing as part of their peace and reconciliation programs, and thus advocate for restorative, not punitive, justice. Healing together is the key, and churches should make it a priority that membership includes the right to enjoy life and live it to the fullest without fear. Violence, discrimination, and restricted civil liberties do not only hurt women, but they hurt the families and faith communities that women uphold everywhere around the world.

Reflection Questions

1) A chronic lack of data and knowledge is a fundamental problem in ending violence against women and girls worldwide. What can Christians do to educate themselves on this issue and take action to combat it? Reflect particularly on churches' track record of overlooking violence against women, and issues related to scripture and gender-based violence.
2) Examine how patriarchal and patrilineal traditions are connected to the exploitation of women. How have governing structures in different countries played a role in perpetuating violence against women? How aware do you think Christians are of the systemic causes of violence against women and girls? Does the church have a role in addressing gender inequalities in reproductive health, political empowerment, and the labor market?
3) Describe some of the measures that Christian organizations have taken to combat gender-based violence, such as the WCC's Thursdays in Black campaign. In your opinion, how effective are these measures? What impact might Christians have to address these issues in the areas of law, government, and policy?

Works Cited

Berman, Sidney K. (2015). Of God's image, violence against women and feminist reflections. *Studia Historiae Ecclesiasticae*, 41(1), 122–137.

Bidegain, Ana María (1989). Women and the theology of liberation. In: *Through Her Eyes: Women's Theology from Latin America* (ed. Elsa Tamez). Maryknoll, NY: Orbis Books.

Breiding, Matthew J., Smith, Sharon G., Basile, Kathleen C., Walters, Mikel L., Chen, Jieru, and Merrick, Melissa T. (2014). Prevalence and characteristics of sexual violence, stalking, and intimate partner violence victimization — national intimate partner and sexual violence survey, United States, 2011. *Morbidity and Mortality Weekly Report: Surveillance Summaries*, 63(8), 1–18.

Burge, Ryan (2018). Which religions support gun control in the US? (ed. Jana Riess), Religion News. https://religionnews.com/2019/08/29/which-religions-support-gun-control-in-the-us (accessed 24 May 2022).

Carroll, Seforosa (2021). Speaking up! Speaking out! Naming the silences. In: *Contemporary Feminist Theologies* (ed. Kerrie Handasyde, Cathryn McKinney, and Rebekah Pryor), 9–20. Abingdon, Oxon: Routledge, Taylor & Francis Group.

Chisale, Sinenhlanhla S. (2018). Domestic abuse in marriage and self-silencing: pastoral care in a context of self-silencing. *HTS Teologiese Studies/Theological Studies*, 74(2), 4784.

Claiborne, Shane and Martin, Michael (2019). *Beating Guns: Hope for People Who are Weary of Violence*. Grand Rapids, MI: Brazos Press, a division of Baker Publishing Group.

Conceição, Pedro (2019). *Human Development Report 2019: beyond income, beyond averages, beyond today: inequalities in human development in the 21st century*. New York: UNDP.

de Rocchietti, Aracely E. (1989). Women and the people of God. In: *Through Her Eyes: Women's Theology from Latin America* (ed. Elsa Tamez), 96–117. Maryknoll, NY: Orbis Books.

Decade Festival of the Churches in Solidarity with Women (1998). From solidarity to accountability: letter to the eighth assembly of the World Council of churches from the women and men of the Decade Festival of the Churches in Solidarity with Women. World Council of Churches. https://www.oikoumene.org/resources/documents/from-solidarity-to-accountability (accessed 28 April 2022).

Essayag, Sebastián (2017). *From commitment to action: policies to end violence against women in Latin America and the Caribbean: regional analysis document*. Panama: United Nations Development Programme and United Nations Women.

European Union Agency for Fundamental Rights (2014). *Violence against Women: An EU-Wide Survey*. Luxembourg: Publications Office of the European Union.

Eves, Richard (2012). Christianity, masculinity and gender violence in Papua New Guinea. State, Society and Governance in Melanesia Discussion paper 2012/2, 1–17.

Filemoni-Tofaeono, Joan and Johnson, Lydia (2016). *Reweaving the Relational Mat: A Christian Response to Violence against Women from Oceania*. New York: Taylor and Francis.

Fortune, Marie M. and Enger, Cindy G. (2005). Violence against women and the role of religion. Applied Research Forum, National Online Resource Center on Violence Against Women.

Gallagher, Sarita D. and Gallagher, Luisa J. (2019). Pentecostalism in Papua New Guinea. In: *Asia Pacific Pentecostalism* (ed. Denise A. Austin, Jacqueline Grey, and Paul W. Lewis), 325–346. Leiden: Brill.

Gebara, Ivone and Bingemer, Maria Clara (2004). *Mary, Mother of God, Mother of the Poor*. Eugene, OR: Wipf and Stock.

General Assembly Resolution 48/104 Declaration on the Elimination of Violence against Women (1993). 23 Feb. A/48/PV.85. New York: United Nations.

Georgetown Institute for Women, Peace and Security (2022). Women, peace and security index 2021/2022. https://giwps.georgetown.edu/the-index (accessed 24 May 2022).

Global Consultation for Women in International Christian Leadership (2019). Call to all Christians. Amsterdam.

Human Rights Watch (2020). Papua New Guinea: events of 2019. https://www.hrw.org/world-report/2020/country-chapters/papua-new-guinea# (accessed 8 November 2021).

Jeyaraj, Sheela and Anderson-Rajkumar, Evangeline (2019). Gender. In: *Christianity in South and Central Asia* (ed. Kenneth R. Ross, Daniel Jeyaraj, and Todd M. Johnson). Edinburgh: Edinburgh University Press.

Johnson, Todd M. and Zurlo, Gina A. ed. (2022). *World Christian Database*. Leiden/Boston: Brill.

Kamionkowski, Tamar (2021). Violence against women in the Hebrew Bible. In: *The Shalvi/Hyman Encyclopedia of Jewish Women* (ed. Jennifer Sartori), https://jwa.org/encyclopedia/article/violence-against-women-in-the-hebrew-bible (accessed 27 April 2022).

King, Sophie and Sifaki, Eleni (2019). Ending domestic violence: the politics of global norm diffusion. In: *Negotiating Gender Equity in the Global South: The Politics of Domestic Violence Policy* (ed. Sohela Nazneen, Sam Hickey, and Eleni Sifaki), 44–66. London: Routledge.

Langteau, James D. and Dunham, Timothy D. (2021). Sex trafficking and slavery in Southeast Asia: to free captives. *Liberty University Journal of Statesmanship & Public Policy*, 2(1), article 4, 1–14

Magezi, Vhumani and Manzanga, Peter (2019). Gender-based violence and efforts to address the phenomenon: towards a church public pastoral care intervention proposition for community development in Zimbabwe. *HTS Teologiese Studies/Theological Studies*, 75(4), a5532.

McPhillips, Kathleen and Page, Sarah-Jane (2021). Introduction: religion, gender and violence. *Religion and Gender*, 11, 151–165.

Melanchthon, Monica Jyotsna and Whitaker, Robyn J. (2021). *Terror in the Bible: Rhetoric, Gender, and Violence*. Atlanta, GA: SBL Press.

Milenković, Nataša (2018). Nowhere to turn: gender-based violence against Roma women. United Nations Development Programme.

Miles, Glenn et al. (2014). *Stopping the Traffick: A Christian Response to Sexual Exploitation and Trafficking*. Eugene, OR: Wipf & Stock.

Miller, Elizabeth L., Brown, Eva, Fisher, Helene, and Morley, Rachel (2022). Invisible: the gender report 2022. Open Doors International.

Morgan, Rachel E. and Thompson, Alexandra (2021). Criminal victimization, 2020. US Department of Justice, Officer of Justice Programs, Bureau of Justice. NCJ 301775.

Moyo, Fulata L. (2016). A discussion with Fulata L. Moyo, World Council of Churches. Berkley Center for Religion, Peace & World Affairs, Georgetown University. https://berkleycenter.georgetown.edu/interviews/a-discussion-with-fulata-l-moyo-world-council-of-churches (accessed 23 May 2022).

Moyo, Fulata L. (2020). Healing together: mission as a journey of healing traumatic memories. *International Review of Mission*, 109(1), 5–14.

Murphy, Nancy (2003). *God's Reconciling Love: A Pastor's Handbook on Domestic Violence*. Seattle: FaithTrust Institute.

Mwaura, Philomena (2010). Gender based violence: a pastoral challenge for the church in Africa. *Journal of Constructive Theology–Gender, Religion and Theology in Africa*, 16(1), 102–119.

Nason-Clark, Nancy (1996). Religion and violence against women: exploring the rhetoric and response of evangelical churches in Canada. *Social Compass*, 43(4), 515–536.

Nason-Clark, Nancy (2000). Making the sacred safe: woman abuse and communities of faith. *Sociology of Religion*, 61(4), 349–368.

Nason-Clark, Nancy (2003). The making of a survivor: rhetoric and reality in the study of religion and abuse. In: *Challenging Religion: Essays in Honour of Eileen Barker* (ed. James A. Beckford and James T. Richardson), 164–173. London: Routledge.

Nason-Clark, Nancy, Fisher-Townsend, Barbara, and Fahlberg, Victoria ed. (2013). *Strengthening Families and Ending Abuse: Churches and Their Leaders Look to the Future*. Eugene, OR: Wipf & Stock.

Nason-Clark, Nancy, Fisher-Townsend, Barbara, Holtmann, Catherine, and McMullin, Stephen (2018). *Religion and Intimate Partner Violence: Understanding the Challenges and Proposing Solutions*. New York: Oxford University Press.

Nazneen, Sohela (2019). Building strategic relationships with the political elites: the politics of Bangladesh's Domestic Violence Act 2010. In: *Negotiating Gender Equity in the Global South: The Politics of Domestic Violence Policy* (ed. Sohela Nazneen, Sam Hickey, and Eleni Sifaki), 129–151. London: Routledge.

OECD (2022). Violence against women (indicator). doi: 10.1787/f1eb4876-en (accessed 25 April 2022).

Open Doors International (2022a). The 2022 World Watch List: 52 weeks of prayer for persecuted Christians.

Open Doors International (2022b). *WWL 2022 compilation of pressure points and gender SRP profiles for countries ranking 1–76*. World Watch Research.

Operation Lady Justice (2021). *2020 missing American Indian and Alaska Native persons data*. FBI's National Crime Information Center missing person file.

Pellauer, Mary D. (1987). *Sexual Assault and Abuse - a Handbook for Clergy and Religious Professionals*. San Francisco: Harper and Row.

Pepper, Miriam and Powell, Ruth (2022). Domestic and family violence: responses and approaches across the Australian churches. *Religions*, 13(3), 270.

Phiri, Isabel Apawo (2002). Why does God allow our husbands to hurt us? overcoming violence against women. *Journal of Theology for Southern Africa*, 114, 19–30.

Prior, Randall A. (2021). Vanuatu. In: *Christianity in Oceania* (ed. Kenneth R. Ross, Katalina Tahaafe-Williams, and Todd M. Johnson), 100–107. Edinburgh: Edinburgh University Press.

Pullella, Philip (2022). Violence against women insults God, pope says in New Year's message. Reuters, January 1. https://www.reuters.com/world/violence-against-women-insults-god-pope-says-new-years-speech-2022-01-01 (accessed 24 May 2022).

Reed, Lou (2009). When domestic violence knocks: it's all too common but rarely acknowledged. How to minister wisely and well when it shows up in your congregation. *Leadership*, 30(4), Fall, 74–78.

Rosay, André B. (2016). Violence against American Indian and Alaska Native Women and Men: 2010 findings from the national intimate partner and sexual violence survey. https://www.ncjrs.gov/pdffiles1/nij/249736.pdf (accessed 24 May 2022).

Saikia, Nandita, Meh, Catherine, Ram, Usha, Bora, Jayanta K., Mishra, Bhaskar, Chandra, Shailaja, and Jha, Prabhat (2021). Trends in missing females at birth in India from 1981–2016: analyses of 2.1 million birth histories in nationally representative surveys. *The Lancet Global Health*, 9(6), E813–E821.

Siwila, Lilian (2012). In search of a feminist cultural analysis model for effective dialogue on harmful cultural practices. *Journal of Gender and Religion in Africa, Special Issue*, 18(2), 105–120.

Smith, Sharon G., Chen, Jieru, Basile, Kathleen C., Gilbert, Leah K., Merrick, Melissa T., Patel, Nimesh, Walling, Margie, and Jain, Anurag (2017). The National Intimate Partner and Sexual Violence Survey (NISVS): 2010–2012 state report. Atlanta: National Center for Injury Prevention and Control, Centers for Disease Control and Prevention.

Smith, Sharon G., Zhang, Xinjian, Basile, Kathleen C., Merrick, Melissa T., Wang, J., Kresnow, Marcie-jo, and Chen, Jieru (2018). The National Intimate Partner And Sexual Violence Survey: 2015 data brief – updated release. Centers for Disease Control and Prevention.

Sophia Network (2018). *Minding the Gap: Women in the Church: Experiences, Barriers and Hopes.*

Tamez, Elsa (1989). Introduction: the power of the naked. In: *Through Her Eyes: Women's Theology from Latin America* (ed. Elsa Tamez). Maryknoll, NY: Orbis Books. 1-14.

Trible, Phyllis (1984). *Texts of Terror: Literary-Feminist Readings of Biblical Narratives*. Philadelphia: Fortress Press.

UN General Assembly (2009). Promotion and protection of all human rights, civil, political, economic, social and cultural rights, including the right to development. A/ HRC/11/2.

United Nations Department of Economic and Social Affairs (2022). Goal 5: achieve gender equality and empower all women and girls. https://sdgs.un.org/goals/goal5 (accessed 26 April 2022).

United Nations Statistics Division (2020). Global SDG indicators database. https://unstats.un.org/sdgs/indicators/database (accessed 26 April 2022).

United Nations Women (2020). Impact of COVID-19 on violence against women and girls in Latin America and the Caribbean. BRIEF v 1.1. 23.04.2020.

United Nations Women (2021). Christian communities in Fiji use faith-based approaches to prevent violence against women. Impact Story.

UNODC (United Nations Office on Drugs and Crime) (2020). *Global Report on Trafficking in Persons 2020*. Vienna: United Nations publication, sales no. E.20.IV.3.

UNODC (United Nations Office on Drugs and Crime) (2021). *Global Report on Trafficking in Persons 2020*. New York: United Nations.

UNODC (United Nations Office on Drugs and Crime) (2022). Human trafficking FAQs. https://www.unodc.org/unodc/en/human-trafficking/faqs.html (accessed 23 May 2022).

UN Women (United Nations Entity for Gender Equality and the Empowerment of Women) (2019). UN Women Global Database on Violence against Women. New York. http://evaw-global-database.unwomen.org (accessed 26 April 2022).

Vegter, Abigail and Kelley, Margaret (2020). The Protestant ethic and the spirit of gun ownership. *Journal for the Scientific Study of Religion*, 59(3), 526–540.

Violence Policy Center (2021). When men murder women: an analysis of 2019 homicide data. http://www.vpc.org/studies/wmmw2017.pdf (accessed 23 May 2022).

Wachsmuth, Melody J. (2017). Roma Pentecostals in Croatia and Serbia. *Spiritus*, 2(1–2), 99–118.

WomenStats Project (2018). Comprehensive scale of rape. https://www.womanstats.org/substatics/LRW-SCALE-11-2018.png (accessed 26 April 2022).

WomenStats Project (2019a). Physical security of women. https://www.womanstats.org/substatics/MULTIVAR-SCALE-1-2019-2.png (accessed 26 April 2022).

WomenStats Project (2019b). Governmental participation by women. https://www.womanstats.org/substatics/GP-SCALE-1-2019.png (accessed 26 April 2022). Governmental participation by women examines national legislative bodies and cabinet positions (not judiciaries due to lack of available data).

WomenStats Project (2019c). Trafficking of women. https://www.womanstats.org/substatics/TRAFF-SCALE-1-2019.png (accessed 26 April 2022).

World Watch Research (2022a). Afghanistan WWL 2022 Full Country Dossier.

World Watch Research (2022b). China WWL 2022 Full Country Dossier.

15

Christian Women and Ecology

"We shall awaken from our dullness and rise vigorously toward justice. If we fall in love with creation deeper and deeper, we will respond to its endangerment with passion."

Hildegard of Bingen (1098–1179)

Kiribati is an island nation in the Pacific Ocean, consisting of 32 atolls and one raised coral island. Half of the country's 122,000 people live on the Tarawa atoll. Christianity first arrived in 1856 via the American Board of Commissioners for Foreign Missions with personnel from Hawai'i, followed by a Samoan with the London Missionary Society in 1870 and Catholic missionaries in 1888. All of Kiribati was Christian by the turn of the century, and today it is 97% Christian (Johnson and Zurlo 2022). Islanders are particularly concerned about rising waters, with portions of the country only six feet above sea level. More than other groups, climate change impacts society's most vulnerable as well as those heavily reliant on the environment. Women bear a greater burden of environmental challenges: having less access to decision-making processes compounds inequalities and prevents them from full participation in climate-related planning, policymaking, and implementation.

Most global environmental political scholars and policymakers do not seriously consider gender in their work (Detraz 2017). Generally left out of discussions on climate policies, women lack access to funds to combat change, and are not among the highest ranks of decision-makers, either nationally or internationally. The 2021 United Nations Climate Change Conference (COP26) stressed the importance of involving people of faith, especially those who are indigenous, to help solve the climate crisis. Religious leaders can shape public opinion on environmental issues and share practical steps to address them. An increasing number of faith leaders recognize the religious imperative of protecting the Earth and are participating in social movements and theological reflection to ensure a greater quality of life. COP26 also included a Gender Day, where many countries pledged to further integrate gender into their climate finance plans – although, notably, only 10 of the 140 leaders at COP26 were women.

Women are victims of environmental degradation, but they are also powerful agents of renewal. Despite prescribed roles for women from both Christianity and culture, women around the world are taking the challenges of climate change seriously and are acting from their faith to ensure the survival of their communities today and their flourishing tomorrow. This chapter discusses the intersection of climate change advocacy and the ecotheologies of Christian women worldwide, identifying the inextricable connection between climate action and women's empowerment. Christian women choose many paths for environmental activism, from faith-based approaches at the local level to working with large secular international justice organizations. Some women's advocacy is political in nature, while others' is theological. Some are overt in the connection between their faith and their activism, others less so. All are concerned about the ecological future of the planet, and all recognize the urgency of climate activism.

Photo 15.1 A member of the Church of Sweden protests during Youth and Public Empowerment Day at COP26 in Glasgow, Scotland (2021). *Source:* LWF/Albin Hillert.

Global Ecological Challenges

Climate change, food insecurity, natural disasters, land issues, and a host of other environmental challenges are not new to the twenty-first century, but they have been exacerbated by increased industrial output, overreliance on limited natural resources, and intense political debates. The global scientific community unanimously agrees that global warming and climate change are real. The evidence is irrefutable:

- The Earth's temperature has risen by 0.14ºF per decade since 1880. Over the last 40 years, the rate has been even faster: 0.32ºF per decade. 2020 was the second warmest year on record, and the other nine records have all occurred since 2005 (Lindsey and Dahlman 2021).
- Sea levels have risen 8–9 inches since 1880 and 3.6 inches since 1993, reaching a record high in 2020 (Lindsey 2022).
- In 2020, the Annual Greenhouse Gas Index, developed by the National Oceanic and Atmospheric Administration, reported a 47% increase in greenhouse gas emissions since 1990. Carbon dioxide accounts for 80% of the increase (Lindsey 2021).
- Since the first measurements were taken in the 1970s, Arctic sea ice has decreased in all recorded months and virtually everywhere it exists. In 1985, very thick ice accounted for 33% of all Arctic ice; in 2020, it was less than 5% (Lindsey and Scott 2021).

Other evidence includes ocean acidification, decreased snow cover, extreme weather patterns, decline in crop outputs, coastal erosion, increased poverty, and forced migration (both rural to urban and cross-national). If not addressed, the effects of climate change could push an additional 35–122 million people into poverty by the year 2030 (Rozenberg and Hallegatte 2015). Much of this ecological change is caused by human activities, such as burning fossil fuels (coal, oil, natural gas), industrial agricultural practices, and increased urbanization (Reid 2014). Wealthy, industrialized nations are largely responsible for these changes, placing the burden of impact on smaller and poorer countries.

The 2015 Paris Agreement (also called the Paris Accord or Paris Climate Accords) is a legally binding international treaty on climate change that covers mitigation efforts, adaptation, and financial aspects of global environmental challenges. Negotiated by 196 countries at the United Nations Climate Change Conference near Paris, France, its goal, according to its website, is to "limit global warming to well below 2ºC, preferably 1.5ºC, compared to pre-industrial levels," with a major emphasis on reducing greenhouse gas emissions. The Agreement was a watershed moment for global climate advocacy, yet progress toward the Agreement's goals has been slow, and by 2022, the world was not on track for meeting them. The Intergovernmental Panel on Climate Change (IPCC) 2022 report raised alarms particularly for policymakers, where progress has been consistently stymied due to political in-fighting. The IPCC working group called for big, governmental actions, stating that, "It is clear now that minor, marginal, reactive or incremental changes won't be sufficient" to reverse the impact of climate change (IPCC 2022).

Gendered Impacts of Ecological Challenges

The poorest, most marginalized groups have the fewest opportunities to combat the impact of climate change in their communities. In much of the global South, men work away from the home, while women care for small plots of land to provide food for their families. Women make up 43% of the agricultural workforce in developing countries, but they have unequal access to land and other necessary resources like fertilizers, seeds, and labor (United Nations Human Development Programme 2019). In nearly all regions, more women than men work in vulnerable kinds of employment, defined as unpaid work, family contributions, or self-employment.

In Africa, women contribute 40% of food and crop production (Christiaensen and Demery 2018; Palacios-Lopez, Christiaensen, and Kilic 2017), account for nearly half of all farm labor (Raney et al. 2011), and 70% of food processors (Malabo 2021). In Libya, women make up 70% of the economically active population in agriculture, and in Lesotho, they make up 67% (Alexander, Nabalamba, and Mublia 2011). Yet, women only own 15% of land in Africa (Habtezion 2012), and their land tends to be less fertile than that of men.

Women are also the main users and carriers of water, making water sanitation a gendered human rights issue. In Bangladesh, local sources of freshwater are being contaminated with salt water from natural disasters and new weather patterns, forcing women to travel longer distances to find freshwater. The added time impacts their other duties, such as making food, which can in turn lead to husbands becoming violent with their wives for not properly performing their household chores. Women in Africa carry 71% of the burden of drinking water collection (United Nations 2012), and as the primary child bearers and family providers, they especially feel the effects of poor water supply and quality (Hellum, Kameri-Mbote, and van Koppen 2015). A 2020 study on the association between water access and intimate partner violence (IPV) in Nepal found that lower quality water in a household consistently elevates women's exposure to all forms of IPV (Choudhary et al. 2020). In Fiji, women walk 1–3 miles each way to access clean water to bathe, wash, and drink, and must walk even longer during drought, which is especially dangerous for young girls. Water rights are clearly connected to other rights: the right for food, health, life, safety, and equality.

In a study of 141 countries, natural disasters and their impacts between 1981 and 2002 killed more women than men (Reid 2014). In fact, women and children are 14 times more likely than men to die during a natural disaster (United Nations Women n.d.). Addressing gender inequalities not only helps women, but entire communities. According to the United Nations, "closing the gender gap in agricultural productivity would increase crop production by 7–19 percent in Ethiopia, Malawi, Rwanda, Tanzania, and Uganda" (United Nations Human Development Programme 2019, p. 163). In many places, the impact of climate change and violence against women are intricately bound. Threats to rural economies, of which women play a major role, force young women to leave their farms and migrate to urban centers. In search of employment, some have no choice but prostitution, which is often illegal and leads to violence and poor health. The greater threats to agricultural life, the more women experience exacerbating gender disparities.

Identifying the gendered dynamics of environmental challenges is important, not only because women are disproportionately impacted by these challenges, but because sustainability requires understanding a wide range of perspectives and experiences to adequately stop undesired environmental change (Detraz 2017). Considering women's experiences brings another set of questions to the problems, demanding more inclusive solutions. The term "ecofeminism" was coined by French writer and activist Françoise d'Eaubonne in 1974 to identify an emerging movement of women around the world working to save the environment (see section below). While not all women activists around the world identify with the term "ecofeminism," seeing feminism as a Western ideology, they are nevertheless working at the intersection of gender rights and environmental activism. Taking a gendered approach to sustainability and ecological issues helps move away from the domination narratives that encourage (primarily) men to conquer the Earth and exploit it for supposed human benefit. Instead, women – especially indigenous women – perceive a much closer connection between humans and ecosystems; the Earth gives life and should be respected as such. Capitalistic growth at all costs is ultimately detrimental to the environment (Detraz 2017).

Christian Responses to Ecological Challenges

Churches around the world have not been silent on ecological issues, though some Christian traditions have been more outspoken than others. Many churches have made definitive statements and steps toward environmental justice, the most notable of which was Pope Francis's encyclical, *Laudato Si': On Care for Our Common Home* (2015). Calling on the example of St. Francis of Assisi, the patron saint of animals and ecology, Pope Francis stressed the necessity of repairing humanity's relationship with the Earth. Much of his letter is theological and advocates for a re-reading of the creation narrative in Genesis. Instead of humans having dominion over the Earth, Pope Francis emphasized the tilling and keeping of land, which he reinterpreted as caring, protecting, overseeing, and preserving the Earth – not dominating it.

Evelyn Tucker, codirector of the Forum on Religion and Ecology at Yale University, has emphasized religion's moral force in advocating for vulnerable populations disproportionately affected by climate change (Council on Foreign Relations 2020). Tucker and other activists have called for "ecological conversions" and an "integral ecology" that align with both the biblical and moral mandates to care for creation. A joint statement from Greek Orthodox Ecumenical Patriarchate Bartholomew I, Pope Francis, and Archbishop of Canterbury Justin Welby (Anglican) made theological arguments for the moral imperative of protecting creation, citing the God-given responsibility of stewardship, the disproportionate impact of climate crises on the world's poor, and the utmost necessity of addressing this crisis now for the sake of future generations. Together, they stated,

> This is the first time that the three of us feel compelled to address together the urgency of environmental sustainability, its impact on persistent poverty, and the importance of global cooperation. Together, on behalf of our communities, we appeal to the heart and mind of every Christian, every believer and every person of good will. We pray for our leaders … to

decide the future of our planet and its people. Again, we recall Scripture: "choose life, so that you and your children may live" (Dt 30:19). Choosing life means making sacrifices and exercising self-restraint.

(Bartholomew, Francis and Welby 2021, n.p.)

The world's largest ecumenical body, the World Council of Churches, has numerous initiatives that address environmental issues, and has held multiple consultations on the topic since the 1970s, including discussions on the intersection of gender and climate change. Initiatives include the Working Group on Climate Change, the Ecumenical Water Network, an Eco-School on Water, Food and Climate Justice, and Economic and Ecological Justice.

Ecofeminism and Ecofeminist Theology

Canadian theologian Heather Eaton describes ecofeminism:

Ecofeminism is about connections between ecological and feminist concerns. It is a way of discerning associations of many kinds between the feminist and ecological movements, and between the oppression and domination of women and the oppression and domination of the earth. Ecofeminism is an insight, an exposition of current problems, and an eco-political strategy. It refers to critical analyses, political actions, historical research, intuitions and ideals.

(Eaton 2005, pp. 2–3)

A new world emerged for the first generation of feminist theologians to critique, analyze, and ask new questions as theologians broadened their conversation partners from philosophy to include the social sciences in the 1960s and 1970s (Eaton 2003). The core of ecofeminist theology was a realignment of power dynamics, as both the ecological and feminist movements opposed "'power-over' relationships which promote dualistic and hierarchical oppression among all beings" (Kyung 1994, p. 176), such as the oppressive power of men over women and that of humans over the environment. Ecofeminist theology exposes harmful attitudes and practices toward the environment and scrutinizes traditions for anti-woman and anti-Earth perspectives. It re-evaluates existing doctrine in light of ecological sensitivities. American ecofeminist theologian Sallie McFague (1933–2019), for example, argued that a new understanding of the Triune God is needed to restore Christian understandings of our relationship to the Earth. The idea of God as the all-powerful victorious king has led to human domination over nature and the marginalization of certain peoples. Instead, McFague suggested a greater emphasis on divine power as kenotic, self-emptying love. She further emphasized God as Mother to illustrate creation as "bodied forth" from God, rendering an intimate relationship. In doing so, a new worldview emerges where creation of the world is itself the body of God and Jesus is the face of the image of God in his self-emptying love (what she calls "radical incarnationalism" in McFague 2017, p. 117; see also McFague 2007).

Intersectional ecofeminists highlight the importance of race, class, and gender to understand the relatedness of patriarchy, feminism, and environmental degradation. Like other contextual theologies that have developed since the twentieth century, ecofeminist theology arose as a critique of Western theologies that subscribed to – either overtly or otherwise – misogyny, patriarchy, and dominion over the Earth. Theologians began to realize that aspects of certain Western theologies were simply ecologically destructive. Women's theology from the global South realizes the interconnectedness between the physical and spiritual worlds, revering the land, sea, and God. These cultural realities make global South women uniquely poised to help lead the way for all Christians to reimagine their relationship with the Earth. Ecofeminist theology is similar to the perspectives of indigenous peoples, in that both emphasize a right relationship with creation. Indigenous communities affirm the centrality and sacredness of land (often, land as mother), holistic perspectives that remove the distinction between sacred and secular, and belief that the whole world is the temple of God (Longchar 2013). This chapter does not delve into the intricacies and debates of ecofeminist theology (see, for example, Moe-Lobeda 2013; Sideris 2003; Eaton 2005; McFague 2007; Ruether 1975, 1992). Instead, it briefly discusses some ecotheologies and activities of Christian women responding to environmental crises in their own communities, for the benefit of all communities, grounded in their Christian faith.

Africa

Reflecting on climate change, mother of African feminist theology Mercy Oduyoye described in a letter to her niece a desire to "join in saving the world" for future generations (Oduyoye 2017, p. 81). "If we are to leave a beautiful world for you and your grandchildren," she stated, "we have to take seriously the fact that creation does not belong to us; we are part of creation" (Oduyoye 2017, pp. 82–83). Africa lags most of the world concerning sustainable development and the ability to combat climate change. An estimated 460 million Africans will remain poor by the year 2030; in other words, eight in ten of the world's poor will live in Africa, two-thirds in rural areas (Twinoburyo et al. 2021). There is a strong correlation between access to water and poverty, as well as access to energy and poverty. Just 61% of people in sub-Saharan Africa utilize basic clean drinking water, 31% have basic sanitation, and 45% have access to electricity (Twinoburyo et al. 2021). There are many challenges in this region, yet governmental initiatives, multinational corporations, small faith-based organizations, local churches, and numerous others are working to improve conditions. However, well-intentioned development projects do not always consider the gendered impacts of their work. Consider the following example:

> A Kenyan reforestation initiative provides another example of faulty gendered assumptions leading to the failure of a development project. Development officials had consulted with male village leaders about the project. They were told that it would be best to plant hardwood trees, since they produced the best wood for their furniture-making endeavors. Hardwood trees were planted, but the trees died shortly thereafter. A subsequent investigation revealed the cause. Both the local men and the development specialists had assumed that the women of the village would take care of the trees. However, the women preferred softwood trees because they grow much more quickly than hardwood trees and can be used for things like firewood for cooking. Because the women saw no value in the hardwood trees, they did not take care of them. Failure to take into account gender-specific roles and needs resulted in the project's failure.
>
> *(Flintan 2003, cited in Campbell et al. 2010, p. 221)*

The Circle of Concerned African Women Theologians has been at the forefront of scholarship to reimagine African religion, culture, tradition, and society in Earth-friendly ways (see Chisale and Bosch 2021; Chirongoma and Kiilu 2022). African ecofeminist and ecowomanist (the terms are used interchangeably) theologians work at the intersection of the environment, gender, liberation theology, and de-colonization. Climate change, a direct consequence of modern colonization, will continue to have a major impact on African women, which demands feminist critical hermeneutics to help move African churches toward liberation (Chirongoma and Mombo 2021). African feminist theologians make explicit connections, for example, between Jesus as redeemer of the world and the redemption of ecosystems, as well as recognize the similarities between African women and Mother Earth – giving life, nurturing, healing, hosting.

Photo 15.2 Attendees of a woman's workshop in the United Church of Christ in Zimbabwe, focusing on environmental stewardship and tree-planting (2012). *Source:* ARC – The Alliance of Religions and Conservation/Flickr/CC BY 2.0.

Among the most notable of African Christian ecofeminists is Wangari Maathai (1940–2011), a Catholic convert and the first woman in East and Central Africa to obtain a PhD (1971, University of Nairobi) (see Maathai and Rollason 2012). She was also the first African woman and the first environmentalist to win the Nobel Peace Prize (2004) for her work in development, democracy, and peace. She founded the Green Belt Movement in 1977 under the auspices of the National Council of Women in Kenya, an African grassroots organization that promotes environmental conservation, builds climate resilience, and empowers communities, especially their women.

Asia

Harmony and wholeness are important themes in Asian cultures and theologies and have been the approach of the Federation of Asian Bishops' Conference to address environmental issues. Vietnamese Catholic theologian Peter Phan stated, "It is out of this sense of universal harmony and wholeness that concern for ecology is born and nourished," as Asians seek harmony "with God, with oneself, with others, and with nature" (Phan 2020, p. 155). Typical of Asian theologies is an emphasis on restoring broken relationships with God, humanity, and nature; salvation is comprehensive healing (Chung 2017). East Asian religions – shamanism, Daoism, Buddhism – embrace the sacredness of nature and typically reject dualism of the spiritual and physical worlds. Many Western missionaries did not understand Asian spiritual cosmologies and only preached other worldly salvation, failing to fully integrate concerns of this life into their eschatology. As a result, Asian Christians are now filling the gaps left behind by their Western influences, drawing direct connections between salvation of body, mind, spirit, and nature. Ecofeminism in this context, according to Korean systematic theologian Meehyun Chung, "promotes a comprehensive, healing-oriented salvation" (Chung 2017, p. 235).

Many groups in Asia have made ecological concerns a critical part of their Christian and feminist identities. For example, the Asian Catholic feminist forum, Ecclesia of Women in Asia (EWA), assists women to engage in research, writing, and reflection that "is inculturated and contextualized in Asian realities; builds on the spiritual experience and praxis of the socially excluded; promotes mutuality and the integrity of creation; dialogues with other disciplines, Christian denominations and religions/faiths" (EWA 2002). Their bi-annual conferences have provided space for Asian Catholic women to respond to current events, such as the 2022 virtual gathering that discussed the COVID-19 pandemic and its impact on women's work, the environment, and spiritual life (see Bong 2017 for an EWA response to Pope Francis's *Laudato Si'*). Renemsongla Ozukum of the Baptist Church Council of Nagaland, India, is a member of the ecology working group of the National Council of Churches in India as well as the World Council of Churches Ecumenical Water Network. Women in her caste-based, male-dominated society have little public influence. As a theologian, she makes poignant connections between women and water. "Gendered water," she says, "is a source of life and vitality, a symbol of pain and hard work, and tool of economic oppression as it has now become an expensive commodity" (Ozukum 2019).

In the Philippines, environmental degradation takes the form of water and air pollution, increased greenhouse gas emissions, the destruction of coral colonies, and the lack of environmental law enforcement. The Philippines is one of the most dangerous countries in the world to be an activist; the human rights NGO Global Witness ranked it as the country with the highest number of murdered land and environmental defenders in 2018. Many protest open-pit mining for copper, gold, nickel, and other mineral deposits, especially by foreign businesses. The Catholic Church has long opposed large-scale mine ownership by foreign bodies because of its negative impact on local people and the natural environment (Mercer 2017). A pioneer of Asian feminist theology, Filipina Catholic Sister Mary John Mananzan was empowered to meld faith and activism after attending the inaugural meeting of the Ecumenical Association of Third World Theologians (EATWOT) in Dar es Salaam, Tanzania (1978). She has protested various problems in Filipino society, including mining, former President Rodrigo Duterte's war on drugs, and forced displacement from ancestral lands. She founded and served as president of the Institute of Women's Studies at St. Scholastica College in Manila, where she developed modules on ecofeminism and courses on creation-centered spirituality. She also formed a Filipino political party, the GABRIELA Women's Party, an acronym for General Assembly Binding Women for Integrity, Reform, Equality, Leadership, and Action.

Latin America and the Caribbean

Land temperatures are rising, the oceans are becoming warmer, and extreme weather is becoming increasingly common across Latin America and the Caribbean. In 2020, temperatures in the region ranged between 0.6ºF and 1ºF higher than in 1981–2010; drought and active fires in southern Amazonia and the Pantanal were the worst they had been in 60 years. Glaciers in the Andes are rapidly retreating, and small island states are facing threats from ocean acidification, sea level rise, and more frequent and intense storms (World Meteorological Organization 2021). 2020 saw a record-setting 30 storms, including Category 4 hurricanes Eta and Iota that made landfall in Central America just two weeks apart, causing widespread devastation. Women make up 48% of Latin America's rural population and they are directly impacted by these environmental challenges, although only 30% of rural women own agricultural land (Biermayr-Jenzano and Paz 2020). Women are more likely to work in the informal economy (often in unpaid labor), making them more vulnerable to economic crises caused by extreme weather and other climate changes.

Like elsewhere in the world, women are important for addressing these challenges and are increasingly becoming leaders in activist movements. Though early liberation theology failed to address ecological concerns, it quickly became clear that ecology and the oppression of the poor were intricately linked. Thus, pioneering Brazilian liberation theologian Leonardo Boff released *Ecology & Liberation: A New Paradigm* in 1993 (Portuguese; English edition in 1995), drawing attention to the holism and interdependence of all creation. He argued that the poor should also be concerned about the environment, not just the wealthy (Boff 1995), and stated the need to respond to "the cry of the Earth and the cry of the poor" (Boff 1997). Liberation theologies today promote ecological awareness as important for understanding the social dimension of faith and practice (Lorentzen and Salvador 2006). Costa Rican theologian Elsa Tamez and Brazilian theologian Sr. Ivone Gebara identified ecofeminism as the third stage of feminist theology in Latin America, beginning in the early 1990s. Gebara – the most prominent ecofeminist in the region – stated, "To speak of climate injustice from the perspective of the suffering of women is to highlight a different aspect of the specificity of women's suffering" (Gebara 2017, p. 69). She argued that Pope Francis's *Laudato Si'* did not adequately address the specific suffering of poor women in Latin America because of its foundation in nostalgic and patriarchal theology, including the notion that women are dependent on a male savior. While she applauded the encyclical for tackling the challenge of environmental sustainability, she noted that women do not speak for themselves in the letter, but rather the pope speaks for them, and in doing so, the letter supports the structures that continue to oppress them.

Grassroots Latin American ecofeminism was born in Christian Base Communities – Catholic lay-led small groups that meet for prayer, Bible study, and social service. One such group, Conspirando, formed in 1991 in Chile as a grassroots organization of Christian women interested in feminism and ecofeminism, initially located in Christian Base Communities. Today, it is one of the most visible initiatives, providing summer schools, regular workshops, and a journal titled, *Conspirando: revista latinoamericana de ecofeminism, espiritualidad y teología* (Con-spirando: A Latin American Magazine of Ecofeminism, Spirituality, and Theology). Another woman working at the intersection of gender, the climate crisis, and Christianity is Nancy Cardoso Pereira, an ordained minister in the Methodist Church of Brazil. Her grassroots education among peasant women, *quilombolas* (African Brazilians), and native women focuses on land rights, where she speaks out against relentless global capitalism that seeks to oppress ecological rights. She also makes direct connections between Scripture and empire, where the Bible has been used as a tool of capitalism and oppression, requiring new, radical readings of the text (Pereira 2019).

Europe and North America

Europe is headed toward a future with increased floods, fires, drought, and agricultural decline, yet many Europeans are unaware that they will be personally impacted, believing climate change to be more of a problem for nations in the global South. Russia, the largest country in Europe, has a long history of climate change denial. For instance, it took until 2005 for the Russian Academy of Sciences to publicly acknowledge that climate change is caused by anthropogenic greenhouse gas emissions (Tynkkynen and Tynkkynen 2018). Climate change battles in the political realm are becoming more common as far-right political parties increase throughout Europe, such as in Germany, the Netherlands, the United Kingdom, and France. Reactions against Swedish climate activist Greta Thunberg (b.2003), for example, ranged from complete support to exceptionally harsh critique. In Iceland, 10% of land is covered by glaciers that have been melting since the late nineteenth century (known as the Little Ice Age), accelerating at an unprecedented pace in the twenty-first century. The increase of greenhouse gas concentrations has led to a rise in global temperatures, causing loss of glacial mass. More than 1,800 miles of glacial ice melted between 1890 and 2019 (Aðalgeirsdóttir et al. 2020). Glacial melting is concerning because it contributes to sea level rise, and because glaciers help keep volcanoes cool. Icelandic theologian Arnfríður

Guðmundsdóttir (b.1961) reflects on the concept of sin as a useful way to address the consequences of climate change. She argues that sin – the broken relationship with God, neighbor, and nature – "becomes a sign of hope when it symbolizes a new beginning through repentance toward salvation" (Guðmundsdóttir 2017, p. 154). Saving the planet requires recognizing brokenness, seeking a renewed relationship, and acting toward transformation.

American Catholic feminist theologian Rosemary Radford Ruether (1936–2022) identified Western civilization as the "primary agent of creating and spreading the ecological crisis throughout the world" (Ruether 2006, p. 362). Yet, she argued that solutions to the crisis can be helped by Christian thought and scriptures, identifying a practical eco-justice way forward that focuses on healing domination narratives among sex, class, and race. She linked Jesus Christ with "cosmogonic wisdom" by which "the universe was created, is sustained, redeemed and reconciled with God" (Ruether 2006, p. 371). She further emphasized the interconnectedness between the impoverishment of the Earth and of peoples – healing, she argued, is holistic, and requires an entirely new way of life.

In the United States, women of color are more likely than White populations (both men and women) to be exposed to environmental toxins and contaminated water or be forced off their land because of industrial development. This happens worldwide; since 1990, more than 91% of the world's natural disasters have occurred in poor countries (World Meteorological Organization/World Bank 2022). Womanist theology uncovers the perspectives of women of color and the realities of their injustice and oppression (see Chapter 6). American womanist theologian Melanie L. Harris is director of the Food, Health and Ecological Well-Being Program at Wake Forest University, where she examines the intersection of race, religion, gender, and the environment (see Harris 2017a). She posits that the approach of "spiritual ecology" is like that of womanism, which honors both deconstructive and constructive analyses (Harris 2017b). She describes ecowomanism as "an approach to environmental ethics that centers on the perspectives, theo-ethical analysis, and life experiences of woman of color and specifically women of African descent" (Harris 2017b, p. 241). Ecowomanism links domination to colonial environmental frameworks, upholds all of creation as sacred, recognizes the interconnectedness of life, and makes a direct connection between Mother Earth and mothers as life-givers. Likewise, Jacqueline Patterson, former senior director of the NAACP Environmental and Climate Justice Program, founded The Chisholm Legacy Project in 2021 specifically for Black climate activism, named after the first African American woman in Congress, Shirley Chisholm (in office 1969–1983). Patterson is also on the steering committee for Interfaith Moral Action on Climate (est. 2011), which brings together faith-based organizations for the sake of climate advocacy.

Among the most prominent environmental activists in North America are Native American (United States) and First Nations (Canada) communities. They have led internationally recognized protests, such as at the Standing Rock Indian Reservation in North Dakota, US (2016). Around 15,000 indigenous people and other climate activists protested the proposed Dakota Access Pipeline, which threatens the Sioux tribe's drinking water and disturbs ancient burial grounds. Protesters also addressed the safety of indigenous women and girls who are impacted by encroachment of the oil industry and pipeline construction. The "man-camps" set up in these places are rife with sexual exploitation and trafficking of Native American women, who already lack basic legal protection (Koster 2017). During the South Dakota oil boom (2008–2014), domestic violence increased by 47% and dating violence by 72%, partially driven by population growth in the area but also the ratio imbalance of men vs. women (Koster 2017).

Catholic women have a long history of social activism and responding to the needs of the cultural moment. Green sisters represent a growing movement in the Catholic Church to serve the world's poor via environmental advocacy. At least 50 green sister institutions operate in the United States and Canada (Taylor 2009). The most prominent among them is the Sisters of Earth network, founded in 1994. Influenced by the Passionist priest Thomas Berry (1914–2009), these sisters have established ecological learning centers, community farms, clean water initiatives, and organic companion planting; they advocate for the cultivation of diversity and biodiversity, and model sustainability for others to emulate. Sister Paula González (1932–2016), known as the "solar nun," held a PhD in cellular physiology and advocated for renewable energy, participated in United Nations climate summits, and founded both La Casa del Sol ("The House of the Sun") and EarthConnection, a solar-heated center that combines eco-education and eco-spirituality.

Oceania

Pacific Islanders feel the stress of climate change most acutely, with low-lying areas more susceptible to rising sea levels, flooding, coastal erosion, and unpredictable rainfall. Entire villages could be obliterated by powerful storm surges, and some church buildings and meeting houses are inaccessible during high tide. Seaside cemeteries have been eroded by rising waters in the Marshall Islands, and many islands are projected to be uninhabitable by the mid-twenty-first century. Some Christians are torn between the biblical promise that precludes another global flood and the evidence of climate change, while others are calling their local communities to action. Tragically, the region's rising sea levels are mostly caused by the detrimental industrial output of larger nations such as the United States, China, and India. Deep imbalances such as this will likely remain a challenge for the global Christian community.

Women's theology from Oceania is ecowomanist, contextual, ecumenical, egalitarian, and inclusive. Their Christology is in context with the land, where Christ has become one with creation and thus unites spirit and nature, contrasting with dualism that leads to environmental degradation. Linking Earth (as mother) to Jesus Christ (in the flesh as a man) represents the coming together of feminine and masculine, where the relationality of God in the Trinity is paralleled to the relationality among God, creation, and people. Numerous women (and men) from across the region are working to reinterpret scripture and tradition to engage ecological challenges more seriously. Australian theologian and poet Anne F. Elvey is central in ecological feminist hermeneutics. Her concept of "material transcendence," for instance, reminds worshippers that they encounter the sacraments *through* their bodies, not despite them. She re-embeds the Eucharist in the context of creation, to interpret it "as a sacrament of the Earth (and by extension cosmic) community," where humans can more fully understand the possibility for transformation to live for others (Elvey 2014, p. 188–189). Other ecofeminist scholars from Australia/New Zealand include Vicky Balabanski (Australia), Elaine Wainwright (New Zealand), Deborah Guess (Australia), Kathleen Rushton (New Zealand), and Dianne Rayson (Australia). Seforosa Carroll (Fiji) is a prominent ecofeminist theologian from Pasifika, where her scholarship intersects Christology, migration, and climate justice (see, for example, Carroll 2022, 2020, 2004).

Numerous Christian women from this region are living into their call as stewards of the Earth. Former Catholic nun Claire Anterea with the Sisters of the Good Samaritans became an outspoken advocate for her country's future and cofounded the Kiribati Climate Action Network (KiriCAN) in 2007, the country's first climate change advocacy group. Other Christian women bring their faith to their advocacy, such as Good Samaritan Sister Marella Rebgetz, who works on harvesting rainwater to avoid wasting fresh water, and Thea Ormerod, head of the interfaith organization, Australian Religious Response to Climate Change. Kathy Jetñil-Kijiner, a poet and climate activist from the Marshall Islands, addressed the United Nations Climate Summit in 2014. Her poem, "Dear Matafele Peinem" – a letter to her seven-month-old daughter – described her dedication to fight for her people's survival on their own land and avoid becoming climate refugees. The Pacific Council of Churches (and its related Ecumenical Pacific Youth) named climate change one of its six main areas of focus for the entire organization.

Conclusion

The scientific community has been sounding alarm bells for decades that climate change is exacerbating. The International Panel on Climate Change reported very high confidence that several species are at risk of extinction, food security and nutrition will be stressed, premature death and ill health are all but ensured, and coastline communities will cease to exist, with resultant displacement and severe economic loss (International Panel on Climate Change 2022). Many of these impacts are expected by 2050. The science is irrefutable, but climate change denial is real, and can be found among people of faith. In the United States, for example, polling reports that 65% of Americans believe the government is doing too little to reduce the effects of global climate change (Tyson and Kennedy 2020). Yet, at the same time, Americans rank climate change lowest on a list of governmental priorities; only 5% of Americans say climate change is the most important issue facing their country (Jones, Cox, and Navarro-Rivera 2014). Hispanic and Black Americans report more concern about climate change compared to White Americans, and White Evangelicals are the most likely to report climate skepticism. A poll reported that 77% of White Evangelicals believed recent natural disasters were due to biblical "end times," not climate change (Jones, Cox, and Navarro-Rivera 2014). An abundance of organizations work together to combat climate change from faith-based perspectives. Consider, for example, A Rocha International, founded in the 1980s, which brings together Christian and scientific organizations worldwide to help empower people, especially churches, to be a part of the environmental solution. In partnering with the Convention on Biological Diversity, the International Union for Conservation of Nature, the Lausanne Movement, the World Evangelical Alliance, the Renew Our World Campaign, the Season of Creation, and United Nations gatherings, there are opportunities for anyone to get involved, no matter your theological persuasions.

A common refrain of female activists, whether they are working in Christian or secular organizations, is the urgency of the environmental activist task. Deadly heat, fire, drought, flood, and unpredictable weather patterns will continue to cause havoc and devastation worldwide without immediate large-scale changes from national and international policymakers. Women are looking at a future of irreversible damage to the planet that will directly impact the people, families, and communities they are expected to preserve. Christianity is now a majority global South faith – 67% of all Christians live in Africa, Asia, Latin America, and Oceania – and Christianity continues to grow among the poor, lower class, and marginalized of society, which are most impacted by climate change. These realities point to an obvious need for churches around the world, which are largely female in their makeup, to be at the forefront of ecological activism and change. As this chapter has shown, Christian women worldwide are being driven by both science and faith to speak out in their theological reflections, scholarship, and activism to help save the world. They are founders of grassroots faith-based movements, partner with large-scale international Christian organizations, become activists in the political sphere, and meld faith and science in holistic ways. They recognize the interconnectedness of humans and creation, as well as God's desire for restored relationships with both. Mitigation, adaptation, and resilience are the key.

Reflection Questions

1) The gendered dynamics of environmental challenges are impossible to ignore. Describe some ways that women in the global South are disadvantaged during climate crises. How are Christian women in Africa, Asia, Latin America, and the Pacific Islands theologically and actively responding to ecological issues?

2) How have different Christian communities worldwide advocated for the biblical mandate of environmental justice? Describe the theological approaches, especially ecofeminist approaches, and biblical interpretations that have been most conducive to promoting care for the Earth.

3) How have reactions to Pope Francis's encyclical, *Laudato Si'*, shaped dialogue about Christian environmentalism? How might his address be improved to achieve a more holistic and contextual posture that includes specific concerns of women?

Works Cited

Aðalgeirsdóttir, Gudfinna, Magnússon, Eyjólfur, Pálsson, Finnur, Thorsteinsson, Thorsteinn, Belart, Joaquín M.C., Jóhannesson, Tómas, Hannesdóttir, Hrafnhildur, Sigurðsson, Oddur, Gunnarsson, Andri, Einarsson, Bergur, Berthier, Etienne, Schmidt, Louise S, Haraldsson, Hannes H, and Björnsson, Helgi (2020). Glacier changes in Iceland from ~1890 to 2019. *Frontiers Earth Science*, 8, 523646. doi: 10.3389/feart.2020.523646.

Alexander, Patricia, Nabalamba, Alice, and Mubila, Maurice (2011). The link between climate change, gender and development in Africa. *The African Statistical Journal*, 12, 119–140.

Alvey, Anne (2014). Living one for the other: eucharistic hospitality as ecological hospitality. In: *Reinterpreting the Eucharist: Explorations in Feminist Theology and Ethics* (ed. Carol Hogan, Kim Power, and Anne F. Alvey), 186–206. London: Routledge.

Bartholomew, Patriarchate, Francis, Pope and Welby, Justin (2021). A joint message for the protection of creation.

Biermayr-Jenzano, Patricia and Paz, Florencia (2020). El rol de la mujer rural en el Sistema agroalimentario Latinoamericano. The role of rural women in the Latin American agri-food system. https://a4nh.cgiar.org/2020/10/14/el-rol-de-la-mujer-rural-en-el-sistema-agroalimentario-latinoamericano/?utm_source=CGIAR (accessed 25 May 2022).

Boff, Leonardo (1995). *Ecology & Liberation: A New Paradigm*. Maryknoll, NY: Orbis Books.

Boff, Leonardo (1997). *Cry of the Earth, Cry of the Poor*. Maryknoll, NY: Orbis Books.

Bong, Sharon (2017). Not only for the sake of man: Asian feminist theological responses to *Laudato Si'*. In: *Planetary Solidarity: Global Women's Voices on Christian Doctrine and Climate Justice* (ed. Grace Ji-Sun Kim and Hilda P. Koster), 81–96. Minneapolis, MN: Fortress Press.

Campbell, Patricia J. et al. (2010). *An Introduction to Global Studies*. Chichester: John Wiley & Sons.

Carroll, Seforosa (2004). Weaving new spaces: christological perspectives from Oceania (pacific) and the Oceanic diaspora. *Studies in World Christianity*, 10(1), 72–92.

Carroll, Seforosa (2020). Too late for justice? disappearing islands, migration, and climate justice. In: *Christian Theology in the Age of Migration: Implications for World Christianity* (ed. Peter C. Phan), 221–236. Lanham: Lexington Books.

Carroll, Seforosa (2022). Climate change, faith and theology in the Pacific (Oceania): the role of faith in building resilient communities. *Practical Theology*. doi: 10.1080/1756073X.2022.2097978.

Chirongoma, Sophia and Kiilu, Wayua ed. (2022). *Mother Earth, Mother Africa: World Religions and Environmental Imagination*. Stellenbosch, South Africa. African Sun Media.

Chirongoma, Sophia and Mombo, Esther (2021). Introduction: mother earth, postcolonial and liberation theologies. In: *Mother Earth: Postcolonial and Liberation Theologies* (ed. Sophia Chirongoma and Esther Mombo), 1–12. Lanham: Lexington Books.

Chisale, Sinenhlanhla S. and Robson Bosch, Rozelle ed. (2021). *Mother Earth, Mother Africa and Theology*. Cape Town, South Africa: AOSIS.

Choudhary, Neetu et al. (2020). Sub-optimal household water access is associated with greater risk of intimate partner violence against women: evidence from Nepal. *Journal of Water and Health*, 18(4), 579–594.

Christiaensen, Luc and Demery, Lionel ed. (2018). *Agriculture in Africa: Telling Myths from Facts*. Washington, DC: The World Bank.

Chung, Meehyun (2017). Salvation for all! Cosmic salvation for an age of climate injustice: a Korean perspective. In: *Planetary Solidarity: Global Women's Voices on Christian Doctrine and Climate Justice* (ed. Grace Ji-Sun Kim and Hilda P. Koster), 219–236. Minneapolis, MN: Fortress Press.

Council on Foreign Relations (2020). Religion and climate change. https://www.cfr.org/event/religion-and-climate-change (accessed 22 March 2022).

Detraz, Nicole (2017). *Gender and the Environment*. Cambridge: Polity Press.

Eaton, Heather (2005). *Introducing Ecofeminist Theologies*. London: T&T Clark.

Elvey, Anne F. (2014). Living one for the other: Eucharistic hospitality as ecological hospitality. In Reinterpreting the Eucharist: Explorations in Feminist Theology and Ethics (ed. Anne Elvey, Carol Hogan, an Kim Power), 186–206. Abingdon: Routledge.

Ecclesia of Women in Asia (EWA) (2002). The constitution and by-laws of Ecclesia of Women in Asia. https://ecclesiaofwomenblog.wordpress.com/about/constitution-by-laws (accessed 8 April 2022).

Flintan, Fiona (2003). Engendering Eden Vol. II: women, gender and ICDPs in Africa: lessons learnt and experiences shared. IIED Wildlife and Development Series, no. 17.

Francis, Pope (2015). *Encyclical letter laudato Si' of the holy father Francis: on care for our common home*. Vatican.

Gebara, Ivone (2017). Women's suffering, climate injustice, God, and Pope Francis's theology: some insights from Brazil. In: *Planetary Solidarity: Global Women's Voices on Christian Doctrine and Climate Justice*. (ed. Grace Ji-Sun Kim and Hilda P. Koster), 67–80. Minneapolis, MN: Fortress Press.

Guðmundsdóttir, Arnfríður (2017). The fire alarm is off: a feminist theological reflection on sin, climate change, energy, and the protection of wilderness in Iceland. In: *Planetary Solidarity: Global Women's Voices on Christian Doctrine and Climate Justice* (ed. Grace Ji-Sun Kim and Hilda P. Koster), 135–154. Minneapolis, MN: Fortress Press.

Habtezion, Senay (2012). Gender, climate change and food security. New York: United Nations Development Programme.

Harris, Melanie L. (2017a). *Ecowomanism: African American Women and Earth-Honoring Faiths*. Maryknoll, NY: Orbis Books.

Harris, Melanie L. (2017b). Ecowomanist wisdom: encountering Earth and spirit. In: *Planetary Solidarity: Global Women's Voices on Christian Doctrine and Climate Justice* (ed. Grace Ji-Sun Kim and Hilda P. Koster), 239–248. Minneapolis, MN: Fortress Press.

Hellum, Anne, Kameri-Mbote, Patricia, and van Koppen, Barbara (2015). The human right to water and sanitation in a legal pluralist landscape: perspectives of southern and eastern African women. In: *Women's Human Rights in National and Local Water Governance in Southern and Eastern Africa* (ed. Anne Hellum, Patricia Kameri-Mbote, and Barbara van Koppen), 1–31. Harare Weaver Press.

International Panel on Climate Change (IPCC) (2022). Sixth assessment report: impacts, adaptation and vulnerability.

Johnson, Todd M. and Zurlo, Gina A. ed. (2022). *World Christian Database*. Leiden/Boston: Brill.

Jones, Robert P., Cox, Daniel, and Navarro-Rivera, Juhem (2014). *Believers, sympathizers, and skeptics: why Americans are concerned about climate change, environmental policy, and science*. Washington, DC: Public Religion Research Institute.

Koster, Hilda P. (2017). Trafficked lands: sexual violence, oil, and structural evil in the Dakotas. In: *Planetary Solidarity: Global Women's Voices on Christian Doctrine and Climate Justice* (ed. Grace Ji-Sun Kim and Hilda P. Koster), 155–176. Minneapolis, MN: Fortress Press.

Kyung, Chung Hyun (1994). Ecology, feminism and African and Asian spirituality. In: *Ecotheology: Voices from South and North* (ed. David G. Hallman), 175–178. Geneva, Switzerland: WCC Publications.

Lindsey, Rebecca (2021). Climate change: annual greenhouse gas index. National Oceanic and Atmospheric Administration. https://www.climate.gov/news-features/understanding-climate/climate-change-annual-greenhouse-gas-index (accessed 24 March 2022).

Lindsey, Rebecca (2022). Climate change: global sea level. National Oceanic and Atmospheric Administration. https://www.climate.gov/news-features/understanding-climate/climate-change-global-sea-level (accessed 24 March 2022).

Lindsey, Rebecca and Dahlman, Luann (2021). Climate change: global temperature. National Oceanic and Atmospheric Administration. https://www.climate.gov/news-features/understanding-climate/climate-change-global-temperature (accessed 24 March 2022).

Lindsey, Rebecca and Scott, Michon (2021). Climate change: Arctic Sea ice summer minimum. National Oceanic and Atmospheric Administration. https://www.climate.gov/news-features/understanding-climate/climate-change-arctic-sea-ice-summer-minimum (accessed 24 March 2022).

Longchar, Wati (2013). Indigenous peoples response to eco-justice in Asia. In: *Asian Handbook for Theological Education and Ecumenism.* (ed. Hope Antone, Wati Longchar, Hyunju Bae, Huang Po Ho, and Dietrich Werner), 389–377. Oxford: Regnum Books International.

Lorentzen, Lois A. and Salvador, Leavitt-Alcantara (2006). Religion and Environmental Struggles in Latin America. In: *The Oxford Handbook of Religion and Ecology* (ed. Roger S. Gottlieb), 510–532. Oxford: Oxford University Press.

Maathai, Wangari and Rollason, Jane (2012). *Unbowed*. Harlow: Pearson Education.

Malabo Montpellier Panel Monograph Report (2021). Recipes for success: policy innovations to transform Africa's food systems and build resilience.

McFague, Sallie (2007). *The Body of God: An Ecological Theology.* Cambridge: International Society for Science and Religion.

McFague, Sallie (2017). Reimagining the Triune God for a time of global climate change. In: *Planetary Solidarity: Global Women's Voices on Christian Doctrine and Climate Justice* (ed. Grace Ji-Sun Kim and Hilda P. Koster), 101–118. Minneapolis, MN: Fortress Press.

Mercer, Joyce Ann (2017). Environmental activism in the Philippines: a practical theological perspective. In: *Planetary Solidarity: Global Women's Voices on Christian Doctrine and Climate Justice* (ed. Grace Ji-Sun Kim and Hilda P. Koster), 287–308. Minneapolis, MN: Fortress Press.

Moe-Lobeda, Cynthia D. (2013). *Resisting Structural Evil: Love as Ecological-Economic Transformation.* Minneapolis, MN: Fortress Press.

OCHA (United Nations Office for the Coordination of Humanitarian Affairs) (2020). Latin America & the Caribbean: weekly situation update.

Oduyoye, Mercy Amba (2017). Earth hope. In: *Ecowomanism, Religion, and Ecology* (ed. Melanie L. Harris), 81–86. Leiden: Brill.

Ozukum, Renemsongla (2019). Challenging 'gendered water': an important step towards women's empowerment. The Naga Republic. March 6. http://www.thenagarepublic.com/expressions/challenging-gendered-water-an-important-step-towards-womens-empowerment-by-renemsongla-ozukum (accessed 7 April 2022).

Palacios-Lopez, Amparo, Christiaensen, Luc, and Kilic, Talip (2017). How much of the labor in African agriculture is provided by women? *Food Policy*, 67, 52–63.

Pereira, Nancy Cardoso (2019). The Bible: globalized commodity in the new strategies of neocolonialism. In: *Scripture and Resistance* (ed. Jione Havea), 135–148. London: Rowman & Littlefield Publishing Group, Inc.

Phan, Peter C. (2020). An ecological theology for Asia: the challenges of Pope Francis's encyclical Laudato Si'. In: *Ecological Solidarities: Mobilizing Faith and Justice for an Entangled World* (ed. Krista E. Hughes, Dhawn B. Martin, and Elaine Padilla), 147–165. University Park, PA: Penn State University Press.

Raney, Terri, Anríquez, Gustavo, Croppenstedt, Andre, Gerosa, Stefano, Lowder, Sarah, Matuscke, Ira, Skoet, Jakob, and Doss, Cheryl (2011). The role of women in agriculture. ESA working paper No.

11-02. The Food and Agriculture Organization of the United Nations, Agricultural Development Economics Division.

Reid, Hannah (2014). *Climate Change and Human Development*. London: Zed Books.

Rozenberg, Julie and Hallegatte, Stephane (2015). The impacts of climate change on poverty in 2030 and the potential from rapid, inclusive, and climate-informed development. Policy Research Working Paper; No. 7483. World Bank, Washington, DC. https://openknowledge.worldbank.org/handle/10986/23447 License: CC BY 3.0 IGO.

Ruether, Rosemary Radford (1975). *New Woman, New Earth: Sexist Ideologies and Human Liberation*. New York: Seabury Press.

Ruether, Rosemary Radford (1992). *Gaia & God: An Ecofeminist Theology of Earth Healing*. San Francisco: Harper San Francisco.

Ruether, Rosemary Radford (2006). Religious ecofeminism: healing the ecological crisis. In: *The Oxford Handbook of Religion and Ecology* (ed. Roger S. Gottlieb), 362–374. Oxford: Oxford University Press.

Sideris, Lisa H. (2003). *Environmental Ethics, Ecological Theology, and Natural Selection*. New York: Columbia University Press.

Taylor, Sarah McFarland (2009). *Green Sisters: A Spiritual Ecology*. Cambridge: Harvard University Press.

Twinoburyo, Enock N., Aheisibwe, Ambrose, Sahilu, Tekalign T., Dushime, Olive, Houngbedji, Koffi, Simkoko, Abigail, Kassa, Yigrem, and Ngulube, James (2021). Africa 2030: SDGs within social boundaries: leave no one behind outlook. The Sustainable Development Goals Center for Africa.

Tynkkynen, Veli-Pekka and Tynkkynen, Nina (2018). Climate denial revisited: (re)contextualising Russian public discourse on climate change during Putin 2.0. *Europe-Asia Studies*, 70(7), 1103–1120.

Tyson, Alec and Kennedy, Brian (2020). *Two-thirds of Americans Think Government Should Do More on Climate*. Washington, DC: Pew Research Center.

United Nations (2012). The millennium development goals report 2012. New York: United Nations.

United Nations (2021). *Sustainable development goal 13: take urgent action to combat climate change and its impacts*. Department of Economic and Social Affairs. Sustainable development. https://sdgs.un.org/goals/goal13 (accessed 24 March 2022).

United Nations General Assembly (2017). Resolution adopted by the general assembly on 6 July 2017: work of the statistical commission pertaining to the 2030 agenda for sustainable development.

United Nations Human Development Programme (2019). Human Development Report 2019: beyond income, beyond averages, beyond today: inequalities in human development in the 21st century. New York.

United Nations Women (2020). Poverty deepens for women and girls, according to latest projections. 10 February. https://data.unwomen.org/features/poverty-deepens-women-and-girls-according-latest-projections (accessed 9 April 2022).

United Nations Women (n.d.). SDG13: take urgent action to combat climate change and its impacts. https://www.unwomen.org/en/news/in-focus/women-and-the-sdgs/sdg-13-climate-action#:~:text=Women (accessed 25 May 2022).

World Meteorological Organization (2021). State of the climate in Latin America and the Caribbean. Geneva, Switzerland.

World Meteorological Organization/World Bank (2022). Disaster risk management. https://www.worldbank.org/en/topic/disasterriskmanagement/overview#1 (accessed 25 May 2022).

16

Christian Women and Theological Education

"How much education shall we give the girls?"
"Give your girls just as much education as you do your boys."

Elizabeth Fisher (1885; in Robert 1997, pp. 182–183)

More girls than ever are enrolled in schools, gaining basic literacy, and increasing their earning potential worldwide. However, gaps remain in educational achievement between boys and girls, and the COVID-19 pandemic severely eroded progress in this area. In 2019–2020, the number of young women enrolled in education, employment, or training programs decreased in dozens of countries. In rural areas lacking Internet access and the necessary devices, remote learning was not an option, and an estimated 11 million girls will never return to school after closures related to the pandemic. For every year a girl is out of school, her potential adult earnings decrease by 20% (Azcona and Min 2021). If such challenges exist for providing adequate basic education for girls worldwide, then formal theological education is completely out of reach for most Christian women, especially in the global South, which is now home to the most Christians. Although Christianity has demographically shifted to Africa, Asia, Latin America and the Caribbean, and the Pacific Islands, many aspects of Christianity have not, including theological education.

No global, comprehensive data exist on trends in theological education worldwide, including estimates of what share of Christians have formal theological education. There are especially no exhaustive data on women in theological education. It is entirely unknown how many women matriculate and graduate from theological schools, what degrees they obtain, and what they do with their training. There is no data on where women can attend schools, if they can take the same classes as men, and where they can or cannot be hired as professors. The closest to such data is the World Council of Churches Global Survey on Theological Education (2011–2013) (see Women and theological education worldwide today section below), but it is not exhaustive, and the data were collected over a decade ago.

This chapter focuses primarily on institutions of formal higher education, which is a limited perspective, given the many kinds of education and training that occur in church settings. For example, the African Sisters Education Collaborative (ASEC) formed in 1999 to help educate women religious across Africa. ASEC estimates that of the 40,000 sisters across ten sub-Saharan African countries it serves, 71% have no higher education credentials (ASEC 2022). This kind of educational ministry is not typically considered "formal theological education," yet thousands of Catholic sisters have received undergraduate- and graduate-level training through ASEC's programs.

Women in World Christianity: Building and Sustaining a Global Movement, First Edition. Gina A. Zurlo.
© 2023 John Wiley & Sons Ltd. Published 2023 by John Wiley & Sons Ltd.

Christian education specialist Perry Shaw observed that, "global higher education in general and theological education in particular has been shaped by empiricist, linear-thinking white Western males for empiricist, linear-thinking white Western males" (Shaw 2018, p. 89). That is, formal theological education in the West was simply not created for women of the global South, who are more "networked, holistic, experience-driven, and relational-cooperative" (Shaw 2018, p. 89). A broad spectrum exists for Christians to access theological education, including by extension, virtual degrees, certificate programs, and church-based lay training. This chapter focuses on formal theological education, typically at the graduate level, and women's access to these spaces. It is difficult to make generalized statements about women's involvement in theological education due to a paucity of data, so the regional information in this chapter is uneven in the examples it provides. Nevertheless, these snapshots paint a picture of the challenges women face to obtain the same levels of education as men around the world.

Historical Vignette: Women and Theological Education in the United States

Women have a turbulent history with Christian theological education. Prior to the Second Great Awakening (1790s–1840s), women in America were considered intellectually weaker than men, and apart from some wealthy families, girls did not receive a secondary education. By this same reasoning, women could not attend seminary (Hassey 1985). Yet, due to a massive shift in American culture, by 1850 there were 6,085 seminaries and academies in America, many exclusively for women (Sweet 1985). Americans became convinced that women needed just as much education than men, if not more, partly because mothers were educating the nation's children, and partly to prepare women for a life of "usefulness." By 1880, one in three students in American higher education was a woman (Reeves-Ellington, Sklar, and Shemo 2010).

Although women were highly organized and successful in overseas mission, formal theological training was not available to them for some time. Mary Lyon (1797–1849) founded Mount Holyoke Female Seminary in 1837 in South Hadley, Massachusetts, the first publicly endowed institute for women's advanced education in America (Porterfield 1997). By 1887, 20% of missionary women from the United States had been trained at Mount Holyoke. Oberlin College in Ohio was the first coeducational college in the world, founded in 1833 as a result of revivals led by Charles Finney (1792–1875). It was one of the few places to encourage female – and Black – education at that time. Still, women were not given the same liberties as male students. Finny had allowed women to speak and pray in mixed-gender revival meetings, yet opinions were divided at Oberlin on whether women could publicly speak. The first ordained woman in a mainstream American Protestant church (Congregational), Antoinette Brown (1825–1921), was only permitted to unofficially attend theological lectures while at Oberlin (1846–1847).

By the 1930s, at least 50 Christian schools had been formed by Fundamentalists, the movement that morphed into neo-Evangelicalism and now Evangelicalism. Leaders of these schools were open to educating women, such as D.L. Moody (Moody Bible Institute), A.J. Gordon (Gordon Bible Institute), W.B. Riley (Northwestern Bible Training School), and A.B. Simpson (Christian and Missionary Alliance). Hundreds of women trained to become preachers, church leaders, and overseas missionaries (Carpenter 1997). Generally restricted from official pastoral ministry at home, many women turned their attention abroad to the frontlines of overseas missions. In the 1930s, for every one male recruit, six women volunteered for the mission field. Harold J. Ockenga, pastor of Boston's Park Street Church and neo-Evangelical revival leader, lamented in a lecture at Fuller Theological Seminary: "What's the matter with the young men who say: 'Yes, God, here I am, send my sister?'" (Bendroth 1993, p. 90). Despite their early support, neo-Evangelical men soon became alarmed by the increased enrollment of women in theological education. Fearing

Photo 16.1 Mount Holyoke Seminary teachers, from left to right: Helen M. French, Julia E. Ward, Emily S. Wilson, Elisabeth Blanchard (standing), and Mary A. Evans (1861). *Source:* Wikimedia Commons/Public Domain.

their ecclesial positions could be overtaken, men pushed women out of educational opportunities and formal leadership. For example, President Nathan Wood of Gordon College of Theology and Missions in Boston reduced the number of female students to one-third of the total to keep the school from being overrun with women. By the 1950s, the school was entirely male, even though its founder, A.J. Gordon, supported female preachers (Bendroth 1993). At Dallas Theological Seminary, "A female Bible institute graduate who in 1910 may have pastored a small church or traveled as an itinerant revivalist would by 1940 more likely serve as director of religious education" (Bendroth 1993, p. 140). It was not until the 1970s that American women could again formally enroll in theological training (Bendroth and Brereton 2001).

Women and Theological Education Worldwide Today

The World Council of Churches Global Survey on Theological Education (2011–2013) is the first and only major global survey on the subject.[1] A quarter of its 1,650 respondents were from Asia, 20% from North America, 19% from Europe, 18% from Africa, 9% from Latin America, and 6% from Oceania (WCC 2013). Respondents suggested that Europe and North America had too many schools, and that there were not enough schools where Christianity was growing the fastest: Africa,

---

1 Theological education is "used in the Survey to refer to all forms of education and formation in ministry (both ordained and lay) and to the preparation for research and teaching in theology and religion" (WCC 2013, p. 8).

Latin America (for Protestants/Pentecostals), and parts of Asia. Mainline Protestant and Catholic seminary enrollment were reported on the decline, while Evangelical and Pentecostal/Charismatic education was on the rise. Notably, the survey found that the number of female students was growing in all schools and in every region; in fact, women were outpacing men in enrollment. Women represented 27% of students in all programs ranging from diplomas to doctorates (Table 16.1), most of whom were between 20 and 30 years old. The most popular program for both male and female students was lay training, representing 38% of female students and 48% of male students. Overall, 86% of respondents indicated that theological education is the most important issue for the future of World Christianity and the mission of the church.

The Global Directory of Theological Education Institutions was created with results from the Global Survey on Theological Education combined with user-entry online submissions at the globethics.net website. Of the 7,000+ entries, 577 institutions report information on the size of their faculty. Of these 577 schools, only 163 of them (28%) report data on the number of full-time female faculty members. Among those, the highest number of female faculty are:

- Uppsala University, Department of Theology (Sweden): 35 women out of 60 total (58%)
- Karen Baptist Theological Seminary (Myanmar): 29 women out of 46 total (61%)
- Indonesian Bible Institute (Indonesia): 28 women out of 53 total (53%)
- Fuller Theological Seminary (United States): 25 women out of 81 total (31%)
- Myanmar Institute of Theology (Myanmar): 22 women out of 45 total (49%)

The share of women faculty is generally very low across geographies and theological traditions. Twenty-one schools that report gender of their faculty indicated zero full-time female professors.

No similar global data on theological education has been produced since the 2011–2013 WCC survey. Regional data exist, such as that from the Association of Theological Schools in North America, but no such coordinating body exists for every region to measure trends. Yet, there are many pressing questions related to women and theological education, especially if they represent

Table 16.1   Global Survey on Theological Education, enrollment (2011–2013).

Program	Total students	Number of female students	% of students who are female	% of female students choosing this program	% of all students choosing this program	% of male students choosing this program
Diploma	79,804	25,504	32.0	27.8	23.6	22.0
Bachelor of Theology (BTh)	30,300	9,882	32.6	10.8	9.0	8.3
Bachelor of Divinity (BD)	8,271	2,021	24.4	2.2	2.4	2.5
Master of Arts (MA)	11,950	4,339	36.3	4.7	3.5	3.1
Master of Divinity (MDiv)	14,259	3,333	23.4	3.6	4.2	4.4
Master of Theology (MTh, ThM, STM)	6,292	1,590	25.3	1.7	1.9	1.9
Doctor of Ministry (DMin)	3,863	456	11.8	0.5	1.1	1.4
Doctor of Philosophy/ Theology (PhD, ThD)	4,339	991	22.8	1.1	1.3	1.4
Lay training	152,191	34,685	22.8	37.8	45.0	47.7
Other	26,845	8,883	33.1	9.7	7.9	7.3
Total	**338,114**	**91,684**	**27.1**	**100.0**	**100.0**	**100.0**

Source: Author's analysis of WCC 2013 data.

an increasing share of students: where do women have access to formal theological training, and where are they prohibited from it? Does women's participation vary based on geography, theological tradition, or a combination of both? In the places where women are permitted to attend seminaries and schools of theology, do they have access to all the degrees and courses that men do? And lastly, what share of faculty of these schools are female? These questions will remain unanswered without concerted efforts to collect new data and synthesize available data.

Africa

Zimbabwean theologian Ezra Chitando stated, "The study of religion in Africa has generally been gender blind until very recently" (Chitando 2013, p. 662). It was not until the formation of the Circle of Concerned African Women Theologians in 1989 that female participation in theological education became encouraged. The Circle is now extremely influential in African theological education, with its affiliated women having moved from the margins of Christian institutions to holding important academic and church leadership positions. Nevertheless, the share of African women in religious studies is still very low. Both female and male theologians now support theological education for women and have made calls for increased women's empowerment, but progress has been uneven. In South Africa, for example, Black and women's theologies are at the core of theological education at universities, but this is not the case throughout the continent.

Theological schools have largely sidelined "gender issues" in Francophone Africa (Djomhoue 2013). They report a larger proportion of male students than female and have very few female professors. The gender ratios are reversed in some secular universities, where women outnumber men. Gender studies are common in state universities but eschewed among theological faculties. Patriarchal cultures and discrimination are compounded in theological schools because their curricula are often determined, or at least influenced by, denominations, rather than the school itself. In these influential denominations, women are generally not permitted to pastoral leadership. Therefore, the theological education these churches support does not encourage women's enrollment. Admission to seminaries also requires a church recommendation, which can be a dead-end for women. Women who do enroll face many challenges: pushback from male peers, curricula that does not address their unique needs, and stigmatization as "feminists" influenced by the West (Djomhoue 2013). Sexual harassment is also a problem.

The lack of gender-sensitive curricula in African theological education is a pressing issue. Botswanan theologian James Amanze stated, "Theological institutions need to come up with curricula that will promote and enhance the dignity of women in church, government, theological colleges, university departments, economic institutions, the family and legal institutions both modern and traditional... it is only a radical approach to this problem that will pull women out of the present abyss to a level where their human dignity as people created in the image of God can be truly realised" (Amanze 2013, p. 232). Women need theological education that is relevant to their lives, and everyone needs education that encourages women's full participation in church and society. Malawian theologian Fulata Moyo provides an example from the aMang'anja people, where theological education intersects with indigenous sex education that empowers women and men to transform their communities with scientific knowledge and sound theological teaching (Moyo 2013). In taking this approach, theological education addresses gender justice and sexuality, topics that are inextricably linked in the African context.

Another example of culturally relevant theological education in Africa is the Tamar Campaign, which addresses gender-based violence and HIV/AIDS. It began as a contextual Bible study for South African women in the 1990s to address sexual abuse and grew to reach children and men via Theological Education by Extension (TEE) programs across Africa (Grueter 2013). The campaign was successful due to a contextual Bible study approach that allowed participants, mainly women, to combine biblical scholarship with a kind of "community consciousness" that emerged from the local community's experiential and interpretive resources (West 2013). Women were able to address a difficult text, create space for sharing experiences, and "do theology" together.

Asia

Asian women's involvement in theological education varies depending on the region, though, generally, women did not have access to formal theological education until the 1970s. Organizations such as the Ecumenical Association of Third World Theologians (EATWOT), the Asian Women's Resource Center (AWRC), and the Christian Conference of Asia (CCA) have empowered women through special programs and events. In some theological programs, this has led to higher rates of female than male enrollment, as can be found in the Philippines, Indonesia, and Myanmar (Longkumer 2010). Chinese theological schools have also produced hundreds of ordained female ministers. Yet, in other places, women have very little access to formal theological education, such as in Nepal, Bangladesh, Pakistan, and other countries where Christians are minorities and education for girls is limited. Women have few opportunities for theological education in the Arab world; their participation is not encouraged, as the entire arena is male dominated. The Master of Divinity program at Evangelical Theological Seminary in Cairo, Egypt, for example, prohibits female students entirely. However, the MDiv program at Arab Baptist Theological Seminary near Beirut, Lebanon does permit female students (Arteen 2020). Exceptions to the widespread restriction on female leadership can be found, such as Mary Mikhael, president of Near East School of Theology (Beirut) from 1994 to 2011 (Arteen 2019).

Western models of theological education – formal institutions, White male theology, transplanted imperial models – do not fit the Asian context, especially for women. Courses on feminist theology are rare, despite the proliferation of such scholarship. Developing appropriate curricula (contextual theology, history, preaching, topics) and relevant educational structures that meet the needs of local students are pressing issues throughout the global South. Although Asian women are increasingly obtaining theological degrees, it is difficult for them to climb Western hierarchical ladders into positions of leadership. A compounding problem is that theological degrees from the West are still perceived as superior to those from Asia, causing many to go overseas for higher education. Some contextual theologies of Asia – such as *minjung* (South Korea) and *Dalit* (India) – overlook women's unique struggles and opportunities and are considered secondary in theological curricula. These dynamics make theological education seem out of reach for many people, especially women, the poor, and the marginalized (Longkumer 2010). Women are also disadvantaged because most schools in Asia are denominationally affiliated and often do not permit female pastors. More interdisciplinary pedagogy is needed to fully incorporate Asian women into theological education, not only for their benefit, but so that theological education is more relevant and therefore able to address contemporary issues for entire communities. An expert on theological education, Nagaland-born (Northeast India) theologian Wati Longchar, stated, "The integration of women's perspectives in the process of theological education will create awareness of discriminatory gender realities and help people to do something concrete to change the oppressive structure currently prevalent" (Longchar 2010, p. 416).

Theological education in South Asia is heavily dominated by men. For example, at one point in the association of Protestant schools in India, the Board of Theological Education of the Senate of Serampore College (BTESSC), 80% of theological students, 90% of teachers, and 90% of governing board members are men (Longchar 2010). Between 1970 and 2007, 17 of its 125 graduates were women (14%), and the first woman graduate was not until 1993 (Melanchthon 2010). Under these conditions, it would be difficult for anything specifically related to women to enter the curriculum. Furthermore, it is not enough to simply add gender onto the peripheries of existing programs. Gender justice and women's issues need to be fully integrated to have a true impact on theological education, for both men and women. Despite the many challenges, there is some support for women in theological education. The Association of Theologically Trained Women in India (ATTWI), for example, formed in 1979 in Chennai as an interdenominational organization to uplift Christian women and girls. Its roughly 500–600 members, all of whom are women, must have a degree from a formal institution recognized by the SSC.

Latin America

Colonial powers transplanted European educational systems to Latin America and the Caribbean beginning in the sixteenth century. The first institute of higher education in the Americas, Universidad Santo Tomás de Aquino in the Dominican Republic (1538), was originally a seminary run by Dominican monks and grew into a secular university. Churches in Latin America and the Caribbean have been at the forefront of providing basic, secondary, and higher education to their affiliates. Given the long history of Catholicism, the region is replete with Catholic institutions of theological education, many of which date to the sixteenth century: the Theological Seminary of Bogotá is the oldest Catholic seminary in the Americas, founded in 1581. Central America is home to more than 220 Catholic seminaries, with the most in Mexico (117), the Dominican Republic (35), and Haiti (16). South America is home to 764 seminaries, with the largest numbers in Brazil (303), Colombia (152), and Peru (107) (Kramarek, Gaunt, and Sordo-Palacios 2017). Catholic seminaries do not prepare women for the priesthood, so these schools have a low share of female students. Yet, women religious (Catholic sisters) have made tremendous contributions to education in Latin America and the Caribbean, having established thousands of schools throughout the continent, especially during the expansion of education in the nineteenth and twentieth centuries. Many of these schools were for girls only, thus advocating for gender equity in education (Suárez 2022). Lay women are highly involved in the 130 Catholic new ecclesial movements in Latin America, which have an emphasis on education and social work among vulnerable populations (homeless, youth, immigrants).

In the nineteenth century, Protestant schools existed only in Brazil, Argentina, and Mexico, all sponsored by Lutherans, Baptists, Methodists, and other North Atlantic mission agencies (Duque 2010). Concerns about contextual theological education arose in the 1980s, such as at the Latin American Commission for Theological Education (CLAET) conference in Colombia. Participants recognized that Christian ministry should focus on human rights, dignity, and address exclusion and exploitation, but women were completely absent from discussions on the status and future of theological education in the region (Ulloa 2010).

There are now thousands of Protestant institutions in the region, reflecting a diversity of instruction: distance, extension, residential, and virtual. Protestant theological education aims to cut across denominational differences. One such ecumenical school is the Latin America Biblical University in Costa Rica, which began as the Latin American Biblical Institute in 1923 exclusively for women, founded by Scottish Presbyterian missionary Susan Strachan (George 2007). Half of its 1,500 students are women, offering priority enrollment also to African descendants and indigenous people. La Comunidad de Educación Teológica Ecuménica Latino-Americana y Caribeña (CETELA; the Latin America and Caribbean Ecumenical Theological Education Community) formed in 1988 and brings together 22 institutions from the region, including Reformed, Methodist, Baptist, Mennonite, and broadly Evangelical schools.

Many Protestant theological schools were historically established to train pastors, typically men, but have now grown into broad Christian universities, such as the Methodist Institute of Higher Education (Brazil) and the Evangelical Seminary of Matanzas (Cuba). Ofelia Ortega Suárez was the first Presbyterian woman ordained in Cuba and served as president of Evangelical Seminary of Matanzas from 1996 to 2004. When she arrived at the seminary, only men could study theology; women were restricted to classes on Christian education, but during her tenure she enacted changes for greater gender equity. In the mid-to-late-twentieth century, some churches in the Caribbean began permitting female ordination, requiring an increase in demand for theological training (Titus 2010). New courses were designed specifically for women, though adding a gendered dynamic to existing courses in biblical and doctrinal studies is difficult and the process is ongoing.

Europe

Theological education in Europe has a tremendously long history, even for women, where Catholic nuns received education to engage in full-time vocational ministry as teachers. Women learned languages, history, and became scholars of theology, whether they were permitted to or not. Monastic life provided tremendous opportunities for women outside of marriage and motherhood, including education, and as a result, women became abbesses of monasteries and authored published works.

Russian Orthodox women gained increased access to education beginning in the 1860s, and the daughters of clergy were the first generation of women to receive formal education (Beliakova 2020). Female monasteries in the nineteenth century were well populated, especially by young, unmarried women from lower social classes. In the twentieth century, female monasteries expanded to include formal education for women, teaching them theology and medicine for the sake of ministering to both soul and body. Russian Orthodox theological education suffered, however, with the closing of all schools in 1917, the separation of church and state, the nationalization of church property, and the prohibition on teaching religion in schools. Theological academies in other territories entering the Soviet Union were also closed, such as in the Baltic states. Many seminaries were reorganized after World War II but until 1990 were strictly controlled by the Communist Party (Fedorov 2010). The fall of the Communist regime in 1991 changed everything, with the reopening of schools and a refashioning of Orthodox identity, status, and education.

Photo 16.2 Indonesians Manda Andrian and Ruth Saiya, graduates of the World Council of Churches Ecumenical Institute in Bossey, Switzerland and recipients of the Sarah Chakko Scholarship, named after the WCC's first female president (2020). *Source:* Albin Hillert, used with permission from the WCC.

The "woman question" in Orthodox churches is a relatively recent discussion and remains a gray area. Orthodox theological education extends beyond simply training for clergy; like other Christian traditions, it includes how to make theology relevant for a community, the interpretation of tradition, and exploring the relationship between faith and society. Women were only recently permitted to enter Orthodox theological schools and they generally remain the minority of students. Yet, in Greek Orthodox schools of theology, female students are the majority, they are more consistent students than men, and many go on for higher degrees. However, precious few women become faculty, and those that do tend to teach history, arts, and languages, not theology, patristics, or biblical hermeneutics (Koukoura 2005; Kasselouri-Hatzivassiliadi 2014). Nevertheless, more Orthodox women are receiving formal theological education and entering official positions in church life (Beliakova 2020).

Europe is home to 1,116 Catholic seminaries, representing just 20% of all such institutions in the world (for comparison, 29% are in Asia-Pacific, 27% in South America, 16% in Africa, and 4% in North America) (Kramarek, Gaunt, and Sordo-Palacios 2017).[2] The highest numbers of seminaries in Europe are in Spain (184), Poland (90), and Portugal (85). There is no comprehensive data available on the proportion of women in these schools. One study from Poland reported that women are an increasing share of seminarians, rising from 35% of all students in 1989 to 60% in 2009 (Penner and Kool 2010). Women make up the majority of Protestant students in Denmark, Sweden, and Norway (men are still the majority in Finland). The early ordination of women in Scandinavian churches (1947) and their continued sizable share of ordained ministers naturally leads to a larger proportion of women in that region's training institutes (Haanes 2010).

The European Council for Theological Education (ECTE, formerly the European Evangelical Accrediting Association) represents 75 Evangelical institutions in Europe and some in the Middle East. Of the 24 accredited European member schools, women make up 13% of faculty, 34% of graduate students, and 42% of undergraduate students (Arteen 2020). A 2021 study of these schools found that many wanted to be more gender sensitive, but did not have more female faculty members for some of the following reasons: they wanted to distance themselves from gender quotas (i.e., they wanted to hire the best person for the job, not necessarily a woman), there were few female applicants for teaching positions, they had to abide by mission organization or denominational guidelines that exclude women from leadership, and many female candidates lacked PhDs (Arteen 2021).

North America

The most comprehensive data on theological education in the United States and Canada is from the Association of Theological Schools (ATS), which reports annual statistics of trends in enrollment, faculty, and finances. ATS members are graduate schools of theology and include Protestant, Catholic, Orthodox, and Jewish institutions; these data do not include accredited or nonaccredited Christian undergraduate institutions. In 2021, the 272 affiliate schools (of all statuses: accredited, candidate, and associate) were 69% majority White Non-Hispanic, 56% Protestant, and 58% independent (i.e., not university- or college-affiliated) (ATS 2021). For full-time equivalent enrollment, 38% of member schools have fewer than 75 students, and 32% report between 75 and 150.

Student enrollment in ATS schools is majority male. In 2021, 64% of students in all member schools were male, and just 36% were female (Table 16.2). The female figure is up from 1971, when

---

2 Here, "'seminary' is understood as an institution for educating students on the secondary, undergraduate and/or graduate levels, an institution for males and/or females, and an institution for helping students discern and/or prepare for priesthood and/or religious life in Catholic Church (Kramarek, Gaunt, and Sordo-Palacios 2017, p. 2).

Table 16.2 Headcount enrollment by gender in the Association of Theological Schools, 2021–2022.

	Male	Male % of total	Female	Female % of total	Other	Other % of total	Total
Master of Divinity	19,962	68.6	8,867	30.5	271	0.9	29,100
Master of Arts	14,615	53.0	12,829	46.5	147	0.5	27,591
Master of Theology/Master of Sacred Theology	1,091	81.8	222	16.7	20	1.5	1,333
Doctor of Ministry/Other Doctor	8,741	73.8	3,090	26.1	17	0.1	11,848
Doctor of Philosophy/Theology	3,054	76.0	953	23.7	10	0.2	4,017
Nondegree	2,736	57.6	1,918	40.4	92	1.9	4,746
Total	**50,199**	**63.8**	**27,879**	**35.5**	**557**	**0.7**	**78,635**

Source: Data from ATS 2021.

only 10% of students were female, but growth has slowed in the last 20 years (Gin and Meinzer 2017). More women are enrolled in Master of Arts (MA) programs than any other degree, and women constituted 46% of all MA students. These figures are higher than Master of Divinity (MDiv) programs, the degree that most typically leads to ordination and pastoral ministry. Women were 30% of all MDiv students and 32% of all female students were enrolled in MDiv programs. Women represent 20% of PhD/ThD enrollments and just 3% of female students at ATS member schools were enrolled in these advanced programs (ATS 2021).

White Non-Hispanic male faculty are the norm at ATS schools, representing 54% of all faculty. Not surprising, given the proportion of women in PhD and ThD programs, women make up just 26% of all faculty in ATS member schools (Table 16.3). This figure is up from 1971, when women (of all ethnicities) were a mere 1% of all ATS faculty. At the highest rank of professor, women are only 19%. White Non-Hispanic women constitute 17% of all ATS faculty but for women of color, the statistics are even more bleak:

- Asian or Pacific Islander women: 3% of all ATS faculty
- Black Non-Hispanic women: 4% of all ATS faculty
- Hispanic women: 1% of all ATS faculty
- American Indian, Alaskan Native, or Inuit women: less than 1% of all ATS faculty
- Visa or nonresident alien women: less than 1% of all ATS faculty
- Multiracial women: less than 1% of all ATS faculty

Structural racism is a major problem despite increased enrollment of Black, Latino/a, Asian, and Asian North American students in ATS schools. According to African American theologian Keri Day, "Theological schools must wrestle continually with the emotional carnage left in the wake of institutional racial disenfranchisement" (Day 2021, p. 4). For example, Day describes what is known as "learning to pass," where students of color are expected to master what is considered standard Western subjects (such as the theology of Karl Barth) instead of those more relevant to them (such as the theology of James Cone). That is, students are required to enroll in "classical" courses of Western theological education, but the "contextual" ones are optional. These curricular and pedagogical choices perpetuate structural racism and overlook the preferences, needs, and experiences of people of color.

Table 16.3 Full-time faculty by gender in the Association of Theological Schools, 2021–2022.

	Male	Male % of total	Female	Female % of total	Other	Other % of total	Total
Professor	1,077	81.3	248	18.7	0	0	1,325
Associate Professor	644	72.9	240	27.1	0	0	884
Assistant Professor	406	62.7	242	37.3	0	0	648
Others	152	68.5	70	31.5	0	0	222
Total	**2,279**	**74.0**	**800**	**26.0**	**0**	**0**	**3,079**

Source: Data from ATS 2021.

Among ATS member schools, those with majority female student bodies tend to be associated with mainline Protestantism, have a higher percentage of women in upper-level administration, and have more female faculty (Gin and Meinzer 2017). Schools with majority female faculty are also generally mainline Protestant, have higher numbers of female students, but also have fewer full-time faculty (that is, the smaller faculty, the more women among them). Evangelical schools are the least likely to have female leaders, such as chief executive officers and chief academic officers (Gin 2018). Even in schools where female leaders are permitted, women are not regularly supported, promoted, or funneled into those positions. The biggest factor preventing women's advancement in theological education in North America is the "impenetrable 'boys club'" of upper-level leadership (Gin and Deasy 2018).

Oceania

Fijian Lorini Tevi was the first female General Secretary of the Pacific Conference of Churches (1970–1980), where debates surrounding women in theological education began in conferences of the South Pacific Association of Theological Schools (SPATS) (Halapua 2010). SPATS had no female lecturers in theology in any of its schools at the founding of its women's organization, Weavers, in 1989. Weavers – symbolizing the communal and participatory act of women's weaving – launched new curricula on violence against women and HIV/AIDS. It continues to support women in theological education across the region through scholarship funds, public forums on pertinent theological topics, and fostering relationships between local churches and theological schools to strengthen women's opportunities. Many women have obtained higher theological education in the Pacific Islands, but only a small proportion of them use their training in official pastoral positions. Many serve as pastor's wives. There are inklings of change, however, such as the appointment of Pastor Lima Tura as the first female lecturer – and a single mother – at Seghe Theological College in the Solomon Islands in 2019.

The Association of Oceania Women Theologians formed in New Zealand in 2006 and helped introduce a new way of doing theology across the continent. Influential theologians such as Katalina Tahaafe-Williams (Tonga-Australia), Lydia Johnson (American living and working in the South Pacific), and Joan Alleluia Filemoni-Tofaeono (Samoa) have made an explicit connection between women's leadership and that of Indigenous peoples (Halapua 2010). Theological education in Oceania is rooted in patriarchal theology that makes "women's issues" like gender-based violence (GBV) irrelevant in the curriculum (Filemoni-Tofaeono and Johnson 2016). Graduates of these schools had no opportunity to theologically address such issues, and as a result, have perpetuated the notion that violence is a normal part of life at best; at worst, some graduates have been perpetrators of violence themselves. Men and women are generally not considered equal partners at theological institutions, neither as students nor faculty (Filemoni-Tofaeono and Johnson 2016). The largest theological school in the Pacific Islands is Pacific Theological College (PTC) in Suva, Fiji, founded in 1965 by members of Anglican, Congregational, Uniting, Evangelical Lutheran, Methodist, and Presbyterian churches. Its Women's Programme began in 1980, which now includes a Certificate in Women's Ministry Studies and a Certificate in Women's Ministry consisting of courses in communications, counseling, youth/children's ministry, Bible study, arts, and ministry leadership (for the latter certificate, two additional courses are required in theology and ethics). Discrimination and harassment of women is still a problem at PTC despite its emphasis on social justice and contextual theology. In the 1990s, theologian Lydia Johnson was the first female faculty member at PTC, where she observed "not only institutional patriarchy, but the personal struggles of female students and student wives in the face of a system which limited their horizons and kept them in their subservient place" (Filemoni-Tofaeono and Johnson 2016, p. xvi). Cultural expectations of women's submission continue to hinder achievements in theological education.

Australia has a long tradition of theological education, much like countries in North America and Europe. Catholic seminaries opened in the early nineteenth century, followed by Anglican and Presbyterian, and Pentecostal/Charismatic institutions began to emerge in the 1980s (Sherlock 2010). Founded in 1891, the Australian College of Theology (ACT; Anglican) is the country's largest provider of theological education, with 17 colleges offering bachelor's, master's, and PhD degrees in theology and ministry. The proportion of female ACT students increased from 16% of all graduates in 1916 to 28% in 1991, but in the period 2005–2016, the proportion of women in accredited programs remained steady at 36% (du Toit, Martin, and Hill 2022). Women are more likely to study part-time compared to men (78% vs. 69%). Attrition is worse for women – which can be attributed to more family responsibilities and work-life balance issues – although women generally have higher GPAs than men. In 2016, women comprised just 13% of permanent ACT teaching and research staff, compared to 45% female faculty in general Australian universities (du Toit, Martin, and Hill 2022). Women are more likely than men to be in part-time, adjunct, nonpermanent, and contingent jobs. More women's perspectives are needed in theological education, as well as more role models for younger women to pursue this path.

Conclusion

Theological education has certainly advanced in the global South with the formation of many graduate programs from the 1960s to 1980s (Ferenczi 2016). Numerous prestigious programs, libraries, and faculties are available to serve local students instead of temporarily transplanting them to Europe or North America for higher education, which often results in a costly and potentially theologically irrelevant experience. The need for theological education in the South grows as many theological schools in the North downsize and shut down. Yet, growth has not always been inclusive of the needs of the entire church – meaning, the needs of women in theological education are still generally not met, even as opportunities expand. Women are central to the functioning of churches all over the world, yet they are routinely denied opportunities to further their biblical and ministerial education for the continued flourishing of those churches. Where they are admitted to programs, they often face the same harassment and discrimination as in wider society. Lack of gender consciousness, coupled with gendered cultural expectations, holds back women in theological spaces. Perhaps more so-called "unconventional educational practices" (Ferenczi 2016, p. 56) are needed to equip students more fully for ministry; that is, models informed by local needs, not external models built for needs of the past and structured exclusively around the experiences of men (for more on cross-cultural gendered education, see Feliciana-Soberano and Shaw 2021).

World Christianity is a women's movement when it comes to who self-identifies as Christian, who serves in the churches with the most regularity and gusto, and who sustains Christian faith in a community. However, Christian theological education is not a women's movement. Based on available data, women are generally the minority of students, professors, and administrators. In most cases, women were only permitted to attend these institutions in the last 50 years. In some contexts, they still cannot be full-time students nor take the same classes as men. Curricula are not designed with women's perspectives in mind, even though they represent an increasing share of students. While women have made advancements in this area, the path toward gender equity in formal theological education remains an uphill journey.

Reflection Questions

1) How can churches, Christian schools, and other organizations address the lack of data on women in theological education worldwide? How can institutes in the global South be motivated and equipped to encourage more women's participation in theological education?
2) What unique barriers do women face in Africa, Asia, and Latin America to obtaining theological education? Reflect on the incompatibility of Western models with local realities. How can theological schools develop more gender sensitive curricula for the benefit of both men and women?
3) How can the symbolic gesture of "weaving" from the Pacific Islands be used to characterize the dynamics of women, community, and activism for education? How might this concept be applied elsewhere in the world where women are overlooked for higher theological education?

Works Cited

African Sisters Education Collaborative (ASEC) (2022). *Who we are*. http://asec-sldi.org/who-we-are/index.html (accessed 8 June 2022).

Amanze, James (2013). Theological education in Southern Africa. In: *Handbook of Theological Education in Africa* (ed. Isabel Phiri, Dietrich Werner, Priscille Djomhoue, James Amanze, Kennedy Owino, Chammah Kaunda, and Stephen Phiri), 223–233. Minneapolis: Fortress Press.

Arteen, Grace Al-Zoughbi (2019). Theological perspectives on the theological education of women in the Middle East and North Africa. *InSights Journal for Global Theological Education*, 5(1) 17–32.

Arteen, Grace Al-Zoughbi (2020). *Gender distribution in theological education – thematic analysis*. European Council for Theological Education.

Arteen, Grace Al-Zoughbi (2021). *Gender distribution in theological education – follow up*. European Council for Theological Education.

Azcona, Ginette and Min, Yongyi (2021). *Progress on the sustainable development goals: the gender snapshot 2021*. United Nations Women and United Nations Department of Economic and Social Affairs.

Beliakova, Nadezhda (2020). Women in the church: conceptions of Orthodox theologians in early twentieth-century Russia. In: *Orthodox Christianity and Gender: Dynamics of Tradition, Culture and Lived Practiced* (ed. Helena Kupari and Elina Vuola), 47–79. London: Routledge.

Bendroth, Margaret and Brereton, Virginia L. ed. (2001). *Women and Twentieth-Century Protestantism*. Urbana University of Illinois Press.

Bendroth, Margaret L. (1993). *Fundamentalism and Gender, 1875 to the Present*. New Haven, CT: Yale University Press.

Carpenter, Joel A. (1997). *Revive Us Again: The Reawakening of American Fundamentalism*. New York: Oxford University Press.

Chitando, Ezra (2013). Religion and masculinities in Africa: an opportunity in Africanization. In: *Handbook of Theological Education in Africa* (ed. Isabel Phiri, Dietrich Werner, Priscille Djomhoue, James Amanze, Kennedy Owino, Chammah Kaunda, and Stephen Phiri), 662–670. Minneapolis: Fortress Press.

Day, Keri (2021). *Notes of a Native Daughter: Testifying in Theological Education.* Grand Rapids, MI: William B. Eerdmans Publishing Company.

Dayton, Donald (1976). *Discovering an Evangelical Heritage.* New York: Harper & Row Publishers.

Djomhoue, Priscille (2013). Mainstreaming gender in theological institutions in Francophone Africa: perspectives from Cameroon. In: *Handbook of Theological Education in Africa* (ed. Isabel Phiri, Dietrich Werner, Priscille Djomhoue, James Amanze, Kennedy Owino, Chammah Kaunda, and Stephen Phiri), 639–646. Minneapolis: Fortress Press.

Dries, Angelyn (1998). *The Missionary Movement in American Catholic History.* Maryknoll, NY: Orbis Books.

du Toit, Megan P., Martin, Kara, and Hill, Graham Joseph (2022). *Women in Theological Education in Australia.* Unpublished manuscript.

Duque, Jose (2010). The growth and challenges of theological education in Latin America: notes from pilgrimage. In: *Handbook of Theological Education in World Christianity: Theological Perspectives, Ecumenical Trends, Regional Surveys* (ed. Dietrich Werner, David Esterline, Namsoon Kang, and Joshva Raja), 466–475. Minneapolis: Fortress Press.

Fedorov, Vladimir (2010). Theological education in the Russian Orthodox Church (in Russia, Ukraine, Belarus). In: *Handbook of Theological Education in World Christianity: Theological Perspectives, Ecumenical Trends, Regional Surveys* (ed. Dietrich Werner, David Esterline, Namsoon Kang, and Joshva Raja), 514–524. Minneapolis: Fortress Press.

Feliciano-Soberano, Joanna and Shaw, Perry (2021). Gender issues in cross-cultural teaching. In: *Teaching Across Cultures: A Global Christian Perspective* (ed. Perry Shaw, César Lopes, Joanna Feliciana-Soberano, and Bob Heaton), 83–100. Carlisle: Langham Partnership.

Ferenczi, Jason (2016). Sustaining what matters in theological education. *InSights Journal for Global Theological Education*, 2(1), 48–59.

Filemoni-Tofaeono, Joan and Johnson, Lydia (2016). *Reweaving the Relational Mat: A Christian Response to Violence against Women from Oceania.* London: Taylor and Francis.

George, Sherron K. (2007). Ecumenical theological education in Latin America, 1916–2005. *International Bulletin of Missionary Research*, 31(1), 15–21.

Gin, Deborah H.C. (2018). *Women in Leadership Survey: What We Found May Not Be What You Think.* The Association of Theological Schools, The Commission on Accrediting. Pittsburgh, PA.

Gin, Deborah H.C. and Deasy, Jo Ann (2018). *In Your Own Words: Women in Leadership in Theological Education. The Association of Theological Schools Women in Leadership 20*th *Anniversary Celebration.* Pittsburgh, PA.

Gin, Deborah H.C. and Meinzer, Chris (2017). *Women in ATS schools: 8 Data Points for Conversation.* The Association of Theological Schools, The Commission on Accrediting. Pittsburgh, PA.

Grueter, Verena (2013). Gender, religion and politics in theological education. In: *Handbook of Theological Education in Africa* (ed. Isabel A. Phiri, Dietrich Werner, Priscille Djomhoue, James Amanze, Kennedy Owino, Chammah Kaunda, and Stephen Phiri), 682–688. Minneapolis: Fortress Press.

Haanes, Vidar L. (2010). Theological education in Scandinavian churches. In: *Handbook of Theological Education in World Christianity: Theological Perspectives, Ecumenical Trends, Regional Surveys* (ed. Dietrich Werner, David Esterline, Namsoon Kang, and Joshva Raja), 570–576. Minneapolis: Fortress Press.

Halapua, Winston (2010). Theological education in Oceania. In: *Handbook of Theological Education in World Christianity: Theological Perspectives, Ecumenical Trends, Regional Surveys* (ed. Dietrich Werner, David Esterline, Namsoon Kang, and Joshva Raja), 449–457. Minneapolis: Fortress Press.

Hassey, Janette (1985). *No Time for Silence: Evangelical Women in Public Ministry around the Turn of the Century*. Minneapolis, MN: CBE.

Kasselouri-Hatzivassiliadi, Eleni (2014). Orthodox women and theological education. *The Ecumenical Review*, 65(4), 471–476.

Koukoura, Dimitra (2005). *The Role of Woman in the Orthodox Church and Some Studies of Ecumenical Concern*. Thessaloniki: Sfakianaki Publications (in Greek).

Kramarek, Michal J., Gaunt, Thomas P., and Sordo-Palacios, Santiago (2017). *Global directory of Catholic seminaries*. Center for Applied Research in the Apostolate. Georgetown University, Washington, DC.

Longchar, Wati (2010). The history and development of theological education in South Asia. In: *Handbook of Theological Education in World Christianity: Theological Perspectives, Ecumenical Trends, Regional Surveys* (ed. Dietrich Werner, David Esterline, Namsoon Kang, and Joshva Raja), 405–419. Minneapolis: Fortress Press.

Longkumer, Limatula (2010). Women in theological education from an Asian perspective. In: *Handbook of Theological Education in World Christianity: Theological Perspectives, Ecumenical Trends, Regional Surveys* (ed. Dietrich Werner, David Esterline, Namsoon Kang, and Joshva Raja), 68–75. Minneapolis: Fortress Press.

Melanchthon, Monica Jyotsna (2010). Graduate biblical studies in India. In: *Transforming Graduate Biblical Education: Ethos and Discipline* (ed. Elisabeth Schüssler Fiorenza and Kent Harold Richards), 119–136. Atlanta: Society of Biblical Literature.

Moyo, Fulata (2013). For gaining instructions in wise dealings, righteousness, justice and equity: theological education for gender justice and sexual empowerment. In: *Handbook of Theological Education in Africa* (ed. Isabel A. Phiri, Dietrich Werner, Priscille Djomhoue, James Amanze, Kennedy Owino, Chammah Kaunda, and Stephen Phiri), 648–652. Minneapolis: Fortress Press.

Neely, Alan (1998). Liele, George. In: *Biographical Dictionary of Christian Missions* (ed. Gerald H. Anderson), 400–401. New York: Macmillan Reference USA.

Penner, Peter and Kool, Anne-Marie (2010). Theological education in Eastern and Central Europe. In: *Handbook of Theological Education in World Christianity: Theological Perspectives, Ecumenical Trends, Regional Surveys* (ed. Dietrich Werner, David Esterline, Namsoon Kang, and Joshva Raja), 531–547. Minneapolis: Fortress Press.

Porterfield, Amanda (1997). *Mary Lyon and the Mount Holyoke Missionaries*. New York: Oxford University Press.

Reeves-Ellington, Barbara, Sklar, Kathryn K., and Shemo, Connie A. ed. (2010). *Competing Kingdoms: Women, Mission, Nation, and the American Protestant Empire, 1812–1960*. Durham, NC: Duke University Press.

Robert, Dana L. (1997). *American Women in Mission: A Social History of Their Thought and Practice*. Macon, GA: Mercer University Press.

Shaw, Perry (2018). Culture, gender, and diversity in advanced theological studies. In: *Challenging Tradition: Innovation in Advanced Theological Education* (ed. Perry Shaw et al.), 89–108. Carlisle: Langham Creative Projects.

Sherlock, Charles (2010). Australian theological education: an historical and thematic overview. In: *Handbook of Theological Education in World Christianity: Theological Perspectives, Ecumenical Trends, Regional Surveys* (ed. Dietrich Werner, David Esterline, Namsoon Kang, and Joshva Raja), 458–465. Minneapolis: Fortress Press.

Suárez, Ana Lourdes (2022). Gender. In: *Christianity in Latin America and the Caribbean* (ed. Kenneth R. Ross, Ana María Bidegain, and Todd M. Johnson), 397–407. Edinburgh: Edinburgh University Press.

Sweet, Leonard (1985). The female seminary movement and woman's mission in antebellum America. *Church History*, 54(1), 41–55.

The Association of Theological Schools (ATS) (2021). Annual data tables.

Titus, Noel (2010). Toward a unified and contextual program in theological education in the Caribbean. In: *Handbook of Theological Education in World Christianity: Theological Perspectives, Ecumenical Trends, Regional Surveys* (ed. Dietrich Werner, David Esterline, Namsoon Kang, and Joshva Raja), 490–493. Minneapolis: Fortress Press.

Ulloa, Amílcar (2010). The origins of ecumenical theological education in Latin America and the Caribbean. In: *Handbook of Theological Education in World Christianity: Theological Perspectives, Ecumenical Trends, Regional Surveys* (ed. Dietrich Werner, David Esterline, Namsoon Kang, and Joshva Raja), 476–488. Minneapolis: Fortress Press.

West, Gerald (2013). The Tamar campaign: returning Tamar's testimony to the church. In: *Handbook of Theological Education in Africa* (ed. Isabel A. Phiri, Dietrich Werner, Priscille Djomhoue, James Amanze, Kennedy Owino, Chammah Kaunda, and Stephen Phiri), 671–681. Minneapolis: Fortress Press.

World Council of Churches (WCC) (2013). *Global survey on theological education 2011–2013: summary of main findings for WCC 10th Assembly, Busan, 30 October–8 November 2013*. Geneva.

17

Christian Women and Peacebuilding

> *"From Asia and Africa to the Americas, Europe, and the Middle East, women's rights activists are the longest-standing socially-rooted, transnational groups mobilizing for peace, countering rising extremism, and providing an alternative vision for the future."*
>
> Women's Alliance for Security Leadership Founding Statement

War and conflict have been a part of human experience throughout history. In the twentieth century, an estimated 231 million people died in or because of warfare worldwide, including from starvation, forced labor, exile, and genocide (Leitenberg 2006; Hobsbawm 1994; Brzeziński 1993). Civil wars have been recently fought in Angola (1975–2002), Sudan (1983–2005), Sri Lanka (1983–2009), Nepal (1996–2006), Chad (2005–2010), and Syria (2011–present), among others. Ongoing territorial conflicts continue in Kashmir (beginning in 1947), between Turks and Kurds (beginning in 1978), and between Oromo people and the Ethiopian government (beginning in 1973). In just the first few years of the 2020s alone, conflict continued to rage in the Persian Gulf, Western Sahara, Cameroon, Israel/Gaza, the Democratic Republic of the Congo, Yemen, India, Peru, Iran, Afghanistan, Libya, Mali, Nigeria, Ukraine, and Bahrain. In most cases, local conflicts have global consequences. For example, the Ukrainian-Russian war, which began in 2014 and intensified in 2022, caused a global energy crisis, a spike in oil and gas prices, and record inflation. Further, it brought about a decrease in food production, which impacted supply not just in Ukraine, but in places already teetering on famine such as Yemen and Syria (Tollefson 2022). War and conflict prove the true interconnectedness of the world.

In 2020, global military expenditure rose to $1,981 billion (an increase of 2.6% from 2019), representing 2.4% of global gross domestic product (da Silva, Tian, and Marksteiner 2021). The United States spends the most on its military ($778 billion, up 4.4% from 2019), representing 62% of global military expenditure. Militarism and patriarchy are closely linked, and together reinforce gendered ideologies and attitudes that negatively impact women. Feminist theorist Cynthia Enloe (b.1938) was among the first to suggest that women's oppression is not just a consequence of but rather a fundamental part of militarism. That is, men place women at the bottom of the social ladder, expecting them to be subservient and submissive, in need of protection from brave, fighting men (Enloe 1983). In this way, militarism perpetuates the belief that women are reliant on men for their safety and basic livelihood. A study of 113 countries from 1990 to 2017 found that those with lower levels of income and democracy have strong associations with both militarization and gender inequality. This means poorer countries where women are the most disadvantaged (especially in labor force participation) are the countries most likely to be involved in military conflicts (Elveren and Moghadam 2019). The gendered impacts of war and violence are indisputable. Although wars are typically (though not exclusively) fought by men, it is women and children who disproportion-ately suffer. During times of war, gender inequalities are exacerbated with decreased social spending – upon which women heavily rely – and increased military spending. Boys are valued more than girls as military "necessities."

Despite the unique impact of militarization and war on women, they are grossly underrepre-sented at the international and national levels of peacebuilding efforts. Between 1992 and 2019, women were just 13% of negotiators, 6% of mediators, and 6% of signatories in major peace processes worldwide; 70% of these negotiations did not involve any women at all (United Nations Security Council 2020). In 2020, just 29% of peace agreements included gender provisions (PA-X Peace Agreements Database 2021). Part of this problem is the lack of women's representation in national and international politics. Women made up just 26% of parliamentarians in 2022, and their share is even lower in countries experiencing conflict (IPU Parline 2022; female share is high-est in the Americas, 34%, and lowest in the Middle East and North Africa, 17%). The first female head of state was elected only in 1980 (Vigdís Finnbogadóttir in Iceland), and in 2022, only 27 countries (11.5%) had a female prime minister or president. Women's absence in one arena impacts women's absence in all arenas.

While war, conflict, violence, and tensions have made life very difficult for women across the world, they work behind the scenes, unrecognized, and without fanfare to help achieve peace, secu-rity, and human flourishing. Women of faith, often working invisibly, have pushed back against gendered norms in both religious and secular spaces to show they are not passive victims of vio-lence, but advocates for peace and security. Religious women in peacebuilding often work across barriers – ethnic, gender, and religious. They tend to promote interfaith engagement and under-standing in their quest for peace, and they encourage religious leaders both male and female to engage in the political sphere to solve social problems. They support victims of violence and they provide education on how to attain and sustain peace (Hayward and Marshall 2015). In doing so, these women help raise the profile of their faith communities as actors of positive change in society. Many of these women are routinely dismissed by cultural expectations and theological interpreta-tions of scripture, yet they are inspired by faith to engage in meaningful work. This chapter high-lights efforts of Christian women in select countries and regions at the intersection of peacebuilding and women's rights. They do so by engaging in gender-conscious readings of scripture, theology, political activism, civil resistance, spiritual support, mediation, community development, and inter-religious boundary-crossing in support of women of all faiths in times of conflict.

What is Peacebuilding?

Katherine Marshall and Susan Hayward – experts in global development, policy, gender, and conflict – describe the intersections of peacebuilding, religion, and gender as the following:

> The term *peacebuilding* thus is used increasingly to define the broad, complex, and sustained process of creating, securing, protecting, and consolidating a peaceful order – work that goes far beyond the formal negotiations that seek to end armed conflicts. Peacebuilding overlaps with development and good governance in the greater effort to build successful, prosperous, and resilient societies. It also reaches into social realms where religious institu-tions hold sway. It affects and is affected by the role of women in society generally and in creating peace specifically.
>
> *(Hayward and Marshall 2015, p. 3)*

Peacebuilding is most effective with contributions from numerous societal spheres, including governments, religious groups, traditional leaders, and the media. It involves an agreement of values that are universal to all parties, such as the right to safety, freedom, respect, and basic needs like housing and employment. It requires skills to build relationships across conflict to teach people new ways of relating to one another and educate people on the nature of conflict and violence. At its core, peacebuilding wages conflict nonviolently, reduces direct violence, transforms relationships, and builds capacity for sustaining peace (Schirch 2004).

A wide variety of peacebuilding organizations exist around the world as networks, foundations, nonprofits, charities, and nongovernmental organizations (NGOs). Some are regional or national, others are global; some have specific foci (such as armed conflict or gender) while others are broader. Well-known organizations such as the United Nations Peacebuilding Commission (est. 2005), the International Peace Institute (est. 1970), the Stockholm International Peace Research Institute (est. 1966), Search for Common Ground (est. 1982), and the Peace Alliance (est. 2004) have been working in conflict resolution, grassroots organizing, legislative work, and research related to peacebuilding for many decades. However, religion was largely overlooked in peacebuilding work until the turn of the twenty-first century, perceiving it to be a negative force that drives conflict, not an influencer of positive societal change. While religion can be divisive, most conflicts that appear to be driven by religion involve other factors under the surface, like ethnic, political, or economic tensions. For example, the Yugoslav Wars of the 1990s were fought between Orthodox Serbs, Catholic Croats, and Bosnian Muslims, but they were not religious wars per se, given the close tie between religion and ethnicity in the region. Religion was not the progenitor of the conflict, rather, the wars were driven by ethnic conflict, nationalism, and collapsing regimes across Europe at the breakup of Yugoslavia. Religious leaders have a clear moral influence in their communities and can encourage peace through shared values of reconciliation, forgiveness, and themes of social justice found throughout all religious traditions. Religions for Peace is the world's largest and most representative NGO in this area, founded in 1970 in New York City with regional headquarters worldwide. Its Women's Mobilization Program formed in 1998, and the Global Women of Faith Network launched in 2001 with over 1,000 members from Baha'i, Buddhist, Christian, Hindu, Indigenous, Jewish, Muslim, Sikh, Shinto, Daoist, and Zoroastrian faith communities.

The United Nations Resolution 1325 on Women, Peace and Security (2000) was the first resolution to urge UN member states to increase women's participation at all decision-making levels regarding conflict resolution and peace processes, including appointing more women as representatives and envoys. This affirmed the crucial role of women in the prevention and resolution of conflicts, in peace negotiations, peacebuilding, and humanitarian response. Further, the Resolution demanded respect for international law to protect the rights of women and girls, address gender-based violence, and pay more attention to the unique needs of women and girls in refugee situations. Resolution 1325 was highly generative for women's peace movements and continues to inspire today. Yet, while progress has been made, tremendous gaps still exist. In Afghanistan, for example, women were only 10% of peace talk negotiators in 2020, although they arguably had the most to lose in the eventual Taliban takeover the following year.

Women are incredibly important in peacebuilding efforts. Peace agreements have more long-term sustainability when women are involved, as they tend to focus more on reconciliation and transitional justice than materiality, and they are also excellent grassroots organizers and influential local leaders as the primary caretakers of their families. Put simply, peace is more attainable and long-lasting when women are involved. While women are not more naturally equipped for peacebuilding than men, elements of women's socialization have proven to be a good fit for this kind of work. Women and girls are generally socialized to not publicly show anger or strong emotions (which helps maintain neutrality in negotiating situations), they are encouraged to hone relational skills,

Photo 17.1 Women engage in peacebuilding in Kinshasa at a meeting held by the United Nations Organization Stabilization Mission in the Democratic Republic of the Congo (2022). *Source:* MONUSCO Photos/Flickr/CC BY-SA 2.0.

and they naturally develop problem-solving abilities to combat the discrimination they face in daily life (Schirch 2004). Women have a vested interest in advocating for peace due to the extreme pressures they face in times of conflict, especially sexual and gender-based violence. Women are keenly able to tap into their social networks and influence the adaptation of peace processes, and they can mobilize in different ways than men. Although women generally have less political authority and power, they have substantial relational influence, which is essential for the success of peace efforts. At the most basic level, women account for at least half of all communities, making it imperative that men and women work together for lasting peace.

Christianity and Peace

The prevalence of violence in scripture – presumably ordained, orchestrated, or approved by God in some way – has contributed to the Christian theology of "just war," which holds that violence is necessary and perhaps even positive. It is argued that God uses violence in particular times and places to justify righteousness, make God's glory known, and to punish God's enemies. Just war theory was outlined by Augustine of Hippo (354–430), refined by Thomas Aquinas (1225–1274), and has moved into secular spheres as a major topic in public policy and international relations. Just war is premised on two conditions. The first is *jus ad bellum*, or the justification for engaging in war, often defined as a state's right to self-defense against unjust aggressors. The second is *jus in bello*, the justice arising within war, which addresses justification of how states act in war (Brooks 2013). Just war theory has dominated Christian understandings of conflict and violence since the fifth century. Yet, from some feminist perspectives, just war theory "turned Christian teaching on its head" in its permission for of "Christians to act as citizen soldiers in a way that would have been unthinkable to earlier Christians" (Hurcombe 1996, p. 175). A complete philosophical treatment of just war is beyond the scope of this chapter, but it is difficult for women to see the violence enacted against them in times of war as anything resembling "just."

Peace, non-violence, and pacifism are part of the Christian heritage, though peaceful witness has been marred by Christianity's intertwinement with power and political structures since Roman emperor Constantine's adoption of the faith in the year 312. Jesus promises peace to his disciples with the coming of the Holy Spirit, "Peace I leave with you; my peace I give you. I do not give to you as the world gives. Do not let your hearts be troubled and do not be afraid" (John 14:27 NIV). He later states, "I have told you these things, so that in me you may have peace. In this world you will have trouble. But take heart! I have overcome the world" (John 16:33 NIV). Jesus offers the promise of peace and examples of nonviolent resistance to those who follow him. Other biblical passages support peacebuilding such as the promotion of equality between all peoples, including among Christians, between men and women, and between Jewish people and gentiles. The Hebrew concept of *shalom*, meaning wholeness, wellness, and complete communal well-being, is also a common biblical and aspirational starting point for Christian and interfaith peacebuilding.

Many Christians have focused on the nonviolent aspects of Jesus's life and ministry and have applied them to their interactions in the political realm. The historic peace churches – Anabaptists, Mennonites, Quakers, and Brethren, named as such for their pacifism, nonresistance, and nonviolence – emphasized Jesus's instructions to turn the other cheek, to love and not kill, and to pray for one's enemies. Anabaptists and Mennonites were ruthlessly persecuted in sixteenth-century Europe, with some entire communities wiped out because of these theological beliefs. Unlike Catholics and other Protestant reformers, these Christians refused to pursue formal relationships with the state, instead opting to live Christ's radical love by eschewing violence, war, and political power. Women make up a majority in these peace churches today: Anabaptist/Mennonites are 52% female, Quakers are 54%, and Brethren are 52% (Johnson and Zurlo 2022). Some of the largest populations of these churches are in the global South, such as Quakers in Kenya (925,000) and Mennonites in the Democratic Republic of the Congo (433,000) (Johnson and Zurlo 2022). Notably, American Quaker Emily Greene Balch (1867–1961) won the Nobel Peace Prize in 1946 for her leadership of the Women's International League for Peace and Freedom. Other churches today practice conscientious objection to military service, such as Holiness pacifist traditions, Christadelphians, and Jehovah's Witnesses; some others lean pacifist, such as the Community of Christ and the Churches of Christ. Jehovah's Witnesses are routinely persecuted for conscientious objection, especially in Russia and former Soviet Union states, where they are jailed for refusing mandatory military service. Globally, Jehovah's Witnesses are 55% female, though in some countries female membership is much higher, such as in Estonia (70%), Armenia (68%), and Lithuania (67%) (Johnson and Zurlo 2022).

Numerous feminist perspectives exist on the concept of biblical peace, but one strand throughout them all is a desire to challenge patriarchal structures that condone violence by promoting equality and life-sustaining initiatives (Kenge 2015). Although women can and have been perpetrators of violence, they are far more likely to be victims, to be dominated by men. Feminist readings of scripture critique the narrative of male domination and female submission, one that leads to violence. Women draw from scripture, tradition, and their spirituality to work not only toward the end of war, but for the restoration of the promised *shalom*.

Vignettes: Christian Women in Peacebuilding

Women have a long history of participating in formal peace movements, so much that in many times and places, peacebuilding and women's rights have been intricately connected. In the United States, for example, the Women's Peace Party (now the Women's International League for Peace and Freedom) formed in 1915 to protest the nation's entrance into World War I, as well as advocate for women's suffrage. In the 1920s and 1930s, Catholic activist Dorothy Day (1897–1980) helped found the influential Catholic Worker Movement on the principles of pacifism, nonviolence, and civil disobedience to combat discrimination against the oppressed, including women, the poor, and the working class. The descriptions of Christian women peacebuilders that follow are not meant to be exhaustive, but rather show a range of women's experiences, activism, and faith-based responses to injustice.

Catholics

In Pope John Paul II's address at the World Day of Peace in 1995, he offered a solution to violence in the world – women. He stated, "The work of building peace can hardly overlook the need to acknowledge and promote the dignity of women as persons, called to play a unique role in educating for peace. I urge everyone to reflect on the critical importance of the role of women in the family and in society, and to heed the yearning for peace which they express in words and deeds and, at times of greatest tragedy, by the silent eloquence of their grief" (John Paul II 1995). For Catholics, peacebuilding is a natural extension of Catholic Social Teaching (see Chapter 8), centered on the dignity of all human beings and the equal creation of men and women in the image of God (Love 2015). Catholic women religious are often engaged in this kind of work, especially in war-torn places.

Women religious peacebuilders are largely under the radar from major international organizations, which tend to work with leaders, who, in the case of Catholicism, are male clergy. The work of women religious and Catholic laywomen helps expand the witness of the church and provides social service supports in the form of girls' education, trauma counseling, gender-sensitive training programs for military and other security leaders, and conflict resolution (Love 2015). Women religious are recognized as trustworthy affiliates of the Catholic Church, an institution which is perceived to transcend race, class, ethnicity, and politics. Yet, women can capitalize on their invisibility since their exclusion from official power structures provides them opportunities unattainable for formal leaders. Sisters are nonthreatening actors with higher mobility than men in the Catholic hierarchy. Often, Catholic women's peacebuilding efforts are seamlessly connected to other forms of holistic mission and outreach. Catholic women, both lay and consecrated, are also highly involved in peacebuilding via Catholic NGOs such as Caritas Internationalis, Pax Christi, Catholic Relief Services, and Focolare.

Part of Catholic peacebuilding is the antinuclear movement. The protest movement Plowshares – from the books of Isaiah and Micah, "They shall beat their swords into plowshares" – gained notoriety in the 1980s when several brothers trespassed and damaged nuclear warhead machinery in King of Prussia, Pennsylvania. In 2012, Sister Megan Rice (1930–2021) – 82 years old at the time – and two other activists, illegally entered a high-security nuclear complex in Oak Ridge, Tennessee, the birthplace of the atomic bomb, where they splashed blood on the walls, spray-painted slogans, and lit candles. This was the most extensive security breach in the history of the US's nuclear complex. After her release from two years in prison, she stated, "Good Lord, what would be better than to die in prison for the antinuclear cause?" (Risen 2021). Antinuclear activism continues in the form of civil disobedience, the careful navigation of international law, and creative courtroom strategies, including self-representing nuns in court. These sisters make an explicit connection between civil resistance and what they consider divine obedience to Christian principles of peace (Sargent 2022).

Democratic Republic of the Congo

Peacebuilding in Africa is a major activity of many Christian churches, missions, and NGOs. The continent has suffered substantial ethnic, religious, and political conflict in the twentieth and twenty-first centuries, often driven by the legacy of colonization and the prevalence of corrupt postindependence dictators. The Democratic Republic of the Congo has been in a near-constant state of conflict since independence in 1960, including insurgencies, wars, coup d'états, and widespread attacks of various kinds. Women suffer from a lack of full equality with men in the DR Congo and continuous conflict makes life for women even more precarious. In ethnic conflicts, it is not uncommon for a rival group to enter a village, destroy the crops, kill or run off the men, and rape the women, as they aim to completely debilitate the community. The DR Congo was named the "rape capital of the world" in 2010 by the United Nations Representative for Sexual Violence and Conflict. The country is 95% Christian (Johnson and Zurlo 2022), and most women are sexual abuse survivors. The stigma, shame, and physical/emotional/mental repercussions of sexual violence are widespread and long-lasting. Gender and religion conscious peacebuilding is not optional in the DR Congo, it is essential.

Christian women make their own theological and relational contributions to building sustainable peace, especially among local communities. A study of Christian women and peacebuilding in the Kivu region, for example, revealed that women were empowered by the biblical story of Abigail (1 Samuel 25), the intelligent and beautiful wife of the boorish and wealthy Nabal. Nabal refused to offer food and shelter to David while he was on the run from Saul, insulting him instead. In turn, David vowed to seek bloody revenge on Nabal and his men. Abigail, without permission from her husband, stepped in to ameliorate the situation, providing David and his men food and seeking humble forgiveness on behalf of her husband. David relented and the crisis was averted. Abigail showcased many critical aspects of peacebuilding in navigating the situation: justice, forgiveness, and humility, while avoiding bloodshed and self-avenging (Kenge 2015). Like the Tamar Campaign that addresses gender-based violence (see Chapter 14), new feminist, contextual readings of scripture empower African women to speak up and seek justice. Women organize to bring peace, trauma healing, and transitional justice to the DR Congo. Sister Marie-Bernard Alima, for example, has worked for over two decades to promote women's rights in the DR Congo. In 2001, she founded the Coordination of Women for Democracy in Peace to offer training for female peacebuilders, now with tens of thousands of women across the country trained in human rights, trauma care, political lobbying, election monitoring, and running as political candidates. She was also the first woman to serve as general secretary of the DR Congo Episcopal Bishops' Commission for Justice and Peace (Hayward and Marshall 2015).

Liberia

One of the most well-known Christian peace advocates in Africa is Leymah Gbowee of Liberia, leader of a nonviolent women's interfaith peace movement that hastened the end of the Second Liberian Civil War (1999–2003) against dictator Charles Taylor. Christian and Muslim women held protests on the main highway leading to the Monrovia airport, capturing the attention of the international community. Interfaith activism was critical to address the conflict, given Liberia's religious diversity – 41% Christian, 41% traditional religionist, and 16% Muslim (Johnson and Zurlo 2022). The 2008 documentary, *Pray the Devil Back to Hell*, documented the more than 3,000 women who – in their signature white T-shirts – came together to help end the civil war through grassroots activism, protests, sex strikes, song, and prayer. Leymah Gbowee, Crystal Roh Gawding, and Comfort Freeman founded Women of Liberia Mass Action for Peace in 2003, which led to the election of Africa's first female head of state, Ellen Johnson Sirleaf (2006). The Ecumenical Women Association of Liberia was formally established in 2009, which advocates for vulnerable women and girls throughout the country. It has trained hundreds of rural and urban women with education, empowerment, and agricultural skills; many now run their own small businesses and are engaged in peace work throughout the country. Gbowee won a Nobel Peace Prize in 2011 for her advocacy and continues to work at the intersection of gender, religion, and peace.

South Asia

South Asia is home to a tremendous amount of religious, ethnic, and linguistic diversity; the region is 54% Hindu, 35% Muslim, 4% Christian, and 3% followers of traditional religions (Johnson and Zurlo 2022). To be effective, peacekeeping and conflict resolution in this region must be boundary-crossing. Women typically show a greater willingness to work across demographic divides such as race, class, and religion for the sake of peace. Interreligious peacebuilding efforts are particularly important in this region for minority Christians, since they can find support from women of other religions experiencing similar traumas related to war, conflict, and societal upheaval. One example is the Association of War Affected Women (AWAW) in Sri Lanka founded by Visaka Dharmadasa, which formed in 2000 for mothers of missing soldiers and war widows during the Sri Lankan Civil War (1983–2009). They engage in ritual pilgrimages to Hindu, Buddhist, and Christian sites to draw empowerment and strength from their faith. AWAW was among the initial groups to establish lines of communication with the separatist military group in the north of the country, the Liberation Tigers of Tamil Eelam (Manchanda 2005). AWAW continues to work with the government and various NGOs on topics such as peacebuilding, interreligious dialogue, pandemic response, and building social cohesion. The work of AWAW led to the founding of the Sri Lanka Women Mediators Network, an interfaith group of women – Hindu, Buddhist, and Christian – that provides in-depth training in mediation and conflict resolution.

The Philippines

While the Philippines is Asia's largest Christian country (90%), most of the country's Muslims live in Mindanao, the country's second-largest island. The ongoing Moro conflict began in 1968, an insurgency with roots in American colonization of the Philippines (1898–1946), resistance of the Bangsamoro people against foreign rule, and the dictatorship of Ferdinand Marcos (1965–1986). While peace agreements were signed in 2014 between the Philippine government, the Moro National Liberation Front, and the Moro Islamic Liberation Front, smaller groups continue to exist and tensions remain high. The Mindanao People's Caucus (MPC) formed in 2001 as a grassroots network of indigenous, Bangsamoro, and Christian community leaders to advocate for peace. In 2010, Christian attorney Mary Ann Arnado formed an interfaith women's department (Muslim, Christian, and followers of traditional religions) to participate in the Bantay Ceasefire, an independent effort to monitor the 2002 ceasefire in the region. It was the first time women had organized to engage in peace processes in the region, and they did so unarmed and unaffiliated with United Nations peacekeepers (Jenkins 2015). Their work was highly successful especially because they were local peacekeepers, not foreign, and because the group's religious and linguistic diversity helped ease similar sectarian divides. Women were empowered by participating in an all-female peacekeeping unit, able to collectively work against *machismo* and patriarchy prevalent in Filipino society.

Many Christian churches engaged in resistance during Ferdinand Marcos's regime. Women were powerful, outspoken critics and put their lives in danger to fight against political corruption, martial law (1972–1981), and authoritarianism. Methodist deaconess Filomena "Ka Liway" Asuncion (1954–1983) became a full-time organizer of local farmers in Isabela province to defend their rights; she was captured by the government, abused, and killed. Catholic sisters openly confronted military forces. Franciscan Sister Mariani Dimaranan (1925–2005) led the Task Force Detainees of the Philippines (TFDP) for 21 years, including the entirety of Marcos's 21-year rule. She documented human rights abuses, assisted victims and their families, and protested torture by the government and military officers. Sister Violeta Marcos (1937–2001) cofounded the Augustinian

Missionaries of the Philippines and was a human rights advocate through the TFDP. Sister Mary Christine Tan (1930–2003) led the Association of Major Religious Superior of Women, a very outspoken group of women religious against the dictatorship, while also helping the suffering poor. Among the most well-known Catholic women religious peacebuilders and activists during this time were the 16 sisters who kneeled before moving military tanks on February 23, 1986, during the People Power uprising. As they prayed, soldiers broke rank to join protesters reciting the rosary. The Bantayog ng mga Bayani ("Wall of Heroes") in Quezon City, Manila, includes the names of nine religious sisters, known as the Bantayog Sisters, who were detained or died while fighting for justice and peace during the anti-Marcos movement. The nonviolent democratic revolution led by the Catholic Church helped end Marcos's decades-long hold over the country.

Religious sisters organized again during the presidency of Rodrigo Duterte (in power 2016–2022). Among these was Australian Sister Patricia Fox, deported from the country in 2018 after living and serving there since 1990, for exposing Duterte's dirty war against farmers, minorities, and civilians, especially in Mindanao. In the run-up to the 2022 presidential election, Filipino religious sisters publicly backed former vice president and human rights lawyer Maria Leonor "Leni" Robredo's candidacy, painting large pink murals on convent walls (Robredo's signature campaign color), engaging in rallies, and organizing via social media. Despite her popularity with the Catholic Church and younger generations, Robredo lost the election to Ferdinand Marcos Jr., son of the former dictator.

The Middle East

The Middle East has been the site of numerous wars, conflicts, and crises since the turn of the twenty-first century, including the Iraq War (2003–2011), the Shia insurgency in Yemen (2004–2014), and the Syrian Civil War (2011–present). These have all caused mass casualties with spillover effects in the region and, furthermore, the creation of a large Middle Eastern diaspora. Peace negotiations are ongoing between Israel and Palestine, between Turks and Kurds, and between the Arab League and Israel, many of which have been unsuccessful. The continued violence in the region impacts men and women differently; for women, kidnapping, forced marriage, forced prostitution, and rape are common. The situation is worse for Christian women as members of a minority and often persecuted religion (Christians make up 4% of the region; Johnson and Zurlo 2022). Women, and especially minority Christian women, are often omitted from decision-making bodies regarding peace in the region. For example, the widely-known Muslim-Christian initiative of 2007 authored by Prince Ghazi bin Muhammad bin Talal of Jordan, "A Common Word Between Us and You," was aimed at greater dialogue and engagement between the world's two largest religions. Its signatories comprised 136 men and two women.

Peace negotiations related to the Arab-Israel conflict and the Palestinian-Israel conflict have been ongoing since at least the 1970s. Some peace treaties have been signed, but there is still much to be done. Peacebuilding in this conflict is very gendered, with men typically in the public arena and women on the sidelines; most Israeli and Palestinian men consider the home the appropriate place for women, not the public square (Blanch, Hertzog, and Mahameed 2015). Women's peace activism in this area is at the grassroots level, such as the Israeli movement Women Wage Peace (WWP), founded in 2014 after the Gaza War (Operation Protective Edge). WWP draws inspiration from Leymah Gbowee's interfaith activism in Liberia and regularly offers screenings of *Pray the Devil Back to Hell* to spur women toward peace activism. With more than 44,000 women members – Jewish, Arab, Druze, Bedouin, Christian, secular, religious, rural, urban – they aim to non-violently hasten the end of the Israeli-Palestinian conflict. Hyam Tannous, an Arab Christian peace activist, has been working with WWP in counseling and psychotherapy. She has trained hundreds of Jewish and Arab counselors to encourage education and dialogue between the two sides. In 2004, she helped organize the From Memory to Peace initiative that brought roughly 400 Israeli Arabs and Jews to the Auschwitz concentration camps in Poland to address Holocaust denial and encourage empathy for Jewish suffering.

Pacific Islands

The Pacific Islands are geographically dispersed, covering more than 300,000 square miles of land and millions of square miles of ocean, but their people are intricately connected at the community level. Religion brings islanders together in congregational settings and theological training institutes, making them less isolated than they may appear. Pacific women collaborate in peacebuilding through these networks (see George 2011), which has resulted in increased representation in regional intergovernmental bodies and the founding of the Pacific Women's Resource Bureau in the 1980s. Pacific women work together across national and ethnic boundaries to advocate for peace in their region, especially in protests of nuclear testing (since the 1960s) and to address localized conflicts in Papua New Guinea, Bougainville, Fiji, Tonga, New Caledonia, Palau, and Gaum (George 2011).

Fiji (64% Christian, 28% Hindu, 6% Muslim; Johnson and Zurlo 2022) gained independence from Britain in 1970 and has experienced ethnic conflict and instability, such as the four coup d'états since 1987. The country has extremely high rates of sexual violence (see Chapters 7 and 14) that are exacerbated by political instability. Women have been active in formal peace processes via the National Women's Plan of Action and the Women, Peace and Security Coordinating Committee (Porter and Mundkur 2012). Fijian women also have an active role in United Nations peacekeeping missions in the Pacific Islands and throughout Southeast Asia, helping shape national politics as visible supporters of antinuclear protests, peace vigils, and in peace talks. A prominent Christian Indo-Fijian feminist activist, Sharon Bhagwan Rolls, works at the intersection of gender, media, communications, and peace. She founded FemLINKpacific in 2000 (a woman's media company), coordinated the Pacific Regional Action Plan on Women, Peace and Security (2012–2015), and has participated in numerous United Nations initiatives to campaign for the adoption of UN Resolution 1325.

Photo 17.2 Members of the Solomon Islands Young Women's Christian Association march in support of women's rights during International Women's Day in Honiara (2011). *Source:* Department of Foreign Affairs and Trade/Flickr/CC BY 2.0.

Colombia

The core component of *mujerista* theology in Latin America and the Caribbean is the promotion of justice and peace for women. Cuban American feminist theologian Ada María Isasi-Díaz asserted that liberation is found in *la lucha* – the everyday struggle for women to survive (Isasi-Díaz 1996; see Chapter 5). Latin American countries have suffered numerous military dictatorships where injustices abounded, including executions, disappearances, economic strife, and, for women, rampant sexual and gender-based violence. Yet, women have not been silent in their victimization and they have emerged as powerful advocates for peace and reconciliation.

In Colombia (95% Christian; Johnson and Zurlo 2022), conflict began in 1948 with the assassination of presidential candidate Jorge Eliécer Gaitán, launching the decade-long civil war, *La Violencia*, where at least 200,000 people died (nearly 2% of the country's population). Over a dozen guerilla insurgencies sprang up to address inequalities related to land, distribution of wealth, and rights of rural populations. By the 1990s, five of these had signed peace agreements with the Colombian government. Women represented nearly a quarter (24%) of ex-combatants, 40% of the Revolutionary Armed Forces of Colombia (FARC-EP), and 25%–33% of the National Liberation Army (ELN) (Bouvier 2016).

Colombian peace negotiations in Havana, Cuba, between 2012 and 2016 resulted in a peaceful resolution to the conflict, with an unprecedented amount of women's involvement. Although women were not necessarily at the official table, they were influencing the process from all sides: "Women's minimal presence as lead negotiators is misleading... At the table, around the table, behind the table, and at side tables, women are having their say and shaping the path to peace" (Bouvier 2016, p. 19). Women participated in the process in large numbers via regional working groups and were especially visible in the 2013 National Summit of Women in Peace, where 450 women across regions, politics, and ethnicities came together in Bogotá to demand greater representation in peace negotiations. As a result, a specific gender subcommittee was created in 2014 to ensure women and LGBTQ+ rights were protected in all agreements – the first of its kind in any peace negotiation worldwide. Women in guerrilla groups also participated in peace negotiations. By 2015, 40% of FARC negotiators in Havana were women (Bouvier 2016). Parallel agreements addressed the specific concerns of indigenous women, leading to the creation of the first National Commission of Indigenous Women. In the case of Colombian peace, women across the country, with the help of international networks, inserted themselves into the process to ensure their unique needs were met. Women were on both sides of the negotiating table – guerilla and governmental – yet came together to show the world that women deserve a seat at the table, and that, when denied one, they make their own tables.

Conclusion

Susan Hayward noted, "Despite the advances in understanding and engagement of religious actors and women in peacebuilding, the scholarship at the intersection of women, religion, and peacebuilding remains thin" (Hayward 2015, p. 308). This statement is even truer when investigating the intersection of Christianity, women, and peacebuilding. Women are everywhere at grassroots levels, participating with their communities, whether secular or religious. They may be absent from official decision-making bodies and the formal peace processes, but their influence is not absent on the ground.

Like all forms of women's activism worldwide, women peacebuilders face many challenges related to religious law, tradition, and local culture. They are caught in between national and international male-led political structures that do not encourage women's participation in peace processes. Further, many of their male-led religious communities may not value peacebuilding as a core part of their mission in the world, or do not value women's public service in this way. The barriers are many for Christian women in this work, but they draw from their theological traditions for empowerment and gain inspiration from biblical women like Abigail to stand up to power. They regularly work across religious divides to address conflicts that impact women regardless of their theological beliefs or religious belonging. Their victimization does not preclude them from participating in their own healing, nor that of their communities and nations. Women's strategic invisibility, as well as their well-fought public advocacy, allows them to do the boundary-crossing work necessary to demand justice and peace.

Reflection Questions

1) Describe the gendered impacts of war, militarization, and violence, and juxtapose these realities with the lack of women's representation on the national and international levels of peacebuilding. What impact would greater inclusion of women at these higher levels have on peacebuilding efforts? Describe the unique strengths that women bring to peacebuilding and how their socialization perhaps prepares them for this kind of work.

2) Do you think churches and Christian organizations have a role in national and international peacebuilding efforts? How have perceptions of religion's influence in conflict hindered Christian involvement in peacebuilding? How has the scripture hindered Christian involvement?

3) Reflect on some examples of the intersection of religion, women, and peacebuilding as described in this chapter. What can churches do at the grassroots level to contribute toward peace in their communities? How willing do you think Christians are to work across differences – religious, gender, ethnic – for peace?

Works Cited

Blanch, Andrea K., Hertzog, Esther, and Mahameed, Ibtisam (2015). Women reborn: a case study of the intersection of women, religion, and peacebuilding in a Palestinian village in Israel. In: *Women, Religion, and Peacebuilding: Illuminating the Unseen* (ed. Katherine Marshall and Susan Hayward), 209–229. Washington, DC: United States Institute of Peace Press.

Bouvier, Virginia M. (2016). *Gender and the Role of Women in Colombia's Peace Process*. New York: United Nations Women and United States Institute for Peace.

Brooks, Thom (2013). Introduction. In: *Just War Theory* (ed. Thom Brooks), 1–10. Leiden: Brill.

Brzeziński, Zbigniew (1993). *Out of Control: Global Turmoil on the Eve of the Twenty-First Century*. New York: Simon and Schuster.

da Silva, Diego L., Tian, Nan, and Marksteiner, Alexandra (2021). *Trends in World Military Expenditure, 2020*. Stockholm: Stockholm International Peace Research Institute.

Elveren, Adem Y. and Moghadam, Valentine M. (2019). *The impact of militarization on gender inequality and female labor force participation*. Working paper No. 1307. Dokki, Giza, Egypt: The Economic Research Forum.

Enloe, Cynthia (1983). *Does Khaki Become You? the Militarisation of Women's Lives*. London: Pluto Press Ltd.

George, Nicole (2011). Pacific women building peace: a regional perspective. *The Contemporary Pacific*, 23(1), 37–71.

Hayward, Susan (2015). Women, religion, and peacebuilding. In: *The Oxford Handbook of Religion, Conflict, and Peacebuilding* (ed. Atalia Omar, R. Scott Appleby, and David Little), 307–332. Oxford: Oxford University Press.

Hayward, Susan and Marshall, Katherine (2015). Religious women's invisibility: obstacles and opportunities. In: *Women, Religion, and Peacebuilding: Illuminating the Unseen* (ed. Katherine Marshall and Susan Hayward), 1–28. Washington, DC: United States Institute of Peace Press.

Hobsbawm, Eric (1994). *The Age of Extremes: A History of the World, 1914–1991*. London: Michael Joseph.

Hurcombe, Linda (1996). Peace movement. In: *An A-Z of Feminist Theology* (ed. Lisa Isherwood and Dorothea McEwan), 174–177. London: Bloomsbury Academic.

IPU Parline (2022). Global and regional averages of women in national parliaments. https://data.ipu.org/women-averages?month=1&year=2022 (accessed 15 June 2022).

Isasi-Díaz, Ada María (1996). *Mujerista Theology: A Theology for the Twenty-First Century*. Westminster: John Knox.

Jenkins, Margaret (2015). An all-women peacekeeping group: lessons from the Mindanao People's Caucus. In: *Women, Religion, and Peacebuilding: Illuminating the Unseen* (ed. Katherine Marshall and Susan Hayward), 143–168. Washington, DC: United States Institute of Peace Press.

John Paul II (1995). Message of his holiness Pope John Paul II for the XXVIII World Day of Peace. Women: Teachers of Peace. 1 January. https://www.vatican.va/content/john-paul-ii/en/messages/peace/documents/hf_jp-ii_mes_08121994_xxviii-world-day-for-peace.html (accessed 16 June 2022).

Johnson, Todd M. and Zurlo, Gina A. ed. (2022). *World Christian Database*. Leiden/Boston: Brill.

Kenge, Esther L. (2015). *Towards a theology of peace-building in the Democratic Republic of Congo (DRC): the contribution of Christian women*. PhD dissertation. University of Kwazulu-Natal. Pietermaritzburg.

Leitenberg, Milton (2006). Deaths in wars and conflicts in the 20th century. Cornell University Peace Studies Program. Occasional paper no. 29, 3rd edn.

Love, Maryann C. (2015). Catholic women building peace: invisibility, ideas, and institutions expand participation. In: *Women, Religion, and Peacebuilding: Illuminating the Unseen* (ed. Katherine Marshall and Susan Hayward), 41–69. Washington, DC: United States Institute of Peace Press.

Manchanda, Rita (2005). Women's agency in peace building: gender relations in post-conflict reconstruction. *Economic and Political Weekly*, 40(44/45), 4737–4745.

PA-X Peace Agreements Database (2021). *Version 5. Political settlements research programme*, University of Edinburgh. www.peaceagreements.org (accessed 15 June 2022).

Porter, Elisabeth and Mundkur, Anuradha (2012). *Peace and Security: Implications for Women*. St Lucia, Qld: University of Queensland Press.

Risen, Clay (2021). Sister Megan Rice, fierce critic of U.S. nuclear arsenal, dies at 91. New York Times. October 17. https://www.nytimes.com/2021/10/17/obituaries/megan-rice-dead.html (accessed 21 June 2022).

Sargent, Carole (2022). *Transform Now Plowshares: Megan Rice, Gregory Boertje-Obed, and Michael Walli*. Collegeville, MN: Liturgical Press.

Schirch, Lisa (2004). Women in peacebuilding resource & training manual. West African Network for Peacebuilding and Conflict Transformation Program at Eastern Mennonite University.

Tollefson, Jeff (2022). What the war in Ukraine means for energy, climate and food. Nature. April 5. https://www.nature.com/articles/d41586-022-00969-9 (accessed 15 June 2022).

United Nations (UN) Women (2015). Preventing conflict, transforming justice, securing the peace: a global study on the implementation of United Nations Security Council resolution 1325. Fact sheet: Latin America and the Caribbean Region. https://wps.unwomen.org/resources/r-fact-sheets/GS-FactSheet-LAC.pdf (accessed 18 June 2022).

United Nations Security Council (2020). Report of the secretary-general on women peace and security (S/2021/827), paragraph 15. Data come from the Council on Foreign Relations, Women's participation in peace processes.

Women's Alliance for Security Leadership. N.d. Announcing the formation of a global alliance of women countering extremism and promoting peace, rights & pluralism. International Civil Society Action Network. https://icanpeacework.org/wp-content/uploads/2017/04/WASL-Founding-Statement.pdf (accessed 17 June 2022).

Conclusion

Religion can be a source of strength, identity, wisdom and autonomy, or it can be a challenge to women's aspirations for themselves, their daughters, and their communities.

Ann Braude (Braude 2007, p. 118)

One of the major themes of this book is that despite the struggles, victimization, discrimination, second-class status, and disadvantages Christian women face worldwide, many women have exhibited a remarkable ability to rise above the fray, girded by their faith, to enact change. This volume includes the stories of many of those women, such as Catholic sisters literally praying in the face of military violence, African women producing scholarship to ensure the survival of their communities and the Earth, and female peacebuilders in Colombia forcing their way to the decision-making table to advocate for women's rights in a postconflict society. Every day, Christian women are tirelessly working to uplift girls and pave a better way ahead. Some organizations have been doing this for a long time: the Girls' Brigade, formed in 1893 in Ireland, operates in 50 countries to support girls, enrich their lives, and guide them to faith in Jesus Christ. Other organizations are new: She Saves a Nation, founded in 2016 in Kenya, provides sanitary products to refugee girls in Kenya, Uganda, and Thailand, as well as works in trauma healing, food relief, and leadership development. Women also work informally outside of institutions, often under-resourced and in partnership across religious traditions to hasten peace and security. For example, Christian and Muslim women in Nigeria's Borno State are coming together to pray and fight against the terrorist group Boko Haram.

Women's subordination to men in churches around the world is the result of many compounding factors. In Japan, for instance, the mythological birth began with a woman, limiting her role to folk tales and stories; Confucianism instructed that men are superior to women; Buddhism taught that women are unclean; and Shinto prohibited women's entrance into sacred spaces (Lee 2022). In many places, the arrival of Christianity appeared to provide the promise of greater freedom for women, but those promises went largely unfulfilled with the coupling of Western gender norms with the gospel, translations of scripture that upheld patriarchal hierarchies, and a lack of positive gender consciousness in mission-founded churches. Late twentieth-century feminism contributed to an increase of women's movements worldwide, where their empowerment stems not from mere translations of Western ideals, but rather grassroots initiatives led by local women with local concerns. Feminist theologians Jenny Daggers (United Kingdom) and Grace Ji-Sun Kim (Canada) identified part of the problem that contributes to a lack of full inclusion of women in churches: "*Christian doctrines* and *global gender justice* rarely appear together in the same sentence" (Daggers and Kim 2015, p. 1, emphasis original). Historians, social scientists, and

Women in World Christianity: Building and Sustaining a Global Movement, First Edition. Gina A. Zurlo.

theologians – the three main disciplines in this book – still have work to do to link Christian doctrine and global gender justice.

Historians are slowly coming to terms that women's history *is* Christian history (a la Braude 1997) and are including more female perspectives in their scholarship. However, simply *adding* women to a previously accepted narrative of church history is not the same as a comprehensive reevaluation of history with gender at the center. Sometimes adding women's perspectives will fragment the existing narrative about a movement, people, or place, but such fragmentation might be necessary to have a comprehensive understanding of the ways in which Christians – *all* Christians – have impacted those movements, peoples, or places. The potential fragmenting of history is a small price to pay for deeper knowledge of the past, but it is possible to write history that integrates diversity and fragmentation (Brekus 2007). More social history is needed, especially in the global South, to uncover the contributions of women to the growth and future of Christianity. Projects like the Dictionary of African Christian Biography (DACB) at Boston University School of Theology, for example, are doing this kind of work. The DACB encourages African Christians to write biographies of their own mothers, grandmothers, female evangelists, theologians, and revival leaders for posterity and inspiration.

As stated in the introduction, social norms are difficult to change, but they keep women from full participation in society and the church. Prescribed roles for women and girls in culture and Christianity are major contributing factors to their inequality, but as the many examples in this book illustrate, Christianity can also empower women to enact change. Christianity is declining the fastest in places where women and men are more equal (e.g., Switzerland, Denmark, Sweden, the Netherlands, Australia, New Zealand), and it is demographically shifting to countries where they are less equal (Papua New Guinea, Chad, Central African Republic). More sociological research at the intersection of religion and gender is needed to fully understand what factors prohibit women's complete flourishing in their societies. What barriers do women face in becoming Christians and participating in Christian communities? What attitudes prevent women from advancing in Christian leadership? Do women even *want* to advance in leadership? How does the Bible inform what roles women have in churches in different cultural contexts? This kind of research needs to be culturally sensitive to each place and not represent transplantations of Western methods. For research to be truly global, methods must be contextual; that is, they must be accessible to local researchers, asking questions that make sense to them.

The first generation of African, Latin American liberation, Asian, and South Pacific theology largely overlooked the experiences of women in their attempt to theologize from the "margins" – now the new center. Although they took into consideration a wide range of experiences related to race, colonization, politics, social movements, and history, they failed to recognize the uniqueness of women. Feminist and womanist theology began to rise in the 1960s and 1970s, and now robust theological traditions exist in all geographic areas and across most Christian traditions. For instance, Pacific, Asian, and North American Asian Women in Theology and Ministry (PANAAWTM) continues to pioneer Asian feminist theology. Yet, a lot of this scholarship has not made its way to the global North, where most theological education still occurs. The majority of universally accepted Western Christian doctrines are written from so-called "gender neutral" positions that do not appear to genuinely consider differences between men and women as it relates to their experiences of the Christian faith. Most Western Christian theology does not consider the widespread implications of particular readings of scripture as they pertain to women, the vulnerable, the environment, equality, and justice. Like history, Christian theology needs a reimagining to take women's concerns, especially of global South women, more seriously. The shifting demographics of World Christianity demand that womanist theology, *mujerista* theology, and feminist theologies from Africa, Asia, the Pacific Islands, and hyphenated communities worldwide (Korean American, Indian American etc.) be central to the faith, not peripheral.

Further Research

The lack of high-quality comprehensive quantitative data on women around the world is a major theme of this book. Without good data, it is difficult to know what problems exist, how they should be addressed, and how to make good decisions. Data are needed to analyze trends to ensure the functioning of all Christian organizations, decide proper resource distribution, and form representative decision-making bodies.

Most fundamentally, Christian denominations and networks must have a greater gender awareness of their affiliates. Christian organizations are well versed in collecting and analyzing quantitative data. A massive data collection initiative occurs among most institutions on a regular cycle, often annually. For example, all Catholic bishops are required to answer, by a fixed date every year, a 21-page schedule in Latin and one other language asking more than 100 precise statistical questions concerning their work. Results are then published in the 2,400-page *Annuario Pontificio* the following January. The Catholic Church also releases *Annuarium Statisticum Ecclesiae* (Statistical Yearbook of the Church) with information on Catholic health, welfare, educational, and other activities. Although the latter is the source for the number of Catholic sisters in the world by region and country,[1] neither of these books includes what share of Catholics in a country or parish are women. No single published Catholic resource has definitively provided information to state, for example, "Catholics in Colombia are X percent female." This basic demographic information is surely known to priests and bishops yet is not published in these official documents. The situation is the same for most Christian denominations worldwide.

If it is essentially unknown, or unreported, what share of a congregation, church, denomination, network, or other organization is female, then it is even more difficult to know what women are *doing* in these organizations and what attitudes fuel gender roles. What kind of education or training do women receive? Do they have access to all levels of leadership that men do? Are they able to serve communion? Perform baptisms? Participate in global missions? Lead global missions organizations? The Gender and Congregational Life Survey (2021) provided a snapshot of gendered participation in churches – generally the only positions that are majority female are children's Sunday School teachers, administrative assistants, and intercessors. However, this survey was not globally representative and is just the tip of the iceberg. More high-quality survey work is needed at local and national levels to measure beliefs and attitudes related to gender dynamics.

This book is limited in scope in that it does not address gender fluidity, transwomen, nonbinary people, and LGBTQ+ issues such as same-sex intimacy, marriage, discrimination, and legal status. As a result, it does not discuss the debates of the inclusion, or lack thereof, of these communities in churches, especially as clergy. This is a major unexplored area for World Christianity scholars, given traditional cultures worldwide that still prohibit and discriminate against gender and sexual fluidity, experimentation, and so-called "non-traditional" families.

For any of this future research to take place, Christian men must be more comfortable talking about and to women, working equally alongside them, and respecting them as leaders, both within and outside the church. Women's voices and concerns would be amplified if men joined the chorus, since men make up the vast majority of leaders in Christian organizations.

---

1 These data do not indicate how many sisters in a country are foreign, and how many are indigenous.

World Christianity is a women's movement because it was built and is sustained by women, and the majority of its members, participants, and affiliates are women. It is anticipated they will continue this work, likely longer than men, since women's religious commitment appears to remain high. Christianity is also continuing its southward shift, with 77% of all Christians likely to live in Africa, Asia, Latin America, and Oceania by the year 2050 (Johnson and Zurlo 2022). This combination means that women in the global South will take on increasingly visible leadership roles in the church, despite the barriers they face, grounded by their faith and in service to their present communities and the next generations. The future of World Christianity depends on it.

Works Cited

Braude, Ann (1997). Women's history *is* American religious history. In: *Retelling U.S. Religious History* (ed. Thomas Tweed), 87–107. Berkeley: University of California Press.

Braude, Ann (2007). *Sisters and Saints: Women and American Religion*. New York: Oxford University Press.

Brekus, Catherine A. (2007). Introduction: searching for women in narratives of American religious history. In: *The Religious History of American Women: Reimagining the Past* (ed. Catherine A. Brekus), 1–50. Chapel Hill: University of North Carolina Press.

Daggers, Jenny and Kim, Grace Ji-Sun (2015). Surveying the landscape of doctrinal imagining. In: *Christian Doctrines for Global Gender Justice* (ed. Jenny Daggers and Grace Ji-Sun Kim), 1–16. New York: Palgrave Macmillan.

Johnson, Todd M. and Zurlo, Gina A. ed. (2022). *World Christian Database*. Leiden/Boston: Brill.

Lee, Samuel (2022). *Japanese Women and Christianity*. Amsterdam: Academy Press of Amsterdam.

Appendices

Methodology

This book features quantitative data on Christianity worldwide, primarily sourced from the *World Christian Database* (WCD; Johnson and Zurlo 2022).[1] The starting point of quantifying religious affiliation of all kinds is the United Nations 1948 Universal Declaration of Human Rights, Article 18: "Everyone has the right to freedom of thought, conscience and religion; this right includes freedom to change his religion or belief, and freedom, either alone or in community with others and in public or private, to manifest his religion or belief in teaching, practice, worship and obser-vance." This fundamental right includes the right to claim the religion of one's choice, and the right to be called a follower of that religion and to be enumerated as such. The section on religious freedom in the constitutions of many nations uses the exact words of the Universal Declaration, and many countries instruct their census personnel to observe this principle.

Religious Change

The question of how and why the number of religious adherents change over time is critical to the demography of religion. It is more complex than simply "counting heads" via births and deaths – a well-established area in quantitative sociological studies – but also involves religious conversion and migration. The dynamics of change in religious affiliation can be reduced to three sets of empirical population data that together enable enumeration of the increase or decrease in adher-ents over time: (1) births minus deaths; (2) converts to minus converts from; and (3) immigrants minus emigrants. The first variable in each of these three sets (births, converts to, immigrants) measures increase, whereas the second (deaths, converts from, emigrants) measures decrease. All projections of religious affiliation, within any subset of the global population, accounts for these dynamics, and the changes themselves are dependent on these dynamics.

Births and Deaths

The primary mechanism of global religious demographic change is (live) births. Children are almost always counted as having the religion of their parents. In simple terms, if populations that

---

1 Portions of the methodology are adapted from Johnson and Zurlo 2019. The baseline data in this book are from the United Nations *World Population Prospects* 2019; the 2022 revision was not released in time for publication. Figures in all tables throughout the book have been rounded.

Women in World Christianity: Building and Sustaining a Global Movement, First Edition. Gina A. Zurlo.
© 2023 John Wiley & Sons Ltd. Published 2023 by John Wiley & Sons Ltd.

are predominantly Muslim, for example, have more children on average than those that are predominantly Christian or Hindu, then over time (all other things being equal) Muslims will become an increasingly larger percentage of that population. This means that the relative size of a religious population has a close statistical relationship to birth rates. In general, it is important for the continuation of religion that children are raised in the faith, but it is also important to realize that raising and retaining children in the faith are arguably two different things.

Fertility rates can be compared across different religions or across different traditions within religions. Several studies have shown that increased religiosity correlates with higher fertility rates among women. Historian Philip Jenkins, for example, asserted that, "Tell me the fertility rate of a particular nation, and I can make a reasonable assessment of the strength or weakness of institutional faith in that society" (Jenkins 2020a; Jenkins 2020b). Even as births increase religious memberships, religious communities experience constant loss through the deaths of members. Though this often includes tragic, unanticipated deaths of younger members, it most frequently affects the elderly. Thus, changes in health care and technology can positively impact religious communities if members live longer. Just as differences in birth rates contribute to the growth or decline of religious communities, death rates also have a similar impact. The change over time in any given population is most simply expressed as the number of births into the community minus the number of deaths out of it. Many religious communities around the world experience little else in the dynamics of their growth or decline. Detailed projections rely on several estimated measures, including life expectancy, population age structures, and the total fertility rate. All attempts to understand the dynamics of religious affiliation must be based firmly on demographic projections of births and deaths.

Converts In and Out

It is a common observation that individuals (or even whole villages or communities) change allegiance from one religion to another (or to no religion at all). Early in the twentieth century it was assumed that within a generation all traditional religionists in Africa would become either Muslims or Christians. Although many conversions took place, over 96 million had not converted by 2000. Many countries in sub-Saharan Africa continue to experience competition between Islam and Christianity for those individuals and communities still adhering to traditional religions. In the twenty-first century, one might project continued conversions to Christianity and Islam but be more modest about overall losses among followers of traditional religions.

Conversion plays a vital, but small, role in the growth of religious communities. As demographer Eric Kaufmann observes, conversion must be viewed in tandem with birth and death rates. He states, "No religion can grow without first enlisting converts from the wider society. Later, the two strategies for fundamentalist expansion are external proselytisation and endogenous growth. External proselytisation is quicker, but rapid conversion is often accompanied by rapid exit. Endogenous growth is often more enduring" (Kaufmann 2010, pp. 30–31). He cites the growth of the Church of Jesus Christ of Latter-day Saints as an example of conversion growth accompanied by strong demographic growth. In other words, Latter-day Saints work hard at spreading their message as well as having large families.

Unfortunately, one of the problems in studying conversion is the paucity of information on it. Reliable data on conversions are hard to obtain. Although some national censuses ask people about their religion, they do not directly ask whether people have converted to their present faith. A few cross-national surveys do contain questions about religious switching, but even in those surveys it is difficult to assess whether more people leave a religion than enter it. In some countries, legal and social consequences make conversion difficult, and survey respondents might be reluctant to speak honestly about the topic.

Conversion to a new religion also involves conversion (or defection) from a previous one. Thus, a convert to Christianity is, at the same time, a convert from another religion. In the twentieth and twenty-first centuries, the most converts from Christianity were and continue to be found largely among those in the Western world who have decided to be agnostics or atheists. The net conversion rate in a population is calculated by subtracting the number of defections from the number of conversions.

Migration

Equally important at the international level is how the movement of people across national borders impacts religious affiliation. Christian diaspora groups around the world today range from the large Hispanic Christian population in the United States, to Palestinian Christians outside of Palestine, to Korean Christian communities in West and Central Asia. Diaspora communities face a series of common challenges in assimilation and differentiation with their host countries. International migration has a significant impact on the religious composition of individual countries. One can try to anticipate the way in which expected immigration and emigration trends will affect a country's population over time.

The six dynamics discussed above determine changes in religious demographics. Gains are the result of three positive dynamics: births, conversions to, and immigration. Losses are the result of three negative dynamics: deaths, conversions from, and emigration. The net change in religious demographics is the result of gains minus losses. The balance of dynamics can be reflected in any proportions (for example, mainly births for gains, mainly defections for losses) but can also be represented by pairing the gains and losses by type: births vs. deaths, converts to vs. converts from, and immigrants vs. emigrants. In each case, the net change (either positive or negative) will be the difference between the two. This means that any attempt to understand religious affiliation in the past, present, or future must be firmly based on demographic dynamics. A proper awareness of these dynamics and their significance is thus vital both for undertaking and for interpreting studies of the future of religion.

Quantifying World Christianity

All those who profess to be Christians in government censuses or public-opinion polls are considered Christians. That is, people who declare or identify themselves as Christians, who say "I am a Christian" or "We are Christians" when asked the question "What is your religion?" are Christians. However, not all those who profess to be Christians are affiliated to organized churches and denominations. Therefore, "affiliated Christians" are those known to the churches or known to the clergy and claimed in their statistics, that is, those enrolled on the churches' books or records, with totals that can be substantiated. This definition of "Christians" is what the churches usually mean by the term and statistics on such affiliated Christians are what the churches themselves collect and publish. In all countries, it may be assumed with confidence that the churches know better than the state how many Christians are affiliated to them. This therefore indicates a second measure of the total Christians that is quite independent of the first (government census figures of professing Christians).

The family is by far the most important instrumentality through which individuals acquire personal, cultural, and social self-identification. Children of church members are more likely to remain members than those whose parents are not church members. Children of practicing Christians usually are, to the extent that their years permit, also practicing Christians. However, many churches do not enumerate children under 15 years. One reason is that it has been widely noted that most conversion crises occur in the 13–20-year age group in Christian families or in majority Christian contexts. On this view, therefore, children who have not yet reached 15 cannot reasonably be expected to be practicing and believing Christians. This book takes the opposite view: children and infants also can properly be called Christians and can actively and regularly (to the extent of their ability) practice Christianity. Consequently, where Christian denominations do not count children in their membership rolls, their membership is reported in the research version of the *World Christian Database* (Johnson and Zurlo 2022). A total community figure is calculated (in the absence of any additional information from the denomination) by adding in the average number of children reported in United Nations statistics for the given country. Thus, the total community figures are comparable from one denomination to the next whether they count children in their membership.

Major Sources of Data

Vast efforts are put into the collection of statistics relating to religion in today's world. Four primary sources for data on religious affiliation are (1) censuses in which a religion question is asked; (2) censuses in which an ethnicity or language question is asked; (3) surveys and polls; and (4) data from religious communities.

Censuses in Which a Religion Question is Asked

Since the twelfth century, many governments around the world have collected information on religious populations and their practices. In the twentieth century, approximately half the world's countries asked a question related to religion in their official national population censuses. Since 1990, however, this number has been declining as developing countries have dropped the question, deeming it too expensive (in many countries, each question in a census costs well over $1 million), uninteresting, or controversial. As a result, some countries that historically included a religion question have not included the question in their censuses since 1990. In several countries, such as Nigeria and Sudan, the decision was for political expediency, to avoid offending particular religious constituencies. In other countries, such as Malta and Türkiye, governments simply assume that the population is essentially 100% of a single religion (Catholic or Muslim, respectively) and therefore justify the question's removal. France rejected the use of a religion question as early as the 1872 census. By the twenty-first century, however, this trend had somewhat begun to reverse. For instance, the United Kingdom – which produced the world's first national census of religious affiliation (the Compton Census in 1676), and later had a religion question in the national census of 1851 (though none thereafter) – reintroduced the question in their 2001 census as the best way to obtain firm data on religious minorities. Whether to include a question on a census can be a heavily politicized decision, as illustrated by India's choice to add questions on caste to its 2011 census. This was the first time such questions had been asked since the 1931 Indian census. Even so, answering the questions on caste was optional.

National censuses are the best starting point for the identification of religious adherents, because they generally cover the entire population. Some censuses, such as South Africa's, even provide information on subgroups of major religious traditions (such as Protestant/Catholic or Sunni/Shia). Governments typically take major population censuses around the end of every decade and then require three to five years to publish the data. In addition to the complete results from a single census date, obtaining these data every ten years enable the calculation of relatively accurate growth rates.

Whether respondents feel free to be completely truthful in answering census questions can be affected by methodological decisions, political biases, and social concerns over how the data will be managed. In addition, problems with comparability of census data can arise when the methods of collection vary (even, and perhaps especially, within a single census). Seemingly mundane issues, like the time of the year when the census is taken, are not irrelevant, because the associated environmental and social factors (such as the weather on enumeration days) can influence the results.

As observed previously, the primary drawback of relying on census data for data on religion is that approximately half of recent country censuses do not include a question on religious affiliation. Taking, for example, the specific case of the European Union (EU), 15 of 27 EU recent country censuses included a religious affiliation question: Ireland, Bulgaria, Croatia, Cyprus, Czechia, Estonia, Finland, Germany, Hungary, Lithuania, Netherlands, Poland, Portugal, Romania, and Slovakia. There are many other issues involved in counting individuals in censuses, one of which primarily revolves around who is and is not considered a legitimate resident of the state. In any analysis of religious demography, it is crucial that the entire population is accounted for. This is especially important when "official" statistics leave out an undocumented religious minority, which would be the case with Muslim immigrants in several European countries.

Another shortcoming of censuses is that they sometimes force people to select their religion or their ethnicity from among a set list. This can result in overestimates, when everyone picks a religion regardless of whether they actually practice it. It also has the potential to miss religions that are not recognized by the government, such as the Baha'i faith in Egypt, or that are considered illegal, as is the case with atheism in Indonesia. Issues related to religious self-identification can be particularly challenging in the West. For example, critics of the 2001 and 2011 United Kingdom censuses claim that even people who in other circumstances would not identify themselves as religious will select "Christian" (because they were baptized as infants) when presented with that choice on a list. On the other hand, pollsters note that making absolute measurements of religious adherence is difficult, because for many people religious identity and religious practice are separate matters.

Censuses are not free from political and social bias and controversy. In 2008, for example, Nigerian officials removed the religious affiliation question from the census questionnaire in response to violent and deadly social protests before the census had even started. The country is nearly equally divided between Christians and Muslims, and various constituencies felt that the census results would be biased and show that one or the other religion predominated. The wording of questions related to religion in censuses is not neutral. For example, much controversy surrounded the 2011 Irish census and its question on religion. The question asks, "What is your religion?" and provides options for Roman Catholic, Church of Ireland (Anglican), Islam, Presbyterian, Orthodox, two rows for "other" (write-in) and then "no religion." Following an invitation by the Central Statistics Office, the Humanist Association of Ireland suggested replacing that question with "Do you have a religion?" This suggestion was rejected on the basis it would make historical comparisons difficult. Using the substitute question, however, would maximize the unaffiliated and nonreligious count.

Censuses Where an Ethnicity or Language Question is Asked

In the absence of a question on religion, another helpful piece of information from a census is ethnicity or language. This is especially true when an ethnic group can be equated with a religion. For example, over 99% of Somalis are Muslim, so the number of Somalis in, say, Sweden is an indication of a part of the Muslim community there. Similarly, a question that asks for country of birth can be useful. If the answer is "Nepal" there is a significant chance that the individual or community is Hindu. In each of these cases the assumption is made (if there is no further information) that the religion of the transplanted ethnic or linguistic community is the same as that in the home country.

Using ethnic or language data as surrogates for religion can be helpful when such information is lacking, but it can also be risky. The most common problem, of course, is that the underlying assumption – that people abroad adhere to a particular religion in the same proportion as those their home country – is not always true. For example, the Palestinian Arab population, just under 2% Christian in Palestine, offers considerable variety in the global diaspora. In neighboring Jordan, they are also 2% Christian, but in the United States they are about 30% Christian (Johnson and Zurlo 2022).

Surveys and Polls

In the absence of census data on religion, large-scale surveys, such as the Demographic and Health Surveys (DHS), often include a question about the respondent's religious affiliation. Demographic surveys, though less comprehensive than a national census, have several advantages over other types of general population surveys and polls. As with most reputable general surveys, a demographic survey bases its sample on population parameters from the most recent census. In contrast to other general surveys, a demographic survey completes sufficient household interviews to produce an accurate demographic profile not only of the country but also of its major states, provinces, and/or regions. To provide this coverage, demographic surveys have larger sample sizes and choose more random locations for samples. Sample sizes for demographic surveys range from more than 5,000 to 100,000, depending on the population and complexity of the country. Early demographic surveys, however, generally included women (and later also men) only in the reproductive ages (15–49 for women and 15–59 for men).

General population surveys also provide valuable information on trends related to religious affiliation, belief, and practice. Such surveys include the General Social Survey, the World Values Survey, the Gallup World Poll, the European Social Survey, the International Social Survey Programme, the Afrobarometer as well as other regional Barometer surveys, and cross-national surveys by the Pew Research Center. However, because general population surveys typically involve a small number of respondents, they cannot provide accurate detail on the sizes of smaller religious groups, though they can give accurate and illuminating data on beliefs and attitudes of larger groups, which helps bolster quantitative data on affiliation.

There are a variety of issues related to finding and choosing the best data sources of religious affiliation. Censuses are generally accepted as the most reliable, but there are times when they fail to present the full picture, for example because they omit certain regions of a country or because they do not ask clear or detailed questions about religion. General population surveys can often fill the gap, but, depending on their quality, they may also have some bias. At times, religious groups may have very different estimates of their sizes than are found by censuses and surveys, but for some types of data, such as denominations of Protestantism, estimates by the groups may be the best information available. Finally, for religions such as Islam, Hinduism, Buddhism, and Judaism, subgroup information is routinely missing from censuses and surveys. Estimates for the subgroups of these religions often rely on indirect measures, such as ethnic groups likely to adhere to a particular subgroup or expert analysis of multiple ethnographic and anthropological sources. Thus, it is important to take into consideration many kinds of data in order to arrive at the best estimate of a particular religious population in a country.

Data from Religious Communities

Data collection and analysis from government censuses and social scientific surveys and polls are common in the demography of religion. A less common, though critical, additional source of data are figures collected by religious groups themselves, in particular, from Christian denominations. A denomination is defined as an organized Christian church, group, community of people, and/or aggregate of worship centers/congregations, within a specific country, that considers itself autonomous, distinct from other churches and traditions, and whose constituents are called by the same name. Denominations are defined and measured at the country level, creating many separate denominations within Christian families and Christian traditions. For example, the presence of the Catholic Church in the world's 234 countries results in 234 Catholic "denominations." The typical way for Christians to count themselves is at the local congregational level and then aggregate these totals at the city, province, state, regional and finally, national level. The Center for the Study of Global Christianity (which produces the *World Christian Database*) collects denominational data from Christian organizations every five years, and the denominational data that appear in this volume are for the year 2015. This book was written in 2021–2022, while data collection was underway for the 2020 denominations cycle, delayed by the COVID-19 pandemic.

Religious communities keep track of their members, using everything from simple lists to elaborate membership reports. They annually invest massive sums of money for this decentralized and largely uncoordinated global census of Christians. Christian denominations send out millions of questionnaires in thousands of languages, covering hundreds of religious subjects and socio-religious variables. This collection of data provides a snapshot of the progress or decline of Christianity's diverse movements, offering an enormous body of data from which researchers can track trends and make projections. Statistics collected by religious communities often enable researchers to distinguish between two categories of religionists – practicing and nonpracticing – based on whether they take part in the ongoing organized life of the religion. In relation to Christianity, practicing Christians are affiliated Christians who are involved in or active in or participate in the institutional life of the churches they are affiliated to (or members of); or who are regarded by their churches as practicing members because they fulfill their churches' minimum annual attendance obligations or other membership requirements; or who in some way have a recognized part in the churches' ongoing practice of Christianity.

Differences in adherent numbers contribute to the popular misperception that religious communities tend to exaggerate their membership figures. Perhaps the most convincing evidence comes from two of the most aggressively evangelistic groups in Christianity. The Church of Jesus Christ of Latter-day Saints and the Watch Tower Society (Jehovah's Witnesses) are both diligent in assembling accurate statistics of membership. Sociologist Alan Aldridge states that there is "no reason to doubt that these [Watch Tower statistics] are accurate. They are in line with estimates produced by government agencies and independent scholars. The society reports poor results as well as good ones, which may well be a sign of honesty" (Aldridge 2007, p. 21). No organization (religious or otherwise) can realistically sustain the reporting of inflated numbers. Eventually, there will either be a ceasing of reported growth, or the fraud will be exposed as the numbers reach obviously impossible levels.

Global North and Global South

Global North is defined in a geopolitical sense by five current United Nations regions: Eastern Europe (including Russia), Northern Europe, Southern Europe, Western Europe, and North America. Global South is defined as the remaining 17 current UN regions: Eastern Africa, Middle

Africa, North Africa, Southern Africa, Western Africa, Eastern Asia, Central Asia, South Asia, Southeast Asia, West Asia, Caribbean, Central America, South America, Australia/New Zealand, Melanesia, Micronesia, and Polynesia. According to the United Nations, "The use of the term 'South' to refer to developing countries collectively has been part of the shorthand of international relations since the 1970s. It rests on the fact that all the world's industrially developed countries (with the exception of Australia and New Zealand) lie to the north of its developing countries" (UN 2003).

Quantifying Women in World Christianity

This book was partially inspired by the lack of comprehensive demographic data on gender in World Christianity.[2] The Women in World Christianity Project (2019–2021) attempted to fill this gap in three ways: a comprehensive literature review, a multilingual survey, and a new quantitative dataset on gender in World Christianity down to the denominational level. This project compiled both quantitative and qualitative data to understand the dynamics of church membership in relationship to gender for thousands of denominations in all countries (234). It became abundantly clear from the literature review that quantitative data on gender is severely lacking. The same methods that are used to ascertain how many members are affiliated to denominations around the world – triangulating data from censuses, surveys, and from denominations themselves – were not sufficient to report on the gender makeup of those groups.

Literature Review

The literature review compiled historical, social scientific, and theological books and articles published in between roughly 2000–2022 related to Christian women around the world. When relevant, active websites and initiatives were also cited to capture real-time events and issues, such as the COVID-19 pandemic. To illustrate how much and what type of research had been completed, the sources were gathered according to region and tagged by country, major Christian tradition/ movement, and over twenty topical tags. The tags were directly related to Christian communities, such as church life, ordination, leadership, theology, missions, persecution, interfaith, and were also broader, such as arts, environment, gender-based violence, sexuality, sexism, patriarchy, politics, development, and education. The taxonomy for regions, traditions, movements, and denominations is sourced from the *World Christian Database* (Johnson and Zurlo 2022). The literature review was limited to sources in English.

Quantitative Data

The core of the project, and the focus of the project's first year, was to assign a percent female to every denomination in every country of the world. The foundational data for this was already in place, housed in the *World Christian Database*. In fact, the only reason such an ambitious project like this was possible is because the Center for the Study of Global Christianity had just completed a five-year research project updating membership figures for every denomination in every country (reported in the *World Christian Database* and *World Christian Encyclopedia*, 3rd edn). As a result, the project began with a strong base year of data (2015) on which to build.

---

2 Thanks to Nadia Andrilenas for her assistance with this section.

The method and reporting of the *World Christian Database* demands that no table has a blank cell, meaning every variable is reported for every denomination in every country. Research assistants combed through census data to identify gender makeup by religion. A difficult part of census research was matching a country's census taxonomy to the taxonomy of denominations in the *World Christian Database*. For example, if a census reports the Apostolic Church is 52% female, does this mean the New Apostolic Church, the Armenian Apostolic Church, the Christ Apostolic Church, the Catholic Apostolic Church, the African Born Full Gospel Apostolic Church, the Apostolic Faith Mission, Zion Apostolic Churches, or something else? This kind of confusion is common in denominational research, given similarities among church names. Some censuses only provided gender for major Christian traditions, such as Zambia, which reports Protestants and Catholics, not individual Protestant denominations nor the Orthodox. In a case like this, the Protestant figure was applied to all Protestant, Pentecostal, and Independent groups in the country and created a national Christian average to apply to the Orthodox and any other missing groups. For countries that do not ask a religion question on their census, weighted global averages were created for each major Christian tradition, or reliable survey figures were used (such as the Pew Research Center for the United States, and CONICET for Argentina). For example, a weighted global average was created for Jehovah's Witnesses (JW) based on available national census data and applied to all JW denominations where they appear. These weighted global averages assume that gender is more tradition/denomination specific, not country specific.

For denominational data, research assistants meticulously analyzed the Center for the Study of Global Christianity's existing digital archives of denominational records, looking for membership figures broken down by gender by using a set of gender-specific search terms. This effort turned up very little hard data. Researchers then turned to WorldCat and online resources to search for books, surveys, reports, articles, and any other kind of material that could indicate the gender makeup of denominations. After months of this kind of research, it was realized that, in general, the data simply do not exist. This was one of the most surprising results of the Women in World Christianity Project: the utter lack of denominational-level membership data on gender in Christianity. This is unexpected because most Christian denominations collect data of all kinds, including church membership, attendance, number of pastors, buildings, women's ministries, children's ministries, budgets, and tithes.

The lack of denominational data came as quite a shock, given two realities. First, churches do collect data but do not collect something as seemingly obvious as gender – that is, they have the capacity to collect data on gender but choose not to. Second, most roles within churches are defined by gender, whether purposefully or otherwise. In many churches, it is typical for women to serve in outreach, prayer, nursery, and children's ministries while men serve as deacons, pastors, elders, and adult teaching ministries. Church life, generally, is gendered. Why do so few denominations acknowledge it in their membership reporting?

The research team did discover that some churches and denominations do report on the gender makeup of regular church *attenders*, but not of *members*. Churches often have a much wider membership than people who actually attend with regularity throughout the week or month. This is particularly the case for national churches, such as state Lutheran churches, Orthodox churches, and the Roman Catholic Church, where many infants are baptized as a matter of national identity. Many churches simply do not update their membership records regularly and miss when people leave the church altogether. Attendance data cannot be used as proxy for membership, which is the variable reported in the *World Christian Database*. This is also the reason why surveys were not utilized as frequently in this study, because surveys tend to measure attenders, not affiliates. Consider the following example from Australia's National Church Life Survey (NCLS). Of the four denominations over 500,000 people in Australia, the NCLS reports percent female of attenders for three (Powell, Pepper, and Hancock 2016):

- Catholic Church in Australia: 58% female attenders
- Anglican Church of Australia: 61% female attenders
- Uniting Church in Australia: 63% female attenders

But, according to the 2016 Australian census:

- Catholic Church in Australia: 52% female affiliates
- Anglican Church of Australia: 54% female affiliates
- Uniting Church in Australia: 56% female affiliates

Censuses typically report lower percent Christian female (affiliates) than surveys (attenders); meaning, men and women are generally church members, but women are by far more active participants. Qualitative literature and ethnographic studies of Christianity in specific communities around the world support the higher figures, but they could not be used in this study because of the affiliation vs. attendance issue. Throughout this book, attempts have been made to illustrate this nuance by providing the affiliation data in the tables but supplementing it with qualitative examples of much higher percent Christian female.

Survey

The Gender and Congregational Life Survey provided a more local level of what women are doing in congregations and attitudes of Christians toward men and women in congregational life. The survey built on previous surveys related to women and Christianity to capture nuances in gender dynamics in Christian congregations (see, for example, Androit and Coe 2016). A databank was created of existing relevant questions, and measures were chosen, adapted, or created to investigate both expectations and realities of gendered roles. Questions had to be equally applicable across Christian tradition, cultures, and geographic contexts, which was very challenging. Pilots of the survey resulted in feedback that some questions just were not applicable for some respondents' locations, cultures, or traditions, revealing a limitation of global survey research. The survey was available in English, Chinese, French, German, Korean, Mongolian, Portuguese, and Spanish and administered online using TypeForm from February 2021 to April 2021. These languages were chosen as those most frequently spoken by Christians around the world, and they were the preferred languages of existing networks that would be likely to take and help disseminate the survey (the latter being most true for Mongolian, due to close ties between the Center for the Study of Global Christianity and Christian networks in Mongolia). For their participation, respondents could opt in a drawing for a hard copy of the *Atlas of Global Christianity*. The survey closed with 1,331 responses from 72 countries. The COVID-19 pandemic canceled all the in-personal global conferences where the survey was initially going to be administered in 2020, resulting in a lower response rate than intended.

The Gender and Congregational Life Survey had many limitations. The online survey used a snowball sample to garner results, which was not the intended method but an unfortunate consequence of COVID-19. As a result, the survey is by no means representative of World Christianity; in fact, respondents were the exact opposite of Christianity's geographic makeup, with 67% from the global North and 33% from the global South. The survey title – Gender and Congregational Life – was interpreted by many potential respondents that it was for women only, despite it being designed for both women and men. This is a problem in the wider field of gender studies, which is often interpreted narrowly as women's studies. As a result, 81% of respondents were female and 19% were male.

The section on men and women in congregational roles was especially important, and these findings are reported in Chapters 1–7 of this book. The survey listed 16 specific roles and asked respondents to indicate whether they thought men or women had a better chance of getting that role in general, and then specifically asked if a man or woman holds that role in their congregation. This series of questions was included because studies on gender in Christianity often concentrate on ordained women or women in orders, leaving a gap in data on other ways women participate in congregational life (see Woodhead 2003). Thus, the survey intentionally included a breadth of roles spanning from highly visible, broader decision-making leadership to those that are more hidden, such as intercessor or janitorial positions. In doing so, the survey acknowledged that women are involved in many ways in congregational life, though are disproportionately missing in visible, broader leadership positions across most traditions and denominations. The diversity and prevalence of naming roles across the full spectrum of Christian ecclesiology and in eight languages was formidable. A "not applicable" option was added after the pilot and instructed respondents to choose the first person that came to mind if their congregation had multiple people in a particular role. Translators were also tasked with choosing the most comparative role for a particular term if a direct translation was not available or applicable. The Gender and Congregational Life Survey revealed some potential realities and trends, but the survey should be readministered with more careful selection criteria for respondents to ensure representativeness.

Works Cited

Aldridge, Alan (2007). *Religion in the Contemporary World: A Sociological Introduction*, 2nd edn. Cambridge: Polity Press.

Androit, Angie and Coe, Deb (2016). *Gender and Leadership in the PC(USA)*. PCUSA Research Services.

Jenkins, Philip (2020a). The future of World Christianity is African. The Gospel Coalition. August 7. https://www.thegospelcoalition.org/article/future-christianity-african (accessed 24 June 2022).

Jenkins, Philip (2020b). *Fertility and Faith: The Demographic Revolution and the Transformation of World Religions*. Waco, TX: Baylor University Press.

Johnson, Todd M. and Zurlo, Gina A. ed. (2022). *World Christian Database*. Leiden/Boston: Brill.

Kaufmann, Eric (2010). *Shall the Religious Inherit the Earth? Demography and Politics in the Twenty-first Century*. London: Profile Books, Ltd.

Powell, Ruth, Pepper, Miriam, and Hancock, Nicole (2016). *2011 NCLS Research Collection*, revised edn. North Sydney, Australia: NCLS Research.

United Nations (UN) Development Programme (2003). *Forging a Global South*. New York.

Woodhead, Linda (2003). Feminism and the sociology of religion: from gender-blindness to gendered difference. In: *The Blackwell Companion to the Sociology of Religion* (ed. Richard K. Fenn), 67–84. Malden, MA: Blackwell Publishing Ltd.

Glossary

This glossary is designed to offer brief definitions of certain terms in this book that might be unusual or are used in specific ways in this book.

adherents Followers, supporters, members, believers, devotees of a religion.

Adventists Protestant tradition begun 1844, emphasizing the imminent Second Advent of Christ.

affiliated Followers of a religion enrolled and known to its leadership, usually with names written on rolls.

affiliated Christians Church members; all persons belonging to or connected with organized churches, whose names are inscribed, written, or entered on the churches' books, records, or rolls.

African Independent Churches (AICs) Denominations indigenous to African peoples, begun without outside help; also termed African Indigenous Churches, African Initiated Churches.

agnostics Persons who lack a religion or profess unbelief in a religion. The term includes (1) "classical" agnostics (who hold that it is impossible to know for certain whether God, or deity of any kind, exists); (2) those who profess uncertainty as to the existence of God; (3) other nonreligious persons such as secularists and materialists; and (4) people who do not claim any religious affiliation but do not self-identify as atheists.

Anglicans Christians related to the Anglican Communion, tracing their origin back to the ancient British (Celtic) and English churches; including Anglican dissidents.

atheists Persons professing atheism, the belief that there is no supernatural higher power; atheists might sometimes but not necessarily be hostile or militantly opposed to all religion (antireligious).

Baha'is Followers of the Baha'i World Faith, founded in 1844 by Baha'u'llah in what is now Iran.

Baptists (1) In its widest meaning, all Christian traditions that baptize adults only, in contrast to paedo-Baptists, who baptize infants; (2) The specific tradition of Protestants and Independents calling themselves Baptists.

Bible The whole or complete Bible of 66 books (sometimes plus Apocrypha).

Buddhists Followers of the Buddha, mostly across Asia, including three main traditions: (1) Mahayana (Greater Vehicle); (2) Theravada (Teaching of the Elders); (3) Tibetan (Lamaists); plus (4) traditional Buddhist sects, but excluding neo-Buddhist new religions or religious movements.

Women in World Christianity: Building and Sustaining a Global Movement, First Edition. Gina A. Zurlo.
© 2023 John Wiley & Sons Ltd. Published 2023 by John Wiley & Sons Ltd.

cargo cults Religious movements in Oceania based on prophecies that if appropriate religious rites are performed, God will send ships and aircraft filled with cargo and goods.

Catholic Charismatics Catholics who have come into an experience of baptism or renewal in the Holy Spirit.

Catholics All Christians in communion with the Church of Rome, also known as Roman Catholics. Affiliated Catholics are defined here as baptized Catholics plus catechumens.

Catholics, non-Roman Old Catholics and others in secessions from the Church of Rome since 1700 in the Western world, and other Catholic-type sacramentalist or hierarchical secessions from Protestantism.

Charismatic Renewal The Pentecostal or neo-Pentecostal renewal or revival movement within the mainline Protestant, Catholic, and Orthodox churches characterized by healings, tongues, prophesyings, etc.

Charismatics Baptized members affiliated to non-Pentecostal denominations who have entered into the experience of being filled with the Holy Spirit.

Christian Brethren Independent Fundamentalist Protestant tradition begun in 1828 out of the Church of England; also called Open Brethren.

Christians Followers of Jesus Christ of all kinds: all traditions and confessions, and all degrees of commitment.

church (1) A building set apart for Christian worship, or the services that go on in it; (2) a local congregation or worshipping body.

Confucianists Followers of the teachings of Confucius and Confucianism. Sometimes spelled Confucians.

Congregation (1) A local church or grouping of worshipers; (2) a religious order, society, or institute (mainly Roman Catholic usage).

Congregationalists Protestant tradition with a system of church government in which the local congregation has full control and final authority over church matters within its own area.

continent Any of the United Nations major areas of Africa, Asia, Europe, Latin America, and Oceania, along with the United Nations region of North America.

conversion Change in a person's allegiance or membership in one religion to allegiance or membership in another.

converts Persons who have become followers of a religion, leaving their former religion or nonreligion.

country Term covering both (1) sovereign nations and (2) non-sovereign territories (dependencies or colonies) that are not integral parts of larger parent nations.

Daoists Followers of the philosophical, ethical, and religious traditions of China, sometimes regarded as part of Chinese folk-religion. Also spelled Taoists.

denomination An organized Christian church, tradition, religious group, community of believers, aggregate of worship centers or congregations, usually within a specific country, whose component congregations and members are called by the same name in different areas.

Disciples A Protestant tradition including the Disciples of Christ and Churches of Christ; also known as Restorationist, Restoration Baptist, Campbellite, or simply "Christian."

doubly-affiliated Christians Persons affiliated to or claimed by two denominations at once.

Eastern Orthodox Referring to Chalcedonian Christians and their congregations and denominations that are in communion with the ecumenical patriarch of Constantinople. Excludes Oriental Orthodox.

Eastern-rite Catholics All Catholics in communion with the Church of Rome who follow rites other than the Latin rite.

emigrant A person who leaves a country or region to establish permanent residence elsewhere.

emigration The movement of emigrants from one country to another.

Ethnic religionists Followers of a religion tied closely to a specific ethnic group, with membership restricted to that group; usually animists, polytheists, or shamanists. Also, indigenous religionists or traditional religionists.

ethnolinguistic people A distinct homogeneous ethnic or racial group within a single country, speaking its own language (one single mother tongue).

Evangelicals Subdivision mainly of Protestants consisting of all affiliated church members calling themselves Evangelicals, or all persons belonging to Evangelical congregations, churches, or denominations; characterized by commitment to personal religion (including new birth or personal conversion experience), reliance on Scripture as the only basis for faith and Christian living, emphasis on preaching and evangelism.

evangelization (1) The whole process of spreading Christianity; (2) the extent to which Christianity has been spread; (3) the extent of awareness of Christianity.

evangelism The church's organized activity of spreading Christianity, in circumstances it can control, in contrast to witness, which is the normal term for the informal, spontaneous, unorganized sharing by individual Christians in circumstances they do not control.

expatriate Any person who has citizenship in one country but resides or lives in another country. In general usage, expatriate frequently connotes (1) temporary, often short-term, residence in the foreign country; and (2) higher socioeconomic status, with those of lower socioeconomic status being termed, e.g., "migrants."

faith-based organization (FBO) An activist organization whose values are based on faith, working to address social issues relevant to that faith.

folk-religionists Adherents of local traditions or religions, often rural, in which elements of major world religions are blended with local beliefs and customs.

foreign missionary Full-time Christian workers who work in countries in which they are not citizens but foreigners, for at least two years.

foreign missions Christian outreach carried out in any other countries than where a sending church or mission is based.

fundamentalist Relating to or characterized by extreme conservatism, especially religious conservatism.

immigrant A person who enters a country or region from elsewhere to establish permanent residence there.

immigrant religion A religion absent from a country until brought in by recent immigrants.

immigration The movement of immigrants to one country from another.

Hindus Followers of the main Hindu traditions: Vaishnavism; Shaivism; Shaktism; neo-Hindu movements and modern sects; and other Hindu reform movements.

Holiness, Holiness Christians Protestant tradition originating in Methodism.

home missionaries Full-time missionaries assigned to work in the country in which they are citizens, including those working cross-culturally in their home countries.

Independency The ecclesiastical position rejecting control of churches by centralized denominational headquarters; organizing churches and missions independent of historic Christianity.

Independents Churches or individual Christians separated from, uninterested in, and independent of historic denominational Christianity.

indigenous Originating or developing or produced naturally in a particular land or region or environment; not introduced directly or indirectly from the outside.

indigenous Christianity In a particular region, that type of Christianity which, in contrast to imported or foreign types, is evolved or produced by populations indigenous to that region.

internationals (1) Persons living abroad; workers, laborers, businessman, entrepreneurs, students, and many other categories of persons who live, reside, and work in a foreign country; excluding tourists or other transients. *See also* expatriate; (2) professionals working for United Nations-related agencies or parallel global organizations (as contrasted with national or regional bodies).

interreligious Existing between two or more religions; used of activities or relationships between two or more of the major world religions (Judaism, Islam, Hinduism, Christianity, Buddhism).

Jains Followers of the two Jain traditions, Svetambara and Digambara; originating in India as a reform movement from Hinduism in the fifth or sixth century BCE.

Jehovah's Witnesses An Independent tradition begun in 1872; also called Russellites.

Jews Followers of the various schools of Judaism: in the United States: Orthodox, Conservative, and Reform; in Israel: Haredi, Orthodox, Traditional, Observant, and secular; ethnically, Ashkenazi (Eastern Europe), Mizrahi (Middle Eastern), Sephardic (Iberian Peninsula).

Latin-rite Catholic That part of the Roman Catholic Church that employs Latin liturgies (forms of Christian worship and liturgy utilizing or based on Latin).

Latter-day Saints A generic term for followers of the Church of Jesus Christ of Latter-day Saints, an Independent Christian movement based in Salt Lake City, Utah, or of its break-off groups; also called Mormons.

LGBTQ+ Acronym for lesbian, gay, bisexual, transgender, and queer (or questioning) people. The plus sign recognizes there are additional sexual orientations and gender identities in the LGBTQ community.

literacy The ability to read and write, as measured by the percentage of the adult population who can read and write their own names and a simple statement. A higher level of competence is required for functional literacy.

Lutherans Followers of Martin Luther and the original sixteenth-century German Protestant protesting tradition.

Mahayana The Greater Vehicle school of Buddhism, or Northern Buddhism (China, Japan, etc.).

mainline Christianity Relating to the historic Protestant churches of Northern and Western Europe (such as Methodist, Presbyterian, Lutheran).

martyr Christian who loses his or her life, prematurely, in a situation of witness, as a result of human hostility.

media believers The total community of those persons (with their dependent adults and children, and other adherents) who derive their ongoing corporate Christian life primarily from isolated radio/TV churches or isolated Bible correspondence course student groupings.

megachurch Very large local congregation or church; in a demographic sense, refers to a congregation or church with a membership over 2,000.

members Affiliated (which usually means enrolled with names recorded) adherents of a religion.

Methodists A tradition formed out of the Church of England in 1795. Many Methodist denominations are called "Wesleyan," "Holiness," or "United," although most belong to the World Methodist Council.

migration Geographical or spatial mobility; physical movement by humans from one area to another with the declared intention to reside in or leave a country for at least a year.

mission The dimension of Christian witness concerned with outreach to the world.

missionary societies Local, denominational, national, or international religious organizations dedicated to starting and supporting missionary work. Also known as mission societies and mission agencies.

Muslims Followers of Islam, in two primary branches: (1) Sunni; and (2) Shia. Other, significantly smaller, branches include Kharijite, Sanusi, Mahdiya, Ahmadiyya, Druze, and Sabbateans.

New Religions The so-called Asiatic twentieth-century New Religions, New Religious movements or radical new crisis religions (new Far Eastern or Asiatic indigenous non-Christian syncretistic mass religions, founded since 1800 and mostly since 1945), including the Japanese neo-Buddhist and neo-Shinto New Religious movements, and Korean, Chinese, Vietnamese, and Indonesian syncretistic religions, among others.

New Religionists Adherents of Hindu or Buddhist sects or offshoots, or new syncretistic religions combining Christianity with Eastern religions, mostly in Asia.

nondenominational Unrelated to any denomination or denominations, nor accountable to any.

nongovernmental organization (NGO) a nonprofit organization that operates independently of any government, usually in social work or politics.

nonreligious Persons professing no religion, or professing unbelief or nonbelief, nonbelievers, agnostics, freethinkers, liberal thinkers, nonreligious humanists. In this book, typically used as an umbrella term for atheists and agnostics together.

Oriental Orthodox Christians of Pre-Chalcedonian/Non-Chalcedonian/Monophysite tradition, of five major types: Armenian, Coptic, Ethiopian, Syrian, Syro-Malabarese.

Orthodox In four traditions: Eastern (Chalcedonian), Oriental (Pre-Chalcedonian, Non-Chalcedonian, Monophysite), Assyrian and nonhistorical Orthodox.

p.a. Per annum, per year, each year, every year, annual, yearly, over the previous 12 months.

Pentecostals Followers of Pentecostalism, a Christian movement originating around 1900.

Presbyterian See Reformed.

Protestants Christians in churches originating in, or reformulated at the time of, or in communion with, the sixteenth-century Protestant Reformation. In European languages usually called Evangéliques (French), Evangelische (German), Evangélicos (Italian, Portuguese, Spanish), though not usually Evangelicals (in English).

poll An opinion inquiry taken at a single point in time, from a very small carefully-constructed sample (usually around 1,500–2,500 adults) representative of the entire adult population, to solicit answers to carefully-formulated questions, to derive information applicable to that entire population.

population For an area, the total of all inhabitants or residents of that area; or occasionally, the total number of persons who spend or spent the night in the area.

population census A government survey to obtain information about the state of the population at a given time.

quality of life The effectiveness of social services in a country, measured by indexes such as the United Nations Human Development Index (HDI).

Reformed A major Protestant tradition originating in continental Europe and including the term Presbyterian (originating in English-speaking countries).

religionists Persons professing adherence to any religion, as contrasted with atheists or nonreligious persons.

refugees Persons who have migrated due to strong pressures endangering their continued stay in their countries of origin, and who are unable or unwilling to return, excluding labor and other migrants and also returnees.

region In United Nations terminology, one of 21 areas into which the whole world is divided for purposes of analysis.

religion An organized group of committed individuals that adhere to and propagate a specific interpretation of explanations of existence based on supernatural assumptions through statements about the nature and workings of the supernatural and about ultimate meaning. In this book, religion as used in a demographic sense includes the unaffiliated (i.e., agnostics and atheists).

religionists Persons professing adherence to any religion, as contrasted with the nonreligious (i.e., agnostics or atheists).

religious change Changes from one religion or religious system to another within a certain time period, e.g., in the course of a year.

religious demography The scientific and statistical study of the demographic characteristics of religious populations, primarily with respect to their size, age–sex structure, density, growth, distribution, development, migration, and vital statistics, including the change of religious identity within human populations and how these characteristics relate to other social and economic indicators.

religious diversity The degree to which a population comprises individuals with differing religious adherences. Interreligious diversity describes the degree of over-all diversity of distinct religions (Islam, Hinduism, Judaism, and so on) within a population or geographic area, whereas intra-religious diversity encompasses the diversity found within a given world religion (for example, traditions such as Catholicism, Orthodoxy, and Protestantism within Christianity).

religious liberty Freedom to practice one's religion with the full range of religious rights specified in the United Nations 1948 Universal Declaration of Human Rights.

religious pluralism The peaceful coexistence of different religions or denominations within a particular community.

religious men (brothers) Unordained male members of Catholic religious institutes or orders, living a consecrated life of the Catholic Church. Vows of poverty, chastity, and obedience.

religious women (women religious) Female members of Catholic religious institutes or orders, working on behalf of the Catholic Church in a variety of settings, often social service, and education. Vows of poverty, chastity, and obedience.

Restoration Movement (1) The Churches of Christ, or Disciples, a major US group of denominations; (2) an Independent charismatic para-denomination splitting in 1974 from the Charismatic Renewal within the mainline Protestant churches in Britain and the USA.

Roman Catholics All Christians in communion with the Church of Rome. Affiliated Roman Catholics are defined in this book as baptized Roman Catholics plus catechumens.

rural area De facto areas classified as rural (that is, it is the difference between the total population of a country and its urban population); defined in many countries as an administrative district with a population of under 2,000.

secularism A view of life or of any particular matter holding that religion and religious considerations should be ignored or purposely excluded.

secularization The act or process of transferring matters under ecclesiastical or religious control to secular or civil or lay control; the process whereby religious thinking, practice, and institutions lose social significance.

shamanists Ethnic religionists with a hierarchy of shamans and healers.

Shias Shi'is Followers of the smaller of the two great divisions of Islam, rejecting the Sunna and holding that Mohammed's son-in-law Ali was the Prophet's successor and itself divided into the Ithna-Ashari Ismaili, Alawite, and Zaydi sects.

short-term missionaries Persons serving as foreign missionary personnel for a single period between one week and 24 months only.

Sikhs Followers of the Sikhism, founded by Guru Nanak in the fifteenth century in the Punjab region of the Indian subcontinent. Traditions include Akali, Khalsa, Nanapanthi, Nirmali, Sewapanthi, and Udasi.

Spiritists Non-Christian spiritists or spiritualists, or thaumaturgicalists; high spiritists, as opposed to low spiritists (Afro-American syncretists), followers of medium-religions, medium-religionists.

Sunnis (Sunnites) Followers of the larger of the major branches of Islam, that adheres to the orthodox tradition of the *sunna*, acknowledges the first four caliphs, and recognizes four schools of jurisprudence: Hanafite, Hanbalite, Malikite, Shafiite.

socioeconomic status (SES) A measure of an individual's or group's position in society, based on factors including income, education, and occupation. Sometimes other factors – such as wealth, place of residence, race, ethnicity, and religion – are also used in determining SES.

state religion An established religion, national religion recognized in law as the official religion of a country.

survey A systematic method for gathering information from (a sample of) entities for the purposes of constructing quantitative descriptors of the larger population of which the entities are members.

switching, religious When individuals leave a religion or religious body either to other religions or religious bodies or to no religion (agnosticism, atheism).

Theravada The Teaching of the Elders or the Hinayana school of Buddhists, or Southern Buddhism (in Sri Lanka, India, Myanmar, Thailand, Cambodia, Laos).

tradition An ecclesiastical family or type of denominations sharing historical and/or many common features.

traditional religion Often used of the dominant pre-Christian religion in a country, sometimes described as ethnic or indigenous religion.

unaffiliated Christians Persons professing allegiance and commitment to Christ but who have no church affiliation.

United churches Churches formed from the union of various Protestant denominations (including Anglicans).

urban areas De facto population living in areas classified as urban according to the criteria used by each area or country; often these are agglomerations of 2,500 or more inhabitants, generally having population densities of 1,000 persons per square mile (391 persons per square kilometer).

urbanization The state or extent of urban areas or the process of becoming urbanized, in a particular country.

worldview A general understanding of the nature of the universe and of one's place in it; outlook on the world, ideology, a cosmological conception of society and institutions.

Yazidis (Yezidis) Members of a monotheistic religion that has elements of ancient Mesopotamian religions and combines aspects of Christianity, Judaism, and Islam.

Zoroastrians Followers of a religion founded in Persia in BCE 1200 by the prophet Zoroaster teaching the worship of Ahura Mazda, now followed by Parsis in India and elsewhere.

Index

a

abduction 64, 275
Abigail (biblical) 322, 327
abolition 124, 129
Aboriginal(s) 145–7, 151, 176, 245
abortion 27, 58, 88, 103, 120, 127, 133, 165, 171, 174, 176–7, 193, 267
Abrams, Minnie 65, 110, 237
abuse 63, 88, 105–6, 125, 133–4, 152, 171–2, 177, 245, 258, 265, 267–70, 273–4, 276–8, 304–5, 322–3
activism 4, 8, 29, 86, 100, 112, 114, 128, 146, 150, 169, 176, 205, 245, 248, 272, 284–5, 287, 291, 293, 295, 312, 317, 321–2, 324, 326
activist(s) 117, 124, 129, 150, 169–72, 287, 291–3, 294–5, 321, 324–5
Adam (biblical) 202, 222, 259
adaptation (climate change) 258, 286, 295
administrative assistant(s) 30, 41, 61, 83, 104, 122–3, 144, 332
administrators 65, 134, 170, 222, 312
adoption (children) 173, 225
advocacy 8, 174, 255, 278, 284–6, 293–4, 322, 327
advocates 26, 51, 114, 129, 132, 170, 277, 287, 317, 322, 326
Afghanistan 69, 256, 267, 274, 316, 318
Africa 3–4, 6–7, 14, 24, 27, 29, 31, 35–8, 40–51, 62, 65, 78, 84–5, 91, 97, 122, 128, 139, 144, 160, 166–7, 171–2, 182–3, 193–4, 198–9, 204–6, 211–12, 216, 220–1, 223, 228–9, 232, 234–5, 238, 240–1, 248–9, 255–8, 267–9, 272–5, 279, 286, 289–90, 295, 300
African American(s) 32, 43–4, 254, 293, 309
African Christian(s) 3, 25, 36, 40, 42–4, 48–51, 212, 255, 257, 290, 331
African Christianity 35–6, 40, 44, 48–9, 51, 212
African Independent Christianity 42, 216, 221
African Independent Churches (AICs) 3, 7, 19, 36, 46–8, 51, 215–16, 220–3, 240
African Methodist Episcopal Church 119, 129
African Methodist Episcopal Zion Church 129–30

African Pentecostalism 36, 48
African theology 31, 49, 51, 222
African Traditional Religion(s) (ATR) 24, 37, 44, 49, 98, 240
African women 40, 43, 46–7, 49–51, 171, 173, 189, 229, 289, 322, 304, 330
African(s) 6, 24, 32, 36, 41, 43–6, 49, 91, 98, 105, 108, 119, 128–9, 172, 205, 212, 220–2, 240–1, 289–90, 292, 306, 331
Afro-Catholic religion 99, 109
agency 4, 27, 35, 66, 72, 85–6, 127, 134, 167, 177, 239, 254
Aglipay, Gregorio 68, 225
agriculture 47, 69, 286–7, 291–2, 322
Ajuoga, Abednego Matthew 222
Aladura churches 46, 221–2
Alaska Native women 277, 309
Albania 76, 89, 165, 192, 200, 219, 277
alcohol 46, 101, 111, 223
Alexandria, Egypt 181, 206
Algeria 35–6, 43, 169, 172, 219, 236, 252, 271
American Baptist Church 120, 198, 272
American Baptist(s) 65, 67, 111
American Board of Commissioners for Foreign Missions (ABCFM) 128, 284
American Catholic(s) 62, 109, 125, 127, 171, 293
American Evangelical(s) 128, 257
American Protestantism 124, 128
American Samoa 138–41, 143, 200, 219, 235
Americas 27, 98, 105, 110, 114, 128, 166, 176, 306, 316–17
Amerindian (beliefs) 98, 109
Anabaptists 202, 320
ancestors 1, 44, 47, 49, 62, 91, 108, 125, 224, 291
Andorra 76, 166
angels 27, 65
Anglican Church of Aotearoa, New Zealand, and Polynesia 141, 143, 147, 198, 210
Anglican Church of Australia 141, 143, 210, 343
Anglican Church of Nigeria 23, 40, 200, 201, 253

Anglican Communion   86, 198, 206, 207, 210, 225, 272, 288, 345
Anglican Diocese of Polynesia   211, 278
Anglican(s)   1–2, 31, 39, 40–1, 46, 61, 63, 70, 82–3, 87, 119, 122, 125, 132–3, 141, 144–5, 146–7, 206, 209, 211, 253, 256, 279, 287, 311, 338
Anglicanism   43, 45, 141, 146
Angola   35–8, 40, 42–3, 172, 206, 272, 316
Antigua   97–8, 100, 110
antinuclear movement   150, 321, 325
apostle   42, 63–4, 159, 176, 221–2, 225, 227
Apostolic Faith Mission of South Africa   47, 240
Aquinas, Thomas   87, 319
Aquino, María Pilar   112–13, 306
Arab(s)   18, 32, 63, 165, 236, 305, 324–5, 339
Argentina   23, 97–9, 102–3, 106–7, 109, 162, 166, 168, 172, 174, 208–9, 272, 275–6, 306, 342
armed conflict   275, 317–18
Armenia   54, 64, 82, 185, 188, 194, 320
Armenian Apostolic Church   64, 189, 342
arranged marriage   243, 277
arts   8, 125, 193, 308, 309, 311, 341
Aruba   97–8
Asia   7, 14, 25, 27, 36, 44, 54–8, 62–5, 67–72, 84, 97, 122, 128, 131, 139, 144, 160, 166–7, 170, 173, 198, 204, 206–7, 211, 216, 224, 249, 256, 274–5, 290–1, 295, 305, 312, 316
Asian Christianity   54–6, 67–8, 70–2
Asian feminist theology   31–2, 70–2, 291, 331
Asian(s)   6, 32, 55, 62, 66, 69, 71, 216, 290
Assemblies of God   24, 29, 143, 200, 208, 231, 237, 238–9, 243, 245, 253
Association of Theological Schools (ATS)   308–10
Assyrian Orthodox   182, 349
asylum seeker(s)   90, 170
attendance (church)   3–4, 29, 35, 37, 44, 65, 68, 78, 89, 118, 122, 131, 166, 176, 226, 239, 340, 342–3
Augustine of Hippo   36, 87, 319
Australia   25, 138–41, 143–7, 151–2, 170, 176, 210–11, 227, 237, 245, 267, 294, 310–11, 331, 341–3
Austria   76, 82, 90
authoritarianism   226, 323
authority   47–8, 51, 57, 65, 71, 105, 112, 125, 127, 133, 144, 148, 164, 168, 170, 188, 191, 224–5, 232, 241, 254–5, 257–60, 273, 278–9, 319, 346
autonomy   40, 45, 174, 209, 239
Aylward, Gladys   28, 204
Azusa Street Revival   231–2, 237, 239, 246

b

baby girls   244, 267
Baha'i   55, 318
Bahrain   18, 54, 69, 316
Bangladesh   18, 54–5, 58, 69, 224, 252, 256, 268, 271, 275, 286, 305
baptism of the Holy Spirit   221, 231, 237–8

baptism   44, 46–8, 89–90, 125, 172, 197, 202, 211, 221, 225, 231, 237–8, 240, 243, 332
Baptist(s)   3, 22, 41, 61, 65, 67–8, 78, 82, 85, 103, 110, 119, 122, 133, 144, 197–8, 200–2, 209, 223, 231, 253, 306
Barbados   18, 97, 100, 106, 249, 252
Barbuda   97, 98, 100
Barker, Jen   32, 152
barrenness   26, 215
Barrett, David B.   2–3, 47, 67, 127, 220, 222–3
barrier(s)   2, 5, 8, 206, 232, 277, 312, 317, 327, 331, 333
Batak Christian Protestant Church   65, 207
beating(s)   193, 273
Beattie, Tina   88, 93, 177
Bebbington, David   248, 261
Becquart, Nathalie   88, 169
Bediako, Kwame   44, 49
Bekono, Anastasie   35
Belarus   76, 185, 186, 192, 267
Belgium   45, 76, 84, 252
belief(s)   4–5, 14, 25, 76–8, 80, 89, 97–8, 100–1, 122, 124, 128, 133, 147, 169, 181–2, 189, 192, 197, 208, 221, 227–8, 238, 240, 243, 248, 254, 259, 265, 270, 279, 289, 316, 320, 327, 332, 334, 339
belonging   71, 89, 182, 327
Benedictines   165, 197
Benin   35, 200–1
Bermuda   18, 117, 119, 127
BES Islands   18, 97, 100
Bessey, Sarah   128, 260
Bhutan   54, 200, 219, 236, 252, 271
Bible study   13, 40, 256, 272, 292, 304, 311
bible teacher   30, 84, 133, 145, 210
Bible translation   43, 50–1, 66, 85, 110
Bible women   3, 6, 27, 67, 128, 224
Bible   31–3, 41, 43–4, 47, 49, 56, 61, 66, 68, 78, 82–3, 103, 110, 112, 122, 129–32, 144, 208, 210, 222, 225–6, 229, 248–9, 254, 256–7, 259, 268, 273, 292, 331
Bingen, Hildegard of   84, 165, 284
biology   81, 170
birth control   87, 127, 133
birth rates   14, 24, 50, 78, 269–70, 334–5
birth(s)   8, 14, 24–5, 36, 50, 78, 127, 133, 152, 159, 165, 189, 206, 253, 267, 330, 334, 336, 339
bishops   88, 159, 166, 168–9, 173, 278, 290, 322
Black church(es)   130, 197, 220, 226, 238
Black Protestant(s)   24, 122
blood   226, 321
Boff, Leonardo   112, 292
Bolivia   97–9, 103, 109, 209, 276
Book of Mormon   131, 149
book(s)   3–9, 13–14, 28, 31, 35, 42, 50, 66, 70, 111, 131, 149, 151, 197, 221, 225, 249, 254, 321, 330–2
Bosnia-Herzegovina   76, 272

Botswana   18, 35, 38, 49, 219, 249, 257, 273, 304
Bougainville   149, 325
Braude, Ann   27, 117, 124, 134, 209, 330
Brazil   13, 17, 23, 91, 97, 99, 102–3, 105–6, 108–9,
      111–12, 131, 159, 162–4, 169, 174, 198, 201,
      208–9, 218, 220, 225–6, 231–2, 234–7, 243–4,
      251, 253, 268–9, 275–6,
      292, 306
Brazilian(s)   91, 98, 234, 292
Brethren   122, 320
bride(s)   187, 268, 275
Britain   125, 198, 203, 248, 254, 325
British Empire   206, 254
British mission   28, 43, 45, 65–6, 85–6
Buddhism   253, 256, 290, 330, 339
Buddhist(s)   25, 55, 62, 118, 139
Bulgaria   76, 79, 166, 184–6, 191, 338
Burghardt, Anne   2, 79, 208
Burkina Faso   35–6, 236, 252, 257, 271–2
Burundi   35, 43, 46, 172, 194, 206
Byzantine Empire   181–2, 187

C

Cabo Verde   35, 163, 172
Calvin, John   76, 202
Calvinism   85, 244, 256
Cambodia   18, 35, 44, 54, 200, 236, 252, 275
Cameroon   35, 44, 271, 316
Canada   24, 117–19, 121–2, 125, 127–8, 131, 176,
      198, 209, 255, 268, 278, 293, 308, 330
Canadian(s)   125, 128, 207, 288
capitalism   113, 169, 287, 292
Carey, Dorothy   65, 85
Caribbean   2, 4, 7, 14, 25, 97–114, 131, 174,
      208–9, 219, 252, 275, 291, 300,
      306–7, 326
Caritas Internationalis   88, 169, 321
Carmichael, Amy   28, 85, 204
Carroll, Seforosa   151, 294
catechist(s)   64, 222–3
Catholic Charismatic(s)   19, 68, 100, 108, 112, 231,
      237, 243–4, 246
Catholic Church (Roman)   22, 29, 35, 48, 54, 65,
      85–8, 93, 99–100, 105, 107, 110, 113–4, 119,
      125, 128, 132, 134, 159–60, 164–8, 170–2, 174,
      176–7, 197, 225, 238, 269, 278, 291, 293, 321,
      324, 332, 338, 340, 343
Catholic order(s)   85, 87, 173
Catholic Relief Services   170, 321
Catholic Social Teaching (CST)   127, 169–70,
      176–7, 321
Catholic Women's League   88, 176
Catholic Worker Movement   127, 169, 321
Catholic(s)   1–2, 6–7, 13–14, 19, 22, 25, 27, 29, 35–8,
      40, 42–6, 48, 54, 56, 59–60, 62–5, 67–8, 72, 78,
      80, 84–91, 93, 97–101, 103, 105–8, 110,
      112–14, 117, 119, 122, 125–32, 134, 141, 145,
      147, 149, 159–60, 164–77, 181–2, 185, 197,
      202, 208, 212, 215–16, 220, 225, 231, 234, 243,
      249, 276, 278–9, 290–4, 300, 303, 306–8, 318,
      320–1, 323–4, 330, 332, 337, 342
Catholicism   13, 25, 36, 38, 42, 45, 48, 54, 64, 76–7,
      80, 86, 88, 91, 97–100, 105–6, 108–12, 114,
      126–7, 129, 131, 134, 140, 145–6, 159–60,
      163–4, 166–7, 171–3, 181–2, 185, 189, 198,
      202, 208, 211–12, 306, 321
Cayman Islands   97–9
celibacy   26, 49, 64, 172
censuses   3, 14, 23, 35, 37, 184
Central Africa   46, 198, 206, 290
Central African Republic   35, 38, 252, 267–8,
      270–2, 331
Central America   98, 131, 209, 291, 306, 341
Central Asia   25, 54, 56, 63, 269, 275, 341
Central Europe   77–8, 89
Chad   35, 219, 267–8, 270, 316, 331
charisma   47, 225
charismatic leader(s)   46–7, 182, 216, 221
charismatic movement   46, 215, 241
Charismatic(s)   7, 19, 39, 48, 55, 58, 68, 78, 81, 91,
      93, 98, 100, 108, 111–12, 119, 131, 143, 149,
      208, 216, 231–2, 225, 227–8, 231–2, 234–46,
      253, 256, 258, 303, 311
charitable work   160, 176
chastity   167, 177
child marriage   68, 194, 203, 266, 268, 274
child(ren)   24–7, 30, 37, 41–4, 47, 56, 61, 65, 68,
      82–5, 101, 103–4, 106, 111, 113, 117, 122–3,
      125, 127, 144, 146, 152, 165, 170–3, 181,
      187–9, 193–4, 203–4, 207, 222, 224, 226,
      238–9, 242, 254–6, 266, 268, 272–7, 279, 286,
      288, 301, 304, 311, 317
childbearing   26, 193
Chile   97–100, 102–3, 106–7, 109–11, 166, 171, 208,
      216, 237, 292
China   14, 17, 19, 23, 26, 54–6, 57–8, 60, 63–70, 85,
      126, 150, 173–5, 200, 203–4, 207, 220, 224,
      226, 232, 237–8, 242, 244, 253, 256, 268,
      275, 294
Chinese Catholic Church   54, 60, 64–5
Chinese house church(es)   68, 197, 220, 224,
      253, 256
Chinese Patriotic Catholic Association   65, 68
Cho, David Yonggi   27, 242
Choi, Jashil   27, 68, 242
Christendom   6, 77, 105–6, 145
Christian education   301, 307
Christian school(s)   241, 301, 312
Christology   151, 258, 294
Church Father(s)   36, 187
church history   6–7, 27, 31, 67, 77, 84, 133, 182, 331
church membership   3, 29, 37, 99, 118, 122, 124,
      202, 226
Church Missionary Society   86, 145
Church mother(s)   36, 130, 222, 240
Church of England   86, 93, 242, 254

Church of God in Christ   121, 130, 220, 226, 236–8
Church of God Mission International   48, 241
Church of Jesus Christ of Latter-day Saints   19, 24, 29, 124, 131–2, 215–16, 226, 228–9
Churches of Christ   120, 215, 320
Circle of Concerned African Women Theologians   49, 171, 206, 273, 289, 304
cities   23, 55, 106, 131, 159, 181, 215, 224, 241, 244, 278, 318, 324
citizen(s)   71, 125, 130, 188, 207, 319
civic life   124, 127, 254
civil disobedience   169, 321
civil resistance   317, 321
civil right(s)   129, 190
civil war(s)   63, 316, 322–4, 326
civilization   45, 77, 160, 203, 293
class   4, 26, 70–1, 97, 107, 113, 130, 133, 151, 169, 174, 237, 239, 277, 288, 293, 295, 321, 323
climate activism   285, 293
climate advocacy   286, 293
climate change/crisis   8, 26, 92, 150–1, 284, 292
climate refugees   26, 294
climate   85, 170, 284–5, 290, 292–5
clinic(s)   110, 206, 278
cloister(s)   64, 85, 164, 167, 197
co-pastor(s)   61, 240
Cold War   77, 191
Colombia   23, 97, 99, 102, 110–11, 113, 164, 166, 174, 237, 271, 275, 306, 326, 330, 332
colonization   25, 36, 43, 45, 50, 55, 63, 64, 70–1, 77, 97, 110, 118, 138, 146–7, 149, 151, 204, 223, 249, 289, 321, 323, 331
communication(s)   68, 98, 120, 159, 228, 266, 311, 323, 325
communion   47, 68, 82, 86, 88, 160, 166, 182, 189, 198, 206, 207, 210, 225, 272, 332
Communism   24, 68, 77, 89–90, 93, 190, 192
community   18, 22, 30, 44, 48–9, 67–8, 70, 72, 89, 91, 108, 111–13, 126, 129, 139, 151, 166, 173, 188, 202, 207, 211, 238, 256–7, 260, 270, 272, 274, 278, 285, 293–5, 305–8, 312, 317, 320, 322–3, 325
complementarianism   114, 128, 133–4, 209, 228, 256, 258
Base Ecclesial Communities (Comunidades Eclesiales de Base, CEBs)   107–8, 112, 114
concentration camp   192, 325
concubine(s)   44, 106, 268
conflict resolution   318, 321, 323
conflict(s)   36, 56, 64, 77, 86, 88, 105, 107, 110, 125, 149, 187, 194, 202, 204, 241, 275, 316–19, 321–7
Congregationalist(s)   22, 43
congregations   3, 13–14, 22, 27, 29–30, 41, 59, 77, 82–3, 91, 110, 121–2, 130, 133, 138, 159, 173–4, 177, 184, 197, 205, 209–11, 221, 224, 226, 240–1, 274, 278–9
conquest   25, 45, 62–4, 97, 113, 181

consecrated life   84–5, 159
Constantine   76, 320
contextual theology   31, 114, 150–1, 207, 288, 305, 311
contextualization   50, 59, 70, 238, 249
contraceptive(s)   26, 171, 174, 225
control   5, 26, 47, 87, 106, 127, 133, 211, 266, 268, 278
conversion(s)   14, 24, 26, 43–4, 50, 55, 58, 62, 76–7, 105, 111, 143, 147, 172, 181, 185, 187, 194, 204, 224, 228, 231, 239, 241, 253, 256, 258, 287
convert(s)   24, 26, 35, 40, 42–3, 47, 65–6, 92, 110, 126, 131, 172, 187, 219, 224, 226, 228–9, 234, 239, 248, 253, 256, 274, 290
Cook Islands   138–9, 148
cooking   59, 125, 149, 289
Coptic Orthodox Church   182, 186, 193, 223
Costa Rica   97, 113, 209, 292, 306
Council of Nicaea   181–2
Council on Biblical Manhood and Womanhood   209, 258
counseling   173, 279, 311, 321, 325
coup d'état   322, 325
COVID-19, 56, 171, 266, 275, 277, 291, 300, 340
creation   49–50, 87, 151, 169, 202–3, 256, 287–9, 291–5
Croatia   76, 93, 257, 338
Cuba   97–9, 106, 113, 271, 306–7, 326
Cultural Revolution (China)   68, 173
culture(s)   19, 31, 42–4, 46, 49–50, 54, 63–8, 71–2, 77, 84–6, 89–91, 93, 97, 109, 118, 124–6, 128, 134, 138–9, 146–7, 151–2, 159–60, 170, 174, 181–2, 191, 194, 203–5, 207, 215, 222, 228, 231–2, 238, 243, 248, 256, 265, 273–4, 276, 279, 284, 289–90, 301, 304, 326, 331–2
Curaçao   97–8, 100
curricula   7, 49, 304–5, 310, 312
Cyprus   54, 185, 249, 338
Czechia   18, 76, 79–80, 88–9, 174, 192, 338

d

Dacuycuy, Emelyn   68, 215, 225
Dalit theology   31, 70, 112
Dalit(s)   31, 70, 112, 239, 305
dancing   48, 221, 223, 228, 231, 243
data   2–3, 7–8, 14, 19, 22, 28–9, 37, 54, 78, 84, 99–100, 120, 123–4, 139–40, 160, 166, 183–4, 232, 239, 249, 270, 272, 275, 300–1, 303–4, 308, 312, 332
daughter(s)   71, 84, 113, 164, 176, 187, 210, 222, 225, 232, 243, 255, 257, 268, 294, 307
Day, Dorothy   87, 127, 169, 321
deacon(s)   84, 129, 145, 147, 166–7, 189, 191, 193, 206, 210
death   24–5, 36, 42, 46, 67, 85, 99, 109, 146, 165, 170, 215, 222, 228, 244, 254, 267–8, 275, 295
decolonization   45, 55, 77, 148

degree(s) 8, 61–2, 82, 103, 111, 122, 144, 300–1, 304–6, 306, 309, 311

Democratic Republic of the Congo (DR Congo, DRC) 2, 17, 23, 35, 38, 40, 42, 49, 162, 164, 170, 172, 218–20, 223, 232, 235–7, 267–9, 272, 316, 320, 322

demographic(s) 21, 24, 29, 32, 36, 50, 77, 121, 139, 160, 182, 187, 323, 331–2

demon(s) 46, 49, 111

Denmark 45, 88, 200, 208, 277, 308, 331

Desert Mothers 42, 187

development 36, 88, 169, 257, 289–90, 293, 317, 341

diaconate 167, 182, 189

dialogue 70, 92, 159, 167, 191, 207, 256, 291, 296, 323–5

diaspora 48, 68–9, 113, 139, 182, 190, 238, 324

dictator(s) 106, 322, 324

dictatorship(s) 2, 54, 100, 106–7, 110, 114, 166, 174, 323–4, 326

Diego, Juan 27, 108

dignity 48, 65, 91, 127, 149, 152, 166, 191, 203, 207, 211, 229, 239, 259, 304, 306, 321

dirty war 107, 324

disability 210, 255, 276

disappeared 84, 106–7, 173, 254

disciples 26, 29, 37, 47, 63, 187, 215, 268, 320

discipleship 32, 67, 255

discrimination 8, 56, 58, 63, 70, 72, 90, 130, 173, 193, 209, 265–6, 268, 274, 276–7, 279, 304, 311, 319, 321, 330, 332

disease(s) 125, 146, 165, 170, 267

disestablishment 88, 226

displacement 291, 295

diversity 23–4, 31–2, 40, 54, 56, 63, 70, 77–8, 80, 97–8, 100, 108, 118–19, 124, 128, 130, 171, 176, 197, 205, 210, 215, 223, 226, 228, 232, 246, 294–5, 306, 323, 331

divorce 4, 241, 274

Djibouti 51, 267

Doctrine of Discovery 105, 124–5, 128

doctrines 111, 197, 221, 226, 228, 238, 244, 288, 330–1

domestic violence 64, 149, 152, 243, 245, 267–9, 273, 276–9, 293

domesticity 4, 111, 117, 203, 207

domination 56, 68, 97, 268, 288, 293, 320

Dominica 97, 252

Dominican Republic 97, 103, 106–7, 306

dress code(s) 226, 274

drinking 36, 101, 111, 150, 228, 243, 286, 289, 293

dualism 151, 290, 294

Dyer, Mary 127, 202

e

Earth 105, 150–1, 284, 287–9, 292–4, 296, 330

East Asia 3, 54–6, 170, 275

Eastern Catholic 63–4, 165

Eastern Europe 24, 78, 80, 89–90, 92, 174–5, 187, 192, 194, 208, 275

Eastern Orthodox 1, 27, 63–4, 93, 181–2, 186, 187, 189–90, 194, 207

ecofeminism 287–8, 290–2

ecofeminist theology 288–9

ecology 8, 92, 152, 169, 176, 285, 287–8, 291–3

economic oppression 113–14, 291

economics 5, 92, 97, 128, 130

ecosystems 287, 289

ecotheologies 150, 284, 289

ecowomanism 151, 289, 293–4

Ecumenical Association of Third World Theologians (EATWOT) 70, 92, 291, 305

ecumenical movement 86, 149, 182, 190, 194

Ecumenical Water Network 288, 291

ecumenism 8, 13, 29, 41, 70, 77, 86, 92–3, 107, 148–9, 151, 165, 182, 190–1, 194, 207–8, 274, 287–8, 291, 294, 305–6, 322

Eddy, Mary Baker 203, 221

Edinburgh World Missionary Conference 44, 106, 128

education 3, 5, 7–8, 18, 26, 29, 36, 43, 45, 47–9, 55–6, 58, 64, 66–7, 69–70, 72, 81, 85, 91, 106, 111, 117, 124–5, 127, 133–4, 138–9, 146–7, 159, 167, 170–2, 174, 176, 181, 189, 191, 193, 197, 203–205, 207, 228, 238–9, 242, 244, 249, 257, 259, 265, 268, 272, 274, 277, 300, 302, 305–6, 311, 332

egalitarianism 2, 26, 48, 92, 114, 122, 130, 133, 151, 222, 227, 237–8, 240, 246, 260, 294

Eglise de Jésus-Christ sur la Terre par le Prophète Simon Kimbangu (Church of Jesus Christ on Earth Through the Prophet Simon Kimbangu, EJCSK) 40, 46, 223

Egypt 35–6, 42–5, 106, 185, 186, 193, 267, 271, 305, 338

El Salvador 97, 106–7, 111, 171

Elaw, Zilpha 129, 254

elder(s) 29, 44, 67, 84, 122–3, 126, 144, 151, 206, 209, 224, 226, 245

election(s) 93, 127, 147, 175, 227, 258, 322, 324

emancipation 59, 68, 72, 97, 172, 211

emigration 24–5, 56

Emmanuel, Christiana Abiodun 3, 47

emotion(s) 60, 129, 144, 237–8, 254, 265, 267, 278, 309, 318, 322

empire 42, 45, 63, 77, 105, 181–2, 187, 190, 206, 254, 260, 292

employment 32, 56, 81, 90–1, 138, 193, 194, 228, 274, 276–7, 286–7, 300, 318

empowerment 48, 58, 97, 149, 152, 174, 203–205, 229, 239, 256–7, 260, 266, 279, 284, 304, 322–3, 327, 330

energy 289, 294, 316

England 65, 84–5, 88, 110, 127, 132, 202, 204, 242

enrollment 133, 301, 303–6, 308–9

enslaved people 98, 105, 108, 128–9
environmental activism 284, 287, 293
environmental degradation 151, 284, 288, 291
Episcopal Church USA 134, 167, 198, 210, 216, 225, 242
Equal Rights Amendment 133, 171
Equatorial Guinea 35, 42, 172
Eritrea 35–6, 42, 271
erosion 285, 294
Estonia 18, 76, 79–80, 88, 189, 191–2, 208, 320, 338
Eswatini 13, 35, 38, 219, 235, 257
Ethiopia 17, 23, 35–6, 38, 40, 42, 44–5, 185, 186, 188, 193, 201, 221, 251, 269, 271, 287
Ethiopian Church 45, 221
Ethiopian Orthodox Church 23, 40, 186, 191, 193,
Ethiopian Orthodox Tewahedo Church 42, 193
ethnic minorities 77–8, 81, 91, 93, 106, 110, 256
ethnicity 4, 24, 63, 70–1, 124, 223, 238, 269, 277, 309, 318, 321, 316
Europe 4, 6–7, 14, 19, 24, 31, 36, 55, 62, 76–8, 80–2, 84–9, 97, 105, 117–18, 122, 131, 145–6, 160, 163–4, 166–7, 171, 174–5, 182, 184, 187, 192–3, 197–8, 202, 225–6, 232, 238, 243, 246, 248–9, 254, 260, 267, 275–7, 292, 302, 307–8, 311
European Catholicism 25, 88, 105–6, 108
European Christianity 45, 76–8, 80, 84, 86, 92–3, 146, 207
European Union 91, 276–7
Europeans 14, 63, 90, 98, 105, 128, 221, 292
Evangelical Church Mekane Yesus 201, 253,
Evangelical Church Winning All 200, 253, 259
Evangelical Lutheran Church 79, 86, 88, 205, 207–8, 210, 276, 311
Evangelical Protestant(s) 19, 66, 93, 113, 122, 128, 134, 171, 182, 254, 257, 278
Evangelical(s) 7, 19, 21, 25, 66, 79, 86, 88–9, 93, 98, 100, 113, 122, 127–9, 133–4, 143, 149, 171, 182, 198, 205, 207–8, 210–11, 216, 225, 244–5, 248–9, 252–60, 276–8, 295, 301, 303, 305–8, 310–11
evangélico(s) 19, 25, 98, 100, 131, 208, 249
evangelist(s) 26–7, 29, 43–4, 46–8, 51, 57, 67–8, 72, 123, 129, 133, 139, 145, 148, 188–9, 204, 208, 210, 224, 226, 237, 240, 244, 331
evangelization 40, 45, 67, 85, 108, 113, 126, 128, 145–6, 159, 169, 203, 222, 226, 244, 249, 255, 257–8
Evans, Rachel Held 128, 260
Eve 187, 202, 222, 259
Ewha Womans University 66, 207
exclusion 49, 70, 113, 167, 243, 272, 277, 306, 321
exorcism(s) 48, 258
exploitation 2, 49, 91, 113, 175, 177, 249, 266, 275, 278–9, 293, 306
exploration 31, 105, 111, 147

f
faculty 303–4, 308–11
faith healing 210, 221
faith mission 47, 110, 221, 239–40
faith-based organization(s) 265, 275, 289
family planning 26, 32, 127
family values 82, 128, 133, 171, 203, 206, 278
family 8, 19, 46–7, 58, 60, 87, 90–1, 97, 111, 113, 132–4, 139, 151, 170–1, 173, 188, 191, 193, 203, 206, 211, 220, 222, 224–5, 228, 234, 241–2, 245, 253, 256, 266, 268–9, 272, 274, 277, 286, 304, 311, 321, 336
farms 287, 293, 323–4
Faroe Islands 76, 200
fasting 68, 82, 242
fear 1, 274, 279
feast day(s) 63, 125, 188, 242
female (church) affiliation 78, 100, 218, 237
female bishop 68, 147, 206, 208–10, 225, 244
female evangelist 204, 331
female faculty 303, 308, 310–11
female founder 3, 47, 198, 202, 221
female genital mutilation (FGM) 170, 193, 266–7
female leader 130, 151, 221, 223, 240–41, 245, 305, 310
female minister 151, 209, 211, 244, 305
female missionaries 4, 6, 13, 43, 65–7, 85, 110, 125, 128, 132, 203–4, 257
female ordination 211, 307
female pastor 61, 112, 134, 207, 209, 240, 305
female president 92, 132, 204–5, 209, 222, 244, 255
female student 57, 133, 166, 302–3, 305–8, 309–11
female theologian 2, 7, 32, 132, 151–2
feminism 4, 70–2, 77, 87–9, 91–2, 111, 117, 128, 132–3, 135, 138, 147, 149, 168, 171, 191, 193–4, 209, 256, 258, 287–8, 292, 304, 330
feminist history 124
feminist theology 6–7, 31, 51, 70, 72, 91–2, 113, 132–3, 151–2, 288–9, 291–2, 305, 331
feminization 71, 124, 166
fertility 26, 119
Fiji 138, 140–1, 143, 148–50, 211, 278–9, 286, 294, 311, 325
filial piety 62, 224
Filipino(s) 64, 68–9, 70, 147, 225, 291, 323–4
Finland 76, 86, 207–8, 277, 308, 338
fire 232, 244, 278, 291–2, 295
First Great Awakening 129, 254
First Nations 125, 293
flood(s) 150, 292, 294–5
flourishing 8, 204, 268, 284, 311, 317, 331
Focolare 108, 321
food insecurity 88, 150, 285, 295
food 193, 286, 316, 322, 330
Foote, Julia 129, 254

forced labor   275, 316
forced marriage   266, 272, 275, 324
formation   108, 132, 176, 190, 194, 239, 304, 311
France   3, 17, 45, 76, 79, 82, 84–5, 88, 93, 105, 124,
       162–3, 165, 168–9, 208, 243, 286, 292
Francis of Assisi   85, 287
Franciscans   76, 85, 323
fraud   225, 244, 275
freedoms   138, 224, 254
French Guiana   97–8
French Polynesia   138, 141, 149, 211, 227
friendship   66, 108, 211
future   5, 9, 24–6, 32, 37, 44, 50–1, 55, 63, 71–2,
       92–3, 98, 106, 114, 117, 152, 166, 184, 212,
       223, 231, 245, 260, 285, 287–9, 292, 294–5,
       303, 306, 331–3

g

Gambia   35, 43
gas   285–6, 291–2, 316
Gaza, Palestine   316, 324
Gbowee, Leymah   322, 324
gender gap   4–5, 57, 117, 286
gender ideologies   60, 204
gender imbalance   4, 24, 58, 184, 204, 275
Gender Inequality Index   97, 266, 269
gender inequality   5, 26, 97, 266, 269, 316
gender issue(s)   49, 149, 304
gender justice   49, 86–8, 147, 151, 273, 304–5,
       330–1
gender norms   212, 229, 232, 241, 265, 330
gender parity   191, 206, 276
gender relations   92, 148, 170, 222, 225, 273–4
gender rights   3, 287
gender role(s)   18, 26, 50, 82, 90, 111, 152, 168, 170,
       176, 181, 191, 193–4, 203, 211, 222, 243, 255,
       259–60, 271, 277, 332
gender-based violence (GBV)   8, 41, 49, 56, 69, 86,
       193, 206, 265–7, 270, 272–5, 277–9, 304, 310,
       319, 322, 326
gendered expectations   24, 37, 41, 61, 64, 83, 90,
       103, 122, 144, 151, 181, 194
generations   1, 27, 77, 81, 87, 93, 124, 132, 181, 245,
       287, 289, 324, 333
genocide   77, 105, 114, 125, 190, 204, 316
Georgia (country)   54, 57, 63, 132, 166, 175, 185,
       187–8, 191
Germany   17, 23, 45, 76, 82, 84, 88, 90, 169, 172,
       198, 202, 208, 226, 292
Ghana   35, 38, 42–4, 47–9, 91, 235, 240–1, 272
gifts of the Spirit   98, 223, 231
girl(s)   8, 26, 28–9, 43–4, 56, 58, 63, 66, 125–6, 144,
       146, 165–6, 169–72, 193, 203–4, 211, 221, 224,
       244, 257, 259, 265–8, 270, 275–7, 286, 293,
       300–1, 305–6, 317–18, 321–22, 330–1
glaciers   291–2
global Christianity   2, 6, 13, 249

Global Church Project   32, 152
global gender justice   330–1
global North   7, 14, 19, 31, 97, 139, 160, 163, 166,
       183, 201, 216, 248, 260, 331
global South   4, 6–8, 14, 19, 24, 28–9, 31–2, 70, 80,
       83, 93, 97, 117, 123, 139, 160, 162, 168, 170,
       182–3, 199–201, 211, 217, 228, 231–2, 234,
       239, 246, 248–9, 253, 255, 258, 260, 269, 272,
       286, 288, 292, 295, 300, 305, 311–12, 320, 331,
       333
Global Survey on Theological Education   300,
       302–3
global warming   285–6
God   1, 14, 27, 44–5, 48, 50, 60, 64, 71, 78–9, 82, 110,
       113, 122, 129–31, 133, 151–2, 167–8, 175, 187,
       188, 194, 202, 207, 215, 221, 225–6, 228, 237,
       239–40, 245, 254–5, 257–9, 265, 268, 276, 279,
       287–8, 289–90, 293–4, 301, 304, 319, 321
gods   98, 108, 129
Goldsworthy, Kay   147, 210
government(s)   3, 21, 23, 28, 35, 37, 45, 47, 65, 68,
       107, 110, 125, 131, 146–7, 150, 173–4, 184,
       194, 244, 257, 265, 268, 273, 277, 279, 295,
       304, 316, 323, 326
graduate (education)   7, 300–1, 307–8, 311
grandmothers   90, 113, 125, 189, 331
grassroots activism   114, 146, 322
Greece   76–7, 82, 88, 181, 185–6, 188–9,
       191, 193
Greek Orthodox   182, 188–9, 287, 308
greenhouse gas   285–6, 291–2
Greenland   117, 119, 127
Gross Domestic Product (GDP)   36, 139
Grudem, Wayne   209, 258
Guatemala   2, 97, 99, 102–3, 184–5, 235
Guinea-Bissau   35, 42, 200, 252
Guinea   35, 267
Gulf States   18, 69, 162, 236, 316

h

Haiti   97–8, 100, 106, 270, 306
harassment   209, 265–7, 269, 271, 276,
       304, 311
harmony   203, 290
Harris, William Wadé   46–7
Havea, Sione 'Amanaki   150–1
Hayward, Susan   317, 326
head pastor   30, 62, 84, 104, 123, 248
healer(s)   47–8, 51, 221
healing   46–8, 91, 98, 109, 111–12, 131, 177, 187,
       210, 221, 223, 225, 231, 237, 240–1, 243–4,
       258, 276, 279, 289–90, 293, 322, 327, 330
healthcare   8, 56, 69, 85, 128, 170–2, 174, 190,
       203–4, 266
heaven   64, 132, 159, 221
herding   18, 58
hermeneutics   70, 92, 289, 294, 308

hierarchy   3, 28, 44, 48, 59, 64, 68, 88, 93, 99–100, 105–6, 110–12, 151, 167, 175, 221, 225, 321, 330

higher education   7, 64, 66, 300–1, 305–6, 311

Hildegard of Bingen   84, 165, 284

Hill, Graham Joseph   32, 152

Hindu(s)   25, 55, 68, 118, 139, 173, 204, 218, 224, 256, 318, 323, 325

Hinduism   26, 204, 224, 253, 256

historian(s)   4, 13, 27, 118, 121, 124, 128, 134, 164, 174, 187, 191, 204, 209, 221, 248, 254, 258, 260, 330–1

historic church(es)   19, 48, 63–4, 89, 149, 231

HIV/AIDS   3, 49, 88, 165, 170–1, 194, 257, 304, 310

Holiness churches   22, 31, 41, 61, 83, 103, 122, 129, 144, 237–8, 242, 245, 320

holism   7, 111, 113, 133, 169, 173, 203, 212, 223, 279, 289, 292, 295–6, 301, 321

Holocaust   226, 243, 325

Holy Spirit   48–9, 68, 111–12, 172, 208, 221, 223, 225, 227–8, 231–2, 237–8, 244, 255, 320

home   58, 71, 85–6, 89, 97, 101, 111, 114, 127, 151, 170–1, 188, 192, 204, 224, 231, 241, 254, 276, 279, 286, 301

homemakers   191, 203

Honduras   97, 103, 171

Hong Kong   54, 61, 65, 70, 72, 170, 207, 242

Hoover, May   110, 237

hope   2, 8, 32, 44, 113, 177, 228, 238, 293

hospital(s)   126, 160, 173,175, 206, 241

house church(es)   19, 22, 25, 29, 56–8, 68, 197, 220, 224, 236–7, 253, 256, 260

household(s)   28, 47, 203, 228, 260, 266, 286

housewives   107, 202

human flourishing   268, 317

human right(s)   107, 112, 132, 149, 169–70, 174, 272, 276, 278, 286, 291, 306, 322–4

human trafficking   88, 165, 170, 274–5

humanity   2, 49, 287, 290

Hungary   76, 79, 90, 174, 208, 338

husband(s)   43–6, 63, 65, 84–5, 103, 105–6, 111, 117, 187, 194, 202–3, 207, 220, 221–2, 225, 227, 232, 237, 240–1, 244, 254, 258–9, 265, 268, 277–8, 286, 322

i

Iceland   76, 79, 88, 163, 185, 200, 208, 292, 317

Idahosa, Benson   48, 241

Idahosa, Margaret   48, 241

identity   4, 8, 48, 70–1, 78, 89, 91, 124–6, 127–8, 134, 139, 144, 151, 174, 182, 186, 192, 193–4, 206, 223, 237, 239, 246, 248, 258, 291, 307

illness   47, 65, 111, 215, 240

immigrant(s)   24, 56, 77, 81, 91, 93, 118, 122, 124–5, 130–1, 134, 141, 162, 258, 306

immigration   24, 77–8, 90, 93, 118, 126, 134, 141, 143, 147, 253, 258, 275

imperialism   65, 105, 113–14, 203–4, 228

income   5, 28, 67, 111, 316

inculturation   49, 64, 147, 167

independence   106, 110, 128, 131, 138, 150, 175, 223, 275, 322, 325

Independent Charismatic(s)   19, 112, 225, 231–2, 237, 240–1, 245

Independent Christianity   19, 25, 38, 182, 215–16, 219–26, 228–9, 253

Independent(s)   3, 7, 19, 24, 25, 36–8, 42, 45–8, 51, 57, 60, 67–8, 78, 89, 91, 100, 111–12, 129, 149, 182, 186, 197, 208, 215–16, 219–29, 231–2, 237, 240–1, 244–5, 253

India   2, 14, 26, 28, 31, 55–8, 63–70, 85, 111–12, 118, 150, 165, 172–3, 191, 197, 204, 224, 237–40, 256, 258, 267–8, 271, 275, 291, 294, 305–6, 316

Indian(s)   18, 44, 62–3, 65, 69, 106, 146, 165, 242

indigenous Christianity   44, 65, 68

Indigenous women   106, 125, 151, 176, 277

individualism   49, 70, 148, 169, 254

Indonesia   54–5, 57–8, 60, 65, 68–9, 199, 224, 251, 267, 275, 303, 305

inequality   5, 26, 55, 97, 266, 269–70, 316, 331

infanticide   8, 27, 203, 267

injustice   2, 258, 292–3, 321

institutional history   27, 76, 124, 134

insurgencies   322–4, 326

integral mission   113, 255

Inter Caetera   105, 110

intercessor(s)   27, 30, 41, 47, 61, 83, 104, 123, 145, 332

interfaith activism   320, 322, 324

International Church of the Foursquare Gospel   203, 221, 231

international law   124, 318, 321

Internet   56, 117, 300

interreligious dialogue   207, 323

intersectionality   4, 32, 70, 130, 151, 277, 288

Iran   18, 54, 219, 224, 236, 252, 256, 268, 316

Iraq   54, 63, 90, 181, 275, 324

Ireland   76, 82, 85, 88, 172, 176, 186, 330, 338

Isasi-Díaz, Ada María   6, 28, 113, 326

Islam   25, 58, 62–3, 78, 93, 181, 224, 253, 256, 274, 323

Israel   1, 18, 44, 54–5, 57–8, 63, 149, 268, 272, 316, 324

Italy   17, 23, 43, 45, 76, 78–9, 82, 88, 90–1, 108, 162–4, 165, 168–9, 172, 175, 186, 226, 267

j

Jamaica   18, 97–9, 100, 106, 110, 209, 276

James, Carolyn Custis   210, 259

Japan   54–5, 64, 66–7, 70, 207, 330

Javanese Christianity   60, 207

Jehovah's Witnesses   19, 22–4, 78, 120, 216, 226, 320
Jesuits   64, 76, 147, 167
Jesus   3, 24, 26, 42, 44, 62–3, 65, 71, 84, 92, 105, 113, 159, 168, 170, 177, 181, 187, 188, 202, 225, 248, 254, 256, 258–9, 268, 288–9, 293–4, 320, 330
Jews   55, 92, 118, 127, 132, 165, 243, 268, 318, 320, 324–5
Jordan   54, 207, 271, 324, 339
Judaism   58, 193
Judson, Adoniram   65, 128
Judson, Ann Hasseltine   28, 66, 204

k

Kang, Namsoon   70–1
Kazakhstan   54, 56–7, 175, 192, 271
Kenya   2–3, 35, 38, 40–1, 48–9, 170, 172, 184, 194, 199, 206, 218, 222–3, 235, 240–1, 251–2, 290, 320, 330
killing(s)   267, 272
Kim, Grace Ji-Sun   133, 330
Kingdom of God   24, 91, 112, 220, 225–6
kingdom   2, 23, 42–3, 45, 68, 88, 91, 106, 112, 172, 199, 220, 225–6, 292, 330
Kiribati Climate Action Network   150, 294
Kiribati   138, 150, 211, 284, 294
knowledge   2, 5, 21, 36, 128, 204, 231, 255, 270, 275–6, 279, 304, 331
Kosovo   76, 80, 200–1, 252
Kuwait   54, 69, 162, 163, 236, 275

l

labor market   97, 266, 279
Lancaster, Sarah Jane   210, 237
land   26, 45, 50, 105–6, 124–5, 146–7, 151, 159, 173–4, 187, 191, 207, 259, 266, 285–9, 291–4, 325–6
language(s)   6, 13, 31, 43–5, 54, 62, 64, 70–1, 86, 91–2, 98, 105, 113, 124–5, 129, 146, 166, 181–2, 193, 222, 232, 239, 243–4, 249, 307, 332
Latin America   4, 6–7, 19, 24, 70, 84–5, 91, 97, 105–6, 108–10, 112–13, 122, 131–2, 160, 166, 171, 174, 198, 208, 211, 225–6, 228, 232, 238, 243, 249, 267, 275, 291–2, 295, 306
Latin Mass   48, 197
Latino/a(s)   7, 31, 97, 113–14, 130–1, 226, 237–8, 276, 306, 309
Latvia   76, 175, 192, 208, 277
Laudato Si'   287, 291–2, 296
Lausanne Movement   255–6, 277, 295
laywomen   176, 321
leader(s)   27, 30, 42, 45–7, 51, 57, 61, 67–8, 72, 76, 84, 91–2, 106, 111, 114, 130, 133–4, 139, 145–6, 148–52, 159, 168, 176–7, 205, 207–9, 221–5, 227–8, 232, 239–41, 244–5, 248, 255–6,

270, 276, 278–9, 284, 287, 289, 291, 301, 304, 310, 317–18, 321–3, 331–2
Lebanon   54, 69, 305
Lee, Jarena   129, 248, 254
Lesotho   35, 172, 206, 286
LGBTQ+ people   134, 197, 260, 326, 332
LGBTQ+ rights   8, 128, 260, 326
liberation theology   31, 70, 72, 107, 112–14, 126, 132–3, 147, 174, 276, 289, 291
Liberia   35, 43–4, 47, 163, 238, 270, 322, 324
liberty   169, 266
Libya   35, 268, 286, 316
literacy   36, 43, 56, 66–7, 90, 117, 147, 204, 249, 277, 300
Lithuania   76, 79, 175, 192, 320
liturgy   48, 181, 238
lobbying   170, 322
London Missionary Society (LMS)   147, 211, 284
Luther, Martin   76, 85, 197, 202
Lutheran World Federation   2, 80, 207–8, 272
Lutheran(s)   2, 43, 48, 65, 79–80, 86, 88, 93, 110, 119, 144, 149, 197, 198, 205, 207–8, 210, 221, 231, 244, 254, 272, 276, 306, 311
Luxembourg   76, 84

m

Maasai   27, 172
Macao   54, 64–5
Macedonia   76, 92, 166, 185, 277
machismo   7, 97, 103, 111, 113–14, 208, 276, 323
Magnificat   1–2
mainline Protestant church(es)   12, 122, 204, 209–10, 216, 238, 246, 253, 278, 303, 310
Malawi   35, 43, 49, 240, 273, 287
Malaysia   54, 61, 242
male domination   40, 50, 56, 97, 106, 320
male headship   208, 225, 227
male leadership   48, 84, 111, 130, 134, 151, 221, 223, 228, 232, 239–41, 244–5, 255, 257, 273, 305, 310
male theologian   2, 7, 32, 70, 132, 151–2, 304
Mali   35, 267–8, 272, 316
Mananzan, Mary John   170, 291
Manila Manifesto   255–6
Māori   146–7, 151
marginalization   7, 27, 47, 50–1, 59, 108, 110, 113, 127, 152, 238–9, 258, 260, 268, 274, 286, 295, 305
Marian devotion   27, 159, 176
marital rape   4, 265
marriage   8, 26, 41, 56, 64, 68, 78, 84, 89, 101, 131–2, 134, 171–2, 187–9, 193–4, 202–3, 206–7, 222, 224–5, 228, 243, 260, 265–8, 272–5, 277–8, 307, 324, 332
Marshall Islands   138, 141, 149, 200, 235, 252, 294
Martinique   97–8, 163
martyrdom   26, 44, 63–4, 84, 188, 202

Mary (biblical)   1–2, 27, 42, 85, 91, 105, 108–9, 152, 159, 187, 189, 276, 291

Maryknoll Fathers   125, 175

Maryknoll Sisters   125, 175

masculinity   128, 258

Mass   35, 45, 48, 86, 88, 107, 131, 166–7, 176, 197, 322

maternal mortality   193, 267

matriarchy   46, 279

matrilineal societies   46–7, 223, 273

Mauritania   35, 219, 268, 270–1

McFague, Sallie   132, 288

McPherson, Aimee Semple   27, 203, 221, 244

measurement   35–7

media   48, 71, 134, 160, 225, 239, 244, 318, 324–5

mediation   317, 323

medical mission   65–6

medicine   128, 307

megachurch(es)   36, 55, 68, 225, 245

Melanesia   25, 138–9, 145, 149, 151–2, 198, 211, 228, 269

membership (church)   3, 13–14, 19, 22, 29, 32, 37, 47, 54, 59, 78, 81, 89, 99–100, 108, 118, 122, 124, 130, 141, 163, 202, 208–9, 226, 238, 279, 320

Mennonite(s)   31, 122, 306, 320

menstruation   193, 222

Mestizo   98, 106

Methodism   237, 254

Methodist(s)   22, 31, 43, 46, 48, 66, 70, 83, 110–11, 119, 121, 127–30, 132–4, 147–9, 206, 207–8, 210–11, 215–16, 237, 244, 253, 272, 279, 292, 306, 311, 323

Mexicans   109, 130

Mexico   17, 23, 27–8, 97, 99, 102–3, 106, 108, 110, 112, 131, 162–4, 166, 170, 174, 176, 185, 209, 226, 235–7, 255, 269, 271–2, 275, 306

Micronesia   25, 138–9, 145, 152

Middle East   24, 29, 60, 90, 170, 181–4, 207, 275, 308, 317, 324

migration   18, 24, 69, 93, 131, 139, 149, 176, 185, 187, 194, 285, 294

military dictatorship(s)   54, 106–7, 110, 114, 326

military service   226, 320

military   2, 42, 54, 56, 76, 106–7, 110, 114, 226, 271, 316–17, 320–1, 323–4, 326, 330

minister(s)   45, 49, 60, 85, 100, 111, 122, 129, 133, 138, 145, 151, 202, 208–9, 211, 221–2, 226, 244, 237–8, 292, 305, 308,317

ministries   5, 8, 27, 29, 46, 100, 108, 133–4, 149, 169, 189, 202, 211, 222–3, 227, 239, 240–1, 257

minjung theology   31, 70, 112

miracle(s)   47, 68, 82, 164, 223, 225, 231, 243

misogyny   88, 93, 177, 288

mission church(es)   46–7, 220–2, 234

mission organization(s)   128, 211, 239, 248, 255, 275, 308

mission   4, 7–8, 25, 36, 44–8, 65–8, 71, 77, 85–6, 105–6, 110–11, 113, 125, 128, 132, 149, 160, 167–8, 172, 174, 176, 198, 203–204, 211, 215–16, 220–3, 227–8, 234, 237–42, 244, 248–9, 255, 257, 273, 275, 279, 301, 303, 306, 308, 321, 327, 330

Missionaries of Charity   85, 165, 173

missionaries   2–4, 7, 13, 26–9, 42–6, 49, 50–1, 55, 58, 62–8, 71–2, 76–7, 85–6, 89, 91, 105–6, 108, 110, 114, 121, 125–6, 128, 131–3, 145–50, 152, 165, 167, 172–5, 187, 203–4, 206–7, 211–12, 221–2, 224, 228, 231–2, 237–40, 248, 255–7, 284, 290, 301, 306, 324

missionary order(s)   45, 64

missionary wives   85, 203

mobility   238, 258, 321

mobilization   100, 257, 318

Moldova   76, 78, 88, 185, 192

Monaco   76, 188

monasteries   91, 167, 189–90, 193, 197, 307

monasticism   167, 182, 189–91, 307

money laundering   225, 244

money   82, 225, 244, 275–6

Mongolia   3, 17, 54–5, 57, 61, 163, 200–1

Mongols   58, 62

Montenegro   76, 185, 192, 277

Montgomery, Helen Barrett   67, 204

Moon, Charlotte "Lottie"   28, 65, 204

Moore, Beth   133, 210

morality   88–9, 225, 254, 257

Moravians   43, 110

Mormon Relief Society   131, 149, 228

Mormonism   149, 228

Mother Earth   289, 293

Mother of God   27, 159, 189

Mother Teresa   85, 173

motherhood   8, 84, 127, 149, 189, 194, 207, 307

Mothers' Union(s)   3, 40, 206, 211

Moyo, Fulata   273, 279, 304

Mozambique   35–8, 206, 219, 234

mujerista theology   6, 31, 113–14, 326, 331

Mukti Mission   68, 111, 237, 242

music   111, 130

Muslim(s)   18, 24, 26, 37, 49, 55–6, 60, 63–4, 80, 90, 92–3, 118, 139, 182, 216, 224, 274, 318, 322–5, 330

Mwaura, Philomena   28, 35, 49, 273

Myanmar   54, 57, 61, 65, 67, 204, 256, 275, 303, 305

myth   31, 164

n

National Baptist Convention of America   121, 130, 220, 226

National Baptist Convention USA   121, 130, 220, 226

National Church Life Survey (NCLS)   143–4, 176, 342–3

National Congregations Study   130, 209
Native American women   126, 269, 293
Native Americans   125, 128
natural disaster(s)   26, 69, 285–6, 293, 295
natural resources   147, 266, 285
nature   7–8, 24, 48–9, 70, 81, 127, 129, 151, 176, 223, 237, 245, 285, 288, 290, 293–5, 318
Nauru   138, 141, 211
Nazi(s)   77, 89, 182, 226
neglect   31, 125, 177, 273
Nepal   54–5, 69, 186, 200, 224, 256, 267, 272, 275, 286, 305, 316
Netherlands   45, 76, 84, 92, 166, 172, 202, 292, 331
New Apostolic Reformation   225, 227
New Caledonia   138, 140, 148, 176, 228, 278, 325
new ecclesial movements   108, 112, 306
New Zealand   25, 32, 138–41, 143–7, 151–2, 176, 198, 210, 221, 227, 267–8, 294, 310, 331
Nicaragua   97, 100, 106–7, 208–9
Niger   35, 46, 268, 271
Nigeria   3, 17, 23, 26, 35, 38, 40–2, 45–8, 68, 85, 91, 199–200, 204–6, 222, 226, 240–1, 253, 267, 272, 279, 316, 330
Niue   138–40, 219
Nku, Christinah   47, 240–1
Nobel Peace Prize   165, 290, 320, 322
Non-traditional, house, cell movements   19, 21, 24, 29, 56–8, 68, 197, 216, 219–20, 224, 236–7, 252–3, 256, 260
nongovernmental organizations (NGOs)   193, 265, 291, 318, 321, 323
North Africa   24, 29, 37, 182, 256, 267–8, 274–5, 317
North America   4, 6–7, 14, 24, 27, 31, 36, 55, 62, 97, 111, 117–19, 122–8, 130–5, 145, 160, 175, 183, 197–9, 202, 209–10, 216, 225–7, 232, 238, 244, 246, 249, 260, 267, 275, 277–8, 292–3, 302–3, 308–11, 331
North American Christianity   117, 124, 133–4, 209–10
North Korea   54, 58, 237, 242
North Macedonia   76, 166, 185, 277
Northern Mariana Islands   138, 141, 147, 176
Norway   45, 76, 88, 92–3, 163, 186, 208, 267, 308
nuclear   149, 321, 325
nun(s)   26, 46, 85, 106, 108, 125, 164, 167–8, 174–7, 189–90, 193–4, 197, 211, 307, 321
nurse(s)   106, 172, 211
nursing   126, 146, 176

o

obedience   27, 103, 117, 167, 172, 177, 187, 194, 225, 248, 321
ocean acidification   285, 291
Oceania   2, 7, 14, 25, 36, 55, 97, 138–40, 143–5, 151–2, 166, 170, 176, 198, 216, 227, 229, 232, 245, 249, 279, 294–5, 302, 310, 333
Oduyoye, Mercy Amba   6, 28, 49, 289
oil   18, 54, 162, 236, 285, 293, 316

Okuthe, Lucia   2, 206
one-child policy   25, 275
opportunities   5, 8, 26, 32, 36, 48, 56, 58, 67–9, 84, 89, 92–3, 100–1, 110–12, 122–3, 130–1, 134, 147–8, 166–8, 171–2, 175–7, 189, 197, 205, 207, 210–11, 216, 221–3, 228–9, 239–40, 245, 254, 266, 286, 295, 302, 305, 307, 310–11, 321
oppression   4, 58, 65, 68, 70, 72, 90–1, 97, 106, 112–14, 126, 133, 177, 288, 291–3, 316
ordination   6, 8, 49, 60, 79, 88, 92, 100, 132–33, 147, 151–2, 167–8, 176, 182, 188–9, 191, 197, 204–11, 222–3, 225–6, 239, 245, 258, 292, 301, 305, 307–9, 319
Oriental Orthodox   63–4, 182, 186–7, 191, 193
Ormerod, Thea   170, 294
orphanage(s)   43, 68, 85, 126, 160, 167, 176, 206
orphans   107, 111, 206, 237, 242
Orthodox Christianity   1, 7, 14, 18–19, 24, 27, 36, 38, 40, 42, 55–6, 59–60, 63–4, 69, 76, 78–82, 86, 89–90, 93, 101, 143, 181–94, 201, 210, 215–16, 220, 223, 231, 251, 287, 307–8, 318
Orthodox Christians   81, 100, 182–4, 187, 191–2
Osborn, Sarah   127, 254
Ottoman Empire   45, 190
Our Lady of Aparecida   109, 159
Our Lady of the Good Death   99, 109
outreach   8, 30, 111, 152, 203, 249, 321

p

Pacific Conference of Churches (PCC)   148–9, 150, 152, 310
Pacific Islander(s)   25, 32, 139, 149, 294, 309
Pacific Islands   2, 4, 25, 32, 138–9, 143, 145, 149–50, 152, 211, 216, 227–9, 252, 272, 278–9, 294–5, 300, 309–12, 325, 332
Pacific Theological College (PTC)   148, 311
Pacific, Asian, and North American Asian Women in Theology and Ministry (PANAAWTM)   70, 331
pacifism   202, 320–1
pagan(s)   27, 63, 80, 110, 187
Pakistan   54, 57, 69, 267, 271, 305
Palau   18, 138, 252, 325
Palestine   54, 63, 65, 69, 187, 272, 324
pandemic(s)   46, 56, 170, 266, 275, 291, 300, 323
Papua New Guinea (PNG)   18, 138–41, 143–4, 149–51, 176, 198, 227–8, 268–9, 270, 272, 278, 325, 331
parachurch organization(s)   248, 255
Paraguay   97–8, 101, 106, 162, 163, 276
parenting   44, 130, 152, 187, 206, 224
Parham, Charles Fox   237–8
parish(es)   91, 108, 176, 189, 211, 222, 332
parochial school(s)   64, 126, 165
participation   5, 24, 29, 35–7, 49, 76, 82, 87–8, 93, 107, 131, 152, 166, 181, 191–2, 202, 207–8, 223, 237, 238, 245, 265–6, 268, 284, 304–5, 312, 316, 318, 327, 331–2

partner(s)   86, 152, 265–6, 275, 277–8, 286, 288, 295, 311

partnership   128, 145, 171, 244, 255–6, 272, 330

pastor's wives   48, 60, 224, 228, 240–1, 310

pastor(s)   29–30, 41, 48, 60–1, 68, 84, 104, 123, 144–5, 207, 209, 224–5, 227–8, 238, 240–1, 243–4, 301, 310

pastoral ministry   205, 211–12, 301, 309

patriarchy   4, 49–50, 59, 62, 90, 97, 103, 105, 109, 113, 132, 134, 206–7, 225, 259–60, 273–4, 279, 288, 311, 316, 323, 341

patron saint   165, 187–8, 287

peace agreement(s)   317–18, 323, 326

peace church   111, 320

peace talk(s)   149, 318, 325

peace work   172, 322

peacebuilding   8, 85, 172, 258, 317–18, 320–4, 326–7, 330

Pentecost (biblical)   32, 35, 232

Pentecostal(s)   7, 19, 22, 36, 39, 41, 48, 55, 58, 60–1, 68–9, 78, 81–2, 89, 91, 93, 98–101, 103, 108, 110–12, 122, 131, 143–4, 149, 208, 210, 215–16, 221, 225–8, 231–2, 234, 236–46, 253, 258, 303, 311

Pentecostalism   25, 36, 48, 98, 110–12, 121, 128–9, 231–2, 234, 238–41, 243, 245–6, 277

pentecostalization   98, 111, 149

persecutions   182, 188

Persia   63, 106, 316

Peru   97–8, 102, 110, 112, 166, 306, 316

Phan, Peter   62, 290

Philippines   17, 23, 54, 57–8, 60, 64, 67–9, 141, 162–4, 170, 173, 176, 218, 225, 231, 234–5, 237, 255, 269, 275, 291, 305, 323–4

philosophy   49, 93, 106, 319

Phiri, Isabel Apawo   6, 28, 49

piety   62, 84, 127, 188, 224, 254

pilgrimage(s)   13, 159, 176, 323

Pinochet, Augusto   100, 106–7

Piper, John   209, 258

pluralism   118, 226

Plütschau, Heinrich   65, 197

Poland   17, 76, 79, 82, 89, 162, 163–4, 172, 174, 192, 267, 308, 325

policy   25, 110, 128, 131–2, 193, 266, 275, 278–9, 284, 286, 295, 317, 319

policymakers   284, 286, 295

political activism   29, 112, 205, 317

political power   4, 93, 169, 258, 320

politics   2, 4–5, 7–8, 26–7, 29, 36, 42, 44–5, 58, 63, 65, 69, 76–7, 87–8, 93, 100, 105, 107–8, 110–14, 120, 124, 127, 130, 146, 149, 166, 169–70, 172, 174, 176, 182, 186, 187, 193–4, 197, 205, 220, 223–4, 227, 238, 240–1, 245, 249, 258, 265–6, 276, 279, 284–6, 288, 317, 321, 325–6, 331

polygamy   43, 47, 49, 131, 203, 222–3, 228

Polynesia   25, 138–40, 145, 147, 149, 152, 198, 210–11, 227, 278

Pope Alexander VI   105, 164

Pope Francis   88, 91, 125, 166, 168, 172, 177, 277, 287, 291–2, 296

Pope John Paul II   168–9, 171, 175, 321

Pope John Paul XXIII   86, 165

Pope Leo XIII   125, 169

Pope Paul VI   86, 127, 165, 167

pope   86, 88, 91, 105, 125–7, 159, 164–6, 168–9, 171–2, 175, 177, 223, 277, 287, 291–2, 296, 321

popular religion   28, 108, 226

populations   18, 25–6, 55, 105, 118, 125, 139, 146–7, 172, 176, 183–5, 192, 200, 216, 220, 226–7, 279, 287, 293, 306, 320, 326

Portugal   45, 76, 79, 91, 105–6, 308

post-Christian contexts   77, 91, 139

post-Communist contexts   77, 89, 194

post-denominational Christianity   225, 232

postcolonialism   49–50

poverty   2, 49, 55, 63–4, 69, 71, 85, 90, 108, 111–13, 126, 138–9, 165, 167, 169–72, 174, 177, 187, 194, 223, 239, 243, 249, 258, 267, 276, 285–7, 289, 292–3, 295, 305, 321, 324

power   4–5, 37, 42, 45, 49–50, 56, 78, 89–90, 93, 97, 111–12, 129–31, 134, 151, 164, 169, 209, 221, 225, 231–2, 237–8, 241, 244–5, 258, 270, 276, 288, 319–21, 324, 327

Pray the Devil Back to Hell   322, 324

prayer   2, 4, 14, 24, 29, 35, 46, 50, 58, 68, 78, 82, 85, 101, 111, 113, 122, 128–31, 133, 143, 149, 167, 172, 174, 176, 187, 193, 202–3, 211, 215, 223, 231, 237, 239, 241–2, 254, 256–7, 271, 292, 301, 320, 322, 324, 330

preaching   22, 44, 46–8, 58, 127, 129, 202, 209–10, 215, 237, 242–4, 245, 254

pregnancy   1, 56, 164–5, 267, 275

Presbyterian(s)   41, 43, 47, 54, 61, 68, 83, 103, 110–11, 125, 133, 141, 144, 148, 199, 205, 207–10, 221, 272, 306–7, 311

priest(s)   2, 36, 48, 60, 63, 68, 80, 86, 88–9, 92, 103, 105, 107–8, 119, 125–7, 145, 147, 166–7, 171, 174–7, 188–9, 191–3, 206, 208–11, 225, 293, 332

priesthood of all believers   110, 202

priesthood   45, 49, 103, 110, 127, 131–2, 147, 149, 164, 167–8, 189, 191, 202, 206, 223, 306

prime minister(s)   138, 317

professor(s)   92, 130, 147, 300, 303–4, 309, 312

progress   5, 8, 194, 266–7, 286, 300, 304, 318

prophecy   98, 223, 227

prophet-healing movements   46, 221

prophet(s)   1, 40, 46–7, 51, 131, 221–2, 223, 227, 232, 240, 273

prophetess(es)   42, 46–7, 133, 202, 222, 268

prosperity gospel   48, 112

prosperity theology 48, 245
prosperity 48–9, 112, 241, 245
prostitution 146, 277
protest(s) 222, 258, 285, 291, 293, 321–2,
    325, 338
Protestant Reformation 19, 197–8, 202, 215
Protestant(s) 7, 13, 19, 24, 25, 27, 29, 36–8, 43–4,
    46, 55, 58, 60, 65–8, 72, 78, 80–1, 84–5, 87,
    89, 93, 98, 100–1, 103, 105, 108, 110–14, 117,
    122, 124, 126–8, 131–2, 134, 140, 147–8, 151,
    166, 171, 182, 186, 197–200, 202–12, 215–16,
    220, 222, 225, 231, 234, 239, 257, 276, 278,
    303
Protestantism 25, 36, 45, 65, 67, 93, 98, 107–8,
    110–12, 124, 128, 145, 166, 182, 197–8, 200,
    203, 205, 207, 211–12, 215, 225, 249, 253–4,
    310
public theology 128, 133–4
Puerto Rico 97, 106, 131, 235
Pui-lan, Kwok 6, 54, 70–2
Puritan(s) 124, 127, 202, 244

q
Qatar 14, 18, 54, 69, 162, 163, 186, 236
Quakers (Friends) 22, 202, 320
Queen Nana 63, 187
Queen of Heaven 159, 221
queen(s) 26, 42–3, 63, 77, 84, 105, 146, 159, 165,
    176, 187, 193, 221

r
race 4, 24, 50, 63, 113, 117, 122, 124, 130, 133, 151,
    237, 239, 277, 288, 293, 321, 323, 331
racism 50, 113, 120, 130, 133, 147, 177, 309
radio 91, 239, 244
Ramabai, Pandita 28, 68, 111, 237, 242
rape 2, 4, 64, 105–6, 125, 265, 267–9, 273, 275,
    277, 322, 324
Reformed, Presbyterian(s) 41, 43, 48, 59, 60–1, 68,
    83, 103, 110, 125, 132–3, 142, 144, 148, 198,
    205, 207–10, 221, 272, 306, 311
reformers 197–8, 202, 320
refugee(s) 26, 69, 170, 172, 294, 318
regime(s) 89–90, 106–7, 182, 318
relationship(s) 13, 49, 71, 92, 105, 110, 119, 121,
    133, 146–7, 151, 173, 205, 240–1, 244, 259–60,
    273, 287–8, 290, 293, 295, 308, 310, 318, 320
religious change 3, 24–5, 118
religious marketplace 108, 110
renewal movement(s) 143, 222, 253
renewal 37, 51, 112, 143, 166, 176, 191, 222, 231,
    254, 284
reproductive health 149, 174, 266, 279
reproductive rights 4–5, 138, 265–6
Republic of the Congo 2, 23, 35, 42, 49, 163, 172,
    223, 232, 237, 267–9, 272, 316, 320, 322
research 2–4, 7, 14, 24, 28–9, 36, 78–9, 82, 91–2,
    103, 118, 122, 130–1, 144, 166, 170–1, 176–7,

188, 193–4, 220, 223, 234, 240, 275, 288, 291,
    311, 318, 331–2
respect 170, 177, 204, 223, 258, 279, 318
restoration 45, 124, 147, 177, 227, 279, 320
retail 69, 163
revival(s) 27, 68, 89, 111–12, 127, 129, 131, 149,
    191–2, 216, 222, 227, 231–2, 237–8, 240,
    242–3, 246, 254, 260, 301, 331
rich 1, 55
risk 24, 29, 63, 71, 82, 110, 129, 271, 295
ritual uncleanness 191, 222
ritual(s) 13, 47, 49–50, 89, 109, 112, 148, 188,
    191–2, 215, 222, 241, 256, 323
Robert, Dana 4, 28
Rogers, Mary Josephine 125, 175
Roma people 91, 243, 277
Roman Curia 159–60, 168–9
Roman Empire 77, 181, 260
Romania 76, 79, 174, 184–5, 188, 190–3
Romanian Orthodox Church 89, 182
Rome, Italy 126, 159–60, 166, 170, 182, 188, 260
royal family 165, 228, 241
Ruether, Rosemary Radford 91, 132, 293
rural 18, 56–8, 90, 106, 108, 110–11, 190, 193, 220,
    224, 253, 256–7, 285, 287, 289, 291, 300, 322,
    324, 326
Russia 17, 23, 45, 76, 78–9, 82, 165, 181–5, 187–8,
    190–2, 226, 268–9, 292, 320
Russian Orthodox Church 182, 186
Russian Revolution 175, 191
Rwanda 35, 38, 194, 206, 272, 287

s
Sabbath 46, 193
sacred space 167, 330
sacrifice 26, 64, 84, 117, 127, 172, 193, 248
safety 8, 110, 171, 224, 265, 268, 286, 293, 316, 318
Saint Kitts and Nevis 97, 106, 200, 219
Saint Lucia 97, 100, 106
Saint Pierre and Miquelon 117, 119, 127, 163
Saint Vincent 97, 219
saint(s) 27, 62, 85, 97, 106, 108–9, 119, 125–7, 129,
    131, 165, 176, 181, 187–8, 216, 219, 287
salvation 27, 47, 131, 167, 203, 221, 231, 242, 244,
    256, 279, 290, 293
Samaritan woman (biblical) 176, 188
same-sex relations 78, 91, 103, 120, 188–9, 260
Samoa 138–41, 143, 219, 227–8, 310
sanctification 237, 244
Sanskrit 68, 242
Saudi Arabia 54, 58, 69, 236, 267, 272, 274
Scaraffia, Lucetta 171, 177
schism(s) 47–8, 131, 143, 181, 197, 222, 225
scholarship 6–8, 27, 31–2, 67, 77, 92, 117–18, 124,
    289, 294–5, 305, 310, 326, 330–1
school(s) 7, 30, 41, 43, 45, 56, 61, 64–6, 68, 83–4, 89,
    103–4, 110, 112, 122–3, 125–6, 128, 133, 144,
    147, 160, 165, 167, 171, 173, 193, 204, 206–7,

225, 228, 237, 241–2, 265, 273, 275, 288, 292, 300–12, 331–2
Scranton, Mary   65–6, 207
sea level(s)   25, 150, 284–5, 291–2, 294
Second Great Awakening   27, 127, 131, 254, 301
Second Vatican Council (Vatican II)   45, 86–7, 91–2, 107, 112, 126, 165–8, 176
second-class citizen(s)   189, 207
second-wave feminism   4, 77, 87, 91, 117, 128, 133, 135, 168, 171, 190, 209
secondary education   5, 36, 55, 268, 301
secularization   44, 88–91, 93, 118, 122, 124, 139, 171, 173, 175, 188, 226, 278, 285, 289, 295, 304, 306, 317, 319, 324, 326
self-identification   4, 35, 78, 249
self-sacrifice   84, 127, 193
seminary   31, 49, 133, 175, 301–3, 305–7, 311
senior pastor   41, 145, 245
Serbia   76, 185–6, 190, 226, 243
Serbian Orthodox Church   186, 190
Servants of the Holy Heart of Mary   35, 167
Seventh-day Adventist Church (SDA)   27, 29, 78, 100, 124, 149–50, 202, 221, 279
sewing   66, 125, 206
sex abuse scandal   88, 134
sex education   134, 304
sex trafficking   8, 177
sex-segregated societies   64, 203–4
sex   2–3, 8, 48, 64, 69, 78, 88, 91, 103, 114, 120, 130, 132–4, 151, 172, 177, 188–9, 203–4, 225, 238, 254, 260, 267, 275, 277, 293, 304, 322, 332
sexism   4, 28, 113, 128, 130, 277
sexual abuse   88, 105–6, 125, 133–4, 171, 177, 245, 258, 269, 274, 304, 322
sexual harassment   269, 304
sexual misconduct   134, 258
sexuality   4, 49, 71, 89, 117, 128, 134, 174, 177, 211, 304
Seychelles   35, 43, 172, 206
Shaker   129, 202
shame   71, 186, 265, 272, 274, 322
Sharia law   26, 224
Shinto   55, 318, 330
Sierra Leone   35, 163, 221, 267, 270, 279
Sikh(s)   55, 118, 318
Silk Roads   63, 256
sin   112, 147, 159, 256, 259, 292–3
Singapore   54, 57, 69, 226, 242
Sint Maarten   97–8, 100
sisterhood(s)   66, 99, 190, 245
Sisters of Charity   126, 165, 176, 189
Sisters of Mercy   85, 176, 189
Sisters of the Good Samaritan   176, 294
sisters   2, 13, 26, 45, 48, 64, 85, 106, 110, 113, 125–7, 160, 165, 167, 170–7, 189, 204, 211, 228, 257, 293–4, 300, 306, 321, 323–4, 330

slave trade   36, 45, 105, 110, 128
slave(s)   36, 45, 63, 105, 110, 128–9, 187, 268, 275
slavery   64, 105, 110, 129, 170, 254, 259, 275
Slessor, Mary   85, 204
Slovakia   76, 175, 208
small group leader(s)   30, 62, 84
Smith, Amanda Berry   43, 129, 204, 254
Smith, Sarah   65, 203–4
social exclusion   243, 272, 277
social history   27, 76, 124, 134, 331
social justice   26, 113, 169, 191, 311, 318
social media   134, 239, 324
social norms   5, 29, 265, 331
social science   7, 288
social service   8, 126, 160, 167, 243, 292, 321
social work   205, 306
socialization   81, 318, 327
societies   2, 27, 29, 36, 46, 49, 56, 58, 63–4, 70, 72, 86, 88, 118, 134, 139, 148, 152, 159, 167, 192, 194, 203–4, 206, 228, 273–4, 278–9, 317, 331
sociology   3, 7, 88–9
sola scriptura   202, 249
Solomon Islands   138, 140–1, 147, 150, 211, 278, 310, 325
sons   71, 113, 223, 232, 255
South Africa   35–6, 38, 41, 43–5, 47, 172, 218–21, 232, 235, 240, 255–6, 272, 304
South America   105, 108, 110, 131, 174, 209, 306–8
South Asia   16, 55–6, 258, 267, 275, 305, 323
South Korea   31, 54–5, 57–8, 60–1, 65–6, 68, 70, 112, 173, 218, 251, 305
South Pacific   279, 310, 331
South Sudan   35, 42, 165, 172, 206, 219, 255, 267, 279
Southeast Asia   3, 54, 56, 64, 67–9, 71, 85, 147, 162, 207, 238, 267, 325
Southern Africa   45–6, 206
Southern Baptist Convention (SBC)   133–4, 197, 201, 209, 253, 258, 269
Southern Europe   78, 184–5, 192, 267, 275
Soviet Union (USSR)   24, 78, 192, 226, 307, 320
Spain   17, 22–3, 45, 76, 79, 82, 105–6, 112, 125, 162–4, 169, 268, 308
Spiritism   98–9
spirits   47, 129, 228, 272
spiritual authority   112, 127, 188, 254, 259
spiritual leader   47, 72, 127, 240–1
spiritual mothers   187, 189, 222
spiritual power   37, 49, 111, 129, 232, 238, 241, 245, 258
spiritual realm(s)   48, 203, 220, 238
spirituality   80, 84, 89, 92, 127, 129, 148, 165, 242, 254, 278, 291–2, 294, 320
Sri Lanka   54, 65, 239, 256, 316, 323
Stanley, Brian   204, 260
state church   19, 88
statistics   1, 3, 29, 37, 79, 85, 132, 190, 209, 266–8, 308–9, 332

stigma   170, 265, 322
student(s)   3, 7, 57, 66, 133, 160, 166, 188, 237,
    301–12
sub-Saharan Africa   3, 6, 24, 27, 31, 36, 38, 40, 45,
    48, 50, 78, 85, 91, 139, 160, 166, 171, 194, 216,
    220, 236, 258, 268, 289, 300, 335
submission   117, 132, 134, 208, 255, 274, 311,
    316, 320
subordination   84, 132, 193, 202–3, 245, 256, 330
successor(s)   47, 118, 159, 215
Sudan   35, 42, 165, 172, 206, 219, 255, 267, 271, 274,
    279, 316
suffering   5, 56, 65, 70–1, 169, 177, 249, 265–6,
    273–4, 292, 317, 322, 324–5
Summaria, Catia   88, 169
Suriname   97–8, 103
survey(s)   3, 7, 23, 29, 41, 61, 80, 82–3, 85, 103, 123,
    141, 143–4, 166, 174, 176, 190, 207, 240, 249,
    277, 300, 302–303, 332
survival   8, 63, 113, 125, 127, 182, 192, 284, 294, 330
survivor(s)   107, 165, 171, 273, 276, 278, 322
Sweden   45, 76, 84, 90, 208, 221, 303, 308, 331
switching (religious)   24, 212, 219
Switzerland   76, 92, 255, 331
Syria   54, 64–5, 69, 90, 106, 181, 186, 189,
    203–4, 316

t

Tahaafe-Williams, Katalina   152, 310
Taiwan   54, 207, 242–3
Tajikistan   54, 56–7, 219, 271, 275
Taliban   69, 275, 318
Tamar Campaign   274, 304, 322
Tamez, Elsa   97, 276, 292
Tanzania   27, 35, 38, 40, 48–9, 172, 194, 205–6, 251,
    268, 272, 287, 291
teacher(s)   29–30, 41, 44–6, 61, 83–4, 103–4, 106,
    128, 133, 144, 172, 188–9, 193, 203–4, 210,
    227, 259, 305, 307, 332
television   225, 239, 241, 244
temperature(s)   8, 285, 291–2
Tertullian   36, 187
Tetteh, Christie Doe   240–1
Thailand   18, 54, 65, 69, 207, 249, 275, 330
theologian(s)   2, 7–8, 28, 32, 44, 49–51, 70–2, 79, 84,
    88, 91–2, 112–14, 117, 132–4, 139, 150–2, 159,
    165, 170–1, 177, 188–91, 194, 206, 208, 248,
    258, 260, 273, 276, 279, 288–94, 304–5,
    309–11, 330–1, 326
theological school(s)   300, 303–12
Theotókos   1, 186–7
Three-Self Patriotic Movement   68, 207
Thursdays in Black   86, 272, 276, 279
Timor-Leste   54, 173
Togo   35, 47, 206
Tokelau   138–9
Tonga   138, 143, 147, 172, 219, 227–8, 310, 325

Tongan(s)   139, 147–8, 150, 152, 228
tongues   48, 98, 131, 221, 231–2, 237–8, 242
Torres Strait Islanders   145, 147
torture   254, 323
tourism   69, 275
traditional gender role(s)   26, 82, 90, 170, 194,
    243, 277
traditional religion(s)   24, 36–7, 44, 49, 98, 126, 170,
    194, 240, 243, 277, 322–3
training   47–8, 60, 90, 110, 133, 173–4, 190, 193,
    204, 206, 211, 222, 224, 237, 256–7, 300–4,
    307–8, 310, 321–3, 325, 332
transformation   66, 108, 169, 207, 223, 293–4
trauma(s)   175, 267, 272, 277, 279, 321–3, 330
trend(s)   5, 7, 14, 23, 26, 29, 32, 55, 63, 81, 92–3, 118,
    135, 139, 150, 152, 211, 239, 300, 303,
    308, 332
Trible, Phyllis   132, 268
Trinity   19, 151, 226, 294
Trump, Donald J.   133, 258
Türkiye   54, 106, 181, 276
Turkmenistan   54, 56–7, 163, 268
Turks   181–2, 316, 324
Tuvalu   138–9, 200
Twitter   133, 225

u

Ubuntu   49, 279
Uganda   35, 38, 40–1, 43, 48, 194, 199, 201, 206, 253,
    287, 330
Ukraine   17, 76–7, 79, 82, 175, 185–7, 191, 226, 316
Ukrainian Orthodox Church   81–2, 185–6
unaffiliated Christians   19, 21
uncleanness   188, 191, 222, 330
United Arab Emirates   54, 69, 162–3, 236
United Kingdom   17, 23, 45, 76, 79, 82, 88, 91, 106,
    172, 200–1, 292, 330
United Nations Decade for Women   86, 272
United Nations Resolution 1325   318, 325
United Nations (UN)   5, 8, 14, 19, 36, 86, 117,
    266–8, 270, 272, 275, 284, 286–7, 294–5,
    317–18, 322–3, 325
United States of America (US)   4, 23–4, 44–5, 63,
    66–7, 69, 91, 105, 108, 110, 112–13, 117–18,
    121–2, 125–8, 130–1, 133, 139, 149–50, 163–5,
    167, 170–2, 175–6, 184, 190, 197–9, 201,
    203–5, 209–10, 218, 220–1, 225–6, 231–2,
    235–8, 239, 244, 248–9, 251, 253, 255, 257–8,
    260, 269, 272, 277–8, 293, 301, 321
Uniting churches   125, 141, 211, 311
Universal Church of the Kingdom of God
    (UCKG)   24, 91, 112, 220, 225
universities   3, 31, 66, 304, 306, 311
upheaval(s)   26, 63, 77, 197, 323
urban   18, 57, 89, 108, 110–11, 220, 238, 253, 285,
    287, 322, 324
urbanization   48, 106, 249, 256, 286

Ursuline(s)   106, 125
Uruguay   97, 103, 170–1, 209, 276
US-Mexico border   108, 131, 170
Uzbekistan   54, 56–7, 191, 271

V

Vanuatu   138, 140, 143, 200, 228, 235, 249,
      252, 278
Vatican   65, 88, 93, 109, 125, 159, 164–71,
      173–4, 177
Venezuela   97, 99, 102, 109, 208, 268
vernacular scripture   44, 222
victim(s)   86, 88, 107, 134, 165, 171, 211, 267,
      269–70, 272, 275–6, 277–9, 284, 317,
      320, 323
victimization   50, 273, 326–7, 330
Vietnam   54, 57–8, 60, 62, 65, 176, 226, 271
Virgin Mary   27, 65, 85, 105, 108–9, 152, 159, 276
Virgin of Guadalupe   28, 109
virginity   159, 165, 187, 268
virtue(s)   64, 127, 165, 167, 203
vision(s)   27, 47, 84, 164, 202, 215, 221–2, 231–2,
      240, 245
vocation(s)   58, 72, 108, 126, 172, 175–6, 191, 194,
      202, 206, 307

W

Wallis and Futuna Islands   138, 163, 176, 201
war(s)   26, 36, 45, 63, 67, 69, 77, 86, 105, 107–8, 125,
      149, 169, 174–5, 186, 189, 191, 194, 204, 228,
      291, 307, 316–18, 319–24, 326–7
ward(s)   22, 64, 87, 149
warfare   71, 105, 112, 265, 316
weaker sex   48, 254, 301
wealth   48–9, 105, 117, 326
weapon(s)   147, 278
weather   8, 285–6, 291, 295
welfare   149, 160, 238, 332
wellness   268, 320
Welsh Revival   237, 254
Wesley, John   127, 237, 254
Wesleyans   45, 129, 147, 221, 244
West Africa   35, 43, 47, 98, 128, 206, 221, 240
West Asia   25, 54–6, 62–3, 66, 256, 274
West, the   4, 31, 44, 49, 54, 62, 67, 70, 92, 105, 181,
      301, 304–5, 338
Western Christianity   46, 49, 67, 181, 222
Western Europe   31, 78, 139, 170, 203
Western theology   43, 49, 51, 71
White Evangelicalism   128, 258, 278, 295
White, Ellen G.   27, 202, 221
wholeness   113, 279, 290, 320
widow(s)   67–8, 87, 107, 111, 125–6, 189, 206, 237,
      242, 244, 323
wisdom   127, 151, 186, 225, 231, 268, 293
witchcraft   49, 82, 105–6, 152, 203, 215, 223, 272
witness   2, 114, 187–8, 202, 238, 277, 291, 320–1

wives   29, 48–9, 51, 60, 84–5, 90, 103, 106, 111, 117,
      125, 131, 134, 151, 165, 173, 187, 189, 202–4,
      211, 221–6, 228, 240–1, 245, 254–5, 265, 268,
      273, 277, 286, 310–11, 322
womanist theology   31, 133, 293, 151, 293, 331
women in leadership   19, 160, 167–8, 207, 223,
      255–7, 277
women in mission   85–6, 198, 204, 222, 255
Women in World Christianity Project   3–4, 341–2
women of color   92, 121, 124, 293, 309
women religious   36, 85, 119, 125, 127, 166–8,
      170–4, 177, 300, 306, 321, 324
women's activities   2, 7, 29, 90, 106, 149, 188, 193,
      198, 211, 241
women's history   6, 27, 124, 331
women's issues   90, 128, 189, 191, 306, 310
women's leadership   49, 60, 67, 208–9, 220, 244, 310
women's liberation   72, 112, 132, 138, 254
women's ministry   30, 212, 255, 311
women's movement   3–4, 7, 9, 88, 90, 132, 209, 272,
      312, 330, 333
women's ordination   6, 147, 152, 168, 176, 188, 191,
      205–7, 209–11, 222–3, 225
women's representation   317, 327
women's rights   4, 65, 120, 124, 170–1, 194, 204,
      209, 242, 258, 317, 320, 322, 330
women's role(s)   4–7, 31, 59, 61, 83, 88, 91, 103, 114,
      121–2, 144, 165, 182, 191, 206, 208, 212, 221,
      222–3, 229, 240, 246, 259–60
women's stories   7, 76, 91, 121
Women's Commission of the Ecumenical
      Association of Third World Theologians
      70, 92
workforce   82, 89, 168, 286
World Christianity   3–4, 6–9, 13–14, 18–19, 27–9,
      31–2, 36, 50, 69, 92, 117, 139, 198, 215–16,
      220, 228, 231, 246, 303, 312, 331–3
World Council of Churches (WCC)   86, 91–2,
      190–1, 272–4, 276, 279, 288, 291, 300, 302–3
World Evangelical Alliance (WEA)   255, 277, 295
World War I   77, 86, 108, 149, 174–5, 191, 321
World War II   86, 108, 149, 174–5, 191, 228, 307
worldview(s)   108, 255, 288
worship   5, 22, 27, 30, 41, 43, 48, 61, 69, 78, 82, 84,
      103, 111–12, 122, 144, 159, 188, 193, 215, 221,
      224–5, 232, 238, 244–5, 256, 265, 270

X

Xavier, Francis   64, 125

y

Yemen   54, 270–1, 316, 324
Yoido Full Gospel Church   27, 68, 242
Yoruba   46, 98, 221
young women   150, 171, 189, 224, 255, 287, 300
Young Women's Christian Association (YWCA)   3,
      29, 149–50

youth pastor   41, 84, 144
Yugoslavia   189, 192, 318

Z

Zambia   35–6, 47, 172
Zedong, Mao   68, 173

zenana missions   66, 86, 204, 256
Ziegenbalg, Bartholomäus   65, 197
Zimbabwe   24, 35, 38, 215, 219, 235, 268, 273
Zionist churches   46–7, 129, 221, 342
Zoroastrian(s)   55, 62, 318

Printed in the USA
CPSIA information can be obtained
at www.ICGtesting.com
JSHW061557270823
47217JS00007B/93